FOURTH EDITION

Striking a Balance

A COMPREHENSIVE APPROACH TO

early literacy

Nancy Lee Cecil
CALIFORNIA STATE UNIVERSITY, SACRAMENTO

Holcomb Hathaway, Publishers
Scottsdale, Arizona

Library of Congress Cataloging-in-Publication Data

Cecil, Nancy Lee.
  Striking a balance : a comprehensive approach to early literacy / Nancy Lee Cecil. —
4th ed.
      p. cm.
  Includes bibliographical references and index.
  ISBN 978-1-934432-14-3
  1. Reading (Primary)—United States. 2. Literacy—United States. I. Title.
  LB1525.C34 2011
  372.6—dc22

                                                        2011014703

To Landon and Katrina. You inspire me!

Photo credits: *front cover,* Cathy Yeulet/123 RF *(top left),* Cathy Yeulet Jonathan Ross/Dreamstime *(left),* Dmitriy Shironosov/123 RF *(right); back cover,* Dmitriy Shironosov/123 RF; *spine,* Jose Manuel Gelpi Diaza/123 RF; *pg. iii,* Thomas Perkins/123 RF; *pg. v,* Andres Rodriguez/123 RF; *pg. xiii,* Thomas Perkins/123 RF; *pg. xv,* Tatiana Gladskikh/123 RF; *pg. xx,* Ljupco Smokovski/123 RF; *pg. 1,* Cathy Yeulet/123 RF *(top),* iofoto/123 RF *(bottom); pg. 7,* Digital Vision; *pg. 8,* PhotoDisk; *pg. 15,* Dmitriy Shironosov/123 RF *(top),* Jose Manuel Gelpi Diaz/123 RF *(bottom); pg. 18,* Dynamic Graphics *(top); pg. 24,* Kyolhin/Dreamstime *(bottom); pg. 7,* Digital Vision; *pg. 8,* PhotoDisk; *pg. 35,* Juriah Mosin/123 RF *(top),* Gennadiy Poznyakov/123 RF *(bottom); pg. 40,* PhotoDisk; *pg. 46,* Digital Vision; *pg. 57,* PhotoDisk; *pg. 61,* Banana Stock; *pg. 65,* Dmitriy Shironosov/123 RF *(top),* Bruce Shippee/123 RF *(bottom); pg. 67,* PhotoDisk; *pg. 72,* PhotoDisk; *pg. 83,* Elena Shchipkova/123 RF *(top),* Andy Dean/123 RF *(bottom); pg. 85,* Banana Stock; *pg. 96,* doctorkan/123 RF; *pg. 97,* Marcel Braendli/123 RF; *pg. 104,* Brand X Pictures; *pg. 108,* Cathy Yeulet/123 RF; *pg. 111,* Sonya Etchison/123 RF *(top),* Thomas Perkins/123 RF *(bottom); pg. 116,* Banana Stock; *pg. 119,* Jose Manuel Gelpi Diaz/123 RF; *pg. 129,* Image 100 Ltd.; *pg. 133,* Banana Stock *(top),* Szocs Jozsef/123 RF *(bottom); pg. 137,* Dynamic Graphics; *pg. 153,* Benis Arapovic/123 RF; *pg. 157,* Yuri Arcurs/123 RF *(top),* Jose Manuel Gelpi Diaz/123 RF *(bottom); pg. 161,* Banana Stock; *pg. 175,* Martinmark/Dreamstime; *pg. 176,* Banana Stock; *pg. 183,* Flashon Studio/123 RF *(top),* Jose Manuel Gelpi Diaz/123 RF *(bottom); pg. 185,* PhotoDisk; *pg. 203,* Brand X Pictures; *pg. 205,* Cathy Yeulet/123 RF; *pg. 209,* Dmitriy Shironosov/123 RF *(top),* Jose Manuel Gelpi Diaz/123 RF *(bottom); pg. 211,* Brand X Pictures; *pg. 219,* Banana Stock; *pg. 228,* Dmitriy Shironosov; *pg. 226,* Cathy Yeulet/123 RF *(top),* Stephen Denness/123 RF *(bottom); pg. 231,* Banana Stock; *pg. 235,* Thomas Perkins/123 RF; *pg. 238,* Andrey Stratilatov/123 RF *(top),* iofoto/123 RF *(bottom); pg. 253,* Cathy Yeulet/123 RF *(top),* Olga Sapegina/123 RF *(bottom); pg. 261,* Xavier Gallego Morell/123 RF; *pg. 264,* Dmitriy Shironosov/123RF; *pg. 273,* Matthew Antonino/123RF; *pg. 277,* Kai Chiang/123 RF *(top),* Jose Manuel Gelpi Diaz/123 RF *(bottom); pg. 289,* Dmitriy Shironosov/123 RF; *pg. 291,* Cathy Yeulet/123 RF; *pg. 304,* Varina and Jay Patel/123 RF; *pg. 307,* PhotoDisk; *pg. 309,* Marcel Braendli/123 RF; *pg. 313,* Pavel Losevsky/123 RF *(top),* Larisa Lofitskaya/123 RF *(bottom); pg. 316,* Brand X Pictures; *pg. 318,* PhotoDisk; *pg. 328,* Dynamic Graphics; *pg. 331,* Yuriy Kobets/123 RF *(top),* Thomas Perkins/123 RF *(bottom); pg. 333,* Banana Stock; *pg. 335,* Banana Stock; *pg. 337,* Banana Stock; *pg. 339,* Cathy Yeulet/123 RF; *pg. 340,* Thomas Perkins/123 RF; *pg. 413,* M.G. Mooij/123 RF; *pg. 423,* Marcel Braendli/123 RF; *pg. 441,* Xavier Gallego Morell/123 RF; *pg. 445,* Oleksandr Pekur/123 RF

Please note: The author and publisher have made every effort to provide current website addresses in this book. However, it is inevitable that some of the URLs listed here will change following publication of this book.

Holcomb Hathaway, Publishers, Inc.
8700 E. Via de Ventura Blvd., Suite 265
Scottsdale, Arizona 85258
(480) 991-7881
www.hh-pub.com

ISBN 978-1-934432-14-3

10 9 8 7 6 5 4 3 2 1

Printed in the United States of America.

Brief Contents

Contents

List of Activities

Preface

Striking a Balance: A Comprehensive Approach to Early Literacy, Fourth Edition, like its predecessors, fully explores a comprehensive program of balanced literacy instruction. In such a program, young children can learn the basics of cracking the code of reading and writing through systematic explicit instruction; in addition, with caring teachers and well-chosen strategies, they will enjoy learning to become literate through ample practice with authentic literacy experiences. The need for balance is especially critical in early literacy, and this edition makes an even stronger case for why both decoding (or word identification) and meaning making (or comprehension) are linchpins of beginning literacy instruction. In keeping with the current consensus in the field of literacy, I believe that children are best served when they receive direct skill and strategy instruction in conjunction with motivating contexts for real reading.

Exactly what needs to be "balanced" in early literacy instruction to provide a comprehensive program? This book highlights the need to offer instruction that focuses on the affective dimension of learning and on the cognitive dimension of early literacy. The book balances attention to reading quality literature for enjoyment and reading for information, and it balances narrative and expository writing. It stresses balancing time spent teaching reading and writing and time allowed for children to actually practice these skills. It recognizes the need to nurture the other language arts (speaking, listening, viewing, and visually representing) as valid alternative ways of receiving and expressing information and it provides myriad opportunities to integrate these processes. The book underscores the importance of explicit instruction, modeling, and scaffolding coupled with the gradual withdrawal of teacher support to encourage student independence. It stresses spelling, vocabulary, and phonics skills, but always in the larger context of authentic literacy experiences. A comprehensive and balanced approach takes all aspects of literacy into account.

Since the third edition was published, emphasis on aligning instruction with standards has continued to gather momentum. Educators differ in their opinions about the success or failure of mandates and legislation concerning educational standards; however, it seems that most educators recognize that standards do provide helpful roadmaps for instruction and that it simply makes sense to select teaching practices shown to be effective through replicable research. Thus, I have included in this book only strategies that are compatible with the majority of state standards for the early grades. Additionally, the selected strategies and activities are limited to those found to be effective through empirical research.

The focus of revisions for the fourth edition was to build on the usefulness of the three previous editions, concentrating on the following:

- **A new chapter on literacy and technology.** Reviewers suggested a more thorough incorporation of classroom technology to engage today's tech-savvy children in literacy. This new chapter explores exciting uses for computers and technology in literacy instruction, including blogs, hypermedia/multimodal projects, e-books, and tools such as interactive whiteboards.

- **An in-depth overview of literacy from birth to the primary grades.** Adopters asked to see more of the literacy transition from birth through fluent reader. A new section shows what to expect from children at each stage of literacy development.

- **Response to Intervention.** RTI, a framework first used in the field of special education, is now helping literacy educators. Its implications for classroom teachers are highlighted here.

- **Case examples.** A new boxed feature highlights specific teachers and students, illustrating topics such as RTI in action, helping one child achieve literacy success, and providing explicit instruction of a comprehension strategy.

- **Updated coverage of reforms.** Discussions include national and state standards, including the Common Core Standards movement.

- **A comparison chart of two models of spelling stages.** Previous editions looked at only one spelling stages model; in this edition, readers will benefit from a comparison to a second research model.

- **An expanded children's literature appendix.** The original children's literature appendix now also includes books ideal for enhancing vocabulary, writing skills, and comprehension.

- **Greater emphasis on working with English learners.** In recognition of this growing need in classrooms across the United States, I have incorporated new teaching ideas throughout the text.

- **Updated teacher resources.** The teacher reference appendix has been expanded to reflect the many books published in early childhood education since the last edition.

- **Updated references and research.** To maintain the strong research base, references and research have been updated where appropriate.

SPECIAL FEATURES

Some of the special features of *Striking a Balance* aid the reader in understanding new concepts and vocabulary. Other features are designed to foster reflection and mastery of the material, and to encourage the reader to try out ideas in the field. The following features are particularly noteworthy:

- **The book's chapter on reading and writing informational text.** Research on informational text indicates that even young children enjoy this mode of discourse. This chapter gives teachers the tools to introduce children to expository text early in their academic lives, which will prepare them to succeed in later encounters with content area material.

- **"In the Classroom" feature.** Each chapter begins with a vignette in which readers observe an authentic classroom setting and see how a practicing teacher deals with the subject addressed in the chapter. These small glimpses of literacy instruction build background and trigger the reader's prior knowledge about the chapter's topic. Throughout the chapter and in some of the activities, I refer to the vignette so the reader can make the connection between chapter concepts and classroom instruction.

- **Activities.** Most chapters include activities designed for use in the classroom. These specific procedures allow readers to put the chapter's ideas and strategies into practice, either in their field placement or in their future classrooms.

- **Questions for Journal Writing and Discussion.** Questions at the end of each chapter help readers reflect on and internalize key ideas in the chapter. These questions are suitable for response in journal form or for stimulating lively discussion.

- **Suggestions for Projects and Field Activities.** This special section makes the connection between research and theory and real classroom practice. At the end of each chapter, the reader is offered several suggestions for surveying, interviewing, or observing local classroom teachers to compare strategies presented in the chapter with actual practice. Other activities ask the reader to try out a strategy or activity in the chapter with a small group of primary school children. These activities will be useful as assignments for students in their field placement experiences.

- **A concluding chapter on "orchestration," or putting it all together.** In the final chapter of the book, I provide an intimate view of the urban classroom of an exemplary first-grade teacher who demonstrates many of the procedures, strategies, and ideals presented in the rest of the book. The reader receives a rare insider perspective on how a seasoned teacher makes decisions about classroom climate, materials, and room arrangement, and how to best utilize the limited available instructional time.

- **Glossary.** An extensive book-end glossary is included, allowing readers to review vocabulary highlighted throughout the text.

- **Appendices.** Included at the end of the book are references for children's literature, teacher and parent resources for early literacy, a variety of literacy checklists and other assessment tools for classroom use, and a list of widely used commercial evaluation instruments. An additional appendix highlights websites of special interest to literacy teachers.

- **Ancillaries.** A PowerPoint presentation and an Instructor's Manual are available to adopters of this text. The Instructor's Manual provides several valuable tools: each chapter offers a summary of key concepts, a list of key vocabulary, suggestions for in-class discussions and activities, and a range of assessment devices, including objective and subjective questions.

- **An interactive Companion Website and study guide.** Available to students, this site offers features such as chapter objectives, key concepts, questions and projects, teaching activities, and relevant website links.

ABOUT THE E-BOOK

his book is also available as an e-book. When adopting this book for use in your class, you may inform your students that the e-book version can be purchased on our website, www.hh-pub.com.

The electronic version of the book offers the same colorful layout and matches the print book page for page; this ensures ease of teaching if some of your students use the print book and some use the e-book. In addition, those reading the e-book will find the following interactive features:

- Active web links for all URLs cited in the text.
- Active links to the student website, to conveniently access features such as questions, projects, and teaching activities.
- Instant access to cross-reference links between chapters; for example, readers can link directly to (and from) tools and resources in the appendices as they are discussed.
- Active links to literature being discussed, allowing readers to learn more about the books and see what others have to say.
- Opportunity to respond to chapter-opening questions using digital note-taking and unlimited bookmarking.

ACKNOWLEDGMENTS

many outstanding professionals, friends, family members, and former students have helped me bring my vision to fruition. As before, I would like to thank the extraordinary primary teachers who graciously allowed me to attend their classrooms and share the amazing ways they are balancing skills-based and holistic instruction to teach children to joyfully read, write, and think. The voices of many of these fine teachers permeate this book. I especially wish to thank Maria Ramon, Janet Rodgers, Rita Lehman, Linda Bernard, and Maria Oropeza, the classroom teachers who allowed me to observe how they bring to life the concept of a comprehensive literacy program. I also wish to extend a special thanks to the Phase I and II students in San Juan Center for reading the manuscript and providing suggestions.

Present and prior reviewers of the manuscript offered critical feedback that I welcomed and incorporated into the final book. I am grateful for their help. First, my sincere thanks to Sherron Killingsworth Roberts, University of Central Florida, for her insightful and constructive comments at various stages of the project's creation. I also want to thank the reviewers of this edition for their assistance: Maureen P. Boyd, SUNY Buffalo; Deborah Farrer, California University of Pennsylvania; Kathy Froelich, Florida State University; Jesse Gainer, Texas State University–San Marcos; Ingrid Graves, Tarleton University; Stephanie A. Grote-Garcia, Texas A&M University–Corpus Christi; Jennifer Hathaway, University of North Carolina–Charlotte; Jennifer Lee Johnson, Washington State University Tri-Cities; Stephen B. Kucer, Washington State University Vancouver; Rita E. Meadows, University of South Florida Polytechnic; David Lund, Southern Utah University; Judy Naim, Xavier University, and Kathy Rosebrock, University of San Francisco.

Finally, my continued thanks to reviewers of earlier editions for their help: Merry Boggs, Pamela Campbell, Lois Catrambone, Jeanne Clidas, Deborah Farrer, E. Sutton Flynt, Dana L. Grisham, Susan Harnden, Bonnie Henderson, T. Tana Herchold, Barbara Hershberger, Anita Holmes, Dee Holmes, Timothy L. Krenzke, Priscilla M. Leggett, Susan Davis Lenski, Linda Marriott, Patricia Mulligan, Edward T. Murray, Angela Raines, Laura Schein, and Rebecca Swearingen.

During work on all four editions of this book, my publisher has been supportive and helpful beyond words. Colette Kelly, Editor, shared my vision of a balanced literacy program that creates readers who can read and who want to read.

Finally, I extend heartfelt gratitude to my husband, Gary, who was ever patient as I took time away from him and family activities to write and edit this new edition. Without his unceasing love, support, and unwavering belief in me, I would have given up long ago.

About the Author

nancy Lee Cecil has had a rich and varied background in education, as an elementary school teacher and a literacy specialist in New York, urban Savannah, Georgia, and in the public schools in the U.S. Virgin Islands. As a result of these experiences, she is especially attuned to the needs of linguistically and culturally diverse children. Cecil received her doctorate from the University of Buffalo and currently teaches in the Department of Teacher Education at California State University in Sacramento, where she recently won the prestigious Outstanding Educator Award. She has written nineteen books on literacy, most recently *Phonemic Awareness and Music: A Feast of Rhyme, Rhythm, and Song,* and received the Teacher's Choice award for an earlier book, *For the Love of Language: Poetry for All Learners.* Cecil also has had many articles published in major literacy journals. She has spoken about literacy to groups of educators on local, national, and international levels.

chapter 1

A Child Learns to Read

Process and Product

focus questions

- What are the fundamental processes of reading?

- Why is it important for teachers in the field to understand all aspects of the reading process?

- How is reading defined by researchers and practitioners in the field?

Although this vignette is titled "In the Classroom," in actuality the learning-to-read process begins long before four-year-old Lydia ever enters school. She has developed certain concepts about the function of print from the numerous signs in her urban environment and by observing how readers in her home interact with books, magazines, newspapers, and other reading material. For example, when she sees her older brother scan the fast-food menu and then order a hamburger and fries, she is discovering that those black squiggles carry meaning. When she asks her mother to write her name and her mother sounds it out in front of her, she observes that words are composed of a string of letters and that those letters are composed of sounds that hold meaning.

When she snuggles in her grandma's lap and "reads" the fairy tale she has memorized after hearing it nearly a hundred times, Lydia demonstrates her understanding that many words together can tell a story. She asks for a second story and Grandma complies. She puts a chubby finger on the words as Grandma says them. Lydia is again revealing her understanding of the matching of spoken and written word.

Lydia knows a lot about reading, but can she actually read?

WHAT IS READING?

a t first glance, it would hardly seem worth the trouble to answer the basic question of what reading is because, in a sense, everybody knows perfectly well what it is: most people do it in one form or another every single day! But definitions underlie all intellectual endeavors. Definitions contain assumptions that determine future educational activities. In other words, what teachers do to teach beginning reading will be determined, in large part, by what they believe reading is.

To define reading, we must know exactly what is involved in this activity that sets it apart from other similar activities. It is not enough, for example, to define reading as "a thought-getting process," because we can get thoughts just as easily from a lecture, a conversation, or a film. There are, to put it another way, many similarities between reading a printed page (whether the printed page appears on paper or on an electronic screen) of difficult text and hearing the same text read to us by another person. The problem of comprehension is paramount for both reader and listener.

No one would deny that a major purpose of reading is to get information or enjoyment of some sort from the written words. But since we get information in the same way from spoken words, the purpose of getting information does not define reading in a way that distinguishes it from engaging in conversation. As soon as we understand this point, the problem of definition begins to resolve itself. If we see that meaning is a function of the relationship between the language and the receiver, we might then ask how the written words (which we read) are related to the spoken words (which we hear). If a language composed of sounds carries the meanings, then what is writing? Writing is a device, or a code, for representing the sounds of a language in visual form. The written words of a language are, in fact, just symbols for the spoken words, which are sounds.

So reading, then, becomes the process of turning these printed symbols back into sounds again whether or not audible vocalization of the sounds actually occurs. The moment we say this, however, some reasonable soul is bound to ask, anxiously, "But what about meaning? Can we propose to define reading as just deciphering the words without regard to the meaning?"

The answer is yes, but only partly. **Reading** is, first of all, the mechanical skill of turning the printed symbols into the sounds of our language. Of course, the reason we turn the printed words into sound—in other words, the reason we *read*—is to get at the meaning. We decode the printed symbols to get what the author is attempting to say, and then, more importantly, we make some meaningful connection to the world as we know it (Pearson, 1993).

■ reading

But there is even more to it than that. Reading entails both reconstructing an author's message and constructing one's own meaning using the words on the page as a stimulus. We can think of it as a transaction, or an exchange, among the reader, the text, and the purposes and context of the reading situation. A reader's reconstruction of the ideas and information intended by the author is somewhat like a listener's reconstruction of ideas from the combination of sounds a speaker makes. An artist creates a masterpiece that means one thing to him and a host of different things to different admirers of his piece. Likewise, the reader, like the listener, may create meanings that are different from those intended by the author. What a reader understands from the reconstructed and constructed meanings depends on that reader's prior knowledge, prior experiences, maturity, and proficiency in using language in differing social contexts.

In addition to these traditional descriptions of what reading is, other considerations arise from the ubiquitous new technologies of the twenty-first century. Educators now talk about **new literacies** (Kist, 2005; Kress, 2003) that consist of ways not only to read and write but also to view and visually represent texts in new and exciting ways—especially texts related to technology. These texts are often in electronic rather than conventional printed paper format and can be viewed on many devices, such as computers, mobile devices, tablets/e readers, interactive whiteboards, and so forth. They may also utilize a variety of enhancements, including video and/or audio clips, computer graphics, and digital photos. This type of reading and writing has many unique characteristics, including the way it is organized and discrete features that allow children to actually interact with the text. These new literacies will require children to be proficient in the six language arts (reading, writing, speaking, listening, viewing, and visually representing); in accessing and synthesizing information from a variety of sources—especially the Internet; and evaluating the information's accuracy, relevance, and authenticity (Castek, Bevans-Mangelson, & Goldstone, 2006).

■ new literacies

THEORIES OF READING ACQUISITION

 wo theories regarding how we learn to read are at the heart of the question about how reading should be taught. Each of these theories offers us important insights about how children think about reading.

Nonstage Theory

The earlier theory is a **nonstage theory**, which holds that unskilled and skilled readers essentially use the same strategies to figure out unknown words. This

■ nonstage theory

theory, revisited by Goodman in 1997, posits that readers use predictions based on the context of sentences, as well as the letter–sound correspondence, to determine unknown words. They depend mostly, however, on the grammar (syntax) and semantics (underlying meaning) to decipher the message. In this process, the reader uses strategies to sample and select from the information in the text, makes predictions, draws inferences, confirms or rejects, and regresses when necessary to make corrections in reading. Visual and aural features of the words—the **graphophonic information**—are used as necessary. Such a theory suggests that certain apparent "errors" that children make while reading, such as saying the word *dad* for the key word *father,* offer observers an actual "window into the child's brain"; such **miscues** are not errors at all, according to the theory, but merely deviations from text, occurring because the child is trying to make sense of print.

graphophonic information ▪

miscues ▪

Stage Theory

A study by Juel (1988) indicates that unskilled and skilled readers use different strategies to unlock or decipher unknown words. Unskilled readers become "stuck" with strategies such as guessing or trying to memorize every new word and therefore are not as successful as those learners who have internalized a wide range of helpful strategies. The **stage theory** holds that children go through three stages in acquiring literacy: During the first stage, the "selective cue stage," children might use only the context of surrounding words and illustrations to predict possible meaning for unknown words or might focus on limited components of words to decode them. For example, recognizing only the first and last letters in words. At the second stage, the "spelling–sound stage," they listen for known sounds and letters to determine the meaning of new words. When children have arrived at the final stage, called the "automatic stage," they have reached the fluent or automatic level of reading. At this sophisticated stage, they almost subconsciously scan every feature of a word and compare it instantaneously to patterns with which they are familiar. Very little mental effort needs to be directed toward decoding unknown words, and most of the reader's attention can be focused on obtaining personal meaning from text.

stage theory ▪

CUEING SYSTEMS

perhaps in an attempt to synthesize the above reading acquisition theories, some researchers have suggested that four systems make communication possible: (1) the grapho-phonological system, (2) the syntactic system, (3) the semantic system, and (4) the pragmatic system. Skilled readers must use all four systems at once as they read, write, listen, and speak (Clay, 1991). These **cueing systems** help children create meaning by using language in a way that most English speakers accept as "standard." Effective teachers of beginning literacy are aware of these systems and model and support students' use of them in all areas of communication. The four cueing systems are described briefly below.

cueing systems ▪

The Grapho-Phonological System

There are roughly 44 to 48 sounds (or **phonemes**) in the English language, and children learn to pronounce these sounds in many different combinations as they begin to speak. Teachers support experimentation with how these sounds correspond to letters (**graphemes**) by teaching children how to use temporary or experimental spellings to sound out words; modeling how to pronounce words; calling attention to rhyming words and alliterations; and directly teaching other decoding skills, such as showing how to divide words into syllables. For example, by pointing out the rhyme scheme in "Twinkle, Twinkle, Little Star," the teacher shows children how the words *are* and *star* have similar ending sounds but different beginning sounds.

- phonemes
- graphemes

The Syntactic (Sound Stream of Language) System

The syntactic system, which includes but is not limited to grammar, governs how a language is structured or how words are combined into sentences. Teachers support this cueing system by showing children how to combine sentences; add affixes to root words; use punctuation and inflectional endings; and write simple, compound, and complex sentences. To begin, a teacher might use the nonsensical group of words, "boy fell the down," to show children the importance of order in language. Further, a teacher might show children how to combine the two sentences, "The boy fell down" and "The boy was not watching where he was going," to become "The boy fell down because he was not watching where he was going."

The Semantic System

The major components of the semantic system are meaning-making and vocabulary. An even smaller unit of meaning-making is the **morpheme**, the smallest unit of meaning in English words, highlighted when we use the *s* to make *cats* plural, or the prefix *re* to make *do* into *redo*. Teachers support the semantic system by providing meaningful literature and relevant reading topics; focusing children's attention on the meanings of words; discussing multiple meanings of words; and introducing synonyms, antonyms, and homonyms. For example, a teacher might explain to children that, although they already know the meaning of the word *change*, it can be used very differently in math when we "make change." In the intermediate grades, teaching children dictionary skills, in context, also supports this system.

- morpheme

The Pragmatic System

The final cueing system is pragmatics, which addresses the social and cultural functions of language. People use language for differing purposes, and how they speak or write is determined partly by their purposes and intended audience. Teachers can support the use of this cueing system by showing children how different forms of language are appropriate for different situations. For example, a teacher might discuss how playground language differs in form and content from that of a shared experience in class, or how we use different language for giving directions than we do for conducting a pretend dialogue with a prince.

THE READING PROCESS

the act of reading is composed of two basic parts: the global reading process and the reading product. By *process* we mean a movement toward an end that is accomplished by going through the necessary steps to crack the code and construct meaning from what the author has said. These aspects of the reading process ideally combine to produce the reading *product*.

Skills Used in the Reading Process

Clearly, the beginning reader has many available options for figuring out unknown words. Some of these—such as random guessing—are more inefficient than others. Learning to read, then, involves sorting through a cafeteria of problem-solving choices and discarding those that are ineffective for the situation, while selecting those that allow for success. To make maximum progress, the beginning reader must acquire three closely related skills at approximately the same time (Clay, 1991):

- using letter–sound relationships
- acquiring a sight vocabulary of immediately recognized words
- gaining meaning from context

Using letter–sound relationships

phonics ■

Some experts believe that the most immediate goal of early reading instruction is teaching children **phonics**—how to "crack the code" by associating printed letters with the speech sounds they represent and helping them to immediately apply this knowledge to meaningful text. Every word in spoken English can be represented using only 26 different letter symbols. In general, letters and letter combinations stand for the same speech sounds in thousands of different words. Although there is not a perfect one-to-one correspondence between written/printed letters and the speech sounds they represent, learning to decode depends on a true understanding of the sound–spelling relationship of the English language (Moats, 1995a).

For children to become proficient spellers and fluent readers, they must master the helpful skills of "sounding out" words, using their knowledge of the sound–spelling relationship in a real reading context. The child says to herself (very quickly and unconsciously), "I know that this word says *baby* and this word says *bed.*" Then, pointing to the *b*, she asks herself, "I wonder if it makes the /b/ sound every time?" The child is giving herself a brief lesson in phonics; she is also using excellent inductive reasoning, but many children need to have these sound relationships pointed out to them directly. After children have learned two or three sound–spelling correspondences, such as the sounds for *b, a,* and *t,* a skilled teacher can then teach the children how to blend these sounds into words. The teacher next demonstrates how to move sequentially from left to right through spellings so that children can sound out or say the sound for each spelling. To be most effective, it seems, phonics should be taught to children formally by teachers trained in how to blend and segment sounds and in the appropriate order to teach phonics skills.

Acquiring a sight vocabulary

Many words used frequently in the English language cannot be easily sounded out or decoded, such as the words *the, give, come, to, was, could,* and *once,* to name just a few, because they do not follow any phonics rule (Cunningham, 2009). Such words appear so often in English speech and writing that it would seem wasteful for a child to even try to sound out these words each time they are met. Therefore, words

Is teaching children how to "crack the code" the most immediate goal of early reading instruction?

such as those offered above must be taught whole, using what has been called the "whole word" or "look–say" method. These words are known as **sight vocabulary words**—words that children should recognize about as quickly as they recognize their own names. The repetition of these words many times, in many different ways, fixes them in the child's memory. With enough repetition, recognition of the words then becomes automatic and instantaneous. Coupled with their expanding decoding skills, children will now be able to read simple sentences and stories without undue frustration.

■ sight vocabulary words

    For early readers, one of the most appropriate methods of teaching sight words, as well as general concepts about the written word, is through the use of *shared reading* with *big books* (see Chapter 3), especially those with predictable or familiar texts (Clay, 1991; Holdaway, 1979). Motivational big books with repeated word patterns are ideal resources for helping children memorize sight words. Encouraging **tracking**—having children point to words as they are read—while using such materials is also invaluable. Tracking fosters awareness of printed text as well as understanding and familiarity with differing grammatical phrases.

■ tracking

Gaining meaning from context

When a child is reading for meaning, the **context** (the surrounding information in the sentence) in which an unknown word is met can often be useful in suggesting what that word might be. At times, only a few words could possibly complete the sentence. For example:

■ context

    The girl went swimming at the _____.

    The hungry boy walked to the _____.

    The girl _____ when she won the prize.

In the first example, probably fewer than a dozen words could logically be inserted in the blank space (swimming pool, pool, pond, park, lake, river, ocean, YMCA). If the child possesses rudimentary phonics skills and the word begins with a *p*, the child can further narrow the possibilities. Some choices would also be less logical than others, depending on what has happened in the story prior to this sentence, allowing children to make an "educated guess" as to what the word might be. When children are shown how to use context to aid them in narrowing the possibilities of an unknown word, they have another strategy at their command.

Authors use a number of devices to provide contextual clues that help readers determine the meaning of new words and difficult concepts. One of these is to incorporate a description/definition in the text (Heilman, 2005).

> The [swan] swam in the pond. This [bird] was bigger than any of the other birds in the water.

Other contextual techniques for deciphering unknown words include comparison or contrast and the use of synonyms or antonyms.

> The apple was very [small]. No one but the new boy wanted the apple, because it was so [little].

Solving the pronunciation of the unknown word is made easier by (1) the meaning of the total sentence in which the word occurs and (2) the meaning in the surrounding sentences.

As a reader interacts with a text, meaning is being construed in her mind. The meaning does not lie on the page but in the mind of the reader.

The above approaches to figuring out new words (letter–sound relationships, sight vocabulary, and context) are probably not of equal value in learning how to read, although each is necessary to some degree. Research quite clearly shows that overemphasizing prediction from contextual clues for word recognition can be counterproductive, possibly even delaying the learning process if it is stressed above trying to analyze words by their sound–spelling components (Stanovich, 1992). On the other hand, too little or too much phonics instruction may contribute to the failure to learn to read (Stahl, 2001; Vadasy, Sanders, & Peyton, 2006).

Additionally, it must be kept in mind that different children may benefit from and rely on one method more than others, whereas some approaches, such as pure memorization by the form of the word, have limited usefulness beyond the earliest stages of learning how to read. It seems clear that automatic, fluent reading would not be the result if a child had to go through a series of trial-and-error approaches in which all three approaches were tried out every time a new word was encountered! Efficient readers tend to use all three methods of word recognition instantaneously and simultaneously, lending even more support to a balanced approach to reading instruction in which all strategies are employed (Barone, 1990; Bissex, 2004; Eldredge, 1995).

Characteristics of the Reading Process

The reading process consists of several fundamental characteristics. If we explore these characteristics, a better understanding of the complex nature of the activity emerges (Hyde & Bizar, 1989).

Reading is a holistic process

Reading is not the sum total of the discrete skills that we have children practice in order to teach them to read; rather, reading is a holistic process whereby the various subskills, such as **decoding**, finding the main idea, and locating impor-   ■ decoding
tant details must be integrated to form a smooth, coherent whole. The subskills, though crucial, must be applied to the act of reading by a competent teacher.

If we want children to be thinkers, we must structure our instruction toward active participation in the search for meaning. Children must be given time every school day to read material that is on their own level and that is of interest to them. Children at all grade levels must also be read to. Teachers who read to children and give them the opportunity to discuss and wrestle with ideas and concepts are providing a sophisticated model of the kinds of thinking they must do when reading on their own.

Reading is a constructive process

We have come to think of reading as the construction of meaning from text (Spiro, Bruce, & Brewer, 1980). As readers interact with the text, meaning is being constructed in their minds. The meaning does not lie on the page but in the mind of the reader. Readers use what is in their heads and what is on the page and construct a meaning based on a fusing of the two forces.

Teachers must be aware of the constructive nature of the reading process so that they can help children develop the necessary tools to participate in this meaning-building process. This can be accomplished by providing an opportunity for children to display a wide range of thinking about what they are reading. Asking an abundance of open-ended questions—those for which there is no single "right" answer—encourages and validates children who are struggling to make their own meaning from text.

Reading is a strategic process

Good readers use different strategies, depending on their purposes for reading and the difficulty of the material. The purpose of reading may be purely for entertainment, to memorize a poem, or to discover how to put together some object. Having these different purposes leads us to read in different ways, depending on the nature of the task (Rosenblatt, 2005).

Teachers need to teach children to set their own purposes for reading and then check to see that their purposes are being met. Teachers can teach children to think about their own thinking (**metacognition**) by modeling various strategies as they read aloud to children. They can also do this by discussing how reading rate and strategies change according to the type of reading that is being done.

metacognition ■

Reading is an interactive process

Finally, we have come to think of reading as a process in which readers interact with the text while tapping into their own experience in order to construct meaning. What readers bring to the activity in terms of prior knowledge of content, structure, and vocabulary determines how well they will be able to derive a rich meaning from the text. We have all had the experience of reading something about which we had little or no background knowledge. When this happens, we soon realize that although we may know most of the words, we cannot make sense of the material. We do not have the content knowledge that we need to construct a valid meaning to take with us from the reading.

As teachers, we must provide activities that activate, access, and build on the knowledge of the children with whom we are working. One way to do this is by showing video excerpts or pictures or by reading short informative passages about the study topic. Another way is to simply brainstorm with the group to elicit what the children know about the topic. For example, if the selection to be read is about koala bears, the teacher asks the children to raise their hands and tell the group anything they know about the animals—information the teacher writes on the board. What one child contributes often triggers a response in other children. This process helps bring to the surface everything the children know about the topic and also provides information for those who may know little or nothing about it. The children are now able to attach new information to known information. They are ready for the active search for meaning.

THE READING PRODUCT

the reading *product* should always be meaningful because it is some form of communication—the reader's transaction with the writer's printed ideas (Rosenblatt, 2005). A wealth of knowledge is available to people today because we are able to read what others have written in the past. Americans can read of events and accomplishments that have occurred at other times in other parts of the globe. Knowledge of great discoveries does not have to be laboriously passed from person to person by word of mouth; such knowledge is freely available to all who read (Spiegel, 1992).

As well as being a means of communicating generally, reading is a means of communicating specifically with friends and acquaintances who may or may not be nearby. A note read by a child can tell him his mother has gone shopping, or it can inform a babysitter who to call in an emergency. An email from a teacher can alert parents to events and issues.

Reading can be a way of sharing another person's insights, joys, sorrows, or creative undertakings. Being able to read can make it possible for a person to vicariously visit places she has never visited before, to take advantage of bargains and discounts, or to avoid disaster by heeding warning signs. It is difficult to imagine what life would be like without this vital means of communication!

The rich form of communication described above depends on comprehension, which is affected by all aspects of the reading process. Being able to decipher the code and put sounds to the symbols is essential, but comprehension involves much more than turning the symbols into the appropriate sounds; the reader must derive meaning from these symbols and in some way connect them to experiences or impressions from his own life. Some children may be able to read a passage and pronounce all the words beautifully and still have no idea what they have just read, or they may understand the words but lack the ability to relate the ideas to anything that has happened in their own lives.

Teachers who understand that all aspects of the reading process have an effect on the comprehension of written material will be better able to survey children's reading difficulties and, as a result, create sound instructional programs based on their needs. Poor performance related to any aspect of the reading process may result in a less-than-satisfactory reading ability or an inability to learn to read at all. Three conditions that suggest a child is at risk for poor performance in reading are the following:

1. The child does not see the symbols or letters on the page; he may not be able to recognize them.

2. The child has developed confusions or incorrect associations between a number of sounds and letters; incorrect recognition of words will result, and comprehension will be lessened.

3. The child has little experience with or knowledge of the topic about which she is reading; she will have less comprehension of the passage than one who has had a rich background in the topic.

The bottom line for teachers, then, is to ensure that children are given an abundance of **explicit**, or direct, **instruction** on the graphic symbols or letters that represent the sounds of our language so that they can begin to build a strong association between the letters and the sounds they make. Additionally, to achieve the greatest transaction between author and reader, any decoded message must have some connection to the child's life and experiences. Therefore, the teacher must determine whether children have the necessary background information and knowledge to understand any given material; if this is not the case, the teacher must provide the background by other means, such as discussion, pictures, video excerpts, and so forth, to ensure adequate processing.

■ explicit instruction

SUMMARY

 earning to read is a complicated, rather miraculous process, and for most children, it does not happen without at least some explicit instruction. Because few of us as adults can accurately remember how we managed to accomplish this feat, we are hard-pressed to provide any earthshaking insights into how it is done. Understanding how children learn to read is further complicated by the fact that whenever we observe a teacher instructing a child in reading, we are seeing only one tiny piece of an ongoing process, and even then we cannot see what is really taking place within the reader. Moreover, if we were to watch a particular child as she reads silently, all we can do is try to guess what is going on in her brain from the behaviors she is showing us at the moment; however, if we were to be a fly on the wall in a classroom where this same first-grader was struggling with her burgeoning reading ability over several months, we might get a better overview of the child's perspective of this intricate process. We could listen to and observe the set of strategies she uses to read aloud and how she responds to what she has read, observe how the teacher facilitates the process, and watch as literacy blossoms.

What we do know is that the act of learning to read does not always occur naturally; it may be arduous and time-consuming or quick and immediately gratifying, and we know that it will not be exactly the same for any two youngsters. For some children, much learning about how to read has occurred before they enter school, through supportive interactions in a literate environment where they have been frequently read to and where evidence of the importance of print is everywhere. But it would be wrong to assume such exposure is enough.

Although some children learn to read at home prior to direct school instruction, many children with the same exposure do not. Sometimes formal instruction is needed for children to put together the observations they have made through their experiences with print. For those children who have had few experiences with print, exposure to a print-rich environment in school is not enough. Most children need explicit instruction in letter–sound relationships so that they can figure out unknown words, they must build a basic sight vocabulary of words they recognize immediately, and they must decide on a method of exacting meaning from unknown words through context and other clues. Equally important, they need to understand how to construct meaning by connecting an author's message to their own experiences. They need to be able to strategize how they will adjust their reading and thinking to the demands of the task at hand. Finally, they need to be supported in their use of the four cueing systems that make communication possible and will allow them to create meaning through socially shared situations.

Because we care about them, we give children affection, attention, exercise, and nutritious things to eat; we try to teach them to be polite, good-natured, thoughtful, and fair. We do these things because we believe it is the best way to start them on their way to healthy, happy lives. We must do as much with reading. When a child has learned how to construct his own meaning from text, he soon enters into a considerably richer world—one where he is able to communicate with all sorts of people he may never even meet. He is able to discover a new dimension of ideas, facts, and opinions that may take him anywhere he wishes to go.

questions
for journal writing and discussion

1. What is your definition of reading? How do you think your understanding of reading will affect the methods you choose to teach your students to read?

2. How would you explain the difference between "reading process" and "reading product" to a parent or any person who is not in the education profession? Why might it be important to distinguish between the two concepts?

3. What are your memories of learning to read? Write a list of everything you can recall about initial instruction, favorite books, successes, difficulties, and how you managed to "crack the code." Solicit help from parents, older siblings, and relatives to help reconstruct your early literacy experiences. Why might such memories be important to your teaching?

suggestions
for projects and field activities

1. Try to teach recognition of two words—*they* and *elephant*—to a child who has not yet learned to read and write. Record and compare the difficulties the child encounters with the two words. Which word was easier for the child to remember? Why do you think this was so? What strategies do you feel were most successful in helping children to remember the words?

2. Talk to two first-grade children. Ask the children what reading is and what kinds of things they think they must do to read successfully. Administer An Early Reader's View of the Reading Process (found in Appendix E) to one of the children. What new insights did you gain about how this child views the reading process? Share this information with your college class.

See Appendix E

3. Observe a child who is in the early stages of learning to read. Ask the child to read several sentences aloud. What are some difficulties the child encounters? What do you think the child needs to know to be more successful? Make two columns on a sheet of paper, one labeled "practice" and the other "explicit instruction." Try to determine what skills would best be developed through each of these modes.

chapter

2

A Quest for Balance

Moving Forward

focus questions

- What is the history of reading instruction in the United States?

- What arc the key issues in phonics and whole language instruction?

- How can classroom teachers combine the elements of both approaches to create a rich and balanced comprehensive literacy program?

Mrs. Johnson, a first-grade teacher in Illinois, uses a holistic approach to literacy instruction with her beginning readers. Her pupils spend much of the school day sharing quality children's literature and tend to remember many new words after being engaged with them numerous times through print that is displayed everywhere in the classroom. Mrs. Johnson's students leave her classroom at the end of a year with a deep appreciation for reading and writing. By contrast, Mr. Ruiz, down the hall, teaches his young learners the names and sounds of each letter of the alphabet. The children spend many hours practicing these sounds so they can immediately sound out unfamiliar words. Mr. Ruiz explains that his pupils love to read because they are empowered by their ability to figure out many words quickly. The two colleagues spend the year comparing notes on beginning reading and discussing which approach is more effective for their children; finally they agree to disagree. The same practices and discussions are occurring in schools across the country.

skills-based approach ■
holistic approach ■
look–say method ■

INTRODUCTION

his is an exciting time to be a teacher of literacy. We now have more conclusive evidence about what can be considered "effective literacy instruction" than at any other time in history. Within the last decade, national panels in the United States have completed a greater number of reports about best practices in reading than have been produced in any prior decade (National Institute of Child Health and Human Development, 2000a, 2000b; Sweet & Snow, 2002).

This body of knowledge did not come without challenges. For years, people debated the relative effectiveness of various reading methodologies. A look into the history of reading instruction in the United States will help to shed light on where we have been and where we are now.

THE HISTORY OF EARLY LITERACY

ew educational issues have engendered as much dialogue as the ongoing discussions over a *skills-based* versus a more *holistic* approach to early literacy instruction. It seems such dialogues have quite a history. As long ago as 1844, Horace Mann, considered the "father of public education," wrote a report that was critical of schools that implored teachers to adopt a rigid decoding approach to teaching reading.

For decades afterward, the popular thinking among educators appeared to move back and forth between a **skills-based approach,** akin to phonics instruction, and a **holistic approach** that was more meaning-centered, as stressed in the whole language philosophy. By the 1950s, a strong skills-based (or phonics) movement gained momentum. This was due, in part, to the publication of a widely circulated book called *Why Johnny Can't Read* (Flesch, 1955), in which Flesch took teachers to task for abandoning traditional phonics instruction in favor of the then popular **look–say method,** which was more meaning based and required children to use the context alone to figure out words they did not know. Flesch claimed the reason children were doing so poorly in reading and writing was that they had not been taught that every letter of the alphabet had at least one corresponding sound. Once that was understood, he contended, every child could easily read and spell every word by simply sounding it out.

In the 1960s, however, a movement came along de-emphasizing decoding and discouraging over-reliance on the use of the **basal readers,** the set of leveled textbooks most commonly used to teach reading. Teachers had begun noticing that although children were proficient at decoding, they did not seem to be understanding what they were reading, nor did they seem to be enjoying the activity. The "new" movement, christened the **whole language philosophy** by the National Council of the Teachers of English in 1978, stressed a pedagogy that moved from a rather narrow focus on isolated subskills to one that encouraged teachers to look at reading more holistically, as a part of the total communication process (Beck & Juel, 1995).

■ basal readers

■ whole language philosophy

During this period, the voice of Jeanne Chall, a Harvard professor who spent many years researching the issue of a skills-based approach versus a holistic program, added to the ongoing dialogue regarding reading instruction. Her now classic book *Learning to Read: The Great Debate* (1967) stated that, for early literacy, learning to decode by direct instruction in phonics yielded better reading achievement results than any other method in use at that time. Chall revised her book in 1983; it reaffirmed her earlier findings, as did continuing research by Johnson and Bauman (2001), Williams (1985), Jacobs, Baldwin, and Chall (1990), Samuels and Farstrup (1992), Stahl (1992), and Adams and Bruck (1995).

During the 1980s and 1990s, however, the argument for a more motivational, holistic approach to literacy continued to have great popularity, despite the many published reports supporting the conclusions of Chall's work. Even the federal government became involved in the continuing public discussions. The government commissioned a widely respected independent reading investigator, Marilyn Adams, to restudy and once again report on what was becoming known as "The Great Debate." Adams's published report, *Beginning to Read: Thinking and Learning about Print* (1990), again lent support to Chall's perspective, but even Chall's subsequent critique, published a year later, defending her original findings, did little to resolve the controversy surrounding the issue.

Despite the findings of Chall, Adams, and others, when the whole language movement was predominant in American schools in the 1980s, many educators assumed that learning to read was a "natural" process, much like learning to talk—a set of skills that most children acquire with no direct tutoring and with apparent ease, if not joy. The concomitant practice in many classrooms, therefore, was to create a literacy-rich environment in early childhood classrooms, filled with plenty of signs, books, posters, captions, and language play. It was expected then that reading would simply flourish in a natural way, in the same way that children learned to speak by being spoken to and having their first words and phrases elaborated upon. In truth, some children *do* learn to read in this way— with plenty of print-rich stimulation but no direct instruction. The downside of this unscientific approach to learning to read is that many children who were taught in this way were never successful at cracking the code. They needed more direct instruction.

Science offers compelling reasons why so many young children failed to learn to read using a purely whole language philosophy. The National Institute of Child Health and Development (NICHD) has studied normal reading development and reading difficulties in children for 35 years. NICHD-supported

Regardless of the method of reading instruction, children benefit from a literacy-rich environment at school and at home.

researchers have studied more than 10,000 children, published more than 2,500 articles, and written more than 50 books that present the results of 20 large-scale longitudinal studies and more than 1500 smaller-scale experimental and cross-sectional studies. Some children were studied for 15 years, others for at least five years (Fletcher & Lyon, 2002).

The results of such in-depth scientific research have impacted the way we teach beginning reading. We know from research that reading is a language-based activity. We also know that reading does *not* always develop naturally, and for many children, specific decoding, word recognition, and comprehension strategies must be taught explicitly and systematically. The evidence also strongly suggests that teachers can foster reading development by providing young children with explicit instruction in concepts about print, age-appropriate vocabulary, the structure of the English language, phonemic awareness, phonics, and spelling skills. Indeed, the scientific research that suggests that learning how to read is *not* a natural process is so overwhelming that it caused Keith Stanovich (1994) to write, "That direct instruction in alphabetic coding facilitates early reading acquisition is one of the most well-established connections in all of behavior science" (pp. 285–286).

Then, in 2000, the National Reading Panel (NRP) added another scientific voice to the discussion. They issued a report in response to a congressional mandate to help parents, teachers, and policy makers identify key skills and methods essential for reading achievement. The Panel was charged with reviewing research in reading instruction, focusing on the foundational years between kindergarten and third grade, and identifying methods that were consistently associated with reading success. In addition to identifying effective practices, the Panel identified several components as essential to early reading success:

1. **Phonemic awareness:** the ability to hear and identify sounds in spoken words.
2. **Phonics:** the relationship between the letters of written language and the sounds of spoken language.
3. **Fluency:** the capacity to read text accurately, quickly, and with expression.
4. **Vocabulary acquisition:** the words children must know to communicate effectively.
5. **Comprehension:** the ability to understand and gain meaning from what has been read.

The work of the NRP challenged educators to consider the evidence of effectiveness when teaching the five components as they make decisions about the content and structure of programs designed to promote early literacy.

Influenced by the NRP's report, the No Child Left Behind (NCLB) Act of 2001 mandated higher standards and greater accountability throughout the nation's school systems. This bill also contained a new program called Reading First, designed to help every child to become a successful reader.

The rationale behind Reading First was summarized in a document disseminated by the U.S. Department of Education (U.S. Department of Education, 2006), which reasoned that research has consistently identified the basic skills that young children need to become proficient readers (National Reading Panel, 2000). Additionally, teachers across many states and districts have demonstrated that scientifically based reading instruction can and does work with children, even those considered the most difficult children to teach. Therefore, the initiative called for such approaches to be used to help every child become a reader by the third grade.

Under Reading First, states could receive significant federal funding to improve reading achievement through the establishment of high-quality, comprehensive reading instruction for all children in kindergarten through third grade. "High quality," according to the bill, meant that in such programs, the children were to be taught to read systematically and explicitly by including the five components (phonemic awareness, phonics, fluency, vocabulary acquisition, and comprehension) identified by the Report of the National Reading Panel (2000) as being essential for early reading success.

Some leading experts in the field of literacy, however, believe that the NRP missed an important opportunity to clarify and enumerate the kind of instructional conditions that lead to effective reading development. When the panel failed to discuss the lack of relationship between phonics instruction and reading comprehension beyond first grade (Allington, 2004; Garan, 2004; Krashen, 2004), they may have overemphasized the importance of systematic and explicit phonics instruction to the exclusion of attention to providing ample opportunities for children to practice comprehension strategies by engaging in extensive reading. Indeed, a widespread concern with the NRP report, as well as subsequent policy initiatives, appears to be that reading is treated as a series of skills, with little appreciation for the instructional conditions necessary to promote sustained reading comprehension and enjoyment. Phonics instruction clearly has an important role in early reading instruction, as we shall see in the following chapters, but it should be taught early and only as a means to an end—*never* as an end in itself. The purpose of reading, as we shall see in this text, is not simply to be able to decode fluently, but to gain meaning, enjoyment, and information from all forms of text.

The central thrust of these reform efforts in literacy instruction has been to implement an accountability system based on the specification of content standards, together with the use of high-stakes assessments to monitor students' attainment of these standards. In this way, underperforming schools (and teachers) could be identified and penalized if they failed to respond rapidly to literacy interventions. Although this high-stakes standardized testing doesn't begin until third grade, it has dramatically affected curriculum in early childhood classrooms. In many classrooms, the emphasis on accountability measures has prompted a shift away from a developmentally appropriate focus on intellectual, physical, social, and emotional development in early childhood programs and toward an explicit instruction model limited to discrete skills.

A large number of literacy experts have decried this shift that devotes large amounts of time to teacher-led drill on literacy subskills as being overly academic (Neuman & Roskos, 2005). This instruction includes drill on phonics and isolated sounds as well as vocabulary words (Holdaway, 2005; Venable, 2006). Many children are no longer given the opportunity to learn letter sounds from authentic encounters with language, nursery rhymes, songs, and stories; instead, they receive a diet of decodable text (which incorporates the exact phonics elements children are learning) taught with scripted programs. To monitor student progress, teachers are expected to administer regular assessments of their phonemic awareness, phonics, fluency, vocabulary, and comprehension abilities. In many schools, the five components are taught sequentially, focusing initially on decoding words and reading quickly but ignoring comprehension (Venable, 2006). Phonics instruction clearly has an important role in early reading, but as far as reading comprehension is concerned, the NRP report itself documented that it rapidly reaches a point of diminishing returns after first grade (Cummins, Brown, & Sayers, 2007). Because of the panel's failure to explore the lack of relationship between phonics instruction and reading comprehension beyond first grade, they overemphasized the importance of explicit, systematic phonics teaching and neglected the beneficial nature of extensive reading and comprehension. Although the reforms mandate only "scientifically based" reading instruction, scientific research *does* in fact support the importance of extensive reading (Krashen, 2004), together with an instructional emphasis on reading comprehension (Pressley, Duke, & Boling, 2004), to maximize reading comprehension development.

Literacy practitioners know that the process of becoming literate requires considerably more than phonemic awareness, phonics, fluency, vocabulary, and comprehension. They know that, at its core, reading is a meaning-making endeavor. As an alternative to skills-based instruction, which emphasizes skills out of context—to the detriment of meaning, purpose, and enjoyment—the present text supports a more balanced, comprehensive approach to literacy instruction. My concern that NCLB has the effect of oversimplifying literacy is shared by a number of other practitioners (see e.g., Allington, 2004; Coles, 2003; Cummins et al., 2007; Garan, 2004; Krashen, 2004).

Comprehensive literacy instruction is a complex concept. We are all aware just how difficult it is to maintain a balanced diet in our fast-food society; so it is with a balanced approach to literacy. Balanced literacy instruction must take into account many continua, including authenticity of instruction—how many real-life applications are included—and the teacher's level of assistance, as dictated by students' needs. Balance in curricular control takes into account how much input the children and others are granted in deciding on the curriculum. Balance in classroom talk considers how much of the talk is teacher directed. Balance also needs to be considered when selecting materials: for example, the amount of fiction versus nonfiction text that is used and the blend of both predictable and decodable texts. Advocates of balanced instruction recognize that effective literacy instruction is multifaceted, rather than based on one position (e.g., phonics) or another, and that it necessarily addresses all of the criteria mentioned above.

APPROACHES TO TEACHING READING

Parents and caregivers of children in public schools, other interested citizens, and students new to the field of education may read about the different approaches used to teach reading and form an opinion without really understanding the underlying concepts. Many are not quite sure what is meant by terms such as "phonics" and "holistic." It might be helpful to further explore these concepts.

Phonics Instruction and the Transmission Model

The term "phonics" is much used but not always entirely understood—especially by those not directly involved in literacy education. For centuries, dating as early as the Greek and Phoenician civilizations three thousand years ago, most approaches to early literacy instruction in alphabetic languages have included letter sequences and how such sequences corresponded to speech patterns (Mathews, 1966). Such methods, focusing on sound–symbol relationships, are what educators generally refer to as "phonics." Valentin Ickelsamer, a German teacher, is credited with being the first educator in relatively modern times (the early 1500s) to introduce a phonics approach to early literacy (Balmuth, 1982). Even today, phonics approaches to early literacy instruction show evidence of the influence of Ickelsamer's early ideas.

Phonics instruction has sometimes been associated with the **transmission model** of instruction. In other words, when using this model in its strictest sense, teachers assume the responsibility of directly "transmitting" information, such as the knowledge of letter sounds and symbols, to their students through explicit instruction and systematic teaching of the code that is the foundation of the English alphabet. Other approaches using transmission include rote instruction of sight words and the memorization of lists of word families, such as those words containing "oi": voice, noise, moist, and so forth. Such instruction is also frequently called "skills-based," as its emphasis is on presenting the smallest parts of our language—the letters and sounds—in isolation, often long before showing children the whole picture of how enjoyable the reading act can be.

■ transmission model

Over the years, phonics instruction has at times been perceived negatively due to additional unfortunate practices that included more drills on isolated skills than were necessary and worksheets unrelated to real reading (see Figure 2.1), often to the distress of children who were already proficient readers. Phonics instruction has also been criticized when it has focused on the teaching of a litany of abstract rules, too many of which have limited application in our language and are lost on very young children who can memorize the rules but who have little idea what they actually mean.

The positive role of phonics instruction

Researchers and educators seeking a balance have long been interested in the positive role that the appropriate amount of phonics instruction can play in early literacy. Many studies have been conducted in an effort to determine the

figure   2.1   An early workbook activity.

Lesson 24

MAKING WORDS

1. Choose a letter from the 4 in each box that will make a real word when you put it in the square.

| l s | ☐ ate | | r h | ☐ une |
| t n | ☐ ame | | n t | ☐ ear |

| n m | ☐ eed | | s l | ☐ eat |
| f s | ☐ ace | | b p | ☐ ike |

2. Write a common word with these.

ade   ean   ale   ote
aid   een   ail   oat

Source: Your Child Can Learn to Read by Margaret McEathron. New York: Grosset & Dunlap, 1952.

value of direct instruction in the sounds and letters of the English alphabet when integrated into a total, literature-rich program.

At about the same time that Jeanne Chall was publicizing the results of her studies in *The Great Debate,* the U. S. Office of Education Cooperative Research Program in First-Grade Reading Instruction was initiated (Adams, 1990). Funded by this office, two prominent researchers, Bond and Dykstra (1967), published the results of a landmark research study involving many first-grade classrooms and the literacy methods employed by the teachers. In many ways, this early landmark study was the first of its kind to lend support to a notion that a balance between phonics and a meaning-based approach just might represent ideal literacy instruction. The results of the study suggested that approaches to reading that included, but were not limited to, a form of systematic phonics instruction were somewhat more effective at producing high-word recognition performance in learners than other methods used in the study. The data from the study also indicated that including an emphasis on meaning and a connection to the children's lives produced even greater gains in reading achievement. In addition, writing instruction was found to be an important factor promoting positive results in literacy acquisition, or the ability to read and write. Perhaps the most unexpected finding of the studies, however, was that the crucial factor in teaching a child to read was not the *method* that was used but that instruction was delivered by a committed and competent teacher.

In *Becoming a Nation of Readers,* a report by the Commission on Reading in the 1980s, phonics instruction was still being advocated:

> The purpose of phonics instruction is to teach children the alphabetic principle. The ultimate goal is for this to become an operating principle so that young readers consistently use information about the relationship between letters and sounds to assist in the identification of known words and to independently figure out unknown words. (p. 73)

The Commission continued by stating that children then need to immediately practice reading the new words they have encountered in meaningful context (Anderson, Hilbert, Scott, & Wilkinson, 1985). The work of these researchers suggests that the transmitting of phonics could be followed by use of a transactional instructional strategy, using student-centered group discussion of the reading material. This report also seemed to offer an early nod toward a balanced, comprehensive approach in literacy instruction.

Current leading educators advocate a "less is more" approach suggesting that teachers offer small doses of direct, systematically taught phonics instruction in the primary grades only to those children who need this structure to make sense of print. Many children come to school with a wide repertoire of word-unlocking skills gained from much experience with and exposure to print. Such educators urge teachers to teach a wide range of comprehension strategies, limiting the teaching of phonics generalizations to those that are the most useful and consistent. Instead of having children memorize phonics generalizations, teachers are encouraged to help children discover the recurring spelling patterns in English words. Finally, educators recommend connecting what is learned in phonics to specifically designed books called **decodable texts** that incorporate the exact phonic elements children are learning, providing immediate reinforcement (Shefelbine, 1995). They also encourage teachers to share an abundance of quality children's literature enthusiastically. With this streamlined, less-is-more approach to early phonics instruction, the overall effort is directed toward the goal of developing readers who can learn to figure out words quickly so that attention can soon be focused on meaning and enjoyment (Adams, 1990; Routman & Butler, 1995; Shefelbine, 1995; Stahl, 1992).

■ decodable texts

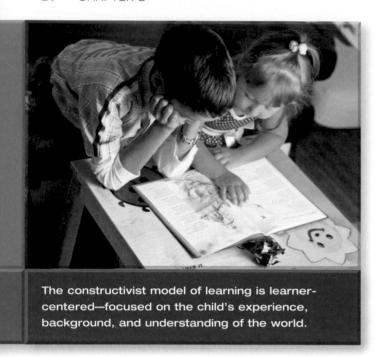

The constructivist model of learning is learner-centered—focused on the child's experience, background, and understanding of the world.

We know now that balance in the teaching of reading is possible only when the teaching of skills does not become an end in itself, but rather a means to an end: reading for personal meaning, acquisition of information, and enjoyment.

Holistic Instruction and the Transactional Model

There have been many terms for and definitions given to holistic approaches throughout the literature on literacy, without a clear consensus about what such terms actually encompass. In reality, whole language, the most recent manifestation of a holistic, meaning-based approach, was not an approach or a practice at all, but rather a perspective or philosophical stance. Whole language teachers were not focused on transmitting knowledge to their students, but rather negotiating with children about their individual ideas concerning what they were reading and writing—in other words, adopting a more collaborative, **transactional model** while integrating the four language modes of reading, writing, listening, and speaking into all the curricular areas. Reading was offered not in stilted basal readers, but in high-quality children's literature. Whole language teachers believed, too, that reading occurs in the brain of the child rather than on the page, as proponents of skills-based instruction seem to suggest. Indeed, whole language as a transactional, child-centered model elevates children to "collaborators in the quest for knowledge" (Goodman, 1986).

transactional model ■

Later, this whole language philosophy began to be recognized as a holistic way of teaching that, unlike phonics (which teaches the sounds of letters and words and then introduces stories), would first get children interested in great literature and then proceed to the parts. Goodman (1986), often considered the father of the whole language movement, argued that skilled reading involves gaining meaning from the context of whole passages rather than simply reading words as individual entities. Smith (1971) concurred and went on to suggest that readers use visual and sound cues only minimally; he believed that visual processing does not take place with every word and that readers do not process each word completely (Smith, 1971, 1992). Readers, according to this view, sample just enough text to get meaning from a passage.

constructivist model of learning ■

Holistic instruction has also often been associated with the **constructivist model of learning** (Au, 1997). This perspective encourages children to "actively construct their own understandings of text material" through personal experimentation with words. Learning, in the constructivist model, is learner-centered, or focused on the child and his experience, background, and understanding of the world. Thus, children become motivated by immediately seeing the large picture of what reading can be, and then they go on to acquire discrete skills as needed. With this model, the teacher continually observes how each child thinks about reading by listening to the child's oral reading. For example, José makes wild guesses about words based solely on the way they look and sound; this practice tells the teacher that José thinks reading is little more than word-calling. Lydia, on the other hand, constantly rereads sentences in a story saying, "That doesn't make sense!" revealing that she sees reading as meaningful but may need help in acquiring specific decoding skills.

In transactional, holistic approaches, quality children's literature is more commonly used for instruction than basals. Literature often takes the form of predictable books that have rhyme, rhythm, and repetition, allegedly allowing children to learn the words by chiming in with their guesses. The stories are often read to children using big books, or those with considerably larger-than-usual format, suitable for reading aloud to a small group of children as they sit cross-legged on the floor. The intent of this exposure to quality literature is not only to increase children's motivation to read but, through its superior story structure, to also provide an excellent model for children's own writing. Children are encouraged to write about topics of their own choosing by using temporary writing or **experimental spelling**—a kind of sounding out of new words. This experimentation with words is supposed to help children learn to decipher the sound and letter relationships of the English language.

■ experimental spelling

Finally, free choice in activities emphasizing reading, writing, listening, viewing, visually representing, together with ongoing assessment, are important aspects of a transactional, holistic approach to literacy. Students' freedom to choose what they wish to read and topics they wish to write about is stressed as a way to ensure that language will always be purposeful and meaningful to each individual. Authentic, ongoing assessment includes observational techniques and analysis of oral reading to determine how children are thinking about reading, what strategies they are employing, and which ones might need to be taught. Such devices are deemed superior to standardized tests because they are individualized and can be interpreted by a teacher who can see the performance in light of *all* the child's strengths and needs. Authentic assessment sometimes includes a **portfolio** that contains many samples of the work the child has done over time, selected in tandem with the student (Clay, 1990).

■ portfolio

Today practitioners are exhorted to avoid "false dichotomies" in reading instruction, such as pitting the transmission phonics approach against a holistic/transactional approach, homogeneous grouping against heterogeneous grouping, or isolated versus contextualized skill instruction. Experts suggest that practitioners can—and frequently do—combine choices rather than choose one over the other. The more important scientific question, according to recent research (and the focus of this text), involves finding the appropriate balance between seemingly opposite viewpoints (Spear-Swerling & Sternberg, 1999).

A Quest for Balance:
Toward a Comprehensive Approach

A comprehensive approach to literacy includes the best elements of a transactional (holistic) and a transmissive (phonics) approach to literacy instruction. Both of these approaches clearly have much to offer for the beginning teacher of young children. It is this author's view that the two can be used together to create a dynamic, synergistic program. Research provides support for the notion that instruction from a committed teacher who can integrate a program of explicit, systematic phonics into a curriculum rich with quality literature, easily decodable text, and many meaningful writing experiences will result in children who not only know how to read but who do so willingly, beyond the classroom doors (Stahl, 1992). Most reading educators have long agreed that a certain amount of instruction in phonics is vital in learning how to decode automatically and that incorporating the basic elements of a holistic, meaning-based program with such instruction will increase children's enthusiasm toward reading as a favored activity (Wink, 2005).

Strong teachers tend to see any new movement in literacy, such as the trend toward a comprehensive approach, not as a pendulum swing, but as a positive spiraling in which more exciting new information about teaching children to read is acquired each time the focus shifts. Echoing this belief, Goodman (1997) muses, "When people talk to me about cycles and pendulum swings, it helps me remember that progress is rarely in a straight line and that knowledge takes a long time to be accommodated, absorbed, and put to work" (p. 596).

More optimism was offered by an interest group of the International Reading Association (IRA) called "The Balanced Reading Group," which advocated a comprehensive approach that incorporates the best of the two perspectives. Former president of the IRA, Susan Glazer (1995), adds that phonics should be considered a critical piece of any holistic, meaning-based system, and that reading has always had three discrete components, or cueing systems: syntax (grammar); phonology (sounds); and semantics (meaning). Glazer maintains that it is clear that these three components cannot be covered by either a skills-based or a holistic approach alone; both are necessary for children to learn to read successfully.

Adding support to the comprehensive approach to literacy is the fact that current thinking on phonics instruction is not as extreme as once perceived. Most phonics proponents today support *streamlined phonics,* in which children are helped to become independent, automatic decoders but are not inadvertently discouraged from reading by an overabundance of worksheets, drills, and abstract rules with little application. Current thinking suggests that efficient phonics instruction that is systematic and explicit gets children decoding quickly so that they can soon turn their attention to more important and enjoyable reading tasks (Shefelbine, 1995; Wink, 2005). Indeed, it appears that thinking has evolved such that the question is now not *whether* to teach phonics but *how* best to teach phonics, within a literature-rich classroom that also stresses background knowledge, comprehension strategies, and an enormous amount of reading (Combs, 2010; Jalongo, 2011).

Stahl (1992) offers nine guidelines for what he considers as "exemplary phonics instruction" to be used in tandem with other more holistic, meaning-based methods. He urges that such balanced instruction should:

- build on a child's rich background in how print functions;
- build on a foundation of sound awareness (phonemics);

- be clear and direct;
- be integrated into a total reading program;
- focus on reading words rather than memorizing rules;
- include the study of beginning sounds and ending sounds;
- include practice with sound symbol relationships through spelling;
- develop word recognition strategies by focusing on the internal structure of words; and
- develop automatic word recognition skills quickly so that children can devote their attention to meaning and enjoyment, not individual words.

There is even more reason to believe that current thinking on reading instruction has evolved from the philosophy first articulated by Goodman in the 1960s. The present text advocates a comprehensive program of broad early literacy curricula that would include phonemic awareness, phonics, rich literature-based activities, and a variety of comprehension strategies. Specifically, such a comprehensive perspective would include:

- a wide range of reading materials on many developmental levels in English and the other languages of the children in the class;
- direct teaching of concepts relating to print;
- explicit instruction in the concept that words are a series of speech sounds;
- cueing systems, including graphophonics, semantics, and syntax;
- explicit instruction in the strategies that skilled readers use;
- critical thinking strategies;
- vocabulary development;
- fluency through encouragement of wide reading at each student's independent reading level; and
- thorough and ongoing assessment to ensure that instruction is compatible with individual needs. (Pearson, Raphael, Benson, & Madda, 2007)

A comparison of three views of literacy instruction (see Figure 2.2) shows how a comprehensive program might be a selection of the best elements of both educational philosophies used to create Mrs. Ramon's first-grade program (outlined in depth in Chapter 15).

On a personal note, through visits to hundreds of primary grade classrooms over the past few years, I have observed that many extraordinary teachers in the field now use and have *always* used phonics skills instruction within a transactional framework. With certain groups of children, such teachers will stress one approach more than others, and for some children, they find it is best to use one approach exclusively. It seems clear to these dedicated professionals that this long-standing pedagogical dialogue will cease only when teachers are treated as knowledgeable authorities regarding their pupils. They must be allowed to decide, based on the individual needs in their classroom, which instructional methods are most appropriate (Bialostok, 1997).

figure 2.2 A comparison of three views of literacy instruction.

PHONICS	HOLISTIC	A COMPREHENSIVE APPROACH
(Skills-Based, Transmission Model)	(Meaning-Based, Transactional Model)	(An Interface Between the Best of Both Stances)
Emphasis on product	*Emphasis on process*	*Emphasis on process and product*
Language broken into bite-sized pieces (letters and words)	Language is kept whole in connected text	Whole–part–whole model
Skills in sequence taught directly	Phonics often taught incidentally	Direct, explicit phonics instruction completed by end of 2nd grade
Phonics taught up to 3rd and 4th grades	Strategies modeled in context	Skills and strategies modeled alone and in context
Word families used for memorization	Real literature used; often no basal text	Phonics based on internal structure of words
Teacher makes curricular decisions	Literature study groups	Skills based on need per assessment
Reading groups based on ability; inflexible	Predictable books and big books used for incidental phonics instruction	Decodable text used for phonics instruction; predictable text for comprehension
Traditional basal texts with controlled vocabulary	Children choose recreational reading material	Quality literature for listening comprehension
Decodable text exclusively	Shared and guided reading for instruction	Free reading time with choice
Discussion questions from teacher or basal text	Paired reading	Shared and guided reading with embedded phonics instruction
Sight words memorized by children	Drama, poetry, and songs used for enjoyment	Emphasis on spelling as a key to phonics
Directed reading of basal text for instruction	Writing topics chosen by children	Word walls, word building, word sorting, word hunts utilized
Writing topics chosen by teacher	Writers' workshop	Writers' workshop
Worksheets for reinforcement of skills	Journals used for response to literature	Direct, explicit instruction in comprehension strategies
Workbooks used for response to basal text	Discussion questions come from children	Drama, poetry, and songs used for phonemic awareness and enjoyment
Traditional spelling programs	Children encouraged to "invent" spelling	Journals for personal writing and literature response; logs for content areas
Growth is quantitatively measured (formal assessment only)	Growth is observable (informal assessment)	Writing as experimentation with sound–letter relationships
		Experimental spelling and instruction in correct spelling
		Flexible grouping systems
		Paired reading, buddy reading, and dyad reading
		Assessment based on measurement and observation (informal and formal)

BALANCE AND TEACHING TO STANDARDS

the standards movement is another development that is affecting education. In most school districts, today's teachers are asked to teach to standards set by their state or district. **Standards,** simply put, are broad curricular goals containing specific grade-level targets or benchmarks. These standards, as they underpin the curriculum, stipulate what the state or district wants children to know and be able to do as a result of schooling. Teachers often ask how addressing standards can lead to a balanced, high-quality literacy program. The answer has to do with commitment. To value and use something in the teaching profession, educators must first understand what it is and what it can mean for them and their students, and then commit to doing it.

■ standards

Historically, curricula in schools have been driven by many influences. Usually an administrator, a committee of teachers, or the principal has chosen the textbooks for a particular grade or subject. Teachers then used the textbook as their resource for delivering instruction. In essence, this gave publishing companies the main responsibility for researching and establishing what is important for children to know and be able to do. Many teachers were dependent upon the adopted basal reader as their blueprint for teaching literacy (see Figure 2.3). This

An excerpt from a basal reader, 1966.   *figure* **2.3**

swing

Here I go, Mark.
See me go up in the swing.
I like this swing.
I like to go up.
I like to go down.
Come on, Daddy, come on.

Source: Outdoors and In by M. O'Donnell and B. H. Van Roekel. California State Series. Sacramento: California State Dept. of Education, 1966.

dependence often made teachers feel compelled to teach page by page; rather than teaching according to true learning goals, some teachers felt their goal was to race to finish the basal reader by the end of the school year. The published basals might have been of excellent quality and based on national standards, but there was an inherent problem with this scenario: Although it established consistency within a district's curriculum, such an approach led to an emphasis on uniform materials, which sometimes resulted in a "cookbook" approach to teaching literacy. Teachers were sometimes left out of the important process of having input into, ownership over, and a thorough understanding of the decisions about the skills and knowledge their particular students needed.

State and district standards have proved problematic because there are many differences in student expectations between states and even between districts in the same states. The quality of the standards have varied widely from state to state. The state standards have now given way to the latest trend in education reform, which is a set of national core standards for education.

The Common Core State Standards Initiative, as it is called, is headed by the National Governors Association and the Council of Chief State School Officers but has had input from teachers, civil rights groups, English-language learners and the College Board, among others. Similar in intent to NCLB, it is an effort to create the next generation of K–12 standards to help ensure that all students are college- and career-ready in literacy by no later than the end of high school. (See www.corestandards.org.)

The standards apply to English language arts, history, social studies, science, and math. They include specific goals, organized by grade and subject. By the end of kindergarten, children are expected to be able to decode simple words with c/v/c (consonant, vowel, consonant) and silent /e/ patterns and to know by sight most of the high-frequency words. As another example, fifth-grade reading standards expect students to be able to explain how similes and metaphors give meaning and rhythm to a poem. By the fourth and fifth grade, students are expected to read books like *Alice's Adventures in Wonderland* and *The Black Stallion*. By ninth and tenth grades, students are expected to be reading William Shakespeare and John Steinbeck or the equivalent (Sacramento Bee, 2010).

In June 2010, a group of educators released the first draft of the proposed set of national core standards for children in kindergarten through twelfth grade. These national standards received support from 48 states, the District of Columbia, two territories, and the Obama administration, but the standards are not without their critics. One concern being expressed by teachers and other practitioners regarding the new standards is that children won't be able to learn at their own speed and according to their own individual development under a set of national core standards. "Once, schools gave youngsters a chance to learn how to read according to their own development. Now, a child who still can't read by the end of first grade is in deep trouble from which it can be hard to emerge," a second-grade teacher recently lamented to me. She added that the standards focus on basic literacy and math, ignoring other essential subjects like the arts and physical education—much the same complaints that teachers had about NCLB.

Skeptics also worried that national standards might result in a "lowest common denominator" approach, but this appears not to be the case. The final product, with some exceptions, has been well received nationally. Education critic E. D. Hirsch, author of *The Schools We Need and Why We Don't Have Them* (2005), submits that the core standards represent a real advance over even the best of existing state standards.

The task placed before literacy teachers today, then, is to be aware of the standards for the grade level they teach and to employ a wide range of instructional strategies, materials, and methods to ensure that all students meet the established learning goals. Again, a balanced, comprehensive approach of imparting the skills of literacy and offering many opportunities to use those skills appears to be the optimal way to meet the learning targets set by such standards.

THE IMPACT OF TECHNOLOGY ON LITERACY

finally, a phenomenon is occurring that must be acknowledged in any text addressing the issue of comprehensiveness in literacy instruction. The computer has become an integral tool in U.S. classrooms and culture (Gambrell, 2005). As the focus has shifted away from an almost exclusive use of story-type reading to using more informational text for early readers, at the same time there has occurred a decided change in the way most people in this country read and obtain their information: they spend time on the Internet that was previously spent in more traditional reading pursuits.

Reading at Risk (National Endowment for the Arts, 2004) decries a decline in the number of books that adults are reading in their leisure time. According to this report, fewer than half the people surveyed reported that they read any literary works at all for pleasure in a year's time. However, Vogt (2004) implored teachers to think more broadly about the possible implications of the findings of this report. Does "reading" entail only reading of "literature"? With personal computers in most homes, schools, and businesses, much time is spent—by children and adults—interacting with vast amounts of information on the Internet. Also, using the Internet and its inherent links often encourages readers to move beyond the original article they are seeking and surf through related articles, blogs, chat responses, and so forth. Reading on the original topic, therefore, may be enhanced by the very nature of the Internet, exposing the reader to multiple versions, reactions to, and interpretations of the original article. It is quite possible that the Internet and its ability to expose ("link," if you will) readers to broader resources may lead to a populace with more reading experience, whose comprehension of any topic they are exploring becomes decidedly richer and deeper.

WWW.

Integrating literacy and technology

http://ctell.uconn.edu/cases.htm

SUMMARY

unlike a purely political debate or any such hypothetical argument pertaining to abstract ideas and theoretical outcomes, the ongoing dialogue about how we should teach our nation's children to read is concrete, crucial, and involves the very core of our future. Educators who have taken sides on this issue have done so with candor and a good deal of questioning, observation of children in classrooms, and a heavy dose of soul-searching.

Most teachers do not take their tasks lightly; the ultimate mission of teachers is, after all, to challenge, assist, and encourage each child in his or her charge to become a good reader, responding to text in meaningful ways, both for enjoyment and for gaining knowledge. With the constant enhancement of knowledge about literacy instruction, we are more than ever realizing the best ways to reach these goals. We have learned that fluent reading requires a basic understanding of the sounds and symbols of our alphabetic language. We are now heeding the substantive body of research suggesting that early, systematic phonics instruction that moves from decoding text to abundant opportunities to read, write, and share ideas can help teachers accomplish their goals of teaching every child to read.

The charge of the teacher of this millennium, then, is to become a wise diagnostician and to provide excellent literacy teaching and intervention for each child. Every child can learn to read and write. The path to literacy may begin with the presence of explicit, systematic phonics instruction and include instruction in phonemic awareness, fluency, vocabulary, and comprehension, but always in the context of a print-rich environment that invites children to explore the world of literature and information while enjoying the thrill of penning their own ideas to be eagerly shared with others. The real question, it seems, is not whether systematic skills instruction should be part of the total program; research continues to strongly support the inclusion of such instruction for beginning readers. More appropriate questions appear to concern how much skills instruction children should receive and under what conditions, and how such instruction can be integrated into a program rich with literature and meaning. This book is an attempt to answer those key questions.

questions
for journal writing and discussion

1. Discuss in your own words the current issues involving the relative merits of phonics and a meaning-based approach to literacy instruction. How would you explain both approaches to the parents of a primary-age youngster? How might you convince them that an ideal program can contain elements from both perspectives?

2. Describe what you remember about your own early reading experiences. Would you characterize the instruction you recall as meaning-based, phonics, or a combination of the two?

3. React to the often-heard statement, "In education, the pendulum constantly swings back and forth from a meaning-based approach to a phonics approach to literacy instruction." What do you think is the impetus for such change when it occurs? Would you characterize the cyclical changes as static "swings" or as progressive "spirals" toward better literacy instruction?

suggestions
for projects and field activities

1. Scan current literacy journals such as *The Reading Teacher* or *Language Arts* for articles on prevalent practices in early literacy instruction. Visit the website for the Common Core State Standards or the standards for your particular state. Summarize your findings and report them to your class. How do the issues raised relate to the issues addressed in this chapter? How do the literacy journals respond to the government mandates on teaching reading?

2. Observe three different first-grade teachers instructing their students in beginning literacy. How might you characterize the methods they are using? In what ways are these educators responding to recent changes in educational methods? How do each of the educators describe the approaches they are using? What are their reasons for making the choices they did?

3. Survey several older adults in your area. Ask them how they think literacy is being taught in the local schools. From where have they obtained their information? Ask them what their recollections are about how they were taught to read. Do they believe the methods used when they were in school were superior to those used today? What conclusions can you draw from this survey?

www.
Common Core Standards
www.corestandards.org

chapter 3

Emergent Literacy

From Birth to Conventional Literacy

focus questions

- What are the stages of language acquisition?

- What are some of the literacy related concepts that come into play when children from birth to kindergarten share in literacy experiences?

- How is emergent literacy defined, and how does this differ from reading readiness?

- What are some of the factors that help determine whether a child will be successful in learning to read and write?

- What are the major influences on children's early literacy development?

  - How can parents and teachers best foster the development of emergent literacy?

Not all plums ripen on the same day, nor are all children able to formally read and write in the same month, year, or day. Just observe three-and-a-half-year-old Sam, on an errand with his mother. "Oh, there's Walmart!" exclaims Sam, as his mother drives into the parking lot of the local discount store. "Hey, there's a car just like ours!" he continues. "It says 'C–h–e–v–r–o–l–e–t'! Does that say 'Chevy,' Mommy?" Later, at home, Sam scribbles on a sheet of paper and informs his mother that he has written a letter to his cousin in Denver. His mother smiles approvingly and admires the child's "writing." Sam's mother feels confident that her child is showing real signs of being ready to learn to read and write.

In another part of town, in the local elementary school, five-year-old Bronson squirms at her desk as the kindergarten teacher, Mrs. McNeil, points out letters in the alphabet. An active, yet shy child, Bronson is busy daydreaming about climbing her favorite tree and is fiddling with the plastic dinosaur she has secreted in her pocket. Her parents worry because, although her older brother and sister caught on quickly to literacy activities, Bronson has never seemed to enjoy being read to nor has she asked how to spell her name. She seldom uses a pencil or crayons and seems to shun any activity requiring fine motor skills.

Can Mrs. McNeil help Bronson become literate along with her classmates, and can she kindle the enthusiasm for learning of her younger contemporary, Sam? Yes. Is Bronson destined to fail at reading and writing? No. We now know that literacy is an active process that can be helped to develop at the child's own rate and not something that happens spontaneously with time, like the aging of fine wine!

INTRODUCTION

reading is a learned set of strategies. For many individuals, it is *not* a spontaneous development (Adams, Treiman, & Pressley, 1997). Children who fall behind in reading at an early age—kindergarten and first grade—have, in the past, tended to fall further behind over time (Fletcher et al., 1994). Such a finding contradicts the once prevalent notion that children begin to learn to read only when they are "ready." But the good news is that most children do not need to lag behind at all in literacy acquisition. There are prerequisite experiences with literacy from which all children—especially children like Bronson—can benefit.

Awareness of language patterns and how sounds go together in the English language can and should be fostered through enjoyable language activities because such awareness is not innately developed (Grossen, 1997). Beginning at birth, virtually every early learner is ready for some positive experiences with spoken and written language. Focusing their attention on sounds, print, words, ideas, and conversations in a playful way can help preschool and kindergarten children to develop the background they will soon need to decode or unlock unknown words. However, if the children who do fall behind do not begin to become aware of sounds in language and are not offered experiences with literacy through active listening and oral reproduction activities, they are likely to fall further behind as the demands of reading become more and more complex.

LANGUAGE ACQUISITION: AN OVERVIEW

he first stage of **emergent literacy** occurs long before any formal reading or writing takes place. Literacy begins with the child's first utterances, as language miraculously begins to support the child's ability to think. A child's first words are among the most frequently documented joys of parenthood. The language acquisition journey, beginning in the womb and continuing throughout a child's school years, is also well documented and appears to follow a similar course regardless of linguistic group.

Of significance in today's multilingual classrooms is the fact that a child's second-language acquisition appears to follow the same path. Like spelling development, which will be explored in Chapter 6, language development can be broken down into a series of stages that tend to be associated with specific age levels: prebirth, infancy, holographic stage, telegraphic stage, preschool to fluency, and primary school.

The stages of language development will be discussed here, with the caveat that the descriptions are to be accepted solely as guidelines, because a degree of variation in language acquisition is normal. Awareness of guidelines for language acquisition is important because, when a child's speech development seems to vary significantly from the norm, it is vital that that child be evaluated by a speech and language expert. (Federal law mandates that school districts provide such service at no cost to parents.) Another reason for the importance of understanding first-language development is that, as mentioned earlier, second-language acquisition appears to follow the same stages.

Prebirth

Even in the womb, infants experience and process a vast array of sensory stimuli that promote neurological development in the brain. Of all these neural sensations, response to the mother's voice is the most apparent (Locke, 1993).

Infancy

From birth through about 9 to 18 months, infants set the stage for later speech through a series of speech production–like utterings. At first the infant cries, burps, and makes other reflexive responses that are often called "vegetative." At around 2 months, the infant becomes more interactive and responds to attention with pleasurable sounds, an activity called "cooing." By 6 months, the infant is making more specific sounds with the mouth, lips, and throat, and is beginning to "babble." Gradually, between 9 and 18 months old, infants begin to imitate sounds heard around them, as if they were actually speaking their own language, often using appropriate rhythm, phrasing, and intonational patterns, although no meaningful words are uttered. This vocal activity is referred to as "nonreplicated babbling." At the same time, children at this age often engage in imitation of real speech that they hear, parroting words and phrases they hear, but again, with little or no understanding of the speech. This parrot-like speech behavior is called "echolalia."

The Holographic Stage

Children move from babbling to authentic speech when they first grasp the concept of the function of speech: to communicate. Occurring at about 12 months, this is referred to as the **holographic stage**. They begin with the traditional "first word," which often represents a person, animal, or pet that captures their interest. For many months they use only one word to represent a whole concept, idea, or complete thought. For example, "kitty" might mean the child sees his

holographic stage

pet, or it might mean he is acknowledging any one of a dozen furry animals that live on his street; similarly, "up" might mean "I want you to pick me up," or "The plane is up in the air." According to Vygotsky (1986), with new opportunities, the words' meanings begin to acquire more and more depth.

The Telegraphic Stage

telegraphic stage ∎   Children in the two-word, **telegraphic stage** (occurring at about 12 to 24 months) are able to perform an amazingly greater repertoire of communicative acts with the simple addition of one more word. They can describe objects and actions ("bad dog"), identify locations ("daddy bye-bye"), and suggest who is doing what ("birdie fly"). Children in this stage have learned some important functions of language, according to Halliday (1975), and can now use it to request something ("Brittany cookie!"), to express interest ("pretty baby!"), and to provide information ("my toy!").

Preschool to Fluency

Children between two and five years old generally experience, quite literally, a "language explosion." They begin to speak in whole sentences and phrases and are able to negate sentences ("She is not my friend anymore"). They are able to use language to ask questions beginning with why, how, and who. They interrupt less often and are able to take turns in conversation. Meaning becomes clearer as the child is able to add the morpheme –*ed* to a verb and suddenly refer to events that occurred in the past, and to indicate quantities by adding –*s* to the end of words. Also, at this stage children are able to recognize when they have not been understood and to rephrase their utterance to assure that their meaning has been communicated.

The Texas Education Agency (TEA) has developed extensive prekindergarten curriculum guidelines for language and early literacy.* The guidelines outline specific goals for prekindergarten children, with the goal of ensuring that all three- and four-year-olds have the opportunity to strive toward these goals. Figure 3.1 is an excerpt from these guidelines regarding speech production and discrimination. Other states have developed similar guidelines. Visit the website for your state's department of education, and look for information about its early childhood program or division.

Primary School

By the time children whose first language is English enter kindergarten, they are able to use, to a greater or lesser extent, all the linguistic constructs in the English language. The greatest communicative skill that separates school-aged children from younger children is their ability to use the passive voice ("The dog was put in the kennel while we were on vacation").

Between the ages of five and eight, the focus on communication is enhanced by a growing appreciation for the ability to communicate as its own reward,

---

*The curriculum guide can be accessed at TEA's website: http://ritter.tea.state.tx.us/ed_init/pkguidelines/index.html

Excerpt from the TEA's pre-K language and literacy curriculum.   *figure*   **3.1**

(2) SPEECH PRODUCTION AND SPEECH DISCRIMINATION

Young children must learn to vocalize, pronounce, and discriminate the sounds and words of language. Although most children in prekindergarten can accurately perceive the difference between similar-sounding words, they continue to acquire new sounds and may mispronounce words quite often in their own speech. The ability to produce certain speech sounds such as /s/ and /r/ improves with age. Just as infants and toddlers develop control over the sounds of their first language, young children in ESL settings gradually learn to pronounce the sounds of the English language.

The child:

- perceives differences between similar sounding words (e.g., "coat" and "goat," "three" and "free," [Spanish] "juego" and "fuego"
- produces speech sounds with increasing ease and accuracy
- experiments with new language sounds
- experiments with and demonstrates growing understanding of the sounds and intonation of the English language (ESL).

which explains why children of this age often find riddles and puns so hilarious. The term **metalinguistic ability** refers to the conscious awareness of the sound, meaning, and practical nuances of language. This ability to evaluate a well formed sentence, recognize an alliteration, or appreciate a well-told story is manifested during this period of the child's early schooling.

- metalinguistic ability

LITERACY'S BEGINNINGS

many fortunate children have literacy encounters very early in their lives, beginning as early as infancy, or as toddlers. Although not all infants and toddlers are involved in literacy experiences with their families, most preschoolers acquire foundational literacy concepts that support later formal understanding of reading, writing, speaking, listening, viewing, and visually representing. At least five crucial literacy-related concepts about books can result when children from birth to kindergarten age share literacy experiences, such as listening to books read to them by parents or caregivers or sharing stories or information on an e-reader or computer (McGee & Richgels, 2004). They are:

- Reading is enjoyable.
- Books and other reading materials should be handled in special ways.
- Story and book sharing, whether traditional or electronic, involve a routine.
- Illustrations represent real things.
- Printed words have meaning.

Even very young children learn important concepts about print when caregivers read to them.

Reading is Enjoyable

Probably the most critical concept that children learn as they are read to while sitting on the lap of a beloved parent or caregiver is the idea that reading is a pleasurable experience. This "lap reading" activity can be one of the most emotionally pleasing activities for children. It often builds fond associations that are remembered for a lifetime. Because this activity involves the adult's total concentration, the activity epitomizes quality time; thus children often choose lap reading over playing with favorite toys.

Books Should Be Handled in Special Ways

Even babies learn important concepts about print (see Figure 3.2 on page 53) by having books read to them. They quickly learn how to hold a book right side up and how to help turn the pages. They see that books are handled with respect and that pages are turned carefully with eager anticipation as to what will be found on the next page. They also begin to understand that books contain stories and are not just for turning pages.

Book Sharing and Story Sharing Involve a Routine

Very young children and those who read to them often develop a shared reading routine. Children may initiate a bedtime story, for example, by finding a book they would like to hear and bringing it to their parent or caregiver. Nestled in the arms of the adult, they learn to focus their attention for a prolonged period of time. As the book is being read, the child learns to show his or her knowledge by answering the question "What is that?" or pointing to objects suggested by the adult. Older children respond to specific questions about characters in the book.

Illustrations Represent Real Things

Well before children are able to decipher words and sentences, they become aware of the representational nature of the illustrations in reading materials. Young toddlers begin to see that pictures are symbols for real objects and actions with which they are familiar. Children learn, for example, that the apples they see in a favorite book are not real apples, but that they suggest apples and even have the same name.

Printed Words Have Meaning

Another decisive outcome of early reading-together routines is the nascent understanding that printed words carry messages. This understanding is the very foundation of children's fluency with later comprehension strategies that, as proficient readers, they will use with ease. Young children begin to use visual cues, including written language cues, to make meaning. When they share books and other reading materials with adults, they attempt to understand the words they hear and the visual symbols they see. Although infants do not look at print and read it as an adult does, they do try to figure out what is going on as the adult reads aloud or talks about the pictures in a story.

READING READINESS: A RETROSPECTIVE

cquiring the above literacy-related concepts is perhaps the first step toward becoming aware of and interested in books. The following sections will explore how children emerge into early readers and writers.

In the past few decades, the most pervasive definitions of **reading readiness** have included: (a) being ready to profit from reading instruction beyond the most basic level (Dechant, 1982); (b) readiness to learn to read, as distinguished from a general readiness to learn (Reutzel, 1992); and (c) having the cognitive ability to meet the specific demands of reading tasks (Ausubel, 1959).

■ reading readiness

In the early 1950s educators believed that children had to reach a certain level of intelligence—a mental age of 6.6—and develop nonreading skills such as perceptual–motor skills and large motor coordination before they could actually learn to read (Durkin, 1966). According to this view, children were not ready to begin reading until they had been instructed in the prerequisite reading abilities, also referred to as "readiness activities." Many parents during this time period were amazed when their child was miraculously able to "read" important words such as "McDonald's" or "Target" without having been formally taught them!

This concept of a formal reading readiness period was accompanied by the related belief that literacy should be taught only in formal school settings. Parents were cautioned not to try to teach their children to read at home, lest the children develop bad habits that would later have to be "untaught" by teachers. It was also believed that writing instruction should occur only after children had learned to read.

These beliefs of the early 1950s resulted in the pervasive idea that early childhood was a time during which a specific set of readiness skills should be taught as a prelude to "real" reading (Teale & Sulzby, 1986a). Accordingly, reading readiness tests were developed to assess children's readiness abilities, and reading readiness programs with workbooks full of perceptual-motor activities (e.g., "Draw a line from the dog to the bone") became popular, although they often had little or nothing to do with reading. Kindergarten and the beginning of first grade were devoted to these kinds of prerequisite skills. Writing activities were postponed until even later, often second or third grade. Such beliefs persisted in many school settings (and in some they continue to persist), mostly fading with the dawning of the whole language movement. At that time, teachers began to see firsthand that readiness was not a simple matter of aging. They found they could actually help children become ready to learn how to read and write by building on the language background their learners already possessed and by providing a print-rich environment and language-play activities (Clay, 1991).

Since the 1970s, the paradigm of a time of "reading readiness" has been largely discarded because preschoolers have demonstrated that, well before any formal instruction, they are able to engage in many activities involving literacy, including not only retelling stories and scribbling but also recognizing environmental print (Morrow & Tracey, 2007).

OVERVIEW OF EMERGENT LITERACY

although the term "reading readiness" has been used for a long time, more recent research has gradually supported a conclusion that such a model is inadequate for studying just how a young child becomes literate. The term "emergent literacy" has been selected to represent a profound change in the way we look at early literacy. Whereas we once defined reading readiness as the prereading period that extends from birth to the time when a child begins to recognize and read words, the term "emergent literacy" proposes the view that literacy begins at birth and continues throughout life (Reutzel & Cooter, 1996).

Use of the Term "Emergent Literacy"

The term *emergent literacy* was introduced in 1966 by New Zealand researcher Marie Clay to describe the behaviors that were seen in young children when they used books and writing materials to imitate reading and writing activities, even though the children cannot actually read and write on a functional level. In the five decades since Clay introduced the term, an extensive body of research has expanded the understanding of emergent literacy. According to current research, children's literacy development begins long before children start formal instruction in elementary school (Beaty & Pratt, 2011; McGee & Richgels, 2003; Morrow & Tracey, 2007; Mullis, Martin, Kennedy, & Foy, 2007). This development is expanded through social interactions with caring adults and exposure to literacy materials, such as children's storybooks (Clay, 2000). It proceeds along a continuum, and children acquire literacy skills in a variety of ways and at different ages. Moreover, instead of reading preceding writing, as educators once believed necessary, there is now abundant evidence that children's skills in reading and writing develop at the same time and are synergistic rather than sequential (Morrow & Tracey, 2007).

This new way of thinking about early literacy supports the notion that very young children, even as young as 2.5 years old, come into early childhood education with a rich yet diverse background of language experiences, including recognizing certain written symbols and having a variety of prewriting efforts from their home and neighborhood environments; for example, most children just entering kindergarten can read *something,* such as their names, Coke, Target, and Toyota. With effective strategies and routines in place for small-group work, this foundation can be used to develop literacy in a formal way in pre-K and kindergarten (Hayes & Creange, 2001). Ollila and Mayfield (1992) stress that emergent literacy includes a language awareness that stems from children's active participation in communicating with those around them. This new concept of literacy places every child on a continuum of readiness in all components of the

Activities for letter recognition

www.starfall.com

language that springs from the child as a result of environmental stimulation. This stage of emergent literacy is said to last until children begin to formally read and write, when they become "beginning" readers and writers.

Literacy, in this current model, embraces not only reading, listening, and speaking, but also writing. During the period when literacy is emerging, children learn to understand and generate words, follow directions, interpret pictures, perceive differences in sight and sound, and acquire a curiosity about how things work. Although such behaviors are related to literacy acquisition, they tell us little about exactly when a given child will begin to formally read and write.

Key Components of Emergent Literacy

Perhaps a more constructive way to look at emergent literacy is to examine a few of its key components as well as some commonly held myths about what constitutes readiness for formal and informal literacy instruction. By developing a better idea about exactly what factors need to be present in children's preliterate development, we are better able to develop a program that successfully assists children in early literacy acquisition. In the body of literature on literacy acquisition accumulated over the past 70 years, the following factors have been most frequently discussed in association with early reading and writing success; revisiting such a list sheds some light on what factors educators once emphasized as compared with current thinking on how a child becomes literate:

- intelligence
- chronological age
- gender
- interest in language
- phonemic awareness

Intelligence

Because learning how to read and write are such complex tasks, it would seem obvious that high intelligence would be correlated with early success in literacy. Research has shown, however, that although some intelligence appears to facilitate progress, a very bright child may not necessarily succeed at the task earlier than a child with average intelligence. Research by Bond and Dykstra (1967) found only a small relationship between reading ability and intelligence. Spache and Spache (1977) discovered that intelligence may be a modest predictor of reading success, but only for children at the extremes; in other words, for those with very high or very low intelligence, there is a positive relationship between intelligence and later success in reading. Finally, a review of reading readiness research by Torrey (1979) indicated that although many early readers who read before kindergarten did well on intelligence tests, the intelligence of the majority of early readers fell into the average and below-average range. These studies suggest that, although high intelligence may be helpful to reading readiness, it clearly is not a deciding factor in predicting which children will do well in early literacy acquisition.

Chronological age

As far back as the 1930s, researchers were attempting to determine if there was an ideal age at which to begin reading instruction for optimal success. In a classic study, Morphett and Washburn (1931) looked at the mental ages of children in first-grade reading programs. These researchers found that children who had reached a mental age of approximately 6.5 did well in beginning reading instruction, whereas those who had not yet reached that level generally experienced more problems. Unfortunately, many educators misinterpreted these results to mean that the *chronological age* of 6.5 was the ideal age to begin reading instruction; thus, educators began to look at the possibility of delaying early reading instruction for all children until they had reached the age of 6.5. In fact, the study had only indicated that a child who is functioning at the cognitive, or intellectual, level of a child 6.5 years old would probably succeed at learning to read—whether that child was 4, 7, or even 10 years old.

Later studies suggested that many children learn to read successfully whether they are taught as early as five, as occurs in Japan, or as late as 7 or 8, as occurs in Denmark and Finland (Harris & Sipay, 1990). These researchers further concluded that many children appear to read successfully regardless of chronological age upon entering school, and that age is, by itself, an inadequate predictor of success in early reading.

Gender

Numerous fallacies surround the differences in linguistic competence between boys and girls. "Girls grow up faster than boys do" chirped a once-popular singing group. Educators, too, once held fast to the belief that boys tended to have a delayed start in general readiness and therefore experienced more problems learning how to read than their female counterparts. Other research suggests that these widely held views may have been misleading (Downing & Thomson, 1977). A landmark study by Dale Johnson (1973) supports a different conclusion. This investigator studied the reading prowess of early readers in the United States, Canada, Nigeria, and England. In most respects, in Nigeria and England the boys tended to score higher in tests of initial reading achievement than the girls. On the other hand, in Canada and the United States the girls scored higher on the very same tests. Based on these findings, Johnson concluded that the girls' relative reading superiority in English-speaking countries may have more to do with how they are acculturated and taught than with their native abilities or natural proclivities toward linguistic success.

Interest in language

Interest is perhaps as important as any other factor in determining when a child is ready to succeed at formal literacy instruction. Because it is not as objectively measurable as, for example, chronological age, interest is a quality that must be assessed by someone who is around the child in many different situations and has a chance to observe the child's interaction with her environment. Questions such as, "What does that word say?" and "How do you spell my name?" or "That story reminds me of another story that I heard. Shall I tell you about it?" or "Please read me a story!"

are all examples of a child with a clear interest in and curiosity directed toward beginning the tasks involved in literacy acquisition (Cecil, 1994d).

Besides being motivated to begin the reading and writing processes, children must have enough confidence to believe that they have a fair shot at succeeding, and they must be emotionally strong enough not to become unduly frustrated when encountering a word or concept that they cannot easily figure out. Coupled with the interest, there must also be an attention span that allows them to attend to literacy instruction and practice for an extended period of time (Pflaum, 1990). Finally, this interest in literacy must be carefully fanned by initiating activities that challenge but do not frustrate. Such activities must reach children at their current level by using their existing knowledge to bring them one step closer to becoming literate.

Interest is an important factor in determining when a child is ready to succeed at formal literacy instruction.

Teachers and caregivers play a major role in encouraging curiosity and interest and developing confidence about reading success.

Phonemic awareness

The ability to speak clearly and express ideas articulately has long been associated with emergent literacy. Thirty years of research into the reading success of early readers indicates that phonemic awareness plays an even larger role in this relationship than was earlier believed. For children to succeed at reading, especially in reading programs where phonics plays a large role, phonemic awareness is *the* most crucial component of emergent literacy (Adams, 1990)—a more potent predictor than nonverbal intelligence, vocabulary, or listening comprehension. To be truly ready to learn how to read and write, children must have an awareness of sounds; that is, an understanding that we speak in a flow of words and that those words contain a sequence of sounds that can be represented by graphic symbols called letters. Later, children must not only be able to discriminate between the sounds of letters, such as /f/ and /v/, but they must also be able to segment, blend, and isolate sounds to manipulate them, or sound them out, into meaningful words (Cunningham & Allington, 2007).

The ability to hear, blend, and discriminate between sounds is also an important part of listening comprehension as well as a factor in helping children understand subtle differences in meaning related to stress, pitch, and intonation in speech (Pearson, 1985). For example, "I wouldn't buy *that* car!" (I'd buy a different model) has a slightly different meaning than "I wouldn't *buy* that car!" (although I might lease it). Another example of the need for accurate discrimination of distinct words is the two-word slang phrase "Jeet yet?" as compared with the four words contained in the query, "Did you eat yet?"

rubber-banding ■   Finally, the ability to segment words, also called **"rubber-banding,"** is helpful as children begin to explore sound–spelling relationships (Calkins, 2000). An example of this occurs when six-year-old Jessica is trying to sound out the word "man" and she stretches the word to *mmmmmmmaaaaaannnnnn* as she laboriously pencils the word onto her paper. Research by Roberts (1975) supports the notion that blending ability seems most necessary in readiness for sounding out words in reading, while the ability to segment sounds into words appears to facilitate early spelling.

Specifically, the following hierarchy of phonemic understandings appears to be necessary for children to experience a smooth transition into formal reading instruction (Juel, 1994):

- ability to distinguish between letter sounds
- ability to hear sounds in words
- ability to hear syllables within words
- ability to identify phonemes
- knowledge about how print works

INFLUENCES ON CHILDREN'S LITERACY DEVELOPMENT

teachers and early childhood educators can promote young children's understanding of reading and writing by helping them build literacy knowledge and skills through the use of engaged learning activities. Children's growth from emergent to conventional literacy, discussed below, is influenced by (1) their understanding of literacy concepts, (2) their developing cognitive skills, and (3) the efforts of parents, caregivers, and teachers to promote literacy, which are discussed subsequently.

Continuing Literacy Development

Children's introduction to literacy begins well before they enter school and continues into adulthood, if not throughout life. It used to be assumed that five-year-olds went to kindergarten to be "readied" for reading and writing instruction, which would not formally begin until first grade. The pervading theory at the time suggested that there was a specific point in children's development when it was the ideal time to teach them to read and write. For children deemed not ready for formal literacy instruction, a variety of "readiness" activities would be then appropriated to prepare them for their eventual reading and writing instruction. This view, popular until the mid-1970s, has been discredited through the observations of both teachers and researchers in the field of early childhood education. Today, researchers and practitioners alike subscribe to a view of literacy attainment suggesting that literacy acquisition begins at birth and should be fostered at every age. This view of literacy will be explored in the following sections.

Emergent literacy

From as early as birth, children experience oral language development and begin to build a foundation for later reading and literacy success. From 2 to

3 years of age, children begin to produce understandable speech in response to books and the written marks they create (Schickedanz & Casbergue, 2007). From 3 to 4 years of age, children show rapid growth in emergent literacy, as Marie Clay(2000) described it: They begin to "read" their favorite books by themselves, focusing mostly on re-enacting the story from the pictures. Eventually, they progress from telling about each picture individually to weaving a story from picture to picture using language that sounds like reading or written language; for example, using the exact dialogue from the story: "'My! What big ears you have!' said Red Riding Hood, as she looked closely as her grandma."

At this time, children also experiment with writing by forming scribbles, letter-like forms, and random strings of letters (Beatty & Pratt, 2011). They also begin to use "mock handwriting" or wavy scribbles to imitate adult cursive writing. Letter-like forms or "mock letters" are the young child's attempt to form alphabetic letters; these forms of writing eventually will develop into standard letters. When using various forms of writing, children maintain their intention to create meaning and will often "read" their printed messages again, using language that sounds like reading (Jalongo, 2011).

Around age 5, children enter school and begin receiving formal literacy instruction. They continue to make rapid growth in literacy skills if they are exposed to literacy-rich environments. Children at this age continue to "read" from books they've heard repeatedly. Gradually, these readings demonstrate the intonation patterns of the adult reader and contain some of the language used in the book. Emergent readers are just beginning to control early reading strategies such as directionality, word-by-word matching, and concepts of printed language. They use pictures to support reading and rely heavily on their knowledge of language (Christie, Enz, & Vukelich, 2011).

Children's writing also develops rapidly during the kindergarten year. Just as children's reading acquisition does not occur in a linear path, children's writing skills also reflect an overlapping development. Children continue to use the variety of writing forms developed earlier, but they typically add random letter strings to their repertoire; in effect, they create strings of letters for their written messages without regard for the sounds represented by the letters (Combs, 2010). At this age, children plan their writing and are able to discuss their plans with others. If encouraged, they begin to use experimental, or temporary, spelling. Whimsical spellings typically represent the most dominant sounds in the words, such as the beginning and ending sounds. Even though children begin applying phonetic knowledge to create invented spellings, there is a lapse in time before they use phonetic clues to read what they write. Often children will try to recall what has been written or will use a picture created with the text to "reread" instead of using the letter clues (Corgill, 2008).

Conventional literacy

At some point during the kindergarten or first-grade year, most children begin to move from emergent literacy into conventional literacy. This process is gradual and cannot be hurried, anymore than a chrysalis can be hurried into a butterfly. Although all aspects of conventional literacy are developing during the emergent period, they become recognizable in conventional literacy. Educators working with young children—as well as parents and legislators—must keep in mind that there is no prescribed grade or age level for reaching conventional literacy. Emergent literacy and conventional literacy are not discrete stages but a continuum of learning that varies with the complexity of each individual's development and internal timeline (Combs, 2010). As children are moving into conventional literacy, they pass through different periods of development in their efforts to become successful readers, just as they did at the emergent level. Many traditional researchers use the terms *early reader, transitional reader*, and *fluent reader* to describe these periods of literacy growth.

Early readers/writers. Most children at the first-grade level are or will soon become **early readers/writers.** They know how to use early reading strategies (such as predicting and using context to help decode new words) and can read appropriately selected text independently after a story introduction given by a teacher. Early readers begin to attend to print and apply the one-to-one correspondence of matching sounds to letters in order to read. They commonly look at beginning and ending letters in order to decode unfamiliar words (Tompkins, 2011). Children in this early reading period also begin to attend to more than one source for cues while reading. Attention is paid to meaning cues, grammatical cues, and prior knowledge on a limited basis (Combs, 2010; Tompkins, 2011). These children are able to recognize a small number of words on sight. In writing, children typically progress through five stages of invented spelling, ranging from writing the initial consonant sound of a word to using conventional spelling.

Transitional readers/writers. Most children at around the second-grade level are **transitional readers/writers.** They are able to read unknown text with more independence than can early readers. Transitional readers use meaning as well as grammatical and letter cues more fully. They recognize a large number of frequently used words on sight and use pictures in a limited way while reading (Corgill, 2008).

In writing, some children continue to use phonetic or invented spelling, but the spelling is easily readable. Sometime during the development from early reader into transitional reader, children's writing also begins to demonstrate characteristics of the transitional speller. Transitional spellers are able to apply spelling rules, patterns, and a variety of other strategies for putting words on paper (Corgill, 2008).

Fluent readers/writers. Children at the third-grade level typically are **fluent readers/ writers.** They are able to use a number of sources of information flexibly to read a variety of unknown texts. Fluent readers are able to read for meaning with less attention to decoding and can independently solve problems encountered in the text (Christie et al., 2011). If the reading materials are appropriately challenging, children's fluency (which includes automatic word recognition, rapid decoding, and checking for meaning) continues to increase (Corgill, 2008).

early readers/writers ■

transitional readers/writers ■

fluent readers/writers ■

Typically, writing develops into mostly conventional spelling, although children may employ transitional and phonetic spellings to spell challenging or infrequently used words. Children at this stage are able to write expressively in many different forms and use an increasingly rich vocabulary and more complex sentences. They often revise and edit their own work.

Understanding of Literacy Concepts

In addition to acknowledging children's developmental acquisition of decoding, comprehension, and writing skills, emergent literacy research emphasizes the changes that occur in children's understanding of literacy concepts. As children have more experience with reading and writing, their understanding of the concepts of reading and writing expand and grow to fit their new knowledge. For instance, Combs (2008) describes categories of children's storybook reading from emergent through conventional reading. She notes that children eventually move from pointing and labeling pictures in a book, to "reading" a story through the illustrations, to telling the story using book language, and finally to reading conventionally using the text of a story.

An important transition occurs when children's "reading" of stories changes from sounding like oral language to sounding like written language. This transition demonstrates a change in ideas from thinking of reading as spoken words to understanding that reading is recreated from written text that uses words in special ways (Combs, 2008; McGee & Richgels, 2003). A similar shift in language can be observed in children's story dictation and in the rereading of their emergent writing (Jalongo, 2011).

Studies indicate that children's ideas about words are quite different from adults' concepts of words. There are differences between how an adult understands reading and writing and how a child understands reading and writing, according to McGee and Richgels (2003). As children progress into conventional literacy, however, their concepts of literacy gradually develop toward more conventional adult conceptualizations.

Developing Cognitive Skills

Because reading and writing are also thinking processes, emergent literacy must be considered in the context of children's developing cognitive skills. The constructionist theories of both Piaget and Vygotsky are relevant to the discussion of emergent literacy and help explain the cognitive concepts formed by young learners. Emergent literacy is partly discovered; children construct their own ideas about literacy as they actively participate in literacy activities (Piaget). Emergent literacy also is based on behaviors modeled and supported by adults (Vygotsky) that encourage children to change and refine their own ideas to more closely match conventional notions. One example of this interface between literacy acquisition and literacy instruction is the child's development of phonemic awareness (awareness that spoken words are made with individual sounds). By playing with language, such as rhyming or substituting sounds in words, some children develop a degree of phonemic awareness on their own, while other children require instruction from adults. Instruction may enable some children to use metacognition (the process of thinking about and regulating one's own learning) to achieve higher levels of sound awareness.

The Role of Teachers, Early Childhood Educators, Parents, and Caregivers

The adults with whom children interact during the transitional years from emergent to conventional literacy play a crucial role in ensuring that children progress successfully in their literacy development. Children's literacy efforts are best supported by adults' interactions with children through reading aloud and conversation and by children's social interactions with each other (McGee & Richgels, 2003). It is imperative that caregivers and educators in all settings are knowledgeable about emergent literacy and make a concerted effort to ensure that children experience literacy-rich environments to support their development into conventional literacy.

Of the most critical importance is reading aloud to children and providing opportunities for them to react to and discuss the stories that they hear. This is especially so during the preschool years. Reading aloud to children not only introduces them to the joy of reading, but also helps them begin to develop in four areas that are important in later formal reading instruction: oral language, cognitive skills, concepts of print, and phonemic awareness. Development of these skills provides a strong foundation to support literacy development during the early school years (Sulzby & Teale, 2003).

Children who are frequently read to also develop background knowledge about a range of topics and build a large vocabulary, all of which assist in later reading comprehension and development of reading strategies. They become familiar with rich language patterns and gain an understanding of what written language sounds like. Moreover, reading aloud to children helps them associate reading with pleasure and encourages them to seek out opportunities to read on their own. Children also become familiar with the reading process by watching how others read, and they develop an understanding of story structure. Repeated readings of favorite stories allow children an informal opportunity to gradually develop a more elaborate understanding of these concepts. By revisiting stories many times, children focus on unique features of a story or text and reinforce previous understandings. In addition, rereadings enable children to engage in emergent reading (Sulzby & Teale, 2003).

Literacy-rich environments, both at home and at school, are fundamental to promoting literacy and preventing reading difficulties. In literacy-rich home environments, parents and caregivers provide children with occasions for daily reading, extended discourse (extensive talking or writing), language play, experimentation with literacy materials, book talk (discussion of characters, action, and plot), and dramatic play. In literacy-rich classrooms, teachers incorporate the characteristics of literacy-rich home environments, but they also use grouping for learning, developmentally appropriate practices, and literacy routines; in addition, they have classroom designs that continue to encourage reading and writing (McGee & Richgels, 2003) through learning centers and engaged-learning activities.

Some children, unfortunately, enter elementary school without a strong foundation for literacy. The children most at risk for developing reading problems are those who begin school with less skill in language, less phonemic awareness and letter knowledge, and less familiarity with literacy tasks and underlying purposes (Beaty & Pratt, 2011). Research in the areas of family risk factors that contribute to children's reading difficulties, of adult–child interactions during story reading, and of delays in language development verifies that successes or struggles with reading can be observed very early in a child's life. To help children develop emergent skills and overcome barriers to literacy, teachers may need to make special efforts to work with children individually and to offer support and encouragement to parents and caregivers who participate in their children's literacy development. Schools also can use a wide variety of literacy intervention programs to minimize identified risk factors and support children in their literacy development.

Special consideration can be given to children who do not have strong skills in oral English. According to Jalongo (2011), non-English-speaking children need adequate preparation before they are taught to read in English. The ability to speak English provides the foundation for learning the alphabetic principle, the structure of the language, and the content of the material they are reading. If children cannot speak English, they can be taught to read and write in their own language while becoming proficient in English. If that is not possible, the initial instructional priority should be developing the children's oral proficiency in English (Jalongo, 2011). Formal reading instruction in English can be started after the child is adequately proficient in oral English.

Literacy development begins very early in a child's life and forms a foundation for the acquisition of conventional literacy. Research consistently supports a conclusion that the more children know about language and literacy before they begin formal schooling, the better equipped they are to succeed in reading. Parents, caregivers, and teachers need to ensure that young children are exposed to literacy-rich environments and receive developmentally appropriate literacy instruction. Such environments and experiences have a profound effect on children's literacy development by providing opportunities and encouragement for children to become successful readers (Tompkins, 2011).

Developmentally appropriate practice (DAP), as defined by the National Association for the Education of Young Children (NAEYC), is "a framework of principles and guidelines for best practice in the care and education of young children, birth through age 8" (NAEYC, 2011). For a detailed description of the DAP framework, see NAEYC's *Position Statement on Developmentally Appropriate Practice* (NAEYC, 2009).

■ developmentally appropriate practice

GUIDELINES FOR SETTING UP A BALANCED, COMPREHENSIVE LITERACY PROGRAM FROM BIRTH TO PRIMARY YEARS

teachers and early childhood educators may choose from many evidence-based practices to ensure that *all* children have an enjoyable and successful journey into literacy. These practices will be explored in the rest of this chapter. The following are general guidelines that teachers may use to set up a balanced and comprehensive literacy program from birth through the primary years.

- Use developmentally appropriate literacy practices that acknowledge children's development, interests, and literacy knowledge.
- Read to children daily and allow them to take turns "reading" the material to each other.
- Use a wide range of literacy materials in class. Allow children to experience a variety of children's books, magazines, newspapers, and online texts. Be sure to include all genres as well as fiction and nonfiction books, and include a wide variety of multicultural books.
- Take time to listen to children to determine their interests, language skills, and areas of need.
- Use children's home cultures and languages as literacy resources.
- Provide multiple rereadings of stories for pleasure and exploration. Invite children to join in the readings, honoring their emergent reading behaviors.
- Provide plenty of appropriate writing materials for children, including differing sizes and types of writing materials and surfaces (e.g., chalk, gel pens, lined and unlined paper, computers).
- Encourage children to compose stories and informational articles in emergent forms; provide opportunities for children to read, share, and display their writing.
- Provide "writing experiences that allow the flexibility to use nonconventional forms of writing at first (invented or phonetic spelling) and over time move to conventional forms."
- As children begin to read conventionally, provide balanced reading instruction to teach both skills and meaning and to meet the reading needs of individual children.
- Share ideas with parents and caregivers on creating an optimal environment to support young children's literacy development.
- Participate in professional development activities to learn and understand more about emergent literacy and appropriate teaching practices.

POSITIVE PRACTICES TO FOSTER EMERGENT LITERACY

In most primary classrooms of future years, teachers will necessarily encounter a heterogeneous garden of children with a multitude of abilities and language backgrounds as well as a diverse set of literacy experiences, such as having been read to and having sung songs. Some will enter the classroom door with many such experiences; others will have had fewer activities directly related to language development in its many forms.

Although individualized instruction seems a logical solution to these diversities, such a course of action is not without a host of problems: Most children are, by nature, social beings who greatly enjoy interaction with other children their own age. We also know from research and past experience that teachers should take an active stance in getting children ready to learn how to read and write, rather than simply waiting for them to become, magically, ready. Three of the factors previously mentioned—interest, development of concepts about print and books, and language experiences—are ones teachers can readily supplement in the classroom in a small or large group setting.

What is first necessary for early literacy experiences to flourish is a teacher who is both sensitive to the physical environment of the classroom and a facilitator of learning. Such a teacher creates a print-rich environment and offers activities to provide a varied, motivational exposure to the English language. Such a teacher must also believe in the power of pre-K and kindergarten experiences to improve the developmental trajectory of children by teaching to what they already bring with them to the classroom (McGill-Franzen, 2005). Chapter 4 offers a host of activities that can be used for direct, explicit instruction in phonemic awareness; the following section in the current chapter allows the teacher to build on what children already know to ready them for more formal reading and writing instruction.

Developing Concepts About Print

As children get ready for formal instruction in literacy, they need to develop some basic understandings of how print works in text; most of these concepts of print have often been mastered before entering first grade. What seems simple may sometimes bewilder children who have never been exposed to it. It is unlikely, for example, that a preliterate child will spot any patterns in a page of print if that child sometimes looks at it from right to left and at other times from left to right. The concepts about (Western) print, listed in Figure 3.2, can be taught directly to children during read-aloud sessions (Clay, 2000).

To reinforce such concepts, teachers can use big books, posters, text posted on an interactive whiteboard, sentence strips in a pocket chart, songs, poetry,

Concepts about print.	*figure* **3.2**

- Print carries meaning.
- Reading of print goes from left to right, top to bottom.
- Print goes from the left page, then proceeds to the right.
- Letters are the black squiggles on the page.
- A word is composed of letters and is surrounded by white space.
- Punctuation marks provide information about inflection and meaning.
- A book has a front and back cover, a title page, an author, and often an illustrator.
- A story has a beginning, a middle, and an end.

or any text that is large enough to share with children. Then before reading the text with children, the teacher can feign forgetfulness and ask children,

Who can show me . . .

    where the cover of the book is?

    which way is right side up?

    where I should start to read?

    where a word is?

    where the end of the story is?

    where a capital (or lowercase) letter is?

On a familiar text, some children may be ready to point to the words as they are read, establishing one-to-one matching of words to print.

Providing Direct and Vicarious Experiences

Providing an adequate background of experience is an integral part of cultivating emergent literacy. Because the child who is intellectually curious reaps the most from his experiences, teachers must take every opportunity to whet his curiosity about unfamiliar activities, ideas, and objects. A broad experiential background is necessary for literacy success because children must be familiar with the concepts and vocabulary they hear and see in written form to gain meaning from them. Indeed, experiences are the foundation for building concepts, and concepts are the foundation for building new vocabulary. Through their experiences children gain an understanding of ideas and concepts and then learn words that go with them. When they later begin to read they will better comprehend because they are able to relate their experiences to the symbols on the page.

Teachers, including preschool teachers, can help children build experiential backgrounds in a variety of ways. As they observe and talk with their pupils, they can see where there are gaps in experience and find ways to fill them. Children can build experience through constructing mobiles and collages, cooking, playing with puzzles, identifying hidden objects, playing language guessing games, singing nursery rhymes, and marching to a Sousa tune. Teachers can invite resource people into the classroom or arrange field trips or virtual field trips on the Internet to places children have never visited.

During "calendar" or "news" time, children gain useful experience observing and discussing the weather, reciting the days of the week and months of the year, and establishing what to do in a fire drill, among other experiences. Because young children love to play, a hidden coin can be a language-learning experience for those studying English (where they must repeatedly ask complete sentences to determine who has the coin); a box becomes a concept-building game when children try to identify the positions of an object placed on it, over it, beside it, or under it. Similarly, children can increase their understanding of the subtleties of vocabulary by responding to invitations to crawl, trot, dash, or stroll.

Experiences may be either direct or vicarious. Children usually remember direct experiences with actual physical involvement best, but such experiences are not always possible. For example, the ideal way to teach about the Laplanders in Scandinavia would be to climb aboard a Lear jet, observe their lives, talk to them firsthand, and spend time in their homes. Because that is not feasible, vicarious experiences, such as television programs about the Laplanders; exhibits; a resource person who has been to Scandinavia; photographs; video excerpts; website stories or articles about their lives will also serve to promote concept and vocabulary development.

Interactive Story Writing

Interactive story writing is a logical extension of either direct or vicarious experiences and is an ideal vehicle through which to reinforce concepts about print. Such story writing can be planned and occur as an introduction to an experience, or it can be the spontaneous result of an experience (Tompkins & Collom, 2004). If the class writes a story after there has been a severe thunderstorm, the children should first discuss the event. By asking carefully selected questions, the teacher can encourage children to formulate valid concepts and to use appropriate vocabulary words. For example, the teacher might ask:

■ interactive story writing

> Who can tell me what the weather was like this morning?
>
> What kinds of things happen during a storm?
>
> How did the storm make you feel?
>
> Why might rain be important to us?

In response to a discussion generated by questions, the children then dictate sentences for the teacher to transcribe onto a chart. The resultant piece of writing might look like the one shown in Figure 3.3, composed by a group of second-graders. The story can be written on chart paper, a whiteboard, or an interactive white board.

An interactive story.	*figure* **3.3**

THE STORM

This morning we didn't have any recess because there was a big storm.

There was loud thunder and bright lightning.

It rained very hard for a long time.

Some children were afraid of the noise.

The storm was scary, but the rain can be good.

We need the rain to make the flowers grow.

Dictated pieces such as this provide an excellent precursor to later use of the language experience approach (see Chapter 9).

Perhaps the most important reason for writing stories in partnership with children, before they are able to write their own, is that they begin to grasp the critical concept that writing is a way to record speech. This awareness occurs as the teacher reads the story back to the children in the words they have just dictated. After repeated readings by the teacher, the children may be able to "read" the story too. The teacher may make copies of the story for the children to take home and share with their families. As a result of this repeated involvement with the story, children may learn to recognize some high-interest words (e.g., "storm" in the story above) and words that were used more than once ("we" and "there"). These understandings are further reinforced when seen in a number of different contexts.

Many literacy skills are reinforced through transcriptions; essentially, children gain an exposure, or bird's eye view, of all the skills involved in literacy. Consider: Children watch as the teacher forms letters that make up the words and she demonstrates how she sounds out the beginning letters. They begin to notice, as the teacher writes, that language consists of separate words that are combined into sentences. They see the teacher begin reading at the left side of the story and move to the right, going from top to bottom. They become aware that dictated stories have titles that tell about the most important idea in the story, and they see that each letter of the title is capitalized. They discover that sentences begin with capital letters and end with a punctuation mark. In addition to becoming familiar with the mechanical conventions of the English language, children develop their thinking skills as the teacher guides them to summarize and organize their thoughts. Finally, as the children recall the events in the order in which they occurred, they become aware of the importance of sequencing ideas.

Reading Aloud to Children: The Importance of Print and Books

Jim Trelease, author of *The New Read Aloud Handbook* (2006), travels around the country exhorting parents to read to their child for fifteen minutes a night to ensure later academic success. The reason he preaches this important message has much to do with emergent literacy: children who have been read to—early and often—develop important concepts about print, such as the fact that a page in a book, whether traditional or electronic, has symbols that stand for words and that there is white space around those words; a physical book has a front and a back; we read from left to right; punctuation at the end of a word lets the reader know when to stop reading and take a small pause. Children who have print and book knowledge can also point to individual words on a page as they read, or track. Advanced understanding of print allows children to identify the first and last word on a page, capital and lowercase letters, and the first and last letters of words—all excellent precursors to the reading process (Clay, 1972, 1993). In a family setting, these understandings are developed naturally through enjoyable exposure to print.

To build on children's knowledge of what is available in print, the teacher should choose a wide variety of reading materials to read aloud to students every day. Reading to children not only builds appreciation of literature and concepts of print; it also develops listening comprehension skills and understanding of various text structures (Beck & McKeown, 2007; Fisher, Flood, Lapp, & Frey, 2004).

When reading aloud to children, teachers share reading materials on a wide range of topics, capture children's attention, and engage them in deep thinking about texts and how one responds to literature (Dickenson, Hao, & He, 1995). Read-aloud materials should be challenging stories or informational texts that provide opportunities to talk about word meanings, to puzzle over characters' motivations, or to explore new concepts (McGee,

Select children's literature from all genres to encourage a wide range of interests.

1998). Read-aloud materials can be chosen to reflect the cultures and ethnicities within the classroom and introduce children to other ones as well. Listening to books being read aloud provides children with opportunities to acquire new vocabulary, extend understandings about the world and themselves, and develop an awareness of story and expository text structures.

Researchers suggest that the most valuable aspect of reading aloud is that it gives children experience with text language that requires them to make sense of ideas that are about something beyond the physical "here and now." The instructive verbal interactions teachers have with children during a read-aloud promote language development and the ability to handle ideas that do not concern the present moment. To optimize this benefit to children, the teacher can initiate **text talk** (Beck & McKeown, 2002), an approach to enhancing young children's ability to build meaning from text. Using this method, the teacher intersperses reading with open-ended questions and follows each story with direct attention to vocabulary. Such questions often begin by repeating and rephrasing the children's answers and then providing generic prompting such as, "What was that all about?" and "Can you tell me more about what you mean by that?" Text talk also includes rereading the relevant portion of text, and then repeating the initial question, if a child's answers seem to be coming only from the pictures or his own background. This approach helps young children focus on the text language as the source for their answers to the questions and thus builds vocabulary and comprehension. Caveat: Too much text talk may disrupt comprehension of the story by interrupting flow and enjoyment.

■ text talk

For heightened enjoyment, it is best to use a variety of well-crafted picture books with large illustrations so that children can observe the action as well as hear what is happening. Big books are commercially available for this purpose. The box on the following page offers guidelines for selecting a big book.

Selecting a big book to read aloud

The criteria for evaluating a big book are the same as the criteria used for selecting any children's book to be read aloud, with the addition of the following features:

1. The book should not be so large that it is difficult to hold on your lap with one hand and turn the pages with the other.

2. The print should be clearly distinguishable from the illustrations. In other words, it should be easy for the children to visually discriminate the units of print from the illustrations.

3. There should be a strong connection between the print and the illustrations; the children should be able to predict what the story is about from the pictures.

4. The print should be large enough to be seen clearly from the back of the group of children.

5. The text of the book should have specific instructional qualities, such as rhythm, a rhyming pattern, a particular phonic element such as an abundance of words beginning with "b," predictability enhanced by repetition, and pictures that support comprehension.

wordless books ■
predictable books ■
See Appendix A ▶

At times the teacher may wish to choose stories with only pictures, or **wordless books** (see Appendix A), so that very young children have a chance to use their imaginations to help tell the story from their everyday experiences and from their experiences with other stories. **Predictable books** (see Appendix A) are other excellent options for reading aloud to children. These are children's books that, through their rhyme, rhythm, and repetition, allow children to participate in the reading and, with the teacher's help, associate the spoken words with the written ones, creating an understanding of one-to-one correspondence between oral and written words.

To acquaint English learners with language variety, the teacher should offer a variety of styles and structures, too. Remember that children do not need to understand every word that is read to them, especially when the text is supported by appropriate illustrations. As with infants acquiring a first language, hearing new words in familiar contexts helps children begin to construct new meanings.

It is helpful to select children's literature from all ethnic groups and all genres—fiction, nonfiction, prose, and poetry—to encourage a wide range of interests.

informational texts ■
See Appendix A ▶

See Appendix E ▶

Recent studies have shown that **informational texts** (see Chapter 10 and Appendix A) are surprisingly scarce in primary classrooms (Duke, 2000). Be sure to seek a variety of informational texts, as such material helps develop important skills and interest in informational reading and writing. Early in the year the teacher can survey students' interests, hobbies, special talents, and country of birth, and then choose stories and nonfiction pieces based on this information (see the interest inventory in Appendix E).

Finally, the teacher should also be sure to share reading materials that he especially enjoys, because pleasure and enthusiasm for reading and books is more effectively "caught" than "taught."

Sharing literature is the perfect experience through which to develop concepts about books and print as they occur naturally in the material being read. Talking about literature with children can also help develop the ideas that the

Classic read-alouds for young readers

The following picture storybooks are "classics" that have withstood the test of time, offering countless children—and adults—enjoyable associations with literature.

Corduroy by Don Freeman
A stuffed bear is rescued from the department store shelf by a little girl who takes him home to be her friend.

From Seed to Plant by Gail Gibbons
A simple introduction to how plants reproduce, discussing pollination, seed dispersal, and growth from seed to plant.

Goodnight Moon by Margaret Wise Brown
Mother Rabbit settles her little one into bed through rhyme by saying goodnight to all the things in the bedroom.

Ira Sleeps Over by Bernard Weber
When he is asked to spend the night at his friend's house, a little boy must decide whether or not to take along his teddy bear.

Make Way for Ducklings by Robert McCloskey
This is the story of the city adventures of Mr. and Mrs. Mallard and their eight ducklings.

Sylvester and the Magic Pebble by William Steig
Sylvester makes a wish on a magic pebble and is unable to undo his wish and return home to his family. The story resolves when Sylvester is reunited with his parents.

The Very Hungry Caterpillar by Eric Carle
An egg hatches into a caterpillar that eats its way through several storybook pages before turning into a beautiful butterfly.

words should make sense; that readers are to be actively involved in thinking about what might happen next; and that the learner brings his or her own knowledge, ideas, and experiences to the text. Prereading discussions about a topic and what the children know about it, the author and illustrator, and a general feeling about what they predict the story might be about will set preliterate children on the road to comprehending text. The modeling of these behaviors by a proficient reader, the teacher, will encourage children to actively construct meaning as they begin to read. The box above offers a list of classic read-aloud books.

Using Drama

Informal dramatic activities create interest in language and stories, develop the imaginations of children, and allow them to use language to express their ideas and feelings. It is especially appropriate for use with those who are learning English, because the action involved supports and reinforces the words, thereby making the meaning accessible for all such students.

Informal drama should be spontaneous and unrehearsed, with children assuming the roles of characters from real life or from stories they have heard. They are free to think, feel, move, react, and speak in accordance with their interpretation of the characters. The drama may begin with simple movements or actions in response to poems or songs the teacher reads (and the horses went clippety-clop, clippety-clop. *Show* me what the horses did, boys and girls!). Later, children may develop their interpretational skills by pantomiming stories or actions after the teacher has read, such as the making of the porridge

Props, masks, and simple costumes can help build interest in acting out stories.

in *Goldilocks and the Three Bears* or dancing the horrific monster dance in *Where the Wild Things Are,* when the "wild rumpus begins."

Acting out stories not only helps build interest in stories but it also develops understandings of the structure of stories. Children can progress to more sophisticated drama that more nearly resembles the entire story. As the teacher reads the story, the children must pay careful attention to the sequence of events, the personalities of the characters, the dialogue, and the mood of the story. Before acting out the story, the teacher can help the children review the events and characters in the story by using a simple organizer such as the one shown in Figure 3.4.

As they act, the children can be encouraged to strive to use appropriate vocabulary, enunciate clearly, and speak audibly. Puppets can be useful with shy children who are reluctant to speak themselves but are often willing to talk through a puppet. Props, such as masks, costumes, scarves, empty food containers, and cardboard boxes, help inspire dialogue. Children often want to act out the stories several times, with different children playing different characters each time. Each successive rereading allows for a deeper appreciation and understanding of the original story.

Dramatic play has many benefits, all prerequisite for learning in literacy. Because children need to carry on conversations, they are practicing their language skills. By interacting with other children, they are developing social and emotional readiness. The teacher can encourage children to use printed words as labels, such as street signs, character names, and package labels. Ambiguous props used in their play can also be labeled—for example, a ball becomes "bowl-

play centers ■ ing ball"—and will later become words recognized on sight. **Play centers** such as the ones described in Figure 3.5 can also facilitate spontaneous dramatic play.

---

figure **3.4**   **A simple story frame.**

Somebody/	Wanted/	But/	So
Goldilocks	to sit	bears	she
	to eat	came	ran
	to sleep	home	away

Examples of play centers. *figure* **3.5**

GROCERY STORE	POST OFFICE
Empty cereal and other boxes	Mail boxes
Pretend money and coins	Stationery
Receipt book for purchasing items	Assorted writing utensils
Paper sacks for bagging groceries	Old stamps or stickers
Calculator or cash register that prints onto tape	Puppets

HOUSE	FARM
Puppets	Stuffed or plastic animals
Telephone	Large boxes or crates for barn
Cardboard boxes for furniture	Burlap bags for pretend feed
Clothing appropriate for different family members	Pails
Kitchen utensils	Plastic plants
Paper and crayons for making props	

By listening attentively to each other, children begin to develop the auditory memory and discrimination necessary for phonemic awareness in an enjoyable package that effectively furthers their learning but seems like play.

SUMMARY

all young children—and everyone else, for that matter—are somewhere on the continuum of proficiency in literacy; therefore, the old question of exactly *when* they will be ready to learn to read becomes irrelevant. The most current understanding of emergent literacy holds that children are emerging as literate persons from birth and continue on this path until death. Success in literacy, then, will depend on a constellation of interlocking factors: it is now deemed to be predicated neither on wholly physical nor on totally intellectual maturation alone, although both of these realms seem to be at least minimally involved. Nor do modern educators believe any longer that success in literacy is something to wait for passively, as educators tended to believe in the early 1950s; we now argue that literacy is a stage onto which a child can be gently guided—and even enticed—when the appropriate methods and activities are offered to that child.

Gender, home environment, and chronological age of children may not be the factors most determinative of who will be literate and when. However, it is helpful to be aware of such factors to understand possible tangential reasons for certain inexplicable behaviors or lack of progress in early literacy acquisition. On the other hand, teachers must guard against preconceived expectations for children, based on gender or chronological age, home environment, or any other nonacademic aspects of the child's life that are not subject to change.

Fortunately, teachers of young children can influence their later literacy success by fostering their awareness of sounds in language—their phonemic awareness. They can affect other areas correlated with success in early literacy as well, such as background experience, interest in literacy, and language development. Teachers can fill in the experiential gaps of the children in their charge with appropriate real-life experiences or well-designed vicarious ones; they can incorporate language-rich activities, such as the transcription of stories, dramatic play, and reading aloud to children into their daily routines. Most of all, teachers have a crucial responsibility to fill their classrooms with plenty of opportunities for pupils to play and experiment with print and language in all their forms. With such print-rich and language-rich experiences at the beginning of their academic lives, children's paths to formalized literacy instruction will no doubt be considerably smoother.

questions
for journal writing and discussion

1. Discuss the prevalent practice of "red shirting"—holding children back a year before sending them to kindergarten. What is your opinion of this practice? How might such a practice stratify our society along socioeconomic lines?

2. What might you say to parents of a kindergarten child who are concerned enough to ask you what they can do at home to help their child become "ready to learn to read"? Explore some websites that discuss emergent literacy. (See Appendix C for some suggestions.) Note the source: Who wrote the information and for what purpose? Share the information you find with the class.

See Appendix C

3. Schools often use a teacher's judgment in addition to the data derived from reading readiness assessments to decide whether or not children are ready to begin formal reading instruction. Do you think these two sources of data are equally reliable? Why or why not? What might be some advantages of each of these forms of evaluation? What might be some limitations?

suggestions
for projects and field activities

1. From the information in this chapter, create a checklist you might use to help determine if a child is ready to learn to read. Include such major factors as language development, interest in reading, and understanding of the English writing system. For each of these main headings, create ways

to evaluate each of the factors. For example, you might say for language development, "Asks many complex questions containing five or more words," or for interest in reading, "Listens attentively when read to" or "Often talks about books he has heard."

2. Spend some time observing in a kindergarten class. Ask the teacher for a list of birthdays of the children in the class. Do there appear to be noticeable differences in the children's involvement in literacy and other behaviors, depending on their earlier or later birthdays? What are these differences? Use the list created for the previous suggestion to consider some other possible factors in the emergent literacy status of this group of children.

3. Research the emergent literacy issues of a country outside of North America. Find out: (1) When do children begin formal reading instruction? (2) What methods are used for instruction? (3) Are there any noticeable differences in achievement levels of boys and girls on standardized reading tests in later years? (4) If there is a discrepancy in test results between girls and boys, to what do educational practitioners attribute this difference? What do you think accounts for the difference?

4. Read a picture book to a child in preschool and observe what he or she seems to understand about the concepts of print. Record your observations using the Concepts About Print Assessment in Appendix E. For those concepts with which the child seems unfamiliar, list several ways parents or preschool teachers can work with the child to help her or him become familiar with the concepts of print.

See Appendix E

chapter 4

Phonemic Awareness

The Sounds of Our Language

focus questions

- What is the relationship between phonemic awareness and phonics?

- How can teachers develop phonemic awareness in their students in motivational ways?

- Why is knowledge of phonemic awareness and the alphabetic principle so important to emergent literacy?

The children in Mrs. Rodgers' kindergarten class are enthusiastically involved in brainstorming about all the foods they can think of while their teacher writes their responses on the board. For every favorite food mentioned, such as "hot dog," the children try to think of a nonsense rhyme that could go with it. "Rot hog!" Aaron exclaims gleefully, and the other children burst into a fit of giggles at this hilarious rhyme, quickly offering a "thumbs up" sign to Aaron. Mrs. Rodgers grins as she writes the letters on the board with the children helping her to sound out the words. The children in Mrs. Rodgers' class enjoy this game immensely. They are oblivious to the fact that they are also engaging in phonemic awareness activities designed to help them tune in to the sounds in the English language. Such activities prepare them to benefit from later phonics instruction.

INTRODUCTION

until fairly recently, the teaching of decoding addressed mostly phonics, or the relationship between spoken sounds and individual printed letters or letter combinations. Now, much greater emphasis is being placed on the understanding and teaching of phonemic awareness. **Phonemic awareness** is the ability to hear, identify, and manipulate individual sounds—phonemes—in spoken words (National Institute for Literacy, 2001). The focus in phonemic awareness is on hearing the sounds in words spoken aloud, and not on the letters or printed words. When children have developed the awareness of sounds in words, they are then able to use the sound–symbol correspondence to read and spell words (Gillon, 2004). A child who possesses phonemic awareness can segment and manipulate sounds in words (e.g., pronounce just the first sound heard in the word "gap"), blend strings of isolated sounds together to form recognizable word forms, and so on (IRA Board, 1998).

Phonemic awareness is really an understanding of oral language—it is not the same as phonics. *Phonics* generally refers to knowing the relationship between specific, printed letters (and combinations of letters) and specific, spoken sounds. With the application of such knowledge, children can use letter sounds and other rules to figure out, or decode, unknown words. Phonemic awareness has been shown to be an important *precursor* to phonics and to the success-

phonemic awareness ■ ful decoding skills critical in reading (Pressley, 2005). Moreover, children who receive instruction in phonemic awareness in kindergarten are better able to produce experimental spellings than those who are not (Tangel & Blachman, 1995). Studies have shown that children who lack experience with phonemic awareness activities often profit less from phonics instruction (Griffith & Olson, 1992).

The current emphasis on the underlying awareness of the sounds in a language has come about as a result of a large volume of research into the problems of numerous children in our schools who do not seem to be learning to read at grade level (Fletcher et al., 1994; Shaywitz et al., 1992; Stanovich & Siegel, 1994). Whereas the majority of children learn to read regardless of the reading methods used by their teachers, the portion of children for whom reading has been a problem has consistently been about 25 percent (Adams, 1990). Early facilitation in phonemic awareness might very well be the instructional component, when integrated into a program rich with language and text, that will enable educators to teach every child to read—including those children who have historically fallen through the cracks.

THE IMPORTANCE OF PHONEMIC AWARENESS

to understand why phonemic awareness is important, it is first necessary to understand a bit about the nature of our language. Linguists describe four separate areas of functioning in the human language system: phonology (sounds), syntax (grammar), semantics (underlying meaning), and pragmatics (usage) (see Chapter 2). The component of phonology is central to eventual success in phonics. **Phonology** is the study of the sound patterns of a language. As we put our ideas into words, it is the phonological part of our language system that puts together the proper sounds of those words in the appropriate sequence; in other words, our canine best friend is a dog and not a god, only because of the precise arrangement of sounds.

■ phonology

Some time ago, Isabelle Liberman and her colleagues (Liberman et al., 1974) suggested that the primary cause for difficulty in learning to read an alphabetic written language (as compared with an ideographic language with meaning-laden characters, such as Kanji or Mandarin) is due to a lack of awareness of the phonology or sounds of the language. The English language employs the **alphabetic principle.** Any alphabetic writing system uses symbols to represent the sounds of a language. Readers must first understand that words can be divided into sounds and that the same basic set of letters can be combined in a great variety of ways. Only then can a child understand that *lake* and *kale,* for instance, have the same letters but represent different words because the particular sequence of the letters—and therefore the sequence of the sounds—is different.

■ alphabetic principle

The ability to hear discrete speech sounds in individual words is elusive for many young children and remains undeveloped—even into adulthood—in a surprisingly large number of people. This is understandable when we consider that sounds are abstract, meaningless in isolation, and often influenced by context. (What does your mouth do when you say the /s/ in *see?* When you say the /s/ in *say?*) However, in the past 30 plus years a large body of research has supported a conclusion that the ability to segment words into individual sounds is an absolute prerequisite to learning how to read in an alphabetic symbol system such as English. Moreover, the degree to which emergent readers are aware of the individual sounds in spoken words very often predicts future reading success. In fact, it has been shown to be a better predictor of reading success than intelligence, parents' educational background, visual or auditory perception, memory, or even eyesight (Blachman, 1991; Wagner, Torgeson, & Rashotte, 1994)! This predictive power has been demonstrated not only among English-speaking children but also among Swedish-speaking children (Lundberg, Olofsson,

Teachers contribute to their students' phonemic awareness by spending a few minutes every day engaging children in stimulating oral language activities that explicitly emphasize the sequence of sounds in language.

for themselves what they do with *their* mouths when producing the sound. The teacher should then ask the children to share orally what their mouths do—in their own words. She should demonstrate how to tell when the /m/ sound is heard in different words by giving some examples. The children will be more likely to succeed in this task as subsequent examples are given for practice.

Second, the teacher must analyze the task to be performed and, initially, keep it as simple as possible. Is the teacher asking the children to listen for syllables or sounds, and exactly which sound should the children be looking for and where in the word will it be found? Also, beginning with very simple two- and then three-phoneme words will help reduce confusion: rather than using a lesson that asks children to listen for the speech sounds in the words *blend, green,* or *brook* (which have blended consonants and other sounds that require more sophisticated discrimination), start with continuous sounds, such as those in *man, sat,* or *nut.*

Finally, for teachers of English learners, there are sounds regularly used in English that are not part of other languages. In general, the sounds listed in Figure 4.1 are not part of the other languages' regular sound systems, although they may occur in certain dialects or sometimes just in the middle positions of words. These sounds are difficult for beginning speakers of English for two reasons. First, children have not had any practice recognizing these sounds or discriminating them from others; native English-speaking children have heard the sounds and have had practice discriminating them since infancy. Second, because children have not used these sounds before, they have had no practice pronouncing them. To help children in these language groups master these sounds in readiness for later phonics instruction, teachers need to point out the discrepant sounds to the children, exaggerate their pronunciation, and help children learn to pronounce them through practice with repetition of each sound used in the beginning, middle, and end positions of words.

figure | **4.1**   **English sounds not occurring in other languages.**

LANGUAGE	ENGLISH SOUNDS NOT PART OF OTHER LANGUAGES										
Chinese	b	ch	d	dg	g	oa	sh	s	th	v	z
French	ch	ee	j	ng	oo	th					
Greek	aw	ee	i	oo	schwa						
Italian	a	ar	dg	h	i	ng	th	schwa			
Japanese	dg	f	i	th	oo	v	schwa				
Spanish	dg	j	sh	th	z						
Native American *(some dialects)*	l	r	st								

Helping non-English speakers

For Spanish Speakers

- Assess children's phonemic awareness in Spanish, not English.
- Allow children to do many language activities in Spanish.
- Continue to develop proficiency in Spanish.
- Help children see similarities in the two language systems.
- Use pictures that have the same sounds in both languages (e.g., gato, cat).

For Non-Alphabetic Language Speakers
(e.g., Arabic, Mandarin)

- Treat children as English speakers who are struggling to "hear" the sounds in English.
- Speak slowly and use lip, mouth, and tongue training in an active, fun approach.
- Intensify instruction three to four times a week, building on children's progress in oral English.

Specifically, teachers can help non-English-speaking children become phonemically aware by following the guidelines shown in the box above. For more information on phonemic awareness and English learners, see Peregoy and Boyle (2008).

From Research to Practice

First of all, it is important to note that not every child needs intensive training in phonemic awareness. In kindergarten, children needing guidance in this area, for example, would be those who cannot rhyme and who don't recognize that *pat* and *pick* start with the same sounds. In first and second grades, children who cannot segment initial sounds or detect different beginning, middle, and ending sounds need additional help. On the other hand, children who already manifest phonemic awareness can be exposed to the phonics and decoding activities presented in Chapter 5.

For children who do need such assistance, there are many research-supported ways to help them develop the spectrum of phonemic awareness skills (Griffith & Olson, 1992; Yopp & Yopp, 2000). Initially, children should be exposed to poems and nursery rhymes, especially those in which the rhymes are the most obvious feature of the poem. At first, the poems should be read for enjoyment and understanding. Then, if the poems are recited with a great deal of emphasis on the words that rhyme, almost to the point of exaggeration, the children's attention will be drawn to that rhyme. Eventually the children should be able to generate their own rhyming words. Engagement in this type of activity should be accompanied by a good deal of humor and poetic license, as "hot dog" is rhymed with "rot hog" in the opening vignette of this chapter. Certain children's literature lends itself to exactly this type of language play. Books such as *The Hungry Thing* by Jan Slepian (1985), for example, engage children in rhyming while having a rollicking good time. Examples of additional appropriate books are found in Appendix A.

See Appendix A

Many phonemic awareness activities can take the form of games or puzzles and can be used in an informal, relaxed setting. For example, children may be

Many phonemic awareness activities can take the form of games or puzzles and can be used in an informal, relaxed setting.

asked to identify pictures for which the beginning sound or the beginning consonant and vowel sound for the picture is the same. Given pictures of a pig, a pin, a pot, and a sun, a child would put the pig, pin, and pot pictures together or tell which picture doesn't fit and explain why on the basis of his perception of sound. When children can do this easily with pictures, they can often listen to just three or four words and tell which ones go together and which ones do not. This can evolve into selecting which middle sounds go together and which ones do not fit (mat, can, lap, bit) and then performing the same tasks with ending sounds (cup, map, lot, pep).

Another game would be to look for objects in the classroom or in magazines whose names begin with a certain sound. Extra challenge and interest can be added by going through the alphabet, finding one thing that starts with /a/, then /b/, and so on. The teacher will need to specify the sound and, if it is a vowel, indicate whether it is long or short.

A similar game is "I Spy with My Eye," except instead of suggesting colors, the teacher declares, "I spy with my eye something beginning with /th/" or "I spy with my eye something ending with /k/," choosing word parts and sounds that the children can handle without too much difficulty.

Children also enjoy counting the number of syllables in words that are pronounced for them in exaggerated fashion. The names of children in the class provide personal examples for this activity. Counting with young children can be done in a variety of ways, such as tapping the table with a pencil, clapping each syllable, or noting the number of times their jaws move up and down as the word is said. It is always most difficult for children to count the syllable in a one-syllable word, as they often attempt to make discrete speech sounds into syllables, so it is helpful to warn them, "Here's a tricky one!"

As children become proficient with activities in which they are asked to recognize how the sounds in words differ, they are often ready to manipulate the sounds themselves. For example, you can give them a word to say (e.g., *bat*) and ask them to say it without the /b/. For children who have difficulty with this, you can begin with compound words, having them leave off one of the syllables, which is a phonologically easier task. For example: "Say *baseball*. Now say it without the *ball*." "Say *baseball*. Now say it without the *base*."

When the children become comfortable with manipulating the sounds in words, but before they have been taught the actual letters, the teacher can begin

sound boxes ■   to use colored markers or small pieces of paper on **sound boxes** to represent the sounds (see Figure 4.2). Each different sound should be represented with a different color, but the same color does not always have to match a particular sound. For example, if you have red, yellow, green, blue, and purple markers, the word

Sound boxes.

figure | **4.2**

map may be represented by blue–green–red, red–purple–yellow, or green–blue–red, as long as each sound has a different color. A word like *pop*, using the same patterning, may be represented by green–blue–green, red–yellow–red, or blue–red–blue, as long as the beginning and ending colors are the same. Using this approach, children may be given problems to solve such as the following:

> If this says /go/ make it say /so/. (Children should replace the first marker with one of another color.)

> If this says /kite/ make it say /cat/. (Children should replace the second marker with one of a different color; silent /e/ is not represented at this early stage; see Figure 4.2.)

Eventually children can progress to deleting a sound:

> If this says /man/, make it say /an/. (Children should remove the first marker.)

When children have learned the sounds and graphic representations (letters) for some consonants and a vowel, they can use letter cards or tiles for these activities, and they will have progressed to reading and spelling words!

Other Phonemic Awareness Activities

The activities presented here are categorized into word beginnings, sound isolation activities, blending activities, and sound substitution activities. The list of activities in this chapter is by no means exhaustive. Teachers may easily modify any of the preceding and following activities by choosing sounds that are developmentally appropriate for their students or discovering similar ways to draw their students' attention to the particular sounds in our language that they are ready to consider. Teachers may also use the websites identified in Appendix C to access many other phonemic awareness activities.

See Appendix C ▶

Rhyming

ACTIVITY

THE SHIP IS LOADED WITH . . . *(Adams et al., 1998)*

Seat children in a circle. To begin the game, say, "The ship is loaded with *bugs.*" Then toss a ball or a beanbag to a child in the circle. That child must produce a rhyme (e.g., "The ship is loaded with *jugs.*") and throw the ball back to you. Repeating the original rhyme, toss the ball to another child. Continue the game this way until children run out of rhymes. Then begin the game again with another rhyme, e.g., "The ship is loaded with *mice.*"

When the children have become good at rhyming, each child can throw the ball to another child instead of back to you. The second child must then continue rhyming with the word suggested by the first child.

WWW.

Rhyming word activities

http://teams.lacoe.edu/
teachers/

> The ship is loaded with bugs. (jugs, mugs, tugs, rugs, etc.)
>
> The ship is loaded with mice. (rice, lice, spice, dice, etc.)
>
> The ship is loaded with cats. (rats, bats, mats, hats, etc.)

Word Beginnings (Onsets)

ACTIVITY

THE SOUND SONG

The lyrics to the following song are sung to the tune of "Mary Had a Little Lamb."

> Taco starts with /t/, /t/, /t/
>
> /t/, /t/, /t/—/t/, /t/, /t/
>
> Taco starts with /t/, /t/, /t/
>
> Other words do too!
>
> It has to start with /t/, /t/, /t/
>
> /t/, /t/, /t/—/t/, /t/, /t/
>
> It has to start with /t/, /t/, /t/
>
> The next word comes from YOU!

The class first sings the song together using a beginning sound chosen by the teacher, then the teacher asks a volunteer to contribute another word that begins with the same sound. To add enjoyment and an extra challenge, the words can be themed, such as all food words or all boys' names or all flowers, and so forth. Finally, when children are adept at discriminating beginning sounds, ending sounds can be targeted using the same song.

CHARADES

Create a 3 × 5 card file that contains pictures of children performing actions (verbs) for every beginning consonant sound (e.g., bat for /b/; walk for /w/; wink for /w/; etc.). Introduce these words using charades for each action and allow children to copy the actions. When several words and their actions have been introduced, include charades as part of your reading lesson routine. Distribute the cards to the children. (If they are unable to recognize their picture, help them identify it.) Invite each child to perform the charade indicated on the card while the remaining children try to guess what the action is by first stating the *word* being acted out, then the *beginning sound* of that word, and finally, the *name of the letter* that makes that sound. (Note: This is an especially effective phonemic awareness activity for English learners, who will increase their speaking vocabulary at the same time.)

Comparing and Contrasting Sounds

A C T I V I T Y

WHAT'S THE SOUND?

Children can be given a word and asked to tell what sound occurs at the beginning, middle, and end of that word. The following song, sung to the tune of "Old MacDonald," asks children to think about the placement of sounds in words.

Beginning Sounds

What's the sound that starts these words:

PAPER, PEN, and POUND?

[wait for a response from children]

/p/ is the sound that starts these words:

PAPER, PEN, and POUND.

With a /p/, /p/, here, and a /p/, /p/, there,

Here a /p/, there a /p/, everywhere a /p/, /p/

/p/ is the sound that starts these words:

PAPER, PEN, and POUND.

Middle Sounds

What's the sound in the middle of these words:

RAIN, LAKE, and CANE?

[wait for a response]

/a/ is the sound in the middle of these words:

RAIN, LAKE, and CANE.

With an /a/, /a/, here, and an /a/, /a/ there,

Here an /a/, there an /a/, everywhere an /a/, /a/

/a/ is the sound in the middle of these words:

RAIN, LAKE, and CANE.

Ending Sounds

What's the sound at the end of these words:

NECK, ROCK, and SEEK?

[wait for a response]

/k/ is the sound at the end of these words:

NECK, ROCK, and SEEK.

With a /k/, /k/, here, and a /k/, /k/, there,

Here a /k/, there a /k/, everywhere a /k/, /k/

/k/ is the sound at the end of these words:

NECK, ROCK, and SEEK.

Blending Sounds

ACTIVITY

SECRET LANGUAGE

Prepare a list of about 30 one-syllable words containing middle or ending vowels. The first 10 should have only two speech sounds (e.g., *go* or *me*); the other 20 should have three phonemes, or speech sounds (e.g., *kite* or *chin*). Explain to the children that you are going to tell them some words in a secret language, and they must try to guess what you are saying. Then say the word in a stretched out manner (e.g., "ch—i—n"), and see if they are able to blend the word back into a whole unit. *Note:* It is sometimes helpful to use a rubber band to graphically illustrate how an item can be stretched out, then snapped back to its normal position and still be exactly the same thing.

Taking this activity to another level of difficulty, make another list of common one-syllable words of two or three phonemes in length. The words should sample a variety of sounds represented by different vowel and consonant combinations. Demonstrate once more how words can be segmented into their sound components, and then invite pairs of children to say each word in the secret language for their partners to guess, as you observe individual success with this task (Griffith & Olson, 1992).

WHAT AM I THINKING OF?

Tell the class you are thinking of an object or an animal. Give them a sound clue: segment each of the sounds of the word, articulating each of the sounds slowly and deliberately. The children, then, must blend the sounds together to discover the animal or object you are thinking of. For higher motivation, and especially to make the game accessible to English learners, the teacher may use picture cards, hiding them from the children; give the segmented clue, and turn the picture around to allow them to check their answers. Finally, real toys or objects in a grab bag heighten suspense when the teacher looks into the bag and says, "I see a d—o—ll in here. Can anyone tell me what I am looking at?"

Substituting Sounds

SPEECH SUBSTITUTION CHANT

A voice projection exercise used by drama students makes an excellent activity to practice consonant substitution while reinforcing a variety of vowel sounds. For this activity, the teacher has the children stand up at their desks. The leader (the teacher, initially) presents a consonant sound or blend such as /d/. Then the children project, at the top of their voices, but without shouting,

Da day dee do doo! [three times]

Another leader is chosen, who gives a different consonant sound. For example /ch/. The children chorus:

Cha chay chee cho choo! [three times]

For musical variety, the chant can be sung using one note, raising the note for every succeeding consonant, or a simple tune can be created for the chant.

Segmenting Sounds

WHAT'S THE SOUND?

Start with beginning sounds (onsets) that can be held for a long period of time, such as /m/, /s/, or /f/, or the parts of the syllable that follow the initial sound (rimes) that are very common, such as /-at/, /-ock/, or /-an/. Introduce the game by saying "I am going to say some words. If you hear one that starts with /m/, show me a thumbs up sign. If it starts with any other sound, show me a thumbs down." Begin mostly with words that start with the target sound. Slowly introduce words with other initial or ending sounds. Have children then volunteer to contribute words that others either accept or reject.

Finish the game by showing children pictures of some objects that have the target sound, inviting children to help you make all the sounds (segment). Discuss similarities and differences in sounds. These pictures can be gathered into a file or bound into a class book.

Manipulating Phonemes

SOUND SWITCH (Fitzpatrick, 1997)

Gather together two sets of large alphabet cards and a wall *pocket chart* (see Figure 4.3). Distribute an alphabet card containing one letter to each child. Place letters in a pocket chart to form a simple one-syllable word (e.g., *get*). Point to each letter in the pocket chart and have children say each sound. Then ask children to blend the sounds together to form the word. Next invite volunteers to create new words by placing their letters over those in the pocket chart, such as placing the letter *b* over

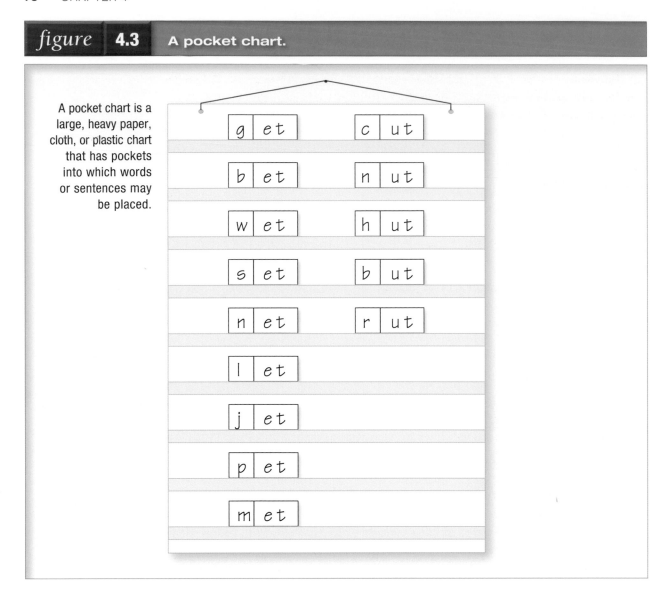

figure **4.3**   A pocket chart.

A pocket chart is a large, heavy paper, cloth, or plastic chart that has pockets into which words or sentences may be placed.

the *g* to form the word "bet." Have children blend the new sounds together and decide whether or not the word is one they know (nonsense words are acceptable). Place a new one-syllable word in the pocket chart, and repeat the process.

RECOMMENDATIONS FOR TEACHING PHONEMIC AWARENESS

honemic awareness activities can be a first step toward literacy for many children, especially for English learners, who are just becoming aware of the sounds in a new language. Such activities enable children to become aware of the sounds that will later help them learn to decode; it is essential that these activities be motivational and appropriate to the developmental level of the learners. For this reason, I include the following five suggestions to ensure that initial instruction in phonemic awareness becomes a joyful entrée into literacy, especially for children who are at risk.

1. **For younger children, do not accompany sound activities with visual cues if it seems that this combination is confusing for them.** Although there is evidence to suggest that presenting sounds for words with their visual counterparts is more effective for children who already know the letters of the alphabet (Hohn & Ehri, 1984; National Institute for Literacy, 2001), children who have not yet reached this level of phonemic sophistication may be better served by concentrating just on the sound units alone (McCracken & McCracken, 1996; Yopp, 1995).

2. **Make the lessons playful—a "treat," not a "treatment."** Children will have a pleasurable experience playing with language if the activities are presented by an enthusiastic, fun-loving teacher, rather than a "drill sergeant" bent on completing exercises and performing rote memorization as quickly and efficiently as possible.

3. **Encourage social interaction wherever possible.** Social interaction tends to heighten language development. Therefore, invite children to learn from one another by asking them to help each other. Provide many opportunities for children to turn to a neighbor and discuss their answers, work with letters and sounds in small groups, and participate in other team-building activities. Make sure the environment is absolutely safe, so there is never the fear of blurting out the "wrong" answer.

4. **Invite children to experiment with language.** When asking for rhyming words, beginning sounds, and other sound units, encourage children to manipulate the sounds and construct their own nonsensical and delightful words and humorous sounds. Demonstrate a sense of playfulness and wonder at the English language, which will be infectious among children.

5. **Support the self-esteem of children.** If the phonemic awareness activities are conducted in group settings, some children will inevitably do better than others. Therefore, a cooperative, relaxed environment is mandatory—no "put-downs" from classmates allowed, *ever!* Also, children for whom hearing sounds is difficult should be given lots of support, demonstrations, and modeling to ensure they, too, have a positive language experience. Above all, the teacher should allow for individual differences and expect a tremendous amount of individual variation in hearing speech sounds. Although many children can achieve phonemic awareness by the end of first grade, not all children do so. In time, however, with continued motivational lessons and practice, most children become adept at this vital precursor to reading.

SUMMARY

Phonemic awareness is the bridge between spoken and written language. Some children construct this bridge for themselves without explicit instruction, but many others do not. Children who lack this bridge often find that written language remains a puzzle; they will try to solve the puzzle for only so long before giving up on the task of learning how to read. It isn't too long before "I can't!" becomes "I won't!"

Experiences must always be provided so that children can understand reading as an activity undertaken for enjoyment, new understandings, and information gathering. But, for that joyful activity to be accessible, learners must also be able to see how the sounds of the language are patterned into words. Extensive research over the past 30 plus years has supported the conclusion that phonemic awareness is the most important prerequisite to understanding the nature of the relationship between letters and sounds. Young children, therefore, must be exposed to experiences that invite them to blend sounds into words and to segment words into sounds before further instruction in the sound–symbol representations—phonics instruction—can take place.

Fortunately, this instruction need not be conducted through a series of repetitious workbook pages or unexciting exercises completed in isolation at the child's desk; rather, these activities can be highly motivational group activities accomplished through enjoyable language play and game-like tasks that are naturally appealing to children. Although many children come to school having had much experience with language through a print- and language-rich environment in their homes, for others such activities may well bridge a gap in their language development and ensure a bright future of success in attaining literacy.

questions
for journal writing and discussion

1. Explain how you would describe the difference between "phonemic awareness instruction" and "phonics instruction" to the parent of a child about to enter school.

2. Examine the scope and sequence of three basal readers used in area elementary schools. Determine which phonemic awareness activities are taught and when. Describe how the three series differ. Based on your knowledge of phonemic awareness, discuss which you prefer and why.

3. The mother of a four-year-old child asks you what she can do, besides reading aloud, to help her child become ready for kindergarten literacy instruction. What can you tell her? Visit some of the websites listed in Appendix C that are appropriate for phonemic awareness and parents. How could such sites encourage parents to help their children become ready for early literacy instruction?

See Appendix C ▶

suggestions
for projects and field activities

1. Look for a folk song, nursery rhyme, or camp song that would be suitable for developing a component of phonemic awareness in young children. Adapt the song as necessary. Teach the song to a small group of kinder-

garten children. What did you observe about the increased awareness of the identified sounds through this exercise?

2. Browse through some children's books in your local bookstore or library without first researching which ones are recommended in Appendix A of this book. With phonemic awareness in mind, identify those books that would help children develop awareness of sounds in our language. Write down the names of the books you have identified, and then compare them with the ones in Appendix A or other lists compiled by literacy professionals.

See Appendix A

3. Interview two kindergarten teachers. Ask them what activities they use to teach phonemic awareness to their students. If possible, observe several of these activities. Summarize your findings for your classmates.

4. Give the Quick Phonemic Awareness Assessment Device in Appendix E to a child in kindergarten. From this assessment, determine which components of phonemic awareness the child has mastered and which he or she needs to develop. Then select three activities from this chapter and from one of the resources (Appendix B) or websites (Appendix C) to enhance the specific needs of the child.

See Appendix E

See Appendix B, C

chapter 5

Phonics, Sight Vocabulary, and Fluency

Why and How

focus questions

- How does direct, systematic instruction in phonics fit into a comprehensive approach to literacy?

- How should sight vocabulary be taught?

- What are the key components of a model phonics program?

- What is fluency, and how does it relate to comprehension?

- What are the most important factors to keep in mind when teaching phonics to beginning readers?

in the classroom

Gina has selected a book from the public library and is sitting cross-legged on the carpet, looking forward to the same enjoyment she has always experienced when she reads in class or when her grandmother reads to her. She puts a chubby finger on the cover of the book and tries to sound out the title: *The Laughing Cow.* Although she knows the beginning sound for the word *laugh* and she is able to sound out the word *cow,* the peculiar spelling of the word *laugh* makes no sense to her. Gina scratches her head and discards the book, having just received a tiny dent in self-confidence for her burgeoning reading ability.

INTRODUCTION

learning to read can be a bewildering experience for children, and teaching reading can be a confounding instructional ordeal for educators. Children become frustrated when they cannot easily figure out the words in a language that is not always "user-friendly." The task is difficult, too, because figuring out new words is an undertaking entirely different from any of a child's other previous experiences.

Literature-loving educators, on the other hand, often become disenchanted when confronted with stilted early basal readers. They are fully aware that constructing meaning from written words is the whole purpose of reading, and yet the material they are asked to use to teach reading, given the limited number of words young children can recognize, is not nearly as exciting as *The Laughing Cow* in the preceding vignette. It seems a contradiction that many children come to school knowing the meanings of most of the words to which they are exposed, yet they still cannot read, because their young brains are still in the process of discovering patterns and analogies in sounds and words. They must first be provided with a compendium of decoding strategies for identifying words that they do not immediately recognize; then they will be able to access the over 60,000 delightful children's books awaiting them in the public library.

The good news is that there is help for both teachers and beginning readers who need to accomplish these tasks together. To help children recognize words as quickly as possible, teachers can systematically show them the relationship between visual cues (letters) and the speech sounds they represent. This is what the teaching of phonics is all about. After words have been identified and have been met many times, they can be recognized automatically, in much the same way as we automatically recognize an old friend or the dilapidated Honda driven by the next-door neighbor. Words that are automatically recognized become part of a

sight vocabulary ■

child's **"sight vocabulary,"** and further strategies for identification are no longer required for those particular words. When a child arrives at this automatic stage with the majority of words she encounters, we can say that she has "learned to crack the code." The child can then move on to more interesting reading tasks.

WHY PHONICS INSTRUCTION?

two of the five essential elements in reading programs, according to the National Reading Panel, are phonics and fluency. Direct phonics instruction provides a clear path to fluent reading. Whereas phonemic awareness instruction concentrates on focusing a child's attention on the way sounds are sequenced in a language, phonics instruction helps children associate letters with those sounds. The purpose of phonics instruction is to teach beginning readers which printed letters and letter combinations represent certain speech sounds heard in words. In themselves the letters are meaningless squiggles. They become meaning-bearing units only when the child applies and adheres to the system of signals. In applying phonic skills, or the system of signals, to unknown words, the reader blends a series of sounds dictated by the order in which particular letters occur in the printed word. When a child is able to do that, she is able to **decode** or unlock the code (Beck & Juel, 1995). A child needs this ability to arrive at the pronunciation of printed word symbols that are not immediately recognized. If the child does recognize the word, however, she will not need to waste time puzzling over the speech sounds represented by the individual letters. Explicit instruction in phonics, then, can lead to fluent reading.

■ decode

The proper use of phonic strategies is one of a number of ways a child may figure out words he does not immediately recognize (Blevins, 2006). Phonics instruction is concerned with teaching letter–sound relationships and patterns as they relate to learning how to figure out unfamiliar written words; such careful attention to the sequence of letters in words can also contribute to spelling ability (Shefelbine, 1995). Because English spelling patterns tend to be deceptive, however, a child sometimes arrives at only a close approximation of the needed sounds. The child may, for example, come upon the word *broad* and pronounce it so that it rhymes with *road* or pronounce *give* so that it rhymes with *five*— both reasonable analyses of these irregular words. If the child is taught to take a flexible attitude with the sounds, however, and if the child is reading for meaning, she will frequently go back and correct these errors. After several such self-corrections, the child will not repeat the same error with these words.

Phonics instruction has long been considered a useful tool in learning how to decode automatically so that children can begin to attend to more interesting reading tasks (Adams, 1990; Beck, 2006; McIntyre & Freppon, 1994; Stanovich & Stanovich, 1995; Vellutino, 1991). Moreover, there exists a large body of strong and persuasive evidence to suggest that children who quickly develop efficient decoding strategies find reading enjoyable and thus read more; on the other hand, those who get off to a slow start in learning to decode words rarely catch up to become strong readers (Stanovich, 1986). In fact, Juel (1994) asserts that children who fall behind in first-grade reading have only a one-in-eight chance of ever catching up to grade level. Stanovich calls this phenomenon the "Matthew effect," where the skilled decoders get better and better through practice while poor decoders lag further and further behind. Although many teachers have great optimism and tend to believe that children

The purpose of phonics instruction is to teach beginning readers which printed letters represent specific speech sounds heard in words.

Phonics skills chart

www2.scholastic.com/
browse/article.jsp?id=4499

who fall behind will catch up in future grades, Clay (2000) concurs with Stanovich; through her own research and experience, she finds that a child's reading level compared with classmates at the end of first grade is pretty much the same level that child will be reading at, relative to classmates, two years later.

Phonics continues to be misunderstood by many educators. The reason for this misunderstanding becomes clear when we look closely at the language. English spelling appears to be imperfect when we look at strange words like *might, cough, should, colonel, sleigh,* and *machine;* and indeed it is challenging, for we use 26 letters to spell 44 to 48 different sounds in more than 250 different ways! This is only one side of the matter, however. If we look at all the words that are spelled regularly (bat, cat, pat, mat; hit, bit, fit), and set about organizing the irregular spellings into groups and patterns suitable for beginning readers (could, would, should), we find that it is not so bad after all. And if we begin instruction with the most regular words, it is not overwhelming for most children to master the exceptions when they are introduced one at a time and continually reinforced. The following statistics support this belief:

- Approximately 50 percent of English words are regular.
- Another 37 percent have only one sound, like the word *could,* that is represented irregularly, and this is usually close enough to connect the written letters and sounds with the actual word.
- The remaining 13 percent (like the word *ocean*) must be memorized as sight words.
- Even irregular words are stored in memory with the letter or letter pattern/sound correspondences (e.g., *light*).

Word and picture activities

www.bbc.co.uk/schools/
wordsandpictures

This brings us to what may at first glance seem a startling contradiction: the "un-phonic" spelling of so many common words constitutes the strongest argument for beginning formal instruction with the regular phonics of English spelling! Why? Simply because if our spelling system is regular a good percentage of the time, it would seem logical to begin with the regular system before taking up the exceptions. When the child learns, at the beginning, one consistent pattern after another, he rapidly gains confidence in understanding of the code. If we were to teach a dozen words only by using rote memorization or by the sight–word method, a child may still confuse *but* and *got;* but when he has been taught all the sounds of the letters, he understands why these particular series of letters spell each word. His recognition of the two words at a glance becomes easier than it would have been if he had memorized each word using only word configuration, without the benefit of previous training in letter sounds. The sight–word method of rote memorization may be appropriate for teaching only those high-frequency words that cannot be easily sounded out, sometimes referred to as "snurks" (see p. 89) or "outlaws."

BEGINNING PHONICS INSTRUCTION

he first few weeks of formal phonics instruction can have some rather remarkable results. Through all the previous reading experiences the child may have had, she may have met many words she did not instantly recognize, and at various times she may have tried one or more of the following strategies:

- skipped the word
- asked someone
- guessed the word
- applied any phonics rules she knew
- sounded out the first letter and then guessed the rest of the word
- tried to figure out the word from the context

Clearly, the beginning reader has many available options for figuring out unknown words. Some of these—such as random guessing—are not always the most efficient choices. Learning to read, then, involves sorting through a cafeteria of choices and discarding ones that are ineffective for the situation, while using others that allow for success. To make maximum progress, the beginning reader must acquire three closely related skills at approximately the same time, as discussed in Chapter 1:

- using letter–sound relationships
- acquiring a sight vocabulary of immediately recognized words
- gaining meaning from context

Essential to early reading instruction is teaching children how to crack the code—how to associate printed letters with the speech sounds they represent. Everything in spoken English can be printed using only 26 different letter symbols. As mentioned in Chapter 1, in general, letter and letter combinations stand for the same speech sounds in thousands of different words. Although there is not always a one-to-one correspondence between letters seen and speech sounds represented, learning to read is facilitated when a child has an understanding of the sound–spelling relationship in English.

Beginning readers read words in four ways: by sight (memorization), by sounding out each letter, by **analog** (comparing patterns to ones already known), and by guessing from the context (Gaskins et al., 1997). To illustrate how word learning works, let's focus on what the child gains by learning one spelling–sound relationship. Assume that the child has already been taught through phonemic awareness exercises or other early literacy activities to:

- analog

- visually recognize the letter *m;*
- associate /m/ with the sound it represents at the beginning of the words *mat, man,* and *mud;*
- differentiate the /m/ sound in *man* from the /p/ in *pan* and the /c/ in *can.*

Phonics instruction then invites the child to become a "word detective," to think to himself in the following way when encountering the unfamiliar word *marker:*

When I see the letter *m* I think of the /m/ sound because this is the same sound that begins the words *mat* and *mud.* It ends with an *er* just like *mother* and *father.*

The middle of the word has an *ark,* just like the word *bark.* The word must be *marker,* a word I have heard before. Yes, it must be, because it's talking about art and drawing, so that makes sense.

Although this process may seem unreasonably slow and tedious, remember that such thoughts go through a child's mind much more quickly than we can read about the phenomenon. As subsequent instruction focuses on other sounds represented by medial vowels and vowel combinations, the child gains new skills that enable her to decode other unfamiliar words, each mastered skill providing a greater degree of independence and **automaticity,** or fluency, in reading. The main point to keep in mind is the eventual goal of making the decoding process almost second nature so that children can expend much more of their time and energy thinking about and enjoying the material they are reading.

automaticity ■

Every new gain the child makes in learning to read will, with sufficient practice, transfer to future authentic reading situations. For instance, after several weeks of early instruction, a child will have encountered some words so frequently that he will recognize them instantly. Once this happens, he will never again have to puzzle over the speech sounds represented by those words. Similarly, with much exposure to reading words that incorporate new phonics patterns to which he has been introduced, he will be capable of detecting and using the pattern for other, similar words (Heilman, 2005).

APPROACHES TO SOUNDING OUT WORDS

research has shown that direct, systematic teaching of phonics elements is more effective than the "hit-or-miss" variety that was once taught only incidentally, when phonics elements happened to be encountered in reading and writing situations (Shefelbine, 1995). With repeated modeling of the following process, children can be taught how to sound out unfamiliar words using phonics. The teacher of emergent readers should start with one or two regular words (never snurks) that contain a targeted sound and model this approach several times every day, using this or a similar script:

Listen. When I say a letter, I'll say its sound. I'll keep saying its sound until I touch the next letter. I won't stop between sounds.

[Example: Sssssaaaaat or Mmmmmaaaaaannnnnnn.]

My turn to sound out this word.

[Put a finger under continuous sounds for 1 to 2 seconds and under stops (sounds that are *not* continuous, such as /b/, /c/, /d/) for just an instant.]

Now you sound out this word with me. Get ready.

[Touch each sound, and say them with the children.]

Your turn. Sound out this word by yourselves. Get ready.

[Touch the word, and let children make the sounds.]

[Encourage individual children to try it with new words.]

When children are able to blend together two or three sounds to make a word, they are ready to tackle more difficult blending tasks through phonics and analog. Although such strategies should be modeled incidentally whenever new words are written on the board, they should also be taught directly by explaining the use of the following approaches:

- Make the first sound. Add the second sound. Put them together before adding the third sound.

  EXAMPLE: "p," "pa," *pan*.

- Make the first sound and add the **rime**.   ■ rime

  EXAMPLE: "b," "oat," *boat*.

- Look at the rime first and put it together backward.

  EXAMPLE: "eam," "dr," *dream*.

- Identify the word parts you know.

  EXAMPLE: "re," "turn," "ing" equals *returning*.

- Ask yourself: What do I know about this word?

  EXAMPLE: *Appointment:* I know the word "point."

- Ask yourself: Do I know any word that looks like this word or any part of it? Does this word make sense?

  EXAMPLE: *Glisten:* I know the word "listen" that looks like this word. Adding a "g" makes it "glisten." That sounds right.

A SEQUENCE FOR TEACHING PHONICS

a phonics program consists of many specific concepts. In any systematic program, the necessary compendium of skills has to be arranged in a teaching sequence that allows the young reader to build confidently on what he already knows. Figure 5.1 presents one possible sequence for teaching phonic skills (Rinsky, 1997). Consult your district or state content standards to determine the exact sequence of skills that teachers in your area are expected to follow.

TEACHING SIGHT VOCABULARY WORDS

a s discussed previously, sight vocabulary is the group of words that the reader recognizes immediately, without having to decode. As children begin learning how to read, they must be taught some common sight vocabulary words known as **"high-frequency words"** at the same time they are   ■ high-frequency
learning how to decode. High-frequency words include *both* very widespread   words
"snurk" words, such as "the," that children are commonly confused by (see Figure 5.2) and should not attempt to decode while reading or "invent" while writing, and easily decodable words such as "but." It is estimated that 50 percent of the words children see are from the 100 to 150 words in the "high-frequency word" group (see Appendix G). The larger the store of words a child can recognize immediately without analysis, the more rapidly and fluently he can read a selection (Burns, Roe, & Ross, 1999).

figure 5.1   A phonics sequence.

KINDERGARTEN

Begin phonemic awareness training during kindergarten and include sounds with and without letters, beginning with consonant sounds; introduce blending and segmentation skills; introduce a few high-frequency sight words; introduce onsets and rimes with a few short vowels. Start with the letters that are dissimilar, the most useful, and introduce the lowercase letters first. An acceptable sequence is:

m, t, a, s, i, f, d, r, o, g, l, h, u, c, b, n, k, v, e, w, j, p, y,

T, L, M, F, D, I, N, A, R, H, G, B, x, q, z, J, E

FIRST GRADE

Review consonants and vowels and letter combinations, and introduce useful rules: endings (ing, er, s), consonant digraphs (two letters that cannot be separated): sh, ch, th, wh, ph; blending and segmentation skills reinforced, frequently used sight words, the final "e" rule, consonant blends (two consonants that can be separated): fl, fr, sl, sm, sn, sw, sc, sk, sp, sq, st; then bl, br, cl, cr, dr, gl, gr, pl, pr, tr, tw; then scr, spl, spr, str; the "ed" ending; then vowel digraphs *(ai, ay, ee, ea, igh, oa, ow, ew, oo, ow, ou, oi, oy, au,* and *aw),* r-controlled vowels *(ar, er, ir, ur,* and *or),* transformations of open and closed syllables *(me* becomes *met; go* becomes *got)* and generalizations for "y" at the end of a word.

SECOND GRADE

Complete highest-frequency words; review and complete single-syllable phonics patterns, then generalizations for *c* and *g* at ends of words; silent consonant clusters: *kn, wr, gn, mb, ght, ng, nk, tch;* continue word parts (prefixes and suffixes, root words) and dividing words into word parts or syllables.

THIRD GRADE

Reinforce syllabication and word parts, and introduce word derivatives (e.g., *interrogative* comes from the word *interrogate*).

Source: Lee Ann Rinsky. Used with permission of the author.

See Appendix G ▶

Become very familiar with a list of high-frequency words, such as Fry's List of Instant Words (see Appendix G), so that you can select meaningful words for classroom activities. Plan activities that focus directly and repeatedly on the words, introducing one or two new words each day and reinforcing them through games, daily stories, and "words of the week." Incorporate new words into reading and writing activities on successive days for review. Each week, the cumulative words should be reviewed.

Abstract words are usually more difficult for children to learn than concrete words, especially for English learners. It is important, therefore, to help children

| figure 5.2 | Common snurks (sight words) for early readers. |

give	woman	word	the	saw	there
what	love	work	of	any	laugh
walk	some	great	to	was	choose
because	does	pear			

associate these words with something meaningful. For example, when teaching the word *of*, one might provide pictures of a piece *of* pie or a box *of* cookies and label the pictures. The children would then be asked to do one of the following activities:

- find or draw their own pictures and label them
- chant or cheer the word (e.g., *of! of! of!*)
- write the word

Finally, four or five words would be selected from the reading each week and added to a **word wall** or bulletin board in the classroom (see Figure 5.3). A word wall or word chart is a listing of high-frequency words that are of particular interest to children or are currently being studied in a reading lesson. These words can be connected by meaning, patterns, or sounds or can simply be words that children hear and want to know how to spell. Such words usually follow a specific pattern in their beginning sound (onsets), vowel sounds, or ending sounds (rimes); other times they are words related to some topic under study. This collection of words can be alphabetized or placed under the corresponding letter of the alphabet. The words should be prominently displayed on the wall or on a bulletin board so that the children may add to the list whenever they think of an appropriate word, and the words may also be used for reference during writing activities. These words should be practiced a few minutes each day at the beginning of a word lesson by having the children (1) stretch them out and read them

■ word wall

| figure 5.3 | A word wall inspired by discussion of the five senses. |

TASTE	LOOK	SMELL	FEEL	SOUND
sweet	dirty	flowery	smooth	squeaky
yummy	round	nasty	rough	loud
sour	pretty	stinky	slimy	soft
yucky	red		dry	
	nice		bumpy	

together, (2) chant or cheer them three times, and/or (3) write them in isolation and context. Also, all words having the same spelling patterns should be starred (Cunningham & Cunningham, 2002).

There is more than one way to set up a word wall, but it should contain these features:

- The wall used should be the wall the children can see most easily when they write.
- The word wall should be dynamic. New words should go up, and old ones should come down on a regular basis.
- Easily confusable words (e.g., *that, what*) can be placed on different colors of paper.
- Children should be encouraged to use the word wall as a resource when they are trying to sound out a word.
- The word wall should be referred to several times as children are reading, writing, speaking, and listening.

The following is a list of activities involving these word walls that should be used on a daily basis (Cunningham, 2009):

- Ask children to use the word wall to find a word that rhymes with the word you say.
- Write the first letter you are thinking of on the board. Say a sentence, leaving out a word that begins with that letter. Have the children find the word on the word wall, and then chant the answer together.
- Dictate a simple sentence using word wall words.
- Play "Be a Mind Reader." Give several clues to the word you are thinking of. Clues should be based on the meaning or function of the word or on the phonic elements. The first clue is always, "It's one of the words on the word wall." Each clue should narrow down the possibilities until the last clue has been given and every child can guess the word.

A MODEL PHONICS PROGRAM

irect phonics instruction with decodable text (see p. 95) is an essential component of a reading and writing program during the early grades, but it is also important that children be involved in authentic reading, writing, speaking, and listening activities as they are acquiring the tools for cracking the code. Without this rich glimpse of literacy, phonics instruction is often ineffective (Freppon & Dahl, 1991). Good teachers use direct, systematic (explicit) but also indirect (embedded or implicit) methods to impart knowledge about decoding words. For example, teachers may use short **minilessons** (5–8 minutes) (see Chapter 9) to introduce specific concepts, skills, and phonics generalizations in a systematic way. Lessons can also take advantage of the **"teachable moments"** that can crop up in any print-rich classroom during the day, providing indirect instruction in decoding through vehicles such as language play, story writing, the language experience approach (see Chapter 9), or

minilessons ■

teachable moments ■

word walls. In general, an effective phonics program consists of all the components described in this section (Stahl, 1992; Trachtenburg, 1990).

Phonemic Awareness

Teachers reinforce understanding of the way sounds form words in our language by having those children who need this reinforcement segment words into their component sounds and by having them blend sounds into words through activities in which they try to discover how to sound out new words. These skills underscore the need for mastery of the subskills of phonemic awareness.

Useful Phonics Generalizations

Teachers teach the phonics concepts, patterns, and generalizations that have the most consistency and utility in helping children decode and spell unfamiliar words. It is best to teach these rules by *showing* children the pattern and having *them* tell what is analogous about the words through word sorting activities (Ehri & Robbins, 1992). The 18 phonics generalizations that have been shown to be most useful to children are presented in Figure 5.4 (Baer & Dow, 2006; Clymer, 1963).

Eighteen useful phonics generalizations.   *figure* **5.4**

1. An *r* gives the preceding vowel a sound that is neither long nor short. *(car)*
2. Words having double *e* usually have the long *e* sound. *(meek)*
3. In *ay* the *y* is silent and gives *a* its long sound. *(say)*
4. When *y* is the final letter in a word, it usually has a vowel sound. *(baby)*
5. When *c* and *h* are next to each other, they make only one sound. *(chair)*
6. *Ch* is usually pronounced as it is in *kitchen*, *catch*, and *chair*, not like *sh*.
7. When *c* is followed by *e* or *i*, the sound of *s* is likely to be heard. *(ceiling)*
8. When the letter *c* is followed by *o* or *a*, the sound of *k* is likely to be heard. *(coat)*
9. When *ght* is seen in a word, the *gh* is silent. *(light)*
10. When two consonants are side by side, only one is heard. *(running, hymn)*
11. When a word ends in *ck*, it has the same last sound as in *look*. *(clock)*
12. In most two-syllable words, the first syllable is accented. *(monkey, lion)*
13. If *a, in, re, ex, de,* or *be* is in the first syllable in a word, it is usually unaccented. *(begin, decide)*
14. In most two-syllable words that end in a consonant followed by a *y*, the first syllable is accented and the last syllable is unaccented. *(baby)*
15. If the last syllable of a word ends in *le*, the consonant preceding the *le* usually begins the last syllable. *(table)*
16. When the first vowel element in a word is followed by *ch, th,* or *sh*, these symbols are not broken when the word is divided into syllables and may go with either the first or second syllable. *(teacher)*
17. When there is one *e* in a word that ends in a consonant, that *e* usually has a short sound. *(bed)*
18. When the last syllable is the sound /r/, it is unaccented. *(runner)*

Whole–Part–Whole Instructional Sequence

To make sure children get the phonics support they need and also understand how these skills are useful to them, teachers use the reading of quality literature (the whole), teach phonics concepts in isolation (the part), and then have **decodable text** ■ children apply these elements immediately into **decodable text** or text that incorporates all the elements with which children are familiar (the second whole).

Coaching

Coaching can be the key to success in helping a child learn to sound out new words (Clark, 2004). For example, if a child is unable to decode the word "reptiles," the teacher can coach by providing the following cues:

- Cover up the *s.*
- The ending is a part of a word family you know *(-ile)*
- The first *e* makes a short sound.
- Break the word into two parts *(rep* and *-tiles).*
- What kind of animals are snakes and crocodiles? Think about the first part of the word *(rep).* What word would make sense here?

Minilessons

Reading games rooms
www.adrianbruce.com/reading/games.htm

Teachers can use short, directed lessons to clearly present concepts about phonics generalizations and skills to those children who, through observation and other forms of assessment, appear to require it. They can then offer opportunities for children to apply these new skills in reading and writing situations.

Application of Phonics Skills

See Appendix A ▶

Through a variety of enjoyable activities such as word play, journal writing (see Chapter 9), word sorts (see Chapter 6), the building of word walls, rhyming books (see Appendix A), and sound matching exercises (see Chapter 4), children reinforce what they are learning about phonics concepts and generalizations.

Use of Different Types of Literature

Three types of literature are necessary for an effective early literacy program, although predictable texts should not be used in phonics instruction:

predictable texts ■

Online stories for phonics
www.theideabox.com

See Appendix A ▶

Predictable texts. **Predictable texts** contain much rhyme, rhythm, and repetition and are used to teach concepts of print and English grammar and to provide an enjoyable language experience when read to young children. Although they have a critical role in a balanced reading program, they *should not be used for direct phonics instruction*. With such texts, children delight in trying to predict or "guess" words, thus delaying the acquisition of important phonics skills. (See Appendix A for a list of predictable books suitable for beginning readers.)

High-quality trade books. High-quality **trade books** are used to build academic knowledge K–12, to build vocabulary, and for enjoyment. There should be a variety of both fiction and nonfiction trade books available. For early literacy instruction, to encourage listening comprehension and enjoyment, teachers should always read such literature aloud and discuss it (see Appendix A).

■ trade books

◀ *See Appendix A*

Decodable texts. Decodable texts are small, beginner-oriented books used to immediately apply phonics elements just taught and needing practice. They provide struggling novices with easy textual experiences because they contain plenty of repetition and fewer complex patterns than trade books (Cole, 1998). Good decodable texts also use many high-frequency words that become sight words (see Appendix A).

■ decodable texts

◀ *See Appendix A*

Teachable Moments

Teachers often give spontaneous phonics lessons as they engage children in literacy lessons prompted by questions children ask about strange words or alliterative sounds, and as they model how to spell the words that come up in brainstorming sessions leading to writing activities.

GENERAL SUGGESTIONS FOR PHONICS INSTRUCTION

a few important constraints should always be considered when planning a phonics lesson. Such behaviors and practices are compatible with exemplary phonics instruction. Although some have been mentioned briefly earlier in the chapter, they are worth discussing here.

■ *Make sure children possess the necessary prerequisites in phonemic awareness for the letter–sound correspondence being introduced.* If children are not able to hear the sequence of sounds in words, training in phonics will be a frustrating and futile experience for them. Therefore, a careful assessment of the phonemic awareness abilities of each learner is vital to any successful phonics program (see phonemic awareness assessment devices in Appendix E). If certain children are deficient in this area, they may be regrouped and should receive special phonemic awareness training.

◀ *See Appendix E*

■ *Always base phonics lessons on knowledge children already have about print.* Children come to school with a variety of language and literacy backgrounds. Some children may have a wide repertoire of rap songs they can chant; others have heard the entire collection of Dr. Seuss books. Being aware of the particular background knowledge of your learners can be a great way to connect, create discussions, and begin instruction (Stahl, 1992).

■ *Focus children's attention on detecting patterns, not memorizing rules.* The human brain is a detector of patterns, not an applier of rules (Cunningham, 1995). Therefore, any phonics lesson should direct children's attention to the letter sequences and particular letter combinations that are similar to ones they already know and to the ones in the words being introduced. By contrast, phonics rules are abstract, and although children may memorize them, true application requires a stage of development beyond that of most young children.

■ *Provide plenty of opportunities for children to experiment with printed words through use of experimental spelling.* Experimenting freely with the way sounds and letters go together in our language is an excellent way for children to reinforce their understanding of and familiarity with the alphabetic principle and how it works (Stahl, 1992).

■ *Be sure that teaching of new letter–sound correspondences is done explicitly and clearly.* Phonics instruction that is direct and clear is characterized by the teacher isolating a particular sound or combination of sounds and showing the child how the sound is associated with a particular letter or combination of letters. Such instruction also includes first showing the child exactly how to blend those sounds together through teacher modeling and then guiding the child's practice.

■ *Provide immediate practice with newly taught letter–sound correspondences through decodable text containing the new letter patterns.* Like any other skill that is being learned, automatic application of phonics skills will not flourish without consistent practice. Therefore, children should be given immediate practice reading materials containing words with the new phonics elements to which they have been introduced. Avoid stilted, contrived decodable material that is limited in motivational appeal (e.g., The fat cat sat on the mat). Also, be sure quality children's literature is used for reading aloud to children and for building listening comprehension many times throughout the day.

■ *Focus on achieving sight vocabulary skills so children can soon concentrate on comprehension and enjoyment.* Teach children strategies to use when encountering an unknown word; these strategies were delineated on pages 88–89. Also, show children what you do when you encounter a new word, by modeling chunking, use of affixes, and comparing patterns in the unknown word to patterns in known words.

Integrate phonics instruction into a total, joyful reading program.

■ *Integrate phonics instruction into a total, joyful reading program.* Phonics instruction is only a small part of reading instruction, and, for many, the least exciting part at that. Phonics should never be considered a goal in itself, but rather a functional *means* to a goal. The ultimate goal of reading instruction should always be to allow children to easily decode the words they encounter so they can not only begin to read for academic purposes but also experience the joy of a most worthwhile pastime (Adams, 1991). An exemplary reading program includes not only phonics instruction but also a variety of strategies for reading and writing and highly motivational activities associated with outstanding examples of children's literature, so children will want to pursue reading far beyond the classroom doors.

Mrs. Rodgers teaches a phonics lesson

Although the sequence shown earlier in Figure 5.1 tells *what* to teach *when,* it gives very little information about *how* to structure a phonics lesson. It might therefore be useful to explain how to orchestrate a phonics lesson by describing how one first-grade teacher, Mrs. Rodgers, designs a typical reading lesson that includes an exemplary phonics component.

1. REREAD YESTERDAY'S STORY FROM A CHART OR FROM A DECODABLE BOOK *(1–2 minutes)*

Children read chorally or in pairs the short story that was introduced on the preceding day. That story allows children to apply a new letter–sound combination immediately in a real reading situation. This **repeated reading** of the story affords deeper comprehension for the child and a chance for the teacher to revisit the story for differing purposes.

2. LEARN A NEW LETTER–SOUND COMBINATION *(1 minute every other day)*

Mrs. Rodgers writes the new letter–sound combination /sp/ on the board with a directional arrow underneath. She points under the letters and pauses. Then she moves her finger under the letters and says the sound. Then she says, "I'll say it again" and repeats the sequence. Next she says, "Now say it with me." She points under the letters and pauses. She says, "Ready?" as she quickly moves her finger under the letters. The children say the blend with her. Then she says, "Your turn." She repeats the process while children look at the letter–sound combination and say the sound.

3. REVIEW ACTIVITY *(2 minutes)*

These first-graders have finished learning about each of the short vowel sounds; they can now identify and write each one. Mrs. Rodgers shows the children pictures of the following five items to remind them of the short vowel sounds: half an <u>a</u>pple, y<u>e</u>llow

jello, an <u>i</u>nch of l<u>i</u>corice, a l<u>o</u>llipop, and b<u>u</u>bble gum. (Each child was given one of each of these food items to eat when they were originally introduced.) The children cheerfully chant the names of each of these food items, exaggerating the vowel sounds in each case. As the food items are shown and the names called out, the teacher asks the children to help her sound out the words as she writes them on the board. For each sound, the children then brainstorm some other words that contain these sounds.

4. ORAL BLENDING AND SEGMENTATION *(2–3 minutes)*

Mrs. Rodgers leads this activity in a very direct yet playful way. The activities in this part of the lesson are carefully sequenced and require a great deal of support for the children. Using a cake mixing analogy, Mrs. Rodgers introduces the consonant blend *sp.* She has written each of the two letters on small squares of white construction paper. She takes the *s* paper and drops it into a bowl, as the children watch and make the /s/ sound; she does the same for the *p* paper. She then pretends to "stir" these two consonants, telling the children to "stir and say" the sounds. Then she dramatically plucks a third paper from the bowl that contains both the letters *sp.* The children say /sp/. The teacher has graphically demonstrated that a blend is two consonant sounds blended together. Children then practice the blending by holding their arms in a bowl shape on their desks. With their writing finger, they then trace each consonant inside their "bowl." They then pull their finger across the letters combining, or blending, the sounds. Mrs. Rodgers then invites them to "stir and say," and they make the /sp/ sound several times (see Figure 5.5).

5. INSTRUCTION IN BLENDING *(2–3 minutes)*

This component is considered the "heart and soul" of any phonics instruction. Children must be taught how to blend sounds together by seeing and hearing the blending process modeled explicitly. Mrs. Rodgers has several words written

(continued)

case example

figure **5.5**   **Stirring the blend.**

on her pocket chart in the reading corner of her classroom. These words, for encoding and decoding, include: *spot, spin, sped, spill,* and *spam.* She says the words aloud, slowly and deliberately, while showing them to the children. Then she writes the onsets on the board and asks for the children's help in providing the last few letters—the rime. Individual children are asked to come up to the board and sound out the last letters of the word while blending it orally.

6. HIGH-FREQUENCY SPELLING *(2–4 minutes)*

Mrs. Rodgers follows this sequence to help children learn and remember high-frequency sight words:

- The children spell the word orally: w–a–s.
- The children read the word: was.
- The children spell the word on their boards: w–a–s.
- The children do a "word cheer": Was! Was! Was!

Mrs. Rodgers also conducts a review of some other high-frequency sight words that have already been taught—*the* and *eat.* These words are then written on a word wall or laminated and put on a word ring so the words can be practiced and reviewed in enjoyable games.

7. WRITING AND SPELLING *(3–5 minutes)*

The children in Mrs. Rodgers' class each write on their individual chalkboards (see Figure 5.6), and they also have their own chalk and a worn-out sock to be used as an eraser. (Individual whiteboards can also be used.) They sit on the floor or at tables for the dictation activity. The children love the chalkboards. Writing with chalk is very tactile; children can actually feel the letters as they write and can correct mistakes or poor letter formations with the help of an old sock. Mrs. Rodgers asks the children to make four panels on their chalkboards and then shows them how to draw three lines in each panel.

She chooses a spelling pattern from the decodable text the children are reading and orally stretches out the blended sounds for the word *mmmmmmaaaannnnnnnn.* She asks the children to help her stretch out the word. Next she asks them, "What is the first sound you hear?" and the children reply, "/m/." She tells them to write that sound on the first line on their chalkboards. Mrs. Rodgers and the class stretch out the word again: *mmmmmmaaaannnn.* She then asks, "What sound do you hear in the middle of the word?" The children chant "/a/." Mrs. Rodgers repeats this process with the ending sound of the word, and soon the children have

figure **5.6**   **Individual chalk-board with four panels.**

written the entire word on their chalkboards. She follows this same procedure with three more words.

8. READING *(10–15 minutes)*

The children in Mrs. Rodgers' class love to read, and the classroom is stocked with plenty of books that include a lot of words containing the sounds they are learning as well as the high-frequency words with which they are already familiar. Now the teacher does a guided reading of their current decodable basal text, enthusiastically discussing pictures with children, who follow along or track in their books, predicting what might happen next. Tomorrow the children will read the same book with their **reading buddies,** with one child summarizing the key points of the page that the other child has just read and then changing roles after every page. When the children are finished reading, they go to sit on the carpet. One child in each pair summarizes the story they have read for the other children in the class.

Mrs. Rodgers listens to each child read every day, jotting down brief notes about the observed difficulties and successes of her learners. She also spends time during the day reading high-quality literature, which the children love to listen to and discuss.

9. JOURNALS AND EXTRA HELP *(10–15 minutes)*

At this time of the school year (March), most children are working independently in their writing journals. Mrs. Rodgers has written a sentence stem on the board:

I like to _____. But I don't like to _____.

This is an excellent time for the children to experiment with the way print works by freely writing their thoughts and feelings. (See Chapter 9 for more information about journals.) They are invited to use experimental spelling to sound out words they do not know. Mrs. Rodgers goes around to each child, encouraging their attempts and praising their efforts. She often shows them the next step in their own emerging literacy odyssey; for example, Hector, a very advanced reader and writer, asks her, "Mrs. Rodgers, is this right?" Hector has written "I like to go to

the post ofis." Mrs. Rodgers replies, "That is exactly the way the word *sounds,* Hector; you did a terrific job sounding it out. This is the way it *looks* when written." Then the teacher proceeds to write the word correctly in pencil for Hector to copy. Because children are working independently, Mrs. Rodgers also takes this time to give some learners extra help they need.

TALK-TO-YOURSELF CHART *(Reinforced Daily)*

A large chart is prominently displayed in Mrs. Rodgers' classroom (see Figure 5.7). This chart helps children self-assess their ability to read and spell new words. This procedure has six steps, which are read and reviewed with children on a daily basis (adapted from Gaskins et al., 1997).

USE OF TECHNOLOGY

Small groups of the children in Mrs. Rodgers' class read **interactive electronic books (e-books)** independently while she is working with other groups; the groups rotate until all have had an opportunity to read the book

figure **5.7**   **A talk-to-yourself chart.**

1. The word is _____.
2. Stretch the word. I hear _____ sounds.
3. I see _____ letters because _____.
4. The spelling pattern is _____.
5. This is what I know about the vowel _____ _____.
6. A word on our word wall with the same vowel sound is ___ _____.

(continued)

on the computer. With these programs, available from Scholastic, Tom Snyder Productions, Computer Curriculum Corporation, Broderbund, and others, the text and illustrations are displayed page by page on the computer screen, and appropriate music accompanies each program. Children who are capable of doing so read the book themselves while the e-book identifies unfamiliar words or reinforces specific sounds. The children can also choose to track along while listening to the e-book, making it ideal for every ability level. (Other suggestions for integrating phonics and technology are found in Appendix C.)

Guidelines for selecting interactive e-books

1. Make sure the e-book format is compatible with your class computers' e-reading program or e-reading device.
2. Choose quality literature in the same way you would choose exemplary books to read aloud to children.
3. Look for helpful features, such as word pronunciation and definitions, and accompanying activities, such as journal questions and opportunities for children to write their own books.
4. Always preview an e-book before buying it.

HOME CONNECTION *(after school)*

Mrs. Rodgers makes up **parent packets** containing cards of any new, high-frequency words that have been introduced during the day; today's words are *sp* words. She also sends home a decodable book for children to re-read, containing words the child can easily decode with the skills that have been introduced and mastered thus far in class. Again, the repeated reading with parents deepens children's comprehension while reinforcing high-frequency words and phonic elements that have been introduced. Children will be expected to read the materials in the packet to a parent or caregiver at home, or even an older brother or sister, to receive the additional practice that helps them to become fluent readers. When this has been accomplished, the child asks the adult or older sibling to sign a form saying the reading has been completed. The child returns the packet to the teacher the next day.

Mrs. Rodgers finds this communication with parents to be a boost to the growth of her students and a way to let parents know what is happening in class and how they can assist in a positive way. (See Chapter 15 for a sample parent packet.)

READING FLUENCY: MAKING DECODING AUTOMATIC THROUGH ORAL READING

the major goal of all literacy instruction is obviously to create proficient readers. Proficient readers, by definition, read quickly, effortlessly, and decode most words automatically. When they read aloud or silently to themselves, they also read with expression, appropriate phrasing, and intonation, inserting pauses as one typically does in conversation, while emphasizing important words.

In the beginning stages of learning to read, a child must depend heavily on his decoding abilities to pronounce words. These decoding abilities include breaking words apart into pronounceable components and putting the appropriate sound with its corresponding symbol(s). In a nutshell, as the child gains repeated practice in performing these requisite reading tasks, he learns to recognize more and more words automatically, accurately, and rapidly and thus becomes what we can call a "fluent reader" (Kuhn & Stahl, 2003).

Fluency, in part, is about developing a large sight vocabulary of words that have either been met and decoded or have simply been memorized during one's academic lifetime (Cecil, 2007). Proficient adult readers, for example, are able to read about 50,000 different words fairly rapidly—words we have seen often enough—through exposure to the roughly 4,000,000 words we read per year—that they are part of our sight vocabulary. On the other hand, struggling readers who are *not* fluent have very few words in their sight vocabulary and thus must spend an exorbitant amount of time and energy sounding out most of the words they read—time and energy that could be more joyfully spent thinking about the personal meaning of the text (Armbruster, Lehr, & Osborn, 2001). Indeed, without fluency and accuracy at the word level, there will always be constraints on comprehension (Adams, 1990; Adams & Bruck, 1995). Fluency instruction, therefore, will ideally focus on helping children to read words and phrases quickly and automatically, with appropriate expression. The hope in this developmental process is that once the child has attained fluency, she can then turn all of her cognitive energy to the ultimate goal of gaining meaning from the printed page—of reading to learn and for enjoyment.

WWW.

Fluency calculator

http://teacher.scholastic. com/browse/article.jsp? id=4433

Why Is Fluency Important?

What exactly is involved in the ability to read a passage fluently, and why do we now consider it so important? Although teachers and researchers have yet to agree on minor elements of reading fluency, most now agree on its essential components. Most researchers agree that there is much more to fluency than simply being able to read a series of words correctly. Rasinski (2003b) defines fluency as "the ability to read accurately, quickly, effortlessly, and with appropriate expression and meaning." Reading researchers currently studying fluency also consider the following features that are often overlooked: (1) accuracy of decoding; (2) appropriate use of pitch, juncture (a pause or other sound feature that indicates a transition or break between sounds), and stress in one's voice; and (3) appropriate text phrasing or "chunking" (Allington, 2009; LaBerge & Samuels, 1974; National Reading Panel, 2000; Perfetti, 1985; Stanovich, 1980, 1986). Thus, a fluent reader should be described as one who can decode the words in the text accurately and with relative ease and, at the same time, read with correct phrasing, appropriate intonation, and at a reasonably rapid rate so as to facilitate comprehension of a text. As children become fluent readers, they will encounter a host of words they do not recognize but can easily figure out and a larger store of other words that they begin to recognize instantly. If readers come to unfamiliar words, they learn to use decoding techniques to hypothesize the pronunciation of the word either orally or silently. Fluency is an equally important issue for English learners. Reports on the most effective instruction for these students, in which fluency is one of the most-addressed issues, indicate that the very same research-based factors identified for native English speakers apply for English learners as well (August & Shanahan, 2006; Goldenberg, 2008).

For the purposes of this book, we will define **fluency** operationally by using the three components of fluency identified by Hudson, Lane, and Pullen (2005). These three critical components of fluency are rate, accuracy, and "prosody,"

■ fluency

---

figure | **5.8** | **Attributes of fluent readers: A summary.**

FLUENT READERS READ:

Effortlessly	With tone and intonation
Smoothly	With appropriate phrasing, or "chunking"
Accurately	With meaning
Quickly	With appropriate pauses and emphasis
With automatic decoding (automaticity)	Without undue laboring over decoding
Flexibly, for different purposes	Following punctuation in text
With appropriate expression	

---

a broad term that encompasses all the rhythmic, expressive, and conversational characteristics of speech contained in Figure 5.8.

Rate

Rapid and effortless decoding strategies are important because when a child reads words with automaticity, the remaining cognitive energy can be used for comprehension, as has been stated previously. Additionally, there is much correlational evidence suggesting that increased reading rate is related to higher levels of comprehension, at least in average and struggling readers (Chard, Vaughn, & Tyler, 2002). But researchers have identified other reasons why reading rapidly is important. Being slower to identify and process visual information puts children at a distinct disadvantage, according to Lovett, Steinbach, and Frijters (2000). They offer that in one second of reading, a fluent reader is able to identify and process about five words of text—which translates to about 300 words per minute—whereas a less rapid reader may only identify and process 230 words per minute, approximately a quarter fewer than the rapid reader. Moreover, children who process all visual material more quickly tend to get more out of the time they spend reading and thus have an easier time developing other reading skills needed to make them proficient readers. So it seems that although speed is not the most important component of becoming a proficient reader, it *does* matter (Rasinski, 2000).

Accuracy

For accurate reading to occur, a child must have a large store of words that can be recognized by sight. She must also possess the ability to figure out unfamiliar words by means of a sequentially executed process in which the reader breaks words into their component parts and then puts corresponding sounds to the letters in each word part. The inaccurate reading of words, resulting from limited sight vocabulary or insufficient decoding strategies, has obvious negative consequences on reading comprehension and fluency. When many words are read incorrectly, it seems logical that the reader is apt to misinterpret text and misunderstand the author's intent. In an oral fluency study (National Assessment Governing Board, 2002), researchers found, not unexpectedly, that when children made errors that affected the meaning of the text, comprehension was affected more than when the errors did not affect the meaning of the text; however, they also noted that children rarely make reading errors that do *not* affect the meaning of text. Therefore, a reader who is able to decode most of the text accurately will be more likely to get meaning from the printed page and, thus, enjoy the activity.

Prosody

When **prosody**, or reading expression, is "correct" in a fluent reader who is reading aloud, it sounds much like conversational speaking. Richards (2000) refers to prosody as "the ability to read in expressive rhythmic and melodic patterns" (p. 535). By contrast, children who are not fluent readers are often described as reading without any expression or with pauses that do not correspond to the natural pauses one takes in normal discourse. It is not clear whether correct prosody is a "cause" or an "effect" of comprehension or whether the relationship is synergistic. But it certainly appears to one who listens to a reader with correct prosody that understanding has occurred, whereas one who listens to a reader who pauses inappropriately and speaks monotonously will be hard-pressed to believe that any comprehension has occurred. Kuhn and Stahl (2003) support this observation by theorizing that prosodic reading is "evidence" that a certain level of comprehension has taken place.

■ prosody

A Brief History of Fluency Instruction

Reading fluency, the ability to read smoothly, at a reasonable rate, and with expression, has historically been acknowledged as an important goal in becoming a proficient and strategic reader (Dowhower, 1991; Hudson et al., 2005; Klenk & Kibby, 2000; National Reading Panel, 2000; Rasinski, 2000, 2003a; Rasinski & Padak, 1996; Reutzel & Cooter, 2008). However, with a shift in emphasis away from proficient oral reading in the early 1900s and toward silent reading for personal purposes, the goal of developing fluent *oral* readers all but disappeared from the reading curriculum. In fact, this was so much the case that it prompted many astute observers to declare oral reading fluency to be an often-neglected goal of reading instruction. These researchers found that many reading methods textbooks and basal reader teacher's manuals in elementary classrooms were providing little or no guidance for developing oral fluency as an important part of comprehensive reading instruction programs. Likewise, visitors to many elementary school classrooms in much of the later twentieth century often observed little attention to oral reading and fluency instruction in daily instruction.

However, elementary schools in California and other states have begun to spend a considerable amount of time on the instruction and assessment of fluency, based on research that suggests that, once a reader becomes so fluent that

As a final step in oral reading lessons, individual children take turns reading sections of the story orally to the class.

all decoding is automatic, he can then can turn his attention to the more important goals of comprehension and true enjoyment of and engagement with text (Carnine, Carnine, & Gersten, 1984; Griffith & Rasinski, 2004; Lesgold & Curtis, 1981). Indeed, one of the primary goals of reading instruction has now become to foster fluency (Wren, 2005).

What Can Be Done to Improve Fluency?

I believe that the optimal way to increase fluency is to help children learn to love reading so that they will choose to do so often in their spare time, both in and away from school. Reading practice, like practice in anything—whether it is typing, skiing, or speaking a second language—will increase fluency in that endeavor. Children will learn to love to read and thus read and practice *more,* if they feel they are successful at doing so and if they are provided with an abundance of texts that match their interests and ability levels. Such recreational reading will provide the reading practice that is indispensible in creating readers who read rapidly and accurately, with appropriate prosody. However, many children will also need some specific, explicit instruction on one or more of these three areas in order to become more fluent, even though they are doing a great deal of recreational reading.

Useful oral reading techniques for increasing fluency include several readings of easy material into a recording device or with a partner, guided oral reading with teacher or partner feedback, and choral reading or oral reading within a reading group. Repeated reading techniques can be particularly valuable as long as the children are able to read the individual words at an acceptable speed. Word-by-word readers and those who sound out words with difficulty may need more basic instruction in fluent application of phonics to single words. The following instructional activities have been found to be effective in helping young children make the transition from emergent readers to fluent readers who read with automaticity (Kemper & Brody, 2001; National Institute for Literacy, 2001). Other activities for increasing fluency can be found on the websites identified in Appendix C.

Activities for Increasing Fluency

A C T I V I T Y

ORAL RECITATION

oral recitation
lessons (ORL) ■

Oral recitation lessons (ORL) offer a group-reading approach to developing fluency (Hoffman, 1985). ORL involves three instructional phases in succession. First, during an explicit instruction phase, the teacher introduces a story, reads it aloud, and then helps children summarize it. Next, children read the story orally as a group, with the teacher offering assistance as needed. Finally, individual children take turns reading sections of the story orally to the class. In a study conducted with second-graders, teachers who used this instructional method improved both the fluency and the comprehension of their students (Reutzel & Hollingsworth, 1993).

REPEATED READINGS

Having a child repeat the reading of a text four times is sufficient to improve fluency, according to research (Samuels, Schermer, & Reinking, 1992). Listening to a recording of an instructional-level text provides children with the necessary motivation to read the text several times or, eventually, read along with the recording. Another authentic form of repeated reading entails having children practice reading a text at their independent reading level, under the guidance of an adult, until they can read it fluently enough to then read it to a group of children at a younger grade level. Similarly, introducing a short, simple poem to children for memorization (I recommend something by Jack Prelutsky or Shel Silverstein) encourages children to read the text again and again until it has been committed to memory.

MODEL FLUENT READING

As you are doing a shared reading activity from a big book (see Chapter 11) or simply reading a story aloud, you can also be building children's reading fluency by modeling fluency and explaining to children why you read phrases and heeded punctuation in the way you did (Clark, 1995). "Did you hear how I made my voice go up in an excited way when I read that last sentence? That was because the exclamation point—this little mark right here—told me that Lilly was *really excited* when she spotted her lost dog." Then you can have children repeat the sentence exactly as you read it. Adult tutors, parents, or classroom helpers can also be encouraged to model fluent reading in this think-aloud fashion with children on a one-to-one basis, asking children to repeat the phrase or sentence after they read it. The activity can also be conducted via partner reading in which a fluent reader is paired with a less fluent reader.

READERS THEATER

Readers theater is a simple and enjoyable way to turn a favorite story into an impromptu oral reading exercise by using the dialogue of the characters in the story. No costumes, props, or makeup are required. A narrator can be used to guide the action of the characters and give clues as to appropriate gestures and other actions. If the children choose to create a script directly from the text, a real purpose of rereading has been generated (Opitz & Rasinski, 1998). The following are steps to create a readers theater script:

■ readers theater

1. Select a story that has sufficient interesting dialogue. If a single episode of a story is used, make sure the episode is self-contained; that is, knowledge of events before and after the episode is not necessary to understand and enjoy the script.

2. Make a photocopy to mark.

Readers theater activities
and evaluation

*www.aaronshep.com/
rt/index.html*

*www.teachingheart.net/
readerstheater.htm*

3. Add narrator parts to identify time, place, scene, or characters, as needed. One narrator can be added for the whole story, or more than one can be used to add variety. A narrator should introduce the script in storylike fashion by introducing the characters and setting with enthusiasm, as if they are "real."

4. Delete lines that are not necessary for the further development of the plot, are peripheral to the main actions of the story, or represent complex imagery or figurative language that is difficult to express.

5. Label character and narrator parts. Most dialogue requires no rewriting for readers theater scripts. Just add the reader's name in the left-hand margin, followed by a colon. It is permissible to give a character advice regarding the speaking of a particular line. These voice directions are placed within parentheses and follow the character's name.

6. Change any lines that are descriptive but could be spoken by a character or would move the story along more easily.

7. When you finish creating the script, ask others to read it aloud. Sometimes listening to the script makes it easier to add voice directions, revise narration, and so forth.

8. Type the completed script. Make sure the lines are easy to read. On the first page type the name of the book, story, or chapter. Then type the author's name followed by "adapted for readers theater by (your name)." On succeeding pages, type the title and page number in the upper right-hand corner of the page. Figure 5.9 shows a partial readers theater script.

---

figure **5.9**   **Partial readers theater script.**

The Boy Who Cried Wolf (in children's manuscript)
Developed by second-graders and their teacher

Narrator:	Once upon a time there was a little shepherd boy who lived in a village with his mother and father. Every morning he went to the hillside to herd his sheep. One day he got bored and decided to play a little joke.
Shepherd boy:	I am tired of looking after these silly sheep. I think I will play a joke. I will get the village people to come and join me. They will keep me company.
Narrator:	So the boy stood up and yelled as loudly as he could:
Shepherd boy:	Wolf! Wolf!
Narrator:	Soon all the village people came running up the hillside to see what was wrong.
Village person #1:	So where is the wolf, young man? I don't see any wolf.
Village person #2:	Yes! We were very busy and you disturbed us. There is no wolf here!
Village person #3:	I don't see any wolf either. Let's go back down the hill. This was a waste of our time.
Narrator:	So the village people went back down the hill. The next day the shepherd boy went to the hillside again. He got bored again. He wondered if his joke would work again.

The necessary rehearsing and the multiple performances of the oral reading activity for peers, parents, or other classes (optional) provide wonderful practice in reading fluency. Additionally, such an activity makes the story immediately accessible to English learners by providing a visual context for the words that are read.

CHORAL READING

Simple poems or predictable stories can be read in unison after you have first modeled how to read them aloud. Less fluent readers, hearing others pronounce the words as all follow along, can practice rapid and accurate reading without the fear of failure. Additionally, children for whom English is a second language become exposed to the cadence and rhythm of the English language through this enjoyable oral language activity.

The following steps can be used to create a choral reading performance with children (Tompkins, 2010):

- Select a poem or verse that is at the children's independent reading level. See Appendix A for suggestions.

See Appendix A

- Copy it onto a chart, interactive whiteboard, or overhead transparency, or make a copy for each child.

- Read the piece to the children with the expression, tempo, and intonation you want them to emulate, while they follow along in the text.

- Brainstorm with the children about how the piece might be divided for multigroup reading. Mark these ideas in the text.

- Read the piece, with the children joining in, several times at a natural speed, enunciating each word carefully. (For the benefit of second language learners, it is sometimes helpful to stand so that these learners can watch how the teacher's mouth forms the words.)

- Guide the children as they read the piece in the agreed-upon groups. Stress proper pronunciation of words, expression, and appropriate speed and volume.

- Optionally, record or video the reading so that the children can listen to their own voices and follow along, possibly deciding also if it is necessary to rearrange the voices in the choral reading.

Interactive Reading with E-Books

Fluency can be enhanced in an enjoyable social context using paired or dyad reading, with children doing several readings of the same text and offering feedback to one another, as described in Chapter 8. E-books can play a similar role and may be instrumental in improving automatic word recognition and providing a "digital language experience approach," reinforcing fluency and the link between written and oral language (Labbo, Eakle, & Montero, 2002).

Many e-books offer children the ability to self-select the amount of assistance they want, thus increasing individual control over their learning environment as they choose for themselves where and when they need help (Leu, 1997). For

WWW.

Teaching fluency through poetry

www.poetry4kids.com/index.php

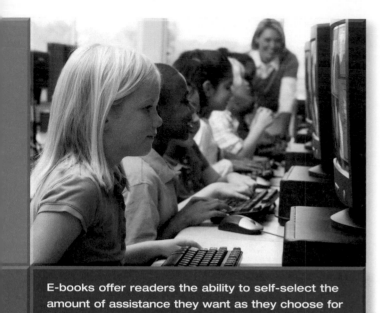

E-books offer readers the ability to self-select the amount of assistance they want as they choose for themselves where and when they need help.

example, when children come to a word or phrase they do not know, they can click on the text to have the word read for them, removing the burden of decoding (McKenna, 1998) to allow for more fluent reading on subsequent attempts. Ultimately, more energy is left to consider the meaning of—and to reap enjoyment from—the text.

The following are helpful guidelines for choosing e-books for use in fostering fluency (adapted from Tompkins, 2010):

1. Select e-books that contain high-quality children's literature.
2. Determine that the e-books are engaging enough to encourage repeated readings.
3. Be sure that the e-book is interactive and offers assistance when children cannot decode a word.

SUMMARY

Phonics instruction can be a vital component of an effective literacy program for early readers. Without any explicit instruction in this component of a comprehensive reading program, children's strategies are limited to guessing at words by their general shape and using clues from illustrations and surrounding words to assist them. Children who know the sounds that letters and letter combinations make have a distinct advantage. Although the deceptive appearance of some words in the English language makes learning the alphabetic code seem confusing at times, there are sufficient words with regular patterns to make instruction in sound–letter correspondence useful for most learners. Moreover, those words that are irregular can be taught as sight words, to be memorized. Through repeated practice with sight words and sound–symbol relationships, children become fluent readers. Such readers read with appropriate speed, accuracy, and expression. Repeated reading activities can help children become fluent readers, but the ideal way to create fluent readers is to instill a love for reading. In this way, children gain reading practice through recreational reading both in and out of school.

Phonics mastery should not be considered an end in itself, but rather the means to an end. The ultimate goal of teaching a child strategies to figure out new words is always to create an enthusiastic learner who loves to read and does so joyfully—in and outside of school. Phonics instruction should always be as brief as possible and be immediately followed by easily decodable text that shows children the reason for such instruction. Above all, phonics instruction must take place within the framework of a total reading program that also includes numerous opportunities to experiment with written language and to share appealing children's literature with the teacher and classmates. The following chapters contain strategies to help teachers instill a love of reading in their learners.

questions
for journal writing and discussion

1. Many words in the English language are not spelled regularly. Present a case for beginning formal reading instruction with the regular phonics of English spelling. Why is this not the contradiction it appears to be?

2. Create a list of 10 decodable words that could ideally be taught using a phonics method. Make another list of 10 irregular words that might be introduced by asking children to pay careful attention to their visual peculiarities. What would you tell children about the differences between these two types of words? How might you teach the irregular words as sight words?

3. Why might a beginning reader naturally confuse the letters *p, b, q,* and *d?* What other activities demanding attention to directionality might have been undertaken before the task of reading? How would you explain this letter confusion to parents who are convinced their child has a severe letter orientation problem, such as dyslexia?

4. Explain in your own words why an increase in fluency—speed, accuracy, and prosody—might be related to an increase in reading comprehension?

suggestions
for projects and field activities

1. Imagine having to learn to read the following printed message:

   3#^   *##^   %#^#*   ^%+^##^   %^^%^#   *^^*##.

   Prepare a list of information and skills that would make this task possible. Prioritize your list so that a teacher might know which skills to teach first, next, and so forth. Share your list with your college class, and defend the order of the introduction of skills.

2. Create a minilesson for first-grade children that encourages them to think of key words. You may want to use themes such as scary words, funny words, exciting words, or sad words. Teach this lesson to a small group of first-graders, having them help you sound out every word they contribute. When a word is not spelled exactly as it sounds, demonstrate to the children that a word can *sound* one way but *look* another. Put the words on a word wall, and see which ones they remember in future visits.

See Appendix E ▶

3. Administer the Phonics Mastery Survey in Appendix E to a first-grade child. From this assessment, make a list of what the child has mastered and another list of what elements the child must still learn. Finally, explain how you would teach one of the needed phonics skills through explicit instruction. Follow up this instruction with a phonics activity from the chapter. Defend your choice.

4. Find a short poem to read with a first-grade student. Pronounce unfamiliar words for the child, and then ask him or her to read the poem aloud while you time the reading. Invite the child to then take the poem home to read to friends and family members. Finally, meet again with the child and ask him or her to reread the poem while you again time the reading. What improvements did you observe in speed? accuracy? prosody?

chapter

6

Spelling

Developing Letter–Sound Correspondence

focus questions

- Why is it important for classroom teachers to be able to identify in their pupils the stages of spelling development?

- What are the important components of an effective spelling program?

- How can experimental spelling be used to help children understand the alphabetic principle?

Chrissy, a child in the third month of first grade, has just drawn an elaborate picture of a princess in an especially ornate ball gown surrounded by a swarthy prince, an adoring fairy godmother, and a lake full of swans. Ms. Sullivan, after offering profuse praise for the effort Chrissy put into her creation, asks the child if she would like to label the characters in her picture. Chrissy shakes her head vehemently, sighing, "I don't know how to write. Can you write it for me?" Ms. Sullivan smiles and urges, "Just have a go. What is the first sound you hear in *Cinderella?*" Chrissy scratches her head and hisses *S,s,s* and then laboriously pens an *s* and, later, an *n*. Chrissy is well on her way toward making the discovery that English writing is an alphabetic system in which letters are used to indicate speech sounds and, subsequently, meaning. She is just beginning to learn how to spell—and how to read and write.

Chrissy and very young children like her are engaged in experimental spelling, which, when carefully analyzed, can tell teachers much about the developmental stages of writing and how beginning readers and writers develop important aspects of the English sound system.

LEARNING AND APPLYING SPELLING SKILLS

there is a synchrony in learning to read, write, and spell. Development in one area generally coincides with advances in the other two areas. All three evolve in stage-like progressions that share important conceptual dimensions (Bear, Invernizzi, Templeton, & Johnston, 2008). Children give evidence of learning to spell by advancing through a sequence of increasingly complex understandings about the organizational patterns of words. Although memory is involved, children learn by progressively inferring the principles by which English words are spelled (Schlagel & Schlagel, 1992). A growing body of research has revealed that knowledge of letter patterns, or orthographic knowledge, develops as a process in children and that this development is reflected in their errors or experimental spelling (Gill & Scharer, 1996). Research also suggests that children also use early spelling experimentation to actually "break the code" of reading (Gentry, 2004).

Just as reading comprehension is enhanced by an ability to recognize words quickly and accurately, children's writing is also supported, according to research, by proficiency in spelling. Along with instruction in the writing process (see Chapter 9), children must be taught letter formation and grade-appropriate spelling skills in order to produce longer, more detailed pieces of writing (Graham et al., 1997). Moreover, research suggests that children can develop correct spelling more quickly if spelling skills are taught beginning in first grade in authentic writing contexts (*Every Child a Reader*, 2000).

Children who are taught spelling explicitly and systematically, and who are also invited to apply their skills in a variety of writing contexts, learn to spell more quickly and accurately than children who are simply given random lists of words to memorize by rote. Additionally, systematic instruction in the following has been found to create more efficient spellers (Gentry, 2008):

1. sound syllable segmentation ("con-tam-in-a-tion")

sound mapping ■ 2. sound–symbol association or **sound mapping**—matching letters and letter combinations with sounds ("Open: /o/ /p/ /e/ /n/.")

3. spelling patterns ("Hmmm, 'glisten' and 'listen' have the same patterns!")

THE STAGES OF SPELLING DEVELOPMENT

I n learning to communicate in written form, a child generally goes through five basic **developmental spelling stages** (discussed below) in roughly the same sequence, despite differences in educational background, although it is not uncommon for a child to evidence elements of two or more of these stages at any one time. It should be noted, however, that rate of progress through the stages varies from child to child. Children first string letters together at random. Then, when they have discovered the alphabetic principle, they begin to "sound out" words. Finally, they progress to one-syllable spelling patterns, syllable combinations, and the spelling of meaningful word parts, or *morphemes* (Bear et al., 2008).

■ developmental spelling stages

A quick assessment device called the "Monster Test" can help teachers determine the approximate developmental spelling stage of their learners (see Appendix E for this and other spelling assessment materials).

◀ *See Appendix E*

Researchers have used various hierarchies to describe the stages children go through as they learn to spell. The next sections will present two ways of looking at the developmental stages of spelling. To familiarize you with these two distinct views, Figure 6.1 compares how the stages of spelling are discussed in the literature, each focusing on differing components of spelling.

Gentry's Stages

According to Gentry (2008), children go through the following stages when learning to encode: precommunicative, prephonetic or preliterate, phonetic or letter-name, transitional or within-word, and conventional spelling or syllable juncture stages.

The precommunicative stage

The initial stage of spelling development is called the **precommunicative stage** and occurs about the time the child learns the alphabet and makes the discovery that words are composed of letters, although the child may have little or no concept at this time of exactly which letter stands for which sound. In this stage, the young child strings scribbles, letters, and letter-like forms together without any particular knowledge of associated phonemes, and the writing may proceed from top to bottom and right to left, or even randomly across the page. A child at this stage might compose a story about an elephant, and to our eyes, the story will be virtually unintelligible and look something like the writing shown in Figure 6.2(a).

■ precommunicative stage

The prephonetic, or preliterate, stage

The second stage of spelling development is called the **prephonetic stage** and evolves when the child begins to understand the alphabetic principle that letters have certain sounds that form words. About this time, too, the child becomes aware of the left-to-right orientation of the English language. This particular stage is somewhat like the stage in very young children's language acquisition when they use one word to symbolize a whole idea or concept, such as "Up!"

■ prephonetic stage

figure   **6.1**   **Stages of spelling development: Two views.**

GENTRY (1985, 2006)	BEAR, INVERNIZZI, TEMPLETON, AND JOHNSTON (2008)
PRECOMMUNICATIVE STAGE	**EMERGENT SPELLING**
Learning the alphabet	Random letters
Scribbles and letter-like forms	Mostly upper-case letters
Mostly unintelligible	Learning directionality
PREPHONETIC STAGE	**LETTER NAME–ALPHABETIC SPELLING**
Alphabetic principle	Alphabetic principle known
Left-to-right orientation emerges	Short vowels and consonants appear
One letter used for dominant sounds	Abbreviated spellings
PHONETIC STAGE	**WITHIN-WORD PATTERN SPELLING**
Refinement of earlier stage	Long vowels and r-controlled words
Basic spelling patterns and families	More complex vowel and consonant patterns
Many sight words known	Awareness of homophones
TRANSITIONAL STAGE	**SYLLABLES AND AFFIXES SPELLING**
Most words spelled correctly	Inflectional endings applied
Aware of visual aspects of words	Can spell multisyllabic words
Vowels in each syllable	Know common affixes
CONVENTIONAL STAGE	**DERIVATIONAL RELATIONS SPELLING**
Mastered English orthography	Aware of Greek and Latin roots
Have a spelling consciousness	Examine etymologies of words
Can apply rules of orthography	Can spell related forms of words and alternative spellings

to mean "I would like you to pick me up, Daddy." Similarly, in this stage, one letter—usually the most dominant sound—is used to represent the entire word. In the previously addressed story about an elephant, a child in this more advanced stage might represent the word "elephant" with an "L" because the name of the letter "L" sounds most like the beginning of the word "elephant." The story might look like the writing in Figure 6.2(b).

The phonetic, or letter-name, stage

phonetic stage ■   The third stage, the **phonetic stage,** is in many ways a refinement of the earlier prephonetic stage. Children continue to use letter names to represent sounds, but at this more advanced stage, they also use consonant and vowel sounds for each spoken syllable. Although certain vowels and silent letters may be omitted,

---

| **Sample illustrations of the stages of spelling development.** | *figure* | **6.2** |

(a) Precommunicative stage.

(b) Prephonetic, or preliterate, stage.

I. W cE.L &

(c) Phonetic, or letter-name, stage.

I wandt to see lafin

(d) Transitional, or within-word, stage.

I want to see the alufints

---

the child seems to have become aware of some of the basic spelling patterns and families in the English language through the visual attention afforded by reading. She may also have memorized some sight words. Now the story about the elephant could look like the writing in Figure 6.2(c).

The transitional, or within-word, stage

The fourth developmental spelling stage, the **transitional stage,** occurs when the child can come close to the spelling of various English words, usually about third grade. Many words are spelled correctly, but irregular words that have not been directly taught still cause confusion. At this stage, children are exposed to a wide range of reading experiences, and they are aware of visual aspects of words that are not detectable to the ear. Vowels are correctly placed in each syllable, and common English letter sequences such as the *ai* in *pain* and *rain* begin to emerge correctly in the child's writing. At this stage the elephant story would look something like the writing in Figure 6.2(d).

■ transitional stage

The conventional spelling, or syllable juncture, stage

When children have mastered the basic principles of English orthography, we say they have arrived at the **conventional spelling stage,** meaning that most words are spelled correctly, as the name implies. Children in this stage are aware of syllables but may still incorrectly spell vowels in the schwa position (e.g., *elavate* for *elevate*). At this stage, children are developing a spelling **"conscience,"** or a concern for spelling all words correctly, as well as a spelling **"consciousness,"** meaning they can generally tell if a word they are trying to spell "looks right."

■ conventional spelling stage

■ spelling "conscience"
■ spelling "consciousness"

Additionally, children learn how to spell homonyms and contractions and become adept at doubling consonants and adding affixes to words; they also learn that there are alternative spellings to certain words.

Bear, Invernizzi, Templeton, and Johnston's Stages

Bear, Invernizzi, Templeton, and Johnston (2008) view the stages of spelling development as emergent spelling, letter-name alphabetic spelling, within-word pattern spelling, syllables and affixes spelling, and derivational relations spelling; these run parallel to Gentry's stages, with some unique observations (See Figure 6.1).

Emergent spelling

The most range in expression is found in this earliest of stages. Much like Gentry's precommunicative stage, 3- to 5-year-old children in this phase of spelling development generally make random marks anywhere on a page, usually using uppercase letters. While there may be some letter–sound matches, such children are just learning how to make letters and realizing that drawing and writing are two different processes.

Letter-name–alphabetic spelling

At this point, 5- to 7-year-old children are learning the alphabetic principle—that letters represent sounds—and beginning to apply this principle to "sound out" words they are trying to write. Initially, such spelling includes only the surface sounds in the word, as in the prephonetic stage where "E" may represent elephant; but as they begin to progress through this stage, they hear and use more short vowels, as well as blends and digraphs, as they learn about them.

Within-word pattern spelling

In this stage, according to Bear et al. (2008), children of roughly 7 to 9 years become aware of long vowels, r-controlled words, and more complex consonant and vowel structures, such as *tough, piece,* and *boil.* They can spell most one-syllable short vowel words with ease. Often overgeneralization occurs: *caught* becomes *catched,* and *mouse* becomes *mowse.*

Syllables and affixes spelling

At about ages 9 to 11, children enter the stage of spelling development where they are able to use the process of "chunking" to break apart multisyllabic words in order to spell them. As a result of reading and formal instruction, they also learn about inflectional endings, such as

Children can learn to spell fairly easily if they are initially encouraged to experiment freely with the way print works.

-ed, -ing, and -s, as well as how to double consonants or drop the final "e" before adding an inflectional ending, such as in the words *getting* and *racing*.

Derivational relations spelling

Instead of entering a conventional stage, as in Gentry's model, children at this stage are still working on specific aspects of our orthographic system in this final stage. They begin to explore the ways words with similar meanings are spelled when they derived from the same root or base word, such as *sanitary* and *sanitize*. They are also learning about morphemes and Greek and Latin roots and how the etymology of certain words affects their spelling (e.g., the word *bazaar*, from Turkish, or *pasteurize*, after Louis Pasteur.

OBSERVING EXPERIMENTAL SPELLING

When children are first beginning to write, it is best to encourage them to do experimental spelling—to invite them to sound out words they don't know, without asking them to necessarily spell them correctly. At this early phase in emergent literacy, teachers need to be resolute about *not* showing children how to spell each word, or children will not develop the strategy of making a first attempt, thus losing important opportunities to experiment with sound–spelling relationships. Because learning how to spell involves problem solving, all children should be encouraged to attempt to spell a word first, perhaps trying it several ways, and then to check its correctness with a resource (Bolton & Snowball, 1993).

Observations of experimental spellings in early writing can show teachers much about children's knowledge of sound–spelling relationships. These observations can also demonstrate how knowing the names of letters can sometimes be a slight hindrance as well as a help, which we shall see in a later discussion. Additionally, teachers begin to understand how coupling this experimentation with systematic instruction in the visual patterns of our language, starting in the first grade, helps children become adept at using the structural patterns of the English language to learn to spell words correctly.

Children's spellings in the following examples illustrate six important concepts about how children attempt to sound out words they wish to spell.

We see from observing children's experimental spelling that knowing letter names helps children spell when the word contains a long vowel sound. For example, a child will spell words with long vowels in the following ways:

> *mak* for *make*   *kit* for *kite*   *tigr* for *tiger*

The vowels are spelled correctly because they are spelled the way the name of the letter sounds. On the other hand, short vowels, such as those in the words *bad*, *bot*, and *win* are more problematic for children if they are trying to spell them based solely on their knowledge of the names of the letters in the alphabet. A beginner's spelling of these words is often *bed*, *bit*, and *wen*, respectively, because experimental spellers use the vowel name that is closest to the sound in the word when spoken.

When children attempt to sound out words with certain consonant blends, such as *dr* and *tr,* they often represent these sounds with the letters *jr* or *ch* because the sounds are somewhat similar. The way words such as *dress* and *try* are pronounced sheds some light as to why this may be so: A sophisticated speller is aware of how such blends *look* in relation to their sound. Beginning writers, however, are concentrating on what their mouths and tongues are doing as they sound out a word slowly, and these sounds tend to cause a slight friction at the front of their mouths as they articulate the words. Children generate their own rules for these sounds based on their pronunciation; later, with instruction, their focus changes to the similarity of the phonetic features of the beginning sounds to other words they know. Sophisticated writers learn this through instruction in English spelling patterns and how words are supposed to *look*.

Especially at the very earliest stages of experimental spelling, children tend to represent /t/ in the middle of words with a *d*. Again, this outcome of experimental spelling underscores that children pay attention to what they *hear* in the word as they articulate it slowly: *butter (budder),* therefore, is often spelled *budr* by early writers, while *matter (madder)* would be sounded out *madr,* because American English does not clearly articulate these middle sounds. As soon as the child sees and understands the difference between the way we say such a word and the way it is represented, he then consistently incorporates this knowledge into subsequent spellings of words with the consonant *t* in the middle of the word.

Early spellers tend to exclude the first letters of certain consonant pairs that are blended together in their mouths. The words *can't* and *won't,* for example, are generally spelled *cat* and *wot* in experimental spelling because the nasal sound produced when they say the /nt/ sound in these words causes their tongues to stay in only one place—in the front of their mouths. Since they do not need to *move* their tongues when they say each of these sounds, they tend to believe they need only one letter to represent both sounds. Again, they are focusing on what they *hear* and experience and are usually not yet aware of how such words *look*.

The ways early writers represent the final letters that signify past tense, plurals, and third-person singular vowels are very consistent. Proficient readers and writers understand that we add *ed* to the ending of a word to indicate that the action happened in the past, whether the *ed* is pronounced as a discrete syllable or not. Young children have no such knowledge until this visual reality is specifically pointed out. We know, for example, that *wanted* contains a final *ed* to indicate that the *wanting* occurred in the past, but we realize that *hoped* also terminates with an *ed* even though it sounds like a /t/ at the end of a one-syllable word. Children using experimental spelling sound out such words as *hopt, laft,* and *stopt.* Similarly, words with plurals commonly represented by the letter *s* would be spelled with the sound that is more prominently heard: *sez, stayz,* and *criz.*

Tommy's perspective on experimental spelling

Our school's parent survey indicated that several parents remained unconvinced about the benefits of invented [experimental] spelling in their children's writing. So I set out to survey students and gather information to support the necessity for invented [experimental] spelling. I purposefully interviewed students at all performance levels, but my conversation with a second-grader, Tommy, held the essence of all the answers.

"Tommy, what strategies do you use when you want to write a word, but you're not sure how to spell it?" I asked.

"I sound it out or ask the kid next to me," answered Tommy confidently.

"Good. But what if all the words you wrote had to be spelled correctly—you couldn't sound them out and the kid next to you didn't know how to spell them either?"

"Oh, I know what you mean," said Tommy. "Then I use different words, like in my journal. I can't spell 'because,' so I write 'it is' instead. Like I write 'My favorite sport is baseball. It is fun' instead of 'because it is fun.' Get it?"

"Yes, I do—that's a good strategy. So baseball is your favorite sport, huh?" I asked, making conversation while I jotted down Tommy's response.

"No, it's soccer, but the kid next to me can't spell soccer."

Undaunted, I pressed on. "So, what if you were all alone in the room with no one to ask how to spell a word?"

"You mean like if I had to stay in for recess because I had messed around all morning and didn't finish my work?" asked an obviously experienced Tommy.

"Yes, like that."

"And there was no one to ask, right?" He wanted to be sure.

"Right," I answered, "no one. And you can't sound it out. What would you do?"

Tommy thought for just a moment and then said, "Then I would write, 'I do not like sports.' I can spell all that."

Source: Excerpt from Romeo, M. G. (April 1995). On Spelling. *The Reading Teacher, 48*(7), 619. Reprinted with permission of the International Reading Association via Copyright Clearance Center.

In general, children are remarkably consistent in their use of the patterns they have devised in their experimental spellings. This is similar to the overgeneralization that occurs when children are learning their first language. They unconsciously detect the pattern they must use to change the original word when forming a past tense, noticing that *pat* becomes *patted* and *want* becomes *wanted*. They overgeneralize this pattern, however, devising *runned* for *ran* and *goed* for *went*. Likewise, it becomes clear from observing children's initial attempts at spelling that when children devise rules to govern how they will construct words according to their sounds, they tend to follow them routinely.

Children move beyond experimental spelling into predicting spellings on the basis of extensive knowledge—knowledge gained through experience with and instruction in how language works—and by noticing the similar patterns or analogs of the words they meet. The Case Example above offers a report of one child's perspective on experimental spelling and how it helps in the writing process.

UNDERSTANDING OUR ALPHABETIC SYSTEM

ood spelling is more than a literary nicety or icing on the editorial cake. Poorly developed spelling knowledge has been shown to hinder children's writing, to disrupt their reading fluency, and even to interfere with their vocabulary development (Adams et al., 1998; Read, 1986). Although it is appropriate to encourage beginning readers, such as Chrissy in the opening vignette, to use experimental spellings to express their written ideas, programmatic instruction in correct spellings should begin in first grade and continue across the school years (California Department of Education, 1996). In addition, children—as well as many adults!—need to be guided to develop a robust conscience about and consciousness of correct spelling in all their written work.

Research supports the premise that written composition and reading are enhanced by mastery of the component skills of spelling, just as reading comprehension is supported by mastery of fluent word recognition (Gentry, 2006). Fluent, accurate letter formation and spelling are associated with children's production of longer and better-organized compositions (Berninger et al., 1998). Word usage, handwriting, punctuation, and capitalization, as well as spelling, are the necessary conventions of written expression that must be taught alongside strategies for composing. Children learn these skills more readily if they are taught explicitly from the first grade onward and applied within the context of frequent, purposeful writing assignments (Graham et al., 1997).

Children can learn to spell fairly easily if they are initially encouraged to experiment freely with the way print works. With guidance, children will soon discover that all 44 or so phonemes in the English language can be represented by letters or groups of letters. With this understanding and further teaching in the common patterns found in English spellings, children eventually become literate (Tangel & Blachman, 1992, 1995). The word "discover" is used advisedly, however, because children do not learn how print works simply by learning the alphabet, then the letter sounds, and then being told that English is an alphabetic system (Gentry, 2006). Although early educators believed there was little more to spelling than that for many years, current spelling research suggests that to become good spellers, children must understand the phonemic nature of speech by being shown that (1) we speak in a flow of individual words, (2) each word is composed of a number of sounds, and (3) the sounds of speech are expressed graphically in a specific left-to-right sequence (McCracken & McCracken, 1996).

Because one of the initial challenges for teachers is to develop children's phonemic awareness and knowledge of basic letter–sound correspondences, activities designed to meet these goals should begin with short, regular words such as *man, but,* and *can.* Because the major goal of these early sessions is to develop the kind of strategizing necessary for good spelling, these lessons should be enjoyable and exploratory. They should also model the processes literate people use to generate the spelling of words and to make logical guesses when they are stumped by unknown spelling patterns. Gradually, the focus of these spelling lessons should be expanded to more complex spelling patterns and words, moving systematically from pattern to pattern and from two- and three letter words through consonant blends, long vowel spellings, and so on (Gentry & Gillet, 1993). The real challenge is to instill in children an understanding of the underlying logic and regularities of a system that, in many cases, can be highly illogical and irregular, as illustrated by the piece in Figure 6.3, written by a child in early second grade.

An effective spelling program, then, is one in which teachers help children explore and understand the patterns and useful generalizations about the complex relationships within and between words, helping them apply these concepts to each new spelling encounter (Henderson, 1995; Zutell, 1996). Moreover, an informed, developmental analysis of children's efforts as they begin to write will show teachers how to match the features of words to be taught to the students' readiness to discover them.

A program with the above components would be similar to the one described in the following section.

AN EFFECTIVE SPELLING PROGRAM

for children in the early phonetic/early letter name stage, formal instructional strategies should include activities that draw children's attention to the beginning, end, and middle of words, in that order. Whenever possible, children should be involved in spelling the same words they are learning to read.

A second-grader's experimentation with print.	*figure*	**6.3**

Early Phonetic/Early Letter Name Stage
(Kindergarten–early first grade)

The following strategy from Moats (1995a) is especially good for introducing new words to children needing help discerning individual sounds.

1. The teacher pronounces the word: *bat.*
2. The children repeat the word, hearing their own voices and feeling the articulation: b–a–t.
3. The children say the word, sound by sound; after identifying each sound, they say the name of the letter that represents the sound and then write the letter as it is being named on individual chalkboards: *b* /b/; *a* /a/; *t* /t/.
4. The children read back, orally, the word they have written: *bat.*

Sound–symbol correspondence can be reinforced on subsequent days using the following activities:

Word hunts. Using the beginning, ending, or middle sound being studied, the children go around the room searching for other words or objects that begin with the same sound. For example, for the /b/ sound they might find the words *Bill, boat,* and *by.* The teacher writes these words on the board as the children contribute them and help to sound them out.

Picture sorts. The teacher places picture cards among the children and sets up one or two pictures as examples of the beginning, middle, or ending sound being studied. The children take turns coming up and placing their cards with the appropriate example, saying the word as they do so. The teacher makes a list of the words, with the children helping to sound them out.

Word-building activities (Cunningham & Cunningham, 1997). Children use paper or tile letters to form words. The teacher reads a word slowly (e.g., *in*), stretching out each sound. The teacher asks the children to stretch the word out using their imaginary rubber bands. Children are required to listen for beginning, middle, and ending sounds, to notice letter patterns, and to discover how capitalization is used in words as they manipulate letters and sounds through the following example sequence:

in	is	it	hit	sit	nit
tin	tins	Tim	this	thin	things

A pocket chart can be used to highlight words for all children to see. As children work through several lessons, each using a different combination of letters, they begin to internalize common word patterns, letter blends, and digraphs.

Cut, paste, and label. The teacher creates a large poster headed with one or more pictures of things with the same beginning, ending, or middle sound being studied. Children are given magazines, catalogs, scissors, and paste. The children, in small groups, find pictures of items with the same target sound, cut them out,

Ideas for meaningful spelling lists

- A series of words containing a specific phoneme
- Any of the dozens of common spelling patterns: "oo" words, words that end with "y" or "ey," compound words, words with double consonants, words that contain the pattern "ough," and so on
- Words from the decodable text that is being used for reading instruction
- Words with similar meanings: paper, newspaper, wallpaper, papered

- Words that have related roots: photo, photographer, telephoto
- Words from units of study: whale, ocean, tadpole, waves
- Common words we use all the time: it, the, when, my, little
- Place names: Sacramento, California, Ohio, Canada
- Any other grouping that will provide related words for sorting

and paste them on the poster. As the words are said, the teacher writes them on the board, asking the children to help sound them out.

Phonetic/Late Letter-Name and Within-Word Stage
(Late first–third grades)

As children advance to the phonetic/late letter name and within-word phases, generally in late first grade through third grade, more systematic spelling is conducted throughout the week and includes different activities for each day, based on a teacher-selected spelling list. An excellent resource for such grade-level–appropriate lists is *Teaching Spelling* (Henderson, 1995). However, many teachers question the use of commercial lists to teach spelling (especially when the words chosen from lists are unrelated to the words children are seeing in their reading and using in their writing), as research on experimental spelling suggests that spelling is ideally learned through copious reading and writing (Gentry & Gillet, 1993; Wilde, 1992). Words chosen should *always* be those that children can already read, particularly those that children use, but misspell, when writing. Initially, sorting by sight and sound is the most helpful. More ideas for appropriate spelling lists are included in the box above.

Transitional/Syllables and Affixes Spelling Stage

As children enter this stage, some who have had no previous trouble mapping sounds in words become confused when they begin to encounter words with more than one syllable. Distinguishing where one word part or chunk ends and the next chunk begins seems overwhelming to them. Before these larger words appear, such children are usually successful with sound–symbol strategies that fit common spelling patterns, such as CVC, one syllable words (*cat*), or words with a silent "e" (*gate*). But multisyllabic words cannot be sounded out as one entity, and not all children automatically say each syllable as they are spelling each chunk. In such cases, the following instructional strategy must be directly taught.

Spelling in Parts (SIP) (Powel & Aram, 2008), uses sound, visual, and meaning strategies. It can be used to help children break multisyllabic words into smaller chunks to make spelling much easier.

Spelling in Parts (SIP)

(Powel & Aram, 2008)

1. The teacher models the SIP strategy on the board, demonstrating how she would say and spell the word *continent*. She discusses the meaning of the word.
2. The teacher says the word "continent" and has the children say the word and distinctly clap each syllable.
3. The children divide the word into chunks as they pronounce each chunk—/con/tin/ent/.
4. Then, on paper, children write the parts one at a time, leaving a space between the parts, as the teacher checks that the division between chunks is acceptable.
5. The children circle any syllables that may be problematic (e.g., the /i/ sound is a schwa and sounds like a /u/).
6. They "take a picture" of the problematic word part within the word to help them keep a permanent visual memory of the word feature.
7. From memory, children say and write each syllable.
8. Children check their spelling against their initial spelling of the word and repeat the process if necessary.

A Typical Week's Study Plan*

Fresch and Wheaton (1997) have devised an effective week's study plan, as discussed below.

Monday: Pretest

The teacher selects a spelling sound, pattern, or rule that she feels children are ready for, based on the spelling assessment. The pattern might be as simple as the short /a/, or as complex as words that have the /k/ sound. All the words the teacher chooses will contain this pattern. The teacher selects 15 or 20 words that have this pattern or sound for the pretest, such as the following list containing variations of the /k/ sound:

like	think	king	kind	cake
car	call	back	book	pack
bike	kitten	lock	walk	talk

* Adapted from Fresch, M.J., and Wheaton, A. (1997, September). Sort, search, and discover: Spelling in the child-centered classroom. *The Reading Teacher, 51*(1), 20–31. Reprinted with permission of Mary Jo Fresch and the International Reading Association via Copyright Clearance Center. All rights reserved.

She administers a pretest created from these words, and children proofread and correct their own attempts. The teacher then displays another slightly more difficult list of 15 to 20 words containing the sound or pattern:

ticket	camp	nickel	kangaroo	cape
ache	cabin	kingdom	cattle	school
Canada	camel	Kansas	camera	market

Children choose words from this list to study in place of any words spelled correctly in the pretest or, if they are exceptionally skilled spellers, create their own lists based on the spelling concept in the lists (Hong & Stafford, 1999). Alternatively, some children who consistently score above 80 percent on the pretest may develop individual contracts with the teacher regarding either specific words they wish to learn to spell or words they have recently needed for writing stories, reports, letters, or other written pieces (see the next section, "Contract Spelling").

The children then copy their individual word lists three times. One list is sent home to be shared with parents, a second is stapled to the child's writing folder for future reference, and the third is cut up into individual word cards for later sorting activities.

Tuesday: Word sort

Children are asked to use their ears, eyes, and brains to sort out their word cards, either individually or in small groups. Such focused, small-group work on word patterns enhances spelling and aids in reading development (Invernizzi, Abouzeid, & Gill, 1994; Schlagel & Schlagel, 1992). Initially, the children use their ears to listen to the sounds in their words, and sort the words by the sounds they have in common, if different sounds are included in the list. Then, they use their eyes to detect other patterns with the help of the teacher, who is moving from group to group offering assistance. Next, they are told to underline the letters that make the specific sound (e.g., /k/) in each word. Finally, they are asked to use their brains to draw some conclusions, either orally with preliterate children or in written form, about what they have discovered. One pair of students came up with the following list and set of generalizations from their list:

k	c	ch	ck
kingdom	cape	ache	ticket
Kansas	Canada	school	nickel
kangaroo	camera		
market	camel		
	camp		
	cattle		
	cabin		

"There are four different ways to make the /k/ sound. You can spell it *k, c, ch,* and *ck.* The most common way seems to be *c,* followed by *k.* The least common seems to be *ch; c* never seems to come at the end of a word; *ck* never seems to come at the beginning of a word; *ck* is never spelled *kc.*"

At this juncture, the whole class comes together to share their findings. The teacher sorts the words using a pocket chart or overhead. She models how she would sort the words, thinking through her decisions aloud. The children add their insights and generalizations to hers, explaining the bases for their conclusions. All generalizations are written on chart paper and posted in the room for future reference and for periodic review.

Wednesday: Word hunt

To allow children to apply the generalizations or rules they encountered on Tuesday, the pairs or small groups of children are given 10 or 15 minutes to search through any printed or written material they have available and come up with other words that conform to the generalizations. Later, the children reconvene as a whole group to share their lists and create a new word wall that is kept visible and updated by children throughout the day as they find other words that fit the pattern.

Thursday: Using the words in context

The ability to remember how to read and write a specific word comes from understanding its meaning in context. Therefore, children with rudimentary writing skills are asked to create brief sentences—and as they grow in literacy, even stories, poems, riddles, or other text—using their individual word lists. Children are then asked to highlight all the spelling words in the piece. The post-test words (see Friday) will be read directly from this written material.

To write their words in context, children must be taught a set of strategies for figuring out what to do when they can't spell a word. Some strategies will be more efficient when children are composing their text; others will be more useful when they are editing. While they are writing they should learn to take a guess by sounding it out, and the following strategies should be taught and then posted for them to reference during any writing activity:

- Say the word to yourself very slowly; really stretch it out so you can *listen* for the different sounds.
- Think of the beginning sound and write down the letters that make that sound; for help with the beginning sound, think of a word you know that begins with that sound.
- Think of the middle sound and write down the letters that make that sound.
- Think of the ending sound and write down the letters that make that sound.
- Look at the word carefully and see if it looks right. Read it back to yourself out loud and make sure you are able to read it even if it isn't correct.
- Always write *something*, even if it's just one letter, so you can remember the word you wanted.

After they have completed a rough draft, children even at the earliest stages need to get into the habit of editing their writing for spelling. Therefore, the following strategies should also be taught and posted for reference. Before finishing any piece of writing:

- Circle or underline the words you are unsure of.
- Check the spelling of the word, using your personal dictionary, a word wall, a class list, or a proofreading buddy.
- If you still can't find the word, ask your teacher.
- Make the corrections you need.
- Recopy the piece and read it again.

Friday: Paired post-tests

Children give a final post-test to each other in pairs by reading the highlighted words from the contextual material written on Thursday. Pairs may correct each other's post-tests or request that the teacher do so. Children scoring below 80 percent are targeted for future minilessons (see Chapter 5) with the week's spelling patterns. The teacher can retain the lists, writings, and post-tests to provide valuable assessment information about each child's spelling growth.

CONTRACT SPELLING

an alternative approach to spelling instruction for more advanced spellers is **contract spelling** (Hoskisson & Tompkins, 2001), whereby children have a written agreement with the teacher each week to learn specific words. Children who have the opportunity to select the words for their spelling program have a special engagement in their own learning. If they are encouraged to select words from their own writing needs, they are able to see the purpose for their spelling list; the motivation to succeed is thus heightened.

■ contract spelling

For this approach, the teacher has children keep a list of their own spelling mistakes and challenges from each week's writing. This becomes the master list from which the child selects a certain number of words, depending on the child's age and ability, to study for the next week. The teacher and each participating child negotiate as to the appropriate number of words to select. Then the child takes a pretest on the words (these can be administered by the teacher or a spelling partner), fills out a spelling contract on the words, studies the words during the week, and takes a final test to see how well the contract has been met. This information provides the foundation for the new contract the following week (see Figure 6.4).

STRATEGIES FOR ENGLISH LEARNERS

english learners may participate successfully in spelling instruction if they are developmentally ready, learning to read in English, and understand the meanings of the words they are being asked to spell. English learners who are also learning to read in a language other than English may most comfortably participate in spelling instruction by doing so orally, if they wish. The primary focus should be on comprehending spelling vocabulary and developing awareness of English sound patterns and specific spelling patterns.

| *figure* | **6.4** | **A sample spelling contract.** |

Name: _Carmen R._   Grade: _3_

Week: _Sept. 8–12_

SPELLING CONTRACT

Number of words spelled correctly on the pretest: _8_

Number of words to be learned: _2_

Total number of words contracted: _10_

1. _personal_
2. _beautiful_
3. _curious_
4. _obvious_
5. _mascara_
6. _popular_
7. _women_
8. _beginning_
9. _sincerely_
10. _receive_

English learners who are only participating orally should not be required to take formal spelling pre- and post-tests; however, they may be asked to demonstrate knowledge of the meaning of spelling words by drawing pictures of the word or providing brief explanations of the word's meaning.

The strategy described in the "Think, Pair, and Share" activity can be helpful in the spelling acquisition of all children—but particularly for English language learners.

Think, Pair, and Share

ACTIVITY

THINK

Children look at the spelling list (or, for younger children, listen as someone reads the words) and consider what they know about each word. They may write down their ideas, draw pictures, use gestures, or use any means to show what they are thinking.

PAIR

Children sit in pairs facing one another. One child chooses a word to share with the partner and completes the following sentence: "Something I know about [the spelling word] is that. . . ." Children may share drawings, and if their partner speaks the same home language, that language may be used.

SHARE

Children regroup into linguistically heterogeneous small groups and, in English, share and build on the knowledge they acquired in the pairs. They may repeat the pair activity by changing their sentences to: "Something I learned from my partner about [the spelling word] was . . . " or they may do a different activity such as a word sort or a word hunt and discuss their findings in the group. They may also choose to enter the words that reflect the concepts they have been studying for the week into a word study notebook, in columns.

PRACTICES TO AVOID

Certain questionable practices in the instruction of spelling have been around since the one-room schoolhouse. In spite of volumes of research disclaiming some of these practices, many teachers still use the same unsubstantiated teaching formulas used generations ago. Because these dubious practices are widespread and continue to thrive, most books on spelling feel the need to mention those activities teachers should avoid. The following practices are not recommended, because they yield nothing of value and may hinder normal spelling development (Gentry, 1981).

AVOID:

■ *requiring children to write out their spelling words repeatedly.* Writing the words three times appears to be the optimal number for retention; all else is counterproductive and time would be better spent on other applied writing activities. Moreover, practice doesn't always make perfect; if the word is misspelled ten times, practice has most likely been made permanent.

■ *correcting spelling mistakes for children.* Children learn much more by paying careful attention to the exact sequence of letters they have confused so they can write it over correctly. A small check in the margin of the line where there is a misspelled word should be enough to call children's attention to a spelling mistake.

■ *having children unscramble strings of letters to find words.* This is an unusually poor practice because it frustrates the visual recognition that is the single most important skill children can develop for spelling. Word searches are also poor exercises, as the diagonal and

"Think, Pair, and Share" and other activities should encourage students to talk and learn about their spelling words.

right-to-left placement of words reinforce poor orientation skills, especially in beginning readers.

■ *lowering grades on written work solely because of poor spelling*. When children are writing drafts and getting their ideas down, they are in the creative stages of writing. At this stage, the teacher should always respond only to what the writer has to say. Later, when children have had a chance to edit their work, the spelling can be addressed.

■ *giving weekly spelling bees*. Spelling bees are enjoyable for those children who are naturally good spellers, but they provide limited practice for those who are experiencing problems in spelling. Moreover, the "good" spellers tend to get most of the spelling reinforcement, whereas the poorer spellers, who could use the practice, get little but a bruised ego.

■ *spending more than 10 to 15 minutes a day on spelling instruction*. Good spelling is an important convention of writing, but it is only a small part of what makes a child literate. As such, teachers should actively engage children in analyzing and categorizing words and identifying generalizations for a few minutes every day; much more time should be spent applying that information to meaningful writing experiences.

SUMMARY

t**he purpose of spelling is to allow writers to communicate more effectively, so writing is the best way for children to learn how to spell. To become good spellers, then, children need to write a lot, and that means they have to begin by using experimental spelling. During the primary years, children's abilities to spell lag so far behind their abilities to communicate that if they could not initially experiment with new spellings, they simply could not write at all. However, it isn't enough to tell children to use experimental spelling; teachers need to show them how to use strategies to sound out new words, thus helping them discover important concepts about sound–spelling relationships in the English language. By observing and analyzing their experimental spellings, teachers can then determine which new concepts about print their students are ready to incorporate into their spelling.

Learning how to spell is not about merely memorizing words anymore; a more sensible approach to the teaching of spelling is now based on several premises: Children must be taught about print and how it works, and they must be shown strategies that are used by competent spellers. They must be taught directly about the symbols used to represent each sound. They must also be guided to discover common spelling patterns and the generalizations that apply to many words. Most importantly, they must be given numerous opportunities to use their spelling in meaningful and varied writing activities. With a burgeoning spelling consciousness that alerts them when a word is not spelled correctly, and a spelling conscience that makes them *want* to spell correctly, young children will be well on the road to effective written communication.

questions

for journal writing and discussion

1. Describe in your own words the stages of spelling development in young children. Explain how being aware of these stages might help a teacher plan an appropriate spelling program for each learner.

2. In your own words, list the six concepts that can be derived from observing children's experimental spelling. Discuss how knowing letter names can be both a help and a hindrance to young children at the initial phases of writing.

3. The mother of a first-grader asks you why the teacher allows her child to misspell so many words in draft writing. What explanation do you offer her?

suggestions

for projects and field activities

1. Administer the "Monster Test" (see Appendix E) to three first-grade children. From their responses, what stage of spelling development would you say each child is in? List what each child already knows about how print works. What do you think each child needs in order to progress toward the next stage?

   See Appendix E

2. Develop a list of 15 spelling words based on similar or contrasting visual or sound aspects. Invite a small group of second-grade children to sort the words and then make statements about their findings, as demonstrated in this chapter. Present your findings to your classmates.

3. Observe a spelling lesson taught to primary-age youngsters. Through discussion with the teacher and your direct observation, answer the following questions:

   - What strategies are children being taught about how to spell new words?
   - How are children being taught about common patterns that occur in words?
   - How is spelling applied in real writing situations in this classroom?

chapter 7

Acquiring Word Meanings

The Building Blocks of Literacy

focus questions

- What is the most important way children acquire new words? How should this information guide classroom practice?

- What factors comprise an effective meaning vocabulary acquisition program?

- What are the two types of meaning vocabulary instruction, and when should each be used?

- What are guidelines for making vocabulary acquisition more accessible for English learners?

in the classroom

Because words are the building blocks of sentences and thus *all* reading and writing activities, a classroom in which both teacher and children enjoy playing with and discussing new words is most conducive to literacy acquisition. In one such classroom, when seven-year-old Maria chirps, "That story was so *um—memorable,* Ms. Komar!," the teacher and the students are visibly enchanted with this sophisticated new word. They immediately stop what they are doing to comment on the meaning of the word after Ms. Komar profusely congratulates Maria on using such a fine word. The teacher then enlists the students to help her sound the word out as she pens it with a black marker on a large word wall chart toward the front of the room. This prominent chart has been created for just such a purpose: to provide a tangible reminder of the group's love of words and to reinforce new words as they are discovered either through class discussion, as in this example, or through content reading, recreational reading, or other media.

INTRODUCTION

Vocabulary development has been widely researched, and in the past 20 years, a number of studies have examined the impact of vocabulary knowledge on student achievement. One major conclusion of these studies is that the interdependence between reading achievement and vocabulary knowledge is very strong (Beck, McKeown, & Kucan, 2002; Graves, 2006). As a result of this vocabulary acquisition research, three main implications for instruction have come to light:

- A wide range of vocabulary is understood by children.
- There is a significant difference between the vocabulary knowledge of high- and low-achieving children.
- A sustained focus on oral and written vocabulary acquisition in the reading/language arts program is crucial.

Several researchers have offered evidence that strongly links vocabulary deficiencies to academic failure in high-risk youngsters in grades 3 through 12. Although the research does not support a conclusion that any single method of teaching vocabulary is better than others, many comprehensive programs for fostering vocabulary acquisition have produced positive results (Dixon-Krauss, 2002; Nilsen & Nilsen, 2003; Rosenbaum, 2001). Therefore, teachers are well-advised to incorporate daily vocabulary acquisition activities into their literacy programs (Herrell & Jordan, 2006).

WHY ACQUIRING A MEANING VOCABULARY IS IMPORTANT

meaning vocabulary ■

meaning vocabulary is just what the term implies—a child's understanding of the meanings of words. It is first acquired through the child's total oral language experiences and therefore begins to form many years before the child ever enters school. In kindergarten, before children know how to read, they gain their meaning vocabulary primarily through listening to and retelling stories, songs, and poems, and by having adults or older children help them focus on the meaning of new words. As children become literate, their vocabularies are enhanced through explicit instruction and independent reading. By the end of third grade, if all goes according to plan, children are able to decode any word in their meaning vocabulary.

The meaning vocabulary of children grows at an astonishing rate—by some estimates about 3,000 words a year, or approximately seven to ten new words per day (Nagy & Herman, 1985). To master such a large number of words, it would seem reasonable to assume that children acquire this new vocabulary both inside and outside of school. Although many teachers suppose that their students learn most new words through their explicit instruction, children actually learn more new words through recreational reading and writing projects; television has also been known to have a positive effect on vocabulary acquisition (Tompkins, 1997). The number of new words children can acquire from reading, of course, depends on exactly how much they read, and that amount can vary tremendously. As documented by research, a fifth-grader achieving at the 90th percentile in reading on standardized tests reads about 200 times more than does the 10th percentile fifth-grade reader (Nagy, Herman, & Anderson, 1985)! Moreover, capable readers have larger vocabularies and a wider repertoire of strategies for figuring out new words than children who read less often (McKeown, 1985).

Written language places greater demands on children's vocabulary knowledge than does everyday spoken language. If children do not continue to develop vocabulary at a rapid rate, they will be ill-equipped to handle the extensive vocabulary demands presented in fourth grade content-area subjects, such as science and social studies. This problem is compounded for children for whom English is not the home language. Therefore, a swiftly growing vocabulary is indispensible for growth in every area of reading. Although the proportion of difficult words in text is the single most powerful predictor of text difficulty, a reader's general vocabulary knowledge is the best predictor of how well that reader is able to understand text (California Department of Education, 1996). This is undoubtedly why Nagy (1988) asserts that increasing the volume of children's reading in both expository and narrative text is the single most important thing a teacher can do to promote large-scale vocabulary growth.

PRINCIPLES OF EFFECTIVE VOCABULARY DEVELOPMENT

to foster proficient readers and writers, teachers must do everything in their power to expand children's vocabulary. Research and research reviews have supported a conclusion that explicit instruction in vocabulary, using a variety of approaches, can lead to an enriched vocabulary as well as an increase in reading comprehension for children (Boulware-Gooden et al., 2007; Kamil, 2004; Nelson & Stage, 2007). Moreover, this finding holds true both for those who have difficulty reading (Ebbers & Denton, 2008) and for English learners (Schmitt, 2008).

In addition, the extensive vocabulary children need for complex tasks can be acquired if children have access to a bounty of good literature and a variety of well-crafted informational texts on many topics. Moreover, they must be actively engaged with the reading material and must be allowed many opportunities to transfer and apply newly acquired words in different,

Teacher behaviors that enhance vocabulary learning

LINK	Relate children's past experiences with present ones.
ELABORATE	Add more information about familiar content or suggest a rewording of the content.
INPUT	Introduce new vocabulary and reinforce through constant use.
CONNECT	Tie new words to the activity or the activity to the new words.
CLARIFY	Add examples, illustrations, or descriptions.
QUESTION	Stimulate thinking about terms through questioning.
RELATE	Show how new words compare with those children know.
CATEGORIZE	Group new words, ideas, and concepts.
LABEL	Provide names for concepts, ideas, and objects.

meaningful ways. Especially in the early grades, children need to have a great number of opportunities to gain meaning vocabulary through oral language development. This can take place through group reading (see Chapter 11), teacher-directed group reading activities, and read-alouds and by applying new vocabulary through motivational writing activities shared with classmates. Also helpful for acquiring meaning vocabulary are extensive discussions, listening and thinking activities, and oral asking and answering of open-ended questions. The box above provides additional suggestions for vocabulary learning.

Additionally, children need to be encouraged to read widely at home and at school and given plenty of opportunities to do so.

Motivating Children to Read Independently

Independent reading is one of the most essential factors in acquiring new meaning vocabulary. Moreover, research informs us that children who read the most, read the best and score the highest on formal and informal assessments (California Reading Association, 1996). Because this component of a comprehensive reading program is so pivotal for the reading success of all children, a plan for motivating children to read should be undertaken in every classroom of every school.

To encourage reading at home, there should be communication with parents. Inform them that for 10 to 15 minutes every evening, their children are expected to read—with the help of a caregiver for children at the preliterate level—independently as soon as they are able. (*Note:* For children whose home language is not English, reading in the home language with parents should be encouraged.) A classroom library with a variety of materials on many topics on many reading levels is a priority; the children should be able to check out these materials and take them home.

Children can also read on their own during independent work time in the classroom—for example, as another small group is receiving reading instruction or after they have completed one activity and are waiting for another to begin (National Institute for Literacy, 2001). Personal progress charts can be kept by each child so that the teacher can check reading interests and growth; incentives can be offered for specified numbers of books, articles, or other textbooks read.

Listening to the Teacher Read

There may be one more great reason to read to your students, no matter what their grade level. Listening to text has been found to have a significant effect on vocabulary acquisition. Because primary children have limited word recognition capabilities, they usually comprehend stories at a higher level of sophistication when they listen to proficient readers read than when they read themselves. Reading to children, then, may have an even more powerful effect on their vocabulary than their own reading. This relationship is well-supported in the research (Beck & McKeown, 2007; Blachowicz & Fisher, 2006). To enhance the vocabulary gains even more, teachers can take a few minutes after reading aloud to discuss interesting words students heard and their meanings.

Other Factors in Vocabulary Development

Besides extensive reading, other activities are conducive to vocabulary acquisition. The most successful vocabulary-enhancing activities are those that are highly

significant to all children and involve active engagement with words taken directly from their reading. Activities that teach children how to determine the meaning of unknown words themselves (Blachowicz & Lee, 1991) are preferred over traditional methods that have, in the past, demanded that children memorize dictionary definitions of commercial lists of arbitrarily chosen words that children are then asked to use in sentences (Blachowicz, 1987).

A number of other key strands must be present in a reading program that seeks to increase meaning vocabulary. As discussed earlier, above all, to foster vocabulary development, children should be read to as much as possible from a wide variety of quality narrative and expository material. Teachers must also attempt to build upon the vocabulary children already have whenever introducing new reading material. For example, if children already know the word *knife,* it is then easy

Teachers should attempt to build upon the vocabulary students already have when introducing new reading material.

to build upon that knowledge to teach them the word *saber*. Children in such a program should be systematically shown strategies for figuring out the meanings of words they encounter in text and encouraged to apply such strategies independently. Finally, studies by Stahl (1983) and Stahl and Fairbanks (1986) suggest that building background knowledge prior to reading is simply not enough to help children overcome limited vocabulary knowledge; these researchers encourage teachers to teach new words directly by showing children exactly how to use context and other strategies to understand complex concepts.

TYPES OF VOCABULARY INSTRUCTION

formal meaning vocabulary instruction for young children is of two main types with two different purposes. The first type is that in which the teacher provides explicit instruction that helps children acquire new vocabulary words. In the second type of meaning vocabulary instruction, teachers help children develop vocabulary-building strategies they can use on their own during noninstructional, independent reading times. Both types of meaning vocabulary instruction will be explored in the following sections.

Explicit Instruction in Meaning Vocabulary

The vocabulary-enhancing effect of reading can be significantly expanded, especially for English learners and struggling readers, when the teacher takes time to directly explain the meaning of unknown words (Biemiller & Boote, 2006; Hui-Tzu, 2008). This section explores ways teachers can provide direct study in meaning vocabulary for five different instructional situations (Graves, Watts, & Graves, 1998).

Vocabulary instruction

www.vocabulary.com

Vocabulary lesson plans

http://lessonplancentral. com/lessons/Language_ Arts/Vocabulary/

1. Learning new words that represent new concepts
   (e.g., children come to grips with the new concept/word *culture*)
2. Clarifying and enriching the meanings of known words
   (e.g., children learn how *shed* differs from *cabin*)
3. Learning new words for known concepts
   (e.g., children know what *rain* is and now learn the word *precipitation*)
4. Moving words into children's speaking vocabularies
   (e.g., children know the meaning of *selfish* but have never used the word)
5. Learning new meanings for known words
   (e.g., children know the word *change* but not *to make change* as in money)

Learning new words for new concepts

word map ■

Learning both a new word and a new concept at the same time is a complex task but can best be accomplished by comparing both the concept and the word with those that are already familiar. The following activity, creating a **word map** (Duffelmeyer & Banwart, 1993), will be useful in this regard and adds an extra layer of clarification for second-language learners.

A Word Map

1. Define the new word and concept by pointing out its special characteristics. For example, "Spring is a season of the year when it begins to get warm and flowers begin to bloom."

2. Describe what the new word is like and what it is unlike: "In spring, it is getting warm and it is often breezy and everything seems new. It is not snowy or freezing cold; it is not like winter."

3. Give examples of the concept and explain why they are examples: "Spring is in March, April, and May. These are the months when it begins to warm up and buds come on the trees."

4. Give "nonexamples" of the concept and explain why they would be poor examples: "December, January, and February are not examples of spring because it is usually very cold in those months and all the flowers have died."

5. Show examples and nonexamples of the concept and ask children to explain why each was chosen: show a picture of a warm spring day with light green everywhere; show another picture of the middle of winter with snow and trees devoid of leaves.

6. Ask children to find examples and nonexamples and to explain their choices.

Use words and brief descriptions from your discussions with the children to create a word map (also called a word web) similar to the one shown in Figure 7.1.

A word map (also called a "word web").   *figure*   **7.1**

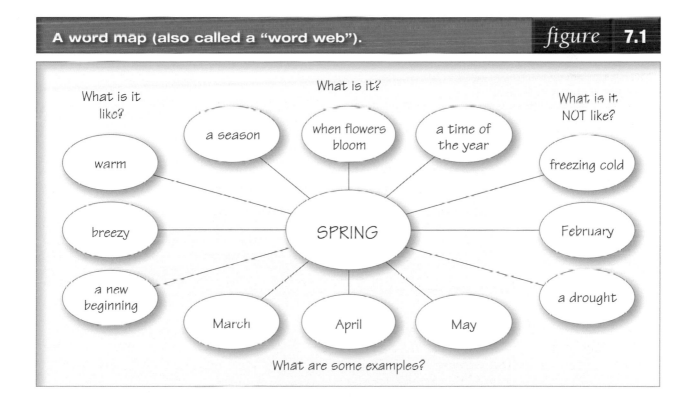

Clarifying and enriching the meanings of known words

semantic maps ■ **Semantic maps** (Johnson & Pearson, 1984), a type of graphic organizer, are important vehicles for helping children put together related information and develop additional words for the same concepts (see Figure 7.2). Maps should be kept on separate sheets in a central location so that children can return to them, add to them, and refer to them over time. Such reinforcement has been found to be particularly important for English learners (Anderson & Roit, 1998). The steps outlined in the activity on the following page are a guide that can be adapted for individual purposes.

figure **7.2**   **A semantic map for *dishwasher*.**

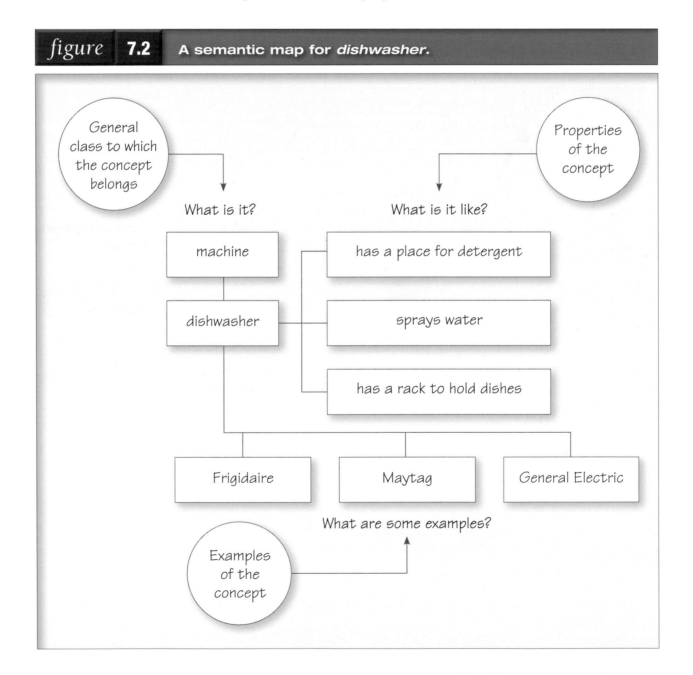

A Semantic Map

1. Choose a key word from a book, story, or passage children will soon be reading.

2. Write the word on a chalkboard, whiteboard, large sheet of chart paper, or overhead transparency.

3. Ask children to think of as many words as they can that are related to the word, as you list them in broad categories. (*Note:* You may want to add any important words that have been overlooked.)

4. Lead children in a discussion of the broad categories and invite them to help you label them. Some words may fit into more than one category.

5. When the map is completed, discuss the categories (such as those for dishwashers in Figure 7.2) and focus attention on those that will be highlighted in the passage to be read.

6. After the reading of the passage, revisit the map and augment it with new words that were not mentioned in the original map making.

Learning new words for known concepts

When children are already familiar with a concept but are acquiring a new word to go with their existing meaning base, a method called the **context–relationship procedure** (Aulls & Graves, 1985) can be used to help children integrate the new word into their meaning vocabularies. The steps of this procedure are outlined in the following activity.

■ context–relationship procedure

Context–Relationship Procedure

1. Write the word (e.g., precipitation) on the board for children and pronounce it for them. Have the children look at the word as they say it several times.

2. Present a paragraph on the board, overhead, or with individual copies, in which the word is used three or four times. Read it with the children.

   EXAMPLE: The newspaper said there was a chance of *precipitation*. Everybody got out their umbrellas to prepare for the rain. *Precipitation* can mean more than just rain. It could be snow or sleet or hail. *Precipitation* means that there will be something wet coming down from the sky.

3. Ask children a question such as the following:

   Precipitation means:

   A. wet weather   B. an earthquake   C. sunshine

4. Read the possible definitions and ask children to choose the best one. Discuss the answers given.

5. Read the word and its definition once again.

Moving words into children's speaking vocabularies

Children can be encouraged to expand their speaking vocabularies, or the words they use in oral language, when appropriate word usage is recognized and praised in the classroom and when plenty of time and support for word play prompts children to experiment with words of their own choosing. The following two activities foster the development of expanded speaking vocabularies.

Semantic Gradient

A C T I V I T Y

1. Allow small groups of children to choose two known words with opposite meanings, such as *good/bad, hot/cold,* or *run/walk.*

2. Have the children put one of the words toward the top of a sheet of paper and the other toward the bottom.

3. Through small-group discussion about word meanings, have children think of words that would fit, meaning-wise, between the two words, and other words that might fit above and below the words. Stress that there are no right or wrong answers.

   EXAMPLE (2nd grade):   perfect

   excellent

   good

   okay

   naughty

   mischievous

   bad

   terrible

   evil

4. Ask children to share their lists and to explain why they placed the words where they did by giving examples of how they would use the words in sentences.

Camouflage

A C T I V I T Y

(Cecil & Lauritzen, 1994)

1. Pass out 3 × 5 word cards, each of which has a word written on it that is in the children's meaning vocabulary but not in their speaking vocabulary. Tell children they may look at their own card but not each other's.

2. Children take turns answering questions generated by other members of the class. For example, a class member might ask an easy personal question such as, "What is your favorite subject?"

3. The child whose turn it is must answer the question while attempting to hide, or camouflage, the word written on the card into the answer.

    EXAMPLE (2nd grade, hiding the word *fond*): "My favorite subject is math. But I also like spelling because my big sister helps me with it. I am *fond* of her even though we often have huge arguments. But I guess I like math best."

4. When the child is finished responding, the other children raise their hands and try to guess which word the child has hidden. If the number of incorrect guesses is greater than the number of correct guesses, the original child wins. (*Hint:* Tell children the best strategy is to use the most "grown-up" words they can think of to throw the other children off.)

Learning new meanings for known words

Many words in the English language are **polysemantic,** having multiple meanings. The word *fast,* for example, has many different meanings, ranging from *abstain from eating,* when used as a verb, to *rapid,* when used as an adjective—and many more meanings when used as a noun or an adverb. If a new meaning for a word does not represent a difficult concept, it can be taught simply by discussing with children their current understanding of the word's meaning, presenting the word's new meaning, and then noting the similarities and differences when the word is used in this new way. If the new meaning is more complex, however, the method outlined in the following activity, ideal for informational text, may be more helpful.

■ polysemantic

Possible Sentences

ACTIVITY

(Stahl & Kapinus, 1991)

1. From an upcoming reading assignment, choose several key words that might be difficult because they are used in an unfamiliar context.

    EXAMPLE: change, spend, left

    Choose a few additional words with which the children are already familiar.

    EXAMPLE: boys, ball, bat, buying

    Write these words on the board or overhead.

2. Provide short definitions for the difficult words or encourage any children who know the words to define them.

3. Ask children to make up sentences using the words in *possible sentences* that might be in the passage they are about to read.

4. Write the sentences the children suggest on the board. Read them together.

5. After the reading of the passage, revisit the sentences the children have written and decide if they could or could not be true based on new information from the passage.

6. If the sentences could not be true, have children help you revise them to make them true.

> EXAMPLE:　The boy will change his bat into a ball. (could not be true)
>
> The boy has change left after buying a ball. (revised)

Strategies to Enhance Independent Meaning Vocabulary Growth

Because, as noted earlier, children by some estimates learn as many as 3,000 words a year, it would seem obvious that it is not possible for every new vocabulary word to be taught individually by the teacher. Therefore, teachers must also explicitly teach strategies to help their pupils become independent word learners through avenues such as the following, which will be explored below:

- using the context
- utilizing word structure
- using the dictionary
- figuring out unknown words
- developing an appreciation for words

Using the context

Arguably the best independent vocabulary-enriching strategy is to use the surrounding information or *context* in a sentence to predict the meaning of an unknown word (see also Chapter 1). Context clues, however, take a variety of forms. Sometimes the word is defined in the sentence (e.g., "When someone *exchanges* something, they trade it for something else"), or it may be defined later in the paragraph. At other times synonyms or antonyms are used, or examples give the reader an idea of the meaning of the word (e.g., "The boy *exchanged*, or traded, the ball for a bat"). Teachers may find a *think-aloud* strategy (see Chapter 8) helpful for modeling how to use context clues. The steps in the following activity provide a guideline.

Using the Context Think-Aloud

ACTIVITY

Sentence: Carla wants to keep her candy, but José wants to exchange his for a new toy.

1. Write the sentence on the board or overhead.
2. Read the sentence aloud, sharing how you think through the problem, as in this example:

"I wonder what *exchange* means? Let's see; the sentence says that Carla wants to keep her candy, but José wants to exchange his. It also says José wants a toy instead. The *but* must mean that José wants to do something different from keeping the candy. When I get something I don't like, I take it back to the store and trade it for something I do like. Maybe that is what José is going to do. I guess *exchange* must mean trade."

3. Provide other unknown words in context and ask student volunteers to verbalize their context usage strategies for the rest of the class or in small groups.

When there is not enough contextual information for children to determine the meaning of an unknown word, the following activity teaches them to make informed guesses about a word's meaning when they are reading independently.

Contextual Redefinition

(Tierney, Readence, & Dishner, 2005)

1. Select two or three unknown words to be pretaught.

2. Write several sentences for each word with enough clues provided for children to guess the meaning of the word. Try to use different strategies such as definitions, synonyms, and antonyms. If the actual text has enough clues to expose the meaning, use that.

   EXAMPLE (1st grade): The boy had played baseball all day long. His arms and legs were very tired. He went to bed early. The boy was *exhausted.*

3. First present the words in isolation. Pronounce the words for the children and have them repeat. Then ask the children to guess what they think the words might mean.

4. Then present the words in context, using the sentences you have created. Read them aloud for the children and have them discuss what the meanings might be from the words around them.

5. Finally, to help the children see the value of contextual information, guide them in a discussion of the difference between trying to guess the meanings of words in context and in isolation.

Utilizing word structure, or morphography

Knowing the meanings of common **prefixes** and **suffixes** and combining them with meanings of familiar root or base words can help children discover the meanings of many new words. For example, if children know the meaning of *heat* and also know that the prefix *pre* means *before,* they can conclude that the word *preheat* means to heat the oven *ahead of time.* Likewise, children can often determine the meaning of **compound words** by combining the meanings of the component parts together: *dollhouse* means a house for dolls. Even the earliest readers can be taught to use word parts as they discover that the simplest, most basic structure of a word, the morpheme, can change the meaning of a word: *dog* with the addition of an *s* becomes more than one dog.

Children can be made aware of the value of word structure through the following activity.

■ prefixes
■ suffixes

■ compound words

Word Hunts

ACTIVITY

(Dear et al., 2001)

1. As you introduce a new prefix or suffix, prepare several flip strips. To create a flip strip, print root words on the front left-hand side of colored strips of construction paper. On the back, print the suffix so that when the paper is folded, a new word appears (see Figure 7.3). Give the flip strips to the children to practice making words using the particular affixes.

2. Using magazines, books, and newspapers, invite children to search for words that have the same structural feature, such as the prefix or suffix that was introduced. For example, children might search for all the words they can find with the suffix *ful*. Provide a time limit.

3. Children write their words in a special word study notebook.

4. Following the word hunt, bring the children back together and record on the board or on chart paper all the words that were discovered.

5. Discuss the meaning of each word with the children. Have them verify that it contains the focus structural element, in this case *ful*.

6. Words that did not contain the element should be put in a "miscellaneous" column, studied closely, and discussed to discover other patterns and word features.

---

figure | 7.3   Flip strips for suffixes.

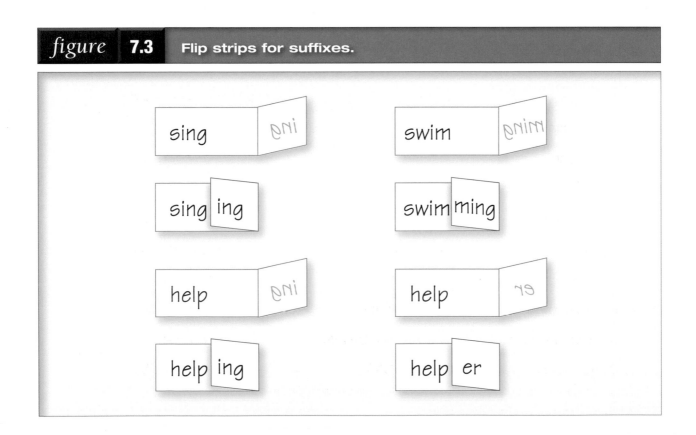

Using the dictionary

The use of the dictionary must be taught in a way that leaves children with a positive attitude toward this important tool. Teaching dictionary skills should begin in kindergarten and proceed through the primary grades until children know and understand the components of a dictionary and can use them effectively. In kindergarten and first grade, the basic concept of a dictionary can be taught using a picture dictionary either online or in book form. As soon as they have some knowledge of the alphabet, children can begin to learn how to locate words or pictures, based on beginning sounds; they can then make picture dictionaries of their own. Older children, or more advanced readers with rudimentary dictionary skills and the ability to alphabetize, can engage in coining their own words with some initial direct teaching of the common word parts shown in Figure 7.4. The "Class Dictionary" activity that follows allows them to coin words in a creative way.

Class Dictionary

A C T I V I T Y

1. Over several weeks, introduce each of the word parts in Figure 7.4 with example words for each.

Common word parts.		*figure* **7.4**
PREFIXES	**ROOTS**	**SUFFIXES**
1. auto (self)	graph (writing)	mania (madness for)
2. anti (against)	phon (sound)	phobia (fear of)
3. tele (far)	hydr (water)	itis (inflammation)
4. bi (two)	therm (heat)	ist (one who)
5. dia (through)	meter (measure)	ic (pertaining to)
6. con (together)	dic (say)	ism (condition of)
7. trans (across)	vit (life)	able (able to)
8. re (again)	port (carry)	ment (state of)
9. in, im, un (not, in)	pen, pun (punish)	er (one who)
10. pre (before)	vert (turn)	ion, tion (act of)

2. Conduct a word hunt as each new part is introduced.

3. Put children in small groups and ask them to form three new words by combining a prefix, a root, and a suffix in new ways.

4. Instruct each group to define each of their new words by considering the meanings of each element. (*Note:* Tell the children the definitions can be humorous or serious.)

5. Encourage a spokesperson for each group to share each of their new words with the other class members, encouraging them to guess the meanings of the new words from their own knowledge of the components.

6. Have each group make an illustration to accompany each of their new words. For example, see the sketch illustrating autohydrable: adj. capable of bathing oneself.

7. As a whole class, help children alphabetize all the words and put them into a class dictionary.

Autohydrable—a child's illustration.

Figuring out unknown words

When children are reading independently, they need a general strategy they can use consistently to unlock the meaning of unfamiliar words they encounter. Getting children into the habit of using such a strategy is not easy, but with a careful introduction and much guided practice, it can be accomplished. The following activity is based on the work of Graves (1986) and has been adapted for beginning readers.

Learning New Words

ACTIVITY

Teach the following procedure by explaining the process and then use a think-aloud to model the steps (see Chapter 8). Offer constant guided practice as children attempt the procedure themselves.

1. When you come to a word you don't know, read to the end of the sentence or paragraph to decide if the word is important to your understanding. If the word is unimportant, just keep reading.

2. If the word *is* important, reread that sentence or paragraph. Try to use the other words around it to figure out what the word means.

3. If the other words are not helpful, look for roots, prefixes, or suffixes that you know.

4. Try to sound out the word. Is it a word you have heard before?

5. If you still don't know the word, ask someone to tell you what it means or ask an older person to look it up for you in the dictionary.

6. Once you think you know the meaning of the word, reread the text and see if it makes sense.

Another activity illustrates the kind of child-centered instruction that encourages independence as well as vocabulary development. Watson (1987) suggests allowing children to select the words that are the focus of instruction. In addition, his technique provides the teacher with an informal assessment of how well the children are reading.

Reader-Selected Vocabulary Procedures (RSVP)

A C T I V I T Y

1. Children are given several strips of paper to use as bookmarks. The strips are cut from letter or notebook paper and are two to three inches wide and three to five inches long.

2. The children are instructed to read as usual, but when they come to a word they do not know and it interferes with their comprehension, they are to place the bookmark there and continue to read. Children are encouraged to continue reading until they reach the end or come to a logical stopping point.

3. At the end of the independent reading time, children are asked to go back to the place where they have placed their markers. They choose the one or two unknown words that *most* affected their comprehension.

4. On their bookmarks, children write down the words and the sentences in which they came across the word and hand these to the teacher.

5. The teacher can use the bookmarks to organize future instruction around the vocabulary problems the children have identified. Children who are having similar problems can be grouped together for small-group instruction planned by the teacher.

Developing an appreciation for words

Teachers who truly find the study of language fascinating can pass this excitement on to their students by constantly directing their attention to words or phrases they find particularly effective in literature, media, the Internet, discussion, or informal conversation (Lane & Allen, 2010). For example, while reading a poem to her class, one teacher stopped when she came to "a plethora of pink poppies" and had the children say it with her. She pointed out the alliteration of the sounds, allowing children to observe how the beginning letters "exploded" on their tongues. Then she eagerly explained the meaning of the words *plethora* and *poppies* to her pupils, who were thrilled to acquire such exciting new vocabulary.

A more direct way of imparting an appreciation for words is to have children collect words and then write them on cards to be stored in their personal word banks or shared on word walls (see Chapter 5). As a precursor to reading a Halloween story, for example, children can participate in a brainstorming session to generate "scary" words. Similarly, children can be encouraged to accumulate "pretty words," "animal words," "summer words," "Arabic words," or words specific to any topic they are studying in a content area.

Technology can also help with vocabulary appreciation through the use of on-screen captions and captioned television programs. Sentences corresponding to the words spoken in videos can be presented on screen, allowing children to actually see the words contextualized by the action. Many captioned videos, such as Reading Rainbow programs, can be obtained from video distributors or educational publishers (Tompkins, 2009). The captioned television broadcast can also be an excellent prereading activity to introduce new vocabulary and build background in an enjoyable way.

Another way to foster children's appreciation for words is to use the following activity, orally for preliterate children and in written form for beginning writers. This activity is especially suitable for classrooms with linguistically diverse children.

Word Aerobics

ACTIVITY

1. Write a simple sentence on the board or overhead. This sentence should contain only a subject and a simple verb or predicate.

2. Read the sentence to the children and then ask them to repeat the sentence.

   EXAMPLE: The man ran.

3. Ask the children to think about how they could make the sentence more vivid by answering questions such as, "Where was the man going?" "What does he look like?" "Why was the man running?"

4. Invite children to think of a revised sentence that would give more information about the sentence.

   EXAMPLE (2nd grade): The tall, thin man ran after the gray cat.

5. Encourage children to share their revised sentences. Discuss how adding descriptive words and phrases helps create a richer sentence.

   Note: This activity can be made accessible to English learners by allowing those who are just beginning to speak to simply repeat the original sentence; more proficient English learners can use one describing word; others can add more complex phrases.

STRATEGIES FOR ENGLISH LEARNERS

english learners come to our classrooms with a wide variety of language levels and vocabulary knowledge. All must struggle, to some degree, with academic language—the vocabulary routinely found in written text but less commonly in everyday conversation. Many English learners lack enough academic language in both their home language and English to be successful with the more complex tasks of reading formal texts (Beck, McKeown, & Kucan, 2008).

Some general guidelines may be followed to make vocabulary acquisition more accessible to English learners, especially when much academic language is involved (Blachowicz & Fisher, 2006). These guidelines, with examples of how to use them, are contained in the following section.

Activate the Schema of the Learners

Very often, English learners have knowledge of a word or concept being taught in their own language but are not familiar with the English word(s) for it. If this is the case, **realia,** such as pictures, brief video clips, or objects can be helpful when introduced in tandem with the new word or concept to build new associations with the English words. Another way to activate prior knowledge is to have English learners consider what they know about the words to be presented. The teacher culls some words that will be in the passage to be read and then asks children, in pairs, to think about the words, discuss them, and put them into three groups: (1) I know this word and can tell you what it means, (2) I know something about the word, and (3) I have never seen this word before. This activity helps English learners monitor their own knowledge, and working with a native English speaker also encourages discussion about the meanings of the words.

■ realia

Focus on Understanding

Although comprehension should be the main focus of any literacy lesson, it is more immediately pressing for English learners simply to get the gist of any passage rather than being able to read it fluently with prosody and appropriate speed. Instructional activities such as dyad or paired reading (see Chapter 8), which asks children to summarize the paragraph a partner reader has just read or to illustrate their understanding of the paragraph if they are not fluent speakers, focus the attention squarely on reading for meaning. For English learners with some proficiency, an activity called "probable passages" can be used (Cecil & Pfeifer, 2011). For this activity, the teacher thoroughly introduces fifteen key words from a passage, pointing out any decoding issues and using realia to explain the meaning. Then (Somebody Wanted But So, see the Structured Listening Activity in Chapter 8) the teacher invites students to create a possible story using the story grammar or frame and the fifteen words. Through the use of this scaffolding device, English learners can write a story using the new vocabulary, and because the words are relevant to the gist of the story, the resultant piece usually closely predicts the author's story.

Scaffold Vocabulary Usage

When parents are raising infants and toddlers, they often unwittingly prop up their child's language with some artful **scaffolding** to teach them new vocabulary through elaboration. When the ten-month-old, using telegraphic speech, exclaims, "Up!" with both arms extended, the mother might respond with something like, "Oh, you want me to pick you up in my arms and carry you for a while," increasing the child's vocabulary acquisition in the most natural of ways. Similarly, when we respond to the emerging language of children at the early stages of English acquisition through elaboration, we extend their English vocabulary. For example, since we are the models of standard English in the classroom, we need only to repeat early English learners' rudimentary messages in standard English, without ever correcting or criticizing them, to increase their vocabulary knowledge. "My dog, he be name Frisco," for example, can be

■ scaffolding

responded to with an accepting nod that immediately acknowledges the content of the message. A restatement can then be offered in standard English, adding elaboration and a question, "Your dog is named Frisco? That is a great name for a dog! Who thought of that name?" Alternatively, having children echo-read passages modeled by the teacher, or reading predictable texts and inviting children to join in on repeated lines are other productive ways to scaffold English vocabulary usage in the classroom.

Use Multisensory and Multimedia Approaches

sheltering ■

When too many words are not comprehensible to English learners in the early stages of second language acquisition, the students are left feeling unconnected to what is going on in the classroom. To rectify the situation, teachers must always bridge the gap by **"sheltering,"** providing meaningful contexts for the words and concepts that are being introduced. In addition to pictures, film clips, charts, and graphs, teachers can also use gestures, charades, and pantomime in providing sheltered instruction to get concepts across. For any verb that is being taught, actions can make it instantly accessible to all. For example, in one second-grade class, when children got to the part where, ". . . the lemmings become *exhausted* from all the swimming," the teacher turned to the class and said, *"Show* me 'exhausted'!" and led them in demonstrating just how an exhausted lemming might appear. Also, graphic novels and comic books often help scaffold new vocabulary for children by simultaneously showing the action that is being discussed. Finally, books in audio and/or video format can support the reading of books for young English learners. Some programs actually read the book while highlighting the text and then invite the child to read along.

Provide Opportunities to Share Home Language

It is important for all the students in a class to honor each child's home language, hear it spoken, and understand that many English learners are already able to speak fluently in languages that others in the class, and perhaps even the teacher, are not able to speak. To respect the fact that learning a second language is difficult and to develop empathy for the challenges the English learner faces, the teacher can offer many opportunities for English learners to share their languages with classmates. At the beginning of the school year, it is important to determine the home languages spoken by each child and to allow each English learner to teach the rest of the class a few common phrases, such as "Good morning!" and "How are you?," in their native tongues, along with a favorite song, poem, or rhyme. This practice instantly elevates the status of each English learner. Additionally, the teacher can encourage English learners to code switch, or to write in either language, when they are doing dialogue journals (see Chapter 9). Finally, an effective writing practice is to use the universal language of poetry to allow children to intersperse words from their home languages and, as they share their poetry with their classmates, to invite them to explain what the words mean through charades, pantomime, art, or other means.

Focus on the Functional Use of Language

"Skill and drill" classrooms, where endless worksheets are completed in isolation, are not places where language learning naturally occurs; second language acquisition happens much more quickly when language is used to communicate for authentic reasons that are important to the language learners. Having children participate in literature circles (see Chapter 11), engaging them in collaborative learning where they are talking about what they are doing, and creating classrooms where children are encouraged to ask classmates when they do not understand something are all examples of instances where language is used purposefully. The various functions of language can be taught in a more formal way in the classroom as well. For example, when children are reading content area texts with much new vocabulary, structured language frames can be used to practice the content vocabulary as well as the specific language functions. For example, an upcoming unit will necessitate students understanding the concept of a "habitat." The teacher then determines an appropriate language function to use for the concept, such as compare/contrast or description. The children can then be given first a simple explanation of each word: "Habitat is a place where something lives." Then provide a sentence frame to help the children practice, in pairs, the new vocabulary with an important language function: "The _____ of a bird is a tree, while the _____ of a deer is the forest." English learners can use the appropriate frames with the new vocabulary before, during, and after the unit to increase language skill and vocabulary knowledge (Donnelly & Roe, 2010).

MODIFYING TRADITIONAL APPROACHES

many activities purporting to develop students' vocabulary accompany most basal readers, but they are not always effective or appropriate. With a few adjustments, however, these approaches can often be made more constructive. Here are some ideas to keep in mind when following basal manual instructions for introducing new meaning vocabulary:

1. Begin instruction with what the children already know. Instead of telling children the meaning of words they may not know, first ask them, "What do you know about these words?" It is never too early to begin to encourage children to take risks by guessing and hypothesizing about new words, based on what they do know.

2. Use as many senses as possible when introducing new words. Instead of always *telling* children the meanings of new words, action words can be acted out by the class ("*Show* me exhausted!") and other words can be sung, drawn, or demonstrated ("This is how you pirouette!").

It is never too early to begin to encourage children to guess and hypothesize about new words based on what they do know.

Also, don't forget the old saying, also true in vocabulary acquisition, that a picture is worth a thousand words—especially for second-language learners, who are especially in need of a visual context for the word.

www.

Vocabulary development
using digital tools

www.techteachers.com/
vocabulary.htm

3. Give children meaningful opportunities to use their new words. Using only the strategy of providing definitions before reading a story or reinforcing new words with workbook pages does not markedly increase meaning vocabulary unless children actually use the words introduced. The words must be used in daily conversations and writing to become part of the children's permanent knowledge.

4. Encourage children to teach each other. Sometimes children are better able to explain new words and concepts to each other than a teacher or a glossary is. Because young children think concretely, they can often present examples of the word that will help others who are not relating the word to anything they already know. This strategy is particularly helpful with children for whom English is a second language.

5. Model curiosity about words and good dictionary habits. For children not yet ready to use a dictionary, observing a respected adult musing, "I wonder what that word means?" and then looking it up and sharing the meaning with the class, would be an excellent introduction.

SUMMARY

Children learn to identify words in order to develop reading fluency and to understand the meanings of words as they add approximately 3,000 words to their vocabularies every year. This chapter has focused specifically on meaning vocabulary and what we know about how it is acquired and how it grows in beginning readers.

Effective meaning vocabulary development strategies include reading aloud to children, helping them appreciate words, encouraging wide reading experiences and application of new words, presenting strategies for independently figuring out new words, and explicit teaching of vocabulary and vocabulary-related skills. The ultimate goal of all vocabulary instruction should be to inspire children to become independent word collectors who enjoy acquiring new words. Such learners become the students who comprehend best and thus read the most, entering into a self-perpetuating cycle of success.

Learning the meanings of many new words is unquestionably an integral part of a balanced comprehensive literacy program for early readers. The more numerous the reading, writing, listening, and speaking experiences young children have, the more they will come into contact with intriguing new words. It is through precisely such experiences that the meaning vocabularies of children grow, just as it is through the excitement of reading and writing that they actually blossom into readers and writers.

questions

for journal writing and discussion

1. Think back to your own early schooling. Do you remember having to look up definitions for vocabulary words? Do you feel you benefited from that experience? How will you teach vocabulary differently?

2. Design and discuss an ideal classroom environment in which meaning vocabulary acquisition could flourish. What, if anything, would you change in your design if you had many English learners in your classroom? Why?

3. How would you explain your approach to vocabulary instruction to parents of your students? Pair up with another member of the class and role-play, presenting your explanation to a parent. Change roles and attempt to make a similar explanation to a teacher who believes only in having children memorize definitions.

suggestions

for projects and field activities

1. Construct a board game that requires players to respond with synonyms or antonyms when they land on certain spaces or draw certain cards. Demonstrate the game to your classmates, asking them to role-play primary-age children, or use the game with second- or third-graders in a regular classroom setting.

2. Ask three 5-year-old children, three 6-year-old children, three 7-year-old children, and three 8-year-old children to tell you the meanings of the following words: *ask, tell, sister,* and *girl.* Record their responses. Were there differences in the children's abilities to give precise definitions for the words? Discuss your findings with your classmates.

3. Select several new terms encountered in this chapter. Decide which ones could be defined, or partially defined, using the context or word parts. Teach these words to a small group of your classmates using one of the vocabulary development activities in this chapter.

chapter

8 Reading Comprehension

Making Sense of Print

focus questions

- How is reading comprehension currently defined by reading researchers and practitioners? How does such a definition inform instruction?

- What strategies do skilled readers employ to help them construct meaning from text?

- What are some components of an effective program for teaching reading comprehension?

Seven-year-old Tiffani reads the words slowly and deliberately to the teacher: "Bobby will go to the party if his sister cleans her room." Tiffani is able to pronounce each of the twelve words in the sentence perfectly. Moreover, since English is her first language, she has probably known the meaning of each of the individual words in the sentence for several years. But Tiffani reports, after reading this sentence, "I get it! The sister went to the party while Bobby cleaned his room!" Mr. Nguyen is rather surprised at this misinformed interpretation of the sentence, but he probably shouldn't be. Simply being able to read the words on a page does not ensure that Tiffani or other beginning readers like her will necessarily understand what they are reading.

Early readers like Tiffani need to be taught directly how language works within the context of a sentence, paragraph, and book. They also need support in acquiring specific strategies that skilled readers use to fully comprehend what they are reading. Then they need plenty of opportunity to use those strategies freely under the watchful eye of a competent and caring teacher.

WHAT IS COMPREHENSION?

Comprehension is currently thought of as the construction of meaning and is the ultimate goal of exemplary, comprehensive reading instruction. Proficient readers, and beginning readers too, construct meaning by making connections—by integrating what they already know about a topic with what they are currently encountering in print. As they establish meaning, skilled readers also use their knowledge about the structure of the text they are reading—*informational* or *narrative*, folk tales or historical fiction—to make predictions about what they expect to discover. They also use problem-solving strategies to monitor their thinking and expand on the text (Barrantine, 1996).

If a child can decode the words in a text but, like Tiffani in the opening vignette, cannot understand what those words mean, is the child actually reading? Scientifically based research suggests that she is not, for reading must be both purposeful and active. To comprehend, a reader must have a specific purpose for reading, whether it is to find out how to fold an origami swan or to discover where the robber hid the gold. A reader must also be actively engaged in thinking as she reads, using her experiences in the world and her knowledge of specific words and the way language works to make sense of the text and receive the author's message. Finally, when a reader does not understand a sentence or paragraph, she needs not only to be aware of it but also to know how to resolve the problem (National Institute for Literacy, 2001).

In a comprehensive literacy program, comprehension is now seen as an interactive process. There *is* meaning and content embedded in the text, but every reader also

comprehension ■ brings particular knowledge and personal ideas to the reading task; comprehension occurs when the reader thinks critically, making meaning by collaborating and negotiating with the author's meaning and then coming to grips with both the text and the writer of the text (Sweet & Snow, 2003). The discerning teacher, then, assumes the role of coach, encouraging the trial and error that accompanies fledgling meaning-making and also moderating unsuccessful attempts without discouraging the child.

AN IDEAL CLIMATE FOR CRITICAL THINKING

an ideal classroom climate for thinking and comprehending in a comprehensive literacy program is one in which children's faces are alive with excitement and every hand is up because every child's imagination is churning and producing ideas about the reading material at hand. Young minds are being stimulated and challenged, and many questions are asked for which there are no right or wrong answers. Immediately upon entering such a classroom, an observer notices how questions and answers proliferate, many of them initiated by the children themselves. Classrooms that embody this kind of enthusiastic interchange strengthen the spirit of children and spark the flames of curiosity. In such classrooms, children respect their own thoughts and ideas and the thoughts and ideas of others; they are open to new experiences and ways to figure things out. Such a classroom climate is most conducive to producing children who feel up to the task of negotiating meaning with texts.

This instructional environment is beneficial for all children, but it holds particular value for children for whom English is a second language. For example, children from Latin cultures are accustomed to working together for the good of the community, a process that is encouraged in their families (Rothstein-Fisch & Trumbull, 2008). They are therefore quite comfortable working in small cooperative groups where a group goal is required. And because English learners often struggle with the academic language used in many textbooks (Vacca & Vacca, 2008), cooperative classroom environments where children help one another through rich conversations about the tasks at hand are not only desirable but also necessary for their success.

One way to foster the willingness and ability of all children to think critically and to comprehend is for the teacher to remove any factors that block—in herself or in her students—the willingness to accept new ideas. To do this, the teacher must in some cases eradicate ingrained patterns of behavior, such as the tendency to evaluate all answers children give to thought questions. In other cases the teacher may need to take more of a direct role than usual and provide children with some rudimentary background knowledge to enable them to think about what they are reading (Cecil & Pfeifer, 2011). Specifically, the teacher–coach in a classroom conducive to thinking and comprehending must consider the following issues: knowledge, think time, and praise.

Knowledge

For children to think about what they are reading, they must have some basis of factual awareness or background knowledge of the topic being considered. This is sometimes called a **"schema"**—or the background of expectations, knowledge, attitudes, feelings, and predictions an individual may hold about a topic. Clearly, children cannot critically examine a topic if they know nothing at all about the subject. For example, a teacher may wish to introduce an expository piece about snakes with a critical question such as, "Why are snakes important to us?" Although this seems to be an excellent open-ended question, it may be a poor first question to introduce the piece, for it is possible that many children do not have enough background knowledge about snakes to formulate an answer. By contrast, after reading children an article about snakes, showing excerpts of videos about snakes, showing pictures of different species of snakes, and discussing them with children—all excellent prereading strategies—children are more able and eager to respond to the original question, backing up their ideas, thoughts, and opinions with facts gleaned from the information they have just

■ schema

received. These activities have helped children create a schema or in some cases enabled them to recall background they already had. Helping children acquire a knowledge base is often a first step in the total process of comprehending text.

Think Time

Thinking through comprehension strategies takes time. Unfortunately, it is often the children who are quick thinkers or vociferous who respond in class to critical-thinking questions, thus getting most of the practice in such skills. Moreover, children from various cultural groups, such as some Southeast Asians, are taught at home to be unfailingly polite and even self-effacing, and they may often be overshadowed by more assertive students. A pattern can be quickly established in the classroom: The teacher demonstrates a comprehension strategy and follows up with a critical-thinking question. Six "eager beavers" have their hands in the air or shout out the answer before the others have even had a chance to consider the question. The other children notice that if they delay raising their hands, the quicker, more assertive children answer and the slower thinkers, or less forthcoming youngsters, are not held accountable for thinking. To avoid this pitfall, it is advisable that the teacher provide as much "think time" as is necessary for *all* children to think through an answer to a critical thinking question.

Praise

A strong (perhaps overly strong) praise response is exemplified by a teacher who responds to a child's answer with, "That's exactly the right answer! Excellent job!" A more tempered response, such as, "Yes, Kay, that is one way to think about the boy's problem," acknowledges the child's thinking rather than the response, and also keeps the window open for different responses by other members of the class.

The use of robust praise is sometimes appropriate—as when working with very young children, second-language learners who are just emerging from their **silent period** (the period during which they are faced with a new language and are not speaking but are developing receptive language skills), children with special needs, or when asking a question of factual or low-level recall, such as, "Raúl, what was the name of the little boy's dog?" On the other hand, when the goal is to have children think critically or creatively about text, the teacher should temper strong praise to student responses because teacher's praise can become the reason children volunteer answers, rather than for the mere sharing of their ideas. The goal should be to help children discover intrinsic sources for their motivation. Overly strong praise tends to encourage conformity, causing children to depend on the praise-giver for the worth of their ideas, rather than on themselves and their own satisfaction with their thinking.

silent period ■

READING STRATEGIES FOR COMPREHENDING

 eading comprehension strategies are among the compendium of skills proficient readers use to connect to and gain personal meaning from literature. Good readers and writers are *always* in the process of creating meaning. They select from among a constellation of appropriate strategies, monitoring their understanding as they read and refining that meaning as they encounter new information in the text.

Unfortunately, teachers do not always spend enough time teaching critical comprehension strategies to children. An ethnographic study of 43 third-grade classrooms found that, on average, the teachers spent little more than a minute on comprehension strategy instruction (Connor, Morrison, & Petrella, 2004), whereas far more time is spent on individual decoding skills in most primary classrooms. Flynt and Cooter (2005) suggest deciding on key comprehension strategies and then spending at least three weeks introducing and reinforcing them in minilessons, an approach they call "marinating."

Some of the most essential comprehension strategies are as follows and are discussed below (Tompkins, 1997):

- making predictions
- tuning in to prior knowledge
- visualizing
- making connections
- monitoring understanding
- generalizing
- evaluating
- asking and answering questions

(The activities later in the chapter will offer ideas for incorporating and modeling these strategies.)

Making Predictions

Proficient readers make mental predictions, or calculated hunches, about what might happen next in the text they are reading. Their hunches are based on what they already know about the topic, what they know about the literary structure the author is using (e.g., is it narrative or expository text? a fairy tale or an autobiographical incident?), and what they have learned thus far in the text. As skilled readers continue, they tend to confirm or nullify their previous hunches, according to new understandings that occur. They often preview informational text to get an overview of what information will be covered, looking through it to see if it matches their expectations. Skilled readers also ask themselves questions for which they hope to find answers as they read, thus asserting their own purposes for reading the text.

Even the youngest readers benefit from comprehension strategies such as making predictions and connections and tuning in to prior knowledge.

Tuning in to Prior Knowledge

Good readers consider what they already know about a topic before they begin reading, and then they assimilate the new information by integrating it with their prior knowledge during the reading process. Such background knowledge may include, but is not limited to, knowledge of the text structure the author is using, familiarity with the literary genre, and the reader's vocabulary and knowledge about the topic. This prior knowledge constitutes a schema for the topic, with which further learning will need to be reconciled.

Visualizing

Proficient readers tend to create pictures in their minds' eye as they read text, especially text containing elaborate imagery or well-developed story characters. Placing themselves in the story as the main character—imagining themselves facing the same trials and tribulations as that character—helps them appreciate, remember, and internalize the story that is unfolding before them. (See the Case Example on visualizing on p. 175.) The experience of mental vision is so personal and intense that readers skilled in this strategy are often disappointed when they see the film version of a story they have read, because the film frequently pales by comparison with what occurs in their rich imaginations.

Making Connections

Proficient readers tend to personalize whatever they are reading by relating it directly to their own lives. They categorize events according to their own sets of experiences and compare story characters to people they know. Experienced readers also compare what they are reading to other literature they have read. Making connections can extend even further when the skilled reader compares books written by the same author or various versions of the same tale or event.

Monitoring Understanding

Proficient readers are continually checking their understanding as they read, making sure what they are confronting conforms to what they already know and assuring themselves they haven't missed something. It is therefore quite normal for skilled readers to make frequent regressions or go back and re-read a sentence or passage to check that they initially "got it right." Such monitoring of understanding occurs, for example, at that moment when a skilled reader is reading an unstimulating text late at night and suddenly realizes that not a word has been understood—a phenomenon to which most readers can relate!

Generalizing

Proficient readers tend to remember important ideas and information they discover throughout a text and bring them together to draw conclusions. Such conclusions then form the "big picture" of the reading material; such a strategy is the basis on which skilled readers are able to summarize what they have read or to articulate the main idea in informational text and separate it from the supporting details. Generalization is also the basis on which readers are able to identify particular underlying themes in literature.

Evaluating

Proficient readers reflect on and form personal opinions about the texts they read; they internalize the meanings certain works have held for them, review ideas frequently, and evaluate what they have read compared with other texts and what they had hoped to gain from the text. Such opinions and reflections about text are not transmitted to the child by a teacher but emanate directly from the child's own thinking about the personal transaction with the material.

Asking and Answering Questions

One of the most valuable ways proficient readers construct text meanings is by asking and answering important questions about the text as they read. They are aware of the difference between "thinking-type" questions and "locating information–type" questions, and they are able to later reflect on the caliber of the questions they have asked themselves.

INSTRUCTIONAL ACTIVITIES FOR
TEACHING COMPREHENSION

Children do not learn to comprehend text just by doing a lot of reading. Teachers must help their students learn how to comprehend by explaining comprehension strategies and then explicitly demonstrating how proficient readers gain meaning using those strategies. Moreover, teachers must then provide authentic reading experiences in which children can apply those strategies (Block & Pressley, 2007). The activities offered in this section incorporate the comprehension strategies discussed in the preceding section. Activities are designated for use during prereading, reading, or postreading, as appropriate. The activities can begin with children as early as kindergarten, when no written response is requested. Written responses can be included as soon as children have the writing proficiency to answer the questions, but oral responses should always be an option. Oral discussions during the activities, accompanied by pictures, objects, or other visuals, have the added benefit of allowing English learners to listen to the way others are thinking and participate as they feel comfortable. Teachers may also visit the websites identified in Appendix C for other activities designed to foster reading comprehension.

Teachers should first explain the process involved in using the strategy and then model it for their students. Then teachers can work with students on activities such as the ones in the section for practice using strategies such as the Knowledge Chart for accessing background knowledge, the Directed Reading–Thinking Activity for predicting, and so forth.

WWW.
Activities for comprehension
www.abcteach.com

See Appendix C

2. As that child reads, the other child listens carefully and then summarizes (orally or in writing) what was in the paragraph. For variation, the second child may simply draw what was read, then describe the picture.

Postreading

3. The reader creates and asks the listener critical comprehension questions.

4. Encourage the children to discuss the answers and, where there is disagreement, to refer to the paragraph to support their answers.

5. Call for children to change roles with succeeding paragraphs.

When children appear ready to practice this activity independently, divide the class into pairs or threesomes. (*Note:* By using a threesome, a child who is an English learner or a nonreader can get the gist of the passage simply by listening to it being read and then summarized.)

Story Prediction

ACTIVITY

Story prediction can be used as a written adaptation of the DRTA to help children develop elaborate predictions about the basal reader or trade book stories they will read (Buckley, 1986). For this activity, pair students or divide the class into small groups. Then follow the sequence below:

Prereading

1. The partners or members of the group leaf through the illustrations in the story in order. Then each partner or group member takes a turn carefully describing what is happening in each illustration. After each illustration is described, the next child in rotation predicts aloud what will happen in that part of the story.

2. After all the illustrations in the story have been discussed in this way, ask each child to write a story predicting what will happen in the story according to what was described in the illustrations. (Younger children can record their predictions.)

3. The partners or group members share their stories with the rest of the class and discuss their opinions about the accuracy of each of the predictions.

During Reading

4. The partners or group members take turns reading the story aloud (or silently) to check their predictions. (For younger children, the teacher may read the story.)

Postreading

5. The partners or group members compare the actual story with their predictive stories and discuss, as a group, who they think came closest to the actual events in the story.

Think-Aloud

A **think-aloud** is one of the most effective ways a teacher can model all the effective comprehension strategies a fluent reader uses to gain meaning from the printed page. You may utilize this activity in the following way:

1. Beforehand, make copies of the text passage that will be demonstrated or prepare it for an overhead projector or interactive whiteboard.

Prereading

2. After looking at the cover or the title and the illustrations in the passage, ruminate aloud as to what the passage might be about.

During Reading

3. Read the passage aloud as the children track. Continually organize images by explaining the passage after every sentence or paragraph.

4. Answer aloud such questions as,

    "What am I reminded of here that I already know?"
    (tapping prior knowledge)

    "What are some ways I can get help in understanding unfamiliar words and/or ideas?" (monitoring understanding)

    "What does this remind me of in my own life?"
    (making connections)

5. After modeling the reading of several paragraphs in this fashion, invite children to add their own problem-solving tactics and personal impressions by reading succeeding passages in pairs.

Think-Aloud Mysteries

(Smith, 2006)

For struggling readers, the teacher can use "think-aloud mysteries" (Smith, 2006). In this think-aloud variation, a small group of children work together to identify the "mystery" solution as they read a short passage written beforehand by the teacher on sentence strips. They look at one sentence at a time and participate in a think-aloud discussion about what "evidence" is provided in each strip. From this evidence, they offer predictions and hypotheses. Initially, the teacher may guide them using typical higher-level comprehension questions. Figure 8.3 shows a partial example (adapted from Smith, 2006) of a think-aloud mystery in which a teacher helps her students identify "hail."

figure 8.3   Sample think-aloud mystery on weather.*

Suddenly I could hear it making noise pounding on the roof of the house.

Teacher: What do you know from your experience that does that?

Student: A storm.

Teacher: Good.

Thunder boomed and lightning flashed.

Teacher: Anything else?

Student: Oh, yeah, still thundering and raining.

Teacher: Yes, I like your noticing details like that.

*   *   *

I could see something bouncing onto the sidewalk and gathering into little white piles.

Student: Still thundering and raining . . .

Teacher: Well, what are those white piles?

Student: Huh? [rereads] Hah. Snow!

Teacher: Really? What does it say besides "white piles"? Is there another clue?

Student: Gathering . . . bouncing? Let's see what the next sentence says.

Teacher: Good thinking! Keep your mind thinking while you read more. This next one might really throw you.

It was summertime, but cold bits were falling from the sky.

Student: Oooh, so it was raining?

Teacher: What makes you think so? Does that fit with what you read right before?

Student: Uh huh.

Teacher: But you said "snow" right before.

Student: Oh, man, snow.

Teacher: Okay, let's review what we've read so far. So you have a storm. What else do you have?

Student: Ice.

Teacher: [laughs delightedly and reads next sentence.]

I've heard that sometimes it could get the size of golf balls or break car windshields.

Student: Oh, I know it . . . but I can't get the word out for it!

Teacher: What's it like?

Student: Hail!

Teacher: You think?! All right, let's see . . .

*   *   *

*This example includes only some of the sentence strips and student interaction from the original.

Source: Adapted from L. A. Smith (May, 2006). Think-Aloud Mysteries: Using structured sentence-by-sentence text passages to teach comprehension strategies. *Journal of Adolescent & Adult Literacy, 49*(8) (764–773). Reprinted with permission of the Intrrenational Reading Association via Copyright Clearance Center.

Reciprocal Teaching

ACTIVITY

reciprocal teaching ■   The **reciprocal teaching** activity has been found to foster comprehension by helping children actively monitor their thinking (Rosenshine, Meister, & Chapman, 1996). During this question-generating activity, the teacher demonstrates how the children can monitor their reading comprehension, observe their thinking process while reading, and determine when they are successfully comprehending and when they are not (Palinscar, Brown, & Martin, 1987). The teacher then asks the children to attempt the same activity on their own, offering them feedback on their performance. The procedure contains five subcomponents—reading, summarizing, questioning, predicting, and clarifying—and is conducted as follows:

1. As the children track, read a paragraph from a passage of text aloud.

2. Model how the paragraph might be summarized. Focus on the main ideas in the paragraph, include the topic sentence, and point out that a summary should be no more than one-third of the original paragraph.

3. Ask the group an important question about the paragraph, one that focuses on the key issues. Solicit other questions from the group.

4. Predict aloud what might be expected in the remainder of the passage. Solicit other predictions from the group.

5. Think aloud about any clarifying information that might be helpful to understand the paragraph more completely. (*Note:* This step is not always necessary for well-written paragraphs that are appropriate for the reader's skill.) Solicit other ideas about what information might be needed.

The Knowledge Chart (also called K-W-L)

ACTIVITY

Teachers can use this activity to show children how to access their background knowledge or their schema for a topic through guided questions; they can then help children identify the new knowledge they gained by reading and place the knowledge on a chart. Modeled after a procedure developed by Ogle (1986), the **knowledge chart** is intended to be used before and after reading or listening to a selection containing factual material. The procedure goes as follows:

▪ knowledge chart

Prereading

1. *Knowledge.* Ask the children: "What do you know about [the topic]?" Record all responses in the first column of a large sheet of chart paper under the heading "What We Know" or "Knowledge."

2. *Questions.* Ask: "What would you *like* to know about [the topic]?" Record the children's responses in the second column of the chart paper under the heading "Questions We Have."

Postreading

3. *New knowledge.* After the reading of the selection, ask: "What have you learned about [the topic]?" Help the children revise the knowledge from the first column, answer the questions from the second column, and list new facts not considered prior to the reading. Place these entries in a third column labeled "What We Learned."

4. *Research.* Distribute student-initiated questions from the second column that have not yet been answered to children interested in researching the answers. Help them find more information on the topic. This information may be added to the chart in a new column, as in Figure 8.4.

| figure | 8.4 | Knowledge chart on lemmings. |

LEMMINGS

What we know	Questions we have	What we learned from reading	What we learned from research	How we feel now
little animals live far away	What do they eat? Good pets? How big? In zoos? Where do you get one?	eat leaves and bugs too wild 4 or 5 inches not in zoos found in Norway	Lemmings drown themselves. No one knows why. Scientists think to keep population down or instinct.	We think it's an interesting mystery!

5. *Evaluation (optional).* Ask a provocative question that will lead children to a personal evaluation of the topic, such as "How did this selection change your feelings about [the topic]?" Place new appreciations in a column labeled "How We Feel Now" or "Evaluation."

Experience–Text Relationship (ETR)

ACTIVITY

Children are not always able to relate their own experiences to a topic before reading about it, even though research confirms that such a skill is indispensible for adequate comprehension and that background must be brought to bear at all phases of the reading process (Cecil, 1995). An effective activity for helping a wide range of learners achieve enhanced comprehension by making their past experiences an integral part of reading involves **experience–text relationship** (Au, 1979). Using Au's method, the teacher asks questions about passages that are difficult for the children due to inadequate background, attempting to fill in the experiential gaps. Through the teacher's questioning, cueing, and prompting, the children are better able to integrate features of the text with their existing experiences. The activity is composed of three phases: (1) an *experience* phase for eliciting existing background; (2) a *text* phase for determining what children are deriving from the text; and (3) a *relationship* phase in which children compare their own experiences with what they have just read. The activity proceeds as follows:

experience–text relationship ■

Prereading

1. *Experience.* Ask the children questions about experiences they have had or ask them to share certain knowledge they have that is in any way related to the selection they are about to read or hear.

During Reading

2. *Text.* After all the children have had an opportunity to share their knowledge or experiences, have them read or listen to short passages of the selection (usually a paragraph or a page at a time), asking them critical thinking questions about the content after each section is read. Listen for responses that reveal lack of understanding due to differing world views or lack of experience with the topic. Add necessary background to correct misunderstandings. This can be in the form of personal anecdotes, pictures, questions, and/or discussion.

Postreading

3. *Relationship.* Attempt to make connections for children between the content of the selection, as discussed in the *text* phase, and their own experiences and knowledge, as shared in the *experience* phase.

Question–Answer Relationships (QARs)

ACTIVITY
■ question–answer relationships

Question–answer relationships (QARs) (Raphael, 1984) help children enhance their comprehension by helping them answer a range of questions and understand each question's relationship to the text, the author, and themselves (see Figure 8.5). With this strategy, children ask themselves, "Where would I find an answer to this question in the text?" and use the hierarchy of questions and answers described below to help them decide.

Literal Question (type 1)

The answer is "right there." This tells the child that the answer to the question is easy to find in the text. In fact, the exact words in the question are contained within the text.

Inferential Question (type 2)

The answer can be found if you "think and search." This tells the child that the answer is in the text, but two ideas will have to be brought together; that is, the words used in the question may be a bit different from the words used in the text, so the answer will be a bit harder to find.

Critical Question (type 3)

The answer is in the mind of "the author and you." The answer is not directly stated in the story, but if readers bring their own ideas to the text and combine them with the opinion the author seems to hold, they will be able to answer the question. There are several possible answers.

Creative Question (type 4)

The answer has to be determined "on your own." The child won't find a direct answer to the question in the text. There is no right or wrong answer to the question; it must emanate from the child's imagination or from information he already has about the topic. There are many possible answers.

Earth adventure activities
www.missmaggie.org

figure **8.5**   **Question–answer relationships (QARs).**

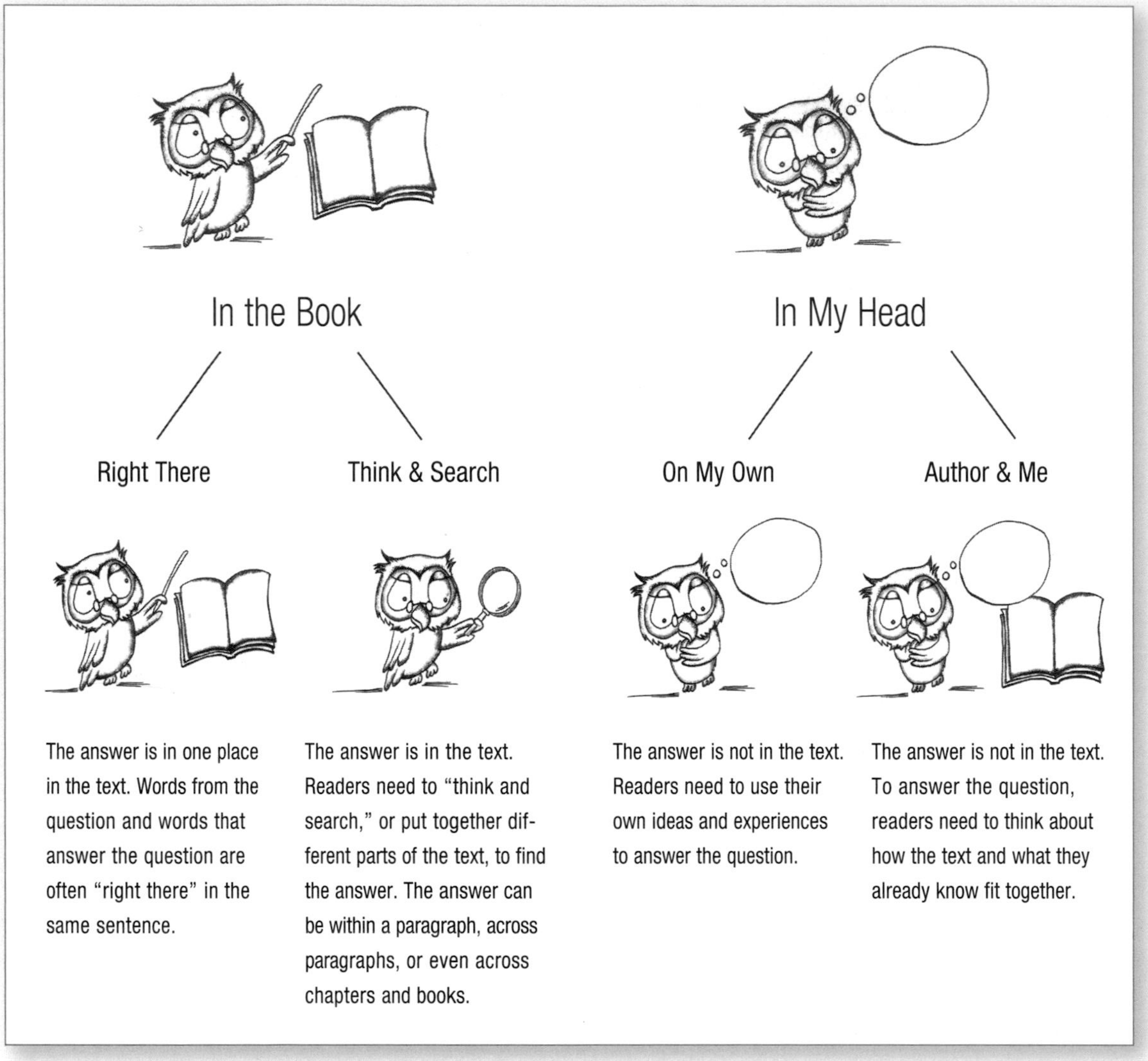

In the Book

In My Head

Right There

Think & Search

On My Own

Author & Me

The answer is in one place in the text. Words from the question and words that answer the question are often "right there" in the same sentence.

The answer is in the text. Readers need to "think and search," or put together different parts of the text, to find the answer. The answer can be within a paragraph, across paragraphs, or even across chapters and books.

The answer is not in the text. Readers need to use their own ideas and experiences to answer the question.

The answer is not in the text. To answer the question, readers need to think about how the text and what they already know fit together.

Source: T. E. Raphael, K. Higfield, and K. H. Au. (2006). *QAR Now.* New York: Scholastic. Reprinted with permission.

The following is an outline of how children can be guided to incorporate the use of these questions to boost their own comprehension:

Prereading

1. Give children four passages with questions for which the question types have already been determined.
2. Using the first passage, model how the answers to each question might be found in the text by identifying the appropriate QAR.

During Reading

3. Read the second passage aloud to children. Ask the questions aloud and ask volunteers to explain which kind of question is being asked and how they would find the answer in the text.

During/Postreading

4. Divide the class into small cooperative groups. Ask them to read the third passage, answer the questions, and identify the appropriate QARs.

5. Have children follow the same procedure individually, as the teacher goes around the classroom offering assistance as needed.

COMPONENTS OF A SUCCESSFUL COMPREHENSION PROGRAM

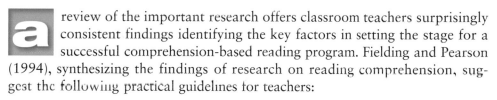 review of the important research offers classroom teachers surprisingly consistent findings identifying the key factors in setting the stage for a successful comprehension-based reading program. Fielding and Pearson (1994), synthesizing the findings of research on reading comprehension, suggest the following practical guidelines for teachers:

- Provide a large block of time for actual text reading.
- Provide explicit instruction in comprehension strategies.
- Provide opportunities for reading in a social setting.
- Provide children with plenty of children's literature.
- Provide opportunities for personal response to text.
- Consider the language and culture of all learners.

Provide a Large Block of Time for Actual Text Reading

As a rule of thumb, children should have more time during the school day to actually practice reading than the combined total allocated for learning about, talking about, or writing about what they are reading. In a truly balanced reading program for primary grades, this is true even for the most fledgling, beginning readers. Such time can be built into the curriculum by having children read on their own during independent work time in the classroom—as another small group is receiving directed reading instruction, for example, or after they have completed one activity and are waiting for another to begin (National Institute for Literacy, 2001).

To ensure that such practice actually translates into enhanced comprehension, however, children should be given some choice about what they read. They should also be provided with reasons to reread some materials to increase fluency, and the material offered should be appropriate in difficulty—that is, not so difficult as to be frustrating but not so easy that nothing challenging is encountered (Fielding & Pearson, 1994).

Encourage greater comprehension

www.bookadventure.com

In the past, the most able readers, because of their ability, were given far less specific, isolated comprehension strategy instruction and were allotted more time to read than other, less able readers. Today researchers are speculating on whether that very discrepancy might have caused an even wider gap between the able and less able readers (Anderson, Wilson, & Fielding, 1988).

From this research, it seems clear that children should be provided with plenty of time during the day to practice reading. Reading material should include texts that are easily decodable so that children can apply recently learned decoding strategies to text. Free time to select from a wide variety of trade books appealing to differing interests and encompassing all independent reading levels in the class should also be a prominent part of the reading program. Additionally, teachers should avail themselves of the wide variety of informational texts now available for young readers. Research suggests that later difficulties with informational reading and writing may be avoided by early experience with such material (Duke, 2000). Finally, teachers should demonstrate the use of the compendium of strategies through the reading aloud of quality children's literature that, although above the decoding level of many of the children in the class, can still be used effectively to spur interest and enhance comprehension.

Provide Explicit Instruction in Comprehension Strategies

A landmark study by Durkin (1979) found that although teachers were spending an inordinate amount of time assessing comprehension through a wide variety of basal workbook pages, only a fraction of instructional time was spent actually showing children how to read strategically for optimal comprehension. The study by Connor, Morrison, and Petrella (2004) cited earlier in this chapter suggests that little has changed since Durkin's study.

Researchers have now attested that children must be taught, directly, what each comprehension strategy is, how and when to use such a strategy, and the circumstances under which they should use it. Each strategy should first be modeled by the teacher, then the children should receive guided practice in applying the strategy, and finally they should use it independently with feedback from the teacher (Duffy, Roehler, & Hermann, 1988) (see the box on the next page for a description of explicit teaching of a comprehension strategy). The strategies offered in this chapter are prototypes of those that, when introduced in this manner, will serve to develop the reading comprehension of students.

Provide Opportunities for Reading in a Social Setting

www.

Children's literature Web guide

www.acs.ucalgary.ca/ ~dkbrown

Children, especially English learners, learn best when they are able to talk about what they are doing and learn from each other. Besides enhancing their knowledge by adding sensory input and vocabulary development provided by oral discussion, social reading, is more enjoyable for most children.

A continuum of reading configurations should be used in a classroom. Shared reading and guided reading (see Chapter 11), in which the teacher is

Jane Waskeiwitz teaches visualizing

Explicit Teaching Begins

"Today we are going to learn another way readers think DURING reading. It's called 'visualizing.'"

"One way good readers visualize during reading is to make pictures in their heads," she continues. "I'm going to show you how, and then it will be your turn. I'll start with one word."

Jane pulls out a card with the word *dog* printed on it and places it beside the word *image* in the pocket chart. Jane then begins her think-aloud.

"I know this is the word *dog.* When I read *dog,* I can make an image in my head of a dog. The dog I see has reddish fur that is long and silky. He is about this big (she holds her hand about three feet from the floor). He has floppy ears and brown eyes. I also have a smell image, because this dog needs a bath!" The kids giggle, and several put their thumbs up.

"Jerry, what are you thinking?" she asks.

"I guessed it is Chester," he says.

"Me, too," says a girl with her thumb up.

"You are right. I was thinking about my dog," Jane says.

"He's a Golden Retriever," a boy adds knowingly.

Jane explains: "I want you to notice HOW I was thinking about the word *dog."* The students seem puzzled. "What were the *visual* images I made in my head?" she coaches.

"You said he was reddish and had brown eyes," a boy responds to the category of color.

"I did have that in my brain image," Jane says. "What else?"

"You said he was silky. That is texture," explains a girl.

"Size! You showed us how big he is," exclaims a boy.

"You could have showed us his shape," adds another boy.

"You are absolutely right, Joshua," Jane says. They are on a roll, and now there are hands up all over. Jane takes another minute to allow students to share and then proceeds.

"Okay, I did the image making in my head, and now it is your turn. I have a new word to read. When I show the card, just read it in your mind, not out loud." Jane shows a card that has the word *cat.*

Scaffolded Practice

"You can close your eyes, if you like. I'll give you suggestions, and you try to make the image in your head. First, make a picture of a cat. Imagine it any color you want." Jane pauses. "Now think the shape of the cat. In your head draw a line around its body like we do with shapes in art prints." She pauses again. "Now visualize how the cat's fur feels, the texture."

Some children are squinting. Others have covered their eyes with their hands. Some are looking up.

"This is our first try. Let's see how you did. Find your Study Buddy and tell each other about your images. Start with whoever is A for this week, and I'll cue you for Person B. Begin."

Text Use and Independent Practice

Jane takes the book *Millions of Cats* from the chalk tray and reads aloud the first sentence. She then does a think-aloud to model her image making. The children then have a go at it and share with their partners. Jane then continues reading without showing any of the pictures, stopping several times for students to share their own mental pictures. These include specifics about the setting, characters (an old man and woman), and more cats.

There is a recess break, and when the children return Jane asks them why they think making images in their heads would help them be good readers. The children reiterate how it is fun and add how it makes them think more. One says it would help them remember ideas. Jane writes down the children's comments on sentence strips and adds them to an ongoing bulletin board labeled "What Good Readers Do." Now it is time for Daily Engaged Independent Reading (DEIR), and Jane reminds students to use all their good reader strategies and to use a sticky note to mark one place in their books where they try visualizing.

Adapted from C. Cornett. (2010). *Comprehension First: Inquiry into Big Ideas Using Important Questions.* Scottsdale, AZ: Holcomb Hathaway.

prominent and works with small groups, are ideal formats for explicit instruction. Other more collaborative approaches include dyad reading, discussed earlier, simple partner reading, and echo reading, with the children repeating the lines the teacher reads. When children begin to possess a modicum of fluency and independence, they can move toward small, independent discussion groups or literature circles where they are in charge of sharing their personal reactions to text.

Provide Children with Plenty of Children's Literature

Quality children's literature is a necessity in beginning literacy instruction. Literature does much more than merely teach children how to read; it also contributes to language development, stimulates the senses, provokes emotional response, and exposes children to a variety of thoughts and ideas (Jalongo, 1988). Although decodable texts are essential for use in reinforcing phonic elements and decoding skills, children's literature is the ideal vehicle for modeling comprehension strategies for children. The primary classroom should be stocked with picture books or books that use both pictures and text to tell the story; award winners, such as the Children's Choice and Newbery medal winners; informational texts and books; predictable books containing phrases that can easily be anticipated by children, such as rhyming patterns, repeating verses, or cumulative verses; and big books, oversized versions of favorite children's books suitable for sharing in small groups. Many books with pictures can also be found online. Besides being used for modeling by teachers, such literature can be used for browsing during free reading time and can be recorded for individual read-alongs.

Leave time for rich, personal discussion of text—the kind of voluntary conversation that is most significant to children.

Provide Opportunities for Personal Response to Text

Not so long ago, it seemed that teachers often became so concerned with assessing comprehension and completing the lists of comprehension questions provided at the end of each basal reader story, that little time was left for rich, personal discussion of text—the kind of voluntary conversation that is the most significant to children. Eeds and Wells (1989) call these two contrasting types of discourses the difference between a "gentle inquisition," a barrage of mainly factual, assessment-oriented questions about text, versus "grand conversations" that ask children to reflect on the personal relevance of the text, much as adults are invited to do in the intimate setting of a book club. Such conversations are vital to developing a genuine love for reading and have the added value of elevating the classroom climate to one of a "community of readers" (Hansen, 2001).

To act on this suggestion, teachers must ensure that they do not limit themselves to factual-type questions and that they allow plenty of time for critical and creative questions for which there is no one "correct" answer and for which every child has an opportunity to voice an opinion. It is also helpful for teachers to sometimes create provocative questions about text for which they themselves do not have an answer, thereby assuring that they will not be "fishing" for the response they have in mind or that is provided by the basal instructor's manual. Moreover, adequate time should be set aside for sharing journal reactions to literature in small interest groups where the atmosphere is safe and conducive to personal conversations about text.

Children can also share responses about books they are reading using a variety of electronic dialoguing techniques. Using a computer, children write their thoughts and feelings about their books and send them to students in other classrooms, to older students, or to preservice students at a university. Using blogs and wikis (see Chapter 12), children can be instantly connected to audiences around the world.

Consider the Language and Culture of All Learners

There are great differences in how rapidly and how well children learn to speak English. When children who are struggling with English are asked to comprehend text in their second language too soon, they can become frustrated and confused. Such children can be encouraged in a supportive classroom where instruction provides for and celebrates differences. Teachers may find it helpful to use a variety of predictable texts, multisensory teaching, and repetition to improve comprehension strategies. Most important, they need to create a language-rich environment and to provide many opportunities for cooperative interaction with English-speaking children (see the box on the next page).

To support English learning, specific language objectives can be incorporated into content area lessons to accommodate second-language learners. Such children can benefit from objectives that incorporate functional language use, such as how to request information, present opinions, negotiate meaning, provide detailed explanations, and so forth. Higher order thinking skills, such as articulating predictions or hypotheses, stating conclusions, summarizing information, and making comparisons, can be tied to language objectives as well (Echevarria, Vogt, & Short, 2010).

Teachers can also improve comprehension in all learners by offering a variety of multicultural reading material that reflects the prior knowledge and background of the diverse learners in the classroom (Wiseman, 1992). For example, classrooms should be supplied with literature that represents a wide range of values, lifestyles, customs, and historical traditions. An example of an effective comprehension activity that encourages multicultural awareness for all children is to compare folktales, such as *Cinderella* with its African counterpart, *Mufaro's Beautiful Daughters* (Steptoe, 1987) or the Chinese *Lon Po Po* (Young, 1990) with its European counterpart, *Little Red Riding Hood*.

Special considerations must be made for children who are learning English as a second language in order for them to fully comprehend, and think critically about, the materials you present. The goal should always be to present quality literature with engaging illustrations; however, consider these additional key elements (outlined by Vardell, Hadaway, & Young, 2006) when matching English learners with books to ensure that they have the best chance to comprehend:

■ **Is the language accessible?** English learners, especially at the initial stages of language acquisition, benefit from predictable books with simple sentences, simple language patterns, and repetitive text. The reader should not be overwhelmed by too many words on a page.

■ **Is a variety of text genres available?** Children for whom English is a second language will benefit by being exposed to a wide variety of writing styles, topics, genres, and patterns of text organization. While this is true of *all* children, it is crucial for those becoming familiar with the way English text is structured.

■ **Are the illustrations accessible?** When children do not have full command of English, it is important for the text to be supported and made comprehensible by the illustrations. Abundant high-quality illustrations will provide cues to help English learners discern the meaning of the text. *Note:* Consider comic books and graphic novels in your classroom library as genres of reading material in which the text is often fully supported by the illustrations. For example, comics on superheroes (Spider-man, Batman, Wonder Woman) and folklore and fairytales such as *Little Lit: Folklore and Fairy Tale Funnies* (Spiegelman & Mouly, 2000) and *The Big Book of Grimm* (Factoid Books, 1999) can make good additions to your classroom library.

■ **Is the content accessible?** When children already have a schema or background knowledge about a topic in their own language, the comprehension of that topic is supported and easier for them to understand.

See the box on the next page for a discussion of selecting multicultural children's literature.

Improving comprehension for English learners

1. Use multisensory materials, such as videos, DVDs, pictures, audio recordings, and other supports.
2. Use gestures and body language.
3. Speak slowly and enunciate clearly.
4. Use longer pauses between phrases and sentences.
5. Use much repetition and review.
6. Use short sentences and simpler syntax.
7. Use fewer pronouns.
8. Exaggerate intonation, especially when introducing phonemic elements.
9. Use high-frequency vocabulary.
10. Use fewer idioms and slang terms.
11. Maintain a low anxiety level.
12. Emphasize cooperative learning.

Selecting multicultural children's literature
FOR KINDERGARTEN THROUGH GRADE 4

To develop positive attitudes about people of all cultures, children need many opportunities to read and listen to quality children's literature that presents accurate and respectful images from a variety of cultures. Unfortunately, relatively few children's books are written from the perspectives of racial and cultural minorities; many that are available include negative racial and cultural stereotypes as well as inaccurate factual information. Therefore, it is helpful to consider the following criteria when selecting quality literature for young children (Temple, Martinez, & Yokota, 2011).

- **Does the book show physical diversity?** For example, one popular children's book shows many pictures of Chinese people of all ages—all of whom look exactly alike, depriving children of an understanding of the rich diversity of Chinese faces.

- **Are the illustrations authentic without being stereotypical?** Every race and culture has positive features that can be highlighted in positive ways. Unfortunately, illustrations may accentuate negative stereotypes.

- **Do the author and illustrator present the culture authentically?** There are many misperceptions of cultures, and a quality book is often written and/or illustrated by a member of the culture and presents an accurate portrayal of the essence of that culture.

- **Is the culture shown to be multidimensional?** A quality multicultural children's book shows a wide array of facets of life for the racial or cultural group being studied.

- **Does the author integrate cultural details in a natural way?** Stories including other races and cultures should avoid misrepresenting diverse people as overly exotic or "quaint."

- **Are the details historically accurate?** Much research is needed in selecting informational text and historical fiction because they are great ways for children to pick up factual information; but they must be accurate for the time period portrayed.

- **Does the book reflect on awareness of the changing status of females?** In the United States as well as the rest of the world, females are now often in positions of power. Reflections of this changing status should be reflected in the text, to include the portrayal of female characters taking active—not only passive and domestic—roles.

- **Are nonwhite characters shown as equals of Anglo characters?** Too often, while a text may include racial diversity, the nonwhite characters are seen in subservient roles or seem to need the Anglo characters to solve problems for them.

- **Does the author avoid offensive vocabulary?** While there may arguably be appropriate times for racially offensive language that was used historically (as in *Huckleberry Finn*), such language is rarely necessary to the integrity of the story, and is never appropriate for younger readers.

- **If dialect is used, does it have a real purpose and appear genuine?** Nonstandard English can be confusing for young children, yet a children's book set in St. Croix would be inauthentic without the characters speaking in a Cruzan dialect. Use of a dialect is appropriate if it makes the characters appear more genuine and if the dialect is truly one that the characters would use.

Some exemplary children's books that contain positive portrayals of cultural diversity are: Sherley Anne William's *Working Cotton* (Harcourt Brace, 1992), which illustrates the hardworking life of a migrant family; Stephanie Stuve-Bodeen's *Babu's Song,* which depicts a loving relationship between a child and her grandmother; Pat Mora's bilingual text, *The Bakery Lady,* which describes close family relationships as they prepare food for the Feast of the Three Kings (Pinata, 2001); and the photographic essay, *Hoang Anh: A Vietnamese American Boy,* by Diane Hoyt-Goldsmith (Holiday House, 1992), which shows the daily experiences in the life of a Vietnamese American child and his family.

SUMMARY

Learning to sound out words through phonics and other word-unlocking strategies is certainly a fundamental skill, but if this component of literacy has been accomplished, can we then say a child has "learned to read"? No. For real reading to occur, the child has to be simultaneously constructing meaning from the words that have been decoded; that meaning must then be assimilated into the child's worldview. This meaning-making is a complex and arduous process best consummated through a program that offers guidance in specific comprehension strategies and many opportunities to apply them with quality literature and with decodable text. The teacher in such a program becomes a kind of coach who is there to model, guide, and provide feedback to learners.

Proficient readers possess a constellation of strategies from which they choose to interact with text and construct meaning. These strategies must be directly taught to developing readers through modeling, guided instruction, and plenty of independent application with actual text. Additionally, they must be given the opportunity to share their personal responses to text with each other in a variety of social settings. For English learners, give special consideration to making a variety of genres available and to ensuring that the texts and illustrations are accessible.

A literacy program myopically focused on meaning-making to the exclusion of instruction in decoding skills may create a rich literacy environment that is, inadvertently, inaccessible to many learners; on the other hand, a program lacking in ways to derive personal meaning from text may well create learners who can read but who choose not to do so. For a literacy program to be truly comprehensive, it must enable learners to decode text, but it must also offer them guidance in strategic reading and ample opportunity to read for meaning and enjoyment.

questions
for journal writing and discussion

1. What is your definition of reading? In what way will your definition determine the importance of comprehension instruction to your total reading program?

2. Think about what you do when you read. What comprehension strategies did you use as you read the beginning of this chapter? Make a list of the strategies you can identify. Then spend several minutes reading a novel or other narrative text. Make a second list of the strategies you used with the narrative text. Compare the two lists. Are there major differences? Why?

3. The parent of one of your students visits your classroom. She expects to see a lot of silent workbook activities. Prepare an argument that you might give to this parent, who wonders why you allow so much time for children to read self-selected material and discuss it in small share groups.

suggestions
for projects and field activities

1. Select one of the comprehension activities outlined in this chapter. Find a selection from a primary basal reader that would be appropriate content for such a strategy. Teach the strategy to a small group of your classmates. Discuss their reactions.

2. Conduct the same activity, or another of your choice, with a small group of third-grade children. What problems did they have with the lesson? What did they like about using the strategy? Discuss your findings with your class.

3. Observe the reading lessons in a primary classroom for an entire week. Make a list of all the activities the teacher and the students engage in during the week and the time spent on each. How much time was spent on the direct teaching of comprehension strategies? What percentage of the total teaching time was spent on teaching comprehension compared with time allotted for the application of these strategies or actual reading by the students? What might you decide to do differently in your own classroom?

chapter 9

Writing-Reading Connections

Reciprocal Paths to Literacy

focus questions

- What are appropriate writing goals for primary-grade children? How can these goals be achieved for every child?

- How can "writers' workshop" be used to help young children learn about print and see themselves as authors?

- In what ways can teachers use modeling and writing structures to encourage emergent writers to acquire the conventions of written language?

in the classroom

Seven-year-old Maria turns to her trusted friend, Josh, to get some objective feedback about her current writing ideas.

"I'm thinking of writing a story about three frogs or maybe about when my dog ran away," Maria declares, showing Josh a paper full of half-formed ideas. "Which one do *you* think I should write about?"

Josh looks up from his own writing and asks Maria what exactly she has to say about the frogs. Maria ponders this for a moment. Then she replies that she really doesn't know much about frogs but that she's read lots of stories that contain three animals, although not necessarily about frogs. Abruptly, Josh poses an insightful question.

"Well, what about your dog running away? Was that a big deal?" "Oh, yes!" replies Maria, her face clouding over with the memory.

Maria begins to tell Josh a woeful tale about a recent time when her dog, Puppy, jumped the fence; the family had thought the dog was gone for good. Josh listens intently and then shrugs; Maria has answered her own question, and both children suddenly realize it.

Talking about her writing before she puts pen to paper has provided Maria with a kind of mental rehearsal for her writing and a clearer picture of what she really wants to talk about.

INTRODUCTION

Like the children in the preceding vignette, most children in the primary grades come to school with excitement and enthusiasm for learning. They tend to be highly motivated and interested in engaging in the reciprocal communicative skills of reading and writing. Their image of being "grown up" and attending school includes involvement in authentic literacy activities such as those they have seen all around them. Most of these young children have probably picked up the idea that they would be learning to write as soon as they entered school.

Farnan, Lapp, and Flood (1992) suggest that early attempts at writing are perfect opportunities for children to experiment with print and extend their understanding of text; Richgels (1995) claims that early writing provides children with invaluable practice with phonic skills, such as blending sounds into words and segmenting words into parts. It is not surprising, therefore, that research in emergent literacy has found that writing—if much experimentation is encouraged—can play a pivotal role in children's learning to read. Rather than developing *after* reading, as educators once assumed, we now know that writing accompanies young children's growing interest in naming letters and reading print. Early-grade teachers would therefore benefit from putting research into practice by accommodating young children's wishes to quickly read and write, providing them with immediate opportunities to participate in real writing along with their initial reading instruction.

WRITING GOALS FOR EARLY READERS

Emergent literacy depends on much more than providing a print-rich environment and then allowing children to "go to it naturally," although there are times when such advice is appropriate. But there must also be literate models—teachers, parents, siblings, or caregivers—to demonstrate the "how-to's" of writing. As with reading, it is important to point out directly the conventions of written language and to answer children's burgeoning questions about print.

184

With these ideas in mind, the following suggested literacy goals are appropriate for fostering the reading–writing connection in kindergarten through third-grade children.

1. Development of oral-language fluency for native English speakers as well as English learners.
2. Development of an awareness that writing is constructing meaning with thoughts and speech in written form.
3. Development of a positive, confident, and conscientious attitude toward writing and its conventions (i.e., spelling, punctuation, and so forth).
4. Development of an awareness and appreciation of self as writer.
5. Development of awareness and appreciation of self as collaborator and evaluator in the writing process.
6. Development of an interest in personal, meaningful writing and experimentation within a widening variety of formats.

The remainder of this chapter is devoted to program attributes and positive practices designed to help teachers reach these early literacy goals.

WRITERS' WORKSHOP AND THE WRITING PROCESS

Writers' workshop is the best way for teachers to organize the teaching of writing and an ideal vehicle through which children can apply the steps of the writing process. They can teach their students how to complete the activities during each stage of the writing process; the children can then practice what they have learned during the writers' workshop. The workshop may

■ writers' workshop

appear loosely structured, but it requires much planning and organization as well as an ongoing, authentic assessment on the part of the teacher (Engel & Streich, 2009).

A writers' workshop for the primary grades should roughly follow this format (also see Figure 9.1): Each session begins with a five-minute minilesson to demonstrate a particular procedure, concept, or skill—such as using dialogue in narrative writing or writing a comparison/contrast paragraph in expository writing— that the teacher has noticed the majority of children are ready to learn. The rest of the workshop is devoted to writing, during which time the teacher circulates, asking questions, providing support, taking anecdotal notes on the children's writing, and providing one-on-one conferences with children. Children do peer-editing of each other's work and keep their written work, in various stages of completion,

Early-grade teachers must provide opportunities for their students to participate in authentic writing experiences.

---

figure 9.1   **Components of writers' workshop.**

Minilesson (5–8 minutes)

This is a short lesson focused on a single, narrow topic that the children need, chosen by the teacher based upon her observation of the children's daily writing. The teacher may see a need in only certain students and invite just them to meet for the lesson.

Status of the class (2–3 minutes)

This is a brief survey by the teacher to find out what each child is working on as well as what stage of the writing process each is in.

Writing time (15–20 minutes)

The children write, choosing topics from their writing folder. The teacher conferences with individual children.

Sharing (5–10 minutes)

Children read what they have written and seek specific feedback from an audience (whole class, small groups, or partners).

---

in writing folders. The session ends with sharing time when children read their pieces to small groups, or to the whole group, and request feedback.

writing process ■ As stated above, through writers' workshop, students apply the steps in the **writing process,** which is a popular way of organizing a writing session in the same way professional writers do. It is based on the premise that writers write best when they write frequently, for extended periods of time, and on topics of their own choosing. It is a set of stages in which a writer engages in activities designed to solve certain problems unique to a particular stage. It is exactly this problem-solving approach that makes the writing process more effective than traditional approaches that tend to focus merely on the completed product. A final product in traditional writing programs is often simply a second draft consisting of a mindless recopying of a teacher's red pen corrections.

The writing process and methods of teaching writing have evolved considerably over the years, but two beliefs have remained consistent: (1) the creation of a piece of writing is a developmental process that takes place over a period of time, and (2) writers engage in different activities depending on their stage of development. The writing process can be introduced to emergent writers as early as kindergarten or first grade.

During writers' workshop, children work through the following stages of the writing process over a period of several days or, sometimes, weeks (Peha, 1996c):

■ prewriting   ■ revising
■ drafting   ■ editing
■ sharing   ■ publishing

Prewriting (Exploring the Topic)

In this initial stage, children think, plan, talk, and take rudimentary notes about something they want to write about. Children are urged to write about topics they know well. Many things qualify as prewriting activities. Some of the most helpful activities for young children are conversations with a friend about the topic, reflecting, drawing, brainstorming, visualizing personal experiences, and jotting down notes.

To ignite the thinking process, it is sometimes helpful for the teacher to offer creative or reflective **writing prompts** or motivational ideas to inspire the children and get their imaginations churning. For example, the teacher might offer a sentence, such as "When I opened my front door, I saw a cute puppy just sitting on my doorstep," and ask children, orally, to add some ideas to turn the sentence into a story. Another prompt might be to brainstorm a "What if?" question with the children— for example, "What if everyone looked exactly alike?" or "What if we could talk to animals?" or "What if we were invisible?" Such prompts, followed by much oral discussion and subsequent brainstorming, make most children eager to write.

■ writing prompts

Drafting (Putting Ideas Down on Paper)

During the drafting stage, formal writing begins. Very young children usually write single-draft compositions, adding words to accompany drawings they have made. (See Figure 9.2.)

The emphasis here is on expressing ideas, never on spelling or handwriting. It is absolutely vital at this stage to respond to what the children have to say

A young writer's draft.   *figure* **9.2**

with positive oral comments or, with older children, written ones. As in the pre-writing stage, it is important that emergent writers are given sufficient time and encouragement to engage in risk-free exploration of their subject matter.

When students are drafting their compositions, a teacher needs to be aware when children are experiencing writer's block so he can provide suggestions, such as the following, to get them beyond the block (Kucer, 2010):

1. Brainstorm possible ideas and jot them down on paper. Select one of the ideas and try it out.
2. Reread what you have written so far and see if an idea comes to mind.
3. Skip ahead to a part where you know what you will write about. Come back to the problem later.
4. Write it as best you can and return later to make it better.
5. Write it several different ways and choose the one that you like the best.
6. Write whatever comes into your mind.
7. Talk about it/conference with a friend.
8. Read other texts to get some ideas.
9. Stop writing for a while and come back to it later.

It may be helpful to introduce the chart shown in Figure 9.3 to the children and then to display it prominently in the room.

---

figure **9.3**   **Writing steps.**

1. Choose a topic. *(Planning)*
2. Discuss your writing with a partner in a comfortable place. *(Planning)*
3. Write down all your ideas for your piece. *(Composing)*
4. Share your writing with a partner, with the class, or with your teacher. Ask your partners questions about your writing. *(Sharing)*
5. Use what your partner says to help you add information, get rid of information, or change words or ideas. *(Revising)*
6. Reread your piece. Correct mistakes you find. *(Proofreading)*
7. Read your piece to the class, a share group, or a partner. *(Presenting)*
8. Store your writing in your folder. Later you may decide to publish it.
9. Choose a new topic and begin again.

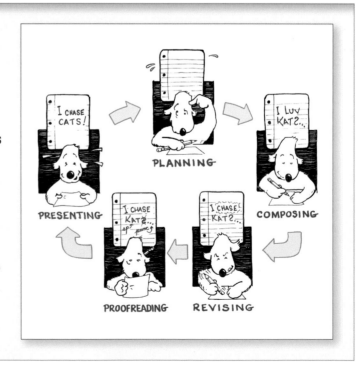

Sharing (Getting Feedback)

Sharing is an integral part of writers' workshop because children are social and want continual feedback on their hard work. However, the feedback need not always come only from the teacher. Writing partnerships of wisely chosen pairs of children can help students to talk constructively and think more deeply about their writing in a social and motivational way (Hsu, 2010). Instead of the teacher answering all questions and offering all the support, children can learn, with careful instruction in the use of response guidelines, to critique and provide suggestions to each other. The sharing phase can occur after each draft or as often as the child desires. In their role as writing partners and, effectively, as peer editors, children possibly learn as much about writing as they do when creating their own pieces.

Children need to be taught to respond to each other's writing in a way that is constructive, helpful, and tactful. The guidelines for responding shown in Figure 9.4 should be introduced to children and used several times with anonymous writing (from other classes or previous years) so children can see which messages are helpful and which ones are not. A blank checklist based on these guidelines is provided in Appendix E. This checklist can easily be entered into a free online survey creator such as SurveyMonkey (www.surveymonkey.com), so students can share feedback electronically.

See Appendix E

Teachers can also use editing forms called Praise, Question, and Polish (PQP) with directions for children to use routinely when reviewing their partner's writing (see Appendix E). PQP uses these three steps:

1. *Praise.* First find something positive and specific to say about the piece. ("I really liked the beginning of your piece. It really grabbed my attention and made me want to keep reading.")

Guidelines for sharing writing with a peer editor.   *figure* **9.4**

1. Ask a partner to listen to your writing.
2. Move quietly to a comfortable place where you can talk in 6" (tiny, inside) voices.
3. Ask your partner questions such as the following:
   - Do you think the opening "grabs" you?
   - Is there any part I should throw away?
   - Did I use any "tired" words?
   - What is the best part of my writing?
   - Is there any part you didn't understand?
   - Do I need a different ending?
   - Are there any sentences I should combine or separate?
   - What do you like best? Why? Least? Why?
4. Return to your seat and decide which, if any, of the suggestions you will use.

2. *Question.* Tell the author something that is not clear in his or her piece. ("How did Josh feel when his dog ran away?")

3. *Polish.* Suggest a way the author can make the piece even better. ("Could you find a better word to describe the boy's father than 'nice'?")

A writing conference with a teacher is a conversation with a clear purpose and a predictable structure. A "conversation" is the best lens through which to view the task of talking about writing (Anderson, 2000). Listed in Figure 9.5 are a few examples of questions a teacher might ask during an author–teacher conference.

Revising (Taking Another Look)

Teachers do not introduce this stage until children have learned the importance of changing their piece to meet the needs of their audience. At first, emergent writers simply reread their writing to see that they have included everything they wanted to say and make very few changes. As they gain more experience, they begin to make changes to clarify their writing and add more information to make it complete.

Editing (Making Corrections)

This stage is also played down until emergent writers have learned conventional spellings for many words and have acquired a rudimentary understanding of punctuation and capitalization rules (check your state or district standards for when this should occur). To introduce editing, the teacher helps children make a couple of corrections by putting a line through the error and writing the correction in pencil above the child's writing, eventually progressing to just a check in the margin of the sentence. As children become more fluent, the teacher encourages them to make more of their own corrections. Children can use the editing checklist (Figure 9.6) to help them proofread their own pieces. Eventually the teacher allows children to read each other's compositions and check for errors, to help them begin to develop a spelling consciousness (see Chapter 6).

figure **9.5** **Guidelines for conferencing (teacher).**

What can I help you with?

How do you think you are doing?

What is the most exciting part of your piece?

How do you want the reader to feel after reading this?

Does your opening sentence get the reader's attention?

What is the most important part of your piece?

Can you tell me more about . . . ?

What makes a good ending?

Does this sound like you talking?

What is happening in this picture?

What were you thinking about when this happened?

What else do you know about this topic/happening?

Editing checklist.   *figure* **9.6**

- ☐ I have read my piece out loud.
- ☐ Every sentence makes sense.
- ☐ Every sentence tells about my topic.
- ☐ I have used lots of details.
- ☐ I have not used tired words (such as "little," "good," or "nice").
- ☐ I have sounded out words or asked someone for help with spelling.
- ☐ Every sentence begins with a capital letter.
- ☐ Every sentence ends with an ending mark.
- ☐ I have capitalized names of people and the pronoun "I."
- ☐ I have checked my spelling.

Publishing (Polishing for Presentation)

Kindergartners and first-graders usually do not recopy their writings, but some-times the teacher types the final copy for the child, editing it and putting it into conventional form (Forseth & Avery, 2002). Children get their piece polished and ready to read to others. They then share their writing and show their draw-ings, often in a special chair labeled and set aside for writers, commonly called the "author's chair" (Graves & Hansen, 1983). Children and the teacher sit in the chair to share books and other texts they have read and written; this is the *only* time anyone sits in the chair. Specifically, children can be taught the steps shown in Figure 9.7 for publishing and sharing.

Publishing steps.   *figure* **9.7**

1. Decide which of your writings you would like to publish.
2. Share your writing with a partner, with the class, or with your teacher. Begin by telling what your piece is about, where you are in the process, and what help you need from the listener.
3. Change your writing if you need to by adding something, getting rid of something, or changing something.
4. Edit your writing for spelling, capitals, punctuation, and correct words.
5. Prepare the paper for your final copy.
6. Add pictures. Rewrite the piece in your best handwriting.

WRITING STRUCTURES

most teachers expect children to begin school with some awareness of narrative or story structure, as a result of being read to and seeing hundreds of stories on television and in movies. However, many primary-grade youngsters have been found to have only a partially developed sense of story. Teaching children about narrative structure using *story frames* has been found to directly improve their reading comprehension as well as their writing ability (Spiegel & Fitzgerald, 1986). Moreover, providing a structure, or template, for expository writing (see Chapter 10), or a literacy scaffold for writing poetry or other patterned pieces (see the activity on page 193) allows English learners and struggling writers to reach a higher level of achievement than is possible *without* the structure (Peregoy & Boyle, 2008).

Story Frames

story frames ■ **Story frames,** also called story grammars, are structured templates that can be used orally as early as kindergarten to help children understand story structure. The following steps can be used to encourage story writing and improve comprehension through the use of the prepared structure:

1. Read children a well-formed story, pointing out the elements that are usually found in a story (i.e., setting, main characters, problem, solution, and ending).

2. Write a story with the children, using the board or overhead. Provide the structure for them, but have them fill in the blanks with what they remember from the story, using a story frame such as the one illustrated in Figure 9.8.

3. When the story is completed, read it to the children and then ask for volunteers to read sentences.

4. Give the children a blank story frame and invite them to write their own original stories. The teacher may want to brainstorm with the whole class to help get them started and then do an original story as a class (see Figure 9.9).

figure **9.8**   **A basic story frame.**

(Story Title)

Once upon a time in _(setting)_ there lived a _(main character)_. (S)he was very _(description)_ and always liked to _(character's favorite activity)_ . One day _(character)_ wanted very much to _(goal)_ . But there was a problem. The problem was _(problem)_ . So _(character)_ tried and tried and finally _(how the character resolved the problem)_ . The story ends when _(resolution and ending)_ .

Example of a story written by a second-grade class using the story frame in Figure 9.8.	*figure* **9.9**

> ### Petey the Lion
>
> Once upon a time in a tiny village in Texas there lived a very strange lion named Petey. He was very shy and quiet and always liked to run and hide when the other lions roared. One day Petey wanted very much to play with the other lions. But there was a problem. The problem was that they didn't like Petey because they thought he was a coward. So Petey tried and tried and finally showed them he wasn't a coward. He saved the life of a baby lion cub who was drowning. The story ends when Petey is playing with the other lions. Now they like him because he is no longer shy but mighty.

See Chapter 10 for a discussion of applying the concept of "frames" to expository text.

Literacy Scaffolds

For struggling writers, especially those for whom English is a second language, writing prose and poetry can be overwhelming, even frightening. This fear can be alleviated with additional structural support. **Literacy scaffolds,** which are temporary frameworks for narrative or expository writing and somewhat looser in structure than story frames, enable all children to achieve success in writing prose and poetry. With a structure provided, children can formulate their ideas in ways that might be difficult, if not impossible, without the framework. Literacy scaffolds offer easy-to-follow patterns or "formulas" for writing, so children can focus on their ideas rather than the mechanics of capitalization and spelling. These scaffolds can be offered as an option so that children with greater ability and more proficiency with the English language are not restricted by their use.

- literacy scaffolds

Many repetitive patterns, such as those found in published poems or songs, can be turned into literacy scaffolds. The activity below is an example of a simple literacy scaffold and the steps for employing it (Cecil, 1994b).

A Simple Literacy Scaffold

ACTIVITY

1. Have the children listen to "These Are a Few of My Favorite Things" from *The Sound of Music.*
2. Have them recall the singer's favorite things as they are listed on the board.
3. Invite them to brainstorm their favorite things and add them to the list.

4. For each of the favorite things, ask the children if they can think of a "down-side" to it; for example, gentle rain is nice, but thunderstorms can be scary.

5. Provide each child with a photocopied sheet containing the following scaffold:

> I Like
>
> I like _ice cream_.
>
> But I don't like _to eat ice cream in the wintertime_.
>
> (Repeat as often as desired.)

6. As a class, write a group piece that includes a response from each child. Read the group effort chorally.

7. Have the children write their own "I Like" pieces.

patterned stories ■   Children also enjoy writing **patterned stories** based on texts such as *Fortunately* by Remy Charlip. Cumulative stories like John Burningham's *Mr. Grumpy's Outing* and *Mr. Grumpy's Motorcar* and Ed Emberley's *Drummer Hoff* offer writing models for children. Additionally, folktales such as *Chicken Little* and *The Little Red Hen* provide repetitive phrases that can be emulated (Tompkins, 1997).

JOURNAL WRITING

there has always been a time for children to engage in some amount of intimate oral communication in the early grades. But until rather recently, there was no place in the literacy curriculum of primary grades for personal writing, leaving a large void in this mode of communication. Journal writing provides the opportunity for personal expression as well as valuable writing practice. Of the variety of journal-writing techniques used in elementary schools, three seem to be well-suited for emergent writers and will be explored here.

Dialogue Journals

dialogue journal ■   In a **dialogue journal,** the teacher and student can carry on a written conversation about any topic of interest to the child. By making written comments in the margins of a notebook in direct response to the child's words, by asking questions, and by providing positive written feedback in response to what the child has written, the teacher helps the student grow as a writer. The frequent writing that occurs in dialogue journals helps promote students' writing fluency, and the reading of the teacher's comments provides valuable reading experience and builds a relationship between teacher and student.

code switch ■   Children just beginning to speak and write English can be encouraged to write in their home language or to **code switch** by using both English for words they know and their home language for words they haven't yet acquired in English.

For preliterate students, the dialogue journal can be used with pictures interspersed with letters, and eventually words, as the child learns them. The teacher can initially ask the child to tell about the pictures. The teacher then transcribes above the picture exactly what the child composes, carefully modeling the sounding out of words until gradually the child begins to use experimental spelling to write down ideas (Cunningham & Allington, 1999).

For some young children, delayed fine-motor coordination can make forming tiny letters in straight lines difficult and painstakingly slow, thus hampering their interest in writing. Their ideas may flow many times faster than their ability to capture them in print. This was the case for seven-year-old Ethan, who took 30 minutes and two large sheets of paper to write a piece about a fictional car he created (see Figure 9.10). Although writing practice fosters dexterity for such children, the teacher may wish to occasionally transcribe the child's ideas to ensure that frustration with the mechanics of writing does not squelch enthusiasm for composing. Also, teaching children keyboarding skills enables them to use word processing programs to more quickly write down their ideas; this can motivate children for whom lack of motor skills is a continuing concern (see Chapter 12).

Reading Response Journals

Young children become interested in literature, for the most part, to the degree that it affects them. Teachers can solicit personal responses to reading by asking children to write in a **reading response journal** a first reaction to something they have read, saying whatever they like without correction (with the exception of simply "I liked it" or "I didn't like it"). Alternatives to traditional book reports in journal format can include responding to a quotation from the book, questioning the author, continuing the story, or writing another version of the story from another character's point of view (Sweeney & Peterson, 1996).

■ reading response journal

This type of journal is an ideal vehicle for personal expression, often called **expressive writing.** Children can write fluently without fear of criticism, because

■ expressive writing

Ethan's composition.   *figure* **9.10**

Ethan's piece translation: The Ferrari Palato has a manual transmission with a 10 cylinder, turbo, V-8 engine, auto seat move, with leather seats.

they are not burdened with the task of polishing their writing for another reader. Journal writers are free to answer the question, "What did I really think of that?" as they read, think, and write.

sentence stems ■ Teachers can adapt reading journals for early writers' use by providing **sentence stems** that ask questions designed to connect what they have read with their own experiences. For example, the following questions can be used after reading a story to prompt journal writing:

1. This character is like me because _____.
2. I like/dislike this character because _____.
3. This story reminds me of _____.
4. If I were _____, I would have _____.
5. I would like the story to have ended this way _____.

Learning Logs

learning log ■ For content area material, children can begin to crystallize their understandings via a **learning log.** This activity requires that children write in their journals immediately after a content area subject lesson, such as social studies. Their journal entry would then include:

■ a summary or examples of what they understand has been presented or read;

■ a summary or examples of what they do *not* understand about what has been presented or read;

■ questions they have about what has been presented or read;

■ a personal reaction to what has been presented or read.

These logs can be interactive if the teacher responds to them regularly, answering children's questions and directing their attention to important concepts. Figure 9.11 shows examples taken from the mathematics learning logs of a third-grade class. The teacher answered the children's thoughtful questions in the margins of the log.

figure **9.11** **Examples from third-graders' learning logs.**

How is multiplication like addition?	You are adding, but you're doing it much more quickly.
How do I know when to divide?	Look for the word "each."
What problems should I watch out for when I am borrowing?	Be sure to cross out the old number and put in the new one so you're not confused.
Why do I need to know the times tables when I have a calculator?	You may not always have a calculator with you!

THE LANGUAGE EXPERIENCE APPROACH

t he **language experience approach (LEA)** is well suited for modeling beginning literacy because it uses children's own language as writing material. Later it can be transcribed by the teacher and read by the children—thus graphically illustrating the connection between the communication processes (Ashton–Warner, 1965; Lee & Allen, 1963; Stauffer, 1980). Because the language patterns utilized are determined by children's own speech and the content is determined by their own experiences, it is relatively easy for children to remember the text of these stories, and they are eager to read them again and again.

■ language experience approach (LEA)

This approach, which stems back to the story and sentence methods of reading instruction that were popular around the turn of the twentieth century, is an ideal way for teachers to demonstrate the interrelatedness of reading, writing, listening, and speaking. Children watch the teacher *write* down their story as they *speak*. They *listen* as the teacher reads the story, and finally they *read* the story themselves. This helps children realize that: (1) what they experience can be talked about; (2) what they talk about can be written down; and (3) what they write can be read. It also helps children grasp the idea that written language often has the same purpose as oral language: the communication of meaning (Allen, 1976; Hall, 1981). As teachers take dictation, they also have an excellent opportunity to demonstrate the conventions of written language: that it proceeds from left to right and from top to bottom, that words have spaces between them, that the first word in a sentence is capitalized, and so forth. The stories can also be illustrated, allowing opportunities for viewing and visually representing.

Steps in the LEA

Language experience compositions can be composed using a chart and chart paper (see Figure 9.12) by groups of children or individuals, and they are ideal for English learners because of the many senses being used simultaneously. The format is the same in either case and includes the following steps (Cecil, 1994d):

1. Provide a stimulus for discussion and writing.
2. Conduct an oral discussion about the stimulus.
3. Brainstorm about the stimulus, creating a word bank.
4. Help children compose the passage.
5. Read the passage aloud; reread several times.
6. Recruit children to read individual sentences.
7. Have the children follow directions and highlight patterns.
8. Have the children name the passage.
9. Conduct a phonics minilesson.
10. Duplicate the passage, and children can provide their own illustrations and reread the passage at home.

figure 9.12   Making a language experience chart.

1. Use regular 24" x 16" (or larger) ruled chart paper, oak tag, or posterboard.
2. Keep a 2" margin on both right and left sides, and a 3" margin on the top of the paper.
3. Use short one-line sentences for beginners.
4. Do not divide a word or phrase at the end of a line.
5. Invite children to illustrate the piece—at the top, bottom, or even the sides of papers—but do not let pictures break up a sentence.
6. Use manuscript writing, with crayon, lettering pen, or felt-tip marker.
7. "Pack" together the letters of each word, leaving the space of an "o" between words.

The Snake

Robert brought a snake to school.
The snake was green and skinny. 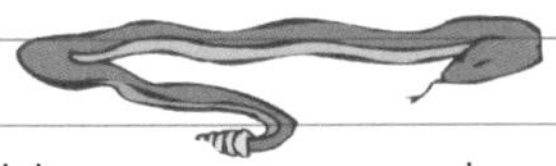
Robert let us hold him but some children were scared.
We thought he would be slimy but he wasn't.
He was dry! We hope the snake enjoyed being in school!

Provide a stimulus for discussion and writing

The stimulus for writing or discussion is usually a concrete object or a current event, but it has been broadened to encompass anything that has recently been experienced by all members of the group. That the object or experience has been witnessed by all children ensures that second language learners will benefit from the later discussion and composing. A language experience story could be written about a snowman made at recess, a seasonal thunderstorm, a television program that everyone happened to see, a story the class just enjoyed listening to, chocolate pudding that all have enjoyed eating, or a garter snake brought in by one of the class members. The single most important criterion is that the subject has captured the interest of the children and they would now like to talk, write, and read about it.

Conduct an oral discussion about the stimulus

Oral discussion is a natural bridge between the sensory stimulus and reading and writing about it. After the stimulus has been experienced, the teacher can encourage the sharing of thoughts and ideas about it. The teacher's role is that of an interested facilitator who is positively and nonjudgmentally responding to comments by discussants and paraphrasing what may be unclear.

Brainstorm about the stimulus

This step gives children the opportunity to think critically and creatively about the stimulus and provides for the word bank words and phrases that will be helpful in writing the passage. The teacher guides the children into categorizing the responses. If, for example, the class were writing a language experience story about a garter snake that a child has brought to class, the brainstorming might proceed as follows:

Associations (nouns). "What kinds of things do you think of when you think of a snake?" *(poison, rattles, grass)* "Why?" *(after each response)*

Description (adjectives). "What words could we use to tell about a snake? How does it look, smell, sound, feel?" *(skinny, slimy, scary)*

Actions (verbs). "What do snakes do?" *(slither, crawl, bite)*

Reactions. "How do snakes make you feel? Why?" *(scared, like running away, curious)*

Similarities (synonyms). "What are some other things that are kind of like snakes? How?" *(worms, spaghetti, sticks)*

Differences (antonyms). "What are some things that are very different from snakes? How?" *(Elephants, because they are big and snakes are small. Note: Almost any answer is acceptable here if children can offer a reasonable explanation for their choice.)*

Phonics element. "What are some words that rhyme with snake?" *(bake, make, take)* or "What words begin like snake?" *(snail, snow, snore)*

The responses to the group brainstorming are written prominently on the board or chart paper as the children help the teacher sound out the words according to their current knowledge.

Help children compose the passage

Referring to the words on the board, the teacher suggests the children write a passage about the stimulus. (*Note:* The word "story" is studiously avoided so that the piece can be written in either expository or narrative format.) The teacher asks for a beginning for the piece and solicits suggestions and continues until children run out of ideas. Finally, the teacher requests an ending and invites children to illustrate the piece. A typical second-grade piece might look like the one shown earlier in Figure 9.12.

During the dictation phase, the teacher should accept the children's ideas verbatim; however, if an unclear sentence or incorrect grammar is offered, the teacher should paraphrase the sentence correctly, keeping the meaning intact by asking a question like "Do you mean . . . ?" This approach, diplomatically employed, can assist an English learner's transition to standard English in a positive way.

Read the passage aloud

Follow the dictation with several readings of the passage, each reading in a different manner. First the teacher reads the passage aloud to the children while they follow along, phrase by phrase, to avoid stilted word-by-word reading. The teacher may then "echo read," or have children repeat every line after she models it. Then the teacher points at each word and deliberately exaggerates the left to right progression and the return sweep to the next line while children read the passage chorally with the teacher. English learners and less able readers are thereby participating in the reading experience by being "fed" the words they hear around them, avoiding the usual embarrassment that can occur with oral reading when every word is not known. Plus, they are able to hear the syntax, rhythm, and cadence of the new language repeatedly.

Recruit children to read individual sentences

All children have read the entire story; now the teacher recruits children to read each individual sentence, thereby focusing the children's attention on the sentence unit as part of the passage. Also, reinforcement is being provided for high-frequency words as well as new ones.

Have children follow directions and highlight patterns

This step is essential for bolstering new vocabulary, providing practice listening, and leading students to look for particular phonic elements and patterns. The teacher gives an oral riddle, incorporating words that contain phonic elements or patterns that the children have previously studied. For example, the teacher might say:

"Can someone come up to the chart and put a circle around the word that has the same ending sound as the word cry?"

Or:

"Can someone come up to the chart and put two stars over the word that has an 'ake' in it, as in 'make'? The word is in the first and the last sentences."

Have children name the passage

Determining the main idea of a paragraph is one of the most difficult comprehension skills. However, with daily practice in selecting the titles for language experience passages, children can soon grasp the idea of honing in on one general thought that conveys the central idea in the passage. Several nominations of titles for the passage should be solicited, followed by a short discussion of why one title does a slightly better job of summarizing the main idea than another. For example, the teacher might want the children to see, through another rereading, why "The Snake" is a more appropriate title for the second-graders' story than "Our Pets," which was also offered.

Conduct a phonics minilesson

After the language experience passage has been written, read, and reread in a different way, the teacher selects six to ten new vocabulary words (depending on the difficulty of the words and the children's grade and ability level) from the passage and/or word bank that incorporate some phonic element that needs reinforcement, for the class as a whole or in small groups. The minilesson proceeds as described in the activity that follows.

A Phonics Minilesson Based on a Language Experience

1. Put the six to ten words you have chosen on the board or in a pocket chart and have the children copy them onto 3 × 5 cards. (Do this for the children if they are preliterate.) Point out specific sounds to be emphasized by underlining those letters, or make them a contrasting color and ask the children to do the same:

   bake   shake   snake
   lake   take   rake

2. Pronounce each word for the children (or ask for volunteers to say them) and stress the sounds being considered, in this case, a review of the *ake* rime or word ending. Ask children what they notice about the ending part (or beginning, or middle) of the words.

3. Ask the children to look closely at the words as they say them and come up and point out the part that is the same for all the words.

4. Invite them to verbalize in their own words what the similarities are.

5. When you feel all the children have made the deduction, ask them to listen as you say more words, with or without the pattern. Have them determine which words fit the pattern. Encourage them to think of more words that fit the pattern

Duplicate the passage

Each passage written by the children in this manner could be carefully duplicated, with space for a personal illustration, so that each child has a copy to reread at home and a copy to compile into a collaborative class book. Passages should be reviewed often with children to reinforce phonic elements, high-frequency words, and new vocabulary. Children will also be proud and eager to read their books to other classes or to create recorded read-alongs for children needing more reinforcement. Every so often the passage can be revisited to allow for further rereadings and review.

Variations on the Basic LEA (Salinger, 1993)

The following group writing activities can be used to vary the standard language experience lesson just presented.

Interactive writing. Interactive writing is a collaborative strategy in which both the teacher and the students work together to create a piece of writing. With help

■ interactive writing

from the teacher, the children dictate sentences about a shared experience, such as a story, a video, or an event (see Chapter 3). The teacher verbally "stretches" each word so children can distinguish its sounds and letters, as children use chart paper to write the letters while repeating the sounds to themselves. After each word is completed, the teacher and children reread it. The children take turns writing letters to complete the words and sentences. The completed charts are put up on the wall so they can reread them or rely on them for standard spelling.

morning message ■   **Morning message.** Each day, the teacher writes a brief **morning message** about the day's weather and upcoming events and records it on a chart (which may be specially made to allow enough space). Sometimes the children dictate the message. This chart provides a model for the children's own daily writing in their journals.

Digital morning message (Labbo, 2005). Using creativity software such as Kid Pix, which supports brainstorming, illustrating, and drafting a writing piece, the teacher can write the morning message digitally. While individual children dictate the sentences, the teacher models using the keyboard to type the children's message. The children then listen and follow along as the voice synthesizer on the computer reads each sentence. Finally, the children read the message chorally, led by the teacher or the class leader of the day.

individual dictation ■   **Individual dictation.** For beginning writers, the teacher may take **individual dictation** from each child and record her work in small notebooks. Transcribing a caption for artwork falls into this category.

Sentence strips. The teacher records transcriptions on long strips of paper or index cards and cuts the **sentence strips** into word cards. Children use these word cards to create sentences at their desks or in pocket charts. Children are encouraged to copy their sentences into a notebook.

sentence strips ■

word bank ■   **Word bank.** Children request individual words from the teacher and keep them in a **word bank** to study on their own, play with, swap with friends, and so forth. Frequently the teacher and students review the words and discard the ones the children cannot read. This strategy complements the sentence strip strategy. The words can also be put on word walls for whole class use.

Content area use. Through LEA strategies, the teacher keeps records of the children's work in content areas such as science and social studies. Observations of experiments, field trips, and even math activities lend themselves to this approach.

ONLINE EXPERIENCES FOR LITERACY AND LEARNING

 any researchers suggest that the Internet is now the major vehicle through which literacy and learning will take place (Hartman et al., 2005). Technology is redefining what it means to be literate. Nowadays, children need to be critical thinkers about what they read in text as well as critical consumers of electronic messages (Valmont, 2003). Thus, it seems self-evident that teachers must fully integrate new technologies in teaching children to love literacy and learning. Motivational online experiences in the classroom can create positive attitudes toward literacy and learning and also develop strong—and increasingly valuable—technology skills.

Castek, Bevans-Mangelson, and Goldstone (2006) offer five ways to make the reading, writing, and technology connection through use of the Internet:

Children *want* to write, to create their own texts in order to make meaning.

1. *Have children collaborate in Internet projects.* For example, primary students can use *The Important Book* (Brown, 1990) to research their own cities or towns on the Internet. They can join classes from around the world that are working on the same project through "My Town Is Important," a collaborative Internet project for K–4 students. The ePals site offers a wide variety of revolving projects.

2. *Have children read or listen to literature on the Internet.* For example, through the Screen Actors Guild Foundation, many actors have volunteered to read exceptional picture storybooks such as *Thank You, Mr. Falker* (Polacco, 1998) on a streaming video at BookPALS Storyline. Young children can explore the read-along stories on the RIF Reading Planet Website.

3. *Add informational websites to your study of literature.* For example, a third-grade class reading *How I Spent My Summer Vacation* (Teague, 1997), a story about a boy who is captured by cowboys, can deviate from the usual personal essay response and instead visit teacher-provided informational links to sound and photo displays of cowboys, rodeos, Western geography, and so forth. (Appendix C includes examples of informational websites.)

4. *Have children join virtual book clubs.* For example, children can participate in discussions, ask questions, and post comments on their favorite books on sites such as the Scholastic "STACKS" site (or search "children's online book clubs").

5. *Encourage children to become authors on the Internet.* The work of revising and editing may become more enjoyable when children know their polished work will be read by a larger audience. As an example, Children's Story Online allows children to collaborate with other same-age peers from around the world. Through this participation, children make deep reading/writing connections and

WWW.

My Town Is Important
www.mrsmcgowan.com/ projects.html

BookPALS Storyline
www.storyonline.com

ePals Projects
www.ePals.com/projects

Read Along Stories
www.Rif.org/readingplanet/ content/read_aloud_stories. mspx

See Appendix C

WWW.

Scholastic STACKS
www.scholastic.com/kids

Children's Story Online
www.childrenstory.com/
stories/index.htm

develop positive attitudes toward the Internet as a vehicle for reading and writing. As an added bonus, they also learn about other cultures.

See Chapter 12 for additional suggestions for online literacy experiences.

OTHER MOTIVATORS FOR EMERGENT WRITERS

even the most reluctant writers can be motivated to write if they are given an initial boost through fixed writing structures, as discussed earlier; a provocative writing prompt; or an outright gimmick (Sweeney and Peterson, 1996). The following teacher-tested ideas contain one or more of these elements and have been used often with emergent writers who have a difficult time getting started (Cecil, 1994b).

Book Making

WWW.
Write a biography
bellinghamschools.org/
sites/default/files/BIO/
Biomaker.htm

One of the most motivational ways for children to publish their individual or group writing is by putting their work into a book. Simple booklets can be constructed by folding a sheet of paper into quarters, like a greeting card. Children write the title on the front cover and use the three remaining sides for their composition and accompanying drawings. Children can also make booklets by stapling sheets of writing paper together and adding covers from construction paper or wallpaper from old sample books. Book covers can be laminated. Figure 9.13 shows a sample of an early first-grade class's literature-response book.

figure   9.13   Sample of a class literature-response book.

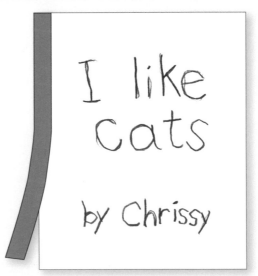

Computer Composing

For early writers, especially those for whom the physical act of producing a neat composition is an onerous chore, using a computer can be an added incentive to writing. In a study of first-graders' use of word processing software, Jones and Pellegrini (1996) found that the technology facilitated the students' writing of narratives. Similarly, in a case study of a five-year-old writer, Cochran-Smith, Kahn, and Paris (1990) noted that the computer provided a mechanism that supported her thoughts rather than her handwriting, letter formation, and word alignment.

Teachers must fully integrate new technologies in teaching children to love reading, writing, and learning.

Not requiring the substantial fine motor coordination needed to write words, word processing allows children to focus on their ideas. As a result, they tend to write more and enjoy seeing the professional-looking results. Using programs designed for early writers, such as *First Writer* (Houghton Mifflin) or *Bank Street Prewriter* (Scholastic), children can more easily revise and edit rough drafts and receive the added bonus of a clean copy every time. Most programs include tutorial lessons ideal for independent small-group work after an initial introduction by the teacher. See Chapter 12 for more information on writing electronically.

Motivational Activities

Teachers may use the following activities to motivate children to begin writing.

Animal Crackers

ACTIVITY

Place an animal cracker on the desk of each child with instructions to look at it and think about it, but not to eat it. Make a list of all the animals represented, sounding them out with children, and brainstorm words that describe each animal. Then, returning attention to each child's animal, discuss the following questions:

    Are these animals alive?

    How do you think your animal felt about being in the box?

    How does it feel to be out of the box?

    What language does your animal speak?

    What does your animal eat?

    Does your animal know it will soon be eaten?

    How does it feel about that?

Finally, have the children write several sentences about their animal, using ideas from the discussion and descriptive words on the board. For less able writers, provide a sentence stem to help them, e.g., "My *(animal)* feels _____." When they are finished, invite them to eat their cracker.

Imagine What Happens!

A C T I V I T Y

Select a picture book such as *The King, the Cheese, and the Mice* by Nancy and Eric Gurney. Read the story aloud and stop at the most exciting point. Ask children to predict what might happen next, using a "predictive web" such as the one shown in Figure 9.14.

Invite children to use one of the brainstormed ideas or one of their own and write (or draw for preliterate children) their version of the ending of the story. Allow children to read or tell about their original endings. Finally, read the author's ending and compare it with the children's predictions.

figure   **9.14**   **Predictive web.**

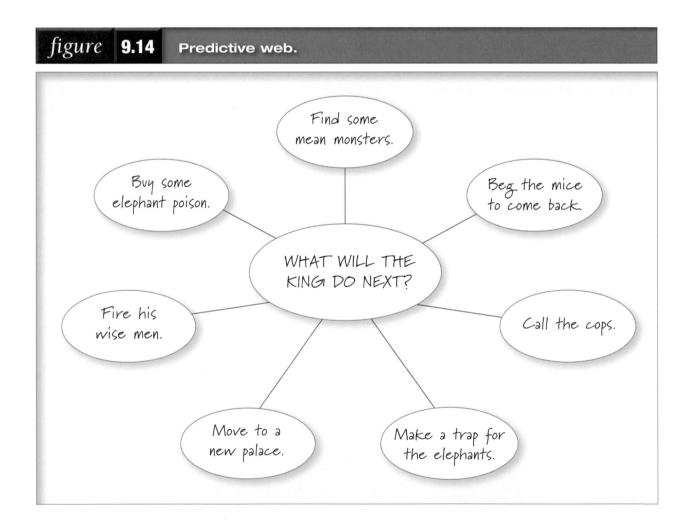

Balloon Sensitivity

Beginning writers are inspired by concrete items they can see, hear, and touch. Help each child blow up and tie a balloon. Divide children into groups of five. Give them time to experiment with the balloons, using their five senses: How do their balloons look, sound, feel, taste, smell? Give each child a sheet with one of the five sentence stems written on it:

My balloon looks _____.

My balloon sounds _____.

My balloon feels _____.

My balloon tastes _____.

My balloon smells _____.

Wishing on a Star

With children's input, write on the board a number of things that can be wished on, such as a wishbone, an eyelash, or a penny thrown into a well. Write the following poem on the board and ask children to recite it chorally with you:

Star light, star bright, first star I see tonight,

I wish I may, I wish I might, have the wish I wish tonight.

Encourage children to share some things they have wished for. Hand out lined paper in the shape of a star and ask children to write about some things they wish for, with every line beginning with "I wish . . ."

SUMMARY

before they began school, most children scribbled on sidewalks, newspapers, and even wallpaper with chalk, crayons, lipstick, pencils, pens—*anything* that would make a mark. The child's mark said, "I am." Whereas in reading children create their meaning from a given text, in writing, children create their own texts in order to make meaning—at first for themselves, and then for other readers. Children *want* to write. They want to write the first day they enter school.

School is merely where the beginning of children's *formal* literacy instruction takes place. The writing process for emergent writers has already begun with the child drawing pictures, and it continues with scribble writing, precursors to the developmental spelling stages that lead to conventional writing. Guided by teacher modeling and inspired by provocative ideas, a fertile imagination, and the freedom to experiment with print, children soon learn to express their own thoughts and feelings in their own language. They gradually evolve into conventional writers and quickly realize the power of the written word to make their thoughts visible to others, graphically illustrated by one little boy's intercepted note to his little classmate that proclaims, "I luv yuw!"

questions

for journal writing and discussion

1. How many ways do you think spoken language can be used in a primary classroom to provide a foundation for writing activities? Make a list and share it with your class.

2. Consider the importance of providing emergent writers with appropriate feedback and encouragement during the process of drafting a piece of writing. Do you or your classmates remember receiving this kind of encouragement? Discuss.

3. Review the suggestions offered in this chapter for connecting reading, writing, and technology. Which of these do you feel you would be most likely to implement in your classroom? Why? Discuss these suggestions with a small group of your classmates. Rate each according to the benefits in the following areas:

   - Amount of writing practice gained.
   - Amount of reading required.
   - Motivational appeal to children.
   - Practice using computer and Internet skills afforded.

suggestions

for projects and field activities

1. Interview two children at different primary grade levels to determine how much writing they say they do in class and how they feel about the writing and themselves as writers.

2. Obtain permission to teach a language experience lesson to a small group of primary-grade youngsters. Bring in a toy or another object to use as a stimulus for discussion, brainstorming, and writing. Follow the steps in this chapter to teach the lesson. Share with your classmates what worked well, what you would do differently next time, and what you learned about the children's ability to compose.

3. Observe a writers' workshop over the period of one week. Ask the children to show you their favorite pieces. Ask them to tell you what they are learning about writing. Finally, ask the teacher what he or she has learned about each of the writing skills of the children in the class through this process. Share your insights with your college class.

chapter

10

Informational Text in the Classroom

Reading and Writing to Learn

focus questions

- Why is informational text important?

- What makes informational text challenging?

- What instructional practices can help children with informational text?

- How can instruction in the structure of informational text help children succeed in writing using this mode of discourse?

209

When several of Mrs. Shreve's second-graders come into the classroom on Monday morning chatting about a film they have seen about sharks over the weekend, the teacher decides to use the children's interest to create a lesson on reading and writing informational text. The next day Mrs. Shreve asks her students, "So . . . what do you know about sharks?" The children eagerly write their answers on sticky notes and place them on the board. Then, as a class, they organize their facts and place them under categories they have identified, including "where they live," "what they eat," "different kinds of sharks," and "behavior." From this list Mrs. Shreve invites the children to create questions, which will serve as their purpose for reading and locating information.

When Hadley asks the popular question, "Do *all* sharks attack people?" the children's eyes widen with curiosity. The teacher, seizing the moment, shows the children how to locate this information in the table of contents (under shark attacks) and the index of an informational book about sharks she has brought for them. She turns to the pages listed and reads the information aloud, modeling how to extract the information that will address the question the child has asked. The teacher then helps children to explore other informational texts about sharks she has amassed from the library and the Internet in order to help them answer such questions as, "What are baby sharks like?" "How big are sharks?" and "What are some other interesting facts about sharks?" This reading activity is followed the next day with a writing activity in which pairs of children use an introduction, a body, and a conclusion to create an informative piece explaining what they have learned about sharks. Included in their paper is a diagram showing the parts of a shark with appropriate labels. They proudly read their pieces aloud to their sixth-grade buddies. Then they publish them in the school newspaper.

WHY INFORMATIONAL TEXT IS IMPORTANT

Instruction created to help children learn new information has always been a primary goal of literacy education, but the information explosion caused by continuing technological advances makes this goal even more important. To become life-long learners, children must learn how to critically sort through all the information now readily available to them. This requires much more than simply acquiring the facts; children must learn *how* to learn by rapidly analyzing the truth and relevance of the information they consume (Rasinski, Padak, & Fawcett, 2010).

Therefore, educational experts and practitioners alike are demanding to see more informational texts in primary classrooms (Moss, 2005). Professional journals and conferences are currently brimming with discussion of the place of informational reading and writing in elementary schools. In addition, accountability for the comprehension of such text is becoming evident on high-stakes assessments. As an example, a component of the No Child Left Behind legislation is the National Assessment of Educational Progress, which audits each state's reading achievement in grades 3 through 8. In one permutation, the test required fourth-graders to read and comprehend narrative material half the time and informational text the other half. By eighth grade, those percentages had changed to roughly 70 percent (Grigg, Daane, Jin, & Campbell, 2003).

The introduction of standards-based education throughout the United States has also helped to heighten interest in children's ability to read informational text: in almost every state, language arts standards related to the reading and writing of informational text are now being used routinely for the primary grades, even including kindergarten (Moss, 2005). The new common core standards have also underscored this effort. Early readers were previously steered toward narrative text almost exclusively (Duke & Bennett-Armistead, 2003; Palmer & Stewart, 2003); but publishers are now responding quickly to this new focus, and informational texts are rapidly becoming available for young readers on increasingly accessible reading levels.

It is becoming clear that there is a mandate to teach children to use informational text at earlier and earlier grade levels, but why is it suddenly at the forefront of so much educational discussion? Reasons for teaching young children to read and write informational text include the following:

Most literacy activities that children will do in their later years in school and beyond will involve comprehending informational text. We live in an increasingly informational world. An expanding focus of U. S. schooling is to develop citizens who can read, write, and critically evaluate informational text and discuss the information they find (Duke, 2000). If we truly value the ability of young readers to deal effectively with this genre, they must be directly taught the necessary foundational skills—and the earlier the better (Moss, Leone, & Depillo, 1997). Moreover, with much reading and research occurring on the Internet, children must learn to access information quickly, sort through volumes of text, and analyze and evaluate the information (Schmar-Dobler, 2003).

Informational literacy helps children to learn content. In the past, educators tended to believe that first the child learned to read and then, in the intermediate grades, they began to read to learn. By using informational text, learning to read and reading to learn can occur simultaneously (Guillaume, 1998). Furthermore, some evidence suggests that children who have more exposure to informational text have an advantage in achievement in science (Bernhardt, Destino, Kamil, & Rodriguez-Munoz, 1995) and other content areas. For some children, engaging with informational text may be the most efficient path to overall literacy, especially for boys and struggling readers and writers (Caswell & Duke, 1998). Often such children have a preference for the concrete nature of such straightforward, factual material.

Informational literacy can be as, if not more, motivational to children than narrative format. Although, as was previously stated, informational text has *not* been found in abundance in most primary classrooms in the past, there is mounting evidence that young children do enjoy—and sometimes prefer—informational text (Caswell & Duke, 1998; Palmer & Stewart, 2003; Pappas, 1993). Indeed, in a series of studies, Kamil (1994) found that, although there was the same proportion of fiction versus nonfiction books in the libraries, children checked out a greater number of informational books than storybooks.

Exposure to informational literacy can help children think clearly and critically. Research, digital skills, and computer literacy skills are finding their way into the earlier grades, and children are increasingly asked to organize and display their work in PowerPoint and similar media formats. By third or fourth grade, children are now expected to read and analyze a great amount of material and

Informational reading and writing help students to learn content.

then write about what they have read in a clear and logical way, integrating several sources and including their prior knowledge (Cazden, 1993). Additionally, although much helpful information may be gleaned from the Internet, children must also learn to evaluate and discard much questionable content. Instruction in and exposure to informational literacy can help young children engage in the kind of critical thinking and research necessary to build meaningful knowledge bases and can foster an ability to think analytically in all the content areas (McMath, King, & Smith, 1998; Parkes, 2003).

WHY INFORMATIONAL TEXT IS CHALLENGING

t here are many reasons why informational text has been long overlooked as a learning genre for early readers and writers. Prominent among these is the perception that informational text is dry, boring, and difficult and that, in order to capture the fancy of beginning readers, teachers must resort to the more appealing storybook or narrative structure. Textbooks, in particular, are thought to be especially difficult for children to read. In truth, many children who have no difficulty reading the basal reader and trade book stories often *do* have more trouble with informational text. However, this difficulty appears to have less to do with motivational factors and more to do with the reader's lack of understanding of the structure and lack of appropriate strategies to comprehend such text (Pages, 2002).

The challenges inherent in informational text include the following:

- Dense content contained in minimal text; a resulting need to reduce reading rate.
- "Facts" versus "plot": the whole text need not always be read to meet reading goals.
- Visual aids (graphs, charts, tables, and the like) that contain much information.
- Unfamiliar technical terms.
- A variety of organizational styles.

Fortunately, many instructional strategies may be used to address the challenges presented by informational text. These will be discussed in the remainder of this chapter.

PRINCIPLES OF USING INFORMATIONAL TEXT

t he ability to gain knowledge from text is indispensible in our current age of exponentially expanding information. From an early age, children must develop the ability to understand the discrete languages of disciplines such as history, science, mathematics, and other content areas. They also must develop the critical-reading abilities to begin to think the way scientists, historians, and mathematicians think. They must understand the information that is being presented to them and be able to evaluate it as well (Moss, 2005). Certain pedagogical tools, discussed below, will help teachers tailor instruction to the interests and capabilities of young children (Richgels, 2002) and thus allow this learning to occur more efficiently.

Teach Previewing

First, make a practice of directly showing children how to preview informational text through the use of study-skill methods that, when taught early, will help them to succeed later, as they encounter more and more informational text in the content areas:

■ Model and provide guided instruction in hypothesizing what the chapter/book/article will be about, based on the title and introductory paragraph.

■ Show children how to use the headings and subheadings to create questions about the text.

■ Explain how reading the summary and previewing the questions and other tools at the beginning and end of a chapter can tell them much about what will be important in the text.

Teachers may use the following activity, along with a grid based on Figure 10.1, with children for previewing an informational book, and a student guide for previewing an informational text is contained in Figure 10.2.

Expectation Grid

ACTIVITY

(DeVries, 2011)

The expectation grid combines reading, writing, viewing, and visually representing. With a student, preview the chapter title, headings, subheadings, pictures, and graphs. Have the reader decide what the main topics are and draw a diagram like the one found in Figure 10.1—if possible, draw it in such a way as to link it to the content. The details are then added as the student reads the passage.

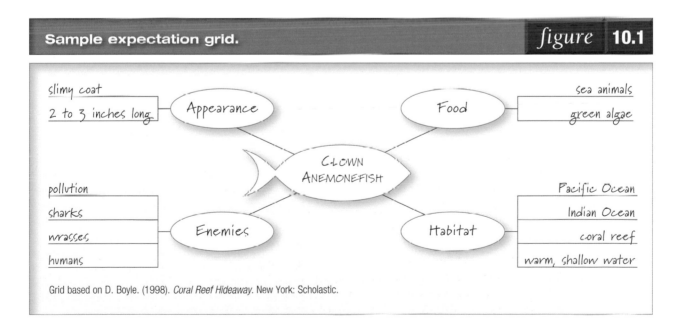

Sample expectation grid.   *figure* **10.1**

Grid based on D. Boyle. (1998). *Coral Reef Hideaway*. New York: Scholastic.

figure **10.2**   **Student guide for previewing informational text.**

Name _____   Date _____

Partner's Name _____

Title of book/article _____

STEP 1.   Read the title and introduction of the book/article.

From the introduction, what do you think this book/article will be about?

_____

_____

STEP 2.   Look at the pictures or diagrams in the book/article.

What do the pictures tell you about the information in the book?

_____

_____

STEP 3.   Read the headings and subheadings.

What are two things you will find out by reading this book/article?

_____

_____

STEP 4.   Read the book summary.

What are two things you should have learned when you finish this book/article?

_____

_____

STEP 5.   Think about the information you wrote for Steps 1–4. Finish this sentence:

I think this book/article will be about

_____

_____

Adapted from *Direct Instruction Reading,* 4th ed. (2003), by D. Carnine, J. Silbert, E. Kameenui, & S. Tarver. Upper Saddle River, NJ: Prentice Hall.

Establish an Authentic Context and Purpose for Reading

Second, make sure that young children's experiences with informational text are authentic and purposeful to them. Do this by modeling how informational texts can be used to help them find answers to many of their common questions, such as "Why do cats purr?" Furthermore, show children how such text can help them find certain bits of information ("What are 'gills'?") even if they cannot read the entire text. Finally, demonstrate to children how informational text often contains pictures and other graphics that can be used to support presentations and discussions; for example, a map of the habitat of different frogs in the world can be copied to help show this concept more expediently than several paragraphs of explanation. Likewise, pictures of different types of frogs can add motivational appeal to a presentation on frogs.

Use in Conjunction with Other Forms of Text

Third, do not use informational text in isolation. Information can be gleaned from many sources besides textbooks. All kinds of environmental print—from signs to recipes and labels—carry information that can help children access this genre of print. Also, Morning Message routines that are typically undertaken in primary classrooms—where the weather, lunch information, and other events of the day are reported—can be used to provide a schema for informational text. In addition, the Internet can expand the information on the topic presented in the book. The Library of Congress website contains information on many topics appropriate for young students. Teachers should show children how to compare the information found on the Internet with that in the book. During this process, they can teach critical-thinking skills as they help students to learn of biases and to evaluate the accuracy of the information. Such instruction is so vital in our highly technological world. However, Malloy and Gambrell (2006) underscore the challenges of teaching about the Internet: "As educators, we need to commit to preparing students for their technological journey . . . [one] toward literacies that grow and change more quickly than we can keep up with them. But by learning together, teachers and students can become fully literate in every sense of the word" (p. 484).

    Finally, an informational book can be paired with a narrative text containing some information about a topic being studied in a content area such as science or social studies (e.g., *The Wall*, about the Vietnam Memorial, can provide motivation, background, and "color" for the lessons). Using the parallel genres, or a narrative and an informational text, can also create an opportunity for the teacher to compare and contrast the two differing ways of presenting information (Richgels, 2002). These **twin texts**, sometimes referred to as paired books, lead children from fiction into nonfiction by pairing related books, one of fiction and one of fact. An authentic way to introduce content material, twin texts form a bridge from reading stories to understanding content from all areas of the curriculum (Camp, 2000).

    The next section explores strategies for teaching children how to gain information and enjoyment from informational text.

WWW.

Awesome library

www.awesomelibrary.org/ student.html

U.S. Library of Congress

www.americaslibrary.gov/ cgi-bin/page.cgi

■ twin texts

TEACHING CHILDREN TO READ INFORMATIONAL TEXT

young children are most often very curious about the world around them. Observe any primary classroom, and it becomes clear that primary youngsters are continually asking questions about how the world works. Young children enjoy learning new things and exploring facts—if the factual information is presented in an accessible and supportive way. Certain instructional strategies implemented by the teacher can provide successful experiences with informational text that will help children feel more strategic and confident with informational text. Such successful experiences and effective instruction can lead to enjoyment of and proficiency with informational text.

Teacher Think-Alouds

The most expedient way to familiarize young children with informational text is for the teacher to read aloud excellent examples of such text and to point out exactly how such text differs from narrative text both in genre and organization. Figure 10.3 offers a simple comparison of narrative and informational texts.

---

figure **10.3**   **Important distinctions between narrative and informational text.**

To help you understand the differences between writing a story and providing information, consider the following terms. When I write a story (narrative), I need a **beginning,** a **middle,** and an **ending.** But papers that share information (expository) have **introductions, body paragraphs** (development), and **conclusions.**

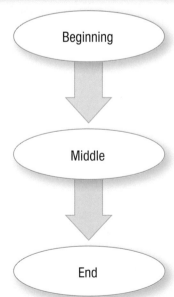

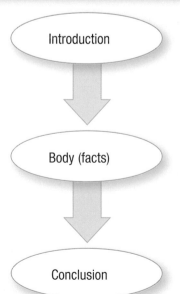

Such read-alouds can be conducted in a "think-aloud" manner, with the teacher addressing the specific organizational patterns and "wondering" out loud why the author may have chosen to use such a particular structure. The reading can be followed by a discussion and critical appraisal of the content. Pages (2002) suggests that teachers start such informational read-alouds with books they themselves enjoy and that they provide background information on the subject to build a knowledge schema before reading, by bringing in artifacts, dramatizing events, sharing current newspaper articles on the topic, and so forth. The following activity will help children explore background information and make predictions about what they will read. Over time, reading aloud informational texts not only familiarizes children with the organizational styles but also helps them learn content and new vocabulary related to the topic (Duke, Bennett-Armistead, & Roberts, 2003). Also, teachers may encourage parents to select informational texts to read to, and with, their children. Appendix A offers a wide variety of informational texts that would be suitable for this purpose.

Background research
on different topics

*www.smithsonian
education.org*

See Appendix A

Making Predictions from Artifacts

ACTIVITY

(Ellermeyer & Chick, 2007)

1. Using an informational picture book (for example, *Smoky Mountain Rose: An Appalachian Cinderella* by Alan Schroeder), choose artifacts to represent the book and place them in a shoebox. For example, for *Smoky Mountain Rose,* you might place a toy high-heeled shoe, a toy mouse or pig, a map of the Smoky Mountains, and a picture of a fiddle.

2. Cover the picture book you selected with brown paper, so students can't see the title or cover. Show students the wrapped book and tell them you will give them some hints about what it is about. Show one artifact at a time from the shoebox and ask students to guess what it might represent in the story. Guesses can be documented on chart paper or the board.

3. After predictions have been made for each artifact, unwrap the book, read the title, and show the cover. Students can again make predictions about each of the artifacts. These guesses can be listed beside the first predictions.

4. Read the book, reminding students to listen for the way each artifact is used in the story. Discuss each artifact, documenting its real purpose in a third list. Have students discuss how close their predictions were to the real purpose of each item.

5. Discuss the history and people of the Appalachians or the region or culture that represents the book you selected.

6. Artifacts can be used to make predictions in any subject area. For example, *Snowflake Bentley* by Jacqueline Briggs Martin would be a good choice for the science classroom.

Explicit Instruction of Organizational Patterns

Once children have become familiar with the basic differences between narrative and informational text, the teacher can explicitly show children the major expository text patterns that authors use when writing informational text. Armed with a schema of the different organizational structures authors can use, children will usually find it much easier to comprehend the informational material being presented. Following are common text patterns used by authors of informational text.

■ *Question and answer.* The content area of social studies often uses a pattern that includes the author's beginning with a question and then answering it in the body of the paragraph.

■ *Description/enumeration.* With enumeration, an author states a concept and then elaborates on it (DeVries, 2011). Words such as *for example, in addition,* and *finally* may be used to help the reader follow the facts or ideas. The author's intent is to describe in such a way that the idea is best understood.

■ *Sequence or chronology.* When time or order is relevant, particularly in content areas such as history, authors may use numbered lists and outline ideas using words such as *first, next, then, after that,* and *finally* to signal the use of sequence or chronology. Sequence may also be used for science experiments, instructions, or the presentation of occurrences that require a number of ordered steps, such as an explanation of how to make bread.

■ *Cause and effect.* One of the most difficult patterns for young readers, the cause and effect pattern, is used to show how one event or fact happens because of another event or fact. Science and social studies texts often use this text pattern and signal the use of such a pattern with words such as *because, as a result,* and *therefore.*

■ *Comparison/contrast.* When two or more ideas, people, animals, facts, or events have both similarities and differences, a common way to portray them in informational text is to compare and/or contrast them. Such a treatment of text can be identified through such words as *however, on the other hand, by contrast, but,* and *whereas.*

When introducing informational text patterns to young children, the following sequence for instruction may be used (adapted from Tompkins, 2002):

1. Introduce the organizational pattern (e.g., comparison/contrast or sequence) by explaining when and why writers would choose this particular structure.

signal words ■
2. Point out the **signal words** or key words associated with a structure (e.g., *because, therefore, as a result*—comparison/contrast; *first, next, after that*—sequence), and share an example of text using these *signal words.* (See Figure 10.4.)

3. Model ways students can determine text structures when signal words are *not* used (e.g., look at the table of contents and headings).

4. Introduce a graphic organizer for the pattern, e.g., an expository frame.

5. Read aloud a section of a book illustrating the text structure.

6. Ask students to listen for and identify the signal words in the selection.

Signal words associated with various expository text patterns.   *figure* **10.4**

SEQUENCE	ENUMERATION	CAUSE/EFFECT	COMPARISON/CONTRAST
First	To begin	Because	Alike
Second	First	Hence	Different
Next	Second	Therefore	Similarly
Then	Also	As a result	In contrast
Last	In fact	If/then	But
Before	For example	Consequently	However
After	Most important		Although
Finally			

7. Using a whiteboard or overhead projector, have the class complete a graphic organizer illustrating the pattern type.

8. Ask students to work in pairs to locate an example of the structure in other informational books.

9. Have students create a graphic organizer for their informational book.

Minilessons

One way that all of the major challenges of reading and comprehending informational text can be directly addressed is through minilessons. For example, to address the issue of dense content in a science textbook, the teacher may do a short lesson on using different reading rates for different purposes; the beginning vignette of this chapter presents a teacher showing children how to find just the needed information from informational sources. A teacher can explain the use of topic sentences by providing examples of interesting introductions, such as those containing provocative questions, quotes, anecdotes, and so forth. Likewise, the importance of visual aids should be noted for children, and they should be shown directly how to gain important information from them. Unfamiliar technical terms—especially multi-meaning words that are used in a differing context—should be explained with abundant examples, such as the word "change," which has different meanings when used in math ("make change") or everyday situations ("change your clothes"). Examples of different organizational styles for informational text can be shown and discussed with children.

A brief minilesson about counting, for example, can help reader comprehension of an informational book.

Other Instructional Strategies for Informational Text

Many other instructional strategies can be used to help children understand and learn from the unique aspects of informational text. Here are a few other specific suggestions for helping children become involved in (and excited by) the many forms of knowledge they will encounter:

- Discuss the content of the text and organize the information using a language experience chart, semantic webbing, KWL chart, or another form of graphic organizer. (See Chapter 8.)

- Read several different informational books on the same topic. Point out how different authors look at the same topic in different ways; for example, one author might be addressing a frog's life cycle while another may be focusing on the different types of frogs and where they are found.

- Compare fiction and informational works on a single topic such as dolphins. Discuss how each genre treats the subject matter differently. See Figure 10.5 for an example comparison of an expository and narrative passage.

- Use the strategy of retelling. The activity on the following page offers steps for retelling.

---

figure **10.5** **Example passage for contrasting expository and narrative writing.**

GIVING INFORMATION
(Explaining)

The dolphin may look like a fish, but this friendly sea creature is really a mammal. First of all, dolphins have lungs just like we do. They must come to the surface of the water to breathe and get oxygen from the air. Fish can take oxygen from the water. Like other mammals, dolphins have backbones and are warm blooded. Finally, they nurse young dolphins on milk just like a cow might nurse a calf. The dolphin's streamlined body and its big, strong tail might resemble a fish, but don't be fooled; it's definitely a mammal.

TELLING A STORY
(A Narrative)

I was excited to see the dolphins, my favorite animal.
"Go closer to the tank," my father said.
I looked into the water and saw the beautiful animals swimming together. Someone was feeding them fish.
"I wish I could swim with the dolphins," I said.
"Maybe someday you will," said my father.
Just then one of the dolphins swam close to us and suddenly we were as wet as could be! We laughed and laughed.

Retelling Informational Texts

(Moss, 2004)

- Involve students in prereading activities such as KWL, brainstorming, or problem solving. Also, encourage children to predict what the text might be about and to predict the order of the text by looking at the table of contents or previewing other aspects of the text.

- The text should then be read aloud by the teacher or silently by the students. Teachers can also make the text come alive with props, pictures, and actual examples of concepts within the story.

- Invite students to create charts, graphs, and other visual aids from the text to help them retell important points of the text. (See Figure 10.6.) Creating a graphic organizer such as this one can help a child remember facts about a topic—for example, the habitat, enemies, appearance, and physical capabilities of a box turtle.

- Ask students what they can remember about the text, and list their responses on the whiteboard. Provide scaffolds and prompts, such as pictures or questions, to help students recall the text. Example questions can include: What did you find out first? What did you learn after that?

- Reread the text or have students reread the text, this time searching for information missed during the first retelling. Add any additional information to the list of previously generated student responses.

- Encourage students to make personal connections between their lives and the concepts within the text. If appropriate, these ideas may also be recorded on the whiteboard.

Graphic organizer: description or enumeration.   *figure* **10.6**

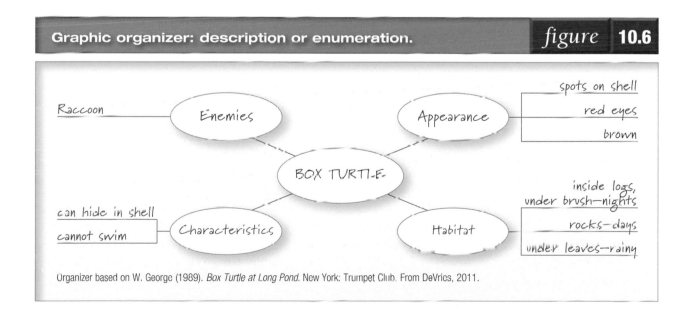

Organizer based on W. George (1989). *Box Turtle at Long Pond*. New York: Trumpet Club. From DeVries, 2011.

WRITING INFORMATIONAL TEXT

informational writing is often called "expository writing" and generally concerns itself with explaining an idea, an object, or a process. The expository paragraph or essay presents a certain amount of information about a topic. The major purpose of the mode of discourse is to explain or inform, to tell readers something they may not know, and to tell them in a way that they will understand.

Given appropriate instruction in the structure of informational text and a topic they find interesting, children are fully capable of coping with the complex organizational challenges that occur when faced with writing informational text. Indeed, children as young as first and second grade can be successful in writing informational text (Read, 2005).

Structuring Informational Writing

Instead of having, loosely, a beginning, a middle, and an end as is found in narrative structure, the expository paragraph has a somewhat more rigid organization and is usually organized according to one of the patterns (question and answer, enumeration, cause and effect, or comparison/contrast) discussed in the last section. Essentially, all expository writing has four main parts to it that children can be taught to include when creating an expository piece. Each piece of expository writing must contain:

- *A topic sentence that clearly tells what the piece is going to be about.* This sentence is the idea statement that tells the reader the reason that the piece is being written. *Example:* Insects differ from spiders in several ways.

- *Transition phrases.* These important words are signals of new ideas, or the "glue" that holds the paragraphs in the piece together. Words and phrases such as *first, second,* and *finally, on the other hand, nevertheless,* and *in a similar way* are all examples of phrases that help the reader to realize that a new idea is being introduced.

- *Examples, evidence, and explanations.* The essence of any expository piece is in the details. The topic sentence has been given, and now the writer must elaborate and make a case for the claim by citing evidence or offering an explanation or by providing examples, reasons, or facts, depending on the organizational structure being used. Using the example mentioned above, in the paragraph on the difference between insects and spiders, a possible supporting sentence may be; "First, insects have six legs while spiders have eight."

- *A conclusion.* The expository piece is usually tied together with a conclusion that reminds the reader of the topic sentence. Because information has been given in the examples, evidence, or explanations, the conclusion is stated slightly differently than in the original topic sentence. For example, "It is easy to tell an insect from a spider because of the many differences between them."

Instructional Strategies for Expository Writing

Expository text frames

Primary-grade children's knowledge of expository structures—content organized around a main idea and supporting details—usually lags far behind their knowledge of narrative structures. This is because almost all children have had less exposure to expository passages and also because the structure of expository text tends to be more complex (Duke, 2000; Englert & Hiebert, 1984). Using **expository frames** can help children understand expository structure by providing a systematic way to write about content material they have read. It is also an effective way to introduce young children to expository writing (Cudd, 1990).

■ expository frames

Expository frames, analogous to story frames that introduce children to narrative structure, provide a scaffold for creating different ways to organize text. They can be used to review and reinforce specific content and to familiarize children with the different ways authors organize informational material. In effect, the frames serve as bridges that help ease the often difficult transition from narrative to expository reading and writing.

By the second semester of first grade, most children can begin working with content area expository frames that are organized sequentially. The sequential pattern appears to be one of the easiest structures for children to recognize and use in their own writing and is a skill taught and reinforced regularly in basals. Moreover, such text structures have been found to increase the comprehension of English learners (Anderson & Roit, 1998). At this point, children are already familiar with signal words, such as *first, next, then,* and *last,* that are used as transitional devices within sequential paragraphs. See Figure 10.4 for additional examples of signal words.

To ensure success in completing expository frames, the teacher begins instruction with a prewritten expository paragraph rather than a blank frame, as in the following activity (Cudd, 1990).

Using Expository Frames

ACTIVITY

1. Write a simple paragraph about a topic that lends itself to sequential ordering, using the signal words *first, next, then,* and *last.*
2. Copy the sentences on sentence strips.
3. With the class, review the topic and logical sequence of events.
4. In a pocket chart, have the children arrange the sentences in correct order.
5. Read the completed paragraph together.
6. Have the children reorder the paragraph on their own and paste it on construction paper in paragraph form.
7. Invite the children to illustrate the details or some important part of the paragraph.

Gradually introduce a sequentially ordered expository frame for the children to complete independently, as in Figure 10.7.

figure 10.7   A child's expository frame for sequence.

Setting the Table

In order to set the table, you need to go step by step. First, you must <u>(get knives, forks, and spoons)</u> . Next, you need to <u>(put napkins under the forks)</u> . After this, you <u>(get glasses of milk for everyone)</u> . Last of all, <u>(you give everybody a plate of food)</u> . When you are finished, <u>(you eat dinner!)</u>

Other frames using different organizational models, such as cause/effect patterns, problem/solution patterns, and comparison/contrast patterns, are also helpful for assisting children in writing expository text. Figure 10.8 is an example of a comparison/contrast pattern, and Figure 10.9 is an example of an enumeration pattern.

Strategies for choosing a topic

It is often easier for young children to choose a topic for informational writing than for narrative writing (Read, 2005). They are less likely to feel "I don't know what to write about!" with so many different topics to explore. Children enjoy

figure 10.8   A child's expository frame for comparison/contrast.

(Title)

Comparing Insects with Spiders

Insects differ from spiders in many ways. First, insects <u>(fly while spiders don't)</u> . Second, insects <u>(don't spin webs but spiders do)</u> . I think the easiest way to tell an insect from a spider is <u>(to count the legs. A spider has eight legs. An insect only has six)</u> .

A child's expository frame for enumeration.

figure **10.9**

Trees are useful in many ways. For example, _____

_____ .

Also, _____ .

In addition, _____ .

Finally, _____ .

researching and then writing about their discoveries in a wide variety of topics, including wild and domestic animals, cars, other countries, volcanoes, and planets. Teachers can show how to use the Internet effectively for researching a topic by leading the student on scavenger hunts. Two sites appropriate for young children are Education World's Scavenger Hunt and Internet Treasure Hunts for ESL Students. However, for expository writing that requires no research, it is sometimes helpful to offer an interesting topic with a proscribed organization for children to follow. The following expository writing activity does just that.

WWW.

Scavenger hunts
www.education-world.com/ a_curr/curr113.shtml

Treasure hunts for ESL students
http://iteslj.org/th

Writing Persuasive Pieces

ACTIVITY

Have children use hypothetical situations to create a four-paragraph, persuasive essay. Hypothetical situations are the kind of rich stimuli that help children turn their fantasies into colorful expository text.

Every so often, pose one of the following situations, or similar ones, to the class:

- What if you could have three wishes?
- What if you could be invisible?
- What if we could talk to animals?
- What if you could read people's minds?
- What if there were no television?
- What if there were only one kind of food?
- What if we could fly?
- What if everyone looked exactly alike?
- What if you could have everything you wanted?
- What if people got younger, not older?
- What if people could live forever?

2. Create a reading lesson using parallel genres, or twin texts, to compare and contrast two different ways to present information. For example, obtain a copy of an informational book such as *Valentine's Day Is . . .* by Gail Gibbons. Find a corresponding narrative text, such as *The Night Before Valentine's Day* by Natasha Wing and Heidi Petach and use it to provide motivation, background, and "color" for the lesson. Or, use Appendix A to select another informational book and find a narrative text on the same topic to create the lesson.

See Appendix A ▶

See Appendix C ▶

3. Log on to three websites suggested in Appendix C to support informational reading and writing. Choose one that you particularly liked and find an informational text for which the website information would be helpful. How might the website information be used to support the text?

chapter 11

Large and Small Group Reading Strategies

Creating a Literate Community

focus questions

- How can shared reading be used to model effective reading strategies?

- How can teachers use guided reading to help children construct personal meanings from text?

- How can the practices of shared and guided reading be kept exciting for both the students and the teacher?

in the classroom

The children are sitting cross-legged on their carpet squares in the back of Mr. Kohl's first-grade classroom, eagerly awaiting the second reading of *The Three Billy Goats Gruff*. Prior to the first reading of this story, children scanned the colorful illustrations of the oversized book and made predictions about what they thought was happening on each page. Several children made comments about similar stories they were reminded of, and one little girl shared that her uncle owned a pygmy goat—much to the delight of the other learners. Mr. Kohl took the opportunity afforded by the story to introduce the children to the /tr/ blend and pointed it out each time it was encountered, as the goats went "trip, trap, trip, trap" across the bridge three times. By the third time the goats reached the bridge, the children were rhythmically and enthusiastically chanting the words "trip, trap, trip, trap" with Mr. Kohl as he pointed to them in the story.

On this day, the day of the second reading of the story, the children brainstorm some ways they might talk to the troll and convince him they really should be allowed to cross the bridge. As the story is read aloud this time, the children turn to each other after every page and take turns summarizing in their own words what has happened on that page. Occasionally, the teacher stops the reading, points to a word, and asks "What is this word? Can anyone raise a quiet hand and tell me?" Eighteen small hands shoot up, and one child is called upon to tell Mr. Kohl that the word is *bridge;* they have seen the word over thirty times now, and they can all recognize it. Mr. Kohl then asks the children to think of some other words that begin with the same blend, the /br/ sound. He writes their answers carefully on the small writing board *(brag, broken, broccoli, brick)* as the children help him to sound out the words.

(Later in this chapter, we'll visit another teacher using *The Three Billy Goats Gruff* for a *shared reading* experience.)

INTRODUCTION

In a comprehensive approach to literacy, teachers use a variety of instructional strategies, from reading aloud to minilessons, to model what fluent readers do and to gradually release the responsibility for reading and constructing meaning to the children (Pearson, 1993).

Mr. Kohl is using *shared reading* with his students, a technique useful in modeling reading for children by reading a book aloud and ultimately inviting the children to join with him. In this chapter we will explore how this strategy, and a similar one requiring more student independence, *guided reading,* can be used to blend comprehension strategies and beginning phonics instruction with strategies that engage the reader in the printed word. Both activities are forms of mediated reading instruction in which the teacher, through modeling and explicit instruction, demonstrates how proficient readers decode and gain meaning from text.

SHARED READING

The mediated reading activity known as **shared reading,** or the *shared book experience,* was developed by Holdaway (1986) as a means of introducing early readers to the use of favorite books, raps, chants, rhymes, and poems in a highly motivational way. In shared reading, children participate in reading, learn important concepts of how print works, and get the feel of the fluency and smoothness of reading without the possibility of error, because the teacher is doing the decoding for them. The teacher reads with fluency and expression and eventually invites the learners to read along. Each reading situation is a relaxed, social one, with emphasis on appreciation of the text. Shared reading is also an excellent technique for allowing children to identify sight words, because it stresses the external features and sounds of individual words while it maintains a focus on meaning. Integrated with a direct and explicit phonics program (see Chapter 5), such a technique can ensure that children not only know *how* to read but also thoroughly enjoy doing so.

The use of the mediated strategy of shared reading is ideal for a teacher wishing to balance meaning-based and skills-based instruction. Through shared reading, the teacher models for children how proficient readers "get" the message the author is trying to communicate and then shows how it can be related to one's own life experiences. Such mediated reading instruction also uses modeling to show how proficient readers sound out words. It is based on the extensive body of research that suggests that young children become accomplished with language through the synergistic processes of talking, listening, experimenting with written language, and interacting with the various language models in their environments (Clay, 1991). These studies found that young children who have learned to read at home before coming to school generally accomplished this task by having their favorite books read aloud to them over and over in a relaxed, joyful atmosphere (Baghban, 1984; Bissex, 2004). Holdaway's (1979) procedure capitalizes on the natural learning processes of young children and builds on their innate curiosity to help them grow into literacy. Many teachers and researchers have used this procedure to successfully engage children of various ability levels and backgrounds in reading (Bridge, Winograd, & Haley, 1983; Harlin, 1990).

Purposes for Shared Reading

Shared reading builds on children's natural desire to read and reread favorite texts, imitating and recreating the intimacy of sitting on a parent's lap listening to a story. Moreover, abundant research supports the effectiveness of shared reading when used with many language-minority populations (Anderson & Roit, 1998). Au (1991) suggests that such reading doesn't have to be simply random rereading, however. Rather, each time a text is reread with the teacher, it can be for an entirely different purpose, although always with the central aim in mind: to extend, refine, and deepen a child's abilities to decode text and construct meaning. Following are six major purposes for shared reading and rereading text (Cooper, 1997):

- to develop print concepts
- to reinforce decoding skills in the context of authentic text
- to explore language
- to think creatively
- to improve comprehension skills through listening
- to foster an appreciation for reading

Developing print concepts

Children at the emergent literacy stage are developing crucial concepts about print through shared reading. Children learn about the conventions of our language—words, letters, sentences, punctuation—as they are discussed in the context of the story being read. For example, in the

Shared reading builds on children's natural desire to read and reread favorite books.

introduction of *The Three Billy Goats Gruff* story (Stimson, 1993), the teacher might have pointed out how quotation marks were used whenever one character talked to another, or how a capital letter always began a sentence (see Figure 11.1).

Reinforcing decoding skills

Another advantage of using this strategy is that children's decoding skills are reinforced in the context of authentic text. With teacher guidance, children learn to figure out unfamiliar words using the various cues provided in the language of the text—context, structure (prefixes, suffixes, inflectional endings), and recurring patterns or phonic elements. Learning to decode involves rereading texts with numerous examples of the exact element to which the children have recently been introduced through explicit instruction. For example, through the reading of the fairy tale, the children were ready to learn the *tr* blend. The teacher pointed out this phonic element in the story, exaggerated it, and asked the children to think of other words beginning with the same sound. Rereading then helped children reinforce that learning.

figure **11.1**   **Excerpt from *The Three Billy Goats Gruff*.**

Source: Joan Stimson, *The Three Billy Goats Gruff*. Illustrated by Chris Russell. Loughborough, UK: Ladybird Books, 1993. Used with permission.

Exploring language

Through shared reading, children are continually engaged in exploring language. By examining unusual or repetitive language patterns, the teacher guides the children in developing a greater appreciation for language while learning about structure and cues that will help them construct meaning. Often the language pattern can serve as a basis for children to then write a new story. For example, in *The Three Billy Goats Gruff*, children explored the language pattern created by the goats tramping across the bridge. They were invited to use the blends they had been studying to make new sounds the goats might have made, using a similar language pattern: The goats went "hip, hop, hip, hop," or the goats went "clip, clop, clip, clop."

Thinking creatively

A fourth by-product of shared reading is that children develop the ability to think creatively. At times, the teacher urges listeners and readers to jump far beyond what an author is saying to formulate original ideas. When this happens, the author's words serve as a trigger that often ignites a new train of thought; children may momentarily stop listening to what an author is saying to ruminate on their own exploding ideas. They may ask themselves, "What can I do with this information? What does this mean in my life? Where can I go with this? What would I do if I were in this character's shoes?" The result of thinking about such questions is often a unique personal invention or a totally original idea.

Improving comprehension skills

Another benefit of shared reading is that children's comprehension skills constantly evolve through intent listening. The teacher begins by reading the text to the group, inviting the children to chime in if they know words or phrases, and asking them to make predictions or to listen for a specific purpose. Sometimes children are encouraged to summarize sections of text by recounting them to another classmate, as occurred in Mr. Kohl's second reading of *The Three Billy Goats Gruff*. Children may at other times be asked to think about the motivation of characters, enumerate episodes in the story, guess outcomes, or share what the text reminds them of in their own lives.

Appreciating reading

Above all, through shared reading children develop an appreciation for reading. The primary reason for a young child to read is, after all, to construct personal meaning; if the child acquires the skill of reading but doesn't care for reading, that child will soon fall into the category of *aliterate,* or one who *can* read but chooses *not* to. Therefore, teachers reading aloud should use methods that encourage children to enjoy texts and to become excited about them. During shared reading, the teacher can talk about the illustrations, the characters, things that happened in the story, things the children liked or didn't like, and how certain events or characters made them feel. All these activities help children form an appreciation for the characters and events in the story. Texts may be re-read many times for this purpose alone. In fact, this appears to be the primary reason that most children choose to reread any story.

Procedures for Shared Reading

Carefully chosen stories in big-book format (see Chapter 3) are perfect for engaging very young children in critical and creative thinking. Stories from quality children's literature (try Newbery Award winners or Children's Choice selections) or literature-based basal readers usually have an easily discernible structure that teaches children what to look for when they encounter a certain structure in their independent reading. Such stories should grab the imagination of young children and stimulate a range of feelings. If wisely chosen, they provide an enjoyable association with reading.

Many educators break the shared reading activity into several related parts: (1) a "warm-up" activity where familiar nursery rhymes, chants, and songs are read and sung, using large print as a guide; (2) introducing the reading selection ("into" the text, or *before* reading); (3) reading and responding to the text ("through" the text, or *during* reading); (4) rereading the text one or more times for various purposes; and (5) extending the text ("beyond" the text, or *post-reading*). The time frames for each of these elements are flexible and can be adapted, shortened, or lengthened, as the teacher sees fit or as time allows (Peetoom, 1986). See the Case Example on pages 235–237 for a detailed look at the procedures as we join a shared reading experience in Mr. Jimenez's classroom.

GUIDED READING

guided reading ■

guided reading is a group reading activity similar in many ways to shared reading. With guided reading, however, the children usually decode the text independently, often silently but sometimes orally, and a major emphasis is put on asking children questions, asking for predictions, and helping them formulate their own questions about the text (Fountas & Pinnell, 1996). Children try to answer these questions after they have read a designated section of the text. The Directed Thinking–Reading Activity (DRTA) (see Chapter 8) is an example of a guided reading activity (Guastello & Lenz, 2005; Schwartz, 2005).

tracking ■

This type of reading is usually initially teacher-led (later done independently) and usually conducted in small groups, giving children the opportunity to develop as individual readers while they participate in a socially supported activity. At the early stages of reading development, children use their fingers to finger-point read. Finger-pointing involves children in **tracking,** or indicating an understanding of the one-to-one correspondence between spoken and written words (Reutzel, 1995). At the conclusion of each section, the children stop and discuss with the teacher the answers to their questions or predictions. At each stopping point, the teacher allows and encourages children to respond to what they have read. The teacher is then able to observe each child's processing of new text. By taking notes on each learner, the teacher becomes aware of what further instruction each child requires in specific phonics elements or other decoding strategies. Peregoy and Boyle (2008) suggest that guided reading is especially effective with ELs because of the teacher scaffolding and smaller groups.

A shared reading experience in Mr. Jimenez's classroom

It's Wednesday morning in Mr. Jimenez's kindergarten classroom. They have just finished a choral reading of a poem from *Poetry Works! The First Verse Complete Set* (1998). Following this warm-up activity, he intends to introduce the book *The Three Billy Goats Gruff* (1993), by Joan Stimson and illustrated by Chris Russell, to his students in a shared reading activity.

"INTO" THE BOOK: INTRODUCING THE TEXT

In Mr. Jimenez's class, the introduction of a text in a shared reading activity meets with a joyous sense of anticipation—beginning with focused attention to the cover. Mr. Jimenez reads the title and asks the children what they think the book might be about. He discusses the author and illustrator and tells the children about any other familiar texts the author and illustrator may have created.

Next, Mr. Jimenez gets the children excited about reading the book by showing a few selected pictures to "whet the children's appetite." This is called a **"picture walk";** he shows each of the pictures, and the children tell what they think is happening in each one. He asks **predictive questions** that encourage children to think about what is going to happen, thus constructing text. Examples of predictive questions he may ask are:

> "Who do you think are going to be the main characters in this story? What do you think is going to happen to them?" (anticipating; predicting)
>
> "Where do you think the goats are going?" (inferring from cover clues)
>
> "What do goats usually eat? Where do they usually live?" (activating prior knowledge)
>
> "Does anyone know what goats' feet are called?" (assessing prior knowledge)
>
> "What kind of sound do you think their hooves make?" (inferring, to prepare students to hear the words *trip, trap*)

Mr. Jimenez records the children's predictions on the board to refer to later. This introduction can take anywhere from 3 to 20 minutes (see Chapter 8 for more information on developing appropriate questions). *Note:*

When Mr. Jimenez reads the shared reading text for the first time, he can record it. Children could then work at a listening center to listen to the story again while tracking along.

"THROUGH" THE BOOK: READING AND RESPONDING TO THE TEXT

In this phase, Mr. Jimenez reads the book aloud to the children as they are gathered around him, holding it so they can see each page clearly. He runs his hand or a pointer along each line of print so that the children develop a sense of the left-to-right orientation of English text and also match speech to print. He invites the children to join in, but for the initial reading, many will just listen.

The first reading is often rather quick, to allow children to get an overview of the story. Mr. Jimenez reads with enthusiasm, modeling the fluency of a proficient reader, yet stopping often to ask predictive questions and to field children's comments and reactions about the text.

At the conclusion of the text, he asks open-ended, prompting questions designed to get children engaged in discussion about the story, such as:

> "How did your predictions match what actually happened in the story?"
>
> "What was your favorite part of the story?"
>
> "What did the story remind you of in your own life?"
>
> "Who was your favorite character? Why?"
>
> "Which billy goat do you think you are most like? Why?"
>
> "How did the story make you feel?"
>
> "What would you have done if you were a billy goat trying to get across the bridge?"
>
> "How would the story have been different if it had been told from the point of view of the troll?"

(continued)

case example

REREADING AND REVISITING THE TEXT FOR VARIOUS PURPOSES

Mr. Jimenez returns to the story and does a second reading, this time encouraging the children to join in, especially with rhyming and repetitious parts. After the second reading the children spontaneously exclaim, "Let's read it again!" which certainly means they have enjoyed the story and having been participants in it. If time permits, Mr. Jimenez will do another reading, because when children are excited about reading, a lifelong love is being kindled.

He may wish to select a variety of purposes for revisiting the story. Children may now be ready to reflect on it in a more individual way. The method Mr. Jimenez uses to encourage responses may vary according to the nature of the story or the wishes of individual children. Some suggestions to elicit reflective responses (but by no means an exhaustive list) are as follows (Hennings, 1992):

- Tell a classmate about a favorite part.
- Retell the story to a partner.
- Write a sentence about the story in your journal.
- Draw a picture about the story with a caption.
- Draw and/or write about a favorite character.
- Explain why you didn't like a certain character.
- Prepare a skit of your favorite scene in the story.

The story can also be revisited to help children visualize the relationships among the story's characters. A **literary sociogram** (Butler & Turbil, 1986; see Figure 11.2) can be used to help children better understand the relationships between story characters and see the differences in feelings that one character may have from another. Mr. Jimenez employs this device by asking children parallel questions about characters. For example, when reading the story *Little Red Riding Hood,* he asked: "How did Mother feel about Red

figure **11.2**   **A literary sociogram.**

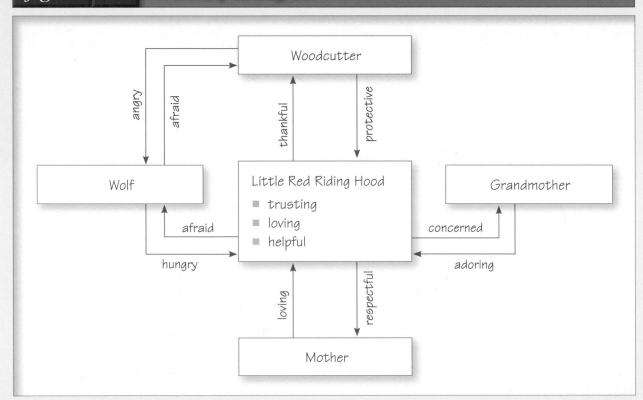

Riding Hood? What evidence do you have?" and "How does Red Riding Hood feel about Mother? What evidence do you have?" After writing down children's responses on arrows, the class discussed why the pairs of characters may have had differing feelings toward each other.

In another session, *The Three Billy Goats Gruff* may be revisited to help children make contact with their feelings through those of the characters. For example, Mr. Jimenez might ask the children:

> "How do you think the last billy goat felt when he was left all alone? Have you ever felt that way?"
>
> "Why was the troll so upset that the goats were going over the bridge?"
>
> "What are some other things the billy goats might have done to keep the troll from being angry?"
>
> "How would you have felt if it had been your bridge?"

In yet another session, Mr. Jimenez used *masking devices* (described later in this chapter) to isolate individual words and focus children's attention on the details of the words. For example, he masked off several words, starting with the blend *tr,* helping the children discover that these words all start with the same sound. Mr. Jimenez uses oral cloze activities, in which he deliberately omits words in the story and pauses for the children to supply the missing words, for promoting prediction and contextual analysis skills:

> EXAMPLE: Now, there was a _____ over the river, and under this bridge lived a very fierce and ugly _____ .

Yet another revisiting of the text might be for the purpose of encouraging children to compare and contrast the present story with another one they have read in the past; for example, Mr. Jimenez used a **Venn diagram** (see Figure 11.3) to have children compare and contrast the story *The Three Billy Goats Gruff* with the story *The Three Little Pigs.* This device of two overlapping circles allows children to view graphically the similarities and differences between two stories or ideas.

"BEYOND" THE BOOK: EXTENDING THE TEXT

The extending phase is really another chance for children to respond to the text; with extension activities, however,

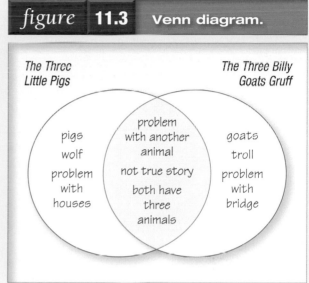

figure **11.3** **Venn diagram.**

The Three Little Pigs — The Three Billy Goats Gruff

pigs / wolf / problem with houses

problem with another animal / not true story / both have three animals

goats / troll / problem with bridge

oral, visual, or written creative expression is the primary focus. Such activities may take place in a small group, or they may be individual efforts and include such experiences as skits, puppet shows, murals, painting, or the creation of a class book from individual statements children have written about the story. Extended activities for Mr. Jimenez's class after several readings of *The Three Billy Goats Gruff* might include the following:

- Singing a song about goats that includes hand actions.
- A dramatization of the story using student-created props.
- A flannel-board retelling of the story with felt cut-outs.
- A group-written poem using the rime from goat—*oat.*
- A tempera paint mural showing the events in order.
- A retelling using three sizes of masks for the goats and three different voices.
- An activity where one child plays the part of the troll and fields questions from other classmates about his motivation.
- Creating another adventure with the same characters.
- Asking a story character some questions.
- Having children explain what they would have done at a particular point in the story if they were the character.

case example

When children are excited about reading, a lifelong love is being kindled.

Purposes for Guided Reading

Guided reading is an ideal strategy when small groups of children need additional support in constructing meaning from text, either because of the text's difficulty or because of the children's limited experience or ability. This approach also allows the teacher to adjust the level of modeling needed for understanding or to **scaffold** according to the children's needs (see Chapter 9). For example, children might read a story about a boy going into a cave. After a brief before-reading survey, the teacher realizes the children have limited backgrounds for this story; most have never been in a cave. Using a scaffolding technique, the teacher would "walk" the group of children through the story, offering helpful information about caves along the way (e.g., "Caves have pieces of limestone

scaffold ■ hanging down that look kind of like icicles. They are called stalactites."), checking their understanding at every point with probing questions (e.g., But *why* do you think the boy's hands were trembling as he entered the cave?") and clarifying concepts as needed.

Guided reading is ideal for use in *literature-based units*. Using this alternative to a basal reader, group-selected literature is read aloud by the children in small groups, and the teacher demonstrates comprehension strategies, clarifies misconceptions, introduces new vocabulary, and takes advantage of "teachable moments" to discuss any other instructional issue that may arise. The small-group arrangement also gives the teacher a chance to observe individual children reading orally, providing an opportunity for informal diagnosis of decoding skills and monitoring comprehension (Tompkins, 2006).

Because of its flexibility, guided reading is a very powerful tool; it should not be overused, however. The teacher can relinquish some control by providing more support at the beginning of the reading and gradually releasing the responsibility to the children as they become more confident with the reading of the story. With guided reading, the teacher can control the amount of scaffolding he provides in the following areas:

1. the types of questions asked before reading and during discussion;
2. the amount of text children read at any one time;
3. the type of discussion held between reading sessions;
4. the number of comprehension strategies modeled by the teacher via think-alouds (see Chapter 8).

When maximum support is needed, for example, the teacher can direct the discussion to underscore a specific fact or idea; then, as children have grasped the idea, the teacher decreases the direction, and the children take more responsibility by carrying out and directing their own discussion with a partner.

Questions play a vital role in guided reading and should always go beyond simply asking children to restate what they have just read. By responding to provocative questions that help them get an overall mental picture, children begin to understand how to construct meaning from text (Beck, 1984; Durkin, 1990). Many of the questions asked should be open-ended—not answerable with a simple "yes" or "no"—and should require critical thinking by the child. The teacher should allow plenty of time for all children to formulate a response. During guided reading, questions should meet the specific criteria discussed next. See Figure 11.4 for examples of each.

Before reading. Questions posed to children *before* the reading of the text should guide children's attention to the key concepts or the most important ideas in the piece to be read. In narrative text, these ideas may include the plot, the theme, the main character, the problem, or the main events. In informational text, children's attention should be focused on the major concept(s) to be presented.

During reading. Questions asked *between* sections of the text should bring together ideas discovered in the reading and are designed to build relationships among facts and ideas.

Typical questions for guided reading.	*figure* **11.4**

BEFORE READING

Narrative text:	Why might [the main character] want to run away from home? Have you ever wanted to run away from home? Why or why not?
Informational text:	Why are trees important to us? What would the world be like without trees?

DURING READING

Narrative text:	What made the boy realize that he cared about his family? Why do you think they welcomed him home and were not angry?
Informational text:	From what you have read, what are some other ways trees are important to us? Why are loggers cutting down the trees?

AFTER READING

Narrative text:	What would you now say to a friend who says he wants to run away? What are some other ways you can solve a family problem?
Informational text:	Why are there fewer trees in our cities? How can we take better care of our trees?

After reading. Questions asked *after* the reading of the text should be designed to help children internalize narrative text by identifying with the main characters or events in the story and, thus, to grow in appreciation of the reading experience; for informational text, the final questions should be created to help children apply the new information to their own lives.

Leveled Texts

leveled books ■

In order to ensure that children are being taught on their appropriate reading level (see Chapter 13), teachers use leveled books such as those published by Rigby, Scholastic, and the Wright Group for instruction in guided reading. **Leveled books** tend to have subtler differences in the difficulty between levels than more traditional "grade-leveled" texts (Fountas & Pinnell, 1999; Schulman & Payne, 2000). Using these texts, teachers may group children according to their individual instructional reading level. The specific level of each text is determined by the following criteria:

- Length of words
- Number of words
- Size of font and layout
- Difficulty of vocabulary and concepts
- Predictability and pattern of language
- Complexity of language and syntax

Figure 11.5 provides a list of books with guided reading book lists, and Figure 11.6 has a list of publishers of leveled books used in guided reading.

Procedures for Guided Reading

The guided reading lesson can be broken into five main parts: (1) the new text or story orientation, (2) the oral or silent reading of the text, (3) story retelling, (4) a "grand conversation" between teacher and class members and/or the

figure **11.5**   **Books with guided reading book lists.**

Fountas, I., & Pinnell, G.S. (2000). *Guided Reading: Good first teaching for all children.* Portsmouth, NH: Heinemann.

Fountas, I.C., & Pinnell, G.S. (2009). *The Fountas and Pinnell leveled booklist, K–8* (2010–2012 ed.). Portsmouth, NH: Heinemann.

Fountas, I., & Pinnell, G.S. (2001). *Guiding readers and writers, Grades 3-6: Teaching comprehension, genre, and content literacy.* Portsmouth, NH: Heinemann.

Schulman, M.B., & Payne, C.D. (2000). *Guided Reading: Making it work.* New York: Scholastic.

Source: DeVries, Beverly A. (2011).

Source: DeVries, Beverly A. (2011).

Publishers of leveled books. *figure* **11.6**

Pearson, www.pearsonschool.com

Rigby, www.rigby.com

Creative Teaching Press,
www.creativeteaching.com

Sadlier-Oxford, www.sadlier-oxford.com

Scott Foresman, http://books.atozteacher
stuff.com/leveled-books

Houghton Mifflin, www.eduplace.com

Sundance, www.sundancepub.com

Newbridge Educational Publishing,
www.newbridgeonline.com

McGraw-Hill, www.mheonline.com

explicit phonics instruction component, as needed, and (5) follow-up activities. As with shared reading, guided reading should be considered flexible and can be expanded, condensed, or modified to meet group needs and the time constraints of the teacher.

New text orientation

Before the new text or story is introduced, the teacher links any new ideas or difficult concepts to the children's prior experience, through a discussion, a visualization of what they are about to read, a video excerpt, or any other technique that will help children, especially English learners, relate to the text.

The teacher then holds up the book and shows the cover, reads the title, and briefly talks about the main idea of the book. Covering the text, the teacher "walks through" the book, discussing the pictures, providing an opportunity for children to make predictions about the text, asking key questions (as discussed earlier), and introducing some of the vocabulary and language structures found in the text—so that children will not find them troublesome when they are reading it independently.

Depending on the children's developmental levels, the first reading is begun by the teacher while the children track with their fingers. Later, the teacher gradually relinquishes responsibility for the first reading to the children by sharing the reading role and then fading into the role of supporter.

Oral/silent reading

When the children are ready to read independently, the teacher gives each child a copy of the text. In some cases, the teacher has a large edition of the book, or a big book (see Chapter 3), or an e-book for display on an interactive whiteboard (see Chapter 12), and the children have smaller versions of the same text. The teacher and children discuss the title, author, and illustrator. Until one-to-one correspondence is established, children should be allowed to point to the words as they read. Repeating the key concept they are to look for, the teacher directs them to read individually at their own pace. While the children are reading, the teacher works with them on an individual basis in the following ways:

1. With children at the very early reading level, the teacher checks for evidence of, and/or prompts for, directionality and one-to-one matching of spoken to printed word. Example: "Who can find the word *is* on this page?"

2. When children have mastered the above skills, the teacher checks for evidence of, and/or prompts for, self-monitoring of understanding ("No, that doesn't make sense."), the ability to search through the repertoire of decoding skills, accuracy, and self-correcting behavior.

Retelling

Children then retell what they have read—to their teacher, to their peers, or to a partner. (See p. 221 for the activity "Retelling Informational Texts.") Typically, the teacher will say, "Can you tell me (or a partner) about what you have just read?" Sometimes the teacher will probe, or further explore, children's answers by asking specific questions to prompt recall. The teacher often takes notes during this phase to record language facility and comprehension of individual children.

Grand conversation and/or explicit phonics instruction

grand conversation ■

The teacher helps the children internalize and appreciate what they have just read through a **grand conversation.** As in any adult book club, appreciation of a book is best created by asking open-ended questions and allowing each child to voice an opinion about what they liked or disliked, what they found humorous, what "grabbed" them, and so forth. A conversational tone is set when the teacher starts with an open-ended question (e.g., "Would you have chosen Leslie for a friend? Why or why not?") and encourages children to ask questions of and respond to each other for the sheer joy of discussing their feelings about the book. The teacher's role, then, becomes that of facilitator, ensuring that all who want to respond are heard—not just the most vociferous.

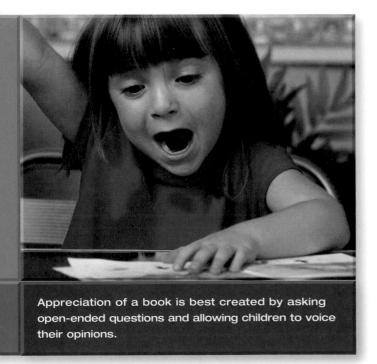

Appreciation of a book is best created by asking open-ended questions and allowing children to voice their opinions.

For children who need it, the teacher may do an additional minilesson (5 to 7 minutes) on some aspect of phonics or structural analysis development that she deems necessary. Such a lesson may be conducted before the piece is read, to increase reading independence, or after, to reinforce patterns that have been introduced previously. This lesson may include: (1) letter/sound association, or focusing children's attention on certain beginning or ending sounds found in the story; (2) word chunks or word patterns, or briefly drawing children's attention to a word chunk used in the story, such as a specific blend, ending, or rime; or (3) reinforcement of high-frequency words, or picking several repeated words from the story and asking children to find, frame, and say them.

Follow-up

The most appropriate follow-up activity to a guided reading lesson is to invite the children to take the finished text home to demonstrate their reading ability to parents, caretakers, or siblings. Such a follow-up not only provides needed practice but also promotes increased confidence and fluency for beginning readers.

GROUPING FOR INSTRUCTION

Children can be placed in temporary, small, homogeneous groups for guided reading instruction based on their knowledge, skills, interest, and experience. Although there should be many times during the day when children come together for whole group reading, there are also times when it is helpful to group together small numbers of children who can read at about the same level and to meet with them three to five days a week. With ongoing assessment of their abilities, these groups should be fluid and frequently changed. To avoid the stigma of low-ability groups, the teacher should maintain other heterogeneous groups during the day for reading aloud, shared reading, discussion groups, writing, and other activities.

The following flexible grouping systems each have a place in a comprehensive literacy program:

- skill groups
- literature circles
- pairs (buddy reading)
- peer-editing groups
- cooperative groups

Skill, or Ability, Groups

Teachers often conduct a guided reading lesson for a homogeneous group of five or six children who are reading at about the same instructional level. This practice helps avoid frustrating a struggling reader or holding back a capable reader from appropriately challenging material. Similarly, small skill groups can be formed when several children are having a problem with a specific skill or strategy and need reinforcement in that area. For example, several children may be having problems with the *ain* word chunk or pattern that was introduced in the day's guided reading lesson. The teacher forms a temporary skill group composed of those children and provides a brief minilesson on words containing *ain*. The group lasts only until the skill is mastered.

Literature Circles

As children grow in independence, there can be time set aside during the day when children with the same reading interest—for example, those interested in mysteries, horse stories, or the books of Judy Blume—come together to read and discuss those texts. Such reading groups can evolve into writing groups as children decide to write letters to the author or add an epilogue to the text. Children in the groups can decide to do *readers theater* (explained in Chapter 5), puppet shows, or murals using the text as inspiration. Literature circles can be temporary or permanent, but often last as long as activities related to the chosen book do.

More about literature circles

Beginning around the second grade, teachers can organize literature circles for readers using the following series of activities.

1. **Select books.** Teachers prepare text sets with five or six titles corresponding to the independent reading levels of the children in the class. They then gather five or six copies of each book. They read the blurb on the back of the book cover to garner interest in each of the books and then ask each child to sign up for the first and second choices, to allow the teacher to select which choice is closer to the reading level of the student.

2. **Form literature circles and assign roles.** Students get together and create a schedule for discussing each chapter or section of the book within the time limits set by the teacher. Students choose discussion roles, which rotate with each chapter or section. Initially, the teacher may want to do minilessons addressing what each role entails and examining text factors (Daniels & Steineke, 2004). For younger children, five roles are suggested:

   ■ Discussion leader: Creates two or three critical-thinking questions about the reading that cannot be answered within the text. Such questions may address personal reactions to what was read or questions about why the events occurred.

   ■ Word detective: Chooses three or four words from the reading, learns as much as possible about the words, and teaches them to the others in the group by acting them out, by illustrating them, or by another way they choose.

   ■ Artist: Draws a picture, sketch, diagram, cartoon, or finds clip art that is related to the chapter. The group discusses how the illustration is related to the text.

   ■ Summarizer: In a one- or two-minute statement, summarizes what the reading was about, focusing on the main ideas of what was read.

   ■ Jewel finder: Locates one or two sentences in the reading that were especially interesting, funny, sad, or important.

3. **Independent reading and role preparation.** Children can read the assigned parts of the book independently at home or using partner reading. Then they complete their assigned role in preparation for the group meeting.

4. **Book discussion.** Children come together and discuss their chosen book, usually beginning with the summary and the discussion leader. Unlike more conventional book groups, where a vociferous individual may dominate the discourse, every child in the literature circle has a voice in the discussion because every child has a role to perform.

5. **Book share.** When the books have been completed, children from each circle can be asked to do a book talk, PowerPoint, or some other presentation to interest their classmates in the book they just read.

Pairs (Buddy Reading)

Because children are social beings, they often enjoy reading aloud to one another. Such partnerships can be formed between cross-age "reading buddies," pairing a sixth-grader from another class with a first-grader, or between friends getting together to take turns reading. Also, pairs of children can participate in dyad reading (see Chapter 8) for the purpose of improving listening and summarizing skills.

Peer-Editing Groups

When children are writing during a writers' workshop or in response to a piece they have read during guided reading, peer editors can offer helpful advice (see Chapter 9). In groups containing no more than two or three children, each child is both writer and editor. As writer, the child obtains feedback on parts of her writing that may not make sense. As editor, the child offers suggestions for improvement in style and word choice and calls attention to mechanical errors that may have been overlooked in self-editing. The children in these groups are rotated in order to obtain different feedback from many editors during the school year.

Cooperative Groups

To foster a collaborative atmosphere in the classroom and to avoid the stigma of low-ability groups, cooperative groups are ideal; they also foster language acquisition for English learners. Typically, teachers assign children to four- or five-member groups mixed in ability (there may be one high achiever, one low achiever, and two average achievers per group), gender, and primary language. The teacher presents a lesson to the entire class and then asks the children to work on follow-up material (workbook pages, spelling words, word sorts, posters) in groups. The children help one another because each is invested in the achievement of the other members since everyone gets credit for the work done by the group.

OTHER PRACTICES FOR GROUP READING

to keep group approaches for early reading instruction fresh and exciting for both the teacher and the students, the following six techniques and tools can be integrated in group activities. Other reading activities can be explored on the websites identified in Appendix C.

◀ *See Appendix C*

- ■ masking
- ■ music
- ■ multimedia packages
- ■ pocket charts
- ■ word walls
- ■ cloze activities

Masking

When the teacher wants children to focus on a particular word or word part, an ideal way to do this is by **masking**, using a sliding frame or stick on notes to call attention to just that part of the word (see Figure 11.7). Usually masking takes place during repeated readings and not during the initial reading of a book. For

■ masking

figure 11.7   Masking device.

DEMONSTRATION SIZE:

1. Starting from the folded edge of a file folder, cut an 8.5 x 6 inch rectangle.

2. Using the remnants of the file folder, start at the fold and cut a 1-inch-wide strip that runs from the fold all the way across the folder.

3. Remove a 2 x 7 inch rectangle from the center of #1. Start cutting at the open edge so the fold remains completely intact.

4. Slide the 1-inch strip over the open ends of the "U" shaped section and staple as indicated.

5. Slide the thin strip back and forth to adjust the frame to the size of the word or letter you are working on.

INDIVIDUAL STUDENT SIZE:

Follow the previous directions with the following changes in dimension:

- The original rectangle cut from the fold should be 5 x 2 inches.
- Remove a .75 x 4 inch rectangle from the center of the 5 x 2 segment.
- Cut a strip .5 x 3 inches, beginning at the fold.
- Staple or tape open edges.

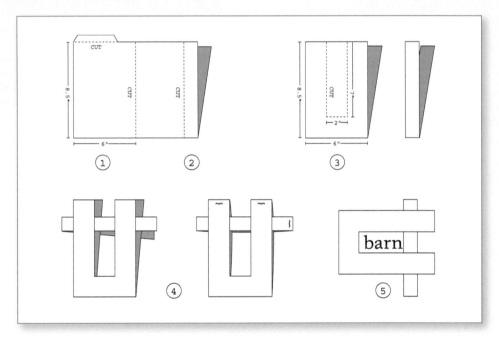

example, if the teacher is reading a story to focus on decoding a specific phonic element, such as the *br* blend, he can use the masking frame to call attention to that particular letter–sound relationship. The teacher may then ask the children to think of other words that begin with that sound.

Music

In a 2004 letter to all U.S. school superintendents, former Secretary of Education Rod Paige wrote, "the arts are a core academic subject." He reminded us of the significant role the arts can play in academic achievement. Music, as one of the fine arts, is no exception and can enhance literacy in a multitude of ways (Paige, 2004).

Carefully selected lyrics can be placed on chart paper in large black letters, with repeated or high-frequency words in color or highlighted. The lyrics can be sung (to the original tune or one with which all are familiar) or chanted. When songs, poems, chants, and raps are chosen for their rhyme, rhythm, repetition, or cumulative sequence, music brings the reading and rereading of text to new heights of motivation (Cecil & Lauritzen, 1994). Young children never seem to tire of singing a catchy tune; thus, songs selected for their patterns can familiarize children with high-frequency sight vocabulary. Songs can also be used to reinforce phonic elements in an enjoyable way, as in the "Old MacDonald" adaptation mentioned in Chapter 4. See the box "Linking Literacy and Lyrics" on the next page for more information.

Multimedia Packages

Sometimes books and media are sold together, allowing teachers to motivate children to sing while repeatedly reading the lyrics, all of which increases fluency (see Chapter 5). One example of such a package is a book of John Denver's "Country Roads," adapted and illustrated by Christopher Canyon (2005) and accompanied with a CD of John Denver's music. The colorful pictures of the journey, coupled with the music, help to stimulate children's interest (while the adults get nostalgic hearing an old favorite). The book and its CD are perfect for shared reading or a community sing with the whole school. Go to http://drscavanaugh.org for excellent collections of e-books for children, such as Aesop's Fables and Clifford Interactive Storybooks, as well as chapter excerpts and educational resources for teachers.

WWW.

Integrate music
with literature

*www.rockhall.com/
education*

Pocket Charts

The use of pocket charts (as discussed in Chapter 4) can help develop children's ability to decode words; they also aid in building children's sight vocabulary. Selected words from a story can be printed on cards, or sentences from the story can be printed on sentence strips. The teacher then has the children "rebuild" the story using the words or sentence strips (McCracken & McCracken, 1986).

Word Walls

As discussed in Chapter 5, a word wall or word chart is a listing of high-frequency words that are of particular interest to children or are currently being studied in a reading lesson. The words should be prominently displayed on the wall or on a bulletin board so that children can add to the list whenever they think of an appropriate word and so they can use them for reference during writing activities. These words should be practiced a few minutes each day at the beginning of a word lesson by having the children (1) stretch them out and read them together, (2) chant or cheer them three times, and/or (3) write using

Linking literacy and lyrics

Music can be used to reinforce print in many ways:

1. Teach children a song by singing the song once (with or without accompaniment) and then inviting the children to sing along with you. Discuss the meaning of the song and any special words that may be unfamiliar to the children. Add motions or drama as appropriate.

2. Link the song to print. Write the lyrics to the song on chart paper. Read the lyrics, inviting the children to join in. Reread the lyrics, with the children reading each word as you point to it.

3. Build phonics skills and reinforce sight vocabulary. Point out words that appear more than once. Select one or two phonic elements or patterns to work with.

Have the children find all words with the same pattern, beginning sound, ending sound, vowel sound, and so forth. Use sentence strips and word cards for matching and sequencing activities.

4. Create new activities based on the song lyrics. Cover words on the song chart and encourage children to brainstorm some new words to fill in the blanks, for example:

> "Mary had a little cat, her fur was black as night."

> Change the pattern of the song, the main character, the outcome, and so on.

Reprinted with permission of the publisher, Teaching K–8, Norwalk, CT. From K. Barclay and T. Coffman (1990). "I Know an Old Lady: Linking Literacy and Lyrics." *Teaching K–8,* May, 47–51.

them in isolation and in context. Additionally, all words having the same spelling patterns should be starred (Cunningham & Cunningham, 1997).

Cloze Activities

cloze procedure ■   In the instructional **cloze procedure,** words or parts of words are blocked out, and the reader uses clues within the text to predict what might complete the blocked portion. This technique can be used, orally or on a recording, during a repeated reading to help children develop sight vocabulary, to practice their use of prediction for decoding unfamiliar words, and to help them construct meaning using all the cueing systems (Cecil, 1994b). For example:

> I had a cat
>
> And I named him Buffy.
>
> His eyes were coal black
>
> And his fur was so _____. (fluffy)

MAKING TEXT ACCESSIBLE FOR ALL LEARNERS

a lthough enabling children to become independent, silent readers is the desired goal of reading instruction, many less-able children and those for whom English is a second language may need extra support or scaffolding to actually read a text by themselves. Mediated reading methods, with their provisions for reading to children and repeated readings, are ideal techniques for providing this support; the following are additional ways to make difficult texts more accessible to less-able readers (Guillaume, 1998; Tompkins, 2006).

Selective Pairing

Pairing an able with a less able reader is a strategy that makes the task of reading more sociable but also more accessible for the less-able reader. If low comprehension is also a problem, the teacher can use dyad reading (see Chapter 8), asking children to summarize sentences or paragraphs and make predictions.

Recorded Books

Many primary classrooms use recordings to accompany favorite books. At listening posts, children follow along by tracking with their fingers to commercially made or teacher/volunteer-made recordings. Although the focus is on reading for enjoyment, repeated listenings and rereadings of favorite stories aid fluency, develop sight vocabulary, deepen comprehension (Routman, 1995), and help English learners to become familiar with the cadence of English. Reading that children cannot accomplish silently on their own can often be achieved with the support of a recording. With this nonthreatening approach, children can be encouraged to repeatedly follow along through a short, troublesome section and then be prepared to read the section orally the next day in a small guided reading group.

Online Books

Increasingly, stories can be found on the Internet to help children explore and appreciate literature and also develop positive attitudes toward technology (Castek, Bevans-Mangelson, & Goldstone, 2006). Children can log on to BookPALS Storyline, an online series of streaming videos, where they can enjoy pieces of wonderful literature read aloud by such actors as Betty White, James Earl Jones, and Amanda Bynes. The site includes classic storybooks such as *The Polar Express* (Van Allsburg, 1985) and *Knots on a Counting Rope* (Martin & Archambault, 1997). For more on e-books, see Chapter 12.

WWW.

BookPALS Storyline
www.storylineonline.net

Echo Reading

For text with a limited number of words, children can "echo" the text as the teacher reads and points to the words while the children repeat them. Such a strategy helps reinforce one-to-one correspondence and is especially appropriate for big books, where all children can see and follow along.

Building Background

Often a text is difficult for some children simply because they have limited background knowledge or prior experience with the topic. If an informal survey of readers suggests this may be the case, a teacher can build background by reading

Information on museum subjects

www.kidscastle.si.edu

Links for thousands of subjects

www.kidsclick.org

a simpler text, providing hands-on experiences, showing a short video excerpt, discussing the topic, brainstorming ideas about the topic, or bringing in objects that relate to the topic before the text is read.

Delaying Independent Reading

If many activities related to the text have occurred before the initial reading of the text, or if the text has been read aloud first, children will be much more familiar with new words and concepts before they are expected to decode them. Therefore, if the teacher believes the material may be excessively difficult, independent reading should be the last activity in which the children engage.

Encouraging a Variety of Responses

Although school life primarily centers on thoughts and ideas, expressions of emotions and feelings should be among the responses teachers encourage in reading. For difficult reading material such as science or social studies, for example, a teacher who elicits the expression of feelings may notice resultant changes in attitudes, curiosity in science, or the ability to look at historical events from another's point of view—all of which would encourage a deeper engagement with the text.

SUMMARY

The goal of a truly comprehensive approach to reading instruction should always be to create young learners who are able to decode fluently, interact meaningfully with text, and read willingly for the sheer enjoyment of the activity. Listening to stories and conversing about them pave the way for the later reading of stories with insight and appreciation. By reflecting before, during, and after listening, children are learning the ways of processing text used by sophisticated readers.

In earlier chapters, the need for explicit instruction in phonemic awareness and a systematic, explicit approach to teaching phonics was explored. Discrete, game-like activities or skill-building exercises can be designed to teach critical and creative thinking as well. Carefully selected children's literature provides many natural opportunities for sharing and thinking reflectively. And when phonics instruction is thoroughly integrated into a literature-rich classroom, children become enthusiastic about reading, because they can do it and because they begin to realize it is enjoyable; many rewarding literary experiences follow.

Shared reading and guided reading, two group reading practices combining appreciation for literature with decoding and constructing meaning from text, are ideal vehicles to help balance an effective reading program for early readers. The skills that have been introduced through explicit instruction in phonics can be reinforced through literature by a skilled and enthusiastic practitioner who enjoys sharing a stimulating story with young learners—learners who are taking giant steps toward becoming literate human beings.

questions
for journal writing and discussion

1. How can shared reading and/or guided reading be used to expand each of the following:

   a. oral language

   b. phonemic awareness

   c. phonics acquisition

   d. literature appreciation

2. Making predictions about what will happen in a story has been found to ensure more engagement with the story and increased comprehension on the part of the learners. Why do you think this is so?

3. How do the similar conversational approaches of shared and guided reading compare with the methods of reading instruction of which you are currently aware? How do they differ from instruction you received when you were learning to read?

suggestions
for projects and field activities

1. Plan a shared or guided reading lesson for a small group of early readers. Record their responses to the lesson. Write a short reflection statement sharing your feelings about student involvement with the lesson.

2. Using the same group of children as in Question 1, read them a story "straight," without using predictive strategies, picture sharing, or any thought-provoking questions. Instead, ask only literal questions requiring factual recall, such as "What was the name of the main character?" What differences in student engagement with the story do you notice between the two lessons?

3. Observe a primary teacher who is conducting two readings of the same story with the same group of learners on successive days. What differences do you notice in the questions the teacher asks during the second reading? In what other ways is the instruction different? Do the children appear to be bored during their second encounter with the text? Why or why not?

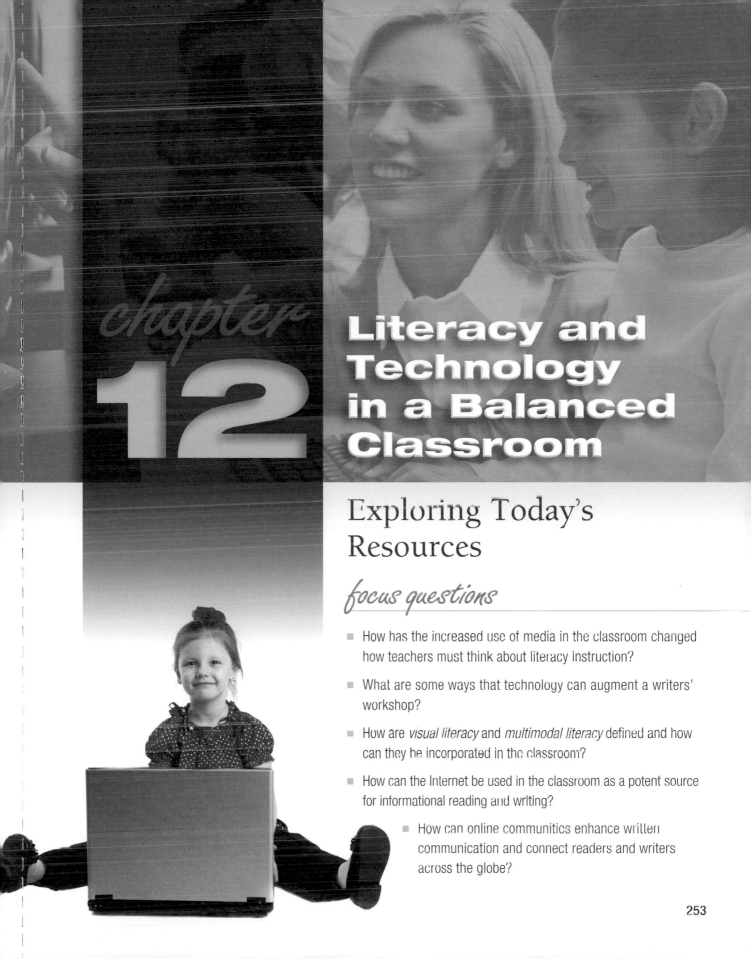

chapter 12

Literacy and Technology in a Balanced Classroom

Exploring Today's Resources

focus questions

- How has the increased use of media in the classroom changed how teachers must think about literacy instruction?

- What are some ways that technology can augment a writers' workshop?

- How are *visual literacy* and *multimodal literacy* defined and how can they be incorporated in the classroom?

- How can the Internet be used in the classroom as a potent source for informational reading and writing?

- How can online communities enhance written communication and connect readers and writers across the globe?

INTRODUCTION

Interest in writing in Ms. Lambating's second grade class has changed dramatically this year with the introduction of eight desktop computers and six laptops, all with Internet access. The teacher smiles and shakes her head as little Quanim uses KidPix to create a drawing of two fierce green dragons in an empty rectangular box and then adds text below, recounting their angry dialogue. A reluctant writer only weeks ago, Quanim now thoroughly enjoys using her imagination to connect her original text to an exciting picture she has created. Without the constraint of her usual labored handwriting, which is large and unfocused, she has become much more prolific, as her thoughts turn almost magically into beautifully formed words, using her growing keyboard skills. Meanwhile Todd, Brittney, and José are collaborating on their Wiki, responding to the latest episode of *Ben 10,* which they will immediately publish and link to several of their favorite *Ben 10* websites. To their great delight, a class of *Ben 10* fans from Connecticut has read their previous entry and commented enthusiastically. The trio is most eager to respond to them and update their newest ideas. Several other students in the class are reading e-books on laptop computers and responding to the readings in personal electronic response journals. Finally, at another computer, Jerome is preparing his latest poem for publication. Another erstwhile reluctant writer, he has recently become fascinated with writing poetry, especially after he learned to middle justify his phrases and select just the right font— and clip art—to make his poetry look polished and professional. Jerome has proudly kept all his poems in a folder and is preparing to publish a book of his poetry on his own poetry blog for a wide audience to read and, hopefully, respond to.

ready or not, technology and education now go hand and hand, offering exciting possibilities for transforming how children experience literacy. In fact, the Internet is the current generation's defining technology for literacy (Coiro & Dobler, 2007). Hancock (2008) suggests that in today's classrooms, not only the Internet but various forms of instructional technologies offer a "new dimension for reader response research" (p. 108), as children incorporate digital literacies with the more traditional literacies of paper, pencil, and text books. Teaching young children to use technology in addition to traditional print is more important than ever so that they are prepared for further education and for the challenges of our increasingly high-tech world. Indeed, the International Reading Association (IRA), the bastion of all methods of instruction related to text, has also recognized the need for a newly broadened concept of literacy that includes the new literacies. The IRA (2002) joins the ranks of those who believe that teachers have a crucial responsibility to integrate these literacies into the classroom so that children may become proficient with these important technological tools, as more and more literacy takes place in front of a computer or online.

Numerous case studies in the literature document just how profoundly various forms of technology can enhance early literacy for those teachers who embrace a social constructivist and transformative approach to teaching, and the effects are particularly intense among low-income and minority students. Studies have shown that properly guided collaborative use of the computer in early elementary classrooms can contribute to pro-social behavior, including positive peer interactions, increased vocabulary, mutual enjoyment, and a heightened understanding of the nature and function of written language when producing and using texts (Van Scoter, 2008). Further, in a study of two elementary schools in high-poverty neighborhoods, Warschaur, Grant, Del Real, and Rousseau (2004), examined how technology-supported teaching practices can lead to increased learning when there is school-wide commitment:

Both schools make highly effective use of technology to promote academic literacy among their students, resulting in sophisticated student products, highly engaged learners, and high standardized test scores in relationship to school demographics. The keys in both cases are a school-wide commitment to excellence, equity, and development of classroom communities of inquiry. Technology is used to apprentice students into academic literacy through promotion of independent reading, support for language scaffolding, involvement in cognitively engaging projects, and student analysis and creation of purposeful texts in a variety of media and genres. (p. 535)

Although academic investigation of twenty-first century literacies is unfortunately not the norm in every school (Leu & Kinzer, 2000), there is, in principle at least, little dispute at the policy level about the need to realign school curricula to promote and take advantage of these emerging literacies. It seems that most educators and legislators now realize that we have moved from an era where print dominated the literacy landscape to one where the various forms of electronic communications are a routine component of literacy development (Leu et al., 2005).

The remainder of this chapter will focus on the potential for positive synergy between literacy and technology that can occur when teachers take an expanded view of literacy for inquiry learning that incorporates technology with the literacy skills of viewing and visually representing and with reading, writing, listening, and speaking. We will explore a number of ways to use technology as a tool to enrich all aspects of literacy learning. Finally, we will identify tools and resources for using technology in teaching literacy to our youngest learners.

VISUAL LITERACY

Visual literacy includes the ability to read and interpret images and icons, video, photographs, graphs, charts, maps, and any other form of visual representation. Children in the United States are inundated by visual as well as auditory media on a daily basis. By some accounts, children from preschool to third grade watch as many as 30 hours of television alone in an average week—and often spend more time playing video and computer games. Though such viewing may be excessive, children do learn much through viewing and visually representing from a very early age, and doing so is an integral part of the most effective approach to learning English as a second language (Krashen, 2004). Moreover, many viewing and visually representing experiences are integral parts of teaching literacy throughout the curriculum. Such experiences can help teach children to view critically; teach media literacy in film, video, and television; and teach literacy in the visual arts and dramatic productions (Cox, 2008). If young children are bombarded with so much visual and auditory stimuli on a daily basis, it logically follows that the literacy curriculum must be used to teach children how to critically sift through it all, thus teaching some fundamental thinking skills along the way. The following sections deal with viewing and visually representing as they relate to technology.

■ visual literacy

Viewing

Children should have positive experiences with quality children's films just as they do with quality children's books. Children can be encouraged to respond to video just as they do to literature, through written responses, drama, discussion art, and other forms of media. Mirroring the "into," "through," and "beyond" model for guided reading, teachers can provide the necessary instruction for the previewing, viewing, and post-viewing phases.

Before viewing a video with children, it is important to do the same kinds of "into" activities teachers generally do before presenting a new book. Teachers must always see the video before showing it to children, checking it for appropriateness of theme and vocabulary and reflecting on just how the concepts in the video can be extended through discussion. A purpose for viewing should always be identified and written on the board, along with several initiating questions for students to keep in mind and to guide their thinking as they are viewing the film.

While viewing a video, it is appropriate to occasionally pause it to point out an important occurrence or an especially confusing part to children. The teacher may want to "think aloud" about how she interprets the clip and to share personal connections she has made. The teacher can then ask for individual reactions from the children as well.

In the post-viewing phase, children can talk about the video in small groups or, using a think, pair, and share activity (see Chapter 6). The children's responses should be the basis for planning further discussion, drawing, writing, drama, or other multimedia activities.

Because children spend such an inordinate amount of time watching television, it seems axiomatic that teachers help them develop the critical-thinking and media literacy skills necessary to analyze what they are watching. To do this, teachers can ask children to keep double-response journals about television programs they frequently watch, with the summary of a program in one column and their critical response to it in the other. See Figure 12.1 for an example of such a journal. Specifically, the teacher can encourage them to consider if what happens on television is in any way different from what, in their experience, happens in real life. Small share groups who have watched the same programs can discuss their reactions to the programs. Children can be guided to use Venn diagrams to contrast original books with their adapted television shows. Finally, teachers can invite children to watch television advertisements and alert them to examples of the following tactics, used mainly by advertisers of products targeted to young children:

- Lots of happy children (friends don't come with the toy)
- Magic (you have to make the plane fly yourself)
- Size distortions (dolls and toy cars are not that large)
- Purposely unclear disclaimers (all sold separately; in specially marked packages; batteries not included; some assembly required)
- Testimonials (Justin Bieber uses it . . . [or does he]?)

Sample of a double-response journal.   *figure* **12.1**

> ## TV Double Response Journal
>
> | Program Summary | Response |
> |---|---|
> | ~~SpongeBob SquarePants~~ SpongeBob SquarePants

SpongeBob and Squidward got stranded in the desert when they were delivering a pizza. ~~Crabber Patty~~ Crabby Patty made him do it. They ran out of gas. The pizza turns into a parachute and then he finds the customer so he gives him the pizza. But he forgot a drink. | It was fun to see SpongeBob on the parashute. But some things don't make any sense. How can you parashute in the water? Theres no desert in the oshun. The desert and the oshun are opisites. Nothing about SpongeBob is real! |
> | Ben 10 Alien Force

Kevin wants Gwen and Ben to help him because somebody came in and took his stuff from his house. Ben has to go alien and turns into ~~chroma~~ Humungator. | I think Ben should of turned into Swampfire because its not always about being bigger. You can be smaller and you can still win. I wish I had an omnatrix and I would fight all the bad guys but theres no such thing in real live. You have to ~~talk about it to~~ just call the polise when you get robbed. |

Visually Representing

Drawing, painting, and other graphic arts have historically been used in the primary classroom to help children visually represent their thoughts and ideas and to extend literacy projects in motivational ways. Now such artwork can also be enhanced via technology. KidPix and similar software allow children to create multimedia works of art by pasting, drawing, altering, and animating with easy-

WWW.

Creating multimedia
projects

mackiev.com/kidpix

to-use tools. This software is also useful for the creation of projects, charts, and presentations. In some classrooms, such vehicles for visually representing are combined with the more traditional technologies of video and photography.

Photography, using either a 35-mm or a digital camera, can be used by young children to enhance written pieces about what they find interesting (their baby sister, a baseball game, a family vacation). For younger children, a tutorial for camera usage, including such components as how to hold the camera, appropriate lighting, and composition, will help them feel successful. They can then photo-illustrate their written pieces. Alternatively, children can shoot the needed pictures and write captions about them. The finished pieces can then be published in slideshow format discussed later in the chapter or in a laminated book to be read to younger classes in the school. In the content areas, children can use photography to take pictures of specific topics of interest (e.g., flowers, cars, food, animals, and so forth) and then research the topics on the Internet. The result can be a photo essay on their chosen area or a topic being studied in science or social studies.

Young children can also create live-action films with a video camera, including documentaries of real events as they occur, original dramas, or the telling of stories, or docudramas, which combine real events with fiction.

Movie Making

After children have been shown the basics of handling the video camera, the teacher can then walk them through the following steps for producing media (adapted from Cox, 2008):

1. *Getting an idea.* Children can get ideas for creating their own videos from books they have read, people who have inspired them, or content material that particularly fascinates them.

2. *Organizing.* Children can clarify their vision by brainstorming, by using a graphic organizer such as a cluster or web, or by using software such as Kidspiration.

3. *Storyboarding.* A helpful way to plan action is by sketching each image with three, six, or nine sequential squares, by folding paper accordingly, with tentative dialogue underneath. (See Figure 12.2.)

4. *Producing.* Children use the storyboard to direct live actors to dramatize the story or event.

5. *Editing.* The story or event is shot in sequence and edited in the camera. (This step is complex and younger children are likely to require teacher assistance.)

6. *Presenting.* Children play their video for classmates, other classes, parents, and for community members, with posters and e-vites announcing the viewing.

Sample storyboard.   *figure* **12.2**

TECHNOLOGY APPLICATIONS FOR LITERACY LEARNING

eachers can choose from numerous ways of incorporating technology in their students' literacy learning as students write, read, research, and communicate and collaborate electronically.

Writing Electronically

Word processing and desktop publishing may be among the most widespread uses of computers in literacy because they provide such positive supports to the fundamental literacy skill of writing (International Society for Technology in Education, 2007), making print instantly legible and professional looking, as the children in the opening vignette of this chapter demonstrate. For this to happen, young children should spend some of their computer literacy time learning keyboarding skills and using word-processing programs.

Although keyboarding skill is not a prerequisite for writing on the computer, it does help make writing more fluent and less frustrating for young children. Just 10 or 15 minutes practice a day using keyboarding software, as the children in Ms. Lambating's class do, can help children develop the skills they need.

"Kids are drawn to technology. They also love a good story. Combining the two can be a powerful educational tool" (p. 35).

Digital Storytelling

(Adapted from DeVries, 2011)

For this activity, students use programs such as PowerPoint, Soundslides, or Photo Story.

- To create digital stories, students begin by writing a story. This story later will be used as the narration for the digitalized story.

- After the story is complete, the author decides how the story will be divided into scenes and which photo or illustration is needed to depict each scene in the storyline. (For planning, sketches of these illustrations can be used in a storyboard similar to the one in Figure 12.2.)

- Have students find photographs, clip art, or draw illustrations that complement each page of text. Any illustration can be scanned so that it is in digital form.

- Next, the student records the story, using expressions that will convey the mood and action and that will captivate the listeners.

- After the story is recorded without any errors, the student is ready to make the "movie." Some students may want to enhance their movie by adding appropriate music and/or sound effects just like a real movie. The next step is to add a title frame, transitions between frames, and rolling credits, citing all the sources for their clip art, photographs, and so on.

- Finally, the student publishes his work by inviting peers to watch his digital story either online or on an interactive whiteboard.

hypermedia projects ■   **Hypermedia projects,** like multimodal projects, combine text, graphics, audio, and video, but they also include hyperlinks in the presentation. Because the presentation includes links, it may not be viewed in a linear sequence. Having children complete hypermedia projects using software such as PowerPoint, Sound Slides, or Photo Story is highly engaging. These projects can be used for learning throughout the curriculum as well as for literacy, as children learn to use written composition skills, oral language, and visual representation and to select content (Garthwait, 2001). Children can read and discuss informational texts, do a KWL, research facts on the Internet, plan and write up a series of slides—each containing some information on the topic—add sound, and then put all the information together using one of the programs mentioned above. This is followed by a highly motivational "carrot," as children become engaged in adding colorful backgrounds, different fonts, and even music or voice-over narration. The results are aesthetically pleasing slides that can be displayed on the computer or an interactive whiteboard or printed out and displayed on a bulletin board, or they can be published in book form. See Figure 12.4 for an example with a hyperlink to a video showing large carousels. Moreover,

when children create such projects collaboratively, they have participated actively in every facet of literacy learning and acquired new informational content.

Online Reading and Researching

Although online reading involves some of the same strategies as reading in closed environments, such as book reading, it also involves other strategies readers need to use. These include:

- having prior knowledge of website structures and Internet search engines;
- self-regulating or directing choices about where to go and in what sequence and how long to spend among the various reading pathways; and
- interacting with new kinds of text, including interactive charts, maps, and diagrams, videos, and so forth, as part of the reading experience (Coiro & Dobler, 2007).

Some of these strategies can be introduced to beginning readers as they are learning how to find information on the Internet.

Evaluating websites

One way to help young children become more directed in their use of the Internet is to show them how to evaluate websites. Teachers and students can use the Internet as a potent resource for doing fascinating research—one that provides instant access to almost anywhere: museums, libraries, governments, schools, and other places all around the world (Henry, 2006). Not all websites, however, are equally worthwhile. Teachers must distinguish between good and poor websites and also assist their students in learning how to select appropriate ones. Harris (2010) provides an effective way to critically assess websites based on their credibility, accuracy, reasonableness, and support. He calls this evaluation technique the CARS Checklist, and it can be adapted for use with young children (see Appendix E). The steps include asking the following questions:

See Appendix E

1. *Credibility.* What is the authority of the author? What are his/her credentials? Is there evidence that peers have judged the site positively? Does the piece exhibit correct grammar and spelling.

2. *Accuracy.* Is the site current, with updated information? Is the information easy to understand and complete? Does the author acknowledge other viewpoints or possible controversies?

3. *Reasonableness.* Does the author present a fair and objective point of view? Does the author appear concerned with the truth?

4. *Support.* Does the author provide documentation for his or her ideas? Are all sources listed? Are there other resources on this topic with similar information? Are these sites mentioned or linked?

Children can also be taught to evaluate websites by showing them both good and poor websites, according to the above criteria, and using a think-aloud approach to demonstrate how they can be judged. After a lesson on discerning fact from opinion in text, the same principles can then be applied to information on websites. Children can be shown to check the websites for currency and to look critically at the author's credentials using child-friendly examples: is a high school student the best source for information about nutrition? Finally, children can compare information in text to that found on the website. Any discrepancies can lead to rich discussion.

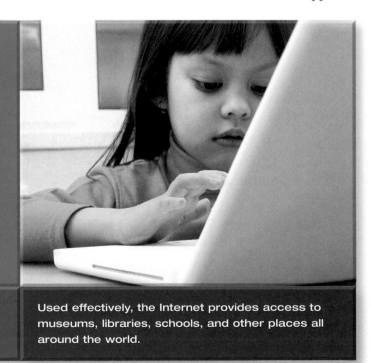

Used effectively, the Internet provides access to museums, libraries, schools, and other places all around the world.

Teaching website navigation

Once students have learned to evaluate websites, show them how to navigate efficiently within a site. This will help them develop knowledge of website instructions and get beyond the random clicking and superficial skimming that often occurs when young children read online. Following is an activity to help students navigate websites.

Website Exploration

(Adapted from Cornett, 2010)

Steps for teaching how websites are structured and how to navigate a site include:

1. Point out the title of the page and the title of the website in the margin at the top of the window.

2. Model a think-aloud about how to scan menu choices. Hold the mouse over the navigational topic menus that often appear down the left frame or across the top of the window, but don't click on them. Use them to help students get a big picture of the information within the site.

3. With the help of students, predict where each of the major links may lead.

4. Explore interactive images, such as animations, or images that change as the mouse is held over them, pop-up menus, and scroll bars that may show additional levels of information within the site.

5. Check author and date. Identify who created the site and when it was last updated. Click on a homepage button labeled "About This Site" to get this information. If it is not available, consider what this indicates about the site.

6. Try out any electronic supports such as an organizational site map or internal search engine.

7. Decide whether information you need will be found at the site, and if so, explore further. If not, return to search results.

8. If you stay on the site, decide which areas to explore first.

Finding information online

Introducing children to use the Internet as a source of information should be just a different, non-print way to engage them in the process of constructing meaning and reading critically. Just as teachers must plan, guide instruction, and assess using books and discussions, so must they plan classroom experiences for finding information on the Internet with the same strategies and goals in mind. A WebQuest is an activity designed to help students locate information on the Internet.

WebQuest

A C T I V I T Y

See Appendix A ▶

Using such an Internet-based inquiry activity, teachers can direct students to various sites on the Internet that present information on a particular topic. A teacher may design a WebQuest around any of the topics covered in the informational books listed in Appendix A or any other text on a topic in which students have expressed interest.

Note: Because of the dynamic nature of the Internet, chosen websites may disappear over time. Thus, always offer plenty of sites from which to choose.

- Present students with a compelling problem or question. If the teacher has used a knowledge chart (see Chapter 8) with students when reading the informational text, she and the class can choose questions from the "Questions we have" column that were not answered in the book for the quest.

- Prepare a list of websites that will provide students with information to answer the question/problem.

- Explain that during the quest, students will be finding information from a number of websites, which they will then need to synthesize.

- Have them record the information in response to the initial question or problem.

- Students can then share their findings with the class, and the teacher can lead a discussion about resolving any discrepancies in the information provided by the various sites.

See Figure 12.5 for a sample WebQuest on frogs in conjunction with *Frogs* (Gibbons, 1994).

Communicating and Collaborating in Online Communities

With increasing access to the Internet, online discussions are becoming more common as a means for teachers to encourage written communication and learner engagement (Hamilton & Cherniavsky, 2006). Meeting the needs of almost any context and user, electronic communications are available in many formats, including e-mail messages and instant messaging, message board discussions, wikis, blogs, and social networking sites. Wikis and blogs, in particular, are more frequently finding their way into the elementary classroom. They require no knowledge of programming, and they are simple to set up using free software (for example, try www.bloggers.com or www.edubloggers.org) with easy-to-use templates. They have the added bonus of being accessible to anyone anywhere in the world.

Figure 12.6 shows the similarities and differences between wikis and blogs so the classroom teacher can make decisions about the relative usefulness of each for his or her instructional purposes.

A FROG'S LIFE

INTRODUCTION

Have you ever wondered how a frog goes from an egg to a full-grown jumping animal? You are a famous scientist who is very interested in frogs, and your job is to research the life cycle of a frog. Then you draw pictures of the life cycle of frogs and, finally, make an origami superfrog. Have fun on your mission!

THE TASK

After reading the book *Frogs* by Gail Gibbons, you will work with a group of 2 to 3 people to do the following:

- discover a description of the life cycle of a frog
- create pictures of the 4 stages in a frog's life cycle and label the stages
- make an origami superfrog

RESOURCES

- computer and access to the Internet
- *Frogs,* by Gail Gibbons (1994). New York: Holiday House.
- two blank pieces of paper, one divided into 4 sections
- Internet sites about the life cycle of frogs
- Internet site for making an origami superfrog

PROCESS

Follow these steps to complete your quest:

1. As a class we will read *Frogs,* by Gail Gibbons.
2. I will divide you into groups. With your group, research these sites for information about the life cycle of frogs:

    www.EnchantedLearning.com/subjects/amphibians/Frogprintout.shtml

    www.tooter4kids.com/Frogs/life_cycle_of_frogs.htm

3. Using one of the blank sheets of paper, evaluate the websites to determine whether the information on the sites will be accurate and unbiased by answering these questions:

    - Who created the site? (Is the person an expert in the field or just someone interested in the topic?)
    - What is the purpose of the site? (If the site is created to promote a product, can the same information be found on any other site?)

(continued)

figure **12.5**   **Continued.**

- Can the same information be found in classroom library books or on any other site(s)? (Always check "facts" from the Web by comparing with other sites.)

4. After reading the information, get a blank piece of paper and divide it into 4 equal squares.

5. In the top left square of your paper, draw a picture of the first stage of a frog's life cycle. Label the stage by writing a sentence(s) about what happens in the first stage.

6. In the top right square of your paper, draw a picture of the second stage of a frog's life cycle. Label the stage by writing a sentence(s) about what happens in the second stage.

7. In the bottom right square of your paper, draw a picture of the third stage of a frog's life cycle. Label the stage by writing a sentence(s) about what happens in the third stage.

8. In the bottom left square of your paper, draw a picture of the fourth and final stage of a frog's life cycle. Label the stage by writing a sentence(s) about what happens in the final stage.

9. Go to this website to play a game about the life cycle of a frog:

    http://www.sheppardsoftware.com/scienceforkids/life_cycle/frog_lifecycle.htm

10. Make an origami jumping frog by following the directions at the site below:

    http://www.origami-fun.com/origami-jumping-frog.html

EVALUATION

You will be evaluated by your teacher on the following:

1. Did the student find the answers to the three questions in item 3 to evaluate the websites for accuracy and credibility?	YES	NO
2. Are the stages of a frog's life cycle in the correct order?	YES	NO
3. Did the student label each stage with the correct information?	YES	NO
4. Did the student demonstrate a knowledge of a frog's life cycle?	YES	NO
5. Did the student work cooperatively with members of the group?	YES	NO
6. Is the student's handwriting legible?	YES	NO
7. Were all directions followed by the student?	YES	NO

CONCLUSION

Congratulations, scientist!! You have completed your assignment successfully. Have fun playing with your origami jumping frog!

Created by Meghan Hickey, Fall 2000 as an independent study project at Bowling Green State University, Bowling Green, Ohio. This WebQuest is part of the CRC Internet Resources WebQuest Children's Literature web page at www.bgsu.edu/colleges/library/crc/page38731.html

Comparison between a wiki and a blog.   *figure* | **12.6**

WIKI	BLOG
A group of interlinked pages appears, each with its own authorship.	Distinct, dated entries are made of news, commentary, notes, or personal reflections.
Suited for collaborative writing, many children can edit each piece.	Suited more for individual authoring, it can also be collaborative.
Wikis are written according to content or any desired order.	Written in reverse chronological order, newest entry is at top.
Children can edit the posts of others.	Only the blogger can edit his or her own post.
Most entries are anonymous.	Usually children sign their names after each entry.
More like a discussion board—others can "talk" about an entry.	Others, such as teacher or peers, can comment on entries—even from a distance.
Previous versions of a post can be saved and retrieved in case of a mistake.	Blogs have no automatic saving function of previous posts.

Wikis

A wiki is a useful collaborative writing tool—a website where the pages can be changed and instantly published using only a web browser. Pages are automatically created and linked to one another. The uses for K–3 classrooms, for both the teacher and the students, include the following:

FOR TEACHERS:

1. *Class activities.* Inform the families about class activities by creating a calendar of events. Upload newsletters and circulars that often get lost in backpacks.
2. *Organizing events.* All members of a faculty committee can work together, remotely, on the planning of events such as book fairs or sports events.
3. *Curriculum planning.* Worksheets, lesson plans, units, and links to resources can all be shared on a wiki.

FOR CHILDREN:

1. *Whole class projects.* Children each make x numbers of pages related to a research project and link it to their classmates' work.
2. *Collaborative story writing.* Children can work together to create a story.

3. *Pen pals.* Connect to classes in China or India on an international project or simply write to individual pen pals from other countries or states.

4. *Group projects.* Small groups of children can collaborate on reports and presentations without having to be physically present.

Teachers can find more information about setting up a wiki by Googling "setting up a class wiki."

Blogs

A blog, by contrast, comes from a combining of the terms "web" and "log." A blog is an online, personal journal that may contain reflections, comments, book reviews, and often, hyperlinks or other websites provided by the author. In simplest terms, a blog is an online diary. But instead of a small locked book, as I remember keeping in my youth, the blog is posted on the Internet so that readers across the globe may read and respond to what the blogger has to say. To begin classroom blogging, two good sites are http://kidblog.org and www.edublogs.org; they provide free blogs for teachers and students with helpful video tutorials.

A blog is perhaps one of the best online tools for encouraging children to express themselves in written form. Blogs provide a unique space for sharing personal opinions, where online communities can converse with one another about any conceivable topic. Often, children dislike writing because it is such a solitary pursuit; the interactive nature of blogging creates enthusiasm for communicating in written form, because it closely resembles a written conversation—with immediate feedback—unlike written composition—with its usual time lag. Also, blogs can give children an understanding of the meaning of personal voice. As children explore their own thinking and learning, their distinctive written voices tend to emerge. As their own voices emerge, the conversation and the thinking behind it become richer. Finally, because a blog is an excellent way to motivate children to write, it also provides an excellent reason to revise and edit: There is the distinct possibility that many others may read and respond to the child's musings. A worldwide audience is an unparalleled motivator for children to try to do their most polished and professional work.

Blogs can also develop higher order thinking (Zawilinski, 2009). As online readers gather information to solve a problem, they often need to analyze information, critically evaluate, synthesize content across multiple texts, and communicate with others using blogs, e-mail, wikis, or other communication vehicles (Leu, 2007). Also, although blogs are often used to report classroom news, to showcase writing or art projects, or to respond to literature, special *mirror blogs* allow children to reflect upon their thinking or about lessons or content that has been introduced.

Blogs can be used by the entire class to discuss a text the class is reading, or on their individual blogs, children can post entries about their interests and outside reading. Other children can visit these posts to gather ideas for new texts to read and to discover new online resources that can provide information about the text and the author. As children gather and share online information about a text or topic, they must synthesize various resources, including other classmates' posts. Blogs can be used for the following purposes:

Setting up student blogs
www.edublogs.org
http://kidblog.org

1. *Autobiographical writing.* Children share their personal thoughts in diary or journal format.

2. *Interactive journals.* Children write their thoughts and ideas or respond to the teacher's prompts.

3. *Book reviews.* Students post comments about a book the whole class, or other classes in other schools, is reading.

4. *Expressive writing.* Children post their prose or poetry and/or constructively critique each other's work.

5. *Digital portfolios.* Children record a body or term of written work by uploading all their documents and images.

6. *Multimedia presentations.* Children add images and sound to their blog entries (Kajder & Bull, 2003).

Interactive Reading: E-Books

Reading fluency and engagement can be enhanced in an enjoyable social context using paired reading—with children doing several readings of the same text and offering feedback to one another. Electronic books (e-books) can play a similar role, and they may be instrumental in improving automatic word recognition and providing a "digital language experience approach" that reinforces fluency and the link between written and oral language (Labbo, Eakle, & Montero, 2002).

Many e-books offer children the ability to self-select the amount of assistance they want, thus increasing individual control over the learning environment as they choose for themselves where and when they need help (Larson, 2008). For example, when children come to a word or phrase they do not know and provide a definition, they can click on the text to have the computer read it for them, removing the burden of decoding and figuring out the meaning of an unknown word, allowing for more fluent reading on subsequent attempts. Ultimately, the children have more energy to consider the meaning of—and to reap enjoyment from—the text.

A further use of e-books is to help the teacher differentiate instruction and provide a wider range of opportunities for all children to interact with text. As all teachers know, children develop their literacy skills at their own rate, in their own time frames. Most teachers deal with children on many different developmental reading levels. While the same level of basal reader is often used to teach all the children in a class, teachers can benefit from e-books as valuable alternative resources to engage children in successful reading at all levels.

Although there are considerable differences in the variety of features offered by e-books, almost all contain audio and graphic animations that allow the characters to talk and seemingly come to life through the use of "hotspots" that produce animation, sound effects, or other features, when a child clicks on them. Most also invite children to highlight an unfamiliar phrase or listen to a reader pronounce a word for them (Lefever-Davis & Pearman, 2005). Some e-storybooks will read the entire book aloud for children, providing an individualized read-aloud with which the child or children can track along, using the mouse.

Choosing Technology Applications

As we have explored throughout this chapter, technology offers great potential to enhance literacy instruction. Software programs and technology-supported learning activities can promote deep understandings when they build upon children's prior knowledge and permit learners to control their own learning. Such tools can also motivate children to engage in extensive reading and writing and help them acquire new vocabulary by communicating with others online (Cummins, Brown, & Sayers, 2007). However, technology should *not* be used merely for its own sake, simply because it is *there*, nor is technology always the best tool for every classroom literacy activity. Any technology use should directly support or add value to the literacy goals that the teacher has already established. Moreover, a teacher must be familiar with available software programs and know how to integrate them effectively with the currently used literacy curriculum. Finally, any software used must be developmentally appropriate in order for it to positively impact children's learning. Reviews of educational software are available online at www.superkids.com. Additionally, ask the following questions when choosing technology applications (adapted from Labbo, Leu, Kinzer, et al., 2003):

- Does it serve the intended purpose? For example, if it claims to improve fluency, can you see that children's fluency is actually improving?
- Can it be used independently by students, or will you need to work with them to facilitate?
- Are there so many sight and sound distractions that children will become overstimulated and lose the literacy focus?
- Does it offer children an opportunity for free choice? (This can be part of the motivation for using technology.)
- Does it use humor? Children tend to prefer these programs and use them more frequently.
- Does it align with conventional literacy goals, district benchmarks, and state standards for literacy?
- Does it address students' individual literacy needs?
- Does it contribute to an overall unit theme or project?

See Appendix E ▶ See Appendix E for a form for evaluating technology applications based on this list.

ENHANCING INSTRUCTION THROUGH TECHNOLOGY

even the way instruction is delivered is getting a new high-tech look. Instead of the traditional writing boards utilizing chalk or colored markers, teachers can now use their computers to connect with their students for instruction that allows everyone to participate. As an example, this year the primary grade teachers in some Sacramento schools are piloting interactive electronic whiteboards. One company that produces the whiteboards offers a website with a wealth of resources for educators: http://smarttech.com/education.

I recently attended an interactive whiteboard training session at one such school, and a world of new possibilities unfolded. This recent technology has the power to transform any elementary classroom!

Interactive whiteboards come with software that allows teachers to create, save, or print any lesson idea they might wish to. There are hundreds of graphic resources that come with the software, including math tools and paper backgrounds such as graph paper. Interactive whiteboards are compatible with Microsoft Office programs, so it is easy to create something in Microsoft Word or PowerPoint and access it through the interactive whiteboard software so that children can interact with it.

Interactive whiteboards offer benefits beyond the typical whiteboard: every file created can then be saved, which is much like having digital charts at your disposal. Moreover, the many interactive opportunities for children using an interactive whiteboard make this tool a great motivator. Most children are engaged during whiteboard lessons, both visually and kinesthetically. Children enjoy coming up to the board to share information and ideas, which also helps develop their public speaking skills.

Teachers I spoke to testify to how easy it is to create materials with children and then go back later to add or make changes as learning progresses. It is relatively simple to add sound and video to create multimedia projects. Since the interactive whiteboard is hooked to a computer, the Internet, and a projector, teachers can use it to easily view and interact with websites. A myriad of websites list other informative websites that work well with the interactive whiteboard, so teachers needn't start from scratch.

Some ways to use interactive whiteboards in the classroom are presented in Figure 12.8.

Since the interactive whiteboard is new to the school I visited, teachers find they are learning along with their students every day, creating a true community of learners. With so many resources available, teachers explain that they are never at a loss for activities or ideas. If you are not yet familiar with interactive whiteboards and don't have access to this technology, I highly recommend visiting a school that does have them.

WWW.

Interactive whiteboards

http://smarttech.com/ education

An interactive whiteboard can be used in a myriad of ways to engage and motivate learners.

TECHNOLOGY AND THE ENGLISH LEARNER

finally, the beauty of technology is that it can be equally accessible to *every* learner, much to the surprise of some teachers who may believe that English learners are "too busy learning English and content material to be receptive to adding bells and whistles," as one teacher recently shared with me. Though I sympathized with her concern, I explained that her fears may

figure **12.8**   **Ways to use an interactive whiteboard in the classroom.**

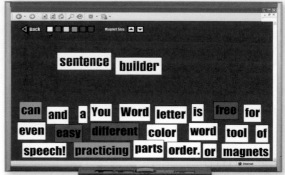

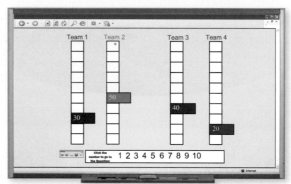

- With morning message. After students read the morning message, the teacher may include a "p.s." that invites them to come up and respond to a question or graph.
- To visit BrainPOP Jr. (www.brainpopjr.com), which features animated online learning resources for various content area topics, and watch a movie and play the quiz.
- To create charts.
- To explore maps and photographs.
- To save lessons for students who were absent.
- To show presentations created by the teacher and students.
- For digital storytelling.
- To teach whole class computer or keyboarding skills.

- To teach editing skills using editing marks.
- To teach how to navigate the Internet.
- To write, illustrate, and narrate a book as a whole class project.
- To allow students to share projects during parent/teacher/student conferences.
- To teach vocabulary.
- To post an interactive word wall.
- To view interactive websites.
- To teach students to evaluate websites.
- To prepare for tests (far more exciting on an interactive whiteboard!).
- With Inspiration software (for class brainstorms, spelling word sorts, and so forth) and Kidspiration software.

Adapted from Interactive Whiteboards in the Classroom. Retrieved August 20, 2010, from http://rmtc.fsdb.k12.fl.us/tutorials/whiteboards.html.

be misguided. Much recent research focusing on the attitude of English learners toward learning as a result of the use of technology has been promising. Often, in traditional classrooms, English learners are unable to follow grade-level curriculum and participate fully in learning for two or three years after starting to acquire English. Therefore, such students usually receive rote instruction addressing low-level skills, such as phonics, vocabulary acquisition, and word pronunciation (LeLoup & Ponterio, 2003). But a study by Meskill & Mossop (2000), as an example, shows encouraging patterns of engagement and investment in learning with the use of technology-supported instruction. English learners in the classrooms they observed were able to participate in classroom activities to the full extent of their intelligence and imagination. The way this emerged is evident in the following excerpt:

> Their [the children's] finished work, whether a word-processed, desk-top published document, an animated story, a multimedia presentation . . . was consistently a source of great pride and, among peers and family members, great admiration. . . . Learners' achievements extended from moment-to-moment successes in editing their work or making decisions to demonstrating to the larger school and community what they could do with technology . . . The ESOL children became adept at using technology in their classes and school. (p. 589)

SUMMARY

When integrated into a balanced and comprehensive early literacy program that includes plenty of high-quality literature to foster reading and writing enjoyment, technology can be a powerful resource for teachers. Word processing programs and multimedia tools can be used to energize writers' workshops, while the Internet provides a plethora of ways to research and critically read about almost any topic children can imagine. Online communities, such as blogs and wikis, can be used to connect learners to other readers and writers across the globe, both as live audiences and learning resources. Literacy skills, such as fluency and reading rate, can be enhanced through the introduction of e-books and programs that give learners autonomy over the amount of help they need. Carefully chosen technology applications can offer teachers a high level of differentiated instruction for learners and the tools to actively engage them in all facets of literacy. All learners, including English learners, can benefit from these technologies. Finally, pedagogy resources such as the interactive whiteboard, can make the delivery of instruction more interactive and the creation of new literacy activities and assessments easier.

Although nothing will ever replace excellent explicit instruction from an adept and dedicated teacher, technological tools can be valuable resources in the early elementary classroom, if chosen wisely and integrated effectively into the literacy curriculum. Perhaps the best reason to use technology to increase literacy skills is the high level of motivation and investment that children bring to literacy tasks completed on the computer. Technology use in the primary classroom can complement and extend traditional literacy learning and enhance student engagement while helping to prepare children for life in the 21st century.

questions
for journal writing and discussion

1. If you were given $1,000 to spend on classroom materials or resources, would you buy computers or spend it in other ways? Justify your response by comparing how you might use the computer with how you would use other types of materials (e.g., book sets) or resources (individual whiteboards).

2. Consider the educational possibilities of technologies other than computers; for example, digital cameras, video cameras, iPods, tablets, and so forth. How might you use these technologies to enhance your students' literacy development?

3. Compare a writers' workshop conducted with word processing software and a writers' workshop without such resources. List five ways that word processing software can make writing more appealing for children. Finally, create a written argument addressed to a school board that would help to convince them that computers and word processing software are necessary for the success of your writing program.

suggestions
for projects and field activities

1. Try out a popular educational software program, such as Kidspiration, according to the instructions. Create your own project. Take notes about what children will need to know about using the program. Share your own project with children in a classroom as a model on which they can base their own.

2. Visit a library media center and ask to preview several children's films for your present or future grade level. Start a resource file of film titles that you feel would enhance the literacy curriculum for that grade level.

3. Create an Internet scavenger hunt for children, based on a topic the children are currently studying, such as spiders. Try it out with children of that grade and report the results back to your class.

chapter
13

Informing Instruction

Assessment of Early Literacy Development

focus questions

- What are the possible types of assessment for early literacy?

- How can literacy assessment be used to inform instruction?

- How does a balance of formal and informal assessment offer a more accurate picture of progress in literacy?

- How can assessment be aligned with state standards?

Emilio and his first-grade teacher, Mr. Steel, are discussing which version of his illustrated report to put in his *showcase portfolio*—his "favorite" or the one he proudly considers his "best." During this conference, the child's teacher takes *anecdotal notes* or written observations to guide Emilio in the self-assessment and reflection he will be expected to attach to his report. In an upcoming end-of-year parent–teacher conference, Mr. Steel and Emilio will show the boy's parents his showcase portfolio, filled with samples of Emilio's written work and Emilio's personal reflections about it. Mr. Steel will also share with the parents the teacher *observational portfolio* he has compiled over the past few months to show Emilio's literacy progress. By explaining some informal assessment data he has collected, Mr. Steel will be able to inform Emilio's parents of his current reading and comprehension levels and exactly which phonics elements he has mastered and which he still needs help with; Mr. Steel will suggest that they can also help reinforce these at home. Finally, Mr. Steel gathers data from a standardized reading test that compares Emilio's reading with that of other children his age. The assessment device, administered in the fall and the spring, also shows numerically how much Emilio has grown as a reader over the school year. Mr. Steel will end the parent–teacher conference by offering to loan several books at Emilio's independent reading level, based on a *reading interest inventory* he recently administered to discover the child's reading preferences.

INTRODUCTION

Ongoing assessment of literacy development refers to the use of various instruments, daily observation, and many work samples to measure progress. It also refers to the ongoing analysis of the data from these instruments and observations concerning individuals, small groups, and the entire class so that the teacher can customize instruction and, when necessary, plan appropriate interventions. The assessment in Mr. Steel's classroom is ongoing and dynamic; it is the basis on which he makes all of his instructional decisions. In an effective primary classroom such as his, all instruction is based on information acquired through valid assessment procedures. Moreover, children in the class, like Emilio, are able to recognize their own strengths and limitations and are encouraged to use strategies designed to increase their literacy competence. Finally, in a strong primary classroom, the teacher is able to use and interpret the results from a variety of informal and formal assessment tools and effectively communicate those results to children, their parents or caregivers, and relevant school personnel. Children know how well they are doing, and so does everyone who cares about them.

WHY ASSESS?

Assessment is more than merely gathering a range of information about a child's literacy progress; it must be data collection with a distinct instructional purpose (Salvia & Yesseldyke, 2000). Effective use of classroom-based assessments depends on the ability of the teacher to select assessments based on instructional goals, frequent and systematic amassing of data, and immediate instructional interventions based on analysis of that data (Risko & Walker-Dahlhouse, 2010). The major reason to spend precious classroom time making assessments of children is to determine how well they are progressing at a given time with respect to a specific aspect of learning; for example: What blends is this child able to recognize? How well is she able to retell a story? What is her attitude toward writing (Sulzby, 1990)? Equally important is to adapt instruction based on assessment that shows learning is not taking place. Other information that can be gained from literacy-related assessments includes the following (Cheek, Flippo, & Lindsey, 1997):

- determining a child's overall reading ability
- examining a child's ability to use graphophonic, semantic, and syntactic cues in reading
- analyzing a child's ability to construct meaning from text
- determining a child's experiential background for content-area material
- determining a child's overall literacy strengths and needs

This basic information can then be used for classroom program planning and decision making, to ensure that classroom instruction and activities are responsive to and appropriate for the current class level. Assessment information indicates who might benefit from special help or need more academic challenge (Afflerbach, 2007).

A second major reason for assessment is to help children take ownership of their learning by allowing them to see how they are doing and to establish equal partnership in fostering literacy growth. By keeping individual progress charts and writing samples over time, for example, children can actually observe their own growth. This leads to a feeling of self-pride that has been found to be surprisingly potent in children. When young children are taught to think about and reflect on their own learning, they become more active partners in the whole endeavor.

Finally, it is important to keep careful progress records for the class as well as each individual child to demonstrate to other school personnel, parents, and the outside community that teachers are doing an effective job teaching children to read and write. The education of children has always been on local, state-wide, and national political agendas, perhaps because every community member has been through the school system and is, therefore, a self-proclaimed "expert" on all subjects related to schools. Hence, it is of utmost importance to be able to inform others and to document progress, especially when new programs and ideas are being initiated.

PRINCIPLES OF ASSESSMENT

for teaching to be effective, there must be a reciprocal, synergistic relationship between assessment and teaching. In other words, teaching and assessing should be continually informing one another. It is on the basis of lesson observation that the teacher finds out what needs to be assessed; reciprocally, the assessment tells the teacher what to teach or, in some cases, reteach. For example, a first-grade class has been discussing the difference between "telling" and "asking," or between a statement and a question. An observer, examining the teacher's lesson plans on the sentence activities, should be able to expect that the ending assessment for the lessons will be very closely aligned with the teacher's learning objectives for those lessons.

Following is a discussion of other assessment principles that can help teachers determine if their assessment plan will complement their instruction (adapted from Cooper, 1997).

The Core of Assessment Should Be Daily Observation

Teachers, who frequently observe and take notes on each aspect of literacy development, know much more about the status of their students than can be obtained from any formal testing, no matter how reliable the testing is purported to be. It is imperative that assessment be a daily event, occurring every time the student reads and writes. Through observing patterns of growth over time, the teacher is in the ideal position to get a clear picture of how the child is progressing.

Children Should Be Actively Engaged in the Assessment Process

Although young children cannot be involved in every aspect of literacy assessment, sometimes asking for input when evaluating their work can be a key factor in encouraging children to take charge of their own learning and inviting ownership of their successes. Because teaching and learning are ideally collaborative processes, we do not want children to view assessment as an uncomfortable practice that the teacher "does" to them. On the other hand, when children and teachers work and think together, assessment becomes a shared responsibility, with children participating enthusiastically as team players in their own learning.

Assessment Should Take Many Different Forms

Different types of assessment tools should be used for different purposes to ensure that a measure of each child's literacy progress is obtained. For example, writing samples, checklists about retellings of stories, and anecdotal notes give insights that are not scientific but based solely on the teacher's judgment. Although data gathered with these tools are essential in effective planning and decision making, the teacher also needs **standardized test** results that have accepted statistical reliability and validity (i.e., they consistently measure what they claim to be measuring). Standardized assessments are generally developed by a publisher or by the school district to allow an objective determination of whether grade-level standards developed by the district or state have been met. To get a truly multidimensional overview of a child's performance in any aspect of literacy, teachers need to look at the data from both sources.

standardized test ■

Assessment Must Avoid Cultural Bias

Children from various cultures, linguistic groups, and backgrounds may have different language issues as well as varied experiences and styles of learning. When planning assessment procedures, and particularly when interpreting and reporting them to others, teachers should consider these factors judiciously.

An example of the importance of considering cultural bias can be found in the case of a little girl in a second-grade class in the Virgin Islands who was diagnosed with a severe reading disability. Upon examining the test, her perceptive teacher realized that the child was certainly *not* reading-disabled. She had scored poorly because she had not known many vocabulary words, such as *chimney* and *caboose*—words that have little meaning for residents of a tiny tropical island!

Assessment should mainly attempt to determine what children *can* do—not what they *cannot* do. When teachers really understand the literacy abilities of their learners, it becomes much easier to decide which new literacy experiences should be offered to help them develop further. Not only is this a more constructive way of looking at learning, but children benefit in other crucial ways. Children are simply able to progress more readily when the atmosphere is one where mistakes are viewed as ways to learn rather than failures to be avoided at all cost.

It would seem axiomatic that the traditional summative biannual reading achievement tests, conducted in whole class settings, would encounter problems when attempting to glean any useful information about the literacy skills of children for whom English is a second language. Even the academic language used in the instructions, for example, may cause confusion and render the test results invalid. To remedy this problem, some researchers suggest that either the test or test procedures be modified to provide increased accessibility to what the instrument is actually testing (Lindholm-Leary & Borsato, 2006). Such tests could include simplified instructional language or easier syntax, with perhaps shorter sentences and fewer clauses. Another possible strategy would be to translate the assessment into the child's home language or provide the child with more time to complete the test. As such accommodations may not always be viable, teachers should certainly balance the questionable test scores by supplementing them with classroom observations and work samples to provide more accurate conclusions about the child's literacy.

TYPES OF ASSESSMENT

teachers have at their disposal an almost overwhelming array of instruments to use as part of the assessment process. Many of these instruments blend naturally into instruction; others provide a separate means to assess literacy progress, either formally or informally. Because so many assessment tools are available, it is impossible to discuss each one in this chapter. Therefore, a sampling of some of the most pervasive assessment devices that are compatible with a balanced early literacy program will be explored here. An example of a comprehensive framework for guiding the assessment process is presented in Figure 13.1.

Assessment can be thought of as informal or formal. **Formal assessments** use standardized tests that are given under controlled conditions so that groups with similar backgrounds can be compared primarily for purposes of program evaluation. **Informal assessments** yield specific information that teachers can use to guide their teaching. Common informal instruments include anecdotal records, checklists, rubrics, portfolios, informal reading inventories, and running records.

■ formal assessments

■ informal assessments

figure 13.1   A framework for guiding the assessment process.

What do I want to know?	How am I going to find out?		
	INFORMAL ← → FORMAL		
	FORMATIVE	SUMMATIVE	
Concepts about print	Observations of book handling & tracking	Checklist of orthographic knowledge	M. Clay's "Concepts About Print"
Phonemic awareness	Observation of songs, rhymes, repetitions Word games	Checklist of phonemic awareness skills	Standardized tests (Torgeson's "Test of Phonemic Awareness")
Phonics	IRI Observation of ability to generate/identify sound/ letter relationships	Running records Shared reading	Miscue analysis Botel phonics survey
Oral reading (fluency)	One-to-one observation Paired reading	Mediated reading Anecdotal notes Running records	DIBELS IRI Miscue analysis
Spelling	Writing samples Pretests	Daily writing Journals	Weekly tests Dictations
Reading comprehension	Retellings QARs Discussions	Paraphrasing Summarizing Class contributions Cloze tests	Standardized tests (Stanford, Metropolitan)
Vocabulary	Writing samples Journals Oral discussions	Formal writing Essays	Word Writing CAFÉ Standardized tests
Writing	Writing samples Journals Quickwrites	Writing samples Daily work Journals	Rubrics (scaled scores) Editing checklist
Reading/writing attitudes	Questionnaire Number of books read/written	Conferences Interest inventories Reading response journals	
Student views of own literacy	Books chosen Attitude survey Reading survey	Portfolio choices Reflection log Dialogue journals	Self-reports Interviews

Assessment can also be thought of as formative and summative. **Formative assessment** refers to the process of ongoing data, usually informally, gathering during instruction that both informs and guides teachers as they make instructional decisions; for example listening for miscues as a child reads and making anecdotal notes or making a checklist of all students who can generate rhyming words are examples of formative assessment. Formative assessment is closely related to the ongoing direct assessment measures used by teachers; it is also referred to as classroom assessment (although not all forms of classroom assessment are formative). Information from formative assessment helps teachers to provide the level of quality feedback learners need and to quickly adjust their instruction if learning is not taking place.

■ formative assessment

Summative assessment, usually more formal, refers to the evaluative assessment or tests that result in a grade or ranking (e.g., a final unit test, end of chapter test, weekly spelling test, or standardized achievement test). Large-scale, high-stakes testing that is prominent in most schools today is also an example of summative assessment. Summative assessments are generally more comprehensive in nature than formative assessments and are designed to include a degree of objectivity and accountability. I offer the following analogy from my own life to describe the difference between formative and summative assessment: When I write a chapter for this text, I subjectively include what I think is appropriate and then reread it and revise it; that is like *formative* assessment. When the editor and reviewers read what I have written, they compare what I have written with their objective standards for what they think the chapter should contain relative to other books they have read or published; this process is analogous to *summative* assessment.

■ summative assessment

Most of the techniques discussed in the remaining portions of this chapter can be used easily on the basis of the information given; others require reviewing an examiner's handbook. Appropriate references are given for those that require more detailed study, and samples of others are presented in Appendices D and E.

◀ *See Appendices D & E*

Three basic types of formative assessments are used in primary classrooms, and each offers a unique perspective for a balanced early literacy program: skills-based assessment, curriculum-based assessment, and process-oriented assessment.

Skills-Based Assessment

Skills-based assessment focuses on the use of tests to measure reading and spelling skills and subskills. These tests are administered by the teacher or reading specialist and sometimes provide numerical scores that represent a child's rank relative to the performance of other children at the same age or grade. The data obtained from these tests can be, but are not always, related to the content of instruction. Examples of skills-based assessments would be systematic appraisals of a child's ability to name letters, the child's knowledge of concepts of print, or the number of vocabulary words the child knows compared with others his age.

■ skills-based assessment

Curriculum-Based Assessment

Curriculum-based assessment ties evaluation directly to the teacher's literacy curriculum to identify instructional needs and to determine what is needed for

■ curriculum-based assessment

a child to "master" a concept. Such assessment may include criterion-based assessment, in which the child's performance is compared against standards deemed appropriate for mastery in a particular area. Scores from such a tool typically offer a number or percentage for the amount of material each child has mastered. These tools are usually administered in the classroom using items and materials derived from the curriculum. Examples of curriculum-based assessment include asking a child to read a passage aloud from the child's basal reader and counting the number of words read correctly per minute, or culminating a thematic unit on dinosaurs by asking children to quickly write down (or tell, for preliterate children) everything they know about dinosaurs.

Process-Oriented Assessment

process-oriented
assessment ◼

Process-oriented assessment refers to a teacher's observations of the child's actual reading and writing abilities. Measures used for such assessment are informal and subjective and are, therefore, usually supplemented by norm-referenced testing that objectively compares a child with others of the same age or grade. In process-oriented assessment, the literacy behavior being examined is documented in the learning context in which it normally occurs. For example, a process-oriented assessment tool could be an informal checklist designed by the teacher to answer such questions as, "Are the child's letters in the proper sequence?" or "Is the child able to spell words correctly in isolation but not in context?" The assessment would be taking place while the child was doing a self-selected writing task, such as writing in a journal (see Chapter 9). An *informal reading inventory* (to be discussed later in this chapter) with miscue analyses also falls under this category.

FORMAL ASSESSMENT PROCEDURES

Using formal assessment devices in the classroom has both advantages and disadvantages. Although formal group tests can be used, in a very broad way, to compare a student's performance with a cross-section of student performances in other areas of the country, such tests provide little or no usable information about the specific diagnostic needs of individual students. As with any assessment device, teachers must first determine what information they are seeking and then decide if the instrument is appropriate to those goals.

Achievement Tests

norm-referenced
achievement tests ◼

grade-level
equivalency score ◼

Norm-referenced achievement tests, often called "surveys," are formal tests, usually administered in a group, that offer the teacher a "ballpark" estimate of their students' reading performance. The results are more helpful in comparing groups than in making judgments about individual children. They provide the teacher with a **grade-level equivalency score** (e.g., 3.7), which supposedly indicates that the child is performing as well as a child in the seventh month of the

An assessment program

Mr. Steel, the teacher we met at the beginning of this chapter, has created an assessment program that incorporates data from a wide variety of assessment tools to evaluate the literacy growth of Emilio and the other children in his class. Those tools are listed here and are further discussed in this chapter.

- Twice a year the children take a norm-referenced achievement test called *"The Stanford Achievement Test"* (The Psychological Corporation) to allow Mr. Steel to obtain general literacy information about his class and an indication of how well the students in his school are doing by comparison with other children of the same age and grade across the nation (skills based).

- At the beginning of the year, children are given an *informal reading inventory* to evaluate each student's reading progress, determine at which level they are reading, and identify specific strengths and needs in comprehension and decoding (process oriented).

- Once a week, Mr. Steel listens to each child read from basal readers and takes *running records* to check their reading fluency (curriculum-based).

- Every day Mr. Steel observes each student and takes *anecdotal notes* monitoring anything he considers significant in their struggles, their successes, and their attitudes; he sometimes uses checklists to make his observations more formal when documenting students' knowledge of sight words, ability to answer a range of comprehension questions, or other skills (process oriented).

- At the end of each basal reader unit, children are given an oral or written *cloze* test to determine their comprehension and understanding of grammar (process oriented).

- Once a week, Mr. Steel listens as children *retell stories* to evaluate their English language fluency, knowledge of story structure, and comprehension skills (process oriented).

- Once or twice a week, the teacher and students examine together and briefly discuss the work in their *writing portfolios* (process oriented).

- Every six to eight weeks, Mr. Steel administers a *phonics survey test* to those children who need it, to measure growth in phonics elements; he also gives a quick *survey of sight words* to determine which words children still need to master (skills based).

third grade on the subskills tested, although such a figure should be considered only a rough estimate of the child's true ability.

Most of these tests, such as the *Gates–MacGinitie Reading Tests* (Riverside Publishing), are general in nature and sample the child's overall literacy achievement. They provide little specific information on a child's literacy strengths and needs, and they can be culturally and linguistically biased. Most reading achievement tests for older children include subscores on vocabulary and comprehension, as well as a total reading score. Readiness tests, such as those normally administered at the end of kindergarten and/or at the beginning of first grade, frequently measure phonemic awareness skills, letter recognition, visual–motor coordination, listening comprehension, and auditory and visual discrimination. *The Test of Early Reading Ability* (PRO-ED), for example, measures knowledge of the alphabet, comprehension, and reading conventions. Clay (1979) offers a more process-oriented tool to assess the emergent literacy development of a young child with her *Concepts About Print Test: Stones* (Heinemann).

One currently popular norm-referenced achievement test, *Dynamic Indicators of Basic Early Literacy Skills* (DIBELS; from Sopris West, www.sopriswest.

com), includes subtests of Oral Reading Fluency, Phonemic Awareness, and Retell Fluency (see Figure 13.2). The Oral Reading Fluency test is standardized and individually administered. Children read a passage aloud for one minute and then the number of correct words per minute is determined to attain the oral-reading fluency rate. The Retell Fluency section is a measure of the child's comprehension and works along with the Oral Reading Fluency assessment. A list of other formal reading and reading readiness tests can be found in Appendix D.

See Appendix D ▶

norming group ■

Norm-referenced tests compare a child's performance with that of a sample group of children, called the **norming group.** This sample group has taken the test under controlled conditions, and their average performance determines the norms, or average performance, for other children who take the test. As mentioned earlier, from a norm-referenced test, teachers receive a numerical grade-level equivalent score for every child. Thus, a score of 2.3 suggests that the child's score was equivalent to that of the average child in the norming group in the third month of second grade. The tests also allow for a percentile rank, enabling the teacher to quickly see how each student's score compares with that of the norming group. Finally, these tests show the range of classroom

stanines ■

scores through the use of **stanines,** which distribute all scores into nine sections, the first three being "below average," the middle three "average," and the top three "above average." Teachers usually find these types of scores more useful for assessment because they represent a wider range of achievement and are better suited to fluctuations that may occur in children's scores.

Scores on norm-referenced tests should be interpreted cautiously, however. Although such tests may compare groups adequately and give a fair sketch of how a class of students is doing, they can be problematic for making major instructional decisions for individual children. Because these tests are administered in groups, and because they are timed, a child who is a powerful but

figure **13.2**   **Components of DIBELS.**

COMPONENTS	GRADE LEVELS				
	K	1st	2nd	3rd	4th–6th
Initial sound (phonemic awareness)	X				
Letter naming	X	X			
Phoneme segmentation	X	X			
Nonsense words	X	X	X		
Oral reading (fluency)	X	X	X	X	X
Retelling (comprehension)	X	X	X	X	X
Word use (vocabulary)	X	X	X	X	X

plodding reader may appear to be less able than she actually is; similarly, an impulsive guesser may do well on a multiple-choice exam and appear to be more skilled than is actually the case. Children from diverse cultural and/or linguistic groups may not have the background to answer the questions at all, though they may be highly literate in their own languages or do well when the context of the question items matches their own experiences.

Standardized norm-referenced tests are administered in a highly circumscribed manner. A teacher's manual, or technical manual, accompanies such tests and describes in detail the procedures for giving and interpreting the test. Included in the manual are the following (adapted from Rupley & Blair, 1990):

1. *Overview and purpose.* This information details the purpose and levels of the test, tells how to select the appropriate level for the child's grade placement, and provides specific information on the literacy areas that are included.

2. *Administration.* This section tells the teacher about time limits for each subtest and exactly what to say to students about how to complete each portion of the test. It also provides sample questions to answer jointly with children to get them familiar with the test's format.

3. *Directions for scoring.* Specific scoring information varies, but most norm-referenced tests now offer the option of either hand-scoring or machine-scoring. The procedures for both are usually provided.

4. *Interpreting the results.* Most norm-referenced literacy tests provide general information for planning literacy instruction based on students' strengths and needs, and such tests suggest specific activities to enhance specific literacy areas. There is often information on how to report classroom scores for administrative purposes.

5. *Technical data.* Selection and characteristics of the norming group, information on how reliable and valid the test is, scaled scores, and test item difficulty are usually described in this section.

Criterion-Referenced Tests (CRTs)

Other standardized tests frequently used to assess children's literacy development are **criterion-referenced tests.** Whereas a norm-referenced test compares a child's performance relative to other children's performances, a commercial criterion-referenced test, such as *Woodcock Reading Mastery Tests* (American Guidance Services), measures specific literacy skills in terms of mastery of those skills. Performance standards are identified as *mastery, review, reteach,* or *lack of mastery.* Many states, and sometimes districts, develop their own CRTs, which are *not* standardized. These tests are created to determine "minimum competency," or the lowest acceptable performance level, and they are considered "mastery tests," designed to test specific district or state standards.

A large number of *behavioral objectives* are often found in commercially published, standardized CRTs; for example, phonics analysis may result in as

criterion-referenced tests

many as 20 to 25 specific behavioral objectives. Such objectives often focus on reading subskill behaviors such as the following:

- Recognizes sound represented by letter *b*
- Recognizes sound represented by the letter *a* in the medial position in a word
- Knows sound represented by the letter *o* in the initial position of a one-syllable word

The major benefit of CRTs is that they are instruction-specific; that is, they reflect children's capabilities with regard to stated objectives, allowing teachers to assess the varying levels of performance in their class and then tailor programs to meet those needs. For example, a CRT might suggest that all but four children in the class can identify all the consonants when they are found in the beginning of words. Two of the remaining children need further help identifying the beginning consonants *p, d,* and *b;* the other two children need help identifying only the initial *r*.

Diagnostic Reading Tests

diagnostic reading tests ■

Many school districts use group **diagnostic reading tests.** They are popular not only because they are easy to administer and interpret but also because, unlike norm-referenced tests, they provide valuable diagnostic information about the strengths and needs of each of the children in the class. Because more diagnostic information is gained from these tools than from norm-referenced tests, some school districts prefer these formal tests, even though they generally cost more and take longer to administer. Districts appreciate the fact that such tests often have subtest scores in areas other than vocabulary and comprehension. *The Stanford Diagnostic Reading Test* (The Psychological Corporation), or SDRT, is one of the most widely used group diagnostic reading tests currently available.

When the teacher needs more detailed information, individual diagnostic tests are often given. These typically are administered by reading specialists trained to provide a more thorough assessment and analysis of a variety of severe reading disorders. Two individual diagnostic reading tests currently being used in school districts are the *Diagnostic Reading Scales* (CTB McGraw-Hill) and the *Durrell Analysis of Reading Difficulties* (The Psychological Corporation).

INFORMAL ASSESSMENT PROCEDURES

the ability to provide meaningful instruction based on the needs of children in a classroom can best be achieved by combining standardized assessment with various informal assessment measures. Informal assessment demands greater teacher knowledge in terms of test administration and interpretation, but the specificity of the information gained makes the assessment well worth the effort.

Informal assessment devices are numerous and include informal reading inventories; interest and attitude inventories; reading, spelling, and writing placement tests; story retelling tasks; phonemic awareness and phonics survey tests; and written teacher observation procedures such as checklists and other anecdotal notes.

Informal Reading Inventory

An **informal reading inventory (IRI)** is one of the most valuable tools for evaluating the reading progress of each child in the class and for diagnosing specific reading strengths and needs. Because they actually hear the child reading aloud, observant teachers are offered a kind of window into the child's brain to see the child's strategies for decoding and constructing meaning. The IRI is an individual diagnostic reading test composed of lists of leveled sight words or sometimes sentences and a set of graded reading passages from preprimer through grade 8 or even 12, with accompanying comprehension questions for each passage. Most basal reading series include their own IRI (sometimes called a student placement test) as part of their evaluation program, but such devices as the *Basic Reading Inventory (BRI)* (Kendall/Hunt) and the *Flynt–Cooter Reading Inventory for the Classroom* (Merrill/Prentice Hall) are also commercially available. In addition, the Texas Education Agency in collaboration with the Center for Academic and Reading Skills developed the *Texas Primary Reading Inventory* specifically to assess a child's early literacy development, including print awareness, phonemic awareness, graphophonemic knowledge, and listening and reading comprehension. Teachers can design their own informal reading inventory by compiling a series of graded passages and using readability formulas and taxonomies for developing appropriate questions.

■ informal reading inventory

The IRI is an invaluable tool because it enables the teacher to:

1. identify each child's instructional, frustration, and independent and listening comprehension levels;

2. determine strengths and needs in decoding and comprehension abilities;

3. understand how children are using syntactic (structure), graphophonic (visual–sound), and semantic (meaning) cues to make sense of reading;

4. compare how a child decodes words in isolation with how that child decodes words in the context of meaningful sentences.

The IRI takes about 20 to 30 minutes to administer and is often recorded; the child reads orally while the teacher notes the child's miscues, or deviations from the actual text, by using a kind of shorthand. After the oral reading, the teacher asks a series of comprehension

The IRI helps teachers assess each child's reading progress and diagnose possible problems.

frustration level ■

reading
capacity level ■

independent level ■

instructional level ■

miscue analysis ■

questions. When the child falls below about 90 percent in word recognition, achieves less than 50 percent in comprehension, or appears frustrated, the test is terminated; the passage level at which this occurs is called the **frustration level.** After the child reaches the frustration level, the teacher reads aloud passages at succeedingly higher grade levels until the child is unable to answer 75 percent of the comprehension questions (this percentage may vary depending on the IRI being used). The purpose of this last step is to determine the child's **reading capacity level,** also called *listening comprehension level.* A reading capacity level is the highest level of material the child can understand when the passage is read to him or her.

Material is at the child's **independent level** (i.e., appropriate for recreational reading), when that child can read the passage without stress and correctly pronounce 99 percent of the words and answers at least 90 percent of the comprehension questions. The passage at which the child can correctly pronounce approximately 90 percent of the words and answer at least 75 percent of the comprehension questions is the child's **instructional level,** the appropriate level of difficulty for classroom instruction in reading (see Figure 13.3).

After analyzing decoding and comprehension miscues to establish what instruction is needed in these skill areas, the teacher also does a **miscue analysis** to determine how the child is using clues to think about reading. The teacher looks for patterns of miscues, such as those that retain the meaning (e.g., *Dad* for *father*), miscues that retain the syntactic pattern (e.g., *being* for *beginning*), or those that simply retain the visual/sound similarities (e.g., *further* for *feather*). Miscues such as repetitions of words or phrases usually do not signify errors but indicate the child may be rereading to try to rework a word or passage that didn't seem to make sense.

Teachers should choose a commercial IRI that corresponds as closely as possible to the instructional materials used in the classroom and to what the teachers consider a text deviation (e.g., a *repetition* is usually considered a positive second search for meaning). Also, by noting the types of comprehension questions, the number asked, and how scoring is handled, teachers can examine how the inventory evaluates comprehension. Teachers should also look at the clarity of instructions for administration, scoring, and interpretation as another basis for selecting the IRI with which they feel most comfortable.

figure **13.3**   **Summary of informal reading inventory percentages.***

	WORD RECOGNITION	COMPREHENSION
Independent level	99% or above	90% or above
Instructional level	90% or above	75% or above
Frustration level	below 90%	below 50%
Listening comprehension level		75% or above

*Percentages may vary among inventories.

Running Record

Another method for analyzing a child's miscues is the **running record** (Clay, 1985), which is comparable to the miscue analysis that often accompanies the IRI but is easier to administer and much more expedient. The IRI is the more thorough evaluation, however, as it generally requires the child to read more than one passage and then compares the child's reading of words in isolation with the reading of words in context. Multiple samples always offer a clearer picture of the child's "true" reading ability, but at times the expediency of the running record makes it more appealing.

■ running record

With the running record, children orally read a passage of text ranging from easy to difficult. Although comprehension is not formally measured, teachers often ask children to do a retelling after the passage is read to check for understanding. Teachers document children's strengths and limitations in the use of various decoding strategies by making a check mark on a piece of paper as a child reads each word correctly and by writing the word diacritically to denote substitutions, repetitions, mispronunciations, or unknown words. Alternatively, teachers can duplicate the pages the child will read and then record errors next to or on top of the text copy (see Figure 13.4).

After identifying the words the child read incorrectly, the teacher calculates the percentage of the words the child read correctly. Teachers use the percentage of words read correctly to determine whether the material is too easy, too difficult, or at the appropriate instructional level for the child at that time, following the same percentages discussed for the IRI determination of reading levels. Additionally, teachers time the student to determine the child's reading rate.

As with the IRI, the teacher can then do a miscue analysis, categorizing the child's miscues according to the graphophonic, semantic, and syntactic cueing systems (see Chapter 1), in order to examine what word identification strategies are being used. Errors can then be classified and charted, and instructional decisions can be made accordingly.

OTHER INFORMAL ASSESSMENT PROCEDURES

many other tools are used for the informal assessment of literacy behaviors, ranging from structured, skills-based tools, such as phonics surveys, to less structured observational procedures based on the teacher's daily interaction with the class and his professional judgment about what he observes. It is not possible to mention all the assessment devices available, nor is it necessary or possible for a teacher to use every device contained in this chapter. Because a teacher has limited instructional time, the choice of tools should be based on the specific literacy needs of his class.

Assessment tools include less structured observational procedures based on the teacher's daily interaction with the class.

figure **13.4**   **An example of a running record.**

| The first thing you must do when you | ✓ | ✓ | ✓ | ✓ | ✓ | ✓ | what / when | ✓ |

The first thing you must do when you ✓ ✓ ✓ ✓ ✓ ✓ what/when ✓

wash your dog is to find him. Some ✓ ✓ ✓ ✓ ✓ ✓ ✓ ✓

dogs do not like to take baths. Use a ✓ ✓ ✓ ✓ ✓ ✓ bats/baths ✓ ✓

hose. Get the dog very wet. Then put   horse/hose ✓ ✓ ✓ ✓ ✓ ✓ ✓

some doggy shampoo on him. Rinse ✓ ✓ shan–/shampoo ✓ Ring/Rinse ✓

him really well. Then dry him off. That ✓ ✓ will/well ✓ ✓ ✓ ✓ ✓

is the part your dog will like the best! ✓ ✓ ✓ ✓ ✓ ✓ ✓ ✓ ✓

Give him a reward for letting you give ✓ ✓ ✓ roar/reward ✓ let/letting ✓ ✓

him the bath. ✓ ✓ ✓

ANALYSIS

Total words: _____67_____   _____Chelsea H._____
Deviations from text: _____8_____   *Name of student*
Accuracy level: _____84%_____   _____67_____
(frustration level)   *WPM (words per minute)*

This child read the text in a halting, word-by-word manner. After reading, the child was able to give the main idea of the text, but was unable to recall details due to the errors in decoding of key words. Her errors were:

Substitutions: what/when   roar/reward   ring/rinse   let/letting
                   horse/hose   will/well   bats/baths

Mispronunciations: shan-/shampoo

Most of her errors affected comprehension because they made no sense, semantically or syntactically, in the sentences. A series of minilessons on using the context to help decode unfamiliar words is recommended.

Anecdotal Notes

Many teachers incorrectly assume that their own observations about a child's literacy status are not as important as the results of formalized tests. Researchers strongly dispute this belief (Cambourne & Turbill, 1990). One of the most powerful and reliable parts of any teacher's assessment and evaluation process, researchers claim, is her daily, systematic observation of the children, using either a clipboard, a tablet or other mobile device, or recording device. Ideally, some observation time should be scheduled every day to focus on particular children and to make brief logs or **anecdotal notes** about those children's involvement in literacy events (Rhodes & Nathenson–Mejia, 1992). Teachers should observe children in every possible literacy context: one-to-one interactions, small-group discussions, and large-class settings. The focus should always be on what children *do* as they read and write; the most useful notes describe specific events, report rather than evaluate, and relate the events to other information about the student. Teachers can make observations about a preliterate learner's concepts about print or an older child's reading and writing activities—the questions they ask, the books they are reading, what they seem to like and dislike in reading, and whether they use strategies and skills fluently or display some confusion. Specific notes can be organized around the literacy areas shown in the box on the following page.

■ anecdotal notes

These records dynamically document children's growth over time; they also direct teachers' attention to problem areas needing explicit instruction for individuals and to possible minilesson topics for small groups.

Sight Words

Teachers may wish to make informal, periodic assessments of their students' recognition of **sight words** or sight vocabulary and keep a running tally for each child. To accomplish this, 3 × 5 index cards can be numbered and arranged in the same order as the words from a list of sight words or high-frequency words, such as Fry's list of "instant words," that are appropriate for the child (see Appendix G). While holding up the cards for the child to respond to, the teacher uses the list to note which words the child recognizes and reads successfully. The child must say the word immediately, with no hesitation or sounding out. For each correct response, the teacher makes a check next to the corresponding word on the word list. For incorrect responses, the teacher writes the mispronunciation or substitution above the word, for later analysis. The child's score is the number of words checked.

■ sight words

◄ *See Appendix G*

Cloze Tests

Cloze is an easy-to-use device that uses a short passage from the basal reader or other reading material, with certain words deleted (and replaced with blanks), to determine a child's ability to comprehend the ideas in the sentences and in the entire passage. Besides establishing whether the basal reader or other text is at the appropriate instructional level for a child, the procedure can also diagnose the child's ability to use context clues in reading. By listing each incorrect

Observable behaviors for anecdotal notes

BOOK HANDLING SKILLS

1. Holds the book appropriately.
2. "Reads" from front to back.
3. Knows the difference between the pictures and the words.
4. Understands the terms "beginning of" and "end of" the book.
5. Understands the term "cover of the book."

CONCEPTS ABOUT PRINT

1. Points to the words and not the pictures while being read to.
2. Is able to touch each word as it is read (one-to-one correspondence).
3. Knows that we read from left to right and top to bottom.
4. Knows that we read a book from front to back.
5. Knows the difference between a letter, a word, and a sentence.

PHONEMIC AWARENESS

1. Can hear and pronounce the sounds of English correctly.
2. Can "stretch" a word out to hear the sounds.
3. Can hear the distinctions between words in continuous speech.

PHONICS: LETTER AND SOUND RELATIONSHIPS

1. Can recognize the visual form and name the letters of the alphabet.
2. Can identify initial consonants in context.
3. Can identify rhyming words.
4. Can recognize spelling patterns and use conventional spelling in writing.
5. Can recognize some high-frequency words (list).

FLUENCY

1. Reads grade level material with accuracy.
2. Reads at reading rate commensurate with grade level.
3. Varies reading rate according to the type of text and reading purpose.
4. Reads with appropriate expression.
5. Reads with appropriate phrasing, attending to punctuation features in text.

VOCABULARY

1. Uses grade-level appropriate vocabulary in written work.
2. Uses grade-level appropriate vocabulary when speaking.
3. Uses available resources to seek meaning of unfamiliar words.
4. Demonstrates curiosity about and interest in unknown words.
5. Incorporates newly taught content area words into writing assignments and oral discussions.

COMPREHENSION

1. Answers literal questions about text.
2. Paraphrases text when asked what it was about.
3. Can give the main idea of a story.
4. Can answer critical questions about text.
5. Asks questions when meaning is not clear.

response made by the child, the teacher can determine if the response makes sense syntactically or semantically. Often, a response may be semantically and syntactically correct without being the exact keyed response (e.g., for "The boy *stroked* the dog" the child substitutes "The boy *petted* the dog"), which would be considered acceptable. The cloze can be designed in written form or orally, in a recording, for preliterate learners.

Writing Folders

The writing folder, whether in printed or electronic form, is the place where children keep all their rough drafts in various stages of the writing process, along with other daily compositions, topics for future pieces they might like to write, and with older children, notes from minilessons (see Chapter 9). Children also include their own assessments and reflections about any piece they have completed. Material from their writing folders is the basis for teacher–student conferences on individual instructional needs, and minilesson topics are chosen from observations during these sessions.

In preparation for special displays, publications, or parent–teacher meetings, the teacher and child often meet together and make collaborative decisions on which piece(s) should be selected to put in a special "showcase portfolio" to be shown to parents. Writing folders are often proudly decorated and personalized by children and kept in a special place in the classroom where they are easily accessible. Anecdotal notes regarding this folder can be important assessment data on the child's writing progress.

Interest and Attitude Inventory

Children's interests and attitudes about reading, writing, and school in general have been found to be highly correlated with success in literacy. The **interest and attitude inventory** assesses these factors and should therefore be included in any comprehensive assessment program. Given the importance of these factors, they should be assessed and monitored both incidentally (using anecdotal notes) and deliberately (through an informal questionnaire, administered orally or in writing, to the whole class or to individuals). A sample *reading interest inventory* and *attitude survey* are found in Appendix E. Teachers can design their own inventories, appropriate to the age and developmental level of their learners. The questions should be designed to solicit at least the following key information, which can be used to determine possible reading and writing interests:

- the subject areas that are motivating to the child
- the child's favorite story or text
- what the child does in his or her spare time
- what sports or hobbies the child enjoys
- the child's favorite television program
- the child's preferred instructional arrangements—for example, teacher-directed, working alone, with a small group, or with one other child
- the child's attitudes toward reading and writing
- what reading materials and experiences the child has been exposed to

■ interest and attitude inventory

◀ *See Appendix E*

Story Retelling

By listening to the **retelling** of a story or expository piece, a teacher can gain diagnostic information about the child's use of language, the child's knowledge of narrative or expository structure, and how the child comprehends or constructs

■ retelling

meaning from text. Therefore, a series of retellings over time assesses progress in these areas and provides important information about each child.

To use this strategy, have the child read a passage aloud or silently (or read the text to a preliterate child). After the reading, ask the child to retell the passage. If needed, provide gentle prompts, such as "Tell me more," or "Keep going; you're doing great." If the child requires further prompting, the teacher asks questions about specific parts of the passage that the child did not mention. If retellings are recorded, the teacher can use the recording to observe the child's oral language and determine how well the child comprehends the passage and organizes ideas. This sample can later be compared with past or subsequent retellings. The teacher can also review and discuss the retelling with the child, using the procedure to develop the same skills that were assessed.

Assessing Phonemic Awareness

Although several norm-referenced phonemic awareness tests are available, such as the *Test of Phonological Awareness* (PRO-ED, Austin, Texas), teachers can informally measure phonemic awareness at frequent intervals to determine which sounds need to be taught or reinforced. In the informal assessment of these important abilities, the teacher gives the student several examples of what he is expected to do in the testing of each skill (see Chapter 4). These phonemic awareness skills appear in order in the box below (adapted from *Phonemic*

Assessing phonemic awareness

Rhyming: "I'll say two words, and you tell me if they rhyme."

EXAMPLES: *boy, toy; go, help; we, me*

Word-to-word match: "I'll say two words, and you tell me if they begin with the same sound."

EXAMPLES: *bat, boy; day, can; run, hop*

Odd word out: "I'll say four words, and you tell me which word ends with a different sound."

EXAMPLES: *bat, hit, make, wet*

(Do the same with beginning sounds.)

Blending: "Tell me what word we would make if we put these sounds together."

EXAMPLES: /a/ /t/; /g/ /o/; /w/ /i/ /n/; /r/ /a/ /n/

Phoneme segmentation: "Tell me what sounds you hear in the words I tell you."

EXAMPLES: *be, pat, got, fish*

Phoneme counting: "Tell me how many sounds you hear in the words I tell you."

EXAMPLES: *in, cat, ship, lake*

Sound-to-word matching: "Answer these questions about what sounds you hear."

EXAMPLES: Is there a /p/ in *pat?* Is there a /n/ in *sun?* Is there a /sh/ in *wash?*

Sound isolation: "See if you can hear these sounds."

EXAMPLES: What is the first sound in *tug?* What is the ending sound in *bat?* What is the middle sound in *cane?*

Phoneme deletion: "Tell me what word would be left if I take away these sounds."

EXAMPLES: Say *cat* without the /c/. Say *hit* without the /h/. Say *bean* without the /n/.

Awareness Assessment, Peddy, 1995, unpublished). Examples are provided for each skill, although teachers often need to create additional examples to ensure that the child completely understands the task; for example, what it means to "rhyme."

Assessing Phonics Skills

The phonic analysis abilities of individual children in the class can be assessed formally, using norm-referenced instruments such as *The Botel Phonics Survey*, but progress in these skills can also be assessed by using an informal inventory of phonics skills (see Chapter 5). Similar to the administration of the phonemic awareness assessment described in the previous section, this procedure also requires that the teacher offer as many examples as are necessary for the child to understand what is being asked. The inventory in the box below can be given to the whole class at one time as a pretest or post-test to discover what skills need to be taught or given individually by having a child read each word orally so the teacher can check knowledge of letter–sound correspondence. Children should be given an answer form with categories and numbers on it to use in recording their responses. Phonics elements mastered, as well as those yet to be learned, can be recorded and analyzed for each child for the purpose of future instructional planning.

Phonics assessment inventory

Consonant sounds (beginning): "Write the beginning letter of each word I say."

> EXAMPLES: *hit, bat, name, just, game, pond*

Consonant sounds (final): "Write the last letter of each word I say."

> EXAMPLES: *man, soft, jam, rub, grass, talk*

Consonant blends (initial): "Write the first two letters of each word I say."

> EXAMPLES: *truck, crab, star, grin, drown, blame*

Consonant blends (final): "Write the last two letters of each word I say."

> EXAMPLES: *back, first, cart, jump, hand, perk*

Consonant digraphs (initial): "Write the first two letters of each word I say."

> EXAMPLES: *shout, child, that, photo, those, chin*

Consonant digraphs (final): "Write the last two letters of each word I say."

> EXAMPLES: *much, ring, cash, moth, sang, luck*

Long and short vowels: "If the vowel in the word I say is short, write short and the vowel. If the vowel in the word I say is long, write long and the vowel."

> EXAMPLES: *sat, hike, same, bone, bless, cot, rug, teet, tin, cube*

Vowel digraphs and diphthongs: "Write the two vowels that go together to form a team—such as /ow/, /ol/, /oy/, and /oo/—in the words I say."

> EXAMPLES: *how, look, oil, ought, boy, mood*

Assessing Fluency

In order to assess reading fluency, teachers need to listen to children read aloud and also make more formal judgments about their progress in the three areas of fluency: rate of reading, reading accuracy, and prosody. The most widely used method to assess, and also increase, a child's reading rate is to ask a child to read a specified passage and determine how much of the passage can be read in one minute (Samuels, 1979). Timed readings differ from traditional silent reading time: in timed reading, the teacher selects the passages, and the children read them and then answer comprehension questions about what they have read (Fox, 2003). The purpose of such an instructional strategy is that children work on increasing their fluency and reading rate, though never at the expense of comprehension.

In assessing accuracy, teachers need to determine if each of their students is able to decode words accurately and if each has a large store of words he or she can recognize automatically, by sight. For determining how a child reads words in context, simply listening to each child's oral reading and counting the number of errors per 100 words can provide valuable information about the child's reading accuracy. This information is helpful for the future selection of texts for individual instructional purposes or for small group instruction. A more thorough assessment providing more detailed information about why a particular child lacks reading accuracy can be obtained through a running record (refer back to Figure 13.4).

Finally, teachers must assess children to consider the following question about prosody: Are each of my students able to chunk words into phrases, heed punctuation, and read with appropriate expression that approximates conversational speech? The best way for teachers to assess a child's prosody is to listen to the child read aloud and use a checklist to determine if the reading contains the qualities that comprise fluent, expressive reading.

The NAEP used four levels to distinguish fluent from disfluent reading (see Figure 13.5). Teachers can use these four levels to determine the reading prosody level of each of the learners in their class. By the end of second grade, children should have reached Level 4. Although most children can benefit from prosody instruction, such instruction would be deemed imperative for those children scoring below Level 4 after second grade (U. S. Department of Education, 1995). Teachers need to be cautioned not to overinterpret the reading-rate norms, however, especially with children for whom English is a second language.

See Appendix E ▶

Besides the assessment procedures mentioned above that involve the teacher, children can be taught to ask their own questions about their reading (see Appendix E). To use these questions, first discuss each of them with the children. Then allow children to record a passage as they read and play it back, listening reflectively to their reading and answering each of the questions.

Assessing Writing and Vocabulary

Evaluating the complexity of a child's writing can provide an insight into the level of difficult words that a child feels comfortable using when composing, but

Oral reading prosody scale.

figure **13.5**

LEVEL 4   Most reading is speechlike and consists of logical phrase groups that vary in length as appropriate. A few repetitions, regressions, and deviations from text may occur but do not change the meaning of the text. Syntax is intact. Most of the text is read with appropriate expression and intonation.

LEVEL 3   Most reading is in phrase groups of three or four words and sometimes fewer, but most phrasing appears appropriate and usually keeps the author's meaning and syntax intact. Little expression or appropriate intonation is noted.

LEVEL 2   Most reading is in two-word phrases, with some three- or four-word groupings. Occasional word-by-word reading is evident. Word groupings are at times awkward and appear not to follow the larger context of the sentence or the passage.

LEVEL 1   Most reading is word-by-word. Occasionally, several-word phrases are used, but these are rare and do not consider the author's meaning or syntax.

Source: Adapted from U.S. Department of Education (1995).

Until recently, no objective assessment of children's word-writing skills could be given to a whole class at one time (Cecil, 2007). Moreover, no assessment device was available that considered children's accuracy, complexity, and fluency in their ability to generate words. A tool called the Word Writing CAFÉ (Leal, 2005; CAFÉ stands for complexity, accuracy, fluency, and evaluation) was developed to allow teachers to objectively evaluate their students' word-writing ability in terms of fluency, accuracy, and complexity in grades 1–6. Through scoring and tracking their students' progress over the school year, teachers can use the assessment data to understand and improve the students' word writing capabilities through explicit instruction.

To administer the Word Writing CAFÉ, each child in the class is given a piece of paper on which three columns of 10 boxes are drawn. Children are then asked to write down as many words as they can think of in 10 minutes (see Figure 13.6 for an example of a completed form). The words are then scored according to the following steps:

- To determine word *fluency:* Count the total number of boxes with any writing in them. Anything counts as a word, except scribbles or pictures. This is the TW (total words) figure.

- To determine *accuracy:* Cross out misspelled words, duplicated words, proper names, and numbers that are not spelled out. This is the CW (correct words) figure.

figure 13.6 — Completed CAFÉ form.

1st/2nd

Name Skylar   Date Oct. 15   Teacher Mr. Nuan

The	l	dad	l	sun	l
see	l	mom	l	~~mun~~	
They	l	two	l	your	l
Then	l	too	l	six	l
~~Thes~~		to	l	ran	l
you	l	grandma	2	~~playd~~	
yes	l	grandpa	2	play	l
no	l	cat ~~hak~~	l	~~sally bally~~	
on	l	day ~~hog~~	l		
can	l	Boo!	l		

TW: __28__   CW: __24__   1S: __22__   2S: __2__

3S: _____   4S: _____   5S: _____   6S: _____

- To determine the *complexity:* Count the number of syllables in each correctly spelled word. Using the blanks provided, fill in the number of one-syllable words (1s) and so on.

Dorothy Leal, the creator of the Word Writing CAFÉ, offers the following important suggestions to consider when administering this helpful assessment tool:

- Use the device to track student progress, not to assign student grade-level abilities.
- Be sure the assessment is administered in a nonprint environment where children cannot copy from word walls or other print displays.
- Use *only* the following prompts to give children ideas of what they can write:
  - "Write words that tell what you like to do and where you like to go."

- "Write words that describe what you can see, hear, smell, taste, and feel."
- "Write words that tell what is in your house or school."
- "Write any word that you know how to read or write."

As national benchmarks have not yet been completed for this pilot assessment device, it can now be used as a criterion-referenced test, to determine progress over time in each of the three areas assessed. National benchmarks are forthcoming. For more information visit http://oak.cats.ohiou.edu/~leal/cafe.htm.

http://oak.cats.ohiou.edu/~leal/cafe.htm

The Word Writing CAFÉ is one way to evaluate fluency accuracy and word complexity. However, word writing is not the only goal of a writing program. Teachers should evaluate for *authentic* writing for *authentic* purposes. As important as it is for teachers to listen to students as they read, it is equally imperative that teachers observe students as they write, in order to provide immediate feedback while children are writing and while they can use it to improve their writing. Anecdotal notes should be taken during writers' workshop to conclude which children easily settle to the task of writing and which children struggle with ideas and writing conventions. In addition to monitoring for children who spend a great deal of time sounding out words and asking for spelling assistance, teachers should also note how easily a child is able to think of writing ideas and complete the writing tasks and how willing he or she is to share written products. For an example of a checklist to facilitate recording observations of each child's writing fluency see Appendix E. A child's writing can also be assessed using the 6 + 1 Trait® Rubric: 5-Point Beginning Writer's Rubric (see Appendix E). The 6 + 1 traits can also be used as a framework for writing instruction. For more information visit http://educationnorthwest.org/traits.

See Appendix E

http://educationnorthwest.org/traits

RESPONSE TO INTERVENTION: BLENDING ASSESSMENT AND INTERVENTION

The 2004 reauthorization of federal legislation IDEA (Individuals with Disabilities Education Act) formalized the process of assessing and teaching struggling learners, but more recently it has gained the interest of reading educators (Fuchs, Fuchs, & Vaughn, 2008). The purpose of **Response to Intervention** (RTI) is not only to provide early intervention for students who are at risk for school failure but also to develop more valid procedures for identifying students with reading disabilities. RTI allows teachers to determine which children need special education instruction in reading, based on whether or not the child can respond to either typical classroom instruction or the more intensive type of support that is also possible in a typical classroom (e.g., brief but intensive small-group intervention on key skills).

Response to Intervention

RTI is a framework that incorporates both assessment and intervention so that immediate benefits come to the student. Assessment data are used to inform interventions and determine their effectiveness. As a result of the intervention-focused nature of RTI, eligibility services shift toward a supportive rather than a sorting function. The purpose of the formalized routine in RTI is to help teachers do what good teachers have always done—make instructional decisions based on their students' needs.

Although RTI is not limited to identifying literacy needs, I will discuss its specific characteristics in relation to literacy. To implement RTI, the following must first be in place:

valid ■
reliable ■

1. ways to measure reading proficiency that are **valid** *(does it measure what it purports to measure?)* and **reliable** *(are the results consistent over time?)* so that children can receive the appropriate type and level of reading instruction for their needs;

2. an assessment program that monitors the children's progress in reading as a result of the instruction they are receiving;

3. various levels, or tiers, of instruction available to children to meet their instructional needs;

4. a data-driven decision-making process in which, once children's level of reading development and instructional needs have been determined, they are placed in the appropriate level and offered the type of scientifically validated literacy instruction that will address their specific needs.

Progress should be monitored regularly to ensure that the instruction children receive is yielding the desired results. Successful RTI schools then routinely transform progress-monitoring data into visual displays such as time-series graphs to share with teachers, intervention team members, parents, and others. These displays demonstrate whether the student is benefiting from the intervention.

In the classroom, RTI instruction has three tiers. Tier 1 instruction is the common core curriculum given to all the children in the class. Most children (typically, around 80 percent) should make adequate progress in reading as a result of Tier 1 instruction. The routine progress monitoring allows teachers to determine who is and who is not progressing with the core curriculum. Children not progressing are placed in Tier 2 instruction, which supplements—but does not replace—Tier 1 instruction. Tier 3 adds an additional layer of instruction as well as instructional intensity for those children who have not progressed with Tier 2 instruction according to assessment results. If this new layer of intensive instruction does not then yield results, individual instruction follows, usually with a reading specialist. If that extra instruction does not prove successful for the child and every other avenue has been exhausted, a decision is made for a special education placement, as deemed necessary.

On the face of it, RTI makes perfect sense in that it strives to meet the needs of all children; however, in order to work efficiently, RTI assumes that the time, the staff, and the financial resources are all available for both the routine assessments and the increasingly complex layers of instructional interventions. Despite these concerns, a growing body of evidence indicates that RTI can work (Haager, Klingner, & Vaughn, 2007; Jimerson, Burns, & VanDerHeyden, 2007) if committed teachers, reading specialists, and administrators think creatively about how to implement it.

RTI in action: Literacy success for Landon

(adapted from Mesmer & Mesmer, 2009)

To illustrate how RTI might work, we will look at a second-grader, Landon, and follow his progress in literacy. This particular vignette shows how a team, including Joan, a reading teacher, Steve, a special educator, and Anthony, Landon's second-grade teacher, worked collaboratively within the RTI framework to foster the literacy progress of one child. Figure 13.7 presents the literacy screening assessments the team used to monitor Landon's needs and progress.

STEP 1: EVIDENCE-BASED LITERACY PRACTICES ARE ESTABLISHED

In September, Landon was given the Phonics Mastery Survey (Appendix E), which assesses a child's ability to identify letters, consonant sounds, rhyming words, more complex consonant and vowel sounds, syllables, and a list of grade 2 words. He was also given a spelling assessment, The Monster Test (Gentry, 1985). These are the measures from which an entry benchmark score is formed. If the benchmark score does not meet the grade-level minimum, then additional, lower diagnostics are administered (preprimer and primer lists, letter naming, letter sounds, concepts about print, phonological awareness). Students also read passages through which accuracy, reading rate, phrasing, and comprehension scores are determined.

In the fall, Landon received a benchmark score of 22 on the first-grade word list and fell below the expected stage of spelling development on the spelling assessment. An expected benchmark score of 30, based on 15 words on the first-grade list, and at least a phonetic stage of spelling development are expected for the beginning of second grade. Specifically, Landon had trouble with all except short vowel sounds, and knew no consonant blends or digraphs. On the QRI, Landon read instructionally at the primer level (1.1) with appropriate phrasing and expression and answered five of six comprehension questions correctly, missing only the critical evaluative question. He read the 120 words in the primer story in 4 minutes and 20 seconds, a rate of about 28 words correct per minute (WCPM) and 20 words below the 50th percentile for second graders in the fall. When follow-up diagnostic assessments were administered, data showed that Landon had mastered alphabetic skills such as phonemic awareness and letters. Anthony wrote in his initial analysis: "Landon seemed to have mastered some basic concepts of reading and his low-level comprehension is good, but he needs more practice at his independent reading level to become fluent and to progress." To begin with, Landon received small-group classroom instruction, including reading daily in on-level materials and working with Anthony on critical comprehension and decoding. In September, October, and November, Anthony took running records on the books that Landon and the other students had been reading. Although the accuracy and book levels of other students

case example

Literacy screening assessments used by Landon's team.   *figure* **13.7**

SCREENING DEVICE	AUTHOR(S)
Dynamic Indicators of Basic Early Literacy Skills (DIBELS)	Good & Kaminski, 2002
Assessments for Phonological Awareness (see Appendix E)	Beilby, 2007
Phonics Mastery Survey (see Appendix E)	Cecil, 2011
Qualitative Reading Inventory (QRI)	Leslie & Caldwell, 2011
The Monster Test (see Appendix E)	Gentry, 1985

were steadily increasing, Landon's accuracy was averaging 90 percent, but only in less difficult books. Anthony explained, "I felt like Landon needed still more help, or he would continue to fall behind."

STEP 2: SCIENTIFICALLY BASED INTERVENTIONS ARE IMPLEMENTED

The team discussed Landon's needs and designed an appropriate intervention. Based on its review of the data, the team determined that accurate, fluent reading in text seemed to be the problem. Landon could easily understand books above his reading level, but his progress was being impeded by slow rate and lack of word-recognition skills. The group decided that an intervention increasing the amount of reading practice for Landon would build up his reading level. The designed intervention comprised the following components: modeling of fluent reading, repeated readings, error correction, comprehension questions, and self-monitoring. They decided that Joan would implement the intervention with three other students in the classroom in 20-minute sessions, three times per week. In addition, Anthony would continue to work with Landon in the classroom during small-group literacy instruction. He had Landon read from the same materials used by Joan to further increase practice opportunities, and she set a daily goal for Landon on comprehension questions. Landon checked his answers each day and provided the results to his teacher at the end of the reading time.

STEP 3: PROGRESS OF STUDENT RECEIVING INTERVENTION IS MONITORED

While the intervention was implemented, Joan monitored Landon's accuracy and fluency in reading passages at the primer through second-grade levels, because the goal was to understand Landon's progress toward grade-level norms. As Landon read these passages weekly, Joan kept track of his accuracy (percentage of words correct) and reading rate (WCPM). Landon demonstrated some gains in accuracy and fluency, but his prog-

ress was not increasing at a rate that would allow him to meet the second-grade literacy goals.

In addition to review of Landon's progress during the six weeks of intervention instruction, Landon's midyear Phonics Mastery Survey and QRI scores were evaluated by the team. The child was found to be reading independently at the primer (1.1) level; barely instructional at the first-grade level, with 14 errors and a reading rate of 42 WCPM; and still unable to read words with consonant blends and digraphs correctly—nor did he fare any better with complex vowel sounds. Despite the increase in Landon's instructional level and fluency, the team remained concerned about the lack of reduction in the number of errors that Landon was making and his lack of knowledge of all but rudimentary vowel and consonant sounds. The team decided that these concerns would ultimately become detrimental to Landon's fluency and comprehension, particularly as texts increased in difficulty. The team determined that individualized intervention was needed.

STEP 4: INDIVIDUALIZED INTERVENTIONS WHEN STUDENT CONTINUES TO STRUGGLE

Results from the Phonics Mastery Survey further revealed that Landon was having difficulty decoding words with more than one syllable and words that contained difficult vowel patterns. This resulted in reduced accuracy and fluency. The team enhanced the intervention by adding practice with problem words. Landon practiced incorrectly read words, received instruction in how to analyze word parts, extended analytic skills to similar words, and practiced through word sorts. Following word sorts, Landon read each word within a sentence. Joan implemented this individualized intervention for 10 minutes each day following the reading practice intervention (discussed earlier).

Landon's reading accuracy and fluency continued to be monitored weekly by Joan. The team determined that the intervention would be implemented for a minimum of 6 weeks, as this time frame would correspond with the end of the school year, although the team recognized that interventions in early literacy often need to run longer—between 10 and 20 weeks. Moreover, Landon's progress was measured each week so that the intervention could be modified if he failed to make adequate gains. Landon quickly responded to the decoding intervention. Data were collected once per week on the percentage of words read correctly from second-grade passages. Landon's response to the intervention contrasted dramatically with his performance when reading unknown words prior to the intervention. By the sixth week, Landon correctly read 100 percent of words presented; before the intervention he was reading only 55 percent to 60 percent accurately. Landon improved in reading fluency as well. Prior to word attack intervention, the effects of the fluency intervention had leveled off. With the addition of the decoding intervention, Landon's fluency steadily improved until he met the second-grade goal. By the end of May, Landon met the grade level goals: he was reading instructionally at second-grade level with comprehension at a rate of about 60 WCPM, according to the latest administration of the QRI.

A graph of Landon's progress was created using PowerPoint so that the team, parents, administrators, and others could have a visual display of the results of all assessments and interventions.

Adapted from Response to Intervention (RTI): What Teachers of Reading Need to Know. *The Reading Teacher, 62*(4), pp. 280–290. Used with permission of the International Reading Association via Copyright Clearance Center.

STEP 5: DECISION-MAKING PROCESS TO DETERMINE ELIGIBILITY FOR SPECIAL EDUCATION SERVICES

Despite falling below the second-grade benchmark in September, Landon demonstrated growth in accuracy, fluency, and decoding as a result of the efforts of school personnel. The team reviewed Landon's intervention data and determined that special education services were not necessary. However, Anthony voiced concerns about Landon and the continued need for support. Although Anthony could see that Landon had made great progress with the extra interventions in addition to the regular curriculum, he was concerned about regression during the summer. He suggested that a meeting be held with Landon's parents to discuss specific summer literacy activities that they could encourage at home. Additionally, Anthony insisted that a meeting with the team be scheduled immediately in September to talk about his need for his third-grade year.

Landon's progress was significant, considering his skills at the beginning of the year. If the interventions had not met Landon's needs, the team would have been charged with determining whether the lack of response was indicative of a learning disability.

COMPILING AND SUMMARIZING ASSESSMENT INFORMATION

t he acts of compiling and summarizing the variety of assessment data help teachers integrate, organize, manage, and keep this information accessible for whenever it is needed. In literacy assessment, information about children is gathered from various formal, informal, and observational sources, with many of the same behaviors appearing in several different appraisals. For example, Mr. Steel has information from writing folders, journal entries, phonics tests, story retellings, IRIs, reading achievement tests, cloze tests, and many anecdotal observations, to name just a few sources. These primary data must be put together to get the big picture of each student's capabilities. Teachers can compile this information into a student profile (see Appendix E). Moreover, as the year progresses, the amount of information proliferates, resulting in far more data than anyone could possibly commit to memory. Two other ways to compile and summarize information are *teacher observational portfolios* for each child and *group profiles* for the entire class.

See Appendix E

Portfolios

Artists use portfolios to demonstrate their skills and achievements; teachers can use portfolios in a similar manner to portray the literacy work and progress of each of the students in their class over an extended period of time (Porter & Cleland, 1995; Valencia, 1990).

There are many options for the contents of portfolios whether they are in hard copy or electronic form; they can be organized in any way that is helpful to teacher, children, parents, and families. Typically, the teacher selects appropriate data, based on observations and informal assessments of children's reading and writing behaviors and accomplishments, and puts these data into a progress file, or a **teacher observational portfolio.** In some cases, the teacher and the child make a collaborative decision about which choice materials will be assembled to go into a showcase portfolio.

teacher
observational
portfolio ■

An alternative vehicle for showcasing children's work is a *video portfolio,* a representation of a child's ongoing reading prowess. Children can be recorded reading aloud during various intervals during the year, or they can be videoed during reading discussion groups. Writer's workshop and special projects such as readers theater can also be videoed to record progress.

Group Profiles

group profiles ■

Group profiles are compilations of individual performances of all the children in the class on one or more assessments. They focus on the range of class literacy behavior and identify clusters or subgroups of children with similar strengths and needs. They also condense information about the whole class's performance onto several worksheets. Unlike individual teacher observational portfolios, student profiles do not cut across different areas, but they summarize one literacy area for the entire class (see Appendix E).

See Appendix E ▶

Group profiles are primarily planning tools that convey the strengths and needs of the entire class so that appropriate activities can be planned to meet them. Instead of generalizing about what the class knows and can do, the group profile graphically shows, for example, that only two children need more direct instruction in phonemic awareness, whereas the majority of the class is ready for formal phonics instruction or, for example, that four children need no phonics instruction but could use specific comprehension strategies (see Chapter 8) to enrich their advanced reading abilities.

USING ASSESSMENT TO INFORM INSTRUCTION

the principles of assessment presented at the beginning of this chapter suggest that there must be a reciprocal, synergistic relationship between assessment and teaching; in other words, teaching and assessing must continually inform one another. Putting this into practice, however, takes skill and shrewd observation on the part of the classroom teacher. Assessing children with no clear plan as to what will be done with the testing results wastes valuable instructional time. The remainder of this chapter consists of practical information, in the form of answers to frequently asked questions, about the choice of assessment tools and what to do with assessment results.

1. When and why might a teacher decide to use a specific assessment tool? Certain assessment tools are mandated by the state or district where the teacher works. So-called **high-stakes assessments** must be administered by teachers usually once or twice a year. These assessments are often used to determine how well children are doing compared with other children in the area, the state, and/ or the nation. The funding of certain programs often depends on how well children do on these tests—hence the moniker "high stakes."

■ high-stakes assessments

Other, more specific diagnostic assessments may be used when a teacher wonders why a child is not progressing as well as expected in a certain area. For example, a teacher may decide to administer a test of phonological awareness (see Appendix E) when she discovers, through observation, that the child is not learning to decode and she fears he may not possess the prerequisite ability to hear discrete sounds in words. A teacher might decide to use the same assessment when a standardized reading test shows that the child is weak in decoding and the teacher is interested in determining the underlying cause. Such time-consuming assessment devices need not be administered to every child in the class, but only to those about whom the teacher requires more specific information.

◀ *See Appendix E*

End-of-chapter and unit tests are examples of assessments that would be used to find out if all children have attained the learning objectives the teacher identified at the beginning of the chapter or unit (e.g., criterion-referenced tests). Other classroom assessments, such as quick writes and random quizzes, are administered during instruction to measure student progress. Such assessments give feedback about students and offer fodder for reflection about areas that might require alternative teaching strategies or different pacing.

Sometimes an assessment tool tells the teacher what *not* to teach or to whom *not* to teach a specific concept or skill. For example, a phonics assessment device administered to all the children in a class might reveal that five children have mastered all the phonics skills and, instead of sitting through lessons on the letters and their corresponding sounds, would be better served by reading material to comprehend and respond to in written form. Similarly, a quick-write at the beginning of a social science unit might reveal that the children in the class already know a great deal about habitats, requiring the teacher to revise and enhance her plans for the unit.

2. If a need is identified, when and how might that need be addressed? When observations or specific assessments show that a large number of children have a specific need, that area can be

Teaching and assessing must continually inform one another.

addressed by reteaching the skill or concept through the vehicle of a minilesson (see Chapter 9) or through explicit instruction during shared or guided reading (see Chapter 11). When several children are found to have the same need, a temporary group can be formed to differentiate instruction and focus on that need; for example, children who need reinforcement in finding the answers to inferential questions, as determined by an informal reading inventory, can become a temporary group working directly with the teacher. Through this type of flexible grouping, individual children can be helped directly through reading conferences, or specific assignments designed to rectify the problem can be sent home with the child if the parents or caregivers are able to help at home. (See the Case Example box showing Chelsea's journey.)

Cross-age tutoring, a program in which older children work with younger ones on specific subject areas such as reading and writing, can be a successful alternative to classroom intervention if tutors are wisely chosen and given some minimal training in the strategy needed. For example, fifth-grade students at Fruitridge Elementary School in Sacramento paired up with first-grade students and were successful in helping the younger children improve their comprehension scores when they listened to the children read stories on their independent reading levels and had discussions afterward that emanated from critical and creative questions designed collaboratively with the fifth-grade teacher.

3. How can assessment and instruction be aligned with state standards? Standards provide a systematic way for educators to ask themselves, "What is it that we want our children to know, and what do we want them to be able to do?" Standards are also an attempt to do away with the often sporadic nature and uncertainty of testing, grading, accountability, and instructional planning. Teachers in nearly every state are now committing time and effort to redesigning curriculum, resequencing courses, aligning materials and resources, redesigning instructional practices, and evaluating and reporting student progress—all in response to standards that are now in place in their states. Many of the state standards are very broad; others not only describe explicitly what the student is expected to know and do but also are accompanied by samples and criteria for assessment (Sargeant & Smejkal, 2000). New common core standards appear more promising.

The alignment of curriculum and assessment with standards is illustrated by a teacher in New Jersey who is teaching her fourth-grade English learners a unit on farm animals. Although the standards she follows are those adopted by New Jersey, the process of aligning curriculum with the standards is the same with every set of standards. This teacher first familiarizes herself with the state standards for her particular grade level and then looks for innovative teaching methods and materials to help her meet those standards. For example, in the New Jersey Core Curriculum Content Standards for Language Arts Literacy, standard 3.2 states:

> All students will listen actively in a variety of situations to information from a variety of sources. Through active listening, students gain an awareness of the role of sound, including intonation, rhythm, pace, enunciation, volume, and quality in combination with words and/or visual presentations to convey meaning.

From diagnosis to intervention to avid reader: Chelsea's journey

DIAGNOSIS

Chelsea H. is a second-grade student in a suburban middle-class school just outside of Sacramento. English is her native language. When she began falling behind in the second month of the school year, her teacher, Mr. Green, reviewed his anecdotal notes about the child's literacy progress. He noticed she seemed distracted in free reading time and resisted reading aloud when asked. Mr. Green administered a running record and determined that Chelsea was reading word by word and made many errors that changed the meaning of the text. Her accuracy level (84 percent) on the second-grade passage revealed that it was at her frustration level. Specifically, Chelsea appeared to have trouble decoding multisyllabic words. Also, a retelling of the passage showed that, while Chelsea got the main idea of the passage, she was not able to recall any details. This retelling supported many earlier observations, suggesting that Chelsea pays little attention to the details of what she reads.

From the Fry's group of instant words **(Appendix G)** that Mr. Green flashed on index cards, Chelsea was able to recognize 120 of 162 words on the first-grade list and fewer than half on the second-grade list.

Chelsea also demonstrated consistent problems with spelling. Although she does surprisingly well on weekly spelling tests, she has trouble, mostly with multisyllabic words, with writing assignments and in her dialogue journal.

An Interest Inventory given at the beginning of the year suggested that Chelsea does not enjoy reading, but likes being read to. When asked how she felt about herself as a reader, Chelsea replied, "I don't care much for reading. I've never read a book I liked. It's hard for me. I can do it when I try, but I'd rather watch television." When Mr. Green asked Chelsea who she thought was a good reader and what good readers do, Chelsea mentioned her 10-year-old sister, Brooke. "Brooke is a really good reader," the little girl mused. "She reads all the time and she reads fast. She read a Harry Potter book in three days!"

INTERVENTION

Mr. Green first spent time with Chelsea during library time. From Chelsea's Interest Inventory, he noticed that she liked the program *Jane and the Dragon.* He selected several similar fantasies on Chelsea's independent reading level and asked her to leaf through them to see if she might like them. She became entranced with these books and soon had read four in the series. Mr. Green made provisions for her to read one to the kindergarten class once a week.

To help Chelsea begin to read more purposefully, Mr. Green paired her with another student and encouraged the two girls to do dyad reading with passages on a daily basis (see Chapter 8). Using this strategy, the two children took turns summarizing the paragraphs the other child read, and both began to pay more attention to details in the passages.

Mr. Green also did explicit instruction of question-answer-relationships (QARs) (see Chapter 8) with Chelsea, teaching her and several other students with the same need how to find the answers to specific kinds of questions in the text.

Mr. Green created an individual progress chart so that Chelsea could keep track of the growth she made in both reading comprehension and accuracy. He also gave her a Sight Word Bingo game to take home to play with her younger brother and older sister. (Chapter 6 in DeVries, 2011, contains a description of this activity, and Appendix D in that book contains sample bingo cards.)

Finally, Mr. Green used the strategy of Spelling in Parts (SIP; see Chapter 6) to help Chelsea break words into chunks in order to decode them and spell them more successfully.

AVID READER

The dyad reading has helped Chelsea to continually be aware of the details of what she is reading, as she now knows she will be accountable for summarizing what she has read.

(continued)

case example

QARs have helped Chelsea see reading in a new light. She is now able to go back in a text and find answers to different kinds of questions and has integrated the four kinds of comprehension (see Chapter 8) into her understanding of the kinds of information she should be gleaning as she reads. Today, when she does a retelling of a passage, she automatically includes the answers to all four kinds of questions.

The SIP strategy has helped Chelsea to both spell and decode multisyllabic words more quickly and effectively. Though she still has problems with "hidden" syllables, like schwas, she is able to break words into pronounceable parts, or chunk them, in order to decode them.

By June, Chelsea is reading at grade level according to a recent running record. As a result of a newly sparked interest in reading (*anything* about dragons!), Chelsea is reading voraciously and looks forward to her sojourns with the kindergarten class. The volume of reading she is now doing, coupled with the repeated readings necessary to prepare for the reading to the kindergarten class, has improved her reading rate, accuracy, and prosody. Additionally, Chelsea admits she now loves to read.

cumulative progress
indicators ■   Each standard, such as the one on page 308, has accompanying **cumulative progress indicators** that help the teacher put the standard in place so that it can be observed when it is demonstrated by the children.

In this particular unit, the teacher's major objective is to have children identify animals found in Latin America, identify the sounds they make, and compare them with farm animals found in the United States. To fulfill this objective, she reads them a story, "The Day the Dog Said Bow Wow!" by David McPhail. Children then compare sounds animals make in both languages, Spanish and English. Using two hula hoops, the students identify and discuss the similarities and differences in animal sounds in Latin America and the United States. The right side of one hoop represents sounds animals make in Latin America; the left side of the other hoop represents sounds animals make in the United States. The middle, where the two hula hoops overlap, represents sounds animals make in both places. Later, together as a class, the children put symbols to the sounds the animals make, using a Venn diagram on an interactive whiteboard and three different colors.

After this lesson, the teacher creates a checklist of the progress indicators for each skill and ability contained in the standard covered by the lesson (see Figure 13.8). Through observation of the participation and discussion inherent in the lesson, she then determines whether individual children are making progress in meeting this standard.

SUMMARY

t he major goal for literacy assessment in a primary classroom is to find out how each child is progressing in a particular area at a given time and to make instructional adjustments more closely attuned to the children's changing needs. The best way to achieve this assessment goal is by using a balance of formal, informal, and observational assessment tools.

The use of formalized reading achievement tests provides important comparative data designed to be valid and reliable, but results do not always provide

Correlating standards with instruction.   *figure* **13.8**

UNIT: "FARM ANIMALS IN TWO COUNTRIES"

Standards Addressed in the Unit

(The following standards should be met by fourth grade, according to the New Jersey Core Curriculum Content Standards.)

Name: _____   Date: _____

Cumulative Progress Indicators:

1.2.1.	Demonstrates performance and participation skills by working and creating individually and with others (Visual and Performing Arts).	NEVER	SOMETIMES	FREQUENTLY	ALWAYS
3.2.2.	Demonstrates comprehension of a story, interview, or oral event or incident (Language Arts Literacy).	NEVER	SOMETIMES	FREQUENTLY	ALWAYS
3.2.3.	Listens for a variety of purposes, such as enjoyment and obtaining information (Language Arts Literacy).	NEVER	SOMETIMES	FREQUENTLY	ALWAYS
3.2.7.	Follows oral directions (Language Arts Literacy).	NEVER	SOMETIMES	FREQUENTLY	ALWAYS
5.6.1.	Compares and contrasts living and nonliving things (Science).	NEVER	SOMETIMES	FREQUENTLY	ALWAYS
6.5.3.	Identifies common elements found in different cultures (Social Studies).	NEVER	SOMETIMES	FREQUENTLY	ALWAYS
7.1.4.	Describes people, places, things, and events using short phrases and simple sentences (Social Studies).	NEVER	SOMETIMES	FREQUENTLY	ALWAYS
7.2.1.	Demonstrates an awareness of culture (World Languages).	NEVER	SOMETIMES	FREQUENTLY	ALWAYS

---

accurate and specific information for individual children, in context. Data from such tests should therefore be interpreted with caution, especially when the test-takers are culturally diverse learners.

Informal assessments and anecdotal information derived from careful observation, though nonscientific, can support or question standardized test results. Informal assessments, if resulting data are compiled frequently and interpreted wisely, can be an excellent method of continually informing instruction.

The value of the assessment devices discussed in this chapter and those contained in Appendix E depends largely on reflective analysis and how the devices are used for communicating about literacy progress and resultant instructional plans with the child, his parents, and others. By recognizing the

See Appendix E

strengths and limitations of different types of assessment devices, a teacher can maximize their value for creating a comprehensive literacy program.

questions
for journal writing and discussion

1. Interview a local primary-grade teacher to determine what assessment strategies he uses, or if you are already teaching, interview a teacher from another school. What and how does the teacher assess? How does the teacher balance formal and informal assessments? Discuss your findings with others in your class to see if similarities, differences, and/or conclusions can be drawn.

2. It is no longer enough to simply give children the opportunity to learn; newspapers and current education journals say that schools must now provide proof that learning has actually taken place. Discuss this pervasive feeling in terms of its implications for literacy assessment.

3. Imagine that, at a parent–teacher meeting, a parent confronts you about your assessment program, complaining that you spend too much time assessing and too little time teaching, considering the brief school day. Role-play the confrontation, defending your position.

suggestions
for projects and field activities

1. Select one of the informal assessment instruments discussed in this chapter and prepare to use it with first- or second-grade children to measure a literacy-related area or skill. Summarize the results and share them with your class. *Note:* Blank copies of some of the assessments are available in Appendix E.

See Appendix E ▶

2. Observe a classroom teacher or reading specialist as he administers an IRI or a running record to a young child. Discuss the interpretation of results with the teacher. Why was the assessment given? What was learned? How will the teacher adapt instruction as a result of the information gained?

3. Examine a standardized reading achievement test that is routinely administered to beginning readers in your area. Review the teacher's manual and technical manual for information about administering and scoring the test. Evaluate the instructions and test items for clarity, and compare the norming population with the children in your area. Examine the items for illustrations of cultural stereotypes and/or bias. Interview school authorities to determine how the information is reported and used to make classroom, school, and district decisions about reading instruction. Finally, peruse Buros's *Mental Measurements Yearbook*, available in the reference section of libraries, for more information on this test and how it compares with others of its kind.

chapter 14

Home as Partner

The Shared Connection

focus questions

- How can teachers help heighten parents' or caregivers' awareness of their critical role in the literacy development of their children?

- What are some appropriate literacy activities that teachers can share with families to help promote literacy development?

- How can teachers best keep families informed about their child's progress in literacy?

Mrs. Nguyen teaches first grade in inner-city Los Angeles. Early in the school year, Mrs. Nguyen collects the personal literacy histories of every child in her class to inform her later instructional decisions. Much as physicians gather the medical history of children they treat, this teacher knows she must learn about the literacy experiences the children have already had, including the kind of literacy materials to which they have been exposed, to get a clear picture of where to begin instruction. She knows that every child has had rich experiences upon which to build, although these experiences may differ from those middle-class youngsters commonly encounter. Over the years, contrary to what she originally expected, she has found that parents are eager to share information about their children and are usually willing to be active participants in their children's reading development.

Because standardized reading test scores suggest that many of her children may be at risk for reading failure, Mrs. Nguyen uses their own community materials as "fodder" for early literacy instruction. For example, she scours the neighborhood for letters on stores and signs with which the children will be familiar, takes pictures of the letters, and brings them into the classroom for instruction. She uses the *M* in McDonald's, the *T* in Taco Bell, the *W* in Walmart, and so forth, to reinforce these letters. Children, then, are encouraged to look for other environmental print when they go home at the end of the day. Parents are invited to share in this literacy scavenger hunt, and many express gratitude that they have been able to be of assistance.

INTRODUCTION

The preceding vignette illustrates a primary aspect of the home–school connection. The example from Mrs. Nguyen's classroom demonstrates the integration of literacies from the children's homes and communities with classroom literacy instruction. It shows a profound regard for parents as partners in the literacy process who have already laid the foundation and are interested in helping in any way they can. *Note:* For the sake of readability, the term "parent" is used throughout this chapter. This term should be understood to encompass the concept of caregiver as well—a family member or other committed adult who may have primary responsibility for the care of a child.

It is often said, and it will be echoed throughout this chapter, that parents are their children's first teachers. Consider: All the experiences children amass, beginning at birth, affect their success in literacy. Moreover, the success of the school literacy program depends, in large part, on the quality of the opportunities for literacy development that occur in the home (Fan & Chen, 2001). Because some children come to school already knowing how to read and write, researchers have extensively studied such children and their home environments (Briggs & Elkind, 1973; Morrow, 1983; Teale, 1978). Although the parents often claim the children began reading and writing "naturally," investigators are now convinced that there is more to it than that, and that much can be done through adult–child interaction and the home environment to enhance the literacy program that exists at school.

Parents can influence their children's literacy development in several ways. The first is through interpersonal interaction with them. This includes the various ways in which all members of the household converse, work, and play with one another. The second is through the climate of the household. When members of the household hold literacy in high esteem and retain high academic expectations for their children, the motivational climate in the household is favorable to literacy development. Finally, the physical environment in the home also has a direct impact on literacy development. When the tools of literacy are easily accessible—books, magazines, newspapers, writing materials, the Internet, and so forth—a subtle yet profound statement is made about the importance of literacy activities.

The following sections offer more specific information, synthesized from current research, on exactly how reading development is enhanced in the home.

RESEARCH ON HOME LITERACY

every teacher hopes for a class full of students whose parents care about and support their literacy growth at home. Teachers know, intuitively and through research, that such children will have a much easier road to becoming readers and writers than those who do not have this background. Indeed, research from the 1970s and 1980s consistently identified strong correlations between parents reading to and with their children and children's later success in literacy (Anderson et al., 1985; Chomsky, 1972; Laosa, 1982; Teale & Sulzby, 1986b). Later research attempted to identify the essential nature of what transpires during parent–child reading interactions to make them so beneficial. Lancy and Bergin (1992) found that children who are most fluent and positive about reading came from parent–child pairs who viewed reading as fun, kept stories moving with a "meaning-seeking" rather than a purely "decoding" orientation, and encouraged questions and humor while reading together.

Teachers have long been telling parents to simply read to their children, but some research suggests this exhortation has been misguided. For example, Lancy, Draper, and Boyce (1989) describe the parents of good readers as using expansionist strategies, such as adding personal information and explanations, or "scaffolding," as their children grapple to understand stories. For example, the parent might start reading a story with the child and then make guesses as to what will happen next, thereby modeling the comprehension strategy of making predictions. Over time, the parent takes a less active role and encourages the child to utilize expansionist strategies themselves when reading. These are especially useful with a story that has been read multiple times. When the child experiences difficulty, the parents of good readers tend to make a mild joke of it, thus diffusing anxiety, whereas the parents of poorer readers treat a decoding error as a serious infraction, sometimes even covering up an illustration to prevent "cheating," according to Lancy et al.

Tracy and Young (1994) studied the home reading behaviors of struggling and more advanced readers and their college-educated mothers. They found no difference in the frequency of children's oral reading during first grade and, indeed, found struggling readers actually did *more* oral reading in second and third grades than did the more proficient readers. Tracy (1995), in a later analysis of videotaped reading sessions with struggling and more advanced readers, noted a striking contrast in the degree to which advanced readers received more physical and verbal attention, support, and extended feedback from their families. In a more in depth study of more than 40 families, Baker et al. (1994) analyzed differences between literacy activities of low- and middle-income families. Low-income families reported doing more reading practices and homework (e.g., flashcards, letter practice) with their kindergarten-aged children than did middle income parents; middle-income parents reported only slightly more book reading with their children than did low-income parents. The middle-income parents reported more enjoyable activities with print, however, as well as more recreational reading on the part of their children. From these studies, it appears that the nature of what actually takes place during literacy events matters a great deal—perhaps more than the mere fact that the parent–child literacy activity occurs.

UNDERSTANDING DIFFERENCES IN HOME PRACTICES

because many teachers come from middle-class backgrounds, they can have the unfortunate tendency to view the home literacy practices that they recall experiencing in their own homes as the only effective ones. The image that most often comes to mind for most teachers is a young child sitting on the lap of a parent—usually a young female—while a large storybook is being read. Such an image sets up the notion that the parent who does not read books to her child while the child sits on her lap is somehow to blame for her child's lack of progress in literacy. It is important, however, that teachers consider the wide range of literacy practices that may occur, so as to more effectively build upon the literacy experiences that children from a host of backgrounds bring with them to school (Thomas, Fazio, & Stiefelmeyer, 1999).

It is helpful for teachers to bear in mind that most parents—regardless of income level or cultural or ethnic background—value education for their children. However, different parents may have differing perceptions of what it means to be literate, and they may not always be aware of the most effective tactics for fostering literacy with their children. Several researchers have reported the high value that many low-income families place on literacy. For example, Delgado-Gaitan (1987) found that the possibility of a better education for their children was cited as a major reason for Hispanic immigration to the United States. Taylor and Dorsey-Gaines (1988), in studying low-income parents whose children succeed in school, noted extraordinary sacrifices and efforts made in the interest of the child's education, despite the parents' limited educational levels. Finally, Fitzgerald, Spiegel, and Cunningham (1991), in a study of low- and high-income parents, reported that low-income families rated the value of education higher than the high-income families.

Another important difference among parents concerns their concepts of literacy. Goldenberg, Reese, and Gallimore (1992) found that low-income Hispanic parents help their children

Every teacher hopes for a class full of students whose parents have fostered literacy growth at home.

acquire literacy mainly by emphasizing letter names and spelling–sound corre-spondences. Similarly, Baker et al. (1994) reported that low income parents spend much time explicitly instructing their children in the work and practice elements of reading, whereas middle-income parents use a more playful approach involv-ing stories and play. Literacy is presented and modeled as an enjoyable pastime and an important lens through which to understand the world. Knowing that this difference might exist, it seems that it would be helpful for teachers to emphasize to all parents that children for whom literacy learning is painful tend to avoid books and reading, whereas children who learn to enjoy reading for its own sake are more likely to ask for books and to read recreationally, thus becoming more successful readers (Baker, Serpell, & Sonnenschein, 1995).

Teachers should be aware that nearly all parents participate in some literacy activities with their children. True, some parents may have problems reading and writing, or English may not be their first language, but nearly all engage in a wide range of literacy activities in the course of their daily lives. In his data, Barton (1997) found many examples of parents who experience difficulties with written communication who nonetheless kept diaries, maintained household accounts, wrote poetry, took phone messages, and sent letters. These parents dealt with shopping lists, bills, forms, recipes, junk mail, and TV schedules. Such parents should not be perceived as unintelligent people living in barren homes "waiting to be filled up by literacy," as the media might lead us to believe. For the most part, adults who admit having problems with reading and writing are ordinary people leading ordinary lives, and if they have children, like everyone else, they are deeply concerned about their children's education.

Key partners in literacy with the schools include mothers, fathers, sib-lings, and other relations and family friends that children cite as important in their literacy lives. In addition, focusing exclusively on parent–child relations excludes important social agencies and community resources that may enhance literacy behaviors. Educators have also moved beyond the notion that parents should read only to young children and have recognized that children of all ages—from infancy up to the teenage years—can benefit significantly from lit-eracy practices carried out at home. Parents can learn from their children, too! Literacy learning can be a symbiotic event within families. Finally, rather than asking parents to replicate what is done in school, educators are now trying to support the practices parents are already doing in their homes to promote literacy (Barton, 1997).

HELPING PARENTS WHO CANNOT READ

More than 44 million adults lack sufficient literacy skills to read a food label, fill out a job application, or even read a simple storybook to their child (National Center for Education Statistics, 2008). The obvious proactive response to this statistic would be to invite illiterate parents to functional literacy classes to prepare them to foster literacy skills in their own children. However, given the life situations of most illiterate parents, who often also are the "working poor"—long hours at work, time restrictions, lack of resources and reliable transportation, to name a few—a great majority of parents enrolled in literacy programs never complete the course. Given the difficulty for these parents of becoming literate in a timely manner, are there still strategies teachers can share with parents so that they can help their children in their own quests for literacy?

Following are some suggestions that can be offered to parents who, though they may have limited English literacy skills, want to help their own children succeed at becoming proficient readers (Cooter, 2006).

dialogic reading ■ **Introduce them to dialogic reading.** In **dialogic reading,** the child selects a picture storybook he or she can read independently. The child then leads a discussion about the pictures in the book. The parent merely listens and uses "what" or "why" questions, elaborates on what the child says, points, and gestures at items on the printed page but takes the position of "follower" in the book conversation (American Library Association, 2005). Ideally, parents should be taught to use a book in this language-rich way. Fortunately, the American Library Association holds parent training sessions and can assist teachers in locating trainers through the Every Child Ready to Read@Your Library program. For more information, log on to their website at www.ala.org.

www.

www.ala.org

Create make-believe-alouds. If parents are not able to read aloud to their children, they can still foster a love for reading and language using this cross between story reading and storytelling. A parent needn't even know the words on a page to take a picture storybook or wordless book and, using the illustrations as a guide, create an imaginative tale that captivates the young reader's attention. Morgan and Goldstein (2004) found that inviting illiterate parents to create stories to accompany picture books in this fashion significantly increased the quality of the language interactions.

Nearly all caregivers, even those who experience difficulties with literacy themselves, participate in some literacy activities with their children.

Build on what the parent can do—talk. Whether in English or the parent's home language, parents can be encouraged to share songs, family stories, oral traditions, and so forth. Simply by talking and listening, parents can do much to help their children with literacy. Also, parents can be urged to speak in longer sentences in any conversation with their children and to use complex or uncommon words to the child, explaining their meaning through demonstrations or pictures. Indeed, the mother's "mean length of utterance" (MLU), or the average words spoken together to the child, has been found to be predictive of that child's later language development (Murray, 1990).

Teachers may offer these suggestions to parents during parent–teacher conferences, workshops, or home visits.

COMMUNICATING WITH PARENTS

good communication between the home and the school right from the start of the school year is essential to any comprehensive literacy program for the early grades. The triangulation of home/school communication must be established early so that families and schools can work collaboratively to benefit the children most effectively. Edwards (2004) suggests that such strong collaborations "involve rethinking the relationship between home and school such that students' opportunities to learn are expanded" (p. 77). This occurs when teachers accept that parents define literacy and their role in supporting it in varying ways. Moreover, such collaborations depend on teachers becoming knowledgeable about the cultural diversity of the families of each of the children they teach and consider how such variations affect parent–teacher relationships.

Conferences

Because most educators are aware of the need for effective communication with parents, many schools schedule several parent–teacher conference days when teachers are available to talk with parents about the progress of their children. The parent–teacher conference can be a fruitful time during which the teacher explains to the parent, in clear terms, the components of the literacy program and how the child is progressing within the program. Moreover, it is the ideal time to communicate to parents that their partnership is needed to reinforce the notion on which a comprehensive literacy program is based: that literacy activities are important in the world and are enjoyable. After hearing about the literacy program, parents typically want to know how they can help their child at home.

What brings the parent to school? When both the school district and individual schools make a concerted effort to let parents know that "We want you, we need you, and we have valuable information to share with you about your child's literacy needs," they will come, if flexible scheduling makes attendance possible. Therefore, schools must take a positive approach and work with the strengths and needs of the families involved. Local radio and television stations as well as newspapers can help publicize the need for caring adults to meet with their children's teachers. In addition, the Chamber of Commerce can be asked to send letters to all area employers requesting that they release parents from work to attend partnership conferences.

Scheduling the conference

Conference scheduling is vitally important. Scheduling strategies should include not only a variety of options for parents but flexibility for teachers as well. It is essential that teachers offer some conference times early in the day, and some late, to accommodate those parents who cannot come to school during the regular school day. For this arrangement to be successful, the district's administrative unit must be fully committed to the partnership concept and arrange for the teachers to receive compensation for their efforts.

Guidelines for effective parent–teacher conferences

Parents are concerned about their children, but they may need reassurance that their concern is appropriate and that they are capable of taking part in the partnership. Consider the following points in this regard:

1. Set up the conference with the comfort of the parents in mind. Rather than sitting behind a desk as an authority figure, create an arrangement in which all adults can sit side by side.

2. Understand that parents and caregivers have a right to their anxiety. It is quite normal for them to wonder how their child compares with his or her peers.

3. Inform parents about their child's strengths and limitations while sympathizing with their concerns. "Don't worry" is a phrase that has little value and should be avoided.

4. Refrain from being judgmental; listen actively to parents, and always seek common ground. Instead of blaming them for what may not have occurred in the home, praise them for their concern and desire to help. This will engender a feeling of true partnership.

5. Focus on specific constructive suggestions rather than vague generalities. "Your child needs help hearing beginning sounds in words" is much more helpful than "Your child is not ready to learn to read."

6. Discuss the child's progress using examples such as progress forms, test results, or samples of the child's work.

7. Accept the parents' questions and provide clear, honest responses.

8. Suggest to the parents specific activities they can do at home, such as those described in a later section, to help the child with any deficiencies or to enhance reading interest and proficiency.

9. Thank the parents for attending and let the parents know that you are available for additional conferences if there are further concerns.

Conducting the conference

Conferences can be productive and pleasant for both the teacher and the parent if the teacher follows a few simple procedures. Begin the conference with a friendly and relaxed greeting to the parent. Adopt a tone of friendly acquaintance with the parent, reinforcing the idea in every way possible that you are both on the same team. If the parent speaks little or no English, arrange to have an aide or community member present who can translate, or invite an older English-speaking sibling to perform this important task. In advance, ask the child to teach you a few polite phrases ("How are you?" or "I am very pleased to meet you.") in her home language, so that you can make the parent feel welcome. Begin and end the conference on a positive note, addressing what is positive and unique about the child.

What parents should know about reading in the early grades

The most common query from parents during conferences crosses all ethnic, cultural, and socioeconomic levels. It is: "What can I do to help my child become a good reader?" The teacher can offer general advice based on practices that research has found to be helpful (as presented in the Research on

Home Literacy section earlier in this chapter), but parents are most interested in specific activities they can do with their children to help them succeed. In the past, teachers often suggested that parents drill children on the alphabet or help them with the sounds of letters. Many well-meaning parents became convinced that formal teaching of skills would help their children get a head start. As mentioned in the earlier section, the newer research on literacy suggests otherwise. When parents provide a rich literacy environment at home, instruction in literacy becomes easier for both the teacher and the child at school. Therefore, this becomes the most important message to deliver to parents. Because most children do not enter public school before age five and preschool before age three, if at all, schools need to take the responsibility of disseminating information in the community so that parents can put it into practice at home.

Parent Workshops

Parents able to attend workshops can benefit from information about activities they can undertake with their children to help build decoding and comprehension skills—and most important, to enjoy reading. Many teachers have had great success conducting two or three workshops during the academic year, each focusing on one activity. (See the following three activities for sample workshop activities.) Refreshments or a parent potluck draw many parents, and a format of simple instructions for the activity followed by practice in small groups bolsters parents' confidence to try the activity at home with their children.

Questioning

ACTIVITY

Encourage parents to follow up on critical-thinking strategies introduced in class by exploring at home the kinds of questions that extend and provoke critical and creative thinking. When children read at home, instruct parents to follow every paragraph or so with a thought-provoking question that cannot be answered with simply "yes" or "no." "Why do you think . . . ?" and "What if . . . ?" questions almost always fulfill these purposes. In a parent workshop, you might begin by brainstorming with parents a list of the kinds of questions that will be the most useful for expanding comprehension and then discuss the kind of responses they are likely to generate. Follow this preparation by giving each attendee a copy of a short story containing several paragraphs. Have parents contribute appropriate questions for each paragraph. Praise correct choices. If a contributed response is not appropriate, accept it, and then rework it into a useful question. For example, if a parent offers, "Did the boy go into the woods?" (and the answer is given in the paragraph), you can accept the answer and then slightly modify it to, "Why do you think the boy went into the woods?" The latter question requires the child to consider the data, compare them with what he or she knows of the world, and create an answer.

Parent Think-Aloud

Parents who already read with their children can extend the reading activity to become a comprehension-modeling practice by utilizing think-alouds. In a parent workshop, explain to parents that in this activity, as its name implies, the parent shares aloud everything he is thinking as a paragraph is read, including:

- making predictions (*"I bet Jerry will ask for his dog back."*)
- imaging (*"Ooh—that meadow reminds me of the field behind Mr. Darrow's farm where we used to hike, remember?"*)
- generalizing (*"So I guess these polar bears hibernate like the grizzlies we were reading about."*)
- using context to figure out the meaning of unknown words (*"It says the pancakes were huge and Tiny had a hard time finishing them. Since Tiny had a hard time eating them, I'll bet 'huge' means really big."*)

Using adult passages, model how a parent might do a think-aloud, slowing your thinking way down and offering a window to the brain for the benefit of the child. Invite parents to add their observations about the passages; praise comments that might lead to think-alouds that would be particularly helpful for children.

Pass out a passage to each attendee and have pairs of parents practice reading a paragraph out loud, sharing their meaning-gaining thought processes as they do so. Have them switch roles after each paragraph so that both parents get a chance to practice the technique. Finally, encourage parents to try this activity at home as part of shared reading. Explain that children can be invited to add their thoughts to those of their parents as they get the gist of the activity.

Dyad Reading

A third activity for parents is one that is especially effective for informational/expository text and, thus, will help parents to be of assistance when their child has reading to do in content areas such as science and social studies. Dyad reading can be explained to parents as a way to have their children read aloud and be sure they are understanding what they are reading. If only one text is available, as is often the case with content area textbooks, the parent and child will sit side by side and take turns reading aloud, rotating after every paragraph. When the reader has finished the paragraph, the reader summarizes it for the listener, who then adds any material that may have been overlooked by the reader. They then switch roles. To introduce this activity to parents, explain the steps as you model them with a partner or attendee who has been briefed in advance. It is helpful to model the activity using one text, as this is the way it will be used at home. However, for the purpose of the demonstration, the passage may be reproduced for the attendees. It may also be helpful to explain to parents that an effective summary is a shortened version of the original—no more than a third in length—that contains the main idea as well as important details. When you have answered questions about the steps of the procedure, hand out new expository passages to pairs of parents and have them practice doing dyad reading, rotating roles after each paragraph. Encourage them to use this technique at home whenever their child brings home homework in the content areas that requires reading.

Other Communication with Parents

Besides regularly scheduled conferences and workshops, teachers can keep parents informed in a variety of other ways, including newsletters, notes, and reading festivals.

Newsletters

A monthly, or even weekly, newsletter, perhaps in the form of an attractive, simply written flyer, can help explain the school's literacy program and help avoid misunderstanding and confusion that can be brought about by a zealous media that sometimes provides negative press about what goes on in the schools. The newsletter can also be a vehicle for conveying or reiterating suggestions for home reading. Additionally, any frequently asked questions can be addressed in the letter.

Progress notes

Progress notes are a more individualized way to keep parents informed about their child. At frequent intervals, short notes can be written about individual children, using a positive, congratulatory tone. A note might be written when a child has completed a book, asked an incisive question, or written an especially interesting piece. Such notes might also include a few open-ended questions for the parent to ask the child about a story that has been read in class or some vocabulary words to review with the child. The parent might also be asked to listen to the child read a passage from a recently finished book so the parent can share in the enjoyable experience of completing a book and celebrating success.

Reading festivals

Reading festivals provide a special opportunity, other than the formal parent–teacher conference, to bring parents to the school. Parents, children, and invited community members come together to share favorite books, articles, and stories. Any number of activities can be planned. Parents can be asked to bring in their favorite children's book to read with the class. Community members—especially those role models that youngsters do not ordinarily associate with reading, such as firefighters, sports figures, or police officers—can be invited to read with small groups of children. Choral reading can be done, with adults and children taking appropriate or reverse roles. Art activities, such as making and playing reading games or constructing dioramas or murals in connection with a favorite text, can be offered.

Reading festivals work well in collaboration with book fairs or book swaps. A book fair can be organized with the help of a local bookstore or a children's paperback book company, such as Scholastic. A book swap, on the other hand, requires less advance planning and can be arranged simply by asking children to bring in old books and magazines from home. Children can then take turns reading aloud the blurbs on the back covers before swapping the books. Teachers work with parents to match books to readers by interest and reading levels.

Family literacy night

family literacy night ∎

Families can come together for a special night of reading and writing together in a variation of the reading festival (Hutchins, Greenfeld, & Epstein, 2008). At a **family literacy night,** parents, relatives, and children read books together and participate in all sorts of reading-related activities. Children can perform readers theater scripts or their original drama, or they can dress up as their favorite book characters and answer questions about the book from the character's perspective. They can give book talks about their favorite texts or read poems, do choral readings, or puppet shows. Teachers can arrange to give away books through programs such as Reading Is Fundamental (RIF) for children to add to their home libraries. Finally, parents and children can write together, with paper products, computers, and other resources provided by the school or local libraries. Teachers can also use the opportunity at such an event to demonstrate one of the three workshop activities described earlier in the chapter.

READING ALOUD TO AND WITH CHILDREN

How to "raise a reader"

www.randomhouse.com/ kids/parents

parents can best help children develop reading literacy by reading to and with them. Research has shown that children who read early generally come from homes where reading materials are readily accessible (Sulzby & Teale, 2010). Additionally, early reading experiences provide children with at least three major concepts about text. These concepts—ultimate reasons for parents to read aloud to their children—should be shared with parents in a straightforward way. First, children come to see reading as pleasurable as they associate it with warm quality time with parents. Second, they learn about language and how it works. Through hearing common language patterns, children imitate new ways of communicating. Finally, children begin to understand that the purpose of reading is to make personal meaning from text and that a message is communicated through each sentence, story, and book. All these concepts are important foundations for literacy.

Teachers can suggest to parents that they provide library corners for their children, preferably in their bedrooms. Texts needn't be new—they can be purchased at garage sales or borrowed from the public library. The reading corner doesn't need to be large; it can even be made from cinder blocks and old wood. Virtually every room can hold reading material that is visible and accessible. Even before children are crawling or walking, books can be brought to their cribs and playpens; waterproof books are available for bath time.

Parents often need information about texts that are appropriate to read to their children. Figure 14.1 offers suggestions of reading materials for every age

AGE	TYPE OF READING MATERIAL
Birth–1 year old	Vinyl or cardboard books; colorful, large pictures; rhymes. Suggestion: *Mother Goose* (Candlewick, 1996).
1–2 years old	Washable cloth; animals and familiar objects; let child turn pages. Suggestion: *Pat the Bunny* (Childs Play, 1995).
2–3 years old	Nonsense, funny books; simple informational books; encourage child to pretend to read. Suggestion: *Henny Penny* (Galdone, 1984).
3–4 years old	Longer stories, fairy tales, folktales; how things work; repeated readings. Suggestion: *Mike Mulligan and His Steam Shovel* (Houghton Mifflin, 1977).
4–5 years old	Variety of books, informative, alphabet, predictable, wordless that tell a story. Suggestion: *Time Flies* (Crown, 1994).
5–6 years old	Predictable books where child can chime in; language play. Suggestion: *I'm a Caterpillar* (Scholastic, 1997).
7–9 years old	More plot development; informational; take turns reading. Suggestion: *Hattie and the Fox* (Bradbury, 1987).

Adapted from Neuman and Celano, 2001.

figure 14.1 Age-appropriate reading materials.

from birth to third grade. Additional suitable texts for parents to share with their children are listed in Appendix A.

See Appendix A

OTHER SUGGESTIONS FOR PARENTS

most of the information and activities presented so far in this chapter focus on books. But books are not the only tools that can encourage children to read, nor do children have to read only books to be considered literate. Following are other ways parents can help promote reading at home:

- Read cereal boxes, menus, place mats, street signs, coupons, junk mail, and other forms of print together.
- Point out and read familiar signs such as "Kmart," "Yield," "Exit," "Beware of Dog!" and so forth.
- Play guessing games such as "I spy with my little eye something beginning with a *b* or a /b/ sound."

Reading aloud to infants and toddlers

Parents often ask teachers and librarians, "When should I begin reading aloud to my child?" The answer is: "From birth!" Parents should be told that reading with their child builds language skills and stimulates the imagination. It introduces children to art through the illustrations, and it instills positive associations with reading. Infants and toddlers who have been read to typically become proficient readers earlier and thus perform better in school.

The following are suggested guidelines for reading with children of various ages. Parents should be aware, however, that each child has his or her own personality and rate of development.

INFANT: 0–6 MONTHS

- Talk to your baby as you go about your day.
- Share lullabies, songs, and rhythmic activities.
- Read aloud with the baby on your lap, in a high chair, or even while the child is lying on the floor.
- Stories should focus on sounds and bold pictures.

INFANT: 6–12 MONTHS

- Select vinyl or sturdy cardboard books. At this age, babies are teething and put everything into their mouths.
- Select books with built-in sound effects, or make your own sound effects. Vary your tone of voice.

- The tactile sense becomes important at this age. Select books with different textures.
- Babies this age like to look at pictures of other babies and familiar objects.
- As the baby can now focus, help guide her hand to point to pictures as you read about them.

TODDLER: 12–18 MONTHS

- Choose participatory texts where the child can chime in with a refrain or help make animal noises.
- Toddlers may be beginning to make the connection between words and what they represent. Label objects and pictures.
- The child can begin to help turn the pages.
- Keep some durable books in a special place where the child can reach them on his own.

TODDLER: 18–24 MONTHS

- Select texts that require more and more participation from the child.
- Point to pictures in books and invite the child to label what she sees.
- Praise correct responses and quickly tell the child a word that she needs or doesn't seem to be able to say.
- Read a favorite book again and again if it is requested.

- Sing songs, nursery rhymes, raps, and chants.
- Share newspapers, magazines, and websites of an appropriate level, and encourage children to pick out certain words from advertisements.
- Provide a quiet time each evening, when TV and video games are not allowed and the child is encouraged to read.

FAMILY LITERACY PROGRAMS

t he ways in which parents interact with their child are paramount to fostering the child's literacy abilities, but some parents may require more assistance than can be offered by teachers in a traditional school-based workshop. Research increasingly supports the notion that the necessary parent–child interactions are often more complex than just reading together and the parent providing the child with literacy materials. In fact, there is evidence to suggest that simply telling a parent to read to a child may be counterproductive and lead to behavior quite different from what the teacher intended, depending on the background of the parent (Mikulecky, 1996).

To address this growing concern, the federal government has begun to set up various family literacy programs, such as Even Start, designed both to increase the literacy skills of the parents and to provide positive strategies and attitudes for fostering their child's literacy at home. Projects involve participants who are speakers of English as a first or second language and are located in a variety of settings, such as libraries, schools, universities, or family centers. A wide variety of activities takes place, ranging from discussions to training in positive parent–child interactions, as well as direct teaching of literacy skills for the parent, leading to the attainment of a high school diploma.

In literacy programs aimed at both children and adults, there are varying perspectives on what family literacy should be. Most initiatives reflect what most adult participants feel they need to help their children become literate, and many also stress the vital role of the community in education. Family literacy, in general, can provide assistance to adults in a way that isn't constrained by intimidating traditions of formal education and, instead, actually draws upon the existing funds of knowledge the family already possesses. Most educators working with families realize that there is no single road to becoming literate and that they must seek the help of the parents to ascertain what positive practices already occur in the home.

It appears that long-term, community-based family literacy programs can be an important adjunct to the relationship the classroom teacher builds with the parent. The classroom teacher can support such programs by acknowledging that literacy's domain is not exclusively in the public schools.

TROUBLESHOOTING

family literacy programs aim to get parents the help they need to develop general literacy interactions at home. But what about parents with whom the teacher has been totally unable to communicate? Certainly, the value of the parent–teacher conference as a venue for discussing specific issues related to the progress of pupils' literacy cannot be underestimated. Therefore, the means for addressing several factors that preclude some parents' attendance at school functions are discussed in the following sections.

Flexible Scheduling

Most schools have several parent–teacher days, during which teachers are available to talk with parents about their child's progress. Although this can be an ideal opportunity to focus on the child's literacy, some parents work during the day and for various compelling reasons are not able to take time off to attend these sessions. Because it is inappropriate—and impossible—for teachers to evaluate parents' priorities and work responsibilities, some schools respond

Today's parents need to be involved in the technologies that play a large role in literacy learning.

to the problem with flexible scheduling. As mentioned earlier in this chapter, scheduling some conference slots later in the day or in the evening (with teachers having the morning to prepare) has been helpful in many schools; these schools report success in reaching parents who had previously not attended conferences because of job conflicts.

Home Visits

Some parents may be reluctant to attend school functions, because they feel uncomfortable in the school environment. They themselves may not have done well in school, and for them anything related to school holds unpleasant memories—much as the dentist's office does for those who suffered painful extractions as a child. Also, parents from certain cultural groups may hold the teacher in such high esteem that they may feel ashamed of being unfamiliar with the language and customs associated with the formal academic environment and fear embarrassing themselves. Because parents in these situations are most often the ones teachers most want to see with regard to their child's literacy habits and attitudes, it can be helpful for the teacher initially to go to the family's home. A handwritten note or brief telephone call saying the teacher will be in the area on a certain day and requesting permission to stop by for a chat is rarely refused. During this visit, nothing educational need be discussed; the teacher should look for common ground with the parent, often found in the adults' common care and concern for the child. A teacher's warm and down-to-earth attitude often forges an initial rapport that makes the parents' attendance at the next conference more likely. If the parents are non–English speakers, a teacher may take along a speaker of the parents' language if available.

Common Language

A third possible barrier for parents is the tendency on the part of many teachers to use the technical "jargon" of literacy with parents. Parents may refrain from attending meetings about their child because they believe they would not be astute enough to understand the teacher's "educated language." It may in fact be true that, in an effort to position the field of education as a "true" profession, educators have acquired a vocabulary of very specific literacy terminology. Lack of "phonemic awareness," for instance, could be replaced in discussions with parents by "a problem hearing sounds in words." Then a clear explanation of the child's problem, how it is being corrected in class, and how the parent might best help the child at home, will ensure the parents' comprehension. Other literacy terms can also be discussed in laymen's terms, of course, with the same result—that the parents understand what the teacher is talking about and feel more able to help. Inviting parents to be true partners in the education of their child requires communication between parents and teachers as equals.

SUMMARY

there is a pressing need for primary classrooms to use children's home literacies as the foundation for literacy instruction. We also need to communicate to parents how much they are needed as valuable partners in their children's literacy growth. Teachers do not always appreciate just how much communication and sensitivity is required to make this relationship work so that there is true synergy between home and school. Teachers often need to be the primary movers, envisioning innovative ways to get parents—from all cultural and linguistic backgrounds—to school. In some cases, a home visit is more appropriate.

Teachers should strive to help parents feel at ease by talking to them in clear terms about the progress of their child and explaining the most effective ways to reinforce the goals of a comprehensive literacy program at home. Be aware of current research that indicates that parents, regardless of income level or educational background, care deeply about their children's success in literacy and need only to be guided to the best practices for augmenting the school's literacy program. Finally, teachers need to explore family literacy programs in their communities that teach parents both to help their children read and write and to further their own educational achievement. Such programs add another dimension to the parent–school partnership, demonstrating for parents and children that the entire community sees literacy as a positive and worthwhile goal.

questions
for journal writing and discussion

1. Interview members of your family or friends who are raising young children. Ask them to discuss specific activities they have done on a daily basis with their children to promote literacy. Collect ideas from other members of your class and put them together in a pamphlet. If possible, arrange to have this pamphlet available at your field placement school to hand out to parents.

2. Develop an argument to counter that of someone who believes that children from poor families always come to school with fewer literacy experiences than middle-class youngsters. Cite research contained in this chapter to bolster your argument.

3. Using the memories of your own family life as a young child, discuss some activities that you feel helped your literacy development. Include any books or materials that you especially remember.

suggestions

for projects and field activities

1. Obtain permission to sit in on one or more conferences between a parent and a teacher in your field experience. Note the following:

   ■ How did the teacher make the parent feel welcome?

   ■ What did the teacher tell the parent about the child's literacy progress?

   ■ What, if anything, did the teacher share with the parent about activities that could be undertaken at home to enhance the child's literacy development?

   ■ What specific questions, if any, did the parent have about her child's literacy development? How were these questions addressed?

2. Using the Internet, search for a parents and literacy website, or use one suggested in Appendix C. Evaluate the contents of the website as to how helpful you think the information might be to parents who wish to help their child with literacy.

See Appendix C ▶

chapter
15

The Early Literacy Classroom

Orchestrating a Comprehensive Program

focus questions

- What are the most important considerations when planning a comprehensive early literacy program?

- What is the best classroom climate for a comprehensive literacy program?

- How can the schedule be arranged so that time for literacy instruction is maximized?

It is the first week of September, and Mrs. Ramon is just getting to know her new class. The 22 children are from four diverse language groups and have entered her first-grade class with an overwhelming array of linguistic, cultural, and socioeconomic backgrounds and emotional needs. For example, Hoa comes from a Vietnamese-speaking home, having arrived in California with her family when she was 13 months old. Her father is deceased, and her mother is currently unemployed and speaks very little English, although she has recently begun attending English classes. Hoa's personal linguistic and cultural data pool is Vietnamese—totally different from most of the class. Responsible for two younger siblings, Hoa has grown up quickly. Although she interacts verbally to a small extent with her mother, her invalid grandmother, and her church community in Vietnamese, the time she spends engaging in language activities in her home language is limited.

On the other hand, Lisa comes from an English-speaking home, and her parents are both professionals in the field of education. She attended a neighborhood preschool for two years before entering public school. Lisa has had a wealth of encounters with English, listening to and interacting with her parents and older brother, singing nursery rhymes at preschool, learning to spell her name, listening to a variety of stories read to her every night, and having all her questions patiently answered and elaborated upon by the many indulgent adults around her.

INTRODUCTION

It is three weeks later, and we re-enter Mrs. Ramon's class. During math and science, where hands-on activities are taking place, Hoa sits in the middle of a small group of English-speaking children who chatter to her about the task at hand—observing air pressure in a balloon. Hoa still knows very little English, but there are three other Vietnamese-speaking children in the class, and during journal writing time, they sit together, conversing in Vietnamese as they draw pictures.

The book *Stone Soup* was the focus of the classroom last week. The teacher read the story several times with much miming and dramatization, once using a flannel board to demonstrate the key events in the story. Even Hoa shyly chimed in on the repetitive refrain, "Soup from a stone? Fancy *that!*" Hoa has picked up the words *stone* and *soup* and the names of an assortment of common vegetables from the repetition afforded by this engaging tale; and these words are showing up in the pictures in her journal, as evidenced when she colors a large purple turnip. When Mrs. Ramon asks Hoa about her pictures, she names some items in English as well as Vietnamese. The entire class stops what they are doing to celebrate Hoa's initial spoken words in English. Mrs. Ramon smiles warmly at the little girl and writes some abbreviated anecdotal notes about her amazing progress on her tablet.

Lisa, in another corner of the room, prefers to labor alone, following her unique writing agenda. She pens the words *cat*, *mat*, and *hat* very neatly in her journal. When asked if she can write a story using some new words on the word wall, she does not answer but begins a second column, chirping to no one in particular, "I'll do *et* words now," as she begins to write the words *wet*, *get*, *met*, and *set*. Then she begins to write a story about a man who met a cat, spelling these words correctly and using the sounding-out strategies she knows to spell mostly the surface sounds of others. When the teacher comes around, Lisa is able to read all the words of her story upon request. Mrs. Ramon grins as she jots anecdotal notes on her tablet about Lisa's current successes, but she also notes that Lisa seems overly concerned that everything she writes must be neat and spelled correctly, thus reducing the growth that occurs when children explore and feel free to take risks.

Hoa and Lisa are developing literacy skills at very different yet appropriate rates, because Mrs. Ramon is supporting their individual growth patterns with self-selection of literacy activities, wise grouping, and careful attention to their unique needs. This teacher knows that Hoa is developing her oral comprehension in English by listening to a group of fluent English-speakers discuss what they are doing with concrete objects. Also, she recognizes that drawing instead of writing allows Hoa to talk about what she knows in two languages. Seeing her participate in the refrain of a story, Mrs. Ramon understands the child is also learning that writing can tell a story—one that she can access because of the entertaining visuals. On the other hand, the teacher is trying to encourage Lisa to move beyond what she can do perfectly and to grow as a writer by taking some risks.

The remainder of this final chapter will explore how Mrs. Ramon provides a balanced, comprehensive, literacy program for *all* of her students by creating a climate conducive to learning, using literacy materials appropriate for her learners, and maximizing the limited available instructional time.

A CLASSROOM CLIMATE CONDUCIVE TO LITERACY

mrs. Ramon is the most requested teacher at the elementary school where she teaches, partly because the children all seem to love her, but mostly because parents are certain their children will learn to read and write by the end of the school year. Although education never comes with a guarantee, Mrs. Ramon stops just short of a promise to teach every child in her class to read and write by June. How does she do it?

The answer to that question lies, at least in part, in the way she makes decisions about classroom instruction. Mrs. Ramon has spent the past few years developing a comprehensive literacy program that includes the systematic, explicit development of decoding skills, yet manages to retain the exploration, engagement, and joy of a more child-centered, holistic approach to instruction. Any changes in her classroom are usually precipitated by a combination of three factors: (1) her ongoing assessment of her learners tells her change is in order; (2) she reads about a strategy or observes an activity that she feels would be beneficial in her class; (3) she has read research in respected literacy journals such as *The Reading Teacher* that provides convincing evidence that a literacy practice she is considering is effective and should be tried. As an example of her responsiveness to research, Mrs. Ramon explains to us that she studiously avoids the following practices that experts say make learning to read more difficult for children.

Teachers are challenged to create a classroom climate that fosters the joy of literacy and learning.

PRACTICES TO AVOID

1. emphasizing only phonics instruction
2. drilling children endlessly on isolated letters or sounds
3. making sure that children perform correctly or not at all
4. focusing on the one "best" answer
5. making perfect oral reading the most important literacy goal
6. focusing on skills at the expense of comprehension
7. using workbooks with every reading lesson
8. always grouping according to ability
9. following the basal without making adjustments
10. expecting children to spell perfectly all the words they read

Another reason Mrs. Ramon is so successful undoubtedly has much to do with the positive classroom climate she has achieved. Four environmental factors immediately stand out when one enters her classroom. Let's examine them.

Print Saturation

The factory-like school building in this urban neighborhood is in desperate need of repair, but the visitor entering Mrs. Ramon's first-grade classroom is struck at once by how enticing it is—in sharp contrast to the grim environment outside. Both bulletin boards in the room are colorfully adorned with the written work and art of the children, and lively mobiles extending from the ceiling attest, in bold print, to the attributes of each learner in the class. Glancing around the room, the visitor observes a wide variety of print, including labels on the arts and crafts work, labels on each item in the room, charts, several word walls, written questions about objects the children have brought in, a diversity of commercially produced books, and even more texts written and published by the children. Visitors are struck, also, by how children are conversing about the tasks at hand at frequent intervals throughout the day. It seems that all day long the children are immersed in reading, writing, listening, speaking, viewing, and visually representing—offering all children an abundance of opportunity to fill their personal linguistic data pools. Mrs. Ramon knows that to be a culturally relevant teacher, she must use knowledge about the social, cultural, and language backgrounds of her students to support their success (Ladson-Billings, 2009; Morrison, Robbins, & Rose, 2008).

Demonstrations

Showing children the intricacies of literacy is a tenet of comprehensive instruction and is far more potent than merely telling them about it (Weaver, 1998). There are many opportunities in Mrs. Ramon's classroom for demonstrations of how language and print work. When the teacher writes a label in front of the children to accompany their latest craft work, she sounds out the word for them, asking them to volunteer sounds they know, and offering explanations about new sounds and sound combinations. When she writes a short story summary in front of the children, thinking aloud as she decides what to say and how to spell the words, she demonstrates how drafts are written, how to deal with unknown spellings, how to scour the environment for words, and how reading, writing, and spelling are interrelated. When she rereads her writing, she shows the children how to edit and proofread and why it is sometimes necessary to rewrite. When Mrs. Ramon conducts a shared reading lesson, she demonstrates how written language is read, what punctuation marks are for, what to do when you don't know a word, what sounds the various symbols make, and so forth. Finally, by reading daily to children, Mrs. Ramon shows that she thinks reading is enjoyable and worth setting aside time for. By selecting informational texts as well as storybooks, she introduces children to different purposes for reading.

High Expectations

Teachers who allow children to make decisions about their own learning are usually more successful than those who make all the decisions autocratically. Mrs. Ramon expects all of her students to learn and to take responsibility for many decisions about their own learning. To enable students to meet her high expectations, Mrs. Ramon gives the children plenty of opportunities to take risks and experiment without fear of failure. She encourages them to be confident and to use the decoding strategies they know to take calculated guesses at unknown words when reading. She often allows them to choose their own writing topics and texts to read during free reading time. She expects them to formulate hypotheses about written language through trial and error and make many mistakes as they experiment with experimental spelling. Although she expects children to be conscientious about checking the spelling of words they have been taught, Mrs. Ramon does *not* presume that children's writing should always be perfect—especially in initial drafts.

Teacher Feedback

Successful teacher–student interactions are probably the key to literacy learning for children from diverse backgrounds (Au, 1997). Mrs. Ramon interacts with all her children about their reading, writing, speaking, listening, viewing, and visually representing in such a way that her feedback is both supportive and instructive to her learners; she also insists that children respond to each other's work in this positive and respectful way. Moreover, this teacher is careful never to communicate that some tasks are achievable by certain children but not others. To that end, Mrs. Ramon uses a flexible grouping system so that children do not feel stigmatized by consistent placement in low-ability groups. At various times during the day, she

Teacher feedback to children about their reading and writing should be positive and supportive.

may have children arranged into skill groups, literature circles, reading buddies, peer editing groups, cooperative groups, and jigsaw groups (see Chapter 11).

Mrs. Ramon's interactions with her students may take the form of a whole-class lesson, a minilesson, a small group activity, or a one-to-one conference. Whatever form the interaction takes, Mrs. Ramon's response is immediate and always emanates from her careful observation of her students.

ORGANIZING THE CLASSROOM ENVIRONMENT

the quality of the classroom environment has received considerable attention in recent years as teachers have become increasingly aware of the need to *invite* children to learn in an organized fashion. The physical arrangement of the classroom is crucial because children must have plenty of room and a range of appropriate materials to be able to experiment with literacy, independently and in small groups. Thus, one of the most immediate concerns of beginning and experienced teachers before their learners ever arrive in September should be the arrangement of the classroom space, so that it is conducive to effective and enjoyable learning. As teachers plan layouts that will suit their classroom activities, they often begin very simply and cautiously. Later, as the need arises, they tend to subdivide the classroom into functional work areas for accomplishing specific literacy tasks and to make more detailed instructional plans.

Room Arrangement

Mrs. Ramon, the first-grade teacher we have been visiting, has several useful areas in her classroom. The largest is a whole-class learning and sharing area. Mrs. Ramon has just brought in a slightly threadbare but brightly colored carpet for children to sit on when they use this area; this new feature has created quite a stir during shared reading time. Other areas in this teacher's classroom are quiet writing and publishing areas, a silent reading area with an overstuffed couch and beanbag chairs, reading conference areas in both corners, appealing display areas for books and artwork, and ample storage areas. Mrs. Ramon sees to it that areas for storing books, magazines, and other reading materials are attractive and well lit. Each area in the classroom is clearly labeled with neatly printed signs. Mrs. Ramon has learned, through experience, that neatness is important, because these very labels become models for children's written products and provide them with an opportunity for environmental reading.

Mrs. Ramon spends several weeks at the end of each summer considering how best to rearrange her classroom. A major objective of the physical design in her classroom has always been to create the optimal physical surroundings

Children thrive on language play, drama, puppetry, and other oral and receptive language activities.

for children to learn from the environment and from each other. Each year she makes physical adjustments in her classroom as she reflects on a grouping arrangement that didn't work well or as she decides to borrow a learning center idea from another teacher. For Mrs. Ramon, the flow of traffic seemed to be a problem last year. Therefore, classroom furnishings in her room this year are expressly chosen and positioned to facilitate easy movement between classroom areas, provide access to necessary materials and a clear view of the whiteboards, and create specific areas for demonstrations and small-group work. (See Figure 15.1 for this room layout.)

Literacy Materials

If teachers make wise choices in the selection of literacy materials, literacy instruction can be made easier. Over the 11 years that she has been teaching, Mrs. Ramon has amassed a rich variety of materials, supplies, and books, and she has carefully organized and stored them so that they are readily accessible to her students. *Manipulative,* or *hands-on, materials* are a standard feature in her classroom, as in most primary classrooms, but in this classroom literacy materials are viewed with equal respect because this teacher is aware that manipulating the tools of literacy production—pencils, paper, books, and the like—is a valuable part of children's early sound-to-symbol learning. Although most furniture, such as tables and desks, is standard in primary classrooms, teachers can sometimes requisition other items they feel would enhance their literacy programs. The materials listed in Figure 15.2 are what Mrs. Ramon considers the "bare essentials" for an emergent literacy classroom.

Mrs. Ramon's classroom.   *figure* **15.1**

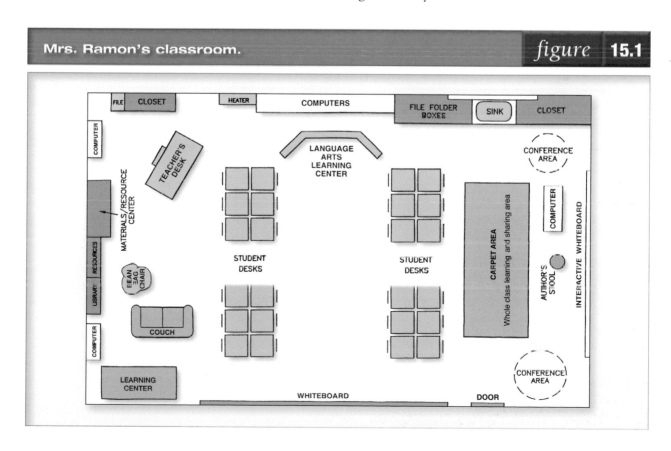

figure **15.2**   **Essentials for an emergent literacy classroom.**

FURNITURE

Teacher's desk and chair and a table
    at which to work privately with the children

Desks or tables and chairs for each child

READING MATERIAL

Trade books at different reading levels

Wordless books and picture storybooks

Multicultural and multiethnic trade books

Phonemic awareness materials

Connected texts at different reading levels

Predictable and patterned texts

Student-authored books

E-books

Song books

Magazines

Other printed material (e.g., catalogs, brochures, menus)

Informational texts

Diagnostic tools

Comic books

ENVIRONMENTAL PRINT/DISPLAY SPACE

Calendar

Teacher- and student-produced charts

Commercially produced charts

Signs and labels designating areas of the classroom

Notices to students and parents

Samples of children's work

Artwork with dictation or written comments

Letter charts with graphic reference material

Rules, class helper assignments, fire drill information,
    and so forth

WRITING SUPPLIES

Many kinds of paper

Old envelopes and stationery

Many kinds of writing utensils

Alphabet stamps

Letter stencils

Staples, tape, and glue for bookmaking

Manipulative letters and letter stencils

Mini-chalkboards or whiteboards

Pocket charts and sentence strips

STORAGE SPACES

Storage space for supplies, accessible to children

Storage space just for teacher

Book storage spaces
- bookcases
- revolving book racks for paperbacks
- crates

Cubbies for children's belongings

Storage space for children's work
- crates for file folders and learning center materials
- teacher file cabinet
- homework cubbies

OTHER SUPPLIES/EQUIPMENT

Objects to observe and write about

Materials for experimentation, observation,
    and writing

Art supplies

Puppets

Flannel board

Digital camera/video camera

Computers

Globes, maps, atlases

Science and math equipment

Easels to hold chart paper, big books

Bulletin boards to display children's work

Educational games and software

TV, DVD player

Whiteboard/interactive whiteboard

Microphone and speakers

DEVISING AN INSTRUCTIONAL PLAN

perhaps the most determinative decisions in setting up the classroom relate to wise use of the limited amount of time available (Allington, 1991). Mrs. Ramon admits that she feels more and more pressured each year to cover the vast amount of material and topics she believes are vital for her learners. Thus, each year she, like most teachers, must adjust her instructional schedule and make weighty decisions about what information to discard and what to add to an already overcrowded curriculum.

When making these decisions, Mrs. Ramon keeps in mind the four components of an emergent literacy curriculum she believes are the keys to her students' success in learning about print; each provides support for her learners' continued growth in reading, writing, listening, and speaking. Mrs. Ramon will not negotiate about or compromise any of the following components:

1. direct systematic instruction in phonics and other supportive reading groups

2. language experience approach stories and expository pieces

3. extensive writing and composing experiences

4. a variety of opportunities for oral discussions, language play, drama, puppetry, and other oral and receptive language activities

With these essentials firmly in mind, Mrs. Ramon sets up a schedule of daily instructional activities. Although unplanned events (fire drills, assemblies, absences, guest speakers, parties) often interfere with this plan, an observer in the room could expect to see a day similar to the one described in the box beginning on the following page. Let's make a hypothetical visit. Some of the strategies and tools discussed previously are boldfaced.

Even young readers and writers benefit from extensive and varied literacy experiences.

A day in Mrs. Ramon's classroom

Mrs. Ramon's class is self-contained and heterogeneously grouped. The instructional day begins at 8:30 and ends at 3:00. No specific time was assigned during our visit for pull-out or special programs such as art, music, physical education, or recess.

8:30–8:40 As we enter the room, we notice the children going about their daily business of communicating with one another and writing notes to each other and to the teacher, which they put in each other's mailboxes designed expressly for this purpose. They also eagerly listen to the digital morning message playing on the interactive whiteboard, written and recorded by Mrs. Ramon before they arrived. Then they read the message chorally. This message tells them about some enjoyable activity they can look forward to during the day or asks them a thought question. This morning's message asks, "Are you more like the sun or the rain?" Children immediately begin discussing this with partners. While these activities are going on, Mrs. Ramon takes a few moments to do a **running record** and **story retelling** with individual children, using a daily rotation.

8:40–9:00 The whole class now congregates on the carpet to discuss the oversized calendar. Using this prop, they discuss the weather; mark in a symbol for rain; and chant the month, the day of the week, and the date. They pledge allegiance to the flag and sing a favorite song of the children's choosing. This day the choice is "Hooray for the World!" by Red Grammer. Every child seems to know the words, but Mrs. Ramon has them written on the whiteboard and points to each one as it is sung, to reinforce the connection between written and spoken language. As the teacher takes attendance, she features the beginning sound of the day—/fr/—and applies it to every child's first name, **"the name game."** For example, *Nancy*

becomes *Francy, Jennifer* becomes *Frennifer,* and so forth. This lively language game is followed by a brief session of **interactive writing.**

9:00–9:05 Before their **shared reading lesson,** Mrs. Ramon does a brief review of the **phonics** components introduced yesterday, two different ways to represent /j/ (*j* and *dge*). The teacher holds up the **word cards** for *jam, badge, jump, ledge, fudge,* and *jar.* She asks for volunteers to say each word. When a child says the word correctly, that child puts the word in the **pocket chart** and then helps Mrs. Ramon sound out **(segment)** the word on the board. Finally, the teacher reads the nursery rhyme "Jack be nimble Jack be quick," asking them to chant it with her, raising a quiet hand every time they hear a word with a /j/.

Tomorrow Mrs. Ramon will have some children do a closed **word sort,** asking partners to sort a series of pictures representing words containing either *j* or *dge.* Other children will look in magazines for pictures containing these two sound representations. After much discussion of the words that have been found and how they fit in the children's chosen pattern, children will then be invited to put their discoveries on the **word wall** under the appropriate column.

9:05–9:55 For the **shared reading lesson,** children in Mrs. Ramon's room move into three different groups; these groups are flexible and change frequently, depending on the activity. Today the teacher is ready to do the first rereading of the **big book** *My Friends* by Taro Gomi, from the first-grade **basal reader** (Macmillan/McGraw-Hill). Four children who need extra reinforcement will be tracking the text as they listen to a recording of *My Friends* at one of the computers; several other children need no further work with this story and are provided with a more challenging trade book that comes with the basal series, *Grandfather Bear Is Hungry,* a Russian folktale retold by Margaret Read MacDonald. These children will **dyad read,** taking turns reading or summarizing a page of text. The remaining 14 children participate in a **shared rereading** of the text in which Mrs. Ramon demonstrates left to right orientation as she reads and points out punctuation marks at the end of sentences. Since this group is preparing to learn the *ap* rime, Mrs. Ramon stops at the page that says, "I learned to nap from my friend the crocodile." She frames the word *nap* with a **word mask,** calling the children's attention to it. They orally stretch out the word and say it several times together. She asks a variety of **comprehension questions** during this rereading, asking how the girl feels about learning to walk from a cat, what they think the girl likes to do best, and so forth.

After finishing the rereading of this book, the children are asked to act out different action words in the book, such as jumping like a dog, marching like a rooster, and napping like a crocodile. This activity not only lends enjoyment and appreciation to the story but also adds new words to the vocabulary of the English learners in the class.

Tomorrow children will be given a small **decodable text** containing many of the same phonic elements, such as the *ap* rime, to read independently and then **partner read.** Such a successful experience with the already introduced phonic elements will help reinforce these sounds in a real reading context, providing valuable practice with easily decoded text.

9:55–10:00 The above lesson ends with a five-minute (usually less) **phonics lesson** on *ap.* The teacher models sounding out several words with the same rime: *nap, map, cap, rap,* and *tap,* stretching out the sounds so the children can easily identify them. After doing this several times, individual children are encouraged to try it.

Tomorrow Mrs. Ramon plans to pass out individual whiteboards on which the children will write the letters as they stretch them out, holding up the whiteboards as they finish, so she can immediately assess how individuals are doing.

10:00–10:35 Writers' workshop is a natural extension of the reading lesson. After children procure their **writing folders** from their cubbies, Mrs. Ramon takes five minutes to do a minilesson on the use of capital letters at the beginning of sentences, as this is an area she has observed to be a concern with almost every child. She conducts this **minilesson** with the entire class, although such a lesson is often conducted for only the small group who has shown a particular need for it.

Mrs. Ramon then puts a writing prompt on the board: "A friend is _____." This sentence stem is not an assignment but only a writing option for those who are searching for a topic. After a very brief discussion about this topic, the children begin the writing process. Several children are in the **prewriting** stage and are researching their topic on the Internet from the list of sites provided by Mrs. Ramon. Some children begin **drafting;** others are illustrating previously written pieces. Some children are writing their pieces using word-processing software and inserting clip art that Mrs. Ramon helps them to download from the Internet, while other children are using Kidspiration to organize their ideas. Some children are sharing their ideas with a partner; others are offering feedback. **Peer editing conferences** and **teacher–student conferences** are occurring at tables set aside for this purpose. Mrs. Ramon, when she is not conferencing with individual children about their work, walks around helping others sound out words, observing, and taking **anecdotal notes** on their progress.

What amazes the observer in this classroom is how engaged the children are and how well they know the boundaries of the activities in which they may participate during writers' workshop. They know they are free to schedule their own time as long as they show progress toward their own goals.

10:35–11:35 Math instruction and practice activities. There is language involved in even this content area. Mrs. Ramon has a child do an addition problem on the board and then queries the other youngsters, "What is another way to think about that?" Four children respond by telling the others their differing ways of thinking about and solving the math problem. Mrs. Ramon shares with us that later in the year children will keep learning logs that summarize, in words, the concept that has been introduced, such as "Tell what you do when you add two numbers."

11:35–12:15 Lunch.

12:15–12:35 After lunch Mrs. Ramon always looks forward to **reading aloud** to her students. For this activity, she selects quality **children's literature** from a variety of genres, cultures, and styles, balancing informational and narrative text.

case example

Today the teacher shares the beautifully illustrated Caldecott medal winner, *Officer Buckle and Gloria* by Peggy Rathmann. Mrs. Ramon feels this is one of the most important times in the day. She is engaging children in a positive experience with literature, introducing new vocabulary, and often thinking aloud about many of her comprehension strategies as she reads. The children clearly enjoy this time too, and they are encouraged to draw as they listen, later sharing how their sketches tell about what is happening in the story.

12:35–1:35 This is the time for social studies, science, computer skills, health, or other content-area and instructional activities. Much speaking, listening, reading, writing, viewing, and visually representing are naturally integrated into these content areas. Today, following on the theme of friendship in the morning's story, Mrs. Ramon leads a multicultural social studies lesson, teaching the children, with the help of her linguistically diverse learners, to say "my friend" in the four different languages represented in the classroom. Children chant these words in the different tongues and then work on a poster showing themselves and a friend involved in an activity that portrays friendship. Finally, Mrs. Ramon shows children pictures taken from the Internet of scenes from cities in each of the four countries. Tomorrow Mrs. Ramon will have the children create a **word web** on friendship, brainstorming ideas and, perhaps, using those ideas in their journals.

1:35–1:45 Drop everything and read (DEAR) time is a critical time in each day. Children quickly and quietly get trade books, magazines, or other reading material from their desks or from the classroom library and begin reading silently. As this is a school-wide program, everyone in the school—from the principal to the janitor—stops what they are doing to read. Afterward, the teacher often invites the children to talk about what they are reading.

1:45–2:15 Mrs. Ramon works on **spelling** and other literacy-related activities. These activities include **drama, word sorts,** word building activities, small- and large-group sharing of writing, learning center activities, or a combination of these experiences. This day, pairs of children give each other a **post-test** on their spelling words for the first 15 minutes. Then students correct their own errors by consulting their primary dictionaries. Many of the children then become involved in a **readers theater** production of *The Boy Who Cried Wolf,* a story the children had very much enjoyed and wish to act out. The children, having heard the story several times for the purpose of acting it out, have now created roles for everyone. Besides the boy, the wolf, the townspeople, the sheep, and the wise man, they have added parents, siblings, and a talking bird that tells the shepherd what to do. Every child has a speaking part that the teacher helps them write down so they have a rough "script" to memorize.

Other children choose to go to the table that has been turned into a **learning center,** with the theme "What is a friend?" In this physically appealing, specialized setting, children work on a series of tasks integrating a content area, such as social studies, with the language arts of reading, writing, listening, speaking, viewing, and visually representing. Through self-selected, individualized activities, the children seek answers to questions independently, such as "What does a friend do?" Each of the activities has been introduced by the teacher, yet the step-by-step instructions are also written on cards next to the individual activities. For example, one gives children the directions for making finger puppet friends. It asks them to create a dialogue with a partner to resolve a problem between two friends. Children later share their product with the larger group.

2:15–2:40 Children write in their **dialogue journals** while Mrs. Ramon goes around the room transcribing text for the few children who are still primarily drawing pictures. She encourages others to sound out the words they are attempting to spell. Mrs. Ramon always carries her tablet to take **anecdotal notes** on children's progress, in this case their understanding of the **alphabetic principle.** The children who finish early love to review previous entries and to revisit their teacher's responses. Mrs. Ramon gives written feedback in each child's journal at least once a week.

2:40–2:50 Mrs. Ramon again **reads aloud** to her students, often finishing a story from the earlier session. Since she completed the early afternoon story, she chooses to read a short expository piece from *Cricket* magazine containing new information about why dinosaurs disappeared from the

Earth. She tries to offer a variety of read-aloud materials, both expository and narrative, including genres from science fiction to folktales, to whet the appetite of these burgeoning readers and expose them to many types of material. To conclude, the teacher asks children to turn to a neighbor and tell one thing they learned about dinosaurs from listening to the piece.

2:50–3:00 Mrs. Ramon calls these final few moments in the school day "the day in review." She asks volunteers to share with the class what they consider to be the highlights of the day. She gains much insight into their young minds and sees, from their perspectives, what worked and what didn't. The children get a final oral language opportunity as Mrs. Ramon observes their comments. Children then do cleanup as necessary and receive their weekly **parent packets,** which contain material corresponding to what they have studied this day. The parents are asked to review the material with their children, sign the packet, and send it back

with their children the following day. This communication with parents enhances the literacy growth of the students, lets parents know what is happening in the classroom, and allows parents to assist in a positive way. The parent packet taken home by most of Mrs. Ramon's children this day is described in Figure 15.3. Other children may have more or less advanced assignments, according to their needs.

After the children have left, we notice that Mrs. Ramon immediately puts anecdotal notes in her children's work **portfolios.** She reflects on how she might offer interventions for the students who need them and how she might provide more challenge to others. Then she approaches to debrief us on her day of teaching, which, she intimates, has been physically and emotionally exhausting, as always. However, this remarkable teacher confesses, "I cannot imagine a profession that is more personally rewarding and more fun than turning children on to the joys of literacy."

case example

An example of a first-grade homework packet. *figure* **15.3**

Help your child practice the vocabulary words from *The Cat Has a Nap,* using the cards in this packet. This can be done in any of the following ways, whichever is most enjoyable for you and your child:

- Show your child the word cards and give them to him/her when they are said correctly.
- Have your child make sentences using the words on the cards.
- Have your child write a story with the words.
- Ask your child to spell the words as you say them.
- Put the cards on the table. Say a word and ask the child to identify the card with that word on it.

Then, please listen as your child reads from the book *The Cat Has a Nap.* Be sure your child's finger is under each word as it is read. Ask the child to read the story twice. Make sure the reading is a "treat," not a "treatment."

As always, please read daily to your child, preferably a text that your child has chosen. Please initial as completed.

Monday _____

Tuesday _____

Wednesday _____

Thursday _____

SUMMARY

throughout this book we have explored ways to teach literacy to early readers and writers. The approach described has been a comprehensive one, in which children receive the explicit, systematic instruction in phonics necessary to help them become automatic decoders. This phonics instruction, however, was presented as a means to an end that allowed children to quickly concentrate on more vital tasks—what reading can mean and how it can make them feel. To that end, many strategies for making text meaningful and using text as a springboard to substantive writing activities were introduced. Yet reading about specific strategies, seeing only individual pieces of the big picture, is not completely satisfactory. Particularly if one has never taught, it is important to see how a real teacher manages to orchestrate all of these elements in a total program for a heterogeneous garden of children with varying strengths and needs. With this in mind, I observed one of the finest teachers I know and invited you, the reader, to see for yourself what such a program might look like.

Though Mrs. Ramon has a challenging situation with a first-grade class composed of a wide range of learners, she will most likely succeed—as she does year after year—at teaching every child in her class not only to read and write, but to enjoy these activities. How does she manage to achieve such lofty goals? Besides creating a comprehensive program of skills-based and holistic methods of teaching literacy, Mrs. Ramon has set up her class in a caring way that is respectful of all the individuals who are in her charge. Her instructional plans emanate from a program of ongoing observation and assessment and are adjusted according to her children's changing needs. She has gathered a host of inviting literacy materials and arranged them in a classroom designed to facilitate the various activities that she plans each day. She has saturated the room with print, so that children are constantly encountering the idea that *print* and *talk* are integrally connected. Additionally, Mrs. Ramon sincerely expects each of her learners to read and write—and they rise to the occasion; her confidence bolsters them when they face a challenging instructional situation. Above all, this teacher's interaction with her learners is continually constructive and positive; she is the consummate cheerleader and encourages the children to offer similar support to one another.

Perhaps the most crucial personal ingredient in Mrs. Ramon's success—and that of so many teachers like her—is her love of and enthusiasm for all aspects of literacy and learning in general. Outside the classroom, Mrs. Ramon is constantly keeping up with new developments in literacy through journals, conferences, and in-service presentations. In her classroom, this teacher often shares her personal writing with children, delightedly looks up words she does not know in front of her students, and has been known to shed a tear or two, unabashedly, while sharing *The Velveteen Rabbit* with her first-graders.

Balance in literacy is possible when a competent and caring teacher creates a comprehensive program of explicit instruction, writing, speaking, listening, viewing, and literature-rich experiences. Mrs. Ramon's classroom is a working example of the achievement of these goals.

questions
for journal writing and discussion

1. Reflect on a teacher you know who seems to be highly effective in teaching literacy to young children. In light of this chapter, what would you say makes this teacher impressive? What do you believe made Mrs. Ramon such an effective teacher of early literacy? What are their similarities? Differences?

2. Brainstorm a list of ways you will ensure that the children in your classroom not only *can* read but do read. Share and discuss this list with others in your class.

3. Discuss the provisions that must be made in a classroom so that linguistically and culturally diverse learners succeed. How do you believe such provisions affect native English-speaking children in the class?

suggestions
for projects and field activities

1. Arrange to observe an early childhood classroom. Make notes about the environment, the classroom climate, and the literacy activities in which the children engage. Your observation summary should be as objective as possible. Compare your experience with those of others in your class, and include in your discussion your personal reactions to the classroom you observed.

2. Interview an early childhood educator. Ask this teacher how she decides on changes in curriculum she needs to make. Which is the most potent factor in changing a classroom practice for this teacher: (1) what research says; (2) what other teachers say; or (3) what the teacher observes?

3. Make a sketch of an ideal classroom, showing the arrangement of furniture, equipment, materials, and storage space that best suits what you believe to be a comprehensive literacy environment. Compare your sketch with the diagram of a literacy classroom in this chapter. How is yours different? Why? Share your sketch with others in your class, discussing the benefits and drawbacks of each design.

Children's Literature References

BOOKS FOR DEVELOPING PHONEMIC AWARENESS

The following books are suitable for use in reinforcing particular letter sounds, patterns, and letter combinations.

Adams, P., and Strop, J. (1986). *Spunky the monkey.* Cleveland, OH: Modern Curriculum Press.

Ahlberg, J., and Ahlberg, A. (1978). *Each peach pear plum.* New York: Scholastic.

Alborough, J. (1992). *Where's my teddy?* Cambridge, MA: Candlewick Press.

Alda, A. (1992). *Sheep, sheep, help me fall asleep.* New York: Bantam Doubleday.

Alda, A. (1994). *Pig, horse, cow, don't wake me now.* New York: Bantam Doubleday.

Bayer, J. (1984). *A my name is Alice.* New York: Dial Press.

Brown, M. (1994). *Pickle things.* New York: Parents Magazine Press.

Brown, M. W. (1983). *Four fur feet.* New York: Doubleday.

Cameron, P. (1961). *"I can't," said the ant.* New York: Coward McCann.

Carlstrom, N. W. (1986). *Jesse bear, what will you wear?* New York: Macmillan.

Carter, D. (1990). *More bugs in boxes.* New York: Simon & Schuster.

Degan, B. (1983). *Jamberry.* New York: Harper & Row.

deRegniers, B., Moore, E., and Carr, J. (1988). *Sing a song of popcorn.* New York: Scholastic.

Fox, M. (1993). *Time for bed.* San Diego, CA: Harcourt Brace Jovanovich.

Galdone, P. (1968). *Henny Penny.* New York: Scholastic.

Galdone, P. (1973). *The three billy goats gruff.* New York: Seabury.

Geraghty, J. (1992). *Stop that noise!* New York: Crown.

Gordon, J. (1991). *Six sleepy sheep.* New York: Puffin Books.

Grossman, B. (1995). *My little sister ate one hare.* New York: Crown.

Guarino, D. (1989). *Is your mama a llama?* New York: Scholastic.

Hague, M. (1993). *Teddy bear, teddy bear: A classic action rhyme.* New York: Morrow Junior Books.

Hawkins, C., and Hawkins, J. (1986). *Tog the dog.* New York: G. P. Putnam's Sons. (See also other books in this series.)

Hoberman, M. A. (2004). *The eensy-weensy spider.* Boston: Little, Brown.

Hutchins, P. (1976). *Don't forget the bacon.* New York: Morrow.

Hymes, L., and Hymes, J. (1964). *Oodles of noodles.* New York: Young Scott Books.

Johnston, T. (1991). *Little bear sleeping.* New York: G. P. Putnam's Sons.

Jorgensen, G. (1988). *Crocodile beat.* New York: Scholastic.

Komaiko, L. (1987) *Annie bananie.* New York: Harper & Row.

Krauss, R. (1985). *I can fly.* New York: Golden Press.

Kushkin, K. (1990). *Roar and more.* New York: Harper Trophy.

Leedy, L. (1988). *Pingo the plaid panda.* New York: Holiday House.

Lewison, W. (1992). *Buzz said the bee.* New York: Scholastic.

Lindbergh, R. (1990). *The day the goose got loose.* New York: Dial Press.

Marzollo, J. (1989). *The teddy bear book.* New York: Dial.

Marzollo, J. (1994). *Ten cats have hats.* New York: Scholastic.

Most, B. (1991). *A dinosaur named after me.* San Diego: Harcourt Brace Jovanovich.

Obligato, L. (1983). *Faint frogs feeling feverish and other terrifically tantalizing tongue twisters.* New York: Puffin.

Ochs, C. P. (1991). *Moose on the loose.* Minneapolis: Carolrhoda Books.

Oppenheim, J. (1989). *Not now! said the cow.* New York: Bantam Books.

Otto, C. (1991). *Dinosaur chase.* New York: Harper-Trophy.

Parry, C. (1991). *Zoomerang-a-boomerang: Poems to make your belly laugh.* New York: Puffin.

Patz, N. (1983). *Moses supposes his toeses are roses.* San Diego: Harcourt Brace Jovanovich.

Philpot, L., and Philpot, G. (1993). *Amazing Anthony ant.* New York: Random House.

Pomerantz, C. (1993). *If I had a paka.* New York: Mulberry.

Prelutsky, J. (1982). *The baby uggs are hatching.* New York: Mulberry.

Prelutsky, J. (1989). *Poems of A. Nonny Mouse.* New York: Knopf.

Provenson, A. (1977). *Old Mother Hubbard.* New York: Crown.

Raffi. (1987). *Down by the bay.* New York: Crown.

Root, P. (2003). *One duck stuck.* Cambridge, MA: Candlewick.

Serfozo, M. (1988). *Who said red?* New York: M. K. McElderry Books.

Seuss, Dr. (1957). *The cat in the hat.* New York: Random house.

Seuss, Dr. (1963). *Hop on pop.* New York: Random House.

Seuss, Dr. (1965). *Fox in sox.* New York: Random House.

Seuss, Dr. (1974). *There's a wocket in my pocket.* New York: Random House.

Shaw, N. (2006). *Sheep in a jeep.* Boston: Houghton Mifflin. (See also other books in this series.)

Slobodkin, E. (1976). *Caps for sale.* New York: Scholastic.

Sowers, P. (1991). *The listening walk.* New York: Harper & Row.

Speed, T. (1995). *Two cool cows.* New York: Scholastic.

Van Allsburg, C. (1987). *The Z was zapped.* Boston: Houghton Mifflin.

Van Laan, N. (1990). *A mouse in my house.* New York: Knopf.

Wadsworth, O. A. (1985). *Over in the meadow.* New York: Penguin.

Wells, R. (1973). *Noisy Nora.* New York: Dial Press.

Winthrop, E. (1986). *Shoes.* New York: HarperTrophy.

Wood, A. (1992). *Silly Sally.* San Diego: Harcourt Brace Jovanovich.

Ziefert, H., and Brown, H. (1996). *What rhymes with eel?* New York: Penguin.

PREDICTABLE BOOKS

The following books are suitable for increasing the listening comprehension of young learners, as they contain rhymes, rhythm, and/or repetition. Children are therefore able to anticipate certain key words and phrases.

Baker, K. (2007). *Hickory dickory dock.* San Diego: Harcourt.

Carle, E. (2005). *A house for hermit crab.* New York: Aladdin.

Carlstrom, N. W. (1986). *Jesse Bear, what will you wear?* New York: Macmillan.

Eastman, P. D. (1960). *Are you my mother?* New York: Random House.

Fox, M. (1986). *Hattie and the fox.* New York: Bantam Doubleday Dell.

Fleming, D. (2006). *The cow who clucked.* New York: Henry Holt.

Galdone, P. (1975). *Henny Penny*. New York: Houghton Mifflin.

Keats, E. J. (1972). *Over in the meadow*. New York: Four Winds.

Kent, J. (1971). *The fat cat*. New York: Scholastic.

Martin, B., Jr. (2007). *Baby bear, baby bear, what do you see?* New York: Henry Holt (See also other books in this series.)

Mesler, J., and Cowley, J. (1980). *In a dark, dark wood*. New Zealand: Wright Group.

Pinkney, J. (2006). *The little red hen*. New York: Dial.

Rosen, M. (2004). *We're going on a bear hunt*. New York: Candlewick.

Seuling, B. (1976). *Teeny tiny woman*. New York: Greenwillow.

Taback, S. (2004). *The house that Jack built*. New York: Puffin.

Tafuri, N. (1984). *Have you seen my duckling?* New York: Greenwillow.

Wood, A. (2007). *Silly Sally*. San Diego: Harcourt.

EASY-TO-READ BOOKS

These books are appropriate for early readers to read independently, as they are written with a controlled vocabulary of limited sight words and easily decodable words.

Bang-Campbell, M. (2002). *Little rat sets sail*. New York: Harcourt.

Bateman, D. M. (2007). *Deep in the swamp*. Watertown, MA: Charlesbridge.

Benchley, N. (1966). *Oscar otter*. New York: Harper & Row.

Bulla, C. R. (1979). *Daniel's duck*. New York: Harper & Row.

Byars, B. (1996). *My brother, Ant*. New York: Viking.

Cazet, D. (1998). *Minnie and Moo go dancing*. New York: DK Ink.

Christelow, E. (2007). *Five little monkeys go shopping*. New York: Clarion Books.

Cole, J., and Calmenson, S. (1990). *Ready . . . set . . . Read!* New York: Doubleday.

Donnio, S. (2007). *I'd really like to eat a child*. New York: Random House.

Eaton, M. (2007). *The adventures of Max and Pinky, best buds*. New York: Knopf.

Friend, C. (2007). *The perfect nest*. Cambridge, MA: Candlewick Press.

Geist, K. (2007). *The three little fish and the bad shark*. New York: Cartwheel.

George, J. C. (2008). *Goose and duck*. New York: HarperCollins.

Gran, J. (2007). *Big bug surprise*. New York: Scholastic.

Grant, J. A. (2008). *Chicken said, "Cluck!"* New York: HarperCollins.

Grey, M. (2007). *Ginger bear*. New York: Knopf.

Griffith, H. V. (1982). *Alex and the cat*. New York: Greenwillow.

Hills, T. (2007). *Duck, duck, goose*. New York: Random House.

Lin, G. (2009). *Ling & Ting: Not exactly the same!* Boston: Little Brown.

Little, J. (2003). *Emma's strange pet* (an I can read book). New York: HarperCollins.

Lloyd-Jones, S. (2007). *How to be a baby, by me the big sister*. New York: Random House.

Lobel, A. (1976). *Frog and toad all year* (and others in the series). New York: Harper & Row.

Manning, M., and Granstrom, B. (2007). *Dino-dinners*. New York: Holiday.

Marshall, J. E. (1982). *Fox and his friends*. New York: Dial.

Milgrim, D. (2003). *See Pip point* (Ready-to Read). New York: Atheneum.

Pomerantz, C. (1993). *Outside dog*. New York: Harper Collins.

Schwartz, A. (1984). *In a dark, dark room*. New York: Harper & Row.

Seeger, L. V. (2008). *One boy*. New York: Roaring Brook.

Seuss, Dr. (1957). *The cat in the hat*. New York: Random House.

Seuss, Dr. (1960). *Green eggs and ham*. New York: Random House.

Seuss, Dr. (1963). *Hop on pop*. New York: Random House.

Steffensmeier, A. (2007). *Millie waits for the mail*. New York: Walker.

Tankard, J. (2007). *Grumpy bird*. New York: Scholastic.

Van Laan, N. (2003). *Busy, busy mouse*. New York: Houghton Mifflin.

Wheeler, L. (2007). *Dino-Hockey*. Minneapolis: Carolrhoda Books.

WORDLESS BOOKS

These books have no words, as the name suggests, and are useful for encouraging language development as children tell the story that goes with the pictures, reinforcing an understanding of story structure. The books are also ideal for English learners who can share the story in their own language.

Aruego, J. (1971). *Look what I can do.* New York: Scribner's.

Berner, R. S. (2008). *In the town all year 'round.* San Francisco: Chronicle.

Day, A. (1985). *Good dog, Carl.* La Jolla, CA: Green Tiger.

dePaola, T. (1978). *Pancakes for breakfast.* San Diego: Harcourt Brace Jovanovich.

Faller, R. (2007). *Polo: The runaway book.* New York: Roaring Book Press.

Geisert, A. (2006). *Oops.* Boston: Houghton Mifflin.

Hutchins, P. (1971). *Changes, changes.* New York: Macmillan.

Hyewon, Y. (2008). *Last night.* Foster/Farrar.

Keats, E. J. (1974). *Kitten for a day.* New York: Watts.

Khing, T. T. (2007). *Where is the cake?* New York: Abrams.

Lehman, B. (2007). *Rainstorm.* Boston: Houghton Mifflin.

Lehman, B. (2008). *Trainstop.* Boston: Houghton Mifflin.

Martin, R. (1989). *Will's mammoth.* New York: Putnam.

McCully, E. (1984). *Picnic.* New York: Harper & Row.

Ormerod, J. (1981). *Sunshine.* New York: Lothrop.

Turkle, B. (1991). *Deep in the forest.* New York: Dutton.

Van Ommen, S. (2007). *The surprise.* Honesdale, PA: Front Street.

Wiesner, D. (1991). *Tuesday.* New York: Clarion.

ALPHABET BOOKS

The following books are useful in introducing the letters and corresponding sounds of the alphabet in an enjoyable and whimsical way.

Brent, I. (1993). *An alphabet of animals.* New York: Little, Brown.

Ehlert, L. (1989). *Eating the alphabet: Fruits and vegetables from A to Z.* New York: Harcourt Brace Jovanovich.

Emberly, E. (1978). *Ed Emberly's ABC.* New York: Little, Brown.

Hague, K. (1983). *Alphabears.* New York: Holt, Rinehart, and Winston.

Hoban, T. (1982). *A, B, See.* New York: Greenwillow.

Hoban, T. (1987). *26 letters and 99 cents.* New York: Greenwillow.

Isadora, R. (1983). *City seen from A to Z.* New York: Greenwillow.

Kellogg, S. (1987). *Aster aardvark's alphabet adventure.* New York: William Morrow.

Kitchen, B. (1984). *Animal alphabet.* New York: Dial.

Lobel, A. (1981). *On market street.* New York: Greenwillow.

MacDonald, S. (1986). *Alphabatics.* New York: Bradbury.

Martin, B., Jr., and Archaumbault, J. (1989). *Chicka, chicka, boom, boom.* New York: Simon & Schuster.

Patience, J. (1993). *An amazing alphabet.* New York: Random House.

Sendak, M. (1990). *Alligators all around: An alphabet.* New York: HarperTrophy.

Seuss, Dr. (1991). *Dr. Seuss's ABCs* (2nd ed.). New York: Random House.

Tallon, R. (1979). *Zoophabets.* New York: Scholastic.

INFORMATIONAL BOOKS

Informational books—that is, nonfiction—can be a valuable part of a young child's reading diet and are often used by teachers to supplement textbooks in the content areas. Informational books are readily available for primary-aged youngsters and are becoming increasingly popular; in fact, in the past few years, publishers' lists have contained nearly as many informational books as fictional titles.

Adler, D. (1989). *Jackie Robinson: A first biography.* New York: Holiday House.

Albert B. (1993). *Windsongs and rainbows.* Illus. by S. Stillman. New York: Simon & Schuster.

Amsel, S. (1992). *A wetland walk.* Illus. by author. Brookfield, CT: Millbrook.

Bare, C. S. (1993). *Never grab a deer by the ear.* New York: Cobblehill.

Baylor, B. (1978). *Everybody needs a rock.* Illus. by P. Parnall. New York: Scribner's Sons.

Berger, M. (1992). *Look out for sea turtles!* Illus. by M. Lloyd. New York: HarperCollins.

Borden, L., and Kroeger, M. (2000). *Fly high: The story of Bessie Coleman.* Illus. by T. Flavin. New York: Simon & Schuster.

Cerullo, M. M. (2000). *The truth about great white sharks.* Illus. by J. L. Rotman. San Francisco: Chronicle.

Christelow, E. (1995). *What do authors do?* New York: Clarion.

Christelow, E. (2000). *What do illustrators do?* Boston: Houghton Mifflin.

Cole, J. (2000). *The new baby at your house.* New York: Morrow/Avon.

Gackenbach, D. (1992). *Mighty tree.* Illus. by author. New York: Harcourt Brace Jovanovich.

Geisert, B. (1998). *Prairie Town.* Illus. by A. Geis. Boston: Houghton Mifflin.

Gibbons, G. (1994). *Frogs.* New York: Holiday House.

Gibbons, G. (2006). *Groundhog Day! Shadow or no shadow?* New York: Holiday House.

Gibbons, G. (2006). *Valentine's Day is . . .* New York: Holiday House.

Glaser, L. (1992). *Wonderful worms.* Illus. by L. Krupinski. New York: Millbrook.

Granger, J. (1982). *Amazing world of dinosaurs.* Illus. by P. B. Ford. Mahwah, NJ: Troll Associates.

Hamilton, K. (2001). *This is the ocean.* Illus. by L. Siomades. Honesdale, PA: Boyds Mills.

Harlow, R. (2002). *Garbage and recycling* (Young discoverers: Environmental facts and experiments). New York: Kingfisher.

Koch, M. (1993). *World water watch.* Illus. by author. New York: Greenwillow.

Markle, S. (2005). *Army ants.* Minneapolis, MN: Lerner.

McNulty, F. (2005). *If you decide to go to the Moon.* New York: Scholastic.

Micklethwait, L. (1993). *A child's book of art.* New York: Dorling Kindersley.

Micklethwait, L. (1994). *I spy a lion: Animals in art.* New York: Greenwillow.

Mills, P. (1993). *Until the cows come home.* Illus. by author. New York: North-South Books.

Nivola, C. A. (2008). *Planting the trees of Kenya: The story of Wangari Maathai.* New York: Farrar, Straus and Giroux.

O'Donnell, E. L. (1991). *The twelve days of summer.* Illus. by K. L. Schmidt. New York: Morrow Junior Books.

Patent, D. H. (2008). *When the wolves returned: The restoring of nature's balance in Yellowstone.* New York: Walker.

Robbins, K. (2005). *Seeds.* New York: Atheneum/Simon & Schuster.

Roop, P., and Roop, C. (1992). *One earth, a multitude of creatures.* Illus. by V. A. Kells. New York: Walker.

Rounds, G. (1999). *Beaver.* New York: Holiday House.

Schulte, J. (2005). *Can you find it inside?* New York: Abrams.

Shelby, A. (1993). *What to do about pollution . . .* Illus. by I. Trivas. New York: Richard Jackson/Orchard.

Sill, C. (1992). *About birds: A guide for children.* Illus. by J. Sill. New York: Peachtree.

Simon, S. (2000). *Seymour Simon's book of trucks.* New York: HarperCollins.

Wootray, K. (1993). *A color sampler.* New York: Ticknor & Fields.

Yolen, J. (1993). *Welcome to the greenhouse.* Illus. by L. Regan. New York: Putnam.

BOOKS FOR INCREASING READING COMPREHENSION

The following books have interesting themes or relatively complex plots and are suitable for developing the comprehension skills of summarizing, visualizing, predicting, connecting to prior knowledge, or getting the main idea when used in small group discussion.

Avi. (2008). *The end of the beginning: Being the adventure of a small snail (and an even smaller ant)*. New York: Harcourt.

Bang, M. (2004). *When Sophie gets angry*. New York: Scholastic.

Bercaw, E. C. (2000). *Halmoni's day*. New York: Dial.

Bunting, E. (1997). *A day's work*. New York: Clarion.

Bunting, E. (1999). *Smoky night*. San Diego: Voyager.

Calmenson, S. (1989). *The principal's new clothes*. New York: Scholastic.

Cameron, A. (1988). *The most beautiful place in the world*. New York: Knopf.

Demi. (1999). *The donkey and the rock*. New York: Henry Holt & Co.

Hall, D. (1994). *I am the dog, I am the cat*. New York: Dial.

Hoffman, M. (1991). *Amazing Grace*. New York: Dial.

Janezcko, P. (2001). *Stone bench in an empty park*. New York: Scholastic.

Paladino, C. (1999). *One good apple: Growing our food for the sake of the earth*. New York: Houghton Mifflin.

Ringgold, F. (2003). *If a bus could talk: The story of Rosa Parks*. New York: Aladdin.

Steig, W. (1990). *Doctor Desoto*. New York: Farrar, Straus & Giroux.

Uchida, Y. (1996). *The bracelet*. New York: Putnam.

Williams, V. B. (1982). *A chair for my mother*. Mulberry.

Winter, J. (2008). *Wangari's trees of peace: A true story from Africa*. San Diego: Harcourt.

Woodson, J. (2001). *The other side*. New York: Putman.

Youme, S. (2005). *That is life: A Haitian story of hope*. El Paso, TX: Cinco Puntos Press.

BOOKS FOR DEVELOPING CONCEPTS AND VOCABULARY

These books use some words and concepts unfamiliar to young children, but through context and with scaffolding by the teacher, the words can be discussed and incorporated into the children's speaking vocabulary.

Asch, F. (2000). *The sun is my favorite star*. New York: Harcourt.

Cleary, B. F. (2003). *Dearly, nearly, and insincerely: What is an adverb?* Minneapolis: Carolrhoda.

Cooney, B. (1982). *Miss Rumphius*. New York: Viking.

Crews, D. (1978). *Freight train*. New York: Greenwillow.

Cumpiano, I. (2008). *Quinito, day and night, Quinito, dia y noche*. New York: Children's Book Press.

Fleischman, P. (1999). *Mind's eye*. New York: Holt.

Gravett, E. (2007). *Wolves*. New York: Simon & Schuster.

Hall, M. (2009). *My heart is like a zoo*. New York: Greenwillow.

Heller, R. (1987). *A cache of jewels and other collective nouns*. New York: Grosset & Dunlap.

Heller, R. (1989). *Many luscious lollipops: A book about adjectives*. New York: Grosset & Dunlap.

Jonas, A. (1989). *Color dance*. New York: Greenwillow.

Lyon, G. E. (1990). *Come a tide*. London: Orchard Books.

McMillan, B. (1989). *Super, super, superwords*. New York: Lothrop, Lee & Shepard.

Seeger, L. V. (2007). *First the egg*. New York: Roaring Brook.

Terban, M. (1986). *I think I thought and other tricky verbs*. New York: Clarion Books.

Ziefert, H. (1997). *Night Knight: A word play flap book*. New York: Houghton Mifflin.

BOOKS TO INSPIRE WRITING

The books in this section are about writers or writing issues and the formats in these books can also be used for rhetorical imitation, or "copy catting." After reading them aloud, the teacher can point out the structure of the story so that children can use this structure to write their own story.

Ada, A. F. (1998). *Yours truly, Goldilocks.* New York: Atheneum.

Barrett, J. (2001). *Things that are the most in the world.* New York: Aladdin Books.

Brown, M. W. (2006). *Another important book.* New York: HarperTrophy.

Cameron, A. (1996). *The stories Julian tells.* New York: Random House.

Clements, A. (2007). *Dogku.* New York: Atheneum.

Estes, E. (1974). *The hundred dresses.* New York: Harcourt Brace Jovanovich.

Fox, M. (1990). *I went walking.* New York: Harcourt.

Langstaff, J. (1974). *Oh, a-hunting we will go.* New York: Simon.

Numeroff, L. J. (1985). *If you give a mouse a cookie.* New York: Harper.

Oakley, G. (1987). *The diary of a churchmouse.* New York: Atheneum.

Pulver, R. (2003). *Punctuation takes a vacation.* New York: Holiday House.

Raschka, C. (2007). *Yo! Yes?* New York: Scholastic.

Rylant, C. (2000). *In November.* New York: Harcourt.

Shannon, G. (1999). *Tomorrow's alphabet.* New York: HarperTrophy.

Shulevitz, U. (2003). *One Monday morning.* New York: Macmillan.

Viorst, J. (1972). *Alexander and the horrible, terrible, no good, very bad day.* New York: Atheneum.

Teacher References for Early Literacy

appendix **B**

RECOMMENDED BOOKS FOR TEACHERS

Adams, M. J. (1990). *Beginning to Read: Thinking and Learning about Print.* Cambridge, MA: MIT Press.

Allington, R. L., Cunningham, P. M., & Cunningham, J. W. (2009). *What Really Matters in Response to Intervention: Research-Based Designs.* Boston: Pearson.

Allington, R. L., Cunningham, P. M., & Cunningham, J. W. (2009). *What Really Matters in Vocabulary: Research-Based Practices Across the Curriculum.* Boston: Pearson.

Beaty, J. J., & Pratt, L. (2011). *Early Literacy in Preschool and Kindergarten* (3rd ed.). Boston: Pearson.

Beauchat, K. A., Blamey, K. L., & Walpole, S. (2010). *The Building Blocks of Preschool Success.* New York: Guilford.

Beck, I. L. (2005). *Making Sense of Phonics: The Hows and Whys.* New York: Guilford.

Brooks, E. (1998). *Just-Right Books for Beginning Readers: Leveled Booklists and Strategies.* New York: Scholastic.

Cecil, N. L. (2004). *Activities for a Comprehensive Approach to Literacy.* Scottsdale, AZ: Holcomb Hathaway.

Cecil, N. L. (2007). *Focus on Fluency: A Meaning-Based Approach.* Scottsdale, AZ: Holcomb Hathaway.

Cecil, N. L., & McCormick, C. W. (2009). *A Feast of Rhyme, Rhythm, and Song: Developing Phonemic Awareness Through Music.* Winnipeg, MB: Portage & Main Press.

Collins, K. (2008). *Reading for Real: Teach Students to Read with Power, Intention, and Joy in K–3 Classrooms.* Portland, ME: Stenhouse.

Columba, L., Kim, C., & Moe, A. J. (2009). *The Power of Picture Books in Teaching Math, Science, and Social Studies, Grades PreK–8.* Scottsdale, AZ: Holcomb Hathaway.

Combs, M. (2010). *Readers and Writers in the Primary Grades: A Balanced and Integrated Approach, K–3* (4th ed.). Boston: Pearson.

Corgill, A. M. (2008). *Of Primary Importance: What's Essential in Teaching Young Writers.* Portland, ME: Stenhouse.

Cramer, R. L. (1998). *The Spelling Connection: Integrating Reading, Writing, and Spelling Instruction.* New York: Guilford Publications.

Cunningham, P. M., & Allington, R. L. (2011). *Classrooms that Work: They Can All Read and Write* (5th ed.). Boston: Pearson.

Cunningham, P. M., & Cunningham, J. W. (2010). *What Really Matters in Writing: Research-Based Practices Across the Curriculum.* Boston: Pearson.

DeVries, B. (2011). *Literacy Assessment and Intervention for Classroom Teachers* (3rd ed.). Scottsdale, AZ: Holcomb Hathaway.

Dickenson, D. K., & Neuman, S. B. (2005). *Handbook of Early Literacy Research.* New York: Guilford.

Dyson, A. H. (1993). *Social Worlds of Children: Learning to Read in an Urban Primary School.* New York: Teachers College Press.

Enz, B. J., & Morrow, L. M. (2009). *Assessing Preschool Literacy Development: Informal and Formal Measures to Guide Instruction.* Newark, DE: International Reading Association.

Flippo, R. F. (2005). *Personal Reading: How to Match Children to Books*. Portsmouth, NH: Heinemann.

Fuhrken, C. (2009). *What Every Elementary Teacher Needs to Know About Reading Tests (From Someone Who Has Written Them)*. Portland, ME: Stenhouse.

Glazer, S. M. (1998). *Assessment Is Instruction: Reading, Writing, Spelling, and Phonics for ALL Learners*. Norwood, MA: Christopher–Gordon.

Graves, M. F., Juel, C., Graves, B. B., Calfee, R., & Dewitz, P. (2011). *Teaching Reading in the 21st Century* (5th ed.). Boston: Pearson.

Gregory, E. (Ed.) (1997). *One Child, Many Worlds: Early Learning in Multicultural Communities*. New York: Teachers College Press.

Gunning, T. C. (1998). *Best Books for Beginning Readers*. Needham Heights, MA: Allyn & Bacon.

Hale, E. (2008). *Crafting Writers, K–6*. Portland, ME: Stenhouse.

Hayes, K., & Creange, R. (2000). *Classroom Routines That Really Work for PreK and Kindergarten*. New York: Scholastic.

Heard, G., & McDonough, J. (2009). *A Place for Wonder: Reading and Writing Nonfiction in the Primary Grades*. Portland, ME: Stenhouse.

Heath, S., & Mangiola, L. (1991). *Children of Promise: Literate Activity in Linguistically and Culturally Diverse Classrooms*. Washington, DC: National Association for the Education of Young Children.

Herrera, S., Perez, D. R., & Escamilla, K. (2010). *Teaching Reading to English Language Learners: Differentiated Literacies*. Boston: Pearson.

Hiebert, E. H., & Raphael, T. E. (1998). *Early Literacy Instruction*. Fort Worth, TX: Harcourt Brace.

Hiebert, E. H., & Taylor, B. M. (1994). *Getting Reading Right from the Start: Effective Early Intervention*. Boston: Allyn & Bacon.

Hughes, M., & Searle, D. (1997). *The Violent E and Other Tricky Sounds: Learning to Spell from Kindergarten Through Grade 6*. York, ME: Stenhouse.

Jalongo, M. R. (2011). *Early Childhood Language Arts* (5th ed.). Boston: Pearson.

Johnston, P. H. (Ed.) (2010). *RTI in Literacy—Responsive and Comprehensive*. Newark, DE: International Reading Association.

Kristo, J. V., & Bamford, R. A. (2004). *Nonfiction in Focus: A Comprehensive Framework for Helping Students Become Independent Readers and Writers of Nonfiction, K–6*. New York: Scholastic.

Lapp, D., Flood, J., Moore, K., & Nichols, M. (2005). *Teaching Literacy in First Grade*. New York: Guilford.

McGee, L. M., & Morrow, L. M. (2005). *Teaching Literacy in Kindergarten*. New York: Guilford.

McGee, L. M., & Richgels, D. (2004). *Literacy's Beginnings: Supporting Young Readers and Writers* (4th ed.). Boston: Allyn & Bacon.

McKenna, M. C., Walpole, S., & Conradi, K. (2010). *Promoting Early Reading: Research, Resources, and Best Practices*. New York: Guilford.

McLaughlin, M. (2010). *Guided Comprehension in the Primary Grades*. Newark, DE: International Reading Association.

McLaughlin, M., & Fisher, L. (2005). *Research-Based Reading Lessons for K–3*. New York: Scholastic.

Meier, D. R. (Ed.) (2009). *Here's the Story: Using Narrative to Promote Young Children's Language and Literacy Learning*. New York. Teachers College Press.

Moore, P., & Lyon, A. (2005). *New Essentials for Teaching Reading in Pre-K–2: Comprehension, Vocabulary, Fluency*. New York: Scholastic.

Moore-Hart, M. A. (2010). *Teaching Writing in Diverse Classrooms K–8: Enhancing Writing Through Literature, Real-Life Experiences and Technology*. Boston: Pearson.

Morrow, L. M. (2005). *Literacy Development in the Early Years: Helping Children Read and Write* (5th ed.). Boston: Allyn & Bacon.

Podhajski, B., Varricchio, M., Mather, N., & Sammons, J. (2010). *Mastering the Alphabetic Principle (MAP): How to Map Speech to Print for Reading and Spelling*. Baltimore, MD: Brookes.

Morrow, L. M., Freitag, E., & Gambrell, L. B. (2009). *Using Children's Literature in Preschool to Develop Comprehension: Understanding and Enjoying Books* (2nd ed.). Newark, DE: International Reading Association.

Moss, B., & Lapp, D. (2010). *Teaching New Literacies in Grades K–3*. New York: Guilford.

Moss, B., & Young, T. A. (2010). *Creating Lifelong Readers Through Independent Reading*. Newark, DE: International Reading Association.

Paratore, J. R., & McCormack, R. L. (2005). *Teaching Literacy in Second Grade*. New York: Guilford.

Preece, A., & Cowden, D. (1993). *Young Writers in the Making: Sharing the Process with Parents*. Portsmouth, NH: Heinemann.

Raphael, T. E., Highfield, K., & Au, K. H. (2006). *QAR Now: A Powerful and Practical Framework that Develops Comprehension and Higher-Level Thinking in All Students.* New York: Scholastic.

Rasinski, T. V., Padak, N. D., & Fawcett, G. (2010). *Teaching Children Who Find Reading Difficult.* Boston: Pearson.

Richards, C., & Leafstedt, J. (2010). *Early Reading Intervention: Strategies and Methods for Struggling Readers.* Boston: Pearson.

Riddle, J. (2009). *Engaging the Eye Generation: Visual Literacy Strategies for the K–5 Classroom.* Portland, ME: Stenhouse.

Rog, L. J. (2007). *Marvelous Minilessons for Teaching Beginning Writing.* Newark, DE: International Reading Association.

Roskos, K. A., Tabors, P. O., & Lenhart, L. A. (2009). *Oral Language and Early Literacy in Preschool: Talking, Reading, and Writing* (2nd ed.). Newark, DE: International Reading Association.

Samuels, S. J., & Farstrup, A. E. (Eds.) (2006). *What Research Has to Say About Fluency Instruction.* Newark, DE: International Reading Association.

Strickland, D. S., & Schickedanz, J. A. (2009). *Learning about Print in Preschool: Working with Letters, Words, and Beginning Links With Phonemic Awareness* (2nd ed.). Newark, DE: International Reading Association.

Szymusiak, K., Sibberson, F, & Koch, L. (2008). *Beyond Leveled Books: Supporting Early and Transitional Readers in Grades K–5.* Portland, ME: Stenhouse.

Temple, C. A., Ogle, D., Crawford, A. N., & Freppon, P. (2011). *All Children Read: Teaching Literacy in Today's Diverse Classrooms* (3rd ed.). Boston: Pearson.

Tompkins, G. E. (2011). *Literacy in the Early Grades: A Successful Start for PreK–4 Readers and Writers.* Boston: Pearson.

Vukelich, C., & Christie, J. (2009). *Building a Foundation for Preschool Literacy: Effective Instruction for Children's Reading and Writing Development* (2nd ed.). Newark, DE: International Reading Association.

Walpole, S., & McKenna, M. C. (2009). *How to Plan Differentiated Reading Instruction: Resources for Grades K–3.* New York: Guilford.

OTHER TEACHER RESOURCES

Auditory Discrimination in Depth. Lindamood, C., and Lindamood, P. Austin, TX: PRO-ED, 1969.

Basic Animated-Literacy English Handbook and Tapes. San Diego, CA: Los Amigos Research Associates. 619-286 3162.

Book Buddies: A Pioneering Program for Early Reading Intervention. Johnston, F. R., Invernizzi, M., and Juel, C. New York: Guilford Publications, 1998, 800-365-7006.

Celebrate Reading: Teacher's Guide, Grade 1, A–F. Glenview, IL: Scott Foresman, 1995.

Daisy Quest & Daisy's Castle. Erickson, E., Foster, K., Foster, D., and Torgeson, J. Austin, TX: PRO-ED. 512-451-3246.

Discovery Phonics: An Integrated Approach to Decoding Strategies. Columbus, OH: Modern Curriculum Press, 1990. 800-321-3106.

Early Success: An Intervention Program, Grades 1 & 2. Boston: Houghton Mifflin, 1995. 800 733-1047

Essential Word Sorts for the Primary Grades. Botsford, CT: Really Good Stuff. 800-366-1920.

Glass Analysis for Decoding Only. Garden City, NY: Easier to Learn, 1970. 516-475-7693.

Interactive Read-Alouds: Grade K–1. Linda Hoyt. Portsmouth, NH: Heinemann, 2006. 800-225-5800. www.interactivereadalouds.com

Interactive Read-Alouds: Grades 2–3. Linda Hoyt. Portsmouth, NH: Heinemann, 2007. 800-225-5800. www.interactivereadalouds.com

It's ALL About Comprehension: Teaching K–3 Readers from the Ground Up (3 DVDs). Newark, DE: International Reading Association, 2009. 800-225-5800.

Leisy's Pan American ABCs: Latino Phonics. Culver City, CA. 310-836 6730.

Literacy-Building Transition Activities, Grades Pre-K–1. Botsford, CT: Really Good Stuff. 800 366-1920.

Literature-Based Mini-Lessons to Teach Writing. Lunsford, S. New York: Scholastic, 1998, 800-724-6527.

More than Words: Activities for Phonological Awareness and Comprehension. Donnelly, K., et al. Tucson, AZ: Communication Skill Builders, 1992.

Mortimer Turns the Alphabet Loose: Early Childhood Alphabet Awareness Kit. Columbus, OH: Modern Curriculum Press. 800-321-3106.

Phonemic Awareness and Phonics Kit. Peru, IL: Open Court. 800-435-6850.

The Phonological Awareness Kit. Robertson, C., and Salter, W. East Moline, IL: LinguiSystems. 800-776-4332.

Phonological Awareness Training for Reading. Torgeson, J., and Bryant, B. Austin, TX: PRO-ED. 512-451-3246.

Poetry Works! The First Verse Complete Set. Columbus, OH: Modern Curriculum Press. 800-321-3106.

Read-Along, Sing-Along Book of Animated Alphabet Songs. San Diego, CA: Los Amigos Research Associates. 619-286-3162.

Read to the Code: A Phonological Awareness and Early Reading Program. Blachman, B. Monterey, CA: Brooks/Cole, 2000.

Reader Rabbit's Interactive Reading Journey: Grades K–2. The Learning Company. 800-852-2255.

Reading Fluency (DVD). New York: Insight Media, 2005. 800-233-9910.

Ready Readers. Columbus, OH: Modern Curriculum Press. 800-321-3106.

Sorting Boxes with a Reading Curriculum Focus. Columbus, OH: Modern Curriculum Press. 800-321-3106.

Sound Foundations. Byrne, B., and Fielding–Barnesley, R. Melbourne, Australia: Peter Leyden Publishing.

Sounds Abound. Catts, H., and Vartianen, T. East Moline, IL: LinguiSystems. 800-776-4332.

The Spanish-Animated Alphabet Handbook and Cassette. San Diego, CA: Los Amigos Research Associates. 619-286-3162.

The Spanish Read-Along, Sing-Along Book of Animated Alphabet Songs. San Diego, CA: Los Amigos Research Associates. 619-286-3162.

Touch Phonics: The Manipulative Multi-Sensory Phonics System. Newport Beach, CA: Touchphonics Reading Systems. 800-928-6824.

Vocabulary Development (DVD). New York: Insight Media, 2005. 800-233-9910.

Waterford Early Reading Program. Provo, UT: Waterford Institute. 800-669-4533.

Words Their Way: Word Study for Phonics, Vocabulary, and Spelling. Bear, D. R., Invernizzi, M., Templeton, S., and Johnston, F. Upper Saddle River, NJ: Prentice Hall. 800-223-1360.

Zoo Phonics. Groveland, CA: Zoo-Phonics. 800-622-8104.

RESOURCES FOR PARENTS

Family Literacy: Connections in Schools and Communities. Morrow, L. M. (ed.) Newark, DE: International Reading Association, 1995.

Fostering the Love of Reading: The Affective Domain in Reading Education. Castle, M., and Cramer, E. (eds.) Newark, DE: The International Reading Association, 1994.

Games for Learning: Ten Minutes a Day to Help Your Child Do Well in School. Kaye, P. New York: Noonday Press, 1992.

Games for Reading: Playful Ways to Help Your Child Read. Kaye, P. New York: Pantheon, 1984.

Home: Where Reading and Writing Begin. Hill, M. Portsmouth, NH: Heinemann, 1989.

Jamie: A Literacy Story. Parker, D. York, ME: Stenhouse, 1997.

Laying the Foundations: A Parent-Child Literacy Training Kit. Push Literacy Action Now, 1332 G Street S.E., Washington, DC 20003.

New Read-Aloud Handbook, The. Trelease, J. New York: Penguin, 2006.

Raising Readers: Helping Your Child to Literacy. Bialostock, S. Winnipeg, Manitoba, Canada: Peguis, 1992.

Reading Begins at Home. Butler, D., and Clay, M. M. Portsmouth, NH: Heinemann, 1987.

Reading, Writing, and Rummy: More than 100 Card Games to Develop Language, Social Skills, Number Concepts, and Problem-Solving Strategies. Golick, M. Markham, Ontario, Canada: Pembroke Publishers, 1986.

Wacky Word Games. Golick, M. Markham, Ontario, Canada: Pembroke Publishers, 1995.

Writing Begins at Home. Butler, D., and Clay, M. M. Portsmouth, NH: Heinemann, 1988.

appendix

Websites for Early Literacy

C

Please note that although we have made every effort to use current information, website addresses change frequently.

C	=	Comprehension	**T**	=	Teachers/lesson plans
P	=	Parents	**PH**	=	Phonics
PA	=	Phonemic awareness	**G**	=	Group reading
F	=	Fluency	**E**	=	Emergent literacy
W	=	Writing	**I**	=	Informational text
V	=	Vocabulary			

C   ABCteach, www.abcteach.com ▪ Great site with much free printable material. Some of the materials work at developing higher-level thinking skills.

G   Author sites: www.eric-carle.com, www.tomiedepaola.com, www.janbrett.com ▪ These sites contain information about the authors of popular picture books and are helpful in planning author studies. Children will enjoy browsing, too.

I   Awesome Library, www.awesomelibrary.org/student.html ▪ This site contains over 26,000 resources. A must-see for information across content areas for teacher and student use. The Talking Library is perfect for English learners, and many sites are available in various languages.

W   Biography Maker, The, bellinghamschools.org/sites/default/files/BIO/Biomaker.htm ▪ This site provides the structure to guide children to write a biography by asking the right questions to draw out a person's life story. Uses the six traits.

C   Book Adventure, www.bookadventure.com ▪ This site is designed to encourage children from K–8 to read more often, for longer periods of time, and with greater comprehension.

C, G   BookPALS Storyline, www.storylineonline.net ▪ An online series of streaming videos where children of all ages can find and appreciate wonderful stories read by famous actors.

I   Children's Book Council (CBC), www.cbcbooks.org/ ▪ Provides lists of outstanding social studies and science trade books for young people.

C, W   **Children's Story Online, www.childrenstory.com/stories**   ■   Allows children to collaborate with peers around the world to develop positive reading and writing connections through the Internet.

T   **Choosing Children's Literature, www.dawcl.com**   ■   Database for award-winning children's literature.

I, G   **Cleveland Rock & Roll Hall of Fame, www.rockhall.com/education**   ■   Offers lesson plans that integrate music with history and literature. Older children can explore the site independently.

I   **Cradle of Aviation, www.cradleofaviation.org/education/index.html**   ■   At this site, simply click on the pictures at the sidebar. The screen will emerge with information and activities about planes, aviation, and related topics.

T   **Crayola, www.crayola.com**   ■   This site includes both a teacher area concerned with integrating art across the curriculum and a site for children. The children's site has an ongoing story with a new chapter every week.

I   **Defenders of Wildlife, www.defenders.org**   ■   The programs addressed on this website focus on the extinction of animal species and the destruction of their environment. The website is committed to protecting endangered plants and wild animals.

T   **Disney Educational Online, http://Disney.go.com/educational**   ■   Part of the Classroom Connect family of online education community resources, this site offers lesson plans for K–12 teachers.

T   **Early Childhood Literacy Technology Project, www.montgomeryschoolsmd.org/departments/earlychi**   ■   Site evaluates early literacy software. Good place for teachers to find out what is available and worthwhile.

I   **Eisenhower National Clearinghouse, www.goenc.com**   ■   This clearinghouse is dedicated to identifying superior curriculum resources, creating high-quality professional development materials, and improving science and math learning in K–12 classrooms.

I   **Endangered Species Coalition, www.stopextinction.org**   ■   This group is the watchdog for the Endangered Species Act of 1973. The website disseminates information and provides discussions about environmental, scientific, and conservation issues related to the ESA Act.

C, W   **EPals Book Club, www.ePals.com/projects**   ■   This site offers children the chance to question and discuss their favorite books. Children may establish free accounts that can be monitored by teachers.

C   **ERIC, www.askeric.org**   ■   This is an excellent website for listening and reading comprehension. Many activities and lessons for beginning readers are offered.

I   **Fish America Foundation, www.fishamerica.org/**   ■   This organization has assisted over 700 grassroots organizations to enhance fish production and increase water quality throughout North America.

T   **Folger Shakespeare Library, www.folger.edu/education/teaching.htm**   ■   Resources, teaching ideas, and lesson plans for teaching Shakespeare through performance with young children.

F   **Funschool.com, www.funschool.com**   ■   Set up for children from preschool to grade 6. Primarily includes games that make learning fun.

I   **Global Exchange, http://globalexchange.org/**   ■   Founded in 1988, this is the site for a human rights organization focused on promoting environmental rights and political awareness around the world.

I Greenpeace, www.greenpeace.org ▪ This activist organization is dedicated to achieving change in environmental and conservationist issues through direct action and international conferences.

I The History Place, www.historyplace.com ▪ This site provides information about history that can be used as resources for any social studies unit, especially good for World War II.

F, PH, PA Idea Box, www.theideabox.com ▪ This is a site for young children that includes online stories as well as song and craft activities for teachers. Lots of activities for teaching the alphabet, phonics, and phonemic awareness.

G Jan Brett (author), www.janbrett.com ▪ Author's site includes lesson plans and reproducible materials to supplement them. These can be used to enhance guided reading, shared reading, and learning centers.

I Journey North, www.learner.org/jnorth/ ▪ This site includes information about an Internet project and resources for the study of seasonal change. Children from all fifty states and Canada have taken part in the project.

P Joys of Parenthood, www.randomhouse.com/kids/parents ▪ Site with good information on raising children, including an excellent section on how to "raise a reader."

I JumpStart, www.jumpstart.com ▪ This site offers activities for teachers, games for students, and links to Knowledge Adventure, for more teaching tools and activities.

P, T K–12.com, http://eprcontent.k12.com/placement/placement/placement_langarts_2.html ▪ This site includes placement tests for phonics assessment.

P Kiddyhouse.com, www.kiddyhouse.com ▪ Resource for parents, children, and teachers. Includes a discussion board and has free worksheets, clip art, and lesson plans.

W Kid Pub, www.kidpub.org/kidpub ▪ Children can publish their original work on this site.

G, I Smithsonian Education, www.smithsonianeducation.org/students ▪ The younger children's version of the Smithsonian Institution website. Includes a picture of the day, activity ideas, and information about all the subjects the 14-museum network encompasses.

G, I KidsClick!, www.kidsclick.edu ▪ This site offers more than 4,000 links for children on subjects such as literature, machines, and mythology. The reading level of each linked site is designated.

I Kids Web Japan, web-jpn.org/kidsweb ▪ Introduces children to Japan, including Japanese lifestyle, pictures, and legends. Managed by the Japan Center for Intercultural Communications.

V, T KinderKorner, www.kinderkorner.com/readalouds.html ▪ This site highlights chapter books and book series for read-alouds, with links for purchase.

W Kidzpage, http://gardenofsong.com/kidzpage ▪ Specialized software programs for poetry writing.

C, T Laura Candler, www.lauracandler.com ▪ This teacher's site offers literary lessons and related tools.

V, T Lesson Plan Central, http://lessonplancentral.com/lessons/Language_Arts/Vocabulary/ ▪ This site includes vocabulary lesson plans.

F Lois Walker's site, www.scriptsforschools.com ▪ For teachers interested in drama, this site offers script packages for beginning readers for a small price.

I Magic School Bus, http://scholastic.com/MagicSchoolBus/index.htm ■ This site includes content area materials and activities for children, as well as a resource area for teachers.

C, I Miss Maggie, www.missmaggie.org ■ Miss Maggie's earth adventures uses puzzles, activities, and games to teach children about environmental issues. The site includes weekly lesson plans, cross-curricular activities, and companion books and articles.

E, P, PH, G MoJo's Musical Mouseum, www.kididdles.com/lyrics/index.html ■ Click on the musical notes displayed by the song titles in this site and hear a music box play the tune while you read the lyrics. Song lyrics may be accessed through a subject index or a searchable database.

W, I Montgomery County Teacher Websites, www.montgomery.k12.ky.us ■ Teachers and students will find many informational links to sound and photo displays of Western subjects (e.g., cowboys and rodeos).

W, T Months of the Year, www.siec.k12.in.us/~west/proj/month ■ Links to activities that relate to every month of the year. Includes projects completed by first-grade children, but other children can share their projects for inclusion on the site.

E, PA, PH, P MotherGoose.com, www.mothergoose.com ■ Free preschool games, crafts, letter-play, and rhyming activities. Over 360 Mother Goose rhymes.

P Mr. Rogers' Neighborhood Online, www.pbskids.org/rogers ■ This site offers the same quality learning experiences as the television show.

I My Hero Project, www.myhero.com ■ This site allows children to read about many heroes and heroines around the world as they come to understand what it means to make a difference.

W My Town Is Important, www.mrsmcgowan.com/projects.html ■ Mrs. McGowan's project allows students to work collaboratively and create projects about their own cities.

P, E Net-Mom's Internet Safehouse, www.netmom.com ■ Great site for preschoolers and their parents. Lots of activities to get young children excited about reading.

I New Literacies, http://ctell.uconn.edu/cases.htm ■ Multimedia cases focused on literacy instruction; created to help teachers improve children's reading achievement.

I New York Philharmonic Kidzone, www.nyphilkids.org/main.phtml ■ Activities on this site include videos about instruments, composing music, games and puzzles.

F Poetry for Kids, www.poetry4kids.com/index.php ■ This site helps teachers use poetry to teach fluency.

P, E PBS Kids, www.pbskids.org ■ Lots of early literacy activities and great information to help parents foster their young children's literacy development.

T Preschool Rainbow, www.preschoolrainbow.org ■ Site is billed as the place where "early childhood teachers find their ideas." Thematically arranged curricula, games, and so forth.

I Rainforest, www.rainforestheroes.com ■ Many environmental ideas, especially about saving the rainforest, can be found here. Contains marvelous color and sound effects that will delight young readers, although it is mainly a teacher resource center.

PA, T, C, W Read, Think, Write, www.readwritethink.org ■ This site offers phonemic awareness games and activities and options allowing children to respond to literature.

F, T Readers theater sites: www.aaronshep.com/rt/index.html, www.teachingheart.net/readerstheater.htm ■ These sites offer scripts and other tools for readers theater programs.

T, E Reading Is Fundamental, www.rif.org ▪ By visiting this site, teachers will get involved with one of the nation's best-known reading initiatives. It includes practical information on books to bring to the classroom and has a program for early readers designed to get child-care providers involved in early literacy.

C, W Reading Planet, www.rif.org/readingplanet/content/read_aloud_stories.mspx ▪ This Reading Is Fundamental site offers ideas and activities to incorporate into the curriculum and keep students interested and motivated.

C, W, T Reading Rubrics, www.mrsmcgowan.com/reading/writing_resources.html ▪ This portion of Mrs. McGowan's site includes rubrics for comprehension, poetry writing, and holistic writing.

P, T Scholastic, www2.scholastic.com/browse/article.jsp?id=4493 ▪ This Scholastic site offers a "teaching with phonics" skills chart for teachers.

F, T Scholastic, www2.scholastic.com/browse/article.jsp?id=4496 ▪ This Scholastic site offers an oral fluency calculator.

P, T Scholastic, http://teacher.scholastic.com/reading/bestpractices/phonics/nonsensewordtest.pdf ▪ This Scholastic site offers a PDF printout of the Nonsense Word Test.

I Smithsonian Education, www.smithsonianeducation.org ▪ This is an extraordinary museum site. Click on History & Culture on the left-hand side under Topics. There you will learn about the Wright Brothers, Black Wing, and World War II aviators.

PA, T Songs for Teaching, www.songsforteaching.com/avni/alliterativebooks.htm ▪ Children's books for teaching phonemic awareness with rhyme, alliteration, and other word play.

E, PH Starfall.com, www.starfall.com/n/level-k/index/play.htm?f ▪ An adult narrator pronounces the name of each capital letter as the child clicks on it, reinforcing letter names. A child narrator says the name of the lowercase letters. Activities and animations are brief, motivational, and support letter recognition and beginning phonics.

PA, T TEAMS Educational Resources, http://teams.lacoe.edu/teachers/index.asp ▪ Rhyming word activities and a wide variety of other phonemic awareness activities.

V, T Tech Teachers, www.techteachers.com/vocabulary.htm ▪ This site offers many links to sites focusing on vocabulary development using digital tools.

I U.S. Library of Congress, http://lcweb.loc.gov/homepage/lchp.html ▪ Here teachers will find a wealth of information for learners of all ages about virtually any informational topic. Click on Kids, Families. Then click on Jump Back in Time to explore any historical era.

V, T Vocabulary.com, www.vocabulary.com ▪ Learning activities and lesson plans to help teachers plan effective vocabulary instruction.

I When They Were Young, www.loc.gov/exhibits/young/young-exhibit.html ▪ This virtual tour of an exhibit at the U.S. Library of Congress shows engrossing photographs of children that cross generations and cultures.

V Word Wizard, www.wordwizard.com ▪ At this amazing site, children can find anything at all pertaining to words.

I Zoobooks series, www.zoobooks.com ▪ This series has a website with pictures, sound effects, games, and information about wild animals.

Commercial Assessment Instruments

CRITERION-REFERENCED READING TESTS

Basic Inventory of Natural Language. San Bernardino, CA: CHECpoint Systems. (Grades K–12)

The Lollipop Test: A Diagnostic Screening Test of School Readiness. Atlanta, GA: Humanistics Limited. (First half of K to grade 1 entrants)

PRI Reading Systems. Monterey, CA: CTB/McGraw-Hill. (Grades K–9)

Reading Yardsticks. Chicago: Riverside Publishing Company. (Grades K–8)

Woodcock Reading Mastery Tests. Woodcock, R. W. Circle Pines, MN: American Guidance Services. (Grades K–12)

FORMAL READING TESTS

Biemiller Test of Reading Processes. Biemiller, A. Toronto, Ontario, Canada: Guidance Centre. (Grades 2–6)

California Achievement Test, Forms C and D. Monterey, CA: CTB/McGraw-Hill. (Grades K–12.9)

Gates–MacGinitie Reading Tests. MacGinitie, W. H. Chicago: Riverside Publishing. (Ages 6 1/2–17)

Iowa Test of Basic Skills: Primary Battery. Chicago: Riverside Publishing. (Grades K–3.2)

Metropolitan Achievement Test. San Antonio, TX: The Psychological Corporation. (Grades K–12.9)

Stanford Achievement Test. San Antonio, TX: The Psychological Corporation. (Grades 1.5–9.9)

Test of Reading Comprehension (TORC). Brown, V., Hammill, J., and Wiederholt, J. L. Austin, TX: PRO ED. (Grades 2–6)

FORMAL TESTS FOR EMERGENT READERS

Clymer Barrett Reading Test. Santa Barbara, CA: Chapman, Brook, & Kent. (Grades K and beginning 1)

CTBS Readiness Test. Monterey, CA: CTB/McGraw-Hill. (Grades K.0 to 1.3)

Metropolitan Readiness Test. Nurss, J. R., and McGauvran, M. E. San Antonio, TX: The Psychological Corporation. (First half of K to beginning Grade 1)

The Primary Language Record: Handbook for Teachers. Portsmouth, NH: Heinemann. (Preschool to Grade 2)

"Sand: Concepts about Print" Tests. Clay, M. M. Portsmouth, NH: Heinemann. (Pre-K to end of K)

Stanford Early School Achievement Test (SESAT). Madden, R., Gardner, E. F., and Collins, C. S. San Antonio, TX: The Psychological Corporation. (Grades K–1.9)

"Stone: Concepts about Print" Tests. Clay, M. M. Portsmouth, NH: Heinemann. (Pre-K to end of K)

Test of Basic Experiences 2 (TOBE2). Moss, M. H. Monterey, CA: CTB/McGraw-Hill. (Pre-K to end of Grade 1)

The Test of Early Reading Ability (TERA). Reid, D. K., Hresko, W. P., and Hammill, D. D. Austin, TX: PRO-ED. (Ages 3 to 7)

INFORMAL READING INVENTORIES

Analytical Reading Inventory. Woods, M. L., and Moe, A. J. Boston: Pearson.

Bader Reading and Language Inventory. Bader, L. A. New York: Macmillan.

Basic Reading Inventory Pre-Primer–Grade Twelve. Johns, J. L. Dubuque, IA: Kendall/Hunt.

Burns/Roe Informal Reading Inventory. Roe, B. D. Boston: Houghton Mifflin.

Classroom Reading Inventory. Silvaroli, N. J., and Wheelock, W. H. New York: McGraw-Hill.

Diagnostic Reading Inventory. Jacobs, H. D., and Searfoss, L. W. Dubuque, IA: Kendall/Hunt.

Ekwall/Shanker Reading Inventory. Shanker, J. L., and Cockrum, W. E. Boston: Pearson.

The Flynt–Cooter Reading Inventory for the Classroom. Flynt, E. S., and Cooter, R. B., Jr. Columbus, OH: Merrill/Prentice Hall.

Qualitative Reading Inventory. Leslie, L., and Caldwell, J. S. Boston: Allyn & Bacon.

Reading Miscue Inventory: Alternative Procedures. Goodman, Y., Watson, D. J., and Burke, C. L. Katonah, NY: Richard C. Owens.

Reading Placement Inventory. Sucher, F., and Allred, R. A. Oklahoma City: The Economy Company.

Retrospective Miscue Analysis: Revaluing Readers and Reading. Goodman, Y., and Marek, A. M. Katonah, NY: Richard C. Owens.

Texas Primary Reading Inventory. Austin, TX: Texas Education Agency.

PHONEMIC AWARENESS TESTS

Auditory Discrimination Test. Wepman, J. Los Angeles: Western Psychological Services.

Comprehensive Test of Reading Related Phonological Processes. Torgeson, J., and Wagner, W. Austin, TX: PRO-ED. 512-451-3246.

Lindamood Auditory Conceptualization Test. Lindamood, C., and Lindamood, P. Austin, TX: PRO-ED. 512-451-3246.

The Phonological Awareness Profile. Robertson, C., and Salter, W. East Moline, IL: LinguiSystems. 800-PRO-IDEA.

Scholastic Ready-to-Use Primary Reading Assessment Kit. Fiderer, A. New York: Scholastic, 1998. 800-724-6527.

Test of Awareness of Language Segments. Sawyer, D. J. Austin, TX: PRO-ED. 512-451-3246.

Test of Phonological Awareness. Torgeson, J., and Bryant, B. Austin, TX: PRO-ED. 512-451-3246.

HOW THE TOOLS IN THIS APPENDIX ARE ORGANIZED

Knowledge of Print

Name _____   Date _____

Interest in Writing

○ Very motivated (enjoys writing)

○ Moderate (writes with prompting)

○ Minimal (only writes if asked to do so)

Awareness of Directionality

○ Consistently writes from left to right and top to bottom

○ Sometimes writes from left to right and top to bottom

○ No awareness of directionality evident

Word Representation

○ Includes a vowel when representing a word

○ Uses several letters to represent a word; not always a vowel

○ Uses a phonetically correct initial consonant for words

○ Can write own name

○ Uses random shapes, letters, and numbers for writing

○ Uses drawings alone to represent writing

Concepts About Print Assessment

Name _____   Date _____

Book Orientation

○ Can point to front of book
○ Can point to back of book
○ Can point to title

Difference Between Illustrations and Print

○ Can point to illustrations
○ Can point to print
○ Can point to where text begins

Directionality of Print

○ Can show directionality of print on page
○ Can point to beginning of text
○ Can point to end of text
○ Can show beginning and end of words on page (knows word boundaries)

Print Terminology

○ Can identify top and bottom of page
○ Can point to a letter
○ Can point to a word
○ Can point to a specific word on request
○ Can point to a specific letter on request
○ Can point to a lowercase letter
○ Can point to an uppercase letter
○ Can identify different punctuation marks on request

Interest Inventory

Name _____   Age _____   Sex _____   Date _____

1. What do you like to do most when you have spare time?

   _____

2. What do you usually do after school?

   _____

   in the evenings?

   _____

   on Sundays?

   _____

   on Saturdays?

   _____

3. How old are your brothers and sisters? _____

   How do you get along with them? _____

   What do you like to do with them?

   _____

4. Do you take any special lessons?

   _____

5. Are your parents/grandparents from another country? _____

   Which one? _____ What language do they speak? _____

6. What kind of food do you like?

   _____

7. Have you ever been to a(n): *(circle all that apply)*

   airport?   circus?   library?   museum?   farm?

   amusement park?   concert?   picnic?   ball game?   zoo?

   swimming pool?   beach?   dairy?   firehouse?

8. Have you ever taken a trip by: *(circle all that apply)*

   airplane?   train?   bus?   boat?

   Where did you go? _____

9. What types of work do you think you would like to do to earn money?

_____

10. What television programs do you like best?

_____

videos?

_____

computer programs?

_____

11. Do you ever listen to the news on TV? _____

12. What songs do you like?

_____

13. Do you have any pets? _____ What kind? _____

_____

What kind of pet would you like to have?

_____

14. Do you have books you read for fun at home? _____

15. Do you like to have someone read aloud to you? _____

16. Do you ever use the Internet by yourself or with your family? If so, what kind of sites do you like to visit?

_____

17. What is your favorite type of story?

_____

18. Are there any books you would like to own?

_____

19. What book is your all-time favorite? *(only one title, please)*

_____

20. Do you enjoy shopping alone or with friends best? _____

21. Which video do you like best?

_____

22. Would you rather spend your relaxation time alone or with others?

_____

An Early Reader's View of the Reading Process

Name _____   Age _____   Sex _____   Date _____

1. Name someone you know who is a good reader. _____
   What makes him/her a good reader?
   _____

2. Do you think (person named in #1) ever comes to a word they don't know
   or an idea they don't understand when they are reading? _____

3. (If yes for #2) When they come to a word they don't know or an idea they
   don't understand, what do you think they do about it?
   _____

4. When *you* are reading and you come to a word you don't know, what do
   you do?
   _____

5. If you knew that someone was having trouble in reading, how would you
   help that person?
   _____

6. What do you think a teacher would do to help that person?
   _____

7. Who helped you learn to read? _____
   How did they help you?
   _____

8. What would you like to be able to do better when you read?
   _____

9. Do you think that you are a good reader?_____
   Why or why not?
   _____

10. What do you like/dislike about reading?
    _____

    Additional notes or comments:
    _____

Response to Literature Checklist

Name _____   Date _____

Responds to teacher's questions

Never	Sometimes	Frequently	Always

Comments on or interprets text

Never	Sometimes	Frequently	Always

Connects text to own life

Never	Sometimes	Frequently	Always

Asks questions about text

Never	Sometimes	Frequently	Always

Makes predictions

Never	Sometimes	Frequently	Always

Shares own background information related to text

Never	Sometimes	Frequently	Always

Strays from topic of text

Never	Sometimes	Frequently	Always

Primary Reading Attitude Survey

Name _____   Date _____

How Do You Feel . . .

1. When you read?

2. About school?

3. About reading in your free time?

4. About going to the library?

5. About reading instead of watching TV?

6. About reading to your family?

7. About reading at your desk in school?

8. About how important reading is?

9. About reading at bedtime?

10. About writing your own stories?

11. About reading to try to learn something?

12. When someone else reads to you?

13. When you come to a new word in a story?

14. About reading in your favorite subject in school?

15. About your reading group in school?

16. About reading out loud?

17. About checking out books from the library?

18. About reading with your teacher?

19. About answering questions about what you read?

20. About taking reading tests?

Primary Reading Attitude Survey Scoring Sheet

Student _____   Grade _____

Teacher _____   Administration Date _____

Scoring guide

☺ 3 points   😐 2 points   ☹ 1 point

Recreational Reading	Academic Reading
1. _____	11. _____
2. _____	12. _____
3. _____	13. _____
4. _____	14. _____
5. _____	15. _____
6. _____	16. _____
7. _____	17. _____
8. _____	18. _____
9. _____	19. _____
10. _____	20. _____

Raw score _____   Raw score _____

Full scale raw score (Recreational + Academic) _____

Percentile Ranks

Recreational _____

Academic _____

Full scale _____

Quick Phonemic Awareness Assessment Device

A high correlation exists between the ability to recognize spoken words as a sequence of individual sounds and reading achievement. Explicit instruction can increase the phonemic awareness of children. To assist in determining the level of phonemic awareness of each child in your class, the following assessment items may be utilized. *Use as many samples as necessary to determine mastery.*

Assessment 1. Isolation of beginning sounds. Ask the child what the first sound of selected words is.

"What is the first sound in *dog?*"

Assessment 2. Deletion of initial sound. Read a word and ask the child to say it without the first sound.

"Say the word *cat.* Say *cat* without the /k/."

Assessment 3. Segmentation of phonemes. Ask the child to say the separate sounds of the word being read.

"What are the two sounds in the word *go?*"

Assessment 4. Blending of phonemes. Slowly read the individual sounds of a word and ask the child to tell what the word is.

"What word am I saying? /d/ /o/ /g/"

Assessment 5. Phoneme manipulation. Read a word and ask the child to replace the initial sound with another. Have the child say the new word.

"In the word *fan,* the first sound is an /f/. If you replace the /f/ with an /m/, how would you say the new word?"

Assessments for Phonological Awareness*

DIRECTIONS FOR USE

Teachers: You will probably not need to complete these assessments for all of your students. Teacher observation and anecdotal records for each child in your class will determine which students need to acquire skills. Description of students to use assessment with:

- difficulty identifying sound elements
- difficulty recognizing when sounds rhyme
- unable to recognize familiar sight words
- nonreaders or emergent readers

For accurate results, follow the guidelines listed here. When completing assessments:

- Make sure children understand concepts being used, such as *beginning, end, first, last, same, sound,* and so on. Use terms they are familiar with.
- Always reinforce task to be completed by modeling or teaching, if necessary, during practice only. Continue until concept is clear or it is apparent the student cannot perform the task. Record practice responses to refer to later.
- Require students to pronounce only sounds asked for, without adding extra sounds.
- A letter between two slash marks, for example /m/, represents the sound that letter stands for. Use during assessment to record student responses.
- A capital letter represents the name of the letter as a response. Record student response, but remind student to say the sounds, not the letter names.
- Put a check ✔ when student responds correctly, or record incorrect response. If an incorrect response is made before correct response, record error first, then put a check.
- When the student waits or hesitates more than 3 seconds, record with a <u>W</u>. Then, record the response, if any, and continue on to the next word.
- If no response is given, say "Try it" and record with a <u>T</u>. Then record the response, if any, and continue on to the next word.

A score of 4/5 or greater on each assessment task generally demonstrates adequate knowledge in this task. Lower scores reflect a need for some instruction in the task. Teach identified tasks using Phonological Awareness Activity Guide at appropriate levels based on results.

*Developed by Katherine Beilby. Used with permission.

Name _____   Grade _____   Date _____

Phonological Awareness: Rhyme

Directions: Responses to rhymes must include more than the ending of the given word (e.g., jam, am is not acceptable). Nonsense words are an acceptable response. Record all responses on the line following each prompt given by teacher, including practice responses. Explain and model tasks during practice only.

Practice: Say "Rhyming words sound the same at the end. I can rhyme with dad: mad, sad. Tell me a word that rhymes with: pin, (_____), fat, (_____), tie, (_____)."

Assessment:

1. sick _____   2. jam _____   3. dog _____   4. wet _____   5. cup _____

SCORE _____

Phonological Awareness: Matching Beginning Sound to Word

Directions: Require student to pronounce only the beginning consonant sound (not letter names). Reinforce correct responses during practice only.

Practice: Say "I'm going to say a sound that you hear at the beginning of a word. I can say the first sound in mug, /m/; the first sound in rug, /r/. Listen closely and tell me the first sound in: man, (_____), sing, (_____), late, (_____)."

Assessment:

1. sun _____   2. not _____   3. like _____   4. five _____   5. mat _____

SCORE _____

Phonological Awareness: Blending Onset–Rimes

Directions: This task demonstrates how sounds can be put together to make words. Onset is the part of the word that precedes the vowel, while rime would include everything from the vowel on.

Practice: Say "Now I will say the first sound and then the rest of the word to make a whole word. I can put these sounds together: /r/ un, run; /s/ et, set. Listen closely and tell me the word I have when I put these sounds together: /m/ op, (_____), /w/ eek, (_____), /s/ ome, (_____)."

Assessment:

1. /m/ ut _____   2. /f/ it _____   3. /n/ ap _____   4. /l/ et _____   5. /s/ ock _____

SCORE _____

Comments:

_____

_____

Phonological Awareness: Segmenting Onset–Rimes

Directions: This task requires the student to take words apart by saying the first sound and then the rest of the word. Reinforce tasks during practice only.

Practice: Say "I can say the sounds in a word: name, /n/ ame; let, /l/ et. Tell me the sounds in coat, (_____), let, (_____), hip, (_____)."

Assessment:

   1. lap _____   2. jet _____   3. fun _____   4. mom _____   5. sit _____

   SCORE _____

Phonological Awareness: Blending Phonemes

Directions: This task requires the student to synthesize or blend each sound in a word. The teacher must pronounce the sounds in a word and have the students say the word quickly. Blending and segmenting tasks require very stretched pronunciation of words without stopping between sounds.

Practice: Say "I'm going to say a word very slowly, and then I'll say it fast: /s/ /a/ /t/, sat. I'll say a word slowly. You say it fast. /h/ /i/ /de/ (_____), /b/ /i/ /g/ (_____)."

Assessment:

   1. /f/ /a/ /t/ _____   2. /k/ /ee/ /p/ _____   3. /t/ /i/ /me/ _____
   4. /p/ /e/ /t/ _____   5. /h/ /o/ /pe/ _____

   SCORE _____

Phonological Awareness: Segmenting Phonemes

Directions: This task requires the student to analyze or segment each sound in a word. Segmenting is the opposite of blending. Each sound must be clearly articulated to receive full credit.

Practice: Say "I can say each sound in a word: came, /c/ /a/ /me/. Tell me each sound in the word sad, (_____), deer, (_____)."

Assessment:

   1. red _____   2. pig _____   3. home _____   4. bus _____   5. cake _____

   SCORE _____

Comments:

_____

_____

_____

_____

_____

Knowledge of Sounds and Letters Checklist

Have child: First: "Read letter names." Second: "Give letter sounds."

n **f** s   n **k** s   n **i** s   n **t** s   n **c** s
○   ○   ○   ○   ○   ○   ○   ○   ○   ○

n **o** s   n **x** s   n **a** s   n **g** s   n **u** s
○   ○   ○   ○   ○   ○   ○   ○   ○   ○

n **z** s   n **p** s   n **j** s   n **v** s   n **q** s
○   ○   ○   ○   ○   ○   ○   ○   ○   ○

n **b** s   n **r** s   n **l** s   n **m** s   n **d** s
○   ○   ○   ○   ○   ○   ○   ○   ○   ○

n **n** s   n **w** s   n **s** s   n **e** s   n **y** s
○   ○   ○   ○   ○   ○   ○   ○   ○   ○

n **h** s   n **ch** s   n **th** s   n **sh** s
○   ○   ○   ○   ○   ○   ○   ○

Key: n   name said correctly   s   correct sound given
           ✔   ✔

Note: If only the long sounds of a, e, i, o, u are given, ask for "another" sound. (Also true of c and g, which also have alternate sounds.) If given, add another check beside circle.

Phonics Mastery Survey

Instructions: Before administering this survey, reproduce letters and words on 3 × 5-inch cards in large, lowercase letters, so the child can see them with ease. This survey should be administered to one child at a time. Use a separate sheet to document each child's progress. In the first section, stop if the child makes more than ten errors. For every other section, stop when child makes five or more errors. When sounds are incorrect, write the sound the child makes above the word.

1. Consonant Sounds

Show the child one card at a time, featuring lowercase consonant letters. Ask the child to tell you what sound the letter makes. On the assessment sheet, circle the letter if an incorrect sound is given. Write the incorrect sound the child gives on top of the letter.

p   b   m   w   f   v   t   s   d   r   j   h   z   n   l   y   k   c   g

If the child is not able to identify at least ten sounds, terminate this assessment and administer the Knowledge of Sounds and Letters Checklist (p. 380).

2. Rhyming Words

Ask the child to read the following words and to say three words that rhyme with each of them. Nonsense words are acceptable.

1. be _____

2. go _____

3. say _____

4. do _____

5. make _____

6. will _____

7. get _____

8. blink _____

9. tan _____

10. bug _____

3. CVC Words

Ask the child to read the following short-vowel, cvc nonsense words. There are four examples of each short vowel sound. Indicate which vowel sounds were read correctly and which were not.

1. nid _____		11. wat _____	
2. gat _____		12. vin _____	
3. bul _____		13. lom _____	
4. rup _____		14. hap _____	
5. sen _____		15. yub _____	
6. nat _____		16. pem _____	
7. det _____		17. dom _____	
8. rit _____		18. kud _____	
9. nup _____		19. wom _____	
10. nop _____		20. zet _____	

4. Consonant Blends

Ask the child to read the following words and nonsense words that contain beginning or ending consonant blends (or both). Indicate any blends the child says incorrectly.

1. blithe _____		11. trink _____	
2. clog _____		12. brind _____	
3. plush _____		13. scup _____	
4. flounce _____		14. stint _____	
5. frisk _____		15. smeat _____	
6. dwelt _____		16. spole _____	
7. skig _____		17. gluck _____	
8. crass _____		18. brame _____	
9. trek _____		19. dredge _____	
10. swap _____		20. lasp _____	

5. Consonant Digraphs

Have the child read the following nonsense words containing consonant digraphs. Indicate any digraphs the child says incorrectly.

1. shan	_____		11. scord	_____
2. thort	_____		12. squean	_____
3. phrat	_____		13. sling	_____
4. chib	_____		14. sprill	_____
5. phant	_____		15. strug	_____
6. yeth	_____		16. splom	_____
7. roch	_____		17. shred	_____
8. lotch	_____		18. squim	_____
9. gresh	_____		19. throbe	_____
10. chass	_____			

6. Long Vowel Sounds

Ask children to read the following nonsense words that contain long vowel sounds. There are four examples of each long vowel sound. Indicate which vowels are read correctly and which are not.

1. stope	_____		11. ploan	_____
2. kade	_____		12. tayne	_____
3. fede	_____		13. sheed	_____
4. gride	_____		14. vied	_____
5. blude	_____		15. trewd	_____
6. kroan	_____		16. whade	_____
7. jaike	_____		17. strean	_____
8. theade	_____		18. blipe	_____
9. smight	_____		19. roke	_____
10. dreud	_____		20. krume	_____

7. Other Vowel Sounds

Have the child read the following words and nonsense words that contain variant vowel sounds. Indicate vowel sounds the child reads incorrectly.

1. nook (oo) _____

2. krouse (ou, ow) _____

3. sar (ar) _____

4. moil (oi) _____

5. noy (oy) _____

6. thirl (ir, er, ur) _____

7. floom (oo) _____

8. gorn (or) _____

9. chaw (aw, au) _____

10. zout (ou) _____

11. larm (ar) _____

12. groil (oi) _____

13. nirl (ir, er, ur) _____

8. Number of Word Parts (Syllables)

Ask the child to read the following words and count the number of word parts or syllables in each word. (Correct answers are in parentheses.)

1. retention (3) _____

2. ride (1) _____

3. panic (2) _____

4. carnival (3) _____

5. monster (2) _____

6. contaminate (4) _____

7. computer (3) _____

8. antagonist (4) _____

9. guess (1) _____

10. consider (3) _____

Peer Editor's Feedback for Writing

Author: _____   Editor: _____

Editor: Please answer these questions about my writing.

1. Do you think the opening grabs you?

   ○ Yes   ○ No

   What would you change?

   _____

   _____

   _____

2. Is there a part I should throw away?

   ○ Yes   ○ No

   Which part?

   _____

   _____

   _____

3. Did I use any tired words?

   ○ Yes   ○ No

   Which ones?

   _____

   _____

   _____

4. What is the best part of my writing?

   _____

   _____

   _____

5. Is there any part you didn't understand?

   ○ Yes   ○ No

   Which part?

   _____

   _____

   _____

6. Do I need a different ending?

   ○ Yes   ○ No

   What would you change?

   _____

   _____

   _____

7. Are there any sentences I should combine or separate? If yes, put the sentence numbers in the box. If no, leave the box blank.

   Combine [_____]

   Separate [_____]

8. What do you like best? Why?

   _____

   _____

   _____

Praise, Question, and Polish (PQP) Form

Title of piece: _____ Date: _____

Author: _____

Peer Editor: _____

Praise: What do you like about the piece? Be specific.

_____

_____

_____

_____

_____

_____

_____

Question: What questions do you have about things you don't understand in the piece?

_____

_____

_____

_____

_____

_____

_____

Polish: What suggestions do you have to make the piece even better?

_____

_____

_____

_____

_____

_____

_____

Beginning Writer's Checklist

Name _____   Date _____

Key: 3 Almost always   2 Sometimes   1 Rarely

Book Orientation

_____ Draws pictures most of the time

_____ Tells about pictures

_____ Draws pictures to accompany writing

Composing/Writing

_____ Generates story ideas orally

_____ Thinks of own ideas and writes them

_____ Uses models or themes in stories

_____ Uses patterns (scaffolds) for writing

Writing Fluency

_____ Uses one- or two-word patterns

_____ Writes two to four lines

_____ Writes easy pattern texts

_____ Writes two to four paragraphs

_____ Writes chapter books

Use of Writing Process

_____ Prewrites (maps, webs, orally rehearses ideas)

_____ Reads writing to others

_____ Does multiple drafts

_____ Offers constructive feedback to others

_____ Makes changes based on feedback

6 + 1 Trait Rubric: 5-Point Beginning Writer's Rubric

1. EXPERIMENTING	2. EMERGING	3. DEVELOPING	4. CAPABLE	5. EXPERIENCED
Ideas	Ideas	Ideas	Ideas	Ideas
Big Idea is unclear; print sense is just beginning	Big Idea is conveyed in a general way through text, labels, symbols	Big Idea is stated in text	Big Idea is clear, but general—a simple story or explanation	Big Idea is clear; topic is narrow, fresh, and original
A Details are missing, or if present, are unclear	Few details are present	Details are relevant to topic and support Big Idea	Details are telling, and sometimes specific to Big Idea	Details are accurate, relevant, high-quality, and support or enrich Big Idea
B Experience with topic is unclear	Some experience with topic is demonstrated	Experience with topic is obvious	Experience with topic is supported by text	Experience with topic is demonstrated clearly
C Pictures, if present, are unclear	Pictures, if present, connect to a few words	Pictures, if present, support topic	Pictures, if present, add descriptive details to topic	Pictures, if present, clarify, enrich, and enhance topic

Key question: Does the writer stay focused and share original and fresh information or perspective about the topic?

Organization	Organization	Organization	Organization	Organization
Beginning/ending is absent	A bare beginning is present	Beginning and middle are present, but no ending	Beginning, middle, and predictable ending are present	Beginning attracts, middle works, ending is present
A Transitions are not present	Transitions are starting to emerge	Transitions rely on connective "and"	Transitions work in predictable fashion	Transitions are somewhat varied
B Sequencing is not present	Sequencing is limited or confusing	Sequencing is adequate	Sequencing is sound	Sequencing is purposeful from start to finish
C Pacing is not evident	Pacing is predictable, monotonous	Pacing is adequate	Pacing moves reader through piece	Pacing is purposeful
D Title (if required) is missing	Title (if required) is attempted	Simple title (if required) works	Title (if required) fits content	Title (if required) is engaging
E Structure is random	Structure is unclear or only starting to emerge	Structure is present and works	Structure matches purpose	Structure clarifies topic

Key question: Does the organizational structure enhance the ideas and make the piece easier to understand?

Voice	Voice	Voice	Voice	Voice
Individual expression is not present	Individual expression is emerging	Individual expression is present	Individual expression is supported by text	Individual expression reflects unique tone
A Writing for audience is not evident	Writing starts to address audience	Writing addresses audience in a general way	Writing connects to audience	Writing clearly engages audience
B Voice is not discernible	Voice is emerging in pictures and/or text	Voice is present	Voice supports writer's purpose	Voice is engaging and enthusiastic for purpose
C Risk-taking is not evident	Risk-taking is limited to "safe" choices	Risk-taking reveals moments of sparkle	Risk-taking uncovers individual perspective	Risk-taking reveals person behind words

Key question: Would you keep reading this piece if it were longer?

	1. EXPERIMENTING	2. EMERGING	3. DEVELOPING	4. CAPABLE	5. EXPERIENCED
	Word Choice	Word Choice	Word Choice	Word Choice	Word Choice
	No words are present— only letters strung together or scribbles	Words are difficult to decode; some are recognizable	General or ordinary words convey message	Favorite words are used correctly	Specific, accurate words are used well
A	Word patters are imitated	Environmental words are used correctly	New words are attempted but don't always fit	New and different words are used with some success	Precise, fresh, original words linger in reader's mind
B	Vocabulary relies upon environmental print	Vocabulary includes phrases, clichés	Vocabulary is limited to safe, known words	Vocabulary is expanding	Vocabulary is natural, effective, and targets audience
C	No awareness of parts of speech exists	Nouns emerge as main word choice	Basic verbs and nouns dominate piece	Modifiers add to mix of words	Variety of parts of speech adds depth
D	Words do not convey meaning of piece	Words begin to convey single idea or topic	Words are mundane, normal, generic for topic	Words clarify topic and convey meaning	Words enhance, enrich, and/or showcase meaning
E	Words do not create mental imagery	Words begin to create mental imagery	Words are grouped in ways that create general mental imagery	Phrases, word groups create specific mental imagery	Strong attempts at figurative language create clear mental imagery

Key question: Do the words and phrases create vivid pictures and linger in your mind?

	Sentence Fluency	Sentence Fluency	Sentence Fluency	Sentence Fluency	Sentence Fluency
	Letters and words are scribbled across page	Words are strung together into phrases	Simple sentences are used to convey meaning	Simple and compound sentences strengthen piece	Consistently varied sentence construction enhances piece
A	Sentences are not used, but instead random words or marks	Sentence parts are present, but not complete	Most simple sentence parts are present; variety in beginnings or length exists	Sentence structure varies; variety in beginnings and length exists	Sentences vary in structure as well as beginnings and length
B	Connective words do not exist	Connective words may appear in sentence parts	Connective words, mostly "and," serve as links between phrases	Connective words are more varied	Connective words work smoothly and enrich fluency
C	Rhythm is not evident	Rhythm is choppy and repetitive	Rhythm is more mechanical than fluid	Rhythm is more fluid than mechanical and is easy to read aloud	Rhythm is fluid and pleasant to read aloud

Key question: Can you feel the words and phrases flow together as you read it aloud?

1. EXPERIMENTING	2. EMERGING	3. DEVELOPING	4. CAPABLE	5. EXPERIENCED
Conventions	**Conventions**	**Conventions**	**Conventions**	**Conventions**
Nearly every convention requires editing	Some conventions are correct, most are not	Half of conventions are correct and half need editing	More conventions are correct than not	Conventions require little editing to be published

	1. EXPERIMENTING	2. EMERGING	3. DEVELOPING	4. CAPABLE	5. EXPERIENCED
A	Spelling is not evident, only strings of letters	Semiphonetic spelling is attempted	Phonetic spelling is used; high-frequency words are still spotty	Spelling is usually accurate for grade-level words	High-frequency words are spelled correctly; spelling is very close on others
B	No sense of punctuation exists	Random punctuation exists	End punctuation is usually correct, experiments with other punctuation	End punctuation is correct; some other punctuation is correct	Punctuation is usually correct and/or sometimes even creative
C	Print sense is still emerging	Upper and lowercase letters are randomly used	Capitals are inconsistent but begin most sentences and some proper nouns	Capitals are more consistent and begin sentences and most proper nouns	Capitals are consistently accurate for sentence beginnings, proper nouns, and title
D	No awareness of grammar and/or usage exists	Part of a grammatical construction is present	A grammatical construction is present	Subject/verb agreement, proper tense are present but the rest is still spotty	Some control is shown over basic grade-level grammar

Key question: How much editing would have to be done to be ready to share with an outside source? (Expectations should be based on grade level and include only skills that have been taught.)

	1. EXPERIMENTING	2. EMERGING	3. DEVELOPING	4. CAPABLE	5. EXPERIENCED
	Presentation	**Presentation**	**Presentation**	**Presentation**	**Presentation**
	No formatting clues are present; placement of text and pictures is totally random	Formatting of text and pictures is starting to come together	Formatting of text and pictures is generally correct	Formatting of text and pictures is clear and thoughtful	Formatting of text and pictures assists comprehension
A	Only scribbles are present	Handwriting shows letters beginning to take shape, though random in placement	Handwriting includes few discrepancies in letter shape; shapes are easily identifiable	Handwriting reveals proper manuscript, spaced and written appropriately	Handwriting is neat and easy to read; proper manuscript or cursive is used
B	Letters and/or words are strung together with no spacing	Spacing between letters and words is attempted	Spacing of words is mostly correct	Words, sentences, and paragraphs have proper spacing	White space is used well within piece and to frame text
C	If pictures are present, they are randomly placed	Pictures are placed appropriately	Pictures fit with text	Pictures add detail, support piece, and are appropriate	Pictures are "balanced" with text and match content
D	No identifiable markers (title, heading, bullets, page numbers) exist	Markers are present but not connected to text	Some markers match some text	Markers clarify, organize, and define text	Markers enrich, enhance, and/or help showcase text
E	No charts, tables, graphs are evident	Charts, tables, graphs are attempted but randomly placed	Charts, tables, graphs match text and are placed properly	Charts, tables, graphs match and clarify text; are placed together properly	Charts, tables, graphs match, clarify, and enrich text and are placed properly

Key question: Is the finished piece easy to read, polished in presentation, and pleasing to the eye?

Fluency Questions for Student Self-Assessment

Name _____   Date _____

- ○ Did my reading sound the way people really talk?
- ○ Would someone understand what the author meant from listening to me read?
- ○ Did I have to work hard to pronounce the words right?
- ○ Did I make many mistakes in my reading?
- ○ When I made a mistake that changed the meaning, did I go back and change it?
- ○ Did I read with good expression?
- ○ Did I change the loudness and softness to show the meaning?
- ○ Did I change the speed when I needed to, to stress certain parts?
- ○ Did I read too slowly?
- ○ Did I read too quickly?
- ○ Did I group the words right as I read?
- ○ Did I make my voice go down for periods?
- ○ Did I make my voice go up for question marks?
- ○ Did I stop a little bit for commas?
- ○ Did I sound excited for exclamation marks?
- ○ Did I stress any words that needed to be stressed?

What is the best thing about my reading?

_____

_____

_____

What should I work on to make my reading better?

_____

_____

_____

Developmental Spelling Test (The "Monster Test")

An easily administered 10-word checklist, such as the following developmental test devised by Gentry (1985), makes it possible for teachers to assess young children's developmental stages of spelling ability.

WORDS	PRECOMMUNICATIVE SPELLINGS	SEMI-PHONETIC SPELLINGS	PHONETIC SPELLINGS	TRANSITIONAL SPELLINGS	CORRECT SPELLINGS
1. monster	random letters	mtr	mostr	monstur	monster
2. united	random letters	u	unitid	younighted	united
3. dress	random letters	jrs	jras	dres	dress
4. bottom	random letters	bt	bodm	bottum	bottom
5. hiked	random letters	h	hikt	hicked	hiked
6. human	random letters	um	humm	humin	human
7. eagle	random letters	el	egl	egul	eagle
8. closed	random letters	kd	klosd	clossed	closed
9. bumped	random letters	b	bopt	bumpt	bumped
10. type	random letters	tp	tip	tipe	type

From Gentry, J. Richard (1985). "You Can Analyze Developmental Spelling." *The Early Years (9)*, 44–45. Reprinted with permission of the author.

Beginning Speller Checklist

Name _____   Date _____

Identification of Words in Context

○ Guesses at words

○ Looks at pictures and then guesses

○ Looks at beginning of word

○ Tries to figure out first sound

○ Uses strategies to sound out word

Pictures and Word Sorts

○ Can sort pictures accurately

○ Can explain why he or she sorted pictures that way

○ Can sort words accurately

○ Can explain why he or she sorted words that way

○ Can sort pictures/words independently

○ Can sort words quickly

Spelling Lists and Tests

○ Recognizes misspelled words

○ Can find words with the same patterns as spelling list words

○ Achieves 80% or better accuracy on spelling post-tests

Spelling in Writing

○ Shows appropriate concern about accuracy

○ Invents spelling when needed

○ Spells learned words correctly

○ Writes with spaces between words

○ "Chunks" syllables and sounds in words

○ Segments (sounds out) words

Running Record Form

Student _____ Date _____

Teacher _____ Reading Level _____

Text _____

Number of Errors _____ Percentage _____

Running Words _____ Level for student: Easy, Instructional, Frustration

Text	Analysis			
	Number		System Used	
	E	SC	E	SC

Website Credibility, Accuracy, Reasonableness, and Support (CARS) Checklist

Name _____   Date _____

Credibility

1. What is the authority of the author?

   _____

   _____

   _____

2. What are his/her credentials?

   _____

   _____

   _____

3. Is there evidence that peers have judged the site positively?
   ○ Yes   ○ No

   Evidence: _____

4. Does the piece exhibit correct grammar and spelling?
   ○ Yes   ○ No

Accuracy

5. Is the site current, with updated information?
   ○ Yes   ○ No

   Evidence: _____

6. Is the information easy to understand and complete?
   ○ Yes   ○ No

   Evidence: _____

7. Does the author acknowledge other viewpoints of possible controversies?
   ○ Yes   ○ No

   Evidence: _____

Reasonableness

8. Does the author present a fair and objective point of view?

   ○ Yes   ○ No

   Evidence: _____

9. Does the author appear concerned with the truth?

   ○ Yes   ○ No

   Evidence: _____

Support

10. Does the author provide documentation for his or her ideas?

    ○ Yes   ○ No

    Evidence: _____

11. Are all sources listed?

    ○ Yes   ○ No

12. Are there other resources on this topic with similar information?

    ○ Yes   ○ No

    Other resources: _____

13. Are these sites mentioned or linked?

    ○ Yes   ○ No

    Example: _____

Adapted from Harris, R. *Evaluating Internet Research Sources*, www.virtualsalt.comevalu8it.htm.

Evaluating Technology Applications

Application _____ Date _____

- ■ Does it serve the intended purpose? For example, if it claims to improve fluency, can you see that children's fluency is actually improving?
  - ○ Yes   ○ No

- ■ Can it be used independently by my students, or will I need to work with them to facilitate?
  - ○ Independently   ○ Teacher help

- ■ Are there so many sight and sound distractions that children will become overstimulated and lose the literacy focus?
  - ○ Yes   ○ No

- ■ Does it offer children an opportunity for free choice? (This can be part of the motivation for using technology.)
  - ○ Yes   ○ No

  How? _____

  _____

- ■ Does it use humor? Chilren tend to prefer these programs and use them more frequently.
  - ○ Yes   ○ No

- ■ Does it align with conventional literacy goals, district benchmarks, and state standards for literacy?
  - ○ Yes   ○ No

  Which ones? _____

  _____

- ■ Does it address my students' individual literacy needs?
  - ○ Yes   ○ No

  Which ones? _____

  _____

- ■ Does it contribute to an overall unit theme or project?
  - ○ Yes   ○ No

  Which ones? _____

  _____

Adapted from Labbo, Lelu, Kinzer, et al., 2003.

Student Profile

Name _____   Date _____

Reading

- ○ Letter names
- ○ Letter sounds
- ○ Decodes words
- ○ Reads words
- ○ Reads sentences
- ○ Reads fluently/comprehends

Writing

- ○ Writes letters
- ○ Copies writing from board
- ○ Writes words using phonics
- ○ Writes sentences
- ○ Writes simple stories
- ○ Writes stories with structure

Speaking

- ○ No verbal response
- ○ Single word responses
- ○ Responds with phrases
- ○ Responds with sentences
- ○ Questions and answers
- ○ Gets in class discussions

Comments:

_____

_____

_____

By Rita Lehmann and Janet Rodgers. Used with permission.

Vocabulary Growth Group Profile

For First Grade

Teacher _____   Date _____

+ = always   x = sometimes   o = seldom/never

STANDARD	STUDENTS															
1. Knows meaning of common words within basic categories																
2. Uses knowledge of individual words in unknown compound words to predict their meanings																
3. Uses reference resources to learn word meanings (e.g., beginning dictionaries and available technology)																
4. Uses knowledge of suffixes (-er, -est, -ful) to determine meanings of words																
5. Develops vocabulary by listening to and discussing both familiar and conceptually challenging selections read aloud																

Source: DeVries, B. (2011). *Literacy Assessment & Intervention for Classroom Teachers,* 3rd ed., p. 461. Scottsdale, AZ: Holcomb Hathaway. Used with permission.

Kid Graph

Directions: Color in the squares for the amount of minutes you spend in recreational reading each day. Ask your parent to sign on the line below, showing that they have checked the amount of time you have spent reading.

	Sun.	Mon.	Tue.	Wed.	Thur.	Fri.	Sat.
15 min.							
14 min.							
13 min.							
12 min.							
11 min.							
10 min.							
9 min.							
8 min.							
7 min.							
6 min.							
5 min.							
4 min.							
3 min.							
2 min.							
1 min.							

My child has read for the actual amount of time noted on the graph.

_____

Rimes and Common Words Containing Them

ack: lack, back, Jack, stack, sack, pack, quack, tack

ail: tail, pail, mail, quail, fail, wail, sail

ain: pain, main, stain, gain, rain, vain

ake: sake, take, bake, lake, wake, fake, rake, cake, make

ale: pale, gale, dale, sale, bale, hale, male

ame: name, game, same, tame, lame, came, dame, fame

an: ran, pan, can, Nan, fan, tan, man, than

ank: sank, thank, bank, tank, stank, dank, shrank

ap: cap, map, lap, sap, gap, nap, zap, tap

ash: dash, cash, stash, lash, mash, gash, trash, crash, flash

at: cat, bat, Nat, mat, pat, sat, at, tat, rat, that, scat

ate: gate, hate, late, sate, plate, slate, crate, fate

aw: saw, paw, claw, law, jaw, straw, raw, flaw

ay: day, play, stay, say, gray, ray, lay, gay, jay, way

eal: seal, meal, steal, heal, deal

eat: meat, beat, heat, cheat, feat, wheat

ell: tell, smell, sell, well, swell, bell, fell, shell

est: test, best, west, vest, jest, nest, pest, chest

ice: nice, mice, rice, lice, spice, twice, vice

ick: pick, Nick, tick, lick, stick, thick, Dick, brick, sick

ide:	side, bride, tide, bide, pride, hide, ride
ite:	kite, bite, sprite
ight:	right, night, tight, flight, might, bright
ill:	bill, hill, kill, thrill, fill, shrill, drill, sill, pill, will, Jill, dill, Lill, mill, quill
in:	chin, fin, bin, win, sin, twin, din, grin, pin, tin
ine:	fine, mine, twine, wine, vine, nine, line
ing:	king, string, sing, thing, ring, wing, bring, swing
ink:	link, think, rink, mink, drink, wink, sink, blink, stink, kink
ig:	big, wig, twig, jig, pig
ip:	lip, skip, sip, flip, whip, dip, drip, trip, tip, hip, ship
ir:	sir, whir, stir, fir
ock:	rock, lock, sock, mock, knock, block, clock
oke:	poke, broke, stroke, Coke, joke, woke, choke
oil:	boil, toil, soil
ook:	book, look, took, hook, crook
op:	chop, mop, crop, top, stop, flop, plop, drop, hop, shop
ore:	sore, tore, more, core, bore, wore, snore, chore, shore, store
uck:	stuck, truck, buck, suck, pluck, struck, duck, luck
ug:	bug, plug, rug, dug, hug, drug
ump:	bump, clump, jump, dump, hump, lump, pump
unk:	junk, bunk, sunk, hunk, stunk, dunk

Fry's List of "Instant Words"

FIRST 100 WORDS (Approx. 1st Grade)

Group 1A

the	a	is	you	to	and	we
that	in	not	for	at	with	it
on	can	will	are	of	this	your
as	but	be	have			

Group 1B

he	I	they	one	good	me	about
had	if	some	up	her	do	when
so	my	very	all	would	any	been
out	there	from	day			

Group 1C

go	we	then	us	no	him	by
was	come	get	or	two	man	little
has	them	how	like	our	what	know
make	which	much	his			

Group 1D

who	an	their	she	new	said	did
boy	three	down	work	put	were	before
just	long	here	other	old	take	cat
again	give	after	many			

From *Reading Teacher's Book of Lists*, 4th ed. by Edward B. Fry, Jacqueline F. Kress, and Dona Lee Fountoukidis. Copyright © 2000, John Wiley & Sons. This material is reprinted with permission of John Wiley & Sons, Inc.

SECOND 100 WORDS (Approx. 2nd Grade)

Group 2A

saw	home	soon	stand	box	upon	first
came	girl	house	find	because	made	could
book	look	mother	run	school	people	night
into	say	think	back			

Group 2B

big	where	am	ball	morning	live	four
last	color	away	red	friend	pretty	eat
want	year	went	got	play	found	left
men	bring	wish	black			

Group 2C

may	let	use	these	right	present	tell
next	please	leave	hand	more	why	better
under	while	should	never	each	best	another
seem	tree	name	dear			

Group 2D

fan	five	read	over	such	way	too
shall	own	most	sure	thing	only	near
than	open	kind	must	high	far	both
end	also	until	call			

THIRD 100 WORDS (Approx. 3rd Grade)

Group 3A

ask	small	yellow	show	goes	clean	buy
thank	sleep	letter	jump	help	fly	don't
fast	cold	today	does	face	green	every
brown	coat	six	gave			

Group 3B

hat	car	write	try	myself	longer	those
hold	full	carry	eight	sing	warm	sit
dog	ride	hot	grow	cut	seven	woman
funny	yes	ate	stop			

Group 3C

off	sister	happy	once	didn't	set	round
dress	tell	wash	start	always	anything	around
close	walk	money	turn	might	hard	along
bed	fine	sat	hope			

Group 3D

fire	ten	order	part	early	fat	third
same	love	hear	yesterday	eyes	door	clothes
through	o'clock	second	water	town	took	pair
now	keep	head	food			

Phonics Terms and Orthography Chart

COMMON PHONICS TERMS

accent (primary) The syllable in a word that receives the strongest and loudest emphasis.

analytic phonics A whole-to-part phonics approach that emphasizes starting with whole words and identifying individual sounds as part of those words. Efforts are generally made to avoid pronouncing the sounds in isolation. Also known as *implicit phonics.*

auditory discrimination The ability to hear similarities and differences between sounds as they appear in spoken words.

base word A word to which prefixes and/or suffixes are added to create new but related words. The simplest member of a word family.

breve An orthographic symbol (˘) placed above vowel graphemes to indicate pronunciation.

circumflex An orthographic symbol (^) placed above vowel graphemes to indicate pronunciation.

closed syllable Any syllable ending with a consonant phoneme. *Examples:* come /m/; love /v/; ran /n/.

compound word A word made up of two or more base words. *Example:* football.

consonant blend Sounds in a syllable represented by two or more letters that are blended together without losing their own identities. *Examples:* green /g/ /r/; swing /s/ /w/; clap /c/ /l/.

consonant cluster Two or more consonant letters appearing together, which when sounded, represent a blend. *Examples:* gr, cr, str.

consonants Sounds represented by any letter of the English alphabet except *a, e, i, o,* and *u.* Consonants are *sounds* that are made by restricting the breath channel.

decoding The process of determining the pronunciation of an unknown word.

deductive instruction Instructional procedure that centers on telling children about generalizations and having them apply those generalizations to specific words. A general-to-specific analysis.

digraph Two letters that stand for a single phoneme or sound. *Examples:* shout /sh/; what /wh/; rang /ng/; meat /ea/. A digraph is a grapheme containing two letters and one sound.

dipthong A single sound made up of two vowel sounds in immediate sequence and pronounced in one syllable. *Examples:* oil /oi/; toy /oy/.

grapheme A letter or combination of letters that represents a phoneme. *Examples:* The phoneme /b/ in *bat* is represented by the grapheme (letter) *b;* the phoneme /f/ in *phone* is represented by the graphemes *p* and *h.*

macron An orthographic symbol, (–), placed over a vowel to show that it is pronounced as a long sound.

onset The consonant sound(s) of a syllable that come before the vowel sound. (See the definition of *rime* for examples of onsets.)

open syllable Any syllable ending with a vowel phoneme. *Examples:* see /e/; may /a/; auto /o/.

phoneme The smallest sound unit of a language that distinguishes one word from another. *Examples:* the phoneme /h/ distinguishes *hat* from *at;* the words *man* and *fan* are distinguished by their initial phonemes /m/ and /f/, respectively.

phoneme blending The process of recognizing isolated speech sounds and the ability to pronounce the word for which they stand.

phoneme segmentation The ability to isolate all the sounds within a word.

phonemic awareness The ability to recognize spoken words as a sequence of individual sounds.

phonetics The scientific study of human speech sounds.

phonics A method in which basic phonetics, the study of human speech sounds, is used to teach beginning reading.

phonogram A letter sequence composed of a vowel grapheme and an ending consonant grapheme(s). *Examples: -it* in *bit, lit,* and *sit,* or *-ain* in *pain, gain,* and *rain.*

r-controlled vowel When a vowel is followed by the letter *r,* it makes the vowel sound neither long nor short. *Example:* in the word *car,* the vowel sound becomes /a/; in the word *more,* it becomes /ô/.

rime The part of a syllable that includes the vowel sound as well as any consonant sound(s) that come after it. The graphic representation of a rime is referred to as a *phonogram. Example:* in the word *cat,* the onset is /c/ and the rime is /at/.

root Often used as a synonym for *base word.*

schwa sound An unstressed sound commonly occurring in unstressed syllables. It is represented by the symbol, ə, and closely resembles the short sound for *u. Examples: i* in *April; io* in *station; u* in *circus.*

silent letter A name given to a letter that appears in a written word but is not heard in the spoken word. *Example: knight* has six written letters but only three are heard; *k, g,* and *h* are "silent."

slash marks Slanting lines (/ /) enclosing a grapheme(s) indicate that the reference is to the sound and not to the letters.

syllable A unit of pronunciation consisting of a vowel alone or a vowel with one or more consonants. There can be only one vowel phoneme (sound) in each syllable.

synthetic phonics A part-to-whole phonics approach that emphasizes the learning of individual sounds, often in isolation, and combining them to form words. Also known as *explicit phonics.*

umlaut An orthographic symbol (¨) placed above vowel graphemes to indicate pronunciation.

visual discrimination The ability to visually perceive similarities and differences. In reading, this means to perceive similarities and differences in written letters and words.

vowels Sounds represented by the graphemes (letters) *a, e, i, o, u,* and sometimes *y* and *w,* in the English alphabet. Vowels are sounds that are made without closing or restricting the breath channel.

AN INTRODUCTION TO ENGLISH ORTHOGRAPHY.

CONSONANTS

		VARIANT CONSONANTS	DIGRAPHS WITH h	DIGRAPHS WITH FIRST SILENT LETTER	DIGRAPH CLUSTER FOLLOWING A SHORT VOWEL	ADDITIONAL DIGRAPH	BLENDS—INITIAL	BLENDS—FINAL	SPECIAL COMBINATION OF CONSONANT AND VOWEL
b	ball	c, g	ch chin	ck neck	dge ledge	ng song	r green	ld held	ci crucial
d	dust		school	gn gnat	tch match		l clear	lk talk	si pension
f	fast	co-	charade	kn know			s spine	nd pond	ti nation
h	hat	cent	gh ghost	wr wren			strap	nk sink	
j	jar		ph phone				tw twine	nt want	
k	kite	get	sh shine						
l	last	giraffe	th thin						
m	man		then						
n	near		wh whale						
p	put		whom						
qu	quack								
r	ran								
t	tack								
v	vase								
w	wall								
x	x-ray								
z	zoo								

VOWELS

	SINGLE—SHORT	DIGRAPHS WITH h	SCHWA ə IN UNACCENTED SYLLABLES	DIGRAPHS/DIPHTHONGS WITH a	DIGRAPHS WITH e	DIGRAPH AND DIPHTHONGS WITH o
a	ă apple		a among	ai as /ā/ pain	ee as /ē/ weed	oa as /ō/ bloat
e	ĕ elephant		e blanket	ay as /ā/ play	ea as /ē/ meat	oi as /oy/ noise
i	ĭ itch		i April	au as /aw/ caution	/ĕ/ dead	oy as /oy/ toy
o	ŏ octopus		o bacon	aw as /aw/ straw	/ā/ great	oo as /ōō/ soon
u	ŭ umbrella				ie as /ē/ belief	/oŏ/ took
	SINGLE—LONG				/ī/ tie	ou as /ow/ trout
	ā ape				ei as /ē/ (after c) receive	/ŭ/ young
	ē event				/ā/ rein	/ō/ soul
	ī ivy				ey as /ē/ monkey	/ōō/ troupe
	ō open				/ā/ prey	ow as /ow/ owl
	ū and ōō uniform crude					/ō/ blow
	SINGLE—THIRD SOUND					
	a ä father (fäther)					
	o ōō move (mōōve)					
	u oŏ bush (boŏsh)					

Fry Readability Graph

Note: This instrument is widely available online.

From the material being assessed, randomly select three average passages of exactly 100 words each. For each passage, count the number of sentences in the 100 words, estimating the length of the fraction of the last sentence to the nearest one-tenth. Count the number of syllables in each passage. If no hand counter is available, put a mark over every syllable *over* one for each word (e.g., a two-syllable word gets one mark); then when you get to the end of the passage, count the number of marks and add 100.

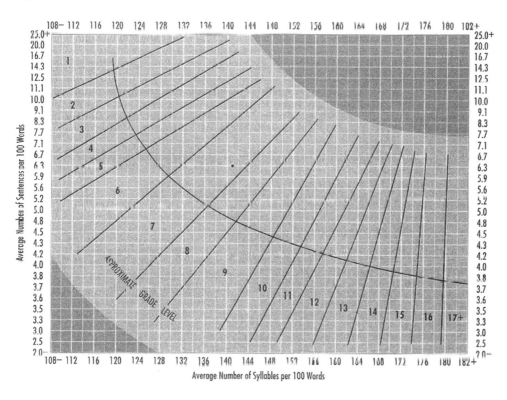

Average Number of Syllables per 100 Words

After you have completed these steps for all three passages, plot the *average* sentence length and *average* number of syllables on the graph. Where the two lines intersect, draw a dot. This point indicates the approximate grade level. The graph on the previous page uses these averages, for example:

	Syllables	Sentences
1st Hundred Words	124	6.6
2nd Hundred Words	141	5.5
3rd Hundred Words	158	6.8
Average	141	6.3

Readability 7th Grade (see dot plotted on graph)

Choose additional passages if great variability is observed among the three original passages, recognizing that the book may have uneven readability.

Glossary

accuracy The ability to recognize words correctly.

achievement test A formalized test that measures the extent to which a person has assimilated a body of information or possesses a certain skill after instruction has taken place.

alliteration A pattern in which all words begin with the same sound.

alphabetic principle The principle that there is a one-to-one correspondence between phonemes (or sounds) and graphemes (or letters); letters represent sounds.

analog A strategy of comparing patterns in words to ones already known.

anecdotal notes Written observations taken by the teacher—usually on a clipboard—of literacy-related behaviors in an authentic literacy context.

antonyms A pair of words that have opposite meanings.

assessment Procedure of evaluating by observing children's growth in the normal course of classroom activities, projects, and units of study.

automaticity Fluent performance without the conscious deployment of attention.

basal readers A coordinated, graded set of textbooks, teacher's guides, and supplementary materials from which to teach reading.

big books An enlarged version of a book used by the teacher for mediated reading instruction so that students can track the print and attention can be focused on particular phonemic elements.

blend A consonant sequence before or after a vowel within a syllable, such as *cl, st,* or *br;* the written language equivalent of a consonant cluster.

camouflage A vocabulary-enriching activity in which learners must try to disguise a chosen word by creating an oral story using several words above their normal speaking vocabulary. The other students must try to guess the hidden word.

closed sort Word sorts that classify words into predetermined categories.

cloze procedure An instructional technique in which certain words are deleted from a passage by the teacher, with blanks left in their places for students to fill in by using the context of the sentence or paragraph.

code switch The use of English for known words and the home language for words not yet acquired in English.

compound word A word made up of two or more base words, such as *football.*

comprehension The interpretation of print on a page into a meaningful message that is dependent upon the reader's decoding abilities, prior knowledge, cultural and social background, and monitoring strategies.

concepts about print Concepts about the way print works, including directionality, spacing, identification of words and letters, connection between written and spoken language, and understanding the function of punctuation.

constructivist model of learning A learning theory suggesting that children are active learners who organize and relate new information to their prior knowledge.

context The surrounding information in a sentence or text.

context–relationship procedure A strategy utilized to help students integrate new words into their meaning vocabularies.

contextual clues The syntactic and semantic information in the surrounding words, phrases, sentences, and paragraphs in a text.

contract spelling Children have a written agreement with the teacher each week to learn specific words.

controlled vocabulary A system of introducing only a certain number of grade-level appropriate words before the reading of each basal story, with periodic review.

conventional spelling stage The final stage of spelling development, in which the child has mastered the basic principles of English orthography and most words are spelled correctly.

correct spelling stage *See* conventional spelling stage.

criterion-referenced test A test for which scores are interpreted by comparing the test taker's score to a specified performance level rather than with the scores of other students.

critical reading Reading to evaluate the material.

cueing systems The four language systems that readers rely upon for cues as they seek meaning from text: graphophonic (based on letter–sound relationships); syntactic (based on grammar or structure); semantic (based on meaning); and pragmatic.

cumulative progress indicators A description of specific activities that accompany curriculum standards to assist the teacher in observing when such standards are being demonstrated by students.

curriculum-based assessment Assessment that ties evaluation directly to the literacy curriculum to identify instructional needs.

decodable text Beginner-oriented books that contain the same letters or word patterns currently being studied, or those previously taught.

decoding The translation of written words into verbal speech for oral reading or mental speech for silent reading.

developmental spelling stages Stage-like progressions that children advance through when learning to spell, characterized by increasingly complex understandings about the organizational patterns of words, including precommunicative, prephonetic, phonetic, transitional, and conventional spelling stages.

developmentally appropriate practice According to NAEYC, "a framework of principles and guidelines for best practice in the care and education of young children, birth through age 8."

diagnostic tests Age-related, norm-referenced assessment of specific skills and behaviors children have acquired compared with other children of the same chronological age.

dialogic reading A strategy in which a child leads the discussion about the pictures in a picture storybook with the parent or teacher taking the position of follower in the book conversation.

dialogue journals Journals that provide a means of two-way written communication between learners and their teachers, in which learners share their thoughts with teachers, including personal comments and descriptions of life experiences, and the teachers, in turn, write reactions to the learners' messages.

direct instruction Teacher control of the learning environment through structured, systematic lessons, goal setting, choice of activities, and feedback.

directionality of print The concept that, in English, writing goes from left to right and from top to bottom. Directionality of print varies among languages.

dramatic play Simulating real experiences with no set plot or goal.

drop everything and read (DEAR) A time set aside each day during which children quickly and quietly get trade books, magazines, or other reading material from their desks or from the classroom library and begin reading silently.

DRTA (directed reading thinking activity) A time-honored format for guiding students as they read selections, usually from basal reading programs.

dyad reading A paired reading activity in which students alternately read aloud or listen and summarize what their partner has read.

early readers/writers Moving from emergent literacy to the first stage of conventional literacy, early readers are able to read appropriately selected text independently after an introduction given by an adult. These readers use early reading strategies; for example, they begin to attend to print and apply the one-to-one correspondence of matching sounds to letters in order to read, and they commonly look at beginning and ending letters in order to decode unfamiliar words. Early writers typically progress through five stages of invented spelling, ranging from writing the initial consonant sound through phonetic and transitional phases.

echo reading A strategy where a lead reader reads aloud a section of text and others follow immediately after it or echo the leader's reading.

EL (English learner) A person who is in the process of acquiring English as a second language.

emergent literacy Behaviors seen in young children when they use texts (both traditional and electronic) and writing tools to imitate reading and writing activities, even though the children cannot actually read and write in the conventional sense.

encoding Transferring oral language into written language.

environmental print Print that is encountered outside of books and that is a pervasive part of everyday living.

ESL (English as a second language) A program for teaching English language skills to those whose native language is not English.

experience–text relationship A lesson format for narrative text that helps students to develop prior knowledge and relate it to what they read.

experiential background The fund of total experiences that aid a reader in finding meaning in printed symbols.

experimental spellings Unconventional spellings, or approximations, resulting from an emergent writer's initial attempts to associate sounds with letters.

explicit instruction Teacher control of the learning environment through structured, systematic lessons, goal setting, choice of activities, and feedback.

expository frame A basic structure for expository text designed to help students organize their thoughts for writing or responding to text.

expository structures Content organized around a main idea and supporting details.

expository text A text written in a precise, factual writing style.

expressive writing Personal writing that expresses emotion such as diaries or letters.

family literacy night An event where relatives and children read books together and participate in a variety of literacy-related activities.

fluency Achieving speed and accuracy in recognizing words and comprehending text, and coordinating the two.

fluent readers/writers Able to use multiple sources of information flexibly to accurately read a variety of unknown texts with appropriate expression and phrasing. Fluent readers are able to read for meaning with less attention to decoding and can independently solve problems encountered in the text. Fluent writing uses mostly conventional spelling and children are able to write expressively using increasingly rich vocabulary and more complex sentences.

formal assessments Standardized tests given under controlled conditions so that specific groups can be compared primarily for purposes of program evaluation.

formal (standardized) test A testing instrument for which readability and validity can be verified; the results of these tests are based on right or wrong answers, and individual scores are interpreted against national norms.

formative assessment During instruction, the process of ongoing data-gathering, usually informal, that informs and guides teachers as they make instructional decisions.

frustration level A level of reading difficulty at which a reader is unable to cope; when reading is on the frustration level, the reader recognizes approximately 90 percent or fewer of the words encountered and comprehends 50 percent or fewer.

grade-level equivalency score A conversion of a score on a test into one that tells how a child compares with others in the same grade; e.g., a grade equivalent score of 4.5 on a reading test would suggest that the child is reading as well as children in the normative sample who are in the fifth month of fourth grade.

graded word list A list of words at successive reading levels.

grand conversation A response to text strategy whereby students share personal connections to the text, make predictions, ask questions, and show individual appreciation.

grapheme A written symbol that represents a phoneme.

graphophonic information Cues based upon sound or visual similarities.

group profile A listing of scores on a specific reading or writing skill that allows the teacher to view the strengths and weaknesses of the whole class for purposes of reteaching and reporting to parents and others.

guided reading procedure A teacher-mediated instructional method designed to help readers improve skills, comprehension, recall, and appreciation of text.

high-frequency words Words common in reading material that are often difficult to learn because they cannot be easily decoded.

high-stakes assessments Assessment tools mandated by the state or district in which the teachers work that are often used to determine how well children are doing compared with other children in the area, state, or nation and whether certain programs will be funded.

holistic approach A whole-to-parts approach where meaning is considered to be more critical than the underlying skills of reading.

holographic stage The earliest language acquisition stage, in which one word is used to represent a concept or idea.

hypermedia projects Like multimodal projects, these projects combine text, graphics, audio, and video, but they also include hyperlinks in the presentation. Because the presentation includes links, they may not be viewed in a linear sequence.

independent level A level of reading difficulty low enough that the reader can progress without noticeable obstructions; the reader can recognize approximately 98 percent of the words and comprehend at least 90 percent of what is read.

individual dictation A strategy in which the student dictates a message while the teacher writes it down, sounding out the words in front of the child.

informal assessments Assessments, often teacher-administered in the classroom, that yield specific information that teachers can use to guide their teaching; these include tools such as checklists, rubrics, portfolios, informal reading inventories.

informal reading inventory An informal assessment instrument designed to help the teacher determine a child's independent, instructional, frustration, and reading capacity levels.

informational texts Nonfiction texts that provide factual information about a topic; expository text.

instructional level A level of difficulty low enough that the reader can be instructed by the teacher during the process; in order for the material to be at this level, the reader should be able to read approximately 95 percent of the words in a passage and comprehend at least 75 percent.

interactive e-books Computerized programs that allow learners to read books on a computer while responding to questions about the text, exploring various aspects or sidelines of the text, and often even adapting the text.

interactive (story) writing A mediated writing experience used to assist emergent readers in learning to read and write. With help from the teacher, children dictate sentences, and the teacher verbally stretches each word so children can distinguish sounds and letters. Children use chart paper to write the letter while repeating the sound.

interest and attitude inventory An informal assessment device that allows teachers to discover how their students feel about reading and about themselves as readers.

interest inventory A list of questions used to assess a person's preferences in a particular area.

intervention The corrective instructional program the teacher devises as a result of assessment.

jigsaw grouping A collaborative learning technique in which individuals become experts on one portion of text and share their expertise with a small group called their home group. Each member of the home group becomes an expert on a different part of the text and shares his or her new knowledge with the group so that each group member will get a sense of the whole text.

journals Journals are kept by children in the same way artists keep sketch books. Children write in them regularly to record life events of their choosing or, for very beginning writers, to complete sentence stems offered by the teacher. At the beginning reader stage, journals are often accompanied by illustrations and are rarely corrected.

knowledge chart (also known as K-W-L) A process intended to be used before and after the reading of an expository selection to document what students already know, what they wish to find out, and then what they have learned after reading the selection.

language arts The global term for reading, writing, listening, and speaking.

language experience approach (LEA) An approach in which reading and the other language arts are inter-related and the experiences of children are used as the basis for the material that is written and then used for reading.

learning center A location within the classroom in which children are presented with instructional materials, specific directions, clearly defined objectives, and/or provisions for self-evaluation.

learning logs Journals students use to summarize a day's lesson and to react to what they have learned.

letter name stage *See* phonetic stage.

leveled books Books that are assigned levels with subtler differences in the difficulty between levels than more traditional "grade-leveled" texts.

literacy The competence to carry out the complex reading and writing tasks in a functionally useful way necessary to the world of work and life outside the school.

literacy scaffolds Structures that provide a template for a writing idea; scaffolds allow the learner to achieve at a higher level than would be attainable without the scaffolds.

literal comprehension Understanding those ideas that are directly stated.

literary sociogram A diagram used to help students understand the complexity of the relationships among characters in a story or chapter.

long vowels Vowels that represent the sounds in words that are heard in letter names, such as the /a/ in ape, /e/ in feet, /i/ in ice, /o/ in road, and /u/ in mule.

look-say method An early meaning-based method of reading instruction requiring children to use the context alone to figure out words they do not know.

masking Using a sliding frame or other device to help children focus on a particular word or part of a word.

Matthew effect The phenomenon that suggests that skilled decoders get better at reading while poor decoders tend to fall further behind.

meaning vocabulary That body of words whose meanings one understands and can use.

mediated reading Large or small group instruction in which the teacher guides the children in selected reading skills.

metacognition A person's awareness of his or her own thinking and the conscious efforts to monitor this awareness.

metacognitive strategies Techniques for monitoring one's own thinking.

metalinguistic ability The conscious awareness of sound, meaning, and the practical nuances of language.

minilesson A short lesson on reading procedures, concepts, strategies, or skills taught based upon teacher observation of the need for it.

mirror blogs Blogs that allow children to reflect upon their thinking or about lessons or content that has been introduced.

miscue An unexpected reading response (deviation from text).

miscue analysis A procedure that lets the teacher gather important instructional information by providing a framework for observing students' oral reading and their ability to construct meaning.

morning message Children observe as the teacher writes a meaningful morning message addressed to all the children on the board about a specific event that is planned for the day or about an interesting question. The morning message is used as an instructional tool for discussing skills children are learning, such as conventions of writing or phonic elements.

morpheme The smallest meaning-bearing linguistic unit in a language.

morphology The aspects of language structure related to the ways words are formed from prefixes, roots, and suffixes (e.g., "re-heat-ing") and are related to each other.

motivation The incentive to do something; a stimulus to act.

multicultural Classrooms are multicultural settings when children from a variety of cultures learn together daily, making it necessary to know how children's perceptions, knowledge, and demeanor are shaped by their experiences at home and in their own community.

multimodal literacy A form of literacy requiring today's students to be literate in multiple modes of communication, including the ability to read, produce, and interpret text, graphics, images, sound, and videos.

narrative text Text that contains the structural features of a story.

new literacies Ways to read and write texts, and also to view and visually represent texts in new and exciting ways, often including enhancements such as video and audio; often in electronic rather than traditional print format and available for viewing on various devices.

nonstage theory A theory that suggests that unskilled and skilled readers use the same strategies to figure out unknown words.

norm-referenced test A test designed to yield results interpretable in terms of the average results of a sample population.

norming (normative) group A large number of students chosen to represent the kinds of students for whom an assessment device is designed.

norms Statistics or data that summarize the test performance of specified groups, such as test takers of various ages or grades.

one-to-one correspondence An awareness that letters or combinations of letters correspond directly to certain sounds in the English language.

onset All the sounds of a word that come before the first vowel.

open sort A type of picture or word sort in which the categories for sorting are left up to the child.

oral recitation lessons (ORL) Three-part lessons designed to increase oral reading fluency.

oral synthesis Hearing sounds in sequence and blending them together to make a word; sounding out.

orthographic knowledge Understanding of the writing system of a language, specifically the correct sequence of letters, characters, or symbols.

parent packets Folders containing early reading and writing reinforcement activities that can be completed at home with a child's parents or caregivers.

partner reading A joint reading event in which a fluent reader is paired with a less fluent reader.

patterned stories Narrative pieces written by students based upon books with clear patterns that can be emulated.

percentile Raw scores are converted to percentiles so that comparisons can be made. Percentiles range from 1 to 99 with 1 being the lowest and 99 being the highest.

phoneme The smallest unit of sound in a language.

phoneme blending Blending individual sounds to form a word.

phoneme counting Counting the number of sounds in a word.

phoneme deletion Omitting the beginning, middle, or ending sounds of a word.

phoneme isolation Identifying the beginning, middle, and/or ending sounds in a word.

phoneme substitution Substituting beginning, middle, or ending sounds of a word.

phonemic awareness The ability to hear, identify, and manipulate individual sounds in spoken words.

phonemic segmentation The process of separating sounds within a word.

phonetic stage The third stage of spelling development, in which consonants and vowels are used for each spoken syllable.

phonics Instruction in the association of speech sounds with printed symbols.

phonics generalizations Rules that help to clarify English spelling patterns.

phonology The study of the sound system of language.

picture sort A precursor to the word sort activity in which children categorize pictures according to their common sounds.

picture walk An instructional strategy in which the teacher guides the children through the text by looking at and discussing the pictures before reading the story.

play centers Areas of the classroom containing inviting props and set aside for spontaneous dramatic play.

polysemantic A word having multiple meanings, such as the word *fast*.

portfolio Place to collect evidence of a child's literacy development. It may include artifacts collected by the child, the teacher, or both.

precommunicative stage The initial stage of spelling development, in which the child scribbles random letters with little concept of which letter makes which sound.

predictable books, predictable texts Books or texts that use repetition, rhythmic language patterns, and familiar patterns; sometimes called pattern books.

predictive questions Questions designed to activate students' prior knowledge before they read in order to focus their attention on key ideas as they read.

prefixes Meaningful chunks attached to the beginnings of words, such as re + play = replay.

preliterate stage *See* prephonetic stage.

prephonetic stage The second stage of spelling development, in which the child becomes aware of the alphabetic principle.

primary language The home language of a child or first language a child learns to speak.

process-oriented assessment Assessment that relies on the teacher's observation of the child's actual reading and writing abilities.

prosody Appropriate expression in oral reading that sounds much like conversational speaking.

QARs (question–answer relationships) A strategy in which students become aware of their own comprehension processes, particularly the importance of the knowledge they bring to text and their role as active seekers rather than passive receivers of information through reading.

r-controlled vowels Vowels that occur in a syllable preceding an *r* and the vowel sound is modified, such as the /r/ in car.

readability An objective measure of the difficulty of written material.

readers theater A form of drama in which participants read aloud from scripts adapted from stories and convey ideas and emotions through vocal expression. This oral interpretation strategy helps children to see that reading is an active process of constructing meaning. Unlike a play, there is no costuming, movement, stage sets, or memorizing of lines.

reading The construction of meaning from coded messages through symbol decoding, vocabulary awareness, comprehension, and reflection.

reading buddies A social reading activity in which students read and reread books with a partner who may help them with unfamiliar words and encourage them to continue reading.

reading capacity level The highest level of material children understand when the passage is read to them.

reading interest inventory An informal assessment device used to determine a child's interests so that the teacher can match appropriate reading material to them.

reading process The steps a reader goes through to construct meaning from what the author has written.

reading product Some form of communication that results from the reading process.

reading rate Speed of reading, often reported in words per minute.

reading readiness The level of preparedness for formal reading instruction.

reading response journal A journal in which readers record their first reactions to something they have read.

realia Pictures, brief video clips, or objects introduced in tandem with a new word or concept to build new associations with the words, especially used for the benefit of English Learners, to provide accessibility to the associated print

reciprocal teaching A technique to develop comprehension and metacognition in which the teacher and students take turns predicting, generating questions, summarizing, and clarifying ideas in a passage.

recreational reading An independent reading activity for motivating voluntary reading interest and appreciation rather than instruction.

reliable Yielding consistent assessment results over time.

reliability A measure of consistency; a test or an assessment is a reliable measure, or possesses reliability, if that assessment produces similar results when given more than once over a short period of time.

repeated readings Students reread a selection for a different purpose and think again about what they have read. Rereading helps improve a young reader's speed, accuracy, expression, comprehension, and linguistic growth.

Response to Intervention (RTI) A framework that incorporates both assessment and intervention with the goal of yielding immediate benefits to the student. Assessment data are used to inform interventions and determine their effectiveness. Using RTI, instruction and intervention shift toward a supportive function that allows teachers to make instructional decisions based upon their students' needs.

retelling Teachers analyze children's retellings of text to gauge their level of comprehension and use of language. In examining the retellings, teachers look for the number of events recalled, how children interpret the message, and how children use details or make inferences to substantiate ideas.

rime The first vowel in a word and all the sounds that follow.

root word A word to which prefixes and/or suffixes are added to create new, but related, words.

rubber-banding The process in which the teacher stretches out all the sounds in a word so learners can pay attention to each phoneme or sound.

running records A procedure for analyzing students' oral reading and noting their strengths and weaknesses when using various reading strategies.

scaffolding A support mechanism by which children are able to accomplish more difficult tasks than they could without assistance.

schema A pre-existing knowledge structure developed about a thing, a place, or an idea; a framework of expectations based upon previous knowledge.

semantic cues Meaning clues.

semantic gradient A vocabulary-enriching activity that allows children to discuss the many shades of meaning of words, beginning with a word and ending with its opposite.

semantic map A graphic representation of the relationship among words and phrases in written material.

sentence stems The first two or three words of a sentence followed by blank spaces offered to students to support initial attempts at writing.

sentence strips Rectangular pieces of tag board or construction paper upon which are written individual sentences from a story students have read.

shared reading A mediated technique whereby the teacher reads aloud while students follow along using individual copies of the book, a class chart, or a big book.

sheltering/sheltered instruction   When teaching English learners, efforts by the teacher to bridge the language gap by providing meaningful contexts for words and concepts being introduced. In providing sheltered instruction, the teacher may use pictures, film clips, charts, and graphs as well as gestures, charades, and pantomime to get concepts across.

short vowels   Vowels that represent the sound of /a/ in apple, /e/ in end, /i/ in igloo, /o/ in octopus, and /u/ in bus.

sight vocabulary words   Words that are recognized by the reader immediately, without having to resort to decoding.

signal words   Those transitional words that signify sequence, such as *first, next,* and *finally.*

silent period   The initial stage in second language acquisition when a learner is increasing receptive vocabulary but not able to express ideas orally.

skills-based approach   A parts-to-whole approach to reading instruction in which all the reading skills are taught sequentially.

skills-based assessment   Assessment focusing on the use of tests to measure reading and spelling skills as well as the subskills of these areas.

sound boxes   Place holders for sounds used by children during phonemic awareness exercises.

sound mapping   Matching letters and letter combinations with sound (sound symbol association).

spelling conscience   A desire to spell correctly as evidenced by a student's proofreading material or using resources to find out how to spell unknown words.

spelling consciousness   The ability to recognize that a word that has been written down is spelled correctly or incorrectly.

SSR   *See* sustained silent reading.

stage theory   A theory that suggests that children go through three stages in acquiring literacy: the "selective cue stage," the "spelling-sound stage," and the "automatic stage."

standardized reading tests   Achievement tests that are published, norm-referenced, group-administered, survey tests of reading ability.

standards   Broad curricular goals containing specific grade-level targets or benchmarks. They represent systematic ways for educators to ask themselves, what do we want our students to know and what do we want them to be able to do?

stanine   A way of reporting test scores that distributes them into nine groups, with 1 being the lowest and 9 the highest.

story frame   A basic outline for a story designed to help students organize their ideas about what they have read.

story grammar   A set of rules that define story structures.

story retelling   *See* Retelling.

structured listening activity   An activity in which students listen to a story accompanied by visuals that support the action in the story and then retell the story with the help of the visuals.

suffixes   Meaningful chunks attached to the ends of words, such as play + ing = playing.

summative assessment   Evaluative assessment or testing that results in a grade or ranking.

sustained silent reading (SSR)   A program for setting aside a certain period of time daily for self-selected, silent reading. During SSR time, each child chooses material to read for a designated period of time, typically 10–15 minutes for beginning readers. Everyone, including the teacher, reads without interruption.

syllabication   Breaking words into syllables; "chunking."

syllable juncture stage   *See* conventional spelling stage.

syllables   The units of pronunciation that include a vowel sound.

synonyms   Groups of words that have the same, or very similar, meanings.

syntactic cues   Clues derived from the word order or grammar of the sentence.

talk-to-yourself chart   A chart to help children self-assess their ability to read and spell new words.

teachable moments   The spontaneous, indirect teaching that occurs when teachers respond to students' questions or when students otherwise demonstrate the need to know something.

teacher observational portfolio   A progress file containing observations and informal assessments of children's reading and writing behaviors and accomplishments.

telegraphic stage   The language acquisition stage in which an idea or concept is represented by two words.

text talk   An approach to read-alouds that is designed to enhance young children's ability to construct meaning from decontextualized language to promote text comprehension and further language development.

think-aloud A strategy in which the teacher models aloud for students the thinking processes used when reading or writing.

think, pair, and share A cooperative learning strategy in which children listen to a question, think of a response, pair to discuss with a partner, and then share their collaboration with the whole class.

tracking Indicating understanding of the one-to-one correspondence of spoken and written words by finger-pointing.

trade books Any books that can be purchased by the general public in book stores, through mail order houses, or at book fairs.

transactional model A perspective of early reading instruction from cognitive psychology and psycholinguistic learning that views children as bringing a rich prior knowledge background to literacy learning.

transitional readers/writers Able to read unfamiliar text with more independence than can early readers. Transitional readers use meaning, grammatical, and letter cues more fully. They recognize a large number of frequently used words on sight and use illustrations in a limited way while reading. Transitional writers may use phonetic or invented spelling, but the spelling is easily readable; writing also begins to demonstrate characteristics of the transitional speller, able to apply spelling rules, patterns, and other strategies.

transitional stage The fourth stage of spelling development, in which the child is able to approximate the spelling of various English words.

transmission model A perspective of early reading instruction from behavioral psychology that views children as empty vessels into which knowledge is poured.

twin texts Books that lead children from fiction into nonfiction by pairing related fiction and nonfiction books to form a bridge from reading stories to understanding factual content.

valid Assessment measures what it purports to measure.

validity The degree to which a test measures what it purports to measure.

Venn diagram A set of overlapping circles used to graphically illustrate the similarities and differences of two concepts, ideas, stories, or other items.

vicarious experiences Indirect experiences, not involving the senses.

visual literacy Ability to interpret and understand images, icons, video, photographs, graphs, charts, maps, and any other form of visual representation of ideas.

vocabulary The knowledge and use of words.

whole language philosophy A pedagogy that moved from a narrow focus on isolated subskills to one that encouraged teachers to look at reading more holistically, as part of the total communication process.

within word stage *See* transitional stage.

word attack An aspect of reading instruction that includes intentional strategies for learning to decode, sight read, and recognize written words.

word bank A collection of sight words that have been mastered, usually recorded on index cards.

word building An activity in which children arrange letter cards to spell words, practicing phonics and spelling concepts.

word hunt An activity in which children search for words that correspond to a certain pattern that has been identified by them or by the teacher.

word map A visual illustration of a word, showing its meaning by offering examples and explaining what it is and what it is not.

word play A child's manipulation of sounds and words for purposes of language exploration, practice, and pleasure.

word sort An activity in which students sort a collection of words into two or more categories.

word wall A chart or bulletin board on which are placed, alphabetically, important vocabulary to be referred to during word study activities.

wordless books Picture books without words.

writers' workshop a regular writing session with the goal of building students' fluency in writing through continuous, repeated exposure to the process of writing. Writers' workshop usually includes a minilesson, writing time, peer editing, student-teacher conferences, and sharing. Students may be encouraged to choose a topic or the teacher may use writing prompts.

writing process A set of recursive stages in which a writer engages in activities designed to solve certain problems unique to a particular stage. For early writers, as with more experienced writers, the writing process typically includes prewriting, drafting, sharing, revising, editing, proofreading, and publishing stages.

writing prompts Motivational ideas or structures that are offered by the teacher to inspire students to write.

References

Adams, C. (2009). Digital storytelling. *Instructor, 119*(3), 35–37.

Adams, M. J. (1990). *Beginning to Read: Thinking and Learning About Print.* Cambridge, MA: MIT Press.

Adams, M. J. (1991).Why not phonics and whole language? In W. Ellis (Ed.), *All Language and the Creation of Literacy.* Baltimore: The Orton Dyslexia Society.

Adams, M. J., and Bruck, M. (1995). Resolving the great debate. *American Educator, 19*(7), 10–20.

Adams, M. J., Foorman, B. R., Lundberg, I., and Beeler, T. (1998). *Phonemic Awareness in Young Children.* Baltimore: Paul H. Brooks.

Adams, M. J., Treiman, R., and Pressley, M. (1997). Reading, writing and literacy. In I. Sigel and A. Renninger (Eds.), *Handbook of Child Psychology, Vol. 4: Child Psychology in Practice.* New York: Wiley.

Afflerbach, P. (2007). *Understanding and Using Reading Assessment, K–12.* Newark, DE: International Reading Association.

Alegria, J., Pignot, E., and Morais, J. (1982). Phonetic analysis of speech and memory codes in beginning readers. *Memory and Cognition, 10,* 451–456.

Allen, R. V. (1976). *Language Experiences in Communication.* Boston: Houghton Mifflin.

Allington, R. (1983). Fluency: The neglected reading goal in reading instruction. *The Reading Teacher, 36,* 556–561.

Allington, R. L. (1991). Children who find learning to read difficult: School responses to diversity. In E. H. Hiebert (Ed.), *Literacy for a Diverse Society: Perspectives, Practices, and Policies.* New York: Teachers College Press.

Allington, R. L. (2004). Setting the record straight. *Educational Leadership, 61,* 22–25.

Allington, R. L. (2009). *What Really Matters in Fluency: Research-Based Best Practices Across the Curriculum.* Boston: Allyn & Bacon/Pearson.

Altwerger, B., Edelsky, C., and Flores, B. M. (1987). Whole language: What's new? *The Reading Teacher, 41*(2), 144–154.

American Library Association. (2005). Background Research: Dialogic Reading for Two- and Three Year-Olds. Retrieved August 16, 2005, from www.ala.org/ala/pla/plaissues/earlylit/researchandeval/dialogicreading.htm/

Anderson, C. (2000). *How's It Going? A Practical Guide to Conferencing with Student Writers.* Portsmouth, NH: Heinemann.

Anderson, R. C., Hilbert, E. H., Scott, J. A., and Wilkinson, I. (1985). *Becoming a Nation of Readers: The Report of the Commission on Reading.* Washington, DC: The National Institute of Education.

Anderson, R. C., Wilson, P. T., and Fielding, L. G. (1988). Growth in reading and how children spend their time outside of school. *Reading Research Quarterly, 23,* 285–303.

Anderson, V., and Roit, M. (1998). Reading as a gateway to language proficiency for language-minority students in the elementary grades. In *Promoting Learning for Culturally and Linguistically Diverse Students: Classroom Applications.* New York: Wadsworth.

Armbruster, B. B., Lehr, E., and Osborn, J. (2001). *Put Reading First: The Research Building Blocks for Teaching Children to Read. Kindergarten Through Grade 3.* Washington, DC: National Institute for Literacy.

Ashton–Warner, S. (1965). *Teacher.* New York: Simon & Schuster.

Atwell, N. (1992). Nancie Atwell talks about teachers and whole language. *Instructor, 102*(4), 48–49.

Au, K. H. (1979). Using the experience–text–relationship with minority children. *The Reading Teacher, 32,* 478–479.

Au, K. H. (1991, June 25). Paper presented at the Notre Dame Reading Conference, South Bend, IN, sponsored by Houghton Mifflin, Boston.

Au, K. H. (1997). *Literacy Instruction in Multicultural Settings.* Orlando, FL: Harcourt Brace.

August, D., and Shanahan, T. (Eds.). (2006). *Developing Literacy in Second Language Learners: Report of the National Reading Panel on Language Minority Children and Youth.* Mahwah, NJ: Erlbaum.

Aulls, M. W., and Graves, M. F. (1985). *Quest: New Roads to Literacy.* New York: Scholastic.

Ausubel, D. P. (1959). Viewpoints from related disciplines: Human growth and development. *Teachers College Record, 60,* 245–254.

Baer, G. T., and Dow, R. S. (2006). *Self-Paced Phonics: A Text for Educators* (4th ed.). Upper Saddle River, NJ: Prentice Hall.

Baghban, M. (1984). *Our Daughter Learns to Read and Write: A Case Study from Birth to Three.* Newark, DE: International Reading Association.

Baker, L., Serpell, R., and Sonnenschein, S. (1995). Opportunities for literacy learning in the homes of urban preschoolers. In L. Morrow (Ed.), *Family Literacy: Connections in Schools and Communities, 236–252.* Newark, DE: International Reading Association.

Baker, L., Sonnenschein, S., Serpell, R., Fernandez-Fein, S., and Scher, D. (1994). Contexts of Emergent Literacy: Everyday Home Experiences of Urban Prekindergarten Children. (Research report.) Athens, GA: National Reading Research Center, University of Georgia and University of Maryland.

Ball, E. W., and Blachman, B. A. (1991). Does phonemic awareness training in kindergarten make a difference in early word recognition and developmental spelling? *Reading Research Quarterly, 26*(1), 49–66.

Balmuth, M. (1982). *The Root of Phonics: A Historical Perspective.* New York: McGraw Hill.

Barclay, K., and Coffman, T. (1990). I know an old lady: Linking literacy and lyrics. *Teaching K–8, 6,* 28–29.

Barone, D. (1990). The written responses of young children: Beyond comprehension to story understanding. *The New Advocate, 44,* 536–541.

Barone, D., and Wright, R. (2009). Literacy instruction with digital and media technology. *The Reading Teacher, 62,* 292–302.

Barrantine, S. J. (1996). Engaging with reading through interactive read-alouds. *The Reading Teacher, 50*(1), 36–43.

Barton, D. (1997). Family literacy programmes and home literacy practices. In D. Taylor (Ed.), *Many Families, Many Literacies: An International Declaration of Principles.* Portsmouth, NH: Heinemann.

Baumann, J. F., and Kame'enui, E. J. (1991). Research on vocabulary instruction: Ode to Voltaire. In J. Flood, J. M. Jensen, D. Lapp, and J. R. Squire (Eds.), *Handbook on Teaching the English Language Arts* (2nd ed.), 604–632. New York: Macmillan.

Bear, D. R. (1991). Learning to fasten the seat belt of my union seat without looking around: The synchrony of literacy development. *Theory into Practice, 30*(3), 149–157.

Bear, D. R., Invernizzi, M., Templeton, S., and Johnston, F. (2004). *Words Their Way: Word Study for Phonics, Vocabulary, and Spelling Instruction* (3rd ed.). Upper Saddle River, NJ: Prentice Hall.

Bear, D. R., Invernizzi, M., Templeton, S., and Johnston, F. (2008). *Words Their Way: Word Study for Phonics, Vocabulary, and Spelling Instruction* (4th ed.). Upper Saddle River, NJ: Merrill/Prentice Hall.

Beaty, J. J., and Pratt, L. (2011). *Early Literacy in Preschool and Kindergarten* (3rd ed.). Boston: Pearson.

Beck, I. (1984). Developing comprehension: The impact of the directed reading lesson. In R. C. Anderson, J. Osborn, and R. J. Tierney (Eds.), *Learning to Read in American Schools: Basal Readers and Content Texts.* Hillsdale, NJ: Lawrence Erlbaum.

Beck, I. L. (2006). *Making Sense of Phonics: The Hows and Whys.* New York: Guilford Press.

Beck, I. L., and Juel, C. (1995). The role of decoding in learning to read. *American Educator, 3.*

Beck, I. L., and McKeown, M. (1991). Conditions of vocabulary acquisition. In R. Barr, M. Kamil, P. Mosenthal, and P. D. Pearson (Eds.), *Handbook of Reading Research, 2,* 789–814.

Beck, I. L., and McKeown, M. G. (2001). Text talk: Capturing the benefits of read-aloud experiences with young children. *The Reading Teacher, 55,* 10–19.

Beck, I. L., and McKeown, M. G. (2007). Increasing young low-income children's oral vocabularies through rich and focused instruction. *Elementary School Journal, 108,* 97–113.

Beck, I. L., McKeown, M. G., and Kucan, L. (2002). *Bringing Words to Life: Robust Vocabulary Instruction.* New York: Guilford Press.

Beck, I. L., McKeown, M. G., and Kucan, L. (2008). *Creating Robust Vocabulary: Frequently Asked Questions and Extended Examples.* New York: Guilford.

Bergeron, B. (1990). What does the term "whole language" mean? Constructing a definition from the literature. *Journal of Reading Behavior, 22,* 301–329.

Bernhardt, E., Destino, T., Kamil, M., and Rodriguez-Munoz, M. (1995). Assessing science knowledge in an English/Spanish bilingual elementary school. *Cognosos, 4,* 4–6.

Berninger, V., Vaughn, K., Abbott, R., Brooks, A., Abbott, S., Reed, E., Rogan, L., and Graham, S. (1998). Early intervention for spelling problems: Teaching spelling units of varying size within a multiple connections framework. *Journal of Educational Psychology, 90,* 587–605.

Bialostok, S. (1997). Offering the olive branch: The rhetoric of insincerity. *Language Arts, 74*(8), 618–627.

Biemiller, A., and Boote, C. (2006). An effective method for building meaning vocabulary in primary grades. *Journal of Educational Psychology, 98,* 44–62.

Bissex, G. L. (2004). *Gnys at Wrk: A Child Learns to Read and Write* (reprint ed.). Cambridge, MA: Harvard University Press.

Blachman, B. A. (1991). Getting ready to read: Learning how print maps to speech. In J. F. Kavanagh (Ed.), *The Language Continuum: From Infancy to Literacy.* Timonium, MD: York Press.

Blachowicz, C., and Fisher, P. (2006). *Teaching Vocabulary in All Classrooms* (3rd ed.). Upper Saddle River, NJ: Prentice Hall.

Blachowicz, C. E. (1987). Vocabulary instruction: What goes on in the classroom? *The Reading Teacher, 2,* 132–137.

Blachowicz, C. E., and Lee, J. J. (1991). Vocabulary development in the whole literacy classroom. *The Reading Teacher, 45,* 188–195.

Blevins, W. (2006). *Phonics from A to Z: A Practical Guide* (2nd ed.). Jefferson City, MO: Scholastic.

Block, C. C. (2004). *Teaching Comprehension: The Comprehension Process Approach.* Boston: Allyn & Bacon.

Block, C. C., and Pressley, M. (2007). Best practices in teaching comprehension. In L. B. Gambrell, L. M. Morrow, and M. Pressley (Eds.), *Best Practices in Literacy Instruction* (3rd. ed.), 220–242. New York: Guilford Press.

Bolton, F., and Snowball, D. (1993). *Teaching Spelling: A Practical Resource.* Portsmouth, NH: Heinemann.

Bond, G., and Dykstra, R. (1967). The cooperative research program in first-grade reading instruction. *Reading Research Quarterly, 2,* 5–142.

Boulware-Gooden, R., Carreker, S. M., Thornhill, A., and Malatesha, J. (2007). Instruction in metacognitive strategies enhances comprehension and vocabulary achievement of third grade students. *The Reading Teacher, 61,* 70–77.

Bridge, C., Winograd, P. N., and Haley, D. (1983). Using predictable materials vs. preprimers to teach beginning sight words. *The Reading Teacher, 36*(9), 884–891.

Briggs, C., and Elkind, D. (1973). Cognitive development in early readers. *Developmental Psychology, 9,* 279–280.

Brown, M. W. (1990). *The Important Book.* Ill. L. Weisgard. New York: HarperTrophy.

Buckley, M. H. (1986). When teachers decide to integrate the language arts. *Language Arts, 63,* 369–377.

Burns, P., Roe, B., and Ross, E. (1999). *Word Recognition and Meaning Vocabulary: A Literacy Skills Primer.* Boston: Houghton Mifflin.

Butler, A., and Turbil, J. (1986). *Towards a Reading and Writing Classroom.* Portsmouth, NH: Heinemann.

Byrne, B., and Fielding–Barnsley, R. (1989). Phonemic awareness and letter knowledge in the child's acquisition of the alphabetic principle. *Journal of Educational Psychology, 81,* 313–321.

California Department of Education. (1998). *Language Arts: Reading, Writing, Listening, and Speaking Standards.* Sacramento, CA: California Department of Education.

California Department of Education. (1996). *Teaching Reading: A Balanced Comprehensive Approach to Teaching Reading in Prekindergarten Through Grade Three.* Sacramento, CA: California Department of Education.

California Reading Association. (1996). *Building Literacy: Making Every Child a Reader.* Sacramento: The California Reading Association.

Calkins, L. M. (2000). *The Art of Teaching Writing.* Boston: Allyn & Bacon.

Cambourne, B., and Turbill, J. (1990). Assessment in whole language classrooms: Theory into practice. *Elementary School Journal, 90,* 337–349.

Cambourne, B., and Turbill, J. (1991). *Coping with Chaos.* Portsmouth, NH: Heinemann.

Camp, D. (2000). It takes two: Teaching with twin texts of fact and fiction. *The Reading Teacher, 53,* 400–408.

Carbo, M. (1988a). An evaluation of Jeanne Chall's response to "debunking the great phonics myth." *Phi Delta Kappan, 71*(4), 152–158.

Carbo, M. (1988b). Debunking the great phonics myth. *Phi Delta Kappan, 70*(8), 226–240.

Cardoso–Martins, C. (1995). Sensitivity to rhymes, syllables, and phonemes in literacy acquisition in Portuguese. *Reading Research Quarterly, 30,* 808–828.

Carnine, L., Carnine, D., and Gersten, R. (1984). Analysis of oral reading errors made by economically disadvantaged students taught with a synthetic phonics approach. *Reading Research Quarterly, 19,* 343–356.

Carr, E., and Wixon, K. K. (1986). Guidelines for evaluating vocabulary instruction. *Journal of Reading, 29,* 588–595.

Castek, J., Bevans-Mangelson, J., and Goldstone, B. (2006). Reading adventure online: Five ways to introduce the new literacies of the Internet through children's literature. *The Reading Teacher, 59,* 714–728.

Caswell, L. J., and Duke, N. K. (1998). Non-narrative as a catalyst for literacy development. *Language Arts, 75,* 108–117.

Cazden, C. B. (1993, May). A Report on Reports: Two Dilemmas of Genre Teaching. Paper presented at the Working with Genre Conference, Sydney, Australia. (ERIC Document reproduction Service No. ED 363593.)

Cecil, N. L. (1994a). *For the Love of Language: Poetry for All Learners*. Winnipeg, Manitoba: Peguis Publishers.

Cecil, N. L. (1994b). *Freedom Fighters: Affective Teaching of the Language Arts*. Salem, WI: Sheffield.

Cecil, N. L. (1994c). Instilling a love of words in children. In E. H. Cramer and M. Castle (Eds.), *Fostering the Love of Reading: The Affective Domain in Reading Education*. Newark, DE: International Reading Association.

Cecil, N. L. (1994d). *Teaching to the Heart: An Affective Approach to Reading Instruction*. Salem, WI: Sheffield Publishers.

Cecil, N. L. (2007). *Focus on Fluency: A Meaning-Based Approach*. Scottsdale, AZ: Holcomb Hathaway.

Cecil, N. L., and Lauritzen, P. (1994). *Literacy and the Arts in the Integrated Classroom: Alternative Ways of Knowing*. White Plains, NY: Longman.

Cecil, N. L., and Pfeiffer, J. E. (2011). *The Art of Inquiry: Questioning Strategies for K–6 Classrooms*. Winnipeg, Canada: Portage & Main.

Chall, J. (1967). *Learning to Read: The Great Debate*. New York: McGraw Hill.

Chall, J. (1989). Learning to read: The great debate (20 years later—response to "debunking the great phonics myth"). *Phi Delta Kappan, 70*(7), 521–525.

Chall, J. (1995). *Learning to Read: The Great Debate* (3rd ed.). New York: McGraw Hill.

Chard, D. J., Vaughn, S., and Tyler, B. J. (2002). A synthesis of research on effective interventions for building reading fluency with elementary students with learning disabilities. *Journal of Learning Disabilities, 35*, 386–486.

Cheek, E. H., Flippo, R. F., and Lindsey, J. D. (1997). *Reading for Success in Elementary School*. Madison, WI: Brown & Benchmark.

Chomsky, C. (1972). Stages in language development and reading exposure. *Harvard Educational Review, 42*, 1–33.

Christie, J. F., Enz, B. J., and Vukelich, C. (2011). *Teaching Language and Literacy: Preschool Through the Elementary Grades*. Boston: Pearson.

Clark, C. H. (1995). Teaching students about reading: A fluency example. *Reading Horizons, 35*, 251–265.

Clark, K. F. (2004). What can I say besides "sound it out"? Coaching word recognition in beginning reading. *The Reading Teacher, 57*, 440–449.

Clay, M. (2000). *Concepts About Print: What Have Children Learned About the Way We Print Language?* Portsmouth, NH: Heinemann.

Clay, M. M. (1972). *Reading: The Patterning of Complex Behavior*. Portsmouth, NH: Heinemann Educational Books.

Clay, M. M. (1979). *Stones. The Concepts About Print Test*. Auckland, New Zealand: Heinemann.

Clay, M. M. (1985). *The Early Detection of Reading Difficulties* (3rd ed.). Auckland, New Zealand: Heinemann.

Clay, M. M. (1990). What is and what might be in evaluation. *Language Arts, 67*(3), 288–298.

Clay, M. M. (1991). *Becoming Literate: The Construction of Inner Control*. Portsmouth, NH: Heinemann.

Clay, M. M. (1993). *An Observation Survey*. Portsmouth, NH: Heinemann Educational Books.

Clymer, T. (1963). The utility of phonic generalizations in the primary grades. *The Reading Teacher, 16*, 252–258.

Cochran-Smith, M., Kahn, J., and Paris, C. L. (1990). Writing with a felicitous tool. *Theory Into Practice, 29*, 235–247.

Coiro, J., and Dobler, E. (2007). Exploring the online reading comprehension strategies used by sixth-grade skilled readers to search for and locate information on the Internet. *Reading Research Quarterly, 42*, 214–257.

Cole, A. D. (1998). Beginner-oriented texts in literature-based classrooms: The segue for a few struggling readers. *The Reading Teacher, 51*, 488–500.

Coles, G. (2003). *Reading the Naked Truth: Literacy, Legislation, and Lies*. Portsmouth, NH: Heinemann.

Combs, M. (2010). *Readers and Writers in the Primary Grades: A Balanced and Integrated Approach, K–3* (4th ed.). Boston: Pearson.

Connor, C., Morrison, F., and Petrella, J. (2004). Effective comprehension instruction: Examining child x instruction interactions. *Journal of Educational Psychology, 96*, 419–427.

Cooper, J. D. (1997). *Literacy: Helping Children Construct Meaning*. Boston: Houghton Mifflin.

Cooter, K. S. (2006). When mama can't read: Counteracting intergenerational illiteracy. *The Reading Teacher, 59*, 698–702.

Corgill, A. M. (2008). *Of Primary Importance: What's Essential in Teaching Young Writers*. Portland, ME: Stenhouse.

Cornett, C. (2010). *Comprehension First: Inquiry into Big Ideas Using Important Questions*. Scottsdale, AZ: Holcomb Hathaway.

Cossu, G., Shankweiler, D., Liberman, I. Y., Tola, G., and Katz, L. (1988). Awareness of phonological segments and reading ability in Italian children. *Applied Psycholinguistics, 9*, 1–16.

Cousin, P. T., Weekly, T., and Gerard, J. (1993). The functional uses of language and literacy by students with severe language and learning problems. *Language Arts, 70*, 548–556.

Cox, C. (2008). *Teaching Language Arts: A Student-Centered Classroom*. Boston: Allyn & Bacon.

Crawley, S. J., and Merritt, K. (2000). *Remediating Reading Difficulties* (3rd ed.). Boston: McGraw-Hill.

Cudd, E. (1990). The paragraph frame: A bridge from narrative to expository text. In N. L. Cecil (Ed.), *Literacy in the '90s: Readings in the Language Arts*. Dubuque, IA: Kendall/Hunt.

Cummins, J., Brown, K., and Sayers, D. (2007). *Literacy, Technology, and Diversity*. Boston: Pearson.

Cunningham, A. E. (1990). Explicit versus implicit instruction in phonological awareness. *Journal of Experimental Child Psychology, 50*, 429–444.

Cunningham, P. M. (1991). *What Kind of Phonics Instruction Will We Have?* Presentation to the National Reading Conference, Palm Springs, December.

Cunningham, P. M. (1992). What kind of phonics instruction will we have? In C. K. Kinzer and D. J. Leu (Eds.), *Literacy Research, Theory, and Practice: Views from Many Perspectives. Forty-First Yearbook of the National Reading Conference*, 17–31. Chicago: National Reading Conference.

Cunningham, P. M. (1995). *Phonics They Use: Words for Reading and Writing* (2nd ed.). New York: Harper-Collins.

Cunningham, P. M. (2007). Best practices in teaching phonological awareness and phonics. In L. B. Gambrell, L. M. Morrow, and M. Pressley (Eds.), *Best Practices in Literacy Instruction*, 159–177. New York: Guilford Press.

Cunningham, P. M. (2009). *Phonics They Use: Words for Reading and Writing* (5th ed.). Boston: Allyn & Bacon.

Cunningham, P. M., and Allington, R. L. (1999). *Classrooms That Work: They Can All Read and Write*. White Plains, NY: Longman.

Cunningham, P. M., and Allington, R. L. (2007). *Classrooms That Work: They Can All Read and Write* (4th ed.). Boston: Allyn & Bacon.

Cunningham, P. M., and Cunningham, D. P. (1997). *Making More Words*. Carthage, IL: Good Apple.

Cunningham, P. M., and Cunningham, J. W. (2002). What we know about how to teach phonics. In A. E. Farstrup and S. J. Samuels (Eds.), *What Research Has to Say About Reading Instruction* (3rd ed.)., 87–109. Newark, DE: International Reading Association.

Daniels, H., and Steineke, N. (2004). *Mini-lessons for Literature Circles*. Portsmouth, NH: Heinemann.

Dechant, E. V. (1982). *Improving the Teaching of Reading* (3rd ed.). Englewood Cliffs, NJ: Prentice Hall.

Delgado-Gaitan, C. (1987). Mexican adult literacy: New directions for immigrants. In S. R. Goldman and H. Trueba (Eds.), *Becoming Literate in a Second Language*, 9–32. Norwood, NJ: Ablex.

deManrique, A. M. B., and Gramigna, S. (1984). La segmentacion fonologica y silabica en ninos de pre-escolar y primer grado [The phonological segmentation of syllables of children in preschool and first grade]. *Lectura y Vida, 5*, 4–13.

Denver, J. (2005). *Take Me Home, Country Roads*. Adapted and illustrated by C. Canyon. Nevada City, CA: Dawn.

DeVries, B. A. (2011). *Literacy Assessment and Intervention for Classroom Teachers* (3rd ed.). Scottsdale, AZ: Holcomb Hathaway.

Diamond, L., and Mandel, S. (1996). *Building a Powerful Reading Program: From Research to Practice*. Sacramento, CA: The California State University Institute for Education Reform.

Dickenson, D., Hao, Z., and He, W. (1995). Pedagogical and classroom factors related to how teachers read to 3- and 4-year-old children. In K. A. Hinchman, C. K. Kinzer, and D. J. Leu (Eds.), *Perspectives on Literacy Research and Practice*. Chicago: Chicago Reading Conference.

Dixon-Krauss, L. (2002). Using literature as a context for teaching vocabulary. *Journal of Adolescent & Adult Literacy, 45*, 310–318.

Donnelly, W. B., and Roe, C. J. (2010). Using sentence frames to develop academic vocabulary for English learners. *The Reading Teacher, 64*, 131–136.

Dowhower, S. L. (1991). Speaking of prosody: Fluency's unattended bedfellow. *The Reading Teacher, 42*, 502–507.

Downing, J., and Thomson, D. (1977). Sex role stereotypes in learning how to read. *Research in the Teaching of English, 11*, 149–155.

Duffelmeyer, F. A., and Banwart, B. H. (1993). Word maps for adjectives and verbs. *The Reading Teacher, 46*, 351–353.

Duffy, G., Roehler, L., and Hermann, B. (1988). Modeling mental processes helps poor readers become strategic readers. *The Reading Teacher, 41*, 762–767.

Duke, N. K. (2000). 3.6 minutes per day: The scarcity of informational texts in first grade. *Reading Research Quarterly, 35,* 202–224.

Duke, N. K., and Bennett-Armistead, V. S. (2003). *Reading and Writing Informational Text in the Primary Grades: Research-Based Practices.* New York: Scholastic.

Duke, N. K., Bennett-Armistead, V. S., and Roberts, E. M. (2003). Bridging the gap between learning to read and reading to learn. In D. M. Barone and L. M. Morrow (Eds.), *Literacy and Young Children: Research-Based Practices,* 226–242. New York: Guilford.

Durkin, D. (1966). *Children Who Read Early.* New York: Teachers College Press.

Durkin, D. (1979). What classroom observations reveal about reading comprehension instruction. *Reading Research Quarterly, 14,* 481–533.

Durkin, D. (1990). Dolores Durkin speaks on instruction. *The Reading Teacher, 43,* 472–476.

Ebbers, S. M., and Denton, C. A. (2008). A root awakening: Vocabulary instruction for older students with reading disabilities. *Learning Disabilities Research and Practice, 23,* 90–102.

Echevarria, J., Vogt, M. E., and Short, D. (2010). *Making Content Comprehensible for Elementary English Learners: The SIOP Model.* Boston: Allyn & Bacon.

Edwards, P. A. (2004). *Children's Literacy Development: Making it Happen Through School, Family, and Community Involvement.* Boston: Allyn & Bacon/ Pearson.

Eeds, M., and Wells, D. (1989). Grand conversations: An exploration of meaning construction in literature study groups. *Research in the Teaching of English, 23,* 4–29.

Ehri, L., and Robbins, C. (1992). Beginners need some decoding skills to read words by analogy. *Reading Research Quarterly, 27,* 13–29.

Eldredge, J. L. (1995). *Teaching Decoding in Holistic Classrooms.* Englewood Cliffs, NJ: Merrill/Prentice Hall.

Elkonin, D. B. (1973). U.S.S.R. In J. Downing (Ed.), *Comparative Reading.* New York: Macmillan.

Ellermeyer, D. A., and Chick, K. A. (2007). *Activities for Standards-Based, Integrated Language Arts Instruction.* Scottsdale, AZ: Holcomb Hathaway.

Engel, T., and Streich, R. (2009). Yes, there *is* room for soup in the curriculum: Achieving accountability in a collaboratively planned writing program. *The Reading Teacher, 59,* 660–679.

Englert, C. S., and Hiebert, E. H. (1984). Children's developing awareness of text structures in expository materials. *Journal of Educational Psychology, 76,* 65–74.

Every Child a Reader: The Report of the California Reading Task Force. (2000). Sacramento, CA: California Department of Education.

Factoid Books. (1999). *The Big Book of Grimm, by the Brothers Grimm as Channeled by J. Vankin and Over 50 top Comic Artists!* New York: Paradox Press.

Fan, X. T., and Chen, M. (2001). Parental involvement and students' academic achievement: A meta-analysis. *Educational Psychology Review, 13,* 1–22.

Farnan, N., Lapp, D., and Flood, J. (1992). Changing perspectives in writing instruction. *The Reading Teacher, 35,* 550–556.

Fielding, L. G., and Pearson, P. D. (1994). Reading comprehension: What works. *Educational Leadership, 2,* 62–68.

Finn, P. J. (1990). *Helping Children Learn to Read.* White Plains, NY: Longman.

Fischer, P. E. (1993). *The Sounds and Spelling Patterns of English: Phonics for Teachers and Parents.* Morrill, ME: Oxton House Publishers.

Fisher, B. (1998). *Bobbi Fisher Classroom Close-Ups: Organization and Management.* Level K–2 (video). White Plains, NY: Longman.

Fisher, D., Flood, J., Lapp, D., and Frey, N. (2004). Interactive read-alouds: Is there a common set of implementation practices? *The Reading Teacher, 58,* 8–17.

Fitzgerald, J., Spiegel, D. L., and Cunningham, J. W. (1991). The relationship between parental literacy level and perceptions of emergent literacy. *Journal of Reading Behavior, 13*(2), 191–212.

Fitzpatrick, J. (1997). *Phonemic Awareness: Playing with Sounds to Strengthen Beginning Reading Skills.* Cypress, CA: Creative Teaching Press.

Flesch, R. (1955, reprinted 1993). *Why Johnny Can't Read.* Cutchogue, NY: Buccaneer Books.

Fletcher, J. M., and Lyon, G. R. (2002). *Reading: A Research-Based Approach.* Palo Alto, CA: Hoover Institute.

Fletcher, J., Shaywitz, S., Shankweiler, D., Katz, L., Liberman, I., Stuebing, K., Francis, D., Fowler, A., and Shaywitz, B. (1994). Cognitive profiles of reading disability: Comparisons of discrepancy and low achievement definitions. *Journal of Educational Psychology, 86*(1), 6–23.

Flippo, R. F. (1997). Sensationalism, politics, and literacy: What's going on? *Phi Delta Kappan, 41,* 301–304.

Flynt, E. S., and Cooter, R. B. (2005). Improving middle grades reading in urban schools: The Memphis comprehension framework. *The Reading Teacher, 58,* 774–780.

Foorman, B., Francis, D., Beeler, T., Winikates, D., and Fletcher, J. (1998). Early interventions for children with reading problems: Study designs and preliminary findings. *Learning Disabilities: A Multi-Disciplinary Journal*.

Forseth, C. A., and Avery, C. (2002). *And with a Light Touch: Learning About Reading, Writing, and Teaching with First Graders* (2nd ed.). Portsmouth, NH: Heinemann.

Fountas, I. C., and Pinnell, G. S. (1996). *Guided Reading: Good First Teaching for All Children*. Portsmouth, NH: Heinemann.

Fountas, I. C., and Pinnell, G. S. (1999). *Matching Books to Readers: Using Leveled Books in Guided Reading, K–3*. Portsmouth, NH: Heinemann.

Fountas, I. C., and Pinnell, G. S. (2006). *The Fountas and Pinnell Leveled Book List, K–8* (2006–2008 ed.). Portsmouth, NH: Heinemann.

Fox, B. J. (2003). *Word Recognition Activities: Patterns and Strategies for Developing Fluency*. Upper Saddle River, NJ: Merrill.

Freppon, P. A. (1991). Children's concepts of the nature and purpose of reading in different instructional settings. *Journal of Reading Behavior, 23*(2), 139–163.

Freppon, P. A., and Dahl, K. L. (1991). Learning about phonics in a whole language classroom. *Language Arts, 68,* 190–197.

Fresch, M. J., and Wheaton, A. (1997). Sort, search, and discover: Spelling in the child-centered classroom. *The Reading Teacher, 51,* 20–31.

Fry, E. (1977). *Elementary Reading Instruction*. New York: McGraw-Hill.

Fuchs, D., Fuchs, L. S., and Vaughn, S. (2008). *Response to Intervention: A Framework for Reading Educators*. Newark, DE: International Reading Association.

Gambrell, L. B. (2005). Reading literature, reading text, reading the Internet: The times they are a' changing. *The Reading Teacher, 58,* 588–591.

Gambrell, L. B., and Almasi, J. F. (Eds.). (1996). *Lively Discussions! Fostering Engaged Reading*. Newark, DE: International Reading Association.

Garan, E. M. (2004). *In Defense of Our Children: When Politics, Profit, and Education Collide*. Portsmouth, NH: Heinemann.

Garthwait, A. (2001). Hypermedia composing: Questions arising from writing in three dimensions. *Language Arts, 78,* 237–244.

Gaskins, I. W., Ehri, L. C., Cress, C., O'Hara, C., and Donnelly, K. (1997). Procedures for word learning: Making discoveries about words. *The Reading Teacher, 50*(4), 312–327.

Gentry, J. R. (1981). Learning to spell developmentally. *The Reading Teacher, 34,* 378–381.

Gentry, J. R. (1985). You can analyze developmental spelling. *Early Years, 9,* 44–45.

Gentry, J. R. (2000). A retrospective on invented spelling and a look forward. *Language Arts, 54,* 318–332.

Gentry, J. R. (2004). *The Science of Spelling: The Explicit Specifics that Make Great Readers and Writers (and Spellers!)*. Portsmouth, NH: Heinemann.

Gentry, J. R. (2006). *Breaking the Code: The New Science of Beginning Reading and Writing*. Portsmouth, NH: Heinemann.

Gentry, J. R. (2008). *Breakthrough in Beginning Reading and Writing: The Evidence-Based Approach to Pin Pointing Students' Needs and Delivering Targeted Instruction*. New York: Scholastic.

Gentry, J. R., and Gillet, J. W. (1993). *Teaching Kids to Spell*. Portsmouth, NH: Heinemann.

Gibbons, G. (1994). *Frogs*. New York: Holiday House.

Gibbons, G. (2006). *Valentine's Day Is . . .* New York: Holiday House.

Gill, C. H., and Scharer, P. L. (1996). Why do they get it on Monday and misspell it on Friday?: Teachers inquiring about their students as spellers. *Language Arts, 73.*

Gillon, G. T. (2004). *Phonological Awareness: From Research to Practice*. New York: Guilford Press.

Glazer, S. M. (1995). Do I have to give up phonics to be a whole language teacher? *Reading Today, 12*(4), 37–43.

Goldenberg, C. (1993). Instructional conversations: Promoting comprehension through discussion. *The Reading Teacher, 46*(4), 316–326.

Goldenberg, C. (2008). Teaching English language learners: What the research does—and does not—say. *American Educator, 32,* 8–19.

Goldenberg, C., Reese, L., and Gallimore, R. (1992). Effects of school literacy materials on Latino children's home experiences and early reading achievement. *American Journal of Education, 100,* 497–536.

Goodman, K. S. (1965). A linguistic study of cues and miscues in reading. *Elementary English, 42,* 639–643.

Goodman, K. S. (1986). *What's Whole in Whole Language?* Portsmouth, NH: Heinemann.

Goodman, K. S. (1990). *What's Whole in Whole Language?* (2nd ed.). Portsmouth, NH: Heinemann.

Goodman, K. S. (1997). Putting theory and research in the context of history. *Language Arts, 74*(8), 595–599.

Graham, S., Berninger, V., Abbott, R., Abbott, S., and Whitaker, D. (1997). The role of mechanics in composing of elementary school students: A new methodological approach. *Journal of Educational Psychology, 89,* 170–182.

Graves, D. H., and Hansen, J. (1983). The author's chair. *Language Arts, 60,* 176–183.

Graves, M. F. (1986). Vocabulary learning and instruction. *Review of Research in Education, 13,* 91–128.

Graves, M. F. (2006). *The Vocabulary Book: Learning and Instruction.* New York: Teachers College Press.

Graves, M. F., Juel, C., and Graves, B. B. (2007). *Teaching Reading in the 21st Century* (2nd ed.). Boston: Allyn & Bacon.

Graves, M. F., Watts, S., and Graves, B. (1998). *Essentials of Classroom Teaching: Elementary Reading* (2nd ed.). Upper Saddle River, NJ: Prentice Hall.

Griffith, L. W., and Rasinski, T. V. (2004). A focus on fluency: How one teacher incorporated fluency with her reading curriculum. *The Reading Teacher, 58*(2), 126–137.

Griffith, P. L., and Olson, M. W. (1992). Phonemic awareness helps beginning readers break the code. *The Reading Teacher, 15*(7), 516–523.

Grigg, W. S., Daane, M. C., Jin, Y., and Campbell, J. R. (2003). *National Assessment of Educational Progress. The Nation's Report Card: Reading 2002.* Washington, DC: U.S. Department of Education.

Grossen, B. (1997). *30 Years of Research: What We Now Know About How Children Learn to Read.* New York: The Center for the Future of Teaching and Learning.

Guastello, E. F., and Lenz, C. (2005). Student accountability: Guided reading kid stations. *The Reading Teacher, 59,* 144–156.

Guillaume, A. M. (1998). Learning with text in the primary grades. *The Reading Teacher, 51,* 476–486.

Gunn, B. K., Simmons, D. C., and Kame'enui, E. J. (2000). *Emergent Literacy: Synthesis of the Research.* Washington, DC: National Center to Improve the Tools of Educators.

Haager, D., Klinger, J., and Vaughn, S. (2007). *Evidence-based Reading Practices for Response to Intervention.* Baltimore, MD: Brookes.

Haggard, M. R. (1986). The vocabulary self-collection strategy: Using student interest and world knowledge to enhance vocabulary growth. *Journal of Reading, 29,* 634–642.

Hall, M. A. (1981). *Teaching Reading as a Language Experience* (3rd ed.). Columbus, OH: Merrill.

Halliday, M. (1975). *Learning How to Mean: Explorations in the Development of Language.* New York: Edward Arnold.

Hamilton, E. R., and Cherniavsky, J. (2006). Issues in synchronous versus asynchronous e-learning platforms. In H. F. O'Neil and S. R. Perez (Eds.), *Web-based Learning: Theory, Research, and Practice,* 87–106. Mahwah, NJ: Erlbaum.

Hancock, M. R. (2008). The status of reader response research: Sustaining the reader's voice in challenging times. In S. Lehr (Ed.), *Shattering the Looking Glass: Challenge, Risk, and Controversy in Children's Literature,* 97–116. Norwood, MA: Christopher Gordon.

Hansen, J. (2001). *When Writers Read* (2nd ed.). Portsmouth, NH: Heinemann.

Harlin, R. P. (1990). *Effects of Whole Language on Low SES Children.* Paper presented at the National Reading Conference, Austin, TX, December.

Harris, A. J., and Sipay, E. R. (1990). *How to Increase Reading Ability* (9th ed.). New York: Longman.

Harris, R. (2010). Evaluating Internet research sources. Retrieved January 6, 2011, from www.virtualsalt.com/evalu8it.htm

Hartman, D., Fogarty, E., Coiro, J., Leu, Jr., D. J. Castek, J., and Henry, L. A. (2005, December). New literacies for learning. Symposium presented at the 55th annual meeting of the National Reading Conference, Miami, FL.

Hayes, K., and Creange, R. (2001). *Classroom Routines that Really Work for Prek and Kindergarten.* New York: Scholastic.

Heilman, A. W. (2005). *Phonics in Proper Perspective* (10th ed.). Upper Saddle River, NJ: Prentice Hall.

Heimlich, J. E., and Pittelman, S. D. (1986). *Semantic Mapping: Classroom Applications.* Newark, DE: International Reading Association.

Henderson, E. H. (1995). *Teaching Spelling* (3rd ed.). Boston: Houghton Mifflin.

Hennings, D. G. (1992). *Beyond the Read Aloud: Learning to Read through Listening to and Reflecting on Literature.* Bloomington, IN: Phi Delta Kappan Educational Foundation.

Henry, L. A. (2006). SEARCHing for an answer: The critical role of new literacies while reading on the Internet. *The Reading Teacher, 59,* 614–627.

Herrell, A. L., and Jordan, M. (2006). *50 Strategies for Improving Vocabulary, Comprehension, and Fluency* (2nd ed.). Upper Saddle River, NJ: Pearson.

Hills, T. W. (1992). Reaching potentials through appropriate assessment. In S. Bredekamp and T. Rosegrant (Eds.), *Reaching Potentials: Appropriate Curriculum and Assessment of Young Children* (Vol. 1). Washington, DC: National Association for the Education of Young Children.

Hirsch, E. D. (2005). *The Schools We Need and Why We Don't Have Them.* Needham Heights, MA: Christopher-Gordon.

Hoffman, J. V. (1985). *The Oral Recitation Lesson: A Teacher's Guide.* Austin, TX: Academic Resource Consultants.

Hohn, W., and Ehri, L. (1984). Do alphabet letters help pre-readers acquire phonemic segmentation skill? *Journal of Educational Psychology, 78,* 752–762.

Holdaway, D. (1986). The structure of natural language as a basis for literacy instruction. In M. L. Sampson (Ed.), *The Pursuit of Literacy: Early Reading and Writing.* Dubuque, IA: Kendall/Hunt.

Holdaway, D. (1979). *The Foundation of Literacy.* Sydney; Portsmouth, NH: Ashton Scholastic, distributed by Heinemann.

Holdaway, D. (2005). *The Foundations of Literacy.* Portsmouth, NH: Heinemann.

Hong, M., and Stafford, P. (1999). *Spelling Strategies that Work: Quick Lessons that Help Students Become Effective Writers.* Jefferson City, NJ: Scholastic.

Honig, B. (1996). *How Should We Teach Our Children to Read: The Role of Skills in a Comprehensive Reading Program, a Balanced Approach.* San Francisco: Far West Lab.

Hoskisson, K., and Tompkins, G. E. (2001). *Language Arts: Content and Teaching Strategies* (5th ed.). Upper Saddle River, NJ: Prentice Hall.

Hsu, C. (2010). Writing partnerships. *The Reading Teacher, 63,* 153–158.

Hudson, R. F., Lane, H. B., and Pullen, P. C. (2005). Reading fluency and assessment: What, why and how? *The Reading Teacher, 58*(8), 702–714.

Hui-Tzu, M. (2008). EFL vocabulary acquisition and retention: Reading plus vocabulary enhancement and narrow reading. *Language Learning, 58,* 73–115.

Hutchings, D., Greenfeld, M., and Epstein, J. (2008). *Family Reading Night.* Larchmont, NY: Eye on Education.

Hyde, A. A., and Bizar, M. (1989). *Thinking in Context: Teaching Cognitive Processes Across the Elementary Curriculum.* White Plains, NY: Longman.

International Reading Association (2002). *Integrating Literacy and Technology into the Classroom: A Position Statement of the International Reading Association.* Newark, DE: Author.

International Society for Technology in Education (2007). ISTE's educational technology standards for students. Retrieved from www.iste,org/Content/Navigationmenu/NETS/For Students/2007standards/NETS_for_students_2007.htm

Invernizzi, M., Abouzeid, M., and Gill, J. T. (1994). Using students' invented spellings as a guide for spelling instruction that emphasizes word study. *Elementary School Journal, 95,* 155–167.

IRA Board. (1998). IRA Board issues position statement on phonemic awareness. *Reading Today, 26,* June/July.

Jacobs, J. (1995). Why Juan and Jenny can't R–E–A–D. *The San Jose Mercury,* August 17.

Jacobs, V., Baldwin, E. L., and Chall, J. (1990). *The Reading Crisis: Why Poor Children Fall Behind.* Cambridge, MA: Harvard University Press.

Jalongo, M. R. (1988). *Young Children and Picture Books: Literacy from Infancy to Six.* Washington, DC: National Association for the Education of Young Children.

Jalongo, M. R. (2011). *Early Childhood Language Arts* (5th ed.). Boston: Pearson.

Jimerson, S. R., Burns, M. K., and VanDerHeyden, A. M. (2007). *The Handbook of Response to Intervention: The Science and Practice of Assessment and Intervention.* New York: Springer.

Johnson, D. D. (1973). Sex differences in reading across cultures. *Reading Research Quarterly, 9*(1), 67–86.

Johnson, D. D., and Baumann, J. F. (2001). Word identification. In P. D. Pearson (Ed.), *Handbook of Reading Research* (3rd ed.). Mahwah, NJ: LEA.

Johnson, D. D., and Pearson, P. D. (1984). *Teaching Reading Vocabulary* (2nd ed.). New York: Holt, Rinehart, and Winston.

Jones, I., and Pellegrini, A. D. (1996). The effects of social relationships, writing media, and microgenetic development of first-grade students' written narratives. *American Educational Research Journal, 33,* 681–718.

Juel, C. (1988). Learning to read and write: A longitudinal study of 54 children from first through fourth grades. *Journal of Educational Psychology, 80,* 437–447.

Juel, C. (1991). Beginning reading. In R. Barr, M. Kamil, P. Mosenthal, and P. D. Pearson (Eds.), *Handbook of Reading Research, 2,* 759–788.

Juel, C. (1994). *Learning to Read and Write in One Elementary School.* New York: Springer–Verlag.

Kajder, S., and Bull, G. (2003). Scaffolding for struggling students: Reading and writing with blogs. *Learning and Leading with Technology, 31,* 32–35.

Kamil, M. (1994, April). Matches between reading instruction and reading task demands. Presentation at the Educational Research Association, New Orleans.

Kamil, M. L. (2004). Vocabulary and comprehension instruction: Summary and implications of the National

Reading Panel findings. In P. McCardle and V. Chabra (Eds.), *The Voice of Evidence in Reading Research*, 213–234. Baltimore, MD: Brookes.

Kamil, M., and Lane, D. (2002, April). Using information text for first grade reading instruction: Theory and Practice. www.stanford.edu/~mkamil/nrc97b.htm

Kemper, L. W., and Brody, S. B. (2001). Advanced decoding and fluency. In S. B. Brody (Ed.), *Teaching Reading: Language, Letters, and Thought.* Milford, NH: LARC Publishing.

Kist, W. (2005). *New Literacies in Action: Teaching and Learning in Multiple Media.* New York: Teacher's College Press.

Klein, P. D., and Olson, D. R. (2001). Texts, technology, and thinking: Lessons from the Great Divide. *Language Arts, 78,* 227–236.

Klenk, L., and Kibby, M. W. (2000). Re-mediating reading difficulties: Appraising the past, reconciling the present, constructing the future. In M. L. Kamil, P. B. Mosenthal, P. D. Pearson, and R. Barr (Eds.), *Handbook of Reading Research,* Vol. 3. Mahwah, NJ: Lawrence Erlbaum.

Krashen, S. D. (2004a). False claims about literacy development. *Educational Leadership, 61,* 18–21.

Krashen, S. D. (2004b). *The Power of Reading: Insights from the Research.* Upper Saddle River, NJ: Pearson.

Kress, G. (2003). *Literacy in the New Media Age.* London: Routledge.

Kucer, Stephen B. Associate Professor of Language and Literacy, Washington State University, Vancouver. Personal correspondence, September 15, 2010.

Kuhn, M. R. and Stahl, S. A. (2003). Fluency: A Review of developmental and remedial practices. *Journal of Educational Psychology, 95,* 3–21.

LaBerge, D., and Samuels, S. J. (1974). Toward a theory of automatic information processing in reading. *Cognitive Psychology, 6,* 293–323.

LaBerge, D., and Samuels, S. J. (1976). Toward a theory of automatic processing in reading. In H. Singer and R. Ruddell (Eds.), *Theoretical Models and Processes of Reading,* 548–579. Newark, DE: International Reading Association.

Labbo, L. D. (2005). From morning message to digital morning message: Moving from the tried and true to the new. *The Reading Teacher, 58,* 782–785.

Labbo, L. D., Eakle, A. J., and Montero, M. K. (2002, May). Digital language experience approach: Using digital photographs and software as a language experience approach innovation. *Reading Online, 5*(8). www.readingonline.org/electronic/elecindex. asp?HREF=labbo2/Back

Labbo, L. D., Leu, D. J., Kinzer, C. J., Teale, W. H., Cammack, D., Kara-Soteriou, J., and Sanny, R. (2003). Teacher wisdom stories: Cautions and recommendations for using computer-related technologies for literacy instruction. *The Reading Teacher, 57,* 300–304.

Ladson-Billings, G. (2009). *The Dreamkeepers: Successful Teachers of African American Children* (2nd ed.). San Francisco: Wiley.

Lancy, D. F., and Bergin, C. (1992). The role of parents in supporting beginning reading. Paper presented at the annual meeting of the American Educational Research Association, San Francisco, CA.

Lancy, D. F., Draper, K. D., and Boyce, G. (1989). Parental influence on children's acquisition of reading. *Contemporary Issues in Reading, 4*(1), 83–93.

Landauer, T. (1995). *The Trouble with Computers.* Cambridge, MA: MIT Press.

Lane, H. B., and Allen, S. A. (2010). The vocabulary rich classroom: Modeling sophisticated word use to promote word consciousness and vocabulary growth. *The Reading Teacher, 63,* 362–370.

Laosa, L. M. (1982). School, occupation, culture, and family: The impact of parental schooling on the parent–child relationship. *Journal of Educational Psychology, 74*(6), 791–827.

Larson, L. C. (2008). Electronic reading workshop: Beyond books with new literacies and instructional technologies. *Journal of Adolescent and Adult Literacy, 52,* 121–131.

Larson, L. C. (2009). Reader response meets new literacies: Empowering readers in online learning communities. *The Reading Teacher, 62,* 638–648.

Leal, D. J. (2005). The Word Writing CAFÉ: Assessing student writing for complexity, accuracy, and fluency. *The Reading Teacher, 59,* 340–350.

Learning First Alliance. (1998). *Every Child Reading: An Action Plan.* Washington, DC: Author.

Lee, D. M., and Allen, R. V. (1963). *Learning to Read Through Language Experience* (2nd ed.). New York: Meredith.

Lefever-Davis, S., and Pearman, C. (2005). Early readers and electronic texts: CD-ROM storybook features that influence reading behaviors. *The Reading Teacher, 58*(5), 446–454.

LeLoup, J. W., and Ponterio, R. (2003, December). Second language acquisition and technology: A review of the research. *CAL Digest.* Washington, D. C. Center for Applied Linguistics.

Lesgold, A. M., and Curtis, M. E. (1981). Learning to read words efficiently. In A. M. Lesgold and C. A.

Perfetti (Eds.), *Interactive Processes in Reading.* Hillsdale, NJ: Lawrence Erlbaum.

Leu, D. J. (1997). Caity's question: Literacy as deixis on the Internet. *The Reading Teacher, 23,* 62–67.

Leu, D. J. (2007). *Teaching with the Internet K–12: New Literacies for New Times.* Norwood, MA: Christopher Gordon.

Leu, D. J., Jr., Castek, J., Coiro, J., Gort, M., Henry, L. A., and Lima, C. O. (2005). *Developing New Literacies Among Multilingual Learners in the Elementary Grades.* Paper prepared as part of the Technology in Support of Young Second Language Learners Project at the University of California Office of the President, under a grant from the William and Flora Hewlett Foundation.

Leu, D. J., Jr., and Kinzer, C. K. (2000). The convergence of literacy construction and networked technologies for information and communication. *Reading Research Quarterly, 35,* 108–127.

Leu, D. J., Jr., Kinzer, C. K., Coiro, J. L., and Cammack, D. W. (2004). Toward a theory of new literacies emerging from the Internet and other technologies. In R. B. Ruddell and N. Unrau (Eds.), *Theoretical Models and Processes of Reading,* 5th ed., 1570–1613. Newark, DE: International Reading Association. Retrieved May 14, 2010, from www.readingonline.org/newliteracies/lit_index.asp?HREF=leu/

Levine, A. (1994). The great debate revisited. *Atlantic Monthly, 27,* 38–44.

Liberman, I., Shankweiler, D., Fischer, F., and Carter, B. (1974). Explicit syllable and phoneme segmentation in the young child. *Journal of Experimental Child Psychology, 18,* 201–212.

Lindholm-Leary, K., and Borsato, G. (2006). Academic achievement. In F. Genesee, K. Lindholm-Leary, W. M. Saunders, and D. Christian (Eds.), *Educating English Language Learners: A Synthesis of Research Evidence,* 176–222. New York: Cambridge University Press.

Locke, J. L. (1993). *The Child's Path to Spoken Language.* Cambridge: Harvard University Press.

Lovett, M. W., Steinbach, K. A., and Frijters, J. C. (2000). Remediating the core deficits of developmental reading disability: A double deficit perspective. *Journal of Learning Disabilities, 33*(4), 334–358.

Lundberg, I., Olofsson, A., and Wall, S. (1980). Reading and spelling skills in the first school years predicted from phonetic awareness skills in kindergarten. *Scandinavian Journal of Psychology, 21,* 159–173.

Malloy, J., and Gambrell, L. (2006). Approaching the unavoidable: Literacy instruction and the Internet. *The Reading Teacher, 59,* 482–484.

Manning, M., and Manning, G. (1993a). Reading. Word or meaning centered. *Teaching PreK–8, 25*(2), 98–99.

Manning, M., and Manning, G. (1993b). They say, you say. *Teaching K–8, 37*(6), 50–54.

Martin, J. B. (1998). *Snowflake Bentley.* New York: Houghton Mifflin.

Martin, Jr., B., and Archambault, J. (1997). *Knots on a Counting Rope.* Ill. T. Rand. New York: Henry Holt.

Mathews, M. M. (1966). *Teaching to Read: Historically Considered.* Chicago: University of Chicago Press.

McAfee, O., and Leong, D. (2007). *Assessing and Guiding Young Children's Development and Learning* (4th ed.). Boston: Allyn & Bacon.

McCracken, M. J., and McCracken, R. A. (1996). *Spelling Through Phonics.* Manitoba, Canada: Peguis.

McCracken, R. A., and McCracken, M. J. (1986). *Stories, Songs, and Poetry to Teach Reading and Writing: Literacy Through Language.* Chicago: American Library Association.

McGee, L. M. (1998). How do we teach literature to young children? In S. Neuman and K. Roskos (Eds.), *Children Achieving: Best Practices in Beginning Literacy.* Newark, DE: International Reading Association.

McGee, L. M. (2007). *Transforming Literacy Practices in Preschool: Research-based Practices That Give All Children the Opportunity to Reach Their Potential as Learners.* New York: Scholastic.

McGee, L. M., and Richgels, D. J. (2004). *Literacy's Beginnings: Supporting Young Readers and Writers* (4th ed.). Boston: Allyn & Bacon.

McGee, L. M., and Richgels, D. J. (2007). *Literacy's Beginnings: Supporting Young Readers and Writers* (5th ed.). Boston: Allyn & Bacon.

McGill-Franzen, A. (2005). *Kindergarten Literacy.* New York: Scholastic.

McIntyre, E., and Freppon, P. A. (1994). A comparison of children's development of alphabetic knowledge in a skill-based and whole language classroom. *Research in the Teaching of English, 28,* 391–417.

McKenna, M. C. (1998). Electronic texts and the transformation of beginning reading. In D. Reinking, M. Mckenna, L. D. Labbo, and R. Kieffer (Eds.), *Handbook of Literacy and Technology: Transformations in a Post-Typographic World,* 45–59. Mahwah, NJ: Erlbaum.

McKeown, M. G. (1985). The acquisition of word meaning from context by children of high and low ability. *Reading Research Quarterly, 20,* 482–496.

McMath, J., King, M., and Smith, W. (1998). Young children, questions and nonfiction books. *Early Childhood Education Journal, 26,* 19–27.

Meloth, M. (1991). Enhancing literacy through cooperative learning. In E. Hiebert (Ed.), *Literacy for a Diverse Society: Perspectives, Practices, and Policies*. New York: Teachers College Press.

Meskill, C., and Mossop, J. (2000). Electronic texts in ESOL classrooms. *TESOL Quarterly, 34,* 585–592.

Mesmer, E. M., and Mesmer, A. E. (2009). Response to intervention: What teachers of reading need to know. *The Reading Teacher, 62,* 114–121.

Mikulecky, L. (1996). *Family Literacy: Directions in Research and Implications for Practice*. Website, January, www.ed.gov/pubs/famLit/appendb

Mikulecky, L., and Lloyd, P. (1995). Parent–Child Interactions in Family Literacy Programs. A paper presented at the National Center for Family Literacy conference, Louisville, KY, May 20.

Mills, H., O'Keefe, T., and Stephens, D. (1991). *Looking Closely: Exploring the Role of Phonics in One Whole Language Classroom*. Urbana, IL: National Council of Teachers of English.

Miramontes, O. B., Nadeau, A., and Commins, N. L. (1997). *Restructuring Schools for Linguistic Diversity: Linking Decision Making to Effective Programs*. New York: Teachers College Press.

Moats, L. C. (1995a). *Spelling: Development, Disabilities, and Instruction*. Timonium, MD: York Press.

Moats, L. C. (1995b). The missing foundation in teacher education. *American Educator, 19,* 43–51.

Moore, M. A. (1991). Electronic dialoguing: An avenue to literacy. *The Reading Teacher, 45,* 280–286.

Morgan, L., and Goldstein, H. (2004). Teaching mothers of low socioeconomic status to use decontextualized language during storybook reading. *Journal of Early Intervention, 26,* 235–252.

Morphett, M. V., and Washburn, C. (1931). When should children begin to read? *Elementary School Journal, 31,* 496–503.

Morrison, K., Robbins, H., and Rose, D. G. (2008). Operationalizing culturally relevant pedagogy: A synthesis of classroom-based research. *Equity & Excellence in Education, 41,* 433–452.

Morrow, L. M. (1983). Home and school correlates of early interest in literature. *Journal of Educational Research, 76,* 221–230.

Morrow, L. M. (1989). Using story retelling to develop comprehension. In K. D. Muth (Ed.), *Children's Comprehension of Text: Research into Practice*. Newark, DE: International Reading Association.

Morrow, L. M. (1995). *Family Literacy Connections in Schools and Communities*. Newark, DE: International Reading Association.

Morrow, L. M., and Rand, M. K. (1991). Promoting literacy during play by designing early childhood classroom environments. *The Reading Teacher, 44,* 396–402.

Morrow, L. M., and Tracey, D. H. (2007). Best practices in early literacy in preschool, kindergarten, and first grade. In L. B. Gambrell, L. M. Morrow, and M. Pressley (Eds.), *Best Practices in Literacy Instruction* (3rd ed.), 57–82. New York: Guilford Press.

Morrow, L. M., Tracey, D. H., and Maxwell, C. M. (Eds.). (1995). *A Survey of Family Literacy*. Newark, DE: International Reading Association.

Moss, B. (2005). Making a case and a place for effective content area literacy instruction in the elementary grades. *The Reading Teacher, 59,* 46–55.

Moss, B. (2004). Teaching expository text structures through information and book retellings. *The Reading Teacher, 57,* 710–718.

Moss, B., Leone, S., and Depillo, M. (1997). Exploring the literature of fact: Linking reading and writing through information trade books. *Language Arts, 74,* 418–429.

Mullis, I. V. S., Martin, M. O., Kennedy, A. M., and Foy, P. (2007). *IEA's Progress in International Reading Literacy Study in Primary School in 40 Countries*. Chestnut Hill, MA: TIMSS & PIRLS International Study Center, Boston College.

Murray, A. D. (1990). Fine-tuning of utterance length to preverbal infants: Effects on later language development. *Journal of Child Language, 17,* 511–525.

NAEYC. (2011). Developmentally appropriate practice. Retrieved February 7, 2011 from www.naeyc.org/DAP

NAEYC. (2009). Position Statement on Developmentally Appropriate Practice. Available at www.naeyc.org/files/naeyc/file/positions/position statement Web.pdf

Nagy, W. E. (1988). *Teaching Vocabulary to Improve Reading Comprehension*. Clearinghouse on Reading and Communication Skills and the National Council of Teachers of English and the International Reading Association. Urbana, IL: ERIC.

Nagy, W. E., and Herman, P. (1985). Incidental vs. instructional approaches to increasing reading vocabulary. *Educational Perspectives, 23,* 16–21.

Nagy, W. E., Herman, P., and Anderson, R. (1985). Learning words from context. *Reading Research Quarterly, 19,* 304–330.

National Assessment Governing Board. (2002). Reading Framework for the 2003 National Assessment of Educational Progress. www.nagb/pubs/reading_framework/tok.html

National Center for Education Statistics. (2008). *The National Adult Literacy Survey*. Washington, DC: Author.

National Endowment for the Arts. (2004). *Reading at Risk: A Survey of Literary Reading in America* (Rep. No. 46). Washington, DC: Author.

National Institute for Literacy. (2001). *Put Reading First: The Research Building Blocks for Teaching Children to Read Kindergarten Through Grade 3*. Washington, DC: Author.

National Institute of Child Health and Human Development. (2000). *Teaching children to read—Summary report of the National Reading Panel*. Washington, DC: U. S. Government Printing Office.

National Reading Panel. (2000). *Report of the National Reading Panel: Teaching Children to Read: An Evidence-Based Assessment of the Scientific Research Literature on Reading and Its Implications for Reading Instruction*. Washington, DC: National Institute of Child Health and Human Development, National Institutes of Health.

Nelson, J. R., and Stage, S. A. (2007). Fostering the development of vocabulary knowledge and reading comprehension through contextually-based multiple meaning vocabulary instruction. *Education and Treatment of Children, 30*, 1–22.

Neuman, S. B., and Celano, D. (2001). Books aloud: A campaign to "put books into children's hands." *The Reading Teacher, 54*, 550–557.

Neuman, S. B., and Roskos, K. (1993). *Language and Literacy Learning in the Early Years: An Integrated Approach*. New York: Harcourt Brace.

Neuman, S. B., and Roskos, K. (2005). Whatever happened to developmentally appropriate practice in early literacy? *Young Children, 60*, 22–26.

Nilsen, A., and Nilsen, D. (2003). A new spin on teaching vocabulary: A source-based approach. *The Reading Teacher, 56*, 436–439.

No Child Left Behind Act of 2001. (2002). PL No. 107-110, 115 Stat. 1425.

Noyce, R. M., and Christie, J. F. (1989). *Integrating Reading and Writing Instruction in Grades K–8*. Boston: Allyn & Bacon.

Ogle, D. (1986). K-W-L: A teaching model that develops active reading of expository text. *The Reading Teacher, 39*, 564–570.

Ollila, L. O., and Mayfield, M. (Eds.) (1992). *Emerging Literacy*. Needham Heights, MA: Allyn & Bacon.

Opitz, M. F., and Rasinski, T. (1998). *Good-bye Round Robin: 25 Effective Oral Reading Strategies*. Portsmouth, NH: Heinemann.

Pages, J. M. (2002, April). Using an author's style and text patterns to support the reading of information. www.kidbibs.com/learningtips/lt39.htm

Paige, R. (2004). Key policy letters signed by the education secretary or the deputy secretary. Retrieved Jan. 3, 2007, from www.ed.gov/policy/elsec/guid/secletter/040701.html

Palinscar, A. S., Brown, A. L., and Martin, S. M. (1987). Peer interaction in reading comprehension instruction. *Educational Psychologist, 22*, 231–253.

Palmer, R. G., and Stewart, R. A. (2003). Nonfiction trade book use in primary grades. *The Reading Teacher, 57*, 38–48.

Palmer, R. G., and Stewart, R. A. (2005). Models for using nonfiction in the primary grades. *The Reading Teacher, 58*, 426–434.

Pappas, C. C. (1993). Is narrative "primary"? Some insights from kindergarteners' pretend readings of stories and information books. *Journal of Reading Behavior, 25*, 97–129.

Parker, D. (1995). Politics and pedagogy: The bookends of California's literacy crisis. *Clips: A Journal of the California Literature Project, 2*(3), 4–9.

Parkes, B. (2003). The power of informational texts in developing readers and writers. In L. Hoyt, M. Mooney, and B. Parkes (Eds.), *Exploring Informational Texts: From Theory to Practice* (pp. 2–7). Portsmouth, NH: Heinemann.

Pearson, P. D. (1985). Changing the face of reading comprehension instruction. *The Reading Teacher, 38*(8), 724–738.

Pearson, P. D. (1993). Teaching and learning reading: A research perspective. *Language Arts, 70*, 502–511.

Pearson, P. D., and Camperell, K. (1994). Comprehension of text structures. In R. B. Ruddell, M. R. Ruddell, and H. Singer (Eds.), *Theoretical Models and Processes of Reading*. Newark, DE: International Reading Association.

Pearson, P. D., Raphael, T. E., Benson, V. L., and Madda, C. (2007). Balance in comprehensive literacy instruction: Then and now. In L. B. Gambrell, L. M. Morrow, and M. Pressley (Eds.), *Best practices in literacy instruction* (3rd ed.), 31–54. New York: Guilford Press.

Peetoom, A. (1986). *Shared Reading: Safe Risks with Whole Books*. Richmond Hill, Ontario, Canada: TAB Publications.

Peha, S. (1996a). *All's Well That Spells Well: A Few Thoughts on the Teaching of Spelling*. Unpublished manuscript.

Peha, S. (1996b). *How the Writing Happens: An Introduction to the Writing Process*. Unpublished manuscript.

Peha, S. (1996c). *Where the Writing Happens: Welcome to Writer's Workshop*. Unpublished manuscript.

Peregoy, S. F., and Boyle, O. F. (2009). *Reading, Writing, and Learning in ESL: A Resource Book for Teaching K–12 English Learners* (5th ed.). Boston: Allyn & Bacon/Pearson.

Perfetti, C. (1985). *Reading Ability*. New York: Oxford University Press.

Petach, H. (2001). *The Night Before Valentine's Day*. New York: Grosset & Dunlap.

Pflaum, S. W. (1990). *The Development of Language and Literacy in Young Children* (3rd ed.). Upper Saddle River, NJ: Prentice Hall.

Pflaum, S. W., Walberg, H. J., Karegianes, M. L., and Rusher, S. P. (1980). Reading instruction: A qualitative analysis. *Educational Researcher, 9,* 12–18.

Polacco, P. (1998). *Thank You, Mr. Falker*. New York: Philomel.

Porter, C., and Cleland, J. (1995). *The Portfolio as a Learning Strategy*. Portsmouth, NH: Heinemann.

Powel, D. A., and Aram, R. (2008). Spelling in parts: A strategy for spelling and decoding polysyllabic words. *The Reading Teacher, 61,* 567–570.

Pressley, M. (1998). *Reading Instruction that Works: The Case for Balanced Teaching*. New York: Guilford Press.

Pressley, M. (2001). What should comprehension instruction be the instruction of? In M. L. Kamil, P. B. Mosenthal, P. D. Pearson, and R. Barr (Eds.), *Handbook of Reading Research*. Mahwah, NJ: Lawrence Erlbaum.

Pressley, M. (2005). *Reading Instruction That Works*. New York: Guilford Press.

Pressley, M., Duke, N. K., and Boling, E. C. (2004). The educational science and scientifically-based instruction we need: Lessons from reading research and policy making. *Harvard Educational Review, 16,* 1–62.

Raphael, T. E. (1984). Question-answering strategies for children. *The Reading Teacher, 36,* 186–190.

Rasinski, T. (1989). Fluency for everyone: Incorporating fluency instruction in the classroom. *The Reading Teacher, 42*(9), 690–693.

Rasinski, T. (1990a). Effects of repeated reading and listening while reading on reading fluency. *The Journal of Educational Research, 83*(3), 147–150.

Rasinski, T. (1990b). Investigating measures of reading fluency. *Educational Research Quarterly, 14*(3), 37–44.

Rasinski, T. (2003a). *The Fluent Reader*. New York: Scholastic.

Rasinski, T. (2003b). Beyond speed: Reading fluency is more than reading fast. *California Reader, 2,* 5–11.

Rasinski, T. V. (2000). Speed does matter. *The Reading Teacher, 54*(2), 146–151.

Rasinski, T. V., and Padak, N. (1996). Five lessons to increase reading fluency. In L. R. Putnam (Ed.), *How to Become a Better Reading Teacher: Strategies for Assessment and Intervention*. Columbus, OH: Merrill/Prentice Hall.

Rasinski, T. V., Padak, N. D., and Fawcett, C. (2010). Developing comprehension with informational text. In T. V. Rasinski, N. D. Padak, and C. Fawcett, (Eds.), *Teaching Children Who Find Reading Difficult,* 187–205. Boston: Allyn & Bacon.

Rasinski, T. V., Padak, N. M., Linek, W., and Sturtevant, E. (1994). Effects of fluency development on urban second-grade readers. *The Journal of Educational Research, 87*(3), 158–165.

Read, C. (1986). *Children's Creative Spelling*. London: Routledge and Kegan Paul.

Read, S. (2005). First and second graders writing informational text. *The Reading Teacher, 59,* 36–44.

Reutzel, D. R. (1992). Breaking the letter a week tradition: Conveying the alphabetic principle to young children. *Childhood Education, 69*(1), 20–23.

Reutzel, D. R. (1995). *Fingerpoint Reading and Beyond: Learning About Print Strategies* (LAPS). Reading Horizons.

Reutzel, D. R., and Cooter, R. B. (1996). *Teaching Children to Read: From Basals to Books* (2nd ed.). Englewood Cliffs, NJ: Prentice Hall.

Reutzel, D. R., and Cooter, R. B. (2003). *Strategies for Reading Assessment and Instruction* (2nd ed.). Upper Saddle River, NJ: Merrill.

Reutzel, D. R., and Cooter, R. B., Jr. (2008). *Teaching Children to Read: From Basals to Books* (5th ed.). Upper Saddle River, NJ: Merrill/Prentice Hall.

Reutzel, D. R., and Hollingsworth, P. M. (1993). Effects of fluency training on second-graders' reading comprehension. *Journal of Educational Research, 86*(6), 325–331.

Rhodes, L. K., and Nathenson–Mejia, S. (1992). Anecdotal records: A powerful tool for ongoing literacy assessment. *The Reading Teacher, 45,* 502–511.

Rhodes, L. K., and Shanklin, N. (1993). *Windows into Literacy: Assessing Learners K–8*. Portsmouth, NH: Heinemann.

Richards, M. (2000). Be a good detective: Solve the case of oral fluency. *The Reading Teacher, 53,* 534–539.

Riches, C., and Genesee, F. (2006). Literacy: Crosslinguistic and crossmodal issues. In F. Genesee, K. Lindholm-Leary, W. M. Saunders, and D. Christian (Eds.), *Educating English Language Learners: A*

Synthesis of Research Evidence, 64–108. New York: Cambridge University Press.

Richgels, D. J. (1995). Invented spelling ability and printed word learning in kindergarten. *Reading Research Quarterly, 30,* 96–109.

Richgels, D. J. (2002). Informational texts in kindergarten. *The Reading Teacher, 55,* 586–595.

Rinsky, L. A. (1997). *Teaching Word Recognition Skills* (6th ed.). Upper Saddle River, NJ: Prentice Hall.

Risko, V. J., and Walker-Dahlhouse, D. (2010). Making the most of assessments to inform instruction. *The Reading Teacher, 63,* 420–422.

Roberts, T. (1975). Skills of analysis and synthesis in the early stages of reading. *British Journal of Educational Psychology, 45,* 3–9.

Rosenbaum, C. (2001). A world map for middle school: A tool for effective vocabulary instruction. *Journal of Adolescent & Adult Literacy, 45,* 44–48.

Rosenblatt, L. (2005). *Making Meaning with Text: Selected Essays.* Portsmouth, NH: Heinemann.

Rosenblatt, L. M. (1983). The reading transaction: What for? In R. P. Parker and F. A. Davis (Eds.), *Developing Literacy: Young Children's Use of Language,* 118–135. Newark, DE: International Reading Association.

Rosenshine, B., Meister, C., and Chapman, S. (1996). Reciprocal teaching: A review of the research. *Review of Educational Research, 64,* 479–530.

Rothstein-Fisch, C., and Trumbull, E. (2008). *Managing Diverse Classrooms: How to Build on Students' Cultural Strengths.* Alexandria, VA: Association for Supervision and Curriculum Development.

Routman, R. (1995). *Invitations: Changing as Teachers and Learners K–12* (2nd ed.). Portsmouth, NH: Heinemann.

Routman, R., and Butler, A. (1995). *Why Talk About Phonics?* Urbana, IL: National Council of Teachers of English.

Rupley, W. H., and Blair, T. R. (1990). *Teaching Reading: Diagnosis, Direct Instruction, and Practice* (2nd ed.). Upper Saddle River, NJ: Prentice Hall.

Salinger, T. (1993). *Models of Literacy Instruction.* New York: Macmillan.

Salvia, J., and Yesseldyke, J. E. (2000). *Assessment* (8th ed.). Boston: Houghton Mifflin.

Samuels, J. S., and Farstrup, A. E. (Eds.). (1992). *What Research Has to Say About Reading Instruction.* Newark, DE: International Reading Association.

Samuels, J. S., Schermer, N., and Reinking, D. (1992). Reading fluency: Techniques for making decoding automatic. In J. S. Samuels and A. E. Farstrup (Eds.), *What Research Has to Say About Reading Instruction,* 124–144. Newark, DE: International Reading Association.

Samuels, S. J. (1979). The method of repeated readings. *The Reading Teacher, 32,* 403–408.

Sargeant, J. W., and Smejkal, A. E. (2000). *Targets for Teachers: A Self-Study Guide in the Age of Standards.* Winnipeg, Manitoba: Peguis Publishing.

Schickedanz, J., and Casbergue, R. (2007). *Writing in Preschool: Learning to Orchestrate Meaning and Marks.* Newark, DE: International Reading Association.

Schlagel, R., and Schlagel, J. (1992). The integrated character of spelling: Teaching strategies for multiple purposes. *Language Arts, 69,* 418–424.

Schmar-Dobler, E. (2003). Reading on the Internet: The link between literacy and technology. *Journal of Adolescent & Adult Literacy, 47,* 80–85.

Schmitt, N. (2008). Instructed second language vocabulary learning. *Language Teaching Research, 12,* 329–363.

Schroeder, A. (1997). *Smoky Mountain Rose: An Appalachian Cinderella.* New York: Puffin.

Schulman, M. B., and Payne, C. D. (2000). *Guided Reading: Making it Work.* New York: Scholastic.

Schwartz, R. M. (2005). Decisions, decisions: Responding to primary students during guided reading. *The Reading Teacher, 58,* 436–443.

Schwartz, R., and Raphael, T. (1985). Concept of definition: A key to improving students' vocabulary. *The Reading Teacher, 39,* 198–205.

Shanahan, T. (1988). The reading-writing relationship: Seven instructional principles. *The Reading Teacher, 41,* 636–647.

Shaywitz, S., Escobar, M., Shaywitz, B., Fletcher, J., and Makuch, R. (1992). Evidence that dyslexia may represent the lower tail of a normal distribution of reading disability. *New England Journal of Medicine, 326*(3), 145–150.

Shefelbine, J. (1995). Learning and using phonics in beginning reading. *Scholastic Literacy Paper, 10,* New York: Scholastic.

Shefelbine, J. (1997). Finding the right balance. *Clip: A Journal of the California Literature Project, 3*(1), 23–24.

Slepian, J., and Seidler, A. (1985). *The Hungry Thing.* New York: Scholastic.

Smith, F. (1971). On the psycholinguistic method of teaching reading. *Elementary School Journal, 71*(4), 10–14.

Smith, F. (1992). Learning to read: The never-ending debate. *Phi Delta Kappan, 73*(4), 432–441.

Smith, L. A. (2006). Think Aloud Mysteries: Using structured, sentence-by-sentence text passages to teach comprehension strategies. *The Reading Teacher, 59,* 764–773.

Smith, N. B. (1986). *American Reading Instruction.* Newark, DE: International Reading Association.

Snider, V. E. (1995). A primer on phonemic awareness: What it is, why it's important, and how to teach it. *School Psychology Review, 24*(3), 443–455.

Spache, G., and Spache, E. (1977). *Reading in the Elementary School* (4th ed.). Boston: Allyn & Bacon.

Spear-Swerling, L., and Sternberg, R. J. (1999). What science offers teachers of reading. *Learning Disabilities, Research & Practice, 16,* 51–57.

Spiegel, D. L. (1992). Blending whole language and systematic direct instruction. *The Reading Teacher, 46,* 38–48.

Spiegel, D. L. (1995). Reinforcement in phonics materials. *The Reading Teacher, 43*(4), 328–330.

Spiegel, D. L., and Fitzgerald, J. (1986). Improving reading comprehension through instruction about story parts. *The Reading Teacher, 39,* 676–682.

Spiegelman, A., and Mouly, F. (Eds.). (2000). *Little Lit: Folklore and Fairy Tale Funnies.* New York: RAW Junior.

Spiro, R. J., Bruce, B. C., and Brewer, W. F. (Eds.). (1980). *Theoretical Issues in Reading Comprehension.* Hillsdale, NJ: Erlbaum.

Stahl, S. A. (1983). Differential word knowledge and reading comprehension. *Journal of Reading Behavior, 15,* 33–50.

Stahl, S. A. (1992). Saying the "P" word: Nine guidelines for exemplary phonics instruction. *The Reading Teacher, 45*(8), 618–624.

Stahl, S. A. (2001). Teaching phonics and phonological awareness. In S. B. Neuman and P. K. Dickinson (Eds.), *Handbook of Early Literacy Research: Vol. 1* (333–347). New York: Guilford.

Stahl, S. A., and Fairbanks, M. M. (1986). The effects of vocabulary instruction: A model-based meta-analysis. *Review of Educational Research, 56,* 72–110.

Stahl, S. A., and Kapinus, B. (1991). Possible sentences: Predicting word meanings to teach content area vocabulary. *The Reading Teacher, 45,* 36–43.

Stahl, S. A., and Shiel, T. G. (1992). Teaching meaning vocabulary: Productive approaches for poor readers. *Reading and Writing Quarterly: Overcoming Learning Disabilities, 8,* 223–241.

Stanovich, K. E. (1980). Toward an interactive-compensatory model of individual differences in the development of reading fluency. *Reading Research Quarterly, 16,* 32–71.

Stanovich, K. E. (1986). Matthew effects in reading: Some consequences of individual differences in the acquisition of reading. *Reading Research Quarterly, 22,* 360–407.

Stanovich, K. E. (1992). Speculation on the causes and consequences of individual differences in early reading acquisition. In P. Gough, L. Ehri, and R. Treiman (Eds.), *Reading Acquisition.* Hillsdale, NJ: Erlbaum.

Stanovich, K. E. (1994). Romance and reality. *The Reading Teacher, 47,* 280–291.

Stanovich, K. E., and Siegel, L. S. (1994). The phenotypic performance profile of reading-disabled children: A regression-based test of the phonological-core variable-difference model. *Journal of Educational Psychology, 86*(1), 24–53.

Stanovich, K., and Stanovich, P. (1995). How research might inform the debate about early reading acquisition. *Journal of Research in Reading, 18*(2), 87–105.

Stauffer, R. G. (1969). *Teaching Reading as a Thinking Process.* New York: Harper & Row.

Stauffer, R. G. (1980). *The Language Experience Approach to the Teaching of Reading* (2nd ed.). New York: Harper & Row.

Steptoe, J. (1987). *Mufaro's Beautiful Daughters: An African Tale.* New York: Lothrop, Lee & Shepard.

Stimson, J. (1993). *The Three Billy Goats Gruff.* Illustrated by C. Russell. Loughborough, UK: Ladybird Books.

Sulzby, E. (1990). Assessment of writing and children's language while writing. In W. H. Teale and E. Sulzby (Eds.), *Emergent Literacy: Writing and Reading.* Norwood, NJ: Ablex Publishing.

Sulzby, E., and Teale, W. H. (2003). The development of the young child and the emergence of literacy. In J. Flood, D. Lapp, M. R. Squire, and J. M Jensen (Eds.), *Handbook of Research on Teaching the English Language Arts* (3rd ed.). Sponsored by the International Reading Association/National Council of Teachers of English. Mahwah, NJ: Erlbaum.

Sulzby, E., and Teale, W. H. (2010). The development of the young child and the emergence of literacy. In J. Flood, D. Lapp, M. E. Squire, and J. M. Jensen (Eds.), *Handbook of Research on Teaching the English Language Arts* (5th ed.). Sponsored by the International Reading Association/National Council of Teachers. Mahwah, NJ: Erlbaum.

Sweeney, J., and Peterson, S. (1996). *350 Fabulous Writing Prompts: Thought-Provoking Springboards for Creative, Expository, and Journal Writing.* New York: Scholastic.

Sweet, A., and Snow, C. (2003). Understanding comprehension: RAND report on comprehension. Washington, DC: RAND.

Sweet, A. P., and Snow, C. E. (2003). Reading for comprehension. In A. P. Sweet and C. E. Snow (Eds.), *Rethinking Reading Comprehension*, 1–11. New York: Guilford Press.

Tangel, D., and Blachman, B. A. (1992). Effect of phoneme awareness instruction on kindergarten children's invented spelling. *Journal of Reading Behavior, 24*, 233–261.

Tangel, D., and Blachman, B. A. (1995). Effect of phoneme awareness on the invented spelling of first-grade children: A one year follow-up. *Journal of Reading Behavior, 27*, 153–185.

Taylor, D. (1997). *Many Families, Many Literacies: An International Declaration of Principles.* Portsmouth, NH: Heinemann.

Taylor, D., and Dorsey-Gaines, C. (1988). *Growing Up Literate: Learning from Inner-City Families.* Portsmouth, NH: Heinemann.

Teague, M. (1997). *How I Spent My Summer Vacation.* New York: Dragonfly Books.

Teale, W. H. (1978). Positive environments for learning to read: What studies of early readers tell us. *Language Arts, 55*, 922–932.

Teale, W. H., and Sulzby, E. (1986a). *Emergent Literacy* Norwood, NJ: Ablex.

Teale, W. H., and Sulzby, E. (1986b). Home background and young children's literacy development. In *Emergent Literacy: Writing and Reading.* Norwood, NJ: Ablex.

Temple, C., Martinez, M., and Yokota, J. (2011). *Children's Books in Children's Hands: An Introduction to Their Literature* (4th ed.). Boston: Pearson.

Tenenbaum, H. A., and Wolking, W. D. (1989). Effects of oral reading rate on intraverbal responding. *The Analysis of Verbal Behavior, 7*, 83–89.

The Sacramento Bee (June, 14, 2010). Big step for level school standards. Editorial. p. A21.

Thomas, A., Fazio, L., and Stiefelmeyer, B. L. (1999). *Families at School: A Guide for Educators.* Newark, DE: International Reading Association.

Tierney, R. J., Readence, J. E., and Dishner, E. K. (2005). *Reading Strategies and Practices: A Compendium* (6th ed.). Boston: Allyn & Bacon.

Tompkins, G. (2002). *Language Arts: Content and Teaching Strategies* (5th ed.). Upper Saddle River, NJ: Merrill/Prentice Hall.

Tompkins, G. (2009). *Literacy for the 21st Century* (5th ed.). Upper Saddle River, NJ: Prentice Hall.

Tompkins, G. E. (1997). *Best Teaching Practices* (video). Boston: Allyn & Bacon.

Tompkins, G. E. (2006). *Literacy for the 21st Century: A Balanced Approach* (4th ed.). Upper Saddle River, NJ: Merrill/Prentice Hall.

Tompkins, G. E. (2010). *Literacy for the 21st Century: A Balanced Approach.* Boston: Allyn & Bacon.

Tompkins, G. E. (2011). *Literacy in the Early Grades: A Successful Start for PreK–4 Readers and Writers.* Boston: Pearson.

Tompkins, G. E., and Collom, S. (2004). *Sharing the Pen: Interactive Writing with Young Children.* Upper Saddle River, NJ: Merrill/Prentice Hall.

Torrey, J. W. (1979). Reading that comes naturally. In G. Waller and G. E. MacKinnon (Eds.), *Reading Research: Advance in Theory and Practice, 1*, 115–144. New York: Academic Press.

Trachtenburg, P. (1990). Using children's literature to enhance phonics instruction. *The Reading Teacher, 43*, 648–654.

Tracy, D. H. (1995). Children practicing reading at home: What we know about how parents help. In L. Morrow (Ed.), *Family Literacy: Connections in Schools and Communities.* Newark, DE: International Reading Association.

Tracy, D. H., and Young, J. W. (1994). Mother–child interactions during children's oral reading at home. In D. Leu and C. Kinzer (Eds.), *Multidimen-sional Aspects of Literacy Research, Theory, and Practice* (Forty-third Yearbook of the National Reading Conference). Chicago: National Reading Conference.

Trelease, J. (2006). *The New Read Aloud Handbook* (6th ed.). New York: Penguin.

U.S. Department of Education. (1995). *Listening to Children Read Aloud.* Washington, DC: National Center for Education Statistics.

U.S. Department of Education. (2006). Questions and answers on No Child Left Behind—Reading. www.ed.gov/nclb/methods/reading/reading.html

Vacca, R. T., and Vacca, J. L. (2008). *Content Area Reading* (9th ed.). Boston: Allyn & Bacon.

Vadasy, P. F., Sanders, E. A., and Peyton, J. A. (2006). Code-oriented instruction for kindergarten students at risk for reading difficulties: A randomized field trial with paraeducator implementers. *Journal of Educational Psychology, 98*, 508–528.

Valencia, S. (1990). A portfolio approach to classroom reading assessment: The whys, whats, and hows. *The Reading Teacher, 43*, 338–340.

Valmont, W. J. (2003). *Technology for Literacy Teaching and Learning.* Boston: Houghton Mifflin.

Van Allsburg, C. (1985). *The Polar Express.* New York: Houghton Mifflin.

Van Scoter, J. V. (2008). The potential of IT to foster literacy development in kindergarten. In J. V. Knezek (Ed.), *International Handbook of Informational Technology in Education,* 149–161. Springer, London.

Vardell, S. M., Hadaway, N. L., and Young, T. A. (2006). Matching books and readers: Selecting literature for English learners. *The Reading Teacher, 59,* 734–741.

Vellutino, F. R. (1991). Introduction to three studies on reading acquisition: Convergent findings on theoretical foundations of code-oriented versus whole-language approaches to reading instruction. *Journal of Educational Psychology, 83*(4), 437–443.

Vellutino, F. R., and Scanlon, D. (1987). Phonological coding, phonological awareness, and reading ability: Evidence from a longitudinal and experimental study. *Merrill–Palmer Quarterly, 33,* 321–363.

Venable, J. (2006). The national reading curriculum's oobleck. *Phi Delta Kappan, 87,* 448–457.

Vogt, M. E. (1997). Whatever happened to comprehension? A review of the literature. Paper presented at the Teacher Education Symposium, Long Beach, CA, January.

Vogt, M. E. (2004, August/September). Book reading drops, says new survey. *Reading Today, 22,* 6.

Vygotsky, L. S. (1986). *Thought and Language* (A. Kosulin, trans.). Cambridge, MA: MIT Press. (Original work published 1934.)

Wagner, R. K., and Torgeson, J. K. (1987). The nature of phonological processing and its causal role in the acquisition of reading skills. *Psychological Bulletin, 101,* 192–212.

Wagner, R. K., Torgeson, J. K., and Rashotte, C. A. (1994). Development of reading-related phonological processing abilities: New evidence of bidirectional causality from a latent variable longitudinal study. *Developmental Psychology, 30,* 73–87.

Walmsley, S. A., and Adams, E. L. (1993). Realities of whole language. *Language Arts, 70*(4), 272–280.

Warschaur, M., Grant, D., Del Real, G., and Rousseau, M. (2004). Promoting academic literacy and technology: Successful laptop programs in K–12 schools. *System, 32,* 525–537.

Watson, D. (1987). Reader-selected miscues. In D. Watson (Ed.), *Ideas and Insights: Language Arts in the Elementary School.* Urbana, IL: National Council of Teachers of English.

Weaver, C. (1998). *A Balanced Approach to Reading: Becoming Successfully and Joyfully Literate* (videotape & facilitator's guide). Bothell, WA: The Wright Group.

Wilde, S. (1992). *You Ken Red This! Spelling and Punctuation for Whole Language Classrooms.* Portsmouth, NH: Heinemann.

Williams, J. P. (1985). The case for explicit phonics instruction. In J. Osborn, P. Wilson, and R. C. Anderson (Eds.), *Reading Education: Foundations for a Literate America,* 206–213. Lexington, MA: Lexington Books.

Wink, J. (1996). Jonathan: Linking critical pedagogy and literacy. *Clip: A Journal of the California Literature Project, 2*(4), 27–30.

Wink, J. (2005). *Critical pedagogy: Notes from the real world* (3rd ed.). Boston: Allyn & Bacon/Pearson.

Wiseman, D. L. (1992). *Learning to Read with Literature.* Boston: Allyn & Bacon.

Wren, S. (2005). Developing research-based resources for the balanced reading teacher: fluency. Austin, TX: www.balancedreading.com/fluency.html

Yopp, H. K. (1992). Developing phonemic awareness in young children. *The Reading Teacher, 45,* 696–703.

Yopp, H. K. (1995). Read-aloud books for developing phonemic awareness: An annotated bibliography. *The Reading Teacher, 48*(6), 538–543.

Yopp, H. K., and Yopp, R. H. (2000). Supporting phonemic awareness development in the classroom. *The Reading Teacher, 43,* 22–28.

Young, E. (1990). *Lon Po Po: A Red Riding Hood Story from China.* New York: Putnam.

Zawilinski, L. (2009). HOT blogging: A framework for blogging to promote higher order thinking. *The Reading Teacher, 62,* 650–661.

Zutell, J. (1996). The directed spelling teaching activity (DSTA): Providing an effective balance in word study instruction. *The Reading Teacher, 50,* 98–108.

Author Index

Adams, M. J., 17, 22, 23, 36, 45, 66, 68, 74, 85, 96, 101, 120, 261
Afflerbach, P., 279
Alegria, J., 68
Allen, R. V., 197
Allington, R. L., 19, 20, 101, 339
American Library Association, 318
Anderson, R. C., 23, 140, 174, 190, 223, 231, 315
Armbruster, B. B., 101
Ashton-Warner, S., 197
Au, K. H., 24, 170, 231, 335
August, D., 101
Aulls, M. W., 141
Ausubel, D. P., 41

Baer, G. T., 93
Baghban, M., 231
Baker, L., 315, 317
Ball, E. W., 68
Balmuth, M., 21
Barclay, K., 248
Barone, D., 9, 260
Barrantine, S. J., 158
Barton, D., 317
Bear, D. R., 112, 113, 116, 146
Beaty, J. J., 42, 47, 51
Beck, I. L., 17, 57, 85, 134, 137, 150, 239
Beilby, K., 303
Bernhardt, E., 211
Berninger, V., 120
Bialostok, S., 27
Biemiller, A., 138
Bissex, G. L., 9, 231
Blachman, B. A., 67
Blachowicz, C. E., 137, 150
Blevins, W., 85
Block, C. C., 163

Blume, J., 244
Bolton, F., 117
Bond, G. L., 22, 43
Boulware-Gooden, R., 135
Boyle, D., 213
Bridge, C., 231
Briggs, C., 314
Brown, M. W., 59, 203
Buckley, M. H., 166
Burningham, J., 194
Burns, P., 89
Butler, A., 236
Byrne, B., 68

California Department of Education, 120, 135
California Reading Association, 136
Calkins, L. M., 46
Cambourne, B., 293
Camp, D., 215
Canyon, C., 247
Cardoso-Martins, C., 68
Carle, E., 59
Carnine, D., 104, 214
Castek, J., 3, 203, 249
Caswell, L. J., 211
Cazden, C. B., 212
Cecil, N. L., 45, 101, 142, 151, 159, 165, 170, 193, 197, 247, 248, 299, 303
Chall, J., 17, 22
Chard, D. J., 102
Charlip, R., 194
Cheek, E. H., 279
Chomsky, C., 315
Christie, J. F., 47, 48
Clark, K. F., 94, 105
Clay, M. M., 4, 6, 7, 25, 41, 42, 47, 53, 56, 86, 231, 285, 291

Clymer, T., 93
Cochran-Smith, M., 205
Coiro, J., 254, 263
Cole, A. D., 95
Coles, G., 20
Combs, M., 26, 47, 48, 49
Commission on Reading, 23
Connor, C., 161, 174
Cooper, J. D., 231, 280
Cooter, R. B., Jr., 318
Corgill, A. M., 47, 48
Cornett, C., 175, 265
Cossu, G., 68
Cox, C., 255, 258
Cummins, J., 20, 272
Cudd, E., 223
Cunningham, P. M., 7, 45, 68, 92, 95, 122, 195, 248

Dechant, E. V., 41

Delgado-Gaitan, C., 316
deManrique, A. M. B., 68
DeVries, B. A., 213, 218, 221, 241, 262
Dickenson, D., 57
Dixon-Krauss, L., 134
Donnelly, W. B., 153
Dowhower, S. L., 103
Downing, J., 44
Duffelmeyer, F. A., 138
Duffy, G., 174
Duke, N. K., 58, 174, 210, 211, 217, 223
Durkin, D., 41, 174, 239

Ebbers, S. M., 135
Echevarria, J., 177
Edwards, P. A., 319

Subject Index

Questioning:
  activity, 321
  vocabulary and, 136
Questions:
  as writing prompts, 187
  asking and answering, 163
  comprehension, 341
  creative, 171–172
  critical, 171–172
  factual vs. critical and creative, 177
  in guided reading, 239
  inferential, 171–172
  literal, 171–172
  open-ended, 9, 159
  predictive, 235
  QARs, 171–173, 309, 310
Quick Phonemic Awareness Assessment
    Device, 376
Quick Writes, 261, 307

Raps, 247
Rate, fluency and, 102
Reactions, as part of language experi-
    ence, 199
Readability, Fry's graph, 411–412
Read-aloud, 216–217
  books, 56–59
  songs, 203
Reader, becoming an avid, 309
Readers (see also Reading):
  early, 48
  fluent, 48
  transitional, 48
Readers theater, 105–107, 244, 342
  family literacy night and, 324
Reader-selected vocabulary proce-
    dures (RSVP), 149
Reading:
  disabilities, identifying, 301–305
  interest inventory, 278
  level, 240–241
  Rainbow, 150
  specialists, diagnostic tests and, 288
  "beyond" the book, 237
  "great debate" regarding, 17–20
  age-appropriate materials, 325
  aloud, 56–59, 200, 315, 324–325,
      341 (see also Read-aloud)
  aloud to infants and toddlers, 326
  and writing as literacy components,
      184–208 (see also Writing)
  appreciating, 233
  approaches to teaching, 20–28
  as constructive process, 9
  as holistic process, 9

as interactive process, 10
as learned strategies, 36
as natural process, 12
as part of phonics program, 99
as strategic process, 9–10
assessing attitudes toward, 282
attitudes, assessment of, 370–375
buddies, 99 (see also Buddy reading)
characteristics of process, 9–10
children's literature and, 176
choosing wide variety of materials,
    52
choral, 107, 323, 324
comprehension, see Reading com-
    prehension
comprehension levels, 290
cueing systems, 4–6
daily independent, 250
defined, 2–3
diagnostic tests, 288 (see also
    Assessment)
dialogic, 318
dyad, 165–166, 322–323, 340
e-books, 271
echo, 249
encouraging responses, 250
establishing authentic context, 215
establishing authentic purpose,
    215
family literacy night and, 324
festivals, 324
fluency, 100–108 (see also Fluency)
fluent/disfluent, 298, 299
formal tests of, 365
grouping for, 243–243
guided, see Guided reading
holistic instruction and, 24–25
in social setting, 174, 176
informational text, 158, 216–221
    (see also Informational text)
interactive/e-books, 107–108, 271
language experience approach and,
    197–202
level, assessing, 411–412
materials, 338
modeling fluent, 105
motivating independent, 136–137
music and, 246–247, 248
narrative, 158
non-book suggestions, 325–326
online, 263–271
oral, 104–105, 241–242, 299, 315
parental influence on, 315–316 (see
    also Home–school connection)
partner, 341

phonemic awareness as predictor
    of success, 67
practices to avoid and, 334
process of, see Reading process
product, 6, 10–11
quest for balance in instruction,
    25–31
readiness, 41–42 (see also
    Emergent literacy; Literacy)
repeated, 97
Response to Intervention and,
    301–305
shared, see Shared reading
signs of poor performance, 11
silent, 241–242
strategies for large and small
    groups, 229–251 (see also
    Shared reading)
studies regarding, 17–19
tests for emergent, 365–366
theories of acquisition, 3–4
tracking and, 7
what parents should know,
    320–321
Reading at Risk program, 31
Reading capacity level, 290
Reading comprehension, 157–181
  activities for teaching, 163–173
  allowing time for reading,
      173–174
  as interactive process, 158
  assessment of, 282, 294 (see also
      Assessment)
  components of successful program,
      173–179
  critical thinking and, 158–160
  defining, 158
  explicit instruction in, 174, 175
  monitoring understanding and,
      162
  observable behaviors and, 294
  praise and, 160
  prediction and, 161
  prior knowledge and, 162
  providing children's literature and,
      176
  story prediction and, 166
  strategies for, 160–163
  think time and, 160
  think-alouds and, 167–168
  visualizing and, 162, 175
Reading First initiative, 19
Reading Is Fundamental (RIF), 324
Reading process, 6–10
  characteristics of, 9–10